'The Greatest Squadron of Them All'

'The Greatest Squadron of Them All'

The Definitive History of 603 (City of Edinburgh) Squadron, RAauxAF

David Ross
Bruce Blanche & Bill Simpson

Volume II
1941 – To Date

GRUB STREET · LONDON

Published by
Grub Street
The Basement
10 Chivalry Road
London SW11 1HT

British Library Cataloguing in Publication Data
The greatest squadron of them all: the definitive history of
   603 (City of Edinburgh) Squadron, RauxAF
   Vol. 2 1941 to date
   1. Great Britain. Royal Auxiliary Air Force. Squadron, 603 – History
   2. Bombers – Great Britain – History 3. Fighter planes – Great Britain – History
   4. World War, 1939-1945 – Aerial operations, British
   I. Ross, David (David M. S.), 1958- II. Blanche, J. Bruce III. Simpson, William
   358.4'00941

ISBN 1 904010 51 2

Typeset by Pearl Graphics, Hemel Hempstead

Printed and bound in Great Britain by
Biddles Ltd, Guildford and King's Lynn

Endpapers: Spitfire VCs of 603 on Malta, 1942.

Frontispiece: From left, S/L Roy Schofield, The Queen, W/C W.G.G Duncan Smith, F/L J. D. A.
Henshaw. Her Majesty, The Queen, Honorary Air Commodore of 603 (City of Edinburgh) Squadron,
presenting The Standard at the Palace of Holyroodhouse on 30 June 1955.

Editor's Note
**The material appearing in this book which has been quoted from letters,
reports, communications and the like has been deliberately left in the style of the
original to preserve their authenticity.**

CONTENTS

Acknowledgements   vii
Equivalent Ranks   x

Foreword   Air Commodore The Right Honourable Lord   xi
                Selkirk of Douglas QCMSP, Honorary Air Commodore
                603 (City of Edinburgh) Squadron RAuxAF

Preface   Wing Commander Alasdair Beaton RAuxAF, Officer   xii
                Commanding 603 (City of Edinburgh) Squadron

Introduction   xiv

Chapter 1   Jim Crows, Rhubarbs, Roadsteads, Circuses and Rodeos!   1
Chapter 2   Return to Hornchurch   15
Chapter 3   The 1941 Offensive Takes its Toll   31
Chapter 4   Withdrawal to Scotland   50
Chapter 5   Rest, Snow and 'Weather Willie'   67
Chapter 6   The First *Wasp* Relief Force   77
Chapter 7   Learning the Malta Form   91
Chapter 8   The Second *Wasp* Relief Force   108
Chapter 9   Consolidation   115
Chapter 10   Summer Heat   125
Chapter 11   Changing Times   145
Chapter 12   The North African Adventure: Convoy Escort   153
Chapter 13   The Ill-Fated Dodecanese Campaign   165
Chapter 14   The Aegean Campaign: Beaufighters and   173
                Rocket Projectiles 1943-1944
Chapter 15   Spit-Bombers!   223
Chapter 16   Peace and Disbandment   272
Chapter 17   Reformation – The New Generation   291
Chapter 18   603 Enters the Jet Age   311
Chapter 19   Disbandment   336
Chapter 20   The Fallow Years   351
Chapter 21   603 (City of Edinburgh) Squadron Reformation   364

Appendices

1.	Life After 603	371
2.	Roll of Honour – 1941-1955	378
3.	Honours and Awards	380
4.	DFC *London Gazette* Entries	381
5.	DFM *London Gazette* Entries	382
6.	Honorary Air Commodores	383
7.	The Squadron Standard and Battle Honours	384
8.	Commanding Officers	385
9.	Selected Pen-Portraits of Commanding Officers	386
10.	Squadron Bases, 1941-Present	396
11.	Summer Camps, 1947-1956	397
12.	Squadron Markings and Codes	398
13.	Operational and Training Aircraft	399
14.	Gifted Spitfires	401
15.	Chronology, 1941 to Date	403
16.	Ground Support Units	405
Map: Offensive Sweeps 1941		406
Selected Bibliography		407
Index of Personnel		410

ACKNOWLEDGEMENTS

A work of this size has taken many years to produce and we are indebted to a great many people for their commitment to helping us. In addition to the RAF and Squadron records, flying log books, personal diaries and letters, first-hand anecdote and testimony have been included as well selected photographs from a unique collection of over 1,000 from the authors collections/603 archive. The faith, support and trust of many Squadron veterans and their families, as well as the family members of those who did not survive, has also been a major factor. Their input has been vital and we therefore hope they share our pleasure on seeing this work come to fruition. As a work of research the history of 603 Squadron is on-going and therefore we look forward to hearing from anyone with information for the 603 archive.

The authors would like to express their gratitude to the following and apologise in advance to anyone who they have inadvertently omitted.

Lord Selkirk of Douglas, Lord James Douglas-Hamilton, PC, QC, MSP, Honorary Air Commodore, 603 Squadron, for his unceasing support of this project and his own expertise on the history of the Edinburgh Squadron and access to private papers and photographs.

Mr C.J. Burnett, Allan Carswell and Edith Philip of the National War Museum of Scotland, Edinburgh Castle; Dr Ann Matheson, Keeper, Mrs Hegarty and Ian McIver of the National Library of Scotland; the staff of Edinburgh Central Library; Joanne Ratcliffe, Anna McIlwaine and Mr Peter J.V. Elliott, Senior Keeper, Department of Research/Information Services, Royal Air Force Museum, Hendon; Alan Thomas, Russell Smith, Flight Lieutenant Mary Hudson, Susan Dickinson and Mike Hatch at Air Historical Branch (AHB) RAF; staff at the Imperial War Museum Library; the staff at the Public Records Office (PRO) at Kew; editor and staff at the *Kent Messenger*; the Commonwealth War Graves Commission, Maidenhead; Mike Oakey, Editor of *Aeroplane Monthly*, and Ken Ellis of *Flypast* for permission to quote, Dr Michael J. Neufeld, Museum Curator of the Space History Division of the Smithsonian National Air and Space Museum in Washington DC; Dr A.J.F. Macmillan of the RAF Centre of Aviation Medicine; Adam Smith, Dawn Kemp and Colin Hendry of the National Museums of Scotland Museum of Flight at East Fortune; a special thank you to the Editor and staff, past and present, of *The Scotsman* and its associated newspapers.

Paul Baillie, Mrs Diana Cameron, Sir Ian T. Campbell, Ross Cormack, Robert Douglas and Andy Douglas, Ernest Hardy, Robin Henderson, Jan P. van't Hoff, Ron Hourston, W/O Bob Lockyer, David Martin, Archie Otto, Mrs Brian Power, Sue Sergeant, Colin Stevens, Scott Swan, Barrie Watson, George West, and Colin and Rose Smith of Vector Fine Art.

The 603 Veterans

The late: Air Commodore Ronald 'Ras' Berry OBE, DSO, DFC and Bar; Group Captain George Denholm DFC, AE; Air Commodore George Gilroy DSO, DFC and Bar, DFC (US), AE; Air Commodore Brian Macnamara CBE, DSO; Flight Lieutenant Bill 'Tannoy' Read AFC; Air Vice-Marshal F. David Scott-Malden CB, DSO, DFC (Bar); F/L Bob Sergeant; Squadron Leader Jack Stokoe DFC; and Sir Hugh Walmsley.

Flight Lieutenant Jack Batchelor; Sgt Harold Bennett, Air Commodore Hugh Chater AFC; John Edgar DFM; Air Chief Marshal Sir Christopher Foxley-Norris GCB, DSO, OBE; Group Captain Mike Hobson CBE, AFC; Tony Holland; Squadron Leader Graham Hunter; W/O Mick Jennings;

Flight Lieutenant Keith Lawrence DFC; F/O Nick Machon; Flight Lieutenant Ludwik Martel; Group Captain Barrington Mason; W/O Eric Mee; Bruce Megone DFC; F/O John Moss; W/O Tom ('Paddy') O'Reilly; F/L Jack Rae; Squadron Leader B.G. 'Stapme' Stapleton DFC, DFC (Dutch); Air Commodore Sir Archie Winskill KCVO, CBE, DFC*, RAF (Ret'd); Wing Commander Geoffrey T. Wynne-Powell DFC, AE; Wing Commander John Young AFC, RAF (Ret'd), Official Historian for the Battle of Britain Fighter Association; and Flight Lieutenant Raymond Baxter of 602 Squadron.

The members of the 603 (City of Edinburgh) Squadron Guardiyen Club, in particular Group Captain Mike Hobson CBE, AFC for permission to quote from his unpublished memoirs; the Rt Hon Lord Monroe of Langham, Joe McCulloch, Don Knight, Frank H. Mycroft, D.M. Smith, Peter M. Spinney, the late George Ballingall, T.A. 'Sandy' Crawford; the late: Wing Commander Roy A. Schofield, Wing Commander Jack Meadows DFC, AFC, AE; W.K. (Bill) Moncur, Tim Ferguson MBE, H.D. Glover, and Captain Duncan McIntosh. Also non-members: Air Commodore R.H. Crompton OBE, BA, the late Miss Marjory Drummond, Dr T.E.H. Lightbody, H.G. Smith, T. McFadyen, J.M. Taylor and Mrs Gillibrand.

The late John Mackenzie, Chairman of the 603 Association, and the following members and non-members: Morris B. Alexander, S. Archer (via D. Archer), E.P. Belford, J. 'Dinger' Bell BEM, C.D.P. Black, Jean Blades (neé Waterston), Duncan Brown, W.R. Campbell, Desmond W. Carbury, Arthur Carroll, Charles 'Chic' Cessford, Reg Cockell, Jean Cunningham, W.G. Darling, Lyn Deans, A. Deas, Betty and Paul Denholm, T.F. Dickson, Mrs Nora Donald (re Bill Donald), Charles Dorward, A. Duff, W.A. Eacott, Cecil Gibson, Pieter Gilroy, John E. Goss, Patricia Hirst, H. Hunter, Joseph Hunter, Arthur Inch, John Inkster, D.K. Kelly, W.G. King, George Knox, Mr Ron Lee, W.D. Lee, the late S. Liddle, Alec Mackenzie, W. Marr, J. Marshall, J.A. Miller, the late Mardi Morton; Roderick Morton, George Mullay Jnr, Mr P. Oliver, Alan Pennie (re E.F. Pennie DFM), Bertie Pringle, the late Philip Reilly, Johnny Reilly, John Rendall, Jim Renwick, W. Ritchie, Wendy Roberts, J.M. Robertson, Harry J. Ross, John Saunders, Jim Skinner, Bill Smith, H. Spencer, Caroline Stanley (née Morton), T. Truesdale, Mary Wale, Mrs H. Whitefield (re K. Whitefield), Bob Wilson, E.E. Wimberger, A.E. Winwood, Norman Wood and the late Alex Wishart.

***

Squadron Leader Peter Brown AFC, RAF (Ret'd); and Group Captain Bob Kemp QVRM, AE, ADC, FRIN, Inspector RAuxAF and Vice President of the 603 Association.

603 (City of Edinburgh) Squadron, RAuxAF, 2003: Wing Commander Alasdair Beaton, Officer Commanding; Squadron Leaders Barry Greenhalgh and Derek Morrison; Flight Lieutenants Graeme Lyall and Barbara Murray RAuxAF and Flight Lieutenant Rachel Newton RAF.

The historians: Henry Boot, M.J.F. Bower, Chaz Bowyer, Henry Buckton, John Coleman, Ken Delve, Alan Foster, Norman Franks, Squadron Leader Chris Goss, Peter Green, James J. Halley OBE, Mike Hooks, Leslie Hunt MBE, AE, Andrew Jeffrey, Dr Alfred Price, the Rev J.D.R. Rawlings, Bruce Robertson, Andy Saunders, Chris Shores, Richard C. Smith, and Squadron Leader Andy Thomas.

Squadron Leader Bruce Blanche would like sincerely to thank the following for their support and assistance in contributing to the history of this prestigious Edinburgh Squadron: Wing Commander A.E. Ross DFC, AE, for his permission to have full access to, and freely quote from his history *The Queen's Squadron* (privately published, 1989); Mr Roy Conyers Nesbit for permission to quote from *The Armed Rovers* (Airlife 1995) and access to photographs; and Air Commodore Graham Pitchfork.

John Davies, Anne Dolamore, Louise King and Luke Norsworthy at Grub Street Publishing for your support and hard work.

Finally to our families who tolerate us. For your love and support: Squadron Leader Cliff Ross RAF (Ret'd), Maureen Ross, Kerry and George Cathro, Alison Bellew; Jean Blanche and Marion Simpson.

Photographic acknowledgements
The photographs in this book collected over many years belong to David Ross and Bruce Blanche with due acknowledgement to the many kind contributors, including: Air Commodore the Rt Hon The Lord Selkirk of Douglas QC, MA, MSP; Mrs Diana Cameron, Air Commodore Hugh Chater DFC, John Coleman, Andy Douglas, Robert Douglas, Group Captain Mike Hobson CBE, AFC, J.A.C. Kirke, Ron Lee, W/O Eric Mee, Roderick Morton, Roy C. Nesbit, Archie Otto, Mrs Brian Power, B. Richardson, Andy Saunders, Mrs Sue Sergeant, Caroline Stanley, W/C G. Swanwick, and the US National Archives.

All maps were provided by Kerry Cathro and David Martin.

**This History is dedicated to all members of 603
(City of Edinburgh) Squadron, Royal Auxiliary Air Force,
who gave their lives in peace and war.**

Marshal of the Royal Air Force	*Generalfeldmarschall*
Air Chief Marshal (ACM)	*Generaloberst*
Air Marshal (AM)	*General*
Air Vice-Marshal (AVM)	*Generalleutnant*
Air Commodore (AC)	*Generalmajor*
Group Captain (G/C)	*Oberst*
Wing Commander (W/C)	*Oberstleutnant*
Squadron Leader (S/L)	*Major*
Flight Lieutenant (F/L)	*Hauptmann*
Flying Officer (F/O)	*Oberleutnant*
Pilot Officer (P/O)	*Leutnant*
Warrant Officer (W/O)	*Stabsfeldwebel*
Flight Sergeant (F/Sgt.)	*Oberfeldwebel*
Sergeant (Sgt.)	*Feldwebel*
Corporal (Cpl)	*Unteroffizier*
Leading Aircraftman (LAC)	*Obergefreiter*
Aircraftman First Class (AC1.)	*Gefreiter*
Aircraftman Second Class (AC2.)	*Flieger*

During the life of 603 Squadron, the official style for abbreviating RAF ranks was, for example: Pilot Officer – 'P/O'. This later became 'Plt Off' and the use of such abbreviations would be correct for the period following it's reformation in 1999. However, the old style has been retained throughout both volumes to maintain continuity.

Times

In this book, many of the accounts of actions and events which took place in the UK during the Second World War are based on official documents such as squadron and station operations record books (ORBs), combat reports, aircrew log books etc. It is worth noting that during the war, Britain operated a system of British Summer Time (BST) and British Double Summer Time (BDST). BST was one hour ahead of Greenwich Mean Time (GMT) and BDST was two hours ahead of GMT. This was to make best use of the hours of daylight. No clear instructions were given to those who compiled the official records as to which regime was to be used and so there is always doubt as to whether times quoted are GMT or one of the BST. (Navigators' logs, however, tended to use GMT.) It is generally accepted that times quoted in the ORBs etc were 'local' time – ie either BST or BDST – not GMT. Similarly, the Germans and Italians used Central European Time (CET), which was one hour ahead of GMT and German Summer Time (GST) which was two hours ahead of GMT. Unless otherwise indicated, the times quoted in this book are those recorded in the ORBs etc which are almost certainly 'local' time. For the record, the times used in Britain during the war were:

From 02.00 hrs	Sunday	16 April 1939	BST
From 02.00 hrs	Sunday	19 November 1939	GMT
From 02.00 hrs	Sunday	25 February 1940	BST
From 02.00 hrs	Sunday	4 May 1941	BDST
From 02.00 hrs	Sunday	10 August 1941	BST

***

Direct quotations from the ORBs are spelt as in the original document but elsewhere the modern spelling is used. Also, the ORBs often use other incorrect spellings of place names and where direct quotations are used, these errors remain.

FOREWORD

603 (City of Edinburgh) Squadron chose as their motto the Doric words 'Gin ye Daur', or 'If you dare'. Anyone who joined the Squadron did so in the knowledge that he might have to face immense challenges.

They were involved from the very outset in the first enemy action of the Second World War on 16 October 1939 when Luftwaffe bombers attempted to bomb naval units in the Firth of Forth. Involved in the action were 603 (City of Edinburgh) Squadron and 602 (City of Glasgow) Squadron, and each Squadron shot an enemy bomber into the sea as part of the same action.

On 28 October, 603 and 602 Squadrons were involved in shooting down the first enemy bomber onto British soil in the Lammermuirs, but the greatest threat of all would come in the Battle of Britain.

The fortunes of war propelled 603 into the very eye of the storm. Sent to Hornchurch in south-east London, the pilots were hopelessly outnumbered in confronting the massed bombing formations of the Luftwaffe, accompanied by huge numbers of fighter aircraft. The Squadron sustained heavy losses in the unrelenting duel high up in the sky, but after each casualty another volunteer came forward, and their morale held. By the end of the Battle of Britain they had emerged as the top scoring squadron in the whole of the Royal Air Force.

Their actions and those of all fighter pilots were immortalised by the wonderful writing in his book *The Last Enemy* by Richard Hillary, a young 603 Squadron pilot, who after a number of successful battles had sustained terrible burns in the Battle of Britain. He conveyed the message that under the shining gleam of medals lies a shadow. Accompanying the courage and heroism, there is also the suffering and sacrifice.

It was not the only great battle or campaign in which 603 Squadron would be involved. Throughout the war their pilots were in the thick of the fighting. Indeed on 10 May 1942, 603, along with other squadrons, won a decisive victory over the Luftwaffe in the Air Battle for Malta. The victory that day represented the turning point in the struggle for the Mediterranean, North Africa and the Middle East.

So who were the young men of valour who had joined 603 (City of Edinburgh) Squadron?

Group Captain Bouchier, who saw them in the Battle of Britain, wrote '603 was composed of a collection of quiet and serious young men; men from the city desks of Edinburgh and the fields of the Lothians, led by one whose quiet personality wrapped his Squadron round as with a cloak and made of them by his concern for them and by his leadership example a great and valiant Squadron'.

Today 603 Squadron is composed of young women as well as young men, and with the onward march of technology they now have much greater technical expertise. Even so the qualities of fortitude, determination, dedication and professionalism which had been shown by their predecessors are every bit as evident today.

At all times both in the past and in the present the Squadron have retained the closest links with the people of Edinburgh and Scotland. And the people of Edinburgh and Scotland are entitled to be deeply thankful to those who have served and are serving their country so well.

The authors have made a very important contribution to the history of the RAF and the Royal Auxiliary Air Force by telling the fascinating, colourful and heroic story of the unit that came to be known as 'The Queen's Squadron'.

James Douglas Hamilton,
Selkirk of Douglas.

Lord Selkirk of Douglas

PREFACE

On 10 March 2000, it was with deep pride as an Edinburgh boy that I was privileged to lead 603 back again, along Princes Street, on our Squadron's Reformation Parade. We marched, exactly on the 43rd anniversary of 603's post World War Two disbandment. Service and civilian dignitaries, current and former members of the Squadron, families and citizens and visitors to Edinburgh proudly witnessed the march-past as Air Chief Marshal Sir Peter Squire, C-in-C RAF Strike Command and Mrs Marion Morton, Deputy Lord Provost of the City of Edinburgh, jointly took the salute. Overhead formations of Nimrod and Tornados from Scotland's RAF stations, flew past, in what was a very deep mark of respect and affection for the return of Edinburgh's own and most famous Royal Auxiliary Air Force Squadron.

Our nation's traditions in peace and war over the last 75 years have been epitomised by the young men and women of the Royal Auxiliary Air Force, and in particular those who served as volunteer members of 603 (City of Edinburgh) Squadron, since the Squadron was formed in 1925 at RAF Turnhouse to its disbandment on 10 March 1957.

In the early years of our history, 603 were directly involved in flying the aircraft of their day. Their expertise, valour and sacrifices are legendary and are now recorded in history together with the names of the many who paid most dearly with their lives. In war they earned the greatest accolade any squadron could achieve within the Royal Air Force – the highest praise and respect of their service chiefs together with that of their fellow airmen. In today's RAF and now looking towards the future, the development and complexity of modern fighting aircraft has required the auxiliary to focus his or her voluntary assistance through ground operational and defensive support roles, leaving the actual operational flying to the current generation of highly skilled young men and women.

But the spirit that grows from being a member of a squadron, in either the Royal Air Force or the Royal Auxiliary Air Force, builds a strength, camaraderie and sense of fun and belonging from which the tackling of any task, however serious, becomes achievable. 603 always had such a spirit. It was very much a 'can-do' Squadron as most volunteer organisations are and certainly will be again in the future 603.

And so, in recommending to Her Majesty Queen Elizabeth II that today's auxiliaries of Edinburgh and throughout Scotland be given the reformed title of 603 (City of Edinburgh) Squadron, Royal Auxiliary Air Force, the Air Force Board of the Royal Air Force not only acknowledged 603's most vital contribution to our nation's past, they also made preparations for our new operational future. They gave today's auxiliaries of Auld Reekie a squadron spirit, and a most honourable foundation upon which to build a new operational future to meet the diverse needs of a modern expeditionary Royal Air Force.

If you were or are a Squadron member, your journey towards the later pages of this book will, I hope, bring back fond memories. Alternatively, if you have no previous links with Edinburgh's auxiliaries, then I am sure that you will find in your reading, the substance from which RAF tradition and respect for such a fine Squadron spirit and reputation was born. In discovering or renewing your interest in the story of 603, enjoy stepping back into military aviation history and in so doing acknowledge the bravery of the men in wartime, both pilots and groundcrews, whose contributions and sacrifices built the foundations for the profound honour and gratitude which is the new 603's inheritance.

Edinburgh's own Royal Auxiliary Air Force Squadron, 603, are back home again.

Gin Ye Daur.

Alasdair Beaton

Alasdair J. Beaton

INTRODUCTION

The authors would like to point out that the title for this book was taken from a quote by Air Commodore Cecil 'Boy' Bouchier CBE, DFC, who, as a Group Captain, commanded RAF Hornchurch from December 1939 until December 1940, during the entire Battle of Britain. It is in no way an attempt to place 603 Squadron any higher in the reckoning than other squadrons. Air Commodore Bouchier's initial assessment of the men of 603 when they arrived at his station followed later by a review of those first impressions appear in this book. His quote is as follows:

> ...As I write, memories come crowding in upon me, and from their store I give you this of 603. They were, I think, the greatest Squadron of them all.

* * *

On 14 October 1925, 603 (City of Edinburgh) Bomber Squadron was formed, so beginning a long and unbroken 78-year link of the Royal Auxiliary Air Force with the city and people of Edinburgh – an association which continues to this day.

The Squadron served with distinction for 32 years before, during and after World War Two, claiming the first enemy aircraft shot down on British soil and the honour of highest scoring squadron in the Battle of Britain.

603 Squadron are perhaps best known for their performance in the Battle of Britain, but their pilots played major and significant roles in other campaigns for the remainder of the war. In 1942, 603 fought heroically during the siege of Malta, a battle that some believe was as significant to the outcome of the war as was the Battle of Britain. Certainly, the defending pilots of 603 and the other squadrons there faced similar huge odds day after day and the airmen, both flyers and the ground crews, lived in conditions of deprivation and hardship that those who fought the Battle of Britain did not have to endure. Further sacrifices were made during the period that the Squadron flew Beaufighters in the maritime strike role in the Mediterranean in 1943 and 1944, and then in 1945 when 603 re-formed in the United Kingdom as a Spitfire squadron operating in the dive-bombing role against V2 launching sites in Holland. This was a particularly dangerous role that receives little acknowledgement elsewhere.

In researching the lives and deaths of the 603 pilots one cannot but marvel at their courage. Whilst there were those who lived to appreciate the time given to them, their colleagues may have suffered instantaneous death by gun or cannon fire or a long slow, painful demise alone with nobody bearing witness to their torrid last few moments on earth. It is with such details in mind that one cannot help but analyse one's own mortality and appreciate the time we ourselves have been given – from a different period in time, in a world still being ravaged by war. In the words of Plato: 'Only the dead have seen the end of war.' The stories of the men of 603 feature in this history and help us to understand their commitment and sacrifice. It is with them in mind that this book was written. In the words of Joseph Conrad:

> A man who is good enough to shed his blood for his country is good enough to be given a square deal afterwards. More than that no man is entitled to, and less than that no man shall have.

Flying 15 different types of aircraft and taking part in eight separate campaigns during the Second World War, the Squadron was disbanded on 10 March 1957, back at the airfield where it had been originally formed, Edinburgh's RAF Turnhouse. Two years later on 1 November 1959, 3603 (City of Edinburgh) Fighter Control Unit (FCU), RAuxAF, a unit which had been set up in 1948 to support 603 Squadron, was also disbanded. On the same day, however, 2 (City of Edinburgh) Maritime Headquarters Unit (MHU), RAuxAF was formed – initially manned by the men and women of the former 3603 FCU. The auxiliaries of 2 MHU thus began a period of maritime operational support to the RAF – a role which it continued for nearly 40 years.

On 1 October 1999, 2 MHU was re-roled to take on the primary task of survive to operate (STO) or force protection with the additional role of mission support continuing its maritime links, directly in support of RAF Kinloss. With the new re-roling also came the award and return of the prestigious 603 (City of Edinburgh) Squadron, RAuxAF number plate. The Air Force Board, in their recommendation to Her Majesty, Queen Elizabeth II, was recognising the long distinguished and meritorious service of Edinburgh's RAuxAF members since 1925 and was setting the scene for the support by auxiliary personnel in Scotland for the RAF of the future.

Today, the members of 603 Squadron are justifiably proud of their heritage and in the 603 Headquarters, practically unchanged since its acquisition in 1926, they rub shoulders with the ghosts of the previous generations who served the unit so proudly. Their spirit is all pervading.

DAVID ROSS, BRUCE BLANCHE, BILL SIMPSON.
MAY 2003

Despite the wintry weather conditions and all pervading mud which caused problems on and off the airfield, limited operational flying continued into the New Year, interspersed with practice flying. New arrivals straight from training units were eager to find their way into the fighting and, bearing in mind the reputations of many of their predecessors, make a name for themselves. Unlike those before them, they would take the fight to the enemy and not just fight to defend their own freedom but regain that of others who had fallen under the advance of the despot. The cycle of training and operational flying continued as they waited for a return to more intense combat where yet more losses were inevitable...

Chapter 1

JIM CROWS, RHUBARBS, ROADSTEADS, CIRCUSES AND RODEOS!

The defensive posture adopted by Fighter Command in 1940 changed in 1941 as more offensive activities were undertaken. 603 were to play a part in these activities and it is relevant to explore and understand the reasons for the change and the effect that it had on the *modus operandi* of Fighter Command and squadrons like 603.

After the *Blitzkrieg* across France and the Low Countries which started on 10 May 1940, Hitler was unenthusiastic about destroying the BEF at Dunkirk (Dunkerque). He felt that Britain and Germany were natural allies and he was hopeful that if the British would recognise the desperation of their situation, they might be willing to come to an accommodation with Germany that would preserve the British Empire and be one less threat that the Third Reich would have to deal with. Ideally, if Britain and its Empire threw in its lot with him the combination would be virtually unstoppable. And he was not without reason to be encouraged. There were those in Britain who would have been in favour of a negotiated settlement.

Hitler's view was that the real threat to Germany's long term survival came from the Soviet Union. He also thought that if Britain was not brought into the sphere of influence of the Third Reich it would get support and succour from that quarter; therefore Russia had to be dealt with. His enthusiasm for an invasion of Britain was waning even whilst the Battle of Britain was being fought and when the Luftwaffe failed to dominate Fighter Command, it was a good enough reason to abandon 'Operation Sealion' and order his generals to prepare the plans for 'Operation Barbarossa'.

American politicians were also in a difficult position at this time. The United States was pursuing an isolationist policy and in the summer of 1940 when things looked as if they couldn't get much worse for Britain, their ambassador in London, Joseph Kennedy, was telling President Roosevelt that Britain was likely to fall. The Americans were very aware that if this happened, Germany might gain control of the ships of the Royal Navy, and the combination of the three navies – Germany, Vichy France and Britain – would dominate the seas leaving the United States even more isolated and threatened. And whilst the President was sympathetic towards Britain, he was presented with an awkward dilemma by Prime Minister Winston Churchill who was pressing him to supply Britain with 50 old and obsolescent US Navy destroyers. Whilst Roosevelt's instinct was to accede, he had to convince the isolationist lobby that this wasn't the thin end of a wedge that would drag America into a European war. Further, he had to reconcile it with the possibility that the ships might ultimately fall under German control and at some point be turned on the United States itself.

But Winston Churchill had no intention of either capitulating or coming to an arrangement with Hitler to ensure Britain's survival and he sent out a very clear signal to both Hitler and Roosevelt to this effect. The Royal Navy's Force H was despatched from Gibraltar to Mers-el-Kebir on the coast of French North Africa where much of the French Fleet was in port. After offering the French sailors the option of throwing in their lot and their ships with the British – which was refused – on 3 July 1940 the Royal Navy opened fire on their erstwhile allies and effectively destroyed their capability as a fighting force.

This single action sent out the same message to both Hitler and the American President. Britain would fight on – alone if necessary – and had no intention of coming to a negotiated settlement with the Third Reich. Much of the French Fleet was destroyed and the Royal Navy would not be allowed to be absorbed into the *Kriegsmarine*. Roosevelt now felt able to supply the 50 destroyers to Britain under the Lend Lease scheme and Hitler concluded that to emasculate Britain, Russia had to be prevented from providing aid. As we know the German invasion of Russia was launched on 22 June 1941.

But in the early days of 1941 none of this was known to Fighter Command. In November 1940, Air Marshal Sholto Douglas replaced Hugh Dowding as AOC Fighter Command and in December Air Vice-Marshal Trafford Leigh-Mallory who had commanded 12 Group during the Battle of Britain, took command of 11 Group in place of Air Vice-Marshal Keith Park and this was to be a significant change. During the summer of 1940, Park and Leigh-Mallory had become embroiled in arguments about the best way to send the defending British fighters in to battle against the Luftwaffe bombers. Leigh-Mallory advocated 'big wings' whereby two or three squadrons flew together to create a large mass of fighters to overwhelm the attacking formations, whereas Park argued that the closeness of the 11 Group airfields to the south coast prevented large numbers of fighters forming up into such wings because of the time that it took to do so. Further, the wings were unwieldy and leading and directing them was not what the squadron commanders were trained for or used to.

As the spring of 1941 approached, there was a general aim to try to take the fight to the enemy and 11 Group started to adopt an offensive rather than a defensive role. Initially small numbers of fighters – often four – would 'sweep' low over the enemy occupied countryside looking for targets. These sorties were known as 'Rhubarbs' and the essence of them was surprise. Often carried out when the weather was marginal with low cloud that was preventing major operations, they generally had a particular target in mind on starting out, but they would attack anything found that looked as if it might hurt the enemy, but by the nature of them – fast, low and in small numbers – they were unlikely to cause more than irritation. At the time, the high-spirited, aggressive pilots saw them as a way of getting back at the enemy and the flying was exhilarating, but just how effective they really were is a matter for debate. But as is frequently the case in such debates, the boost to morale that they brought is often ignored.

Ironically, it soon became clear that if the RAF was going to take the fight to the Germans across the Channel, the roles which the two opposing air forces had assumed in 1940 would be exactly reversed. It would be the RAF fighters operating at the extremes of their range, with the disadvantage that any pilot who had to bale out or crash land was going to be in enemy territory and lost, at best, for many months, not hours. And there would be no quick return to a friendly airfield after combat. It would be the Spitfire pilots who were anxiously watching the fuel gauge on the long return flight back over the sea to the English coast. Further, there was the additional disadvantage that the fighters would be operating at the furthest extent of both radio and radar and so warnings of enemy activities would be much less reliable.

For their part, the Luftwaffe would now be able to recover downed pilots quickly and because they were defending occupied territory, and not Germany, there wasn't the same emotional need to rise to every challenge.

Whilst not ignoring the possibility of another summer of attacks on Britain, Fighter Command now developed offensive tactics and strategies. The aim of each operation was not the same. Sweeps to look for enemy shipping were called 'Jim Crows' (usually carried out by a small number of aircraft); those to attack shipping were known as 'Roadsteads'. 'Rodeos' were larger sweeps by fighters alone, whilst 'Circuses' were designed to draw up the German fighters into combat using a small force of bombers as bait and 'Ramrods' were similar to 'Circuses' but had genuine targets for the bombers to attack.

It was now that the 'big wings' really began to come into their own. In a Circus, the last ditch protection for the bombers was provided by the 'close escort', consisting of two or three fighter squadrons – in a wing – whose job was to stick with the bombers whatever happened and deal with any enemy fighters that reached them. The next layer of protection was the 'escort cover' – another wing – and above that the 'high cover' which might have been a single squadron but with a more roving responsibility to keep the enemy away from the close escort and escort cover layers which were tied strictly to the bomber formation's course, height and timings. The huge accumulations of aircraft were sometimes known as 'beehives'.

But Circuses usually had yet more support. Others wings would operate as 'target support' or 'withdrawal cover' depending on the level of threat the Circus was expected to meet. The target support and withdrawal cover wings were not tied to the main formation, but met them either near the target, or on the way back to base as their names suggest. And yet more support was sometimes provided by other completely separate operations to different targets to try to confuse the German controllers as to what was the real objective.

These offensive operations involved large numbers of fighters – sometimes over a hundred – working together in situations where good control and discipline was vital if the operation was to be successful to precision plans.

The bombers were usually from 2 Group – often Blenheims initially. But 'Hurri-bombers' were sometimes used. The escort fighters were from the wings created in 11 and 12 Groups and comprised three squadrons based at the same airfield or a satellite and commanded by experienced and accomplished pilots given the rank of wing commander. Each squadron would attempt to put up 12 aircraft so a wing comprised 36. The ability of the wing leader to command and control such a large and unwieldy formation was critical to the success of the operations and so it is no surprise that the first wing – established at Tangmere – was commanded by Douglas Bader who together with Leigh-Mallory had been vocal in promoting the concept of the 'big wing' the previous summer from his base at Duxford. Other wings followed – Kenley under John Peel, Biggin Hill under 'Sailor' Malan, North Weald under Ronald Kellett, Hornchurch and so on.

As an example of the numbers involved in one of these operations, consider Circus 27 mounted on Monday 30 June 1941. The core was 18 Blenheims from 18 and 139 Squadrons in 2 Group. The fighter squadrons in the escort wings were 303, 306, 308 and 242. Target support was provided by 54, 603 and 611 Squadrons from Hornchurch and 74, 92 and 609 Squadrons from Biggin Hill. Rear support came from 145, 610, 616, 65, 266 and 485 Squadrons. And as part of the operation, diversionary incursions were made by 1, 258 and 312 Squadrons from Kenley. In summary, the Circus involved two squadrons from Bomber Command and 19 from Fighter Command. The effort involved in planning and mounting such operations was, indeed, colossal.

603 would return to the south in May 1941 as part of the Hornchurch Wing and be there until December.

But what of the Luftwaffe? Once the Germans had invaded Russia in June 1941, the RAF's offensive operations were also seen as a way of helping the hard pressed Soviets by making the Germans retain defending fighters in the west.

For the Luftwaffe on the continent, their main pre-occupation over the winter had been the night 'Blitz'. The fighters, the 109s, sometimes swept over the southern coast of England in small numbers trying to draw up the British and they resorted to fitting bombs to 109s so that they were a threat but could quickly revert to the fighter role if the Spitfires and Hurricanes were met.

Prior to Operation Barbarossa being mounted against Russia in June, some of the Luftwaffe units were transferred to what would be the Eastern Front, but Jagdgeschwaderen 2 Richthofen and 26 Schlageter would remain and face the wings – and 603 – during the summer of 1941.

From 22 August 1940 until 5 December 1941, Jagdgeschwader 26 was commanded by Oberstleutnant Adolf Galland. JG26 was responsible for north-eastern France and Belgium.

During 1941 I Gruppe was based at Brest-Guipavas between 1 April and 1 June then at St Omer-Clairmarais until 17 November before moving to St Omer-Arques. During the year, it was commanded firstly by Hauptmann Rolf Pingel and then Major Johannes Seifert. II Gruppe was at Morlaix between 3 April and 1 June when it moved to Maldegem in Holland until 1 July. It then moved to Moorseele until 15 October when it moved yet again to Wevelgem where it remained until 22 December. It was commanded by Hauptman Walter Adolph and then from September 1941 by Hauptman Jochen Müncheberg.

On 28 November 1940, the Geschwaderkommodore of JG2, Major Helmut Wick was shot down over the Solent having just achieved his 55th 'kill'. He baled out, but was never found and at 25 years of age, the Luftwaffe had lost one of its most successful airmen. Hauptmann Greisert was appointed Geschwaderkommodore in his place, but only on a temporary basis until 16 February when Major Wilhelm Balthasar took over command. During 1941, JG2 was responsible for protecting France – other than the north-eastern part which was protected by JG26. Balthasar was another outstanding fighter pilot, but he was to be killed at the beginning of July in combat with the

RAF and be replaced by Major Walter Oesau, called back from JG3 in Russia.

Tactically, the RAF had still not caught up with the Luftwaffe. The 'rule book' still required the fighters to fly in rigid formations, and in particular to adopt 'line astern' when in escort situations. By now, many pilots knew only too well that the 'finger four' and line abreast pair formations were much better but strictly speaking they were not able to use them.

Some did try to adapt. At Biggin Hill, they adopted a weaving type of line astern formation known as 'the snake' and whilst some of the pilots there felt that it was successful, other pilots could not understand why line abreast was not used when it clearly had so many advantages over the line astern which caused the needless loss and death of many 'tail-end Charlies'. Sixty years on, the spectre of such losses can still raise the emotions of some of the pilots. One said 'Oh how those Luftwaffe boys must have laughed to see us wriggling our way slowly through the skies leaving no. 4 frantically hanging on to the tail. There was only one effective aggressive and yet safe way to operate and that was in line abreast or the near cousin of the finger four.'

The continuation of the struggle between the two opposing fighter arms as always brought with it improvements in the aircraft flown. For the Luftwaffe, it meant the introduction of the Messerschmitt 109F – 'Friedrich' – variant to replace the E – 'Emil'. In appearance the two were different. The struts supporting the Emil's tailplanes disappeared and the Friedrich had rounded wing tips whilst the Emil's were square. The Friedrich also had a retractable tailwheel. There were several sub-variants of the E but those employed during the Battle of Britain were mainly the E-3 and E-4, both powered by a Daimler-Benz 601A engine. The E-3 was armed with two 7.9mm MG17 machine guns mounted on the engine, a single 20mm MG FF cannon which fired through the airscrew spinner and a single MG17 machine gun or 20mm cannon in each wing. The cannon mounted in the engine was found to be unreliable and the E-4 variant reverted to only the cowling-mounted machine guns and the wing armament.

In early 1940, more powerful engines were coming along and a prototype Friedrich was created by installing a 1,200 horsepower DB601E into a standard Emil airframe. From testing and experimental flying, the Friedrich configuration developed. In addition to the obvious visual changes it had improved Frise-surfaced ailerons and plain flaps to replace the slotted ones on the older versions. There were initial problems with the F-1 issued to the units in January 1941 when several crashed after the pilots lost control when they thought the engines were vibrating badly, but it transpired that the fault lay with the tail unit which at certain engine revs, developed a sympathetic oscillation which tore the tailplanes off.

As with the E, there were a number of variants of the F in use. The RAF was fortunate that in July 1941, an F-1 was forced down over Britain and was captured virtually intact which allowed comparison of its performance with the Spitfire. The F-1 carried two MG17 machine guns and a single MG FF cannon whilst the F-2 was similarly armed but with the MG FF cannon replaced by a 15mm MG151. This was a reduction in armament which raised some criticism by some pilots although the *experten* were not so concerned because of the consequent increase in performance. The F-3, the principal variant wasn't in common use until 1942 – although JG26 received its first Friedrichs at the beginning of 1941.

Like the Emil, there was also a fighter-bomber variant of the Friedrich, the F-4/B which could carry a single 250lb bomb mounted on the centreline.

The first indication to the RAF that a new version of the 109 was on its way was during the development phase at the end of 1940 when it appeared in small numbers over the English coast but at altitudes that were higher than the RAF's fighters could match comfortably. Then the 109Fs started carrying out fast, irritating bombing raids across the Channel.

For the RAF, the counter to the Friedrich was the Spitfire V. In appearance it was very similar to the II with only subtle differences. Developed towards the end of 1940 and the beginning of 1941, the V was a direct response to the 109F and could be described as a late variant Mark II with the more powerful Merlin 45 engine and the incorporation of all of the modifications made to the Mark II. But it was more complex than that. A natural developmental successor to the Marks I and II, the Mark III was being worked on by Supermarine and was to have been powered by a new, uprated Merlin – the Mark XX. The Spitfire Mark III should have included a strengthened airframe and undercarriage (which was to be angled two inches further forward) and a reduction in the wing area to improve the roll rate. But whilst the development proceeded, the need for an improved Spitfire to counter the threat from the Bf109F became urgent.

Planned as a temporary measure, the Spitfire V in the end was a strengthened Mark I airframe with a variant of the Merlin XX – the Merlin 45 – installed as the powerplant. This increased performance significantly. The top speed was now 369mph at just over 19,500 feet, the rate of climb 3,469 feet per minute at 14,000 feet and the ceiling increased to 38,000 feet which allowed it to match the new German fighters. In fact, the V would become one of the most widely used versions of the Spitfire and the Mark III was largely overtaken by it. Initially, the armament was eight .303 Browning machine guns fitted to the A wing, but this was quickly superseded by the B wing which took two 20mm cannon and four machine guns. Ultimately, the C or 'Universal' wing was introduced which could carry a mix of machine guns and cannon. Perhaps not surprisingly, the three versions of the Spitfire V were given the nomenclature 'a', 'b', and 'c'.

Jack Rae was a New Zealander who was flying with 485 Squadron from Redhill and Kenley during 1941 and later flew with 603 in Malta in 1942. His recollection was that the Spitfire Vb was 'slightly superior to the Bf109E at top speed and could out-turn it' whereas the 109F 'could outperform us at any altitude above 30,000 feet' but could not out-turn the Spitfire.

603 started to re-equip with the Vs when they arrived at Hornchurch in May 1941. Bill Douglas' log book shows that his first flight in a Spitfire V was on 18 May 1941 in R7299 (XT-F), a Va. It was a patrol lasting an hour and a half and he flew Spitfire Vs from then on, until later marks were introduced.

**

At Drem for the first two days of 1941 there was no flying for 603 Squadron and practice flights began again on the 3rd with the first operational patrol the following day. By the 5th 603 were back in the swing with 'operational and practice flying.'

On 6 January more newcomers reported to 603 Squadron: P/Os Burleigh, Delorme and C.A. Newman arrived fresh from 57 OTU, Hawarden while P/O Archie Winskill departed for 41 Squadron, at Hornchurch, where he later became a flight commander.*

With the Squadron grounded on 7 January due to bad weather Sergeant Pilots Compton, Cook, Lamb, Liddell and McNeill further bolstered the Squadron numbers when they also arrived from 57 OTU.

On 12 January operational and practice flying continued. John Strawson rejoined the Squadron but, along with Jack Stokoe, fell foul of the slope on the aerodrome when he crashed on landing. This incident provides us with the first mention of Strawson in the 603 ORB! Neither pilot was hurt.

On the 14th Sergeant Andy Darling also came a cropper on the Drem slope when he crashed on landing. Possibly as a result of the injury received on 25 October P/O John Soden returned to RAF Hornchurch at his own request. Soden was one of many lost aboard the troopship SS *Laconia*, when it was torpedoed and sunk by a U Boat on 12 September 1942 and is remembered on Column 247 of the Alamein Memorial.

On 18 January, Sgt Liddell was killed at Dyce ferrying an aircraft from Kinloss. Liddell had only moved to 603 seven days earlier.

The ORB reads: 'Operational and practice flying: F/Lt Ritchie I.S., posted from Unit to CUAS, Cambridge.'**

On 23 January Brian Carbury was attached to 603 Squadron from RAF Grangemouth and newly arrived MO, Flying Officer 'Doc' Skene, married Lucy Jamesona Milne in Edinburgh. The following day the Squadron continued with operational and practice flying but there was a buzz of the kind of excitement which had been missing in recent weeks when, at 14.15, 603 were ordered to intercept a hostile aircraft: Sgt Strawson (P7750), P/O Martel (P7359), F/O Berry DFC (P7564), F/L. Boulter (P7597), and Sgt Wilson (P7528). By now Ras was A Flight commander. The ORB reads:

---

*See Appendix 'Life After 603.'
**See Appendix 'Life After 603.'

5 aircraft from B Flight took off from Drem to patrol Turnhouse at cloudbase. They then received several vectors. When 10 miles off E. of May Island, saw Ju88 climbing into cloud behind and to starboard. Squadron did a steep climbing turn but only Blue 3 (Sgt Strawson) was able to fire a 1 second burst at 400 yards without result. E/a was then lost in cloud.

Due to disorientation and lack of fuel, Bolster and Wilson landed at Montrose. After refuelling they returned to Drem. All aircraft were down again by 15.30 except for Sgt Wilson who stooged around for another 45 minutes before landing at Montrose.

For the 25th the ORB reads: 'No Flying. Sgt Stokoe J., discharged from the RAF on appointment to a commission as a Pilot Officer, RAFVR.' According to Jack, his commission had been long overdue, a point which rankled.

On 29 January Brian Carbury was posted to 1 PDC (Personnel Dispersal Centre), Uxbridge. The reference in the ORB to him re-joining 603 Squadron and then moving to 1 PDC, Uxbridge, appeared on record but didn't actually involve him moving from his instructor's post at Grangemouth.

The next day the Squadron carried out 'operational, co-operation and practice flying'. Sgt Compton was injured when he also crashed at Drem while landing.

February 1941

On 1 February, in accordance with a contract issued by the Air Ministry, the artist Cuthbert Orde arrived at Drem to sketch a number of 603's Battle of Britain veterans including George Denholm, Ras Berry, Stapme Stapleton, David Scott-Malden and John Boulter. Brian Macnamara returned to 614 Squadron at Macmerry, a few miles east of Edinburgh.* On 2 February Pilot Officer Kenneth James McKelvie, son of 603 Squadron's first commanding officer, reported to the Squadron for flying duties from 58 Operational Training Unit (OTU) at Grangemouth. Operational, co-operational and practice flying continued throughout the month.

Keen for more frontline action P/O Jack Stokoe departed from 603 on the 3rd to join 54 Squadron which was at Catterick at the time. By that time he had amassed over 365 flying hours and on leaving 603, Squadron Leader George Denholm completed Jack's 'summary of flying assessments on posting' and rated him to be an 'above average pilot and shot.' Praise indeed but, in contrast, under 'any points in flying or airmanship which should be watched,' he added: 'suffers from overconfidence.'**

On 13 February Sgt Hurst was posted from 603 to RAF Drem and Sergeant Pilot H.K. Hall arrived from 54 Squadron. On the 16th tragedy struck. The ORB reads: 'Practice flying. F/Lt J.C. Boulter DFC seriously injured when crashed into by Hurricane at DREM while taking off.' Details of the accident vary. Stapme had flown with Boulter throughout the Battle of Britain and had been in his section during what proved to be his last flight and witnessed events:

> We had just landed at Drem and he was steering his Spitfire across the airfield towards the hangars when another Spitfire, which was in the process of taking off, hit his aircraft side-on, right on the cockpit. The other pilot had not seen him as the slope on the Drem airfield contributed to the lack of visibility. It was a very sad end to a very talented pilot.

The slope at Drem had previously proved to be a problem and this latest accident bore similarities to the accident involving Sheep Gilroy and Sergeant Price on arrival from Rochford the previous December.

With horrific leg and facial injuries Boulter was carefully removed from his cockpit by the very ground-crew members who had served him throughout the Battle of Britain. They recall with some emotion:

> When we reached him his face was a real mess... His legs were practically severed at the knees. Boulter was in the process of *taking off* when he hit the other Spitfire as it taxied

---

*See Appendix 'Life After 603.'
**See Appendix 'Life After 603.'

across the airfield, taking a short cut instead of carrying on after landing and using the peri track thus passing behind Boulter's Spitfire. We had no idea he had died the next day, we just assumed he died from his injuries the same day.

The interpretation of this accident varies with that of Stapme who could be considered the most reliable source as he was flying with Boulter when the accident occurred. There were two other squadrons at Drem at the time of the accident, 43, equipped with Hurricanes, which adds credibility to the entry in the 603 ORB, and 600 Squadron had a detachment of Spitfires at the airfield when the accident occurred adding credibility to the eyewitness accounts. Unfortunately the accident record card has not survived. Boulter was rushed to the nearby hospital at East Fortune, on the site of the World War I and II airfield. Now Scotland's Museum of Flight.

On 17 February P/O Gidman was posted to the unit from 54 Squadron and the sad news came from East Fortune Hospital that John Boulter had died of multiple injuries and shock. The tragic accident had robbed the Squadron of an outstanding and experienced pilot. He was buried in Dirleton Cemetery, near North Berwick town in East Lothian, a small, secluded, high-walled cemetery, which overlooks the site of the airfield from where he last flew. He was 28.

Wartime tragedy inflicted on the Boulter family had not started with the death of John. Before the war John's father had been a civilian worker in France and when the country fell to the advancing Germans he had been slow in leaving and was captured and interned. As the war progressed news reached his wife and children in England that he had fallen ill in captivity and died. John's younger

Dirleton cemetery, East Lothian. The grave of F/L J. C. Boulter.

brother was subsequently killed on operations with Bomber Command leaving just John and his mother. With John's death in February 1941, she had lost her husband and both sons in the war. She later moved from the south to live in Ladybank, Fife, where a number of the wives of 603 Squadron veterans made friends with her and kept in touch, specifically Betty Denholm who made initial contact and was a comfort to her during her grief. Following John Boulter's sitting for Cuthbert Orde two weeks earlier, the artist made the following observations about his subject:

> He seemed to me to be another example of the inherently tough type, though he was slighter in build than others I have mentioned in this connection. He was wiry and had a springy step and I guess him to have been stronger than he looked. He was a quiet and rather diffident person with extremely nice manners. I can visualise his lower lip thrusting forward when things are happening and I can see tenacity and determination.

From 18 to 23 February there was no flying due to bad weather. Practice flying resumed on the 24th but flying was again cancelled on the 27th when the veterans of 603 saw the return of P/O Bill Douglas from 610 Squadron. On the 28th practice flying continued in conjunction with the Squadron's move back to RAF Turnhouse.

Turnhouse March 1941

Depending on the weather practice flying continued. On the 3rd Sergeant Andy Darling was posted from 603 Squadron to 611 at RAF Hornchurch. Sadly, having achieved much success with the Edinburgh Squadron he didn't last long after leaving. The Scot was killed on 26 April 1941, as a sergeant pilot with 91 Squadron. His body was returned to Auchterarder for burial. He was 28.

On 4 March 1941 P/O Bill 'Tannoy' Read left to join 53 OTU at Heston as an instructor.*

On 5 March 1941, Uncle George, his flight commanders and veteran pilots put the inexperienced pilots through their paces during practice flights knowing that they would inevitably be returning to tougher fighting. P/O Newman was discharged from RAF Hospital, Rauceby, and travelled to the Queen Mary Hospital, RAF Halton for a medical examination. Following his accident on 30 January at Drem, Sgt Compton was admitted to Gogarburn Hospital, Gogar, situated on the south of the aerodrome. Sgt Cook was also admitted. On the 8th, 603's Medical Officer, F/O Doc Skene, was posted from 603 to RAF Turnhouse non-effective sick. On the 10th P/O Blackall joined 603 from 57 OTU, Hawarden and the next day Sergeant Pilots McKelvie and Jackman also arrived from 57 OTU. On 12 February F/O T.B. Purdy was attached to 603 from RAF Catterick for 'medical duties.' P/O Newman rejoined the Squadron from RAF Halton after successfully passing a medical board. Sergeants Compton and Cook rejoined the Squadron having been discharged from Gogarburn Hospital. On 14 March Sergeant Compton was posted from 603 to recently formed 485 Squadron at Driffield. On the 15th P/O Gidman was 'attached from unit to RAF Weetem for parachute packing course.' On 17 March Sergeant Hall was posted to 54 Squadron at Hornchurch.

On 19 March P/O Ludwik Martel was posted to 317 Squadron at Acklington. A devotee of 603 who carried out 70 sorties with the Squadron, Ludwik expressed reluctance to leave but despite his protestations the order was not rescinded. Ludwik Martel was awarded the KW, gazetted on 1 April 1941. On January 28 1942, Martel was rested from operational flying when he was sent to 58 OTU at Grangemouth, as an instructor. On 25 August, he returned to 317 Squadron. On 13 February 1943, Martel was sent to West Kirby, to prepare for an overseas move and on 13 March arrived in the Middle East in a C47, along with other Polish pilots sent to form the Polish Fighting Team. Otherwise known as 'Skalski's Circus', the unit was attached to 145 Squadron and operated in the Western Desert from 17 March until 12 May 1943. The Polish unit claimed the destruction of 30 enemy aircraft. On 4 April, Martel claimed a FW 190 damaged and on the 20th destroyed a Bf109 and damaged a Mc200. On returning to the UK, Martel was sent to his former unit, 317 Squadron, on 22 July 1943. On 20 August he went to 16 FTS at Newton as an instructor and on 4 November he once again rejoined 317 Squadron as a flight commander. On 20 September 1944, as 'tour-expired', he was posted to HQ, PAF. Martel received two Bars to his KW (gazetted on 20 December 1943) and was awarded the VM (5th Class), gazetted on 25 September 1944. On 4 March 1945, Martel was attached to the School of Air Support at Old Sarum, whilst undertaking a course. In January 1946, he went to HQ, BAFO, for operations room duties. He served with 131 Wing from 14 October 1946, until January 1947 when as a Flight Lieutenant he was released from the PAF. Ludwik Martel settled in England, attends the occasional London-based Battle of Britain related function, and lives in retirement in Wimbledon.

In 1982, Ludwik was reunited with his former CO of 603 Squadron when they attended the funeral of Black Morton. Ludwik met George and Betty at King's Cross and drove them to the Morton's Hampshire home. Afterwards, before returning the couple to King's Cross for their journey north, Ludwik drove the Denholms back to his flat in Wimbledon for tea. There, for the first time, Sasha Martel thanked George for looking after her husband during the Battle of Britain and making sure 'he was a good boy'!

As operational and practice flying continued, P/O Gidman returned from Weetem on 21 March. On the 24th F/O Stapme Stapleton proceeded to Headquarters Fighter Command for an interview regarding a move. He rejoined the unit the following day. Tour-expired, he was posted to 4 Delivery Flight on 27 March 1941. His wife and baby son, Mike, born in December 1940, went to live with her parents.**

No flying took place on 28 March due to bad weather but further operational and practice flights continued until the end of the month.

---

*See Appendix 'Life After 603.'
**For the full story of S/L B.G. Stapleton DFC, DFC (Dutch), see *Stapme* by David Ross (Grub Street 2002)

April 1941

On 1 April P/O K. J. McKelvie was posted to 603 from RAF Grangemouth and S/L George Denholm was posted to RAF Turnhouse from 603 Squadron. Uncle George had been with the Squadron for almost eight years and remained in command throughout the Battle of Britain. The station CO at Hornchurch, Group Captain Bouchier, recalled the arrival of George Denholm and the other 603 pilots during August 1940: '....with bent shoulders, hands in his pockets, followed by what seemed to me then to be the motliest collection of unmilitary young men I had seen for a very long time.' This was an unfortunate observation because George Denholm expected high standards. With the day's fighting over, he saw the need to keep his men together during the evening and insisted that they changed and washed for dinner, ate together in the mess any night circumstances allowed, and generally behaved in an exemplary manner. This had also given the pilots the opportunity to talk to one another. After dinner, instead of port, once in a while he served a glass of Drambuie to his pilots to remind them that they were in a Scottish squadron. He was always the first up each morning and, whenever possible, always flew the first patrol. He was also very concerned about the ground crew personnel and the others left on the ground. He was asked to pose by wartime portraitist Cuthbert Orde with the top button of his tunic undone, wearing a Fettes/Lorettonian scarf in order to give him a more rakish appearance. This irritated George as it was not an image he was keen to promote and he was always appropriately turned-out. To many, his age and experience of life was his strength.

On 22 October 1940 he had been awarded the DFC and was described by Marshal of the Royal Air Force Sir Arthur (later Lord) Tedder as: 'An outstanding Distinguished Flying Cross'. On 1 April 1941 he was sent to the operations room at Turnhouse and was on duty the night Rudolph Hess baled out of his Messerschmitt Bf110 on what was reputed to be a peace mission to Britain.

He had successfully commanded 603 during the most hectic period of their existence having led the men up at every opportunity. In addition to his flying duties he also had administrative duties to carry out ably assisted by his adjutant, including compiling a list of casualties following his return from a patrol. This he would do for the first hour. Sometimes news came in the form of a phone call from a pilot who had been forced to land at another airfield or who had baled out. On other occasions the call would come from a recovery team who had identified a crashed aircraft and its pilot. The paperwork following the latter, including notification of next of kin, was grim work. Disassociation from the memory of the courageous and eager young pilots who had been in his company just a short time before was essential. Some he had known only weeks, others he had known for many years. He knew they would have been fortunate to have died quickly and painlessly. There had been little time for grief. Desperate to continue to lead his men he was occasionally forced to relinquish leadership due to the mounting paperwork and handed over the task of leading the Squadron into battle to other experienced pilots such as Ken Macdonald and Jack Haig. It is a measure of the man and his belief in his responsibilities that, following 603's return north after the Battle of Britain, George used the leave granted to him to visit the widows and families of those in his Squadron who had perished.*

George Denholm was replaced by Canadian, Squadron Leader Forgrave Marshall Smith. Known as 'Hiram', he was posted to 603 from 72 Squadron at Acklington. Prior to that he had been recovering from wounds and serious burns after being shot down during the Battle of Britain.**

On 2 April P/O Blackall was married. On the 7th P/O Newman was granted leave until the 13th. The following entry was recorded in the ORB for 8 April: 'The flying hours for the Squadron for the week ending noon today were: A Flight 32.30 hours and B Flight 40.15 hours.' On the 10th Flight Lieutenant W.W. Lendon was posted to 603 as adjutant from his temporary post as SAO at Station Headquarters, attached from 13 Group. F/O Alen Wallace replaced Lendon as station adjutant for RAF Turnhouse after nine years with 603 Squadron. Also on that day, P/O Dudley Stewart-Clark returned to 603 from 11 Group Headquarters having recovered from the leg injuries received on 3 September the previous year.

On 13 April Ras Berry was taken off command of A Flight having been assessed as temporarily unfit and joined his former CO when he was attached to the operations room at Turnhouse. P/O 'Pug' Delorme became 'operational by day' with A Flight, which F/O Scottie Scott-Malden had been given

---

*See Appendix 'Life After 603.'
**See Appendix for biography of Hiram Smith.

Above: Standing: S/L R. Berry, F/L D. Stewart-Clark, F/L A. Wallace, S/L G.K. Gilroy, F/L J. Haig and S/L G.C. Hunter. Seated: S/L I. Kirkpatrick, S/L T.C. Garden, S/L G.L. Denholm, G/C E.H. Stevens, S/L I.S. Ritchie and S/L H.M. Pinfold. *Below:* 603 reunion in the garden of George and Betty Denholm's house, in the summer of 1941.

Top: Ras Berry later in the war, in North Africa.
Top right: Pug Delorme, June 1941.
Middle right: P/O Hugh Blackall and his dog.
Right: P/O P.J. Delorme and sweetheart.
Above: 'There's dirty work afoot!' 'Doc' Skene and 'Spy'
Blackbourn.

603 pipe band, Turnhouse, April 1941.

temporary command of in Ras's absence, and Dudley Stewart-Clark 'operational by day and night' with B Flight. The flying hours for the Squadron for the week ending noon on the 13th were: A Flight 110 hours and B Flight 110 hours.' A large increase on the previous week.

On the 16th Sergeant Pilot Hurst returned to duty from sick leave and posted to B Flight. On 17 April F/L Sheep Gilroy assumed command of 603 Squadron when S/L Smith left for a three-day visit of RAF Hornchurch, authorised by the Air Ministry.

The following day Sheep's cousin, P/O J.A.R. Falconer, reported for duty with 603 from 58 OTU and attached to A Flight. 'Hamish' was born to Mr and Mrs J.A. Falconer C.A., of Abingdon Lodge, Barnton, Edinburgh, and educated at Edinburgh Academy, Clifton Hall, Stowe and Cambridge, where he learnt to fly with the CUAS shortly before the war at the age of 19. In May 1940 he had married Charlotte Maxwell Smith, also of Edinburgh.

On the 22nd S/L Smith returned from the south and resumed command of the Squadron. Sheep was granted leave until 3 May and returned home to Tweedsmuir. The ORB states:

F/O H.A.R. Prowse.

> Gilroy anxious to superintend his sheep-farm for lambing – he owns about ninety score and is worried about the wintry weather on the Peebleshire Hills below Broughton. P/O Stewart-Clark appointed Squadron Sports Officer vice A/F/Lt Berry, wef., the 18th.

At 02.30 hours on 23 April, P/O Harry Prowse was in a car being driven by Lieutenant Thompson of the 55th (City of Edinburgh) Light Anti-Aircraft Battery, which drove into the back of one of three stationery lorries on the Turnhouse-Kirkliston road. Although they were returning from a night out it was reported that they had not seen the lorries due to the blackout conditions! Prowse was the only one injured, receiving a cut over his left eye. The entire left-hand side of the car was torn off making the 'escape of these two officers extraordinary.'

On the 25th Ras Berry was posted to operations at Turnhouse with effect from 18 April. The following day B Flight's Sgt Wilson was taken off flying duties by the MO for 48 hours. Total flying times for the week ending noon 27 April: A Flight 107 hours 50 minutes, B Flight 75 hours 55 minutes.

On the 29th Sgt Cook became operational whilst Sgt Jury was taken off flying duties for four days by the MO. The next day S/L Smith flew to Ayr for an investigation into a fatal air accident.

During April Ras was rested and posted to Turnhouse as a Fighter Controller.* He put his success and ability to survive aerial combat down to exceptional eyesight, although he wasn't aware of it at the time, and his short, stocky frame which increased his body's tolerance of g-Force:

> Tall, lean men like Hillary and Peter Pease, handsome fellows, and then there is me, squat and built like a you-know-what. They would black-out far sooner than I would thus allowing me to remain in control and not fall prey to the enemy fighter at that vital moment. There were many better pilots than me but at least I was able to fight in the Spit.

When asked if he had enjoyed shooting down Germans he said:

> That is a hard question to answer. I do know that when I saw Heinkel bombers just unleashing their load onto the poor populace of London it had an effect on me of making me hopping-mad, and I think from that moment on I had the feeling that there was something much more serious than just having dogfights in the air, and perhaps I think from then on it sunk in a bit more solidly than it had done before. I was enraged at that sort of bombing. I acquired what I can only describe as being a 'bloodlust'. Some people don't like killing anybody, I never thought of killing anybody, I just wanted to shoot them down.

By that time he had become one of the more successful pilots in 603. When asked if he had a killer instinct before the conflict he replied:

> Oh no, I was just getting on with my job at first, but then I felt pretty bloody-minded about it, and I kept this attitude, this bloodlust, throughout the war, as far as I could. My biggest feeling is that I was sorry to lose friends, but we had great support including that of the CO who exuded a quiet, but complete control, and I shared his sadness at the loss of all those fellows, they made a tremendous contribution. There were several good Auxiliary Squadrons but I happened to belong to 603, and I am glad that I can look back historically and see that it became the Queen's Squadron. It just adds to my pride of having gone from a little VR sergeant to become a flight commander.

Despite Nancy's illness Ras died before her in 2002. He is remembered as a wonderfully jolly man with a great sense of humour. He was also an outstanding member of the RAF and a brilliant pilot with 14 enemy aircraft destroyed, ten shared, nine probable, 17 damaged and seven destroyed on the ground. A very modest man, he once stated that he knew he had destroyed several more but was quite happy to settle for those he had been credited with.

May 1941

At 16.10 hours on 1 May, A Flight took off for Drem where they underwent one week's night flying under the command of F/O Scott-Malden. Sgt Lamb became operational and on the 2nd S/L Smith returned from Ayr but was '…ordered unfit for flying for a few days by order of the MO, suffering from chill with temperature.'

On 3 May Medical Officer, F/O Doc Skene, left for a course at The Queen Mary Hospital, RAF Halton. Having volunteered for duty overseas Sergeants Strawson and Wilson went on embarkation leave until the 10th when they reported for duty with 260 Squadron at Drem, flying Hurricanes.*

---

*See Appendix 'Life After 603.'

Sgt Pilot D.P. Lamb (left), and P/O P.J. Delorme, (right), known as 'Pug'. The man in the centre is unknown.

On 4 May Pilot Officers McKelvie and Falconer were declared operational. The following day P/O Burleigh was also made operational and Sgt Neill returned from leave and was sent to join A Flight at Drem.

On the 6th P/O Newman joined many of his colleagues from 57 OTU when he also became operational. S/L Smith returned to flying duties following his bout of illness and Sgt Stone returned from sick leave following his motorcycle accident on 13 December 1940 when John Strawson had been riding pillion.

At 15.45 hours Sgt Lamb was flying Spitfire P7288 when the aircraft fouled high tension cables near Dunkeld, north of Perth. Lamb managed to land near Perth where he discovered damage to the propeller and port wing. With that in mind he then took off and flew back to Turnhouse where he landed safely. He was unhurt.

On 8 May by order of the MO, Sgt William McKelvie was taken off flying duties for four days observation suffering from suspected diptheria. It was later diagnosed as tonsillitis.

The 9th saw the Squadron prepare for a return to RAF Drem. Sgt Jackman was made operational by day. The ORB reads: '13 Group say (telephone message from P.2) that we must provide one pilot for overseas, to go with 260 Squadron. No.85939, P/O M.J. Gidman volunteered and was accepted (A Flight).' Gidman joined former 603 colleagues Wilson and Strawson at Drem the following day.

On 11 May A Flight (F/O Scott-Malden, F/O Keith Prowse, P/O McKelvie and Sgt Pilot Jackman) proceeded to Drem.

CHAPTER 2

RETURN TO HORNCHURCH
16 MAY – 12 NOVEMBER 1941

On 12 May the MO, F/O Skene, returned from his course at RAF Halton and Sergeant Pilot Hunter reported for duty with the Squadron from 260 Squadron at Drem in exchange for Sgt John Strawson. The next day all arrangements were completed for the Squadron's move to Drem. For the morning of the 14th the ORB reads:

> Squadron Leader Chater (Officer i/c Operations) informed the Adjutant that the move to Drem had been cancelled and that we were to move to Hornchurch on the 16th.

On the 15th arrangements were carried out for the move, with a rail party from Turnhouse to travel via Waverley Station, Edinburgh, consisting of two flight sergeants, one sergeant, four corporals, 20 airmen and a rail party from Drem, travel via Waverley, consisting of one flight sergeant, one sergeant, one corporal and 24 airmen. All servicing crews were to travel down by air. At approximately 09.00 hours on the morning of 16 May 13 pilots took off from Turnhouse and Drem respectively for Hornchurch. They stopped off to refuel at Church Fenton. Half an hour after departing Turnhouse two Ferry Flight Harrows with 54 NCOs and men took off from Turnhouse and Drem respectively. The rail party left Edinburgh at 22.35 hours.

Nine months earlier 603 Squadron had carried out the same move with many of its pilots, both young and old, unaware of what lay ahead as they went to fight in a veritable cauldron of aerial activity. By the time 603 returned to Hornchurch in 1941 the aerial tactics had changed and the RAF were on the offensive. The 603 veterans of the previous summer had a distinct advantage over the newcomers and were able to pass on much of their experience.

The following morning the Squadron carried out a 'squadron formation' flying exercise. That afternoon S/L Smith led the Squadron on its first patrol in 1941 from Hornchurch.

At 15.00 hours on 18 May, S/L Smith led the Squadron away from the aerodrome. They were accompanied by Hornchurch Wing Commander Flying, A. Douglas Farquar, who many had known when he was the CO of 602 Squadron. Due to low cloud and haze over the Channel the operation was aborted and all pilots landed again safely.

At 17.20 hours on the 21st 11 Spitfires of 603 led by W/C Farquar took off from Hornchurch on a Circus

Top: Sealing the barrel of a cannon gun on a 603 Spitfire. AC1 A. Duff on left.
Bottom: Adjustment and re-loading of a cannon gun. Cpl Gillan (left) and Sgt Thompson.

– providing Channel cover for bomber offensive action. As they patrolled Gravelines at 18,000 feet they encountered a number of Bf109s and P/O Newman fired a short burst with no visible result. All pilots landed again at 18.45. The following day P/O Blackall was taken off flying by the MO and P/O Hamish Falconer was married back home in Edinburgh.

On 23 May, Dudley Stewart-Clark was admitted to hospital with cellulitis.* Sgt Bill McKelvie reported to the Squadron having been discharged from hospital in Edinburgh and was posted non-effective sick to RAF Station Hornchurch pending a medical board. According to the ORB the Squadron carried out three sweeps on the 23rd involving six aircraft. Flying over the Channel south of Ostende and inland over Gravelines the pilots saw no enemy action. Bill Douglas, flying W3123, later recorded flying:

> ...to within four miles of the Dutch coast but low cloud prevented useful observation. F/Lt Gilroy crossed the Belgium coast near Ostende, and inland coming out over Gravelines. Nothing to report owing to bad visibility. He was accompanied by F/O Stewart-Clark who, on landing, was taken off flying by the MO for the reasons stated above. S/Ldr Smith and A/F/Lt Scott-Malden carried out sweep over Channel. Visibility poor nothing to report.

Between 14.04 and 15.51 hours on 26 May the Squadron carried out a Rhubarb operation. The pilots split up over the Channel before crossing the coast at various points – Nieuwport, Dunkerque, Gravelines, Hardelot and west of Ostende in what was a heavy rainstorm. The following pilots were involved: S/L Smith (W3130), F/O Douglas (R7345), P/O Delorme (R7333), P/O Newman (R7229), P/O Mycelia (R7299), P/O Burleigh (X4669), F/O Scott-Malden (R7300) and F/O Prowse (R7339). Although enemy aircraft were spotted they could not be attacked owing to bad weather conditions. During the return flight Blue 1 fired a short burst at a cargo boat in the Channel.

On the 27th Hamish Falconer returned to Hornchurch following his marriage and short honeymoon. The next day F/O Harry Prowse and Sgt Hunter attended a conference on convoys at the Thames Naval Control, Southend. At 18.50 hours 11 aircraft of 603 Squadron, accompanied by W/C Farquar, led aircraft from Nos 54 and 611 Squadrons on a Rhubarb – 'follow-up sweep'. 603 Squadron consisted of: S/L Smith (W3130), Sheep Gilroy (X4669), F/O Scott-Malden (R7300), P/O Burleigh (R7223), P/O Delorme (R7339), P/O Falconer (R7226), P/O Blackall (X4665), P/O Newman (R7272), Sgt Lamb (R7345), Sgt Neill (R7227), and Sgt Cook (R7335).

The formation of 36 Spitfires split up over the Channel, climbed to 25,000 feet over Dungeness and crossed the French coast north of Boulogne. On sighting a number of Bf109s, 603 split into three sections of four aircraft. Flight Lieutenant Scott-Malden led one section and fired at two Bf109s one of which was probably destroyed, the other damaged. Sgt Pilot Cook also fired a short burst with no visible result. The Squadron returned to base on a course which took them over Gravelines at an altitude of 10,000 feet and landed at Hornchurch at 20.10 hours.

On 29 May, as part of his on-going recovery from cellulitis, Dudley Stewart-Clark was granted sick leave until 4 June. The *London Gazette* of 16 May published Dudley's promotion to Flying Officer, w.e.f. April.

June 1941
On 1 June the Squadron practiced formation flying and on the 2nd ten officers and ten sergeant pilots took off from Hornchurch and flew to Debden for a night-flying exercise. The following morning they flew back to Hornchurch and returned to Debden later that day where formation flying was practised. On the morning of the 4th the pilots returned to Hornchurch but then flew back to Debden in the evening before finally returning to Hornchurch on the 5th. Harry Prowse was granted 48 hours leave and Dudley Stewart-Clark returned to 603 Squadron. Also, on the 4th the Squadron adjutant, F/L Lendon, travelled to RAF Halton for a medical board at the CME after which he was granted 48 hours leave. At 12.00 hours 603 took off on a sweep, as recorded in the ORB:

*Cellulitis - a spreading infection of the skin with pus-forming bacteria. It is possible the infection from which he was suffering was the on-going legacy of the bullet wound to his leg received on 3 September 1940.

Top: Essential maintenance, Hornchurch 1941. Sgt Mackie supervising. Willy Wallace is on prop boss and Lamont on his left.
Bottom: 603 ground crew with striking mascot at Hornchurch 1941. Includes: George Mullay, Bill Ridd, George Cook, Arthur Clipstone, 'Tatty' Tate, John White, Olly Mevlin, Jimmy Hay, Vincent Oliver, Chic Cessford, Jock Struthers, 'Shirley' Ingles, Blake.

Top: F/L F.D.S. Scott-Malden DFC.
Bottom: P/O Raymond G. Marland.

10 of our aircraft took off as part of a large formation, from Hornchurch and Biggin Hill. Sweep operations were carried out over N.E. France. All our pilots returned with the exception of Pilot Officer R.J. Burleigh, flying Spitfire XT-O, W3111. Pilot Officer Burleigh (No.81423) was last seen diving through cloud, apparently in pursuit of an enemy aircraft. No further details obtainable up to 16.00 hours. The incident took place over N.E. France vicinity of Boulogne. F/O Douglas proceeded on leave to the 13th June.

That afternoon 603 were on patrol over Barrow Deep. On 6 and 7 June patrols continued with Scott-Malden claiming a 109 damaged on the latter. On the 8th George Denholm visited and accompanied Sheep Gilroy on a 20-minute 'air test' in R7229, XT-M. While George was satisfying his urge to fly a Spitfire again, the Squadron carried out two shipping patrols. For 9 June the ORB reads: 'A/F/Lt. Scott-Malden completed 170 hours operational flying since June 1940.' Five shipping patrols were maintained that day without incident.

On the 11th Sergeant Pilots Ian Paget, a New Zealander, and Desmond Ruchwaldy arrived from 53 OTU, Heston. Sheep Gilroy carried out a competitive 55-minute …'air test v G/C Broadhurst'. Meanwhile the Squadron mounted more shipping patrols. Flying continued well into the evening when 12 Spitfires took off at 20.05 on patrol of the airspace over Dungeness at 25,000 feet.

The following day six shipping patrols took place involving 14 of the Squadron pilots. That evening P/O R.J. Burleigh's brother-in-law, Mr E.G.L. Russell, called at the officers' mess where, according to the ORB: 'We supplied him with all the available information we had with reference to our missing colleague.' On 13 June 603 Squadron carried out 19 sorties involving 12 pilots.

On the morning of 14 June Sheep Gilroy was up early to carry out an air test in R7223 XT-O. At 07.05 hours 12 Spitfires took off from Hornchurch to take part in an offensive patrol from Gravelines to Ostende led by S/L Hiram Smith (W3130): F/L Scott-Malden (R7300), Sgt Jackman (R7227), P/O Delorme (R7333), F/O Douglas (W3110), F/O Stewart-Clark (R7345), P/O Blackall (X4665), Sgt Stone (R7229), F/O Prowse (R7339), P/O Falconer (R7229), F/L Gilroy (W3113 XT-O), Sgt Lamb (R7223).

Scottie, Harry Prowse and Bill Douglas claimed four Bf109s damaged of which two were later allocated to 603 as having been destroyed. All pilots landed safely. Later that same day the ORB provides details of a Rhubarb:

15.05: F/O Stewart-Clark and Sgt Pilot Cook took off proceeding out over Deal and then 25 miles to the North-East. Cloud was 5/10 at 6,000 feet so they returned. Nothing seen and landed at 15.57 hours. F/Lt. Gilroy and Sgt Pilot Lamb went from Dungeness but visibility poor so returned and landed at 16.20 hours. F/O Prowse and Sgt Pilot Neill saw convoy of six ships half a mile off Dunkerque. They attacked a Dutch barge about 2 miles ahead of convoy, coming down to 500 feet they made two attacks each, bullets were seen to hit the deck. There was no return fire.

On the 15th the Squadron carried out a number of shipping patrols without incident. At 18.15 that evening 12 Spitfires of 603 took part in an offensive patrol. Situated above and behind 54 Squadron they flew across the coast of France at Gravelines sweeping inland and over Cap Gris Nez then back to Dungeness where they split up and made a further sweep ten miles south-west of Calais. No enemy aircraft were sighted.

F/O W. A. Douglas.

Rochford

On 16 June 603 had a particularly busy day. According to Sheep Gilroy's log book he flew three sorties. Having already been airborne for ten minutes two successive patrols were cancelled. They were then ordered to move from Hornchurch to Rochford, Southend: 'Thirteen Officers, two W.Os, three Flight Sergeants, five Sergeants, 11 Sgt Pilots, 108 Airmen, a total of 145 with 18 aircraft.' The day's flying was far from over. The ORB provides the details:

Spitfires

Mark Va	Crew	Duty	Time Up	Down	Details of Sortie
W3110	F/O Douglas	Patrols	05.00	06.10	Barrow Deep
R7229	Sgt Hurst		"	"	
R7305	F/O Stewart-Clark		05.45	07.00	
R7272	Sgt Stone		"	"	
R7339	F/O Prowse		06.25	07.30	
R7226	Sgt Cook		"	"	
R7300	F/Lt Scott-Malden		07.05	08.10	
W3123	Sgt Neill		"	"	
X4665	P/O Blackall		07.45	08.45	
R7221	Sgt Salt		"	"	
R7229	Sgt Hurst		11.45	12.00	Dover to Deal
X4665	P/O Blackall		"	"	
W3110	F/O Douglas		"	"	
R7225	F/O Stewart-Clark		"	11.55	
X4669	XT-X F/Lt Gilroy		"	"	
R7272	Sgt Hunter		"	"	
R7300	F/Lt Scott-Malden		11.55	12.05	
R7226	Sgt Cook		"	"	
R7229	F/O Prowse		"	"	
R7227	Sgt Jackman		"	12.10	
R7333	P/O Delorme		"	12.05	
W3123	Sgt Neill		"	"	
X4669	XT-X F/Lt Gilroy		12.40	12.50	Rochford
X4665	P/O Blackall		"	"	
R7229	Sgt Hurst		"	12.55	
W3110	F/O Douglas		"	"	
W3130	S/Ldr Smith		16.40	18.10	
R7300	F/Lt Scott-Malden		"	18.15	
R7339	F/O Prowse		"	18.10	
R7335	Sgt Cook		"	"	
R7333	P/O Delorme		"	18.15	
W3123	Sgt Neill		"	18.10	
R7229	Sgt Hurst		16.45	18.15	
R7305	F/O Douglas		"	"	
X4665	P/O Blackall		17.50	"	
X4669	XT-X F/Lt Gilroy		18.20	"	
R7221	Sgt Salt		"	"	
R7223	Sgt Stone		"	"	
X4669	XT-X F/Lt Gilroy		21.00	21.50	
R7299	P/O Falconer		21.05	21.55	
W3110	F/O Douglas		21.30	22.40	
R7229	Sgt Hurst		"	"	
W3130	S/Ldr Smith		21.35	21.45	
W3132	Sgt Neill		"	"	
X4669	XT-X F/Lt Gilroy		22.20	22.55	
R7299	P/O Falconer		22.25	22.55	

Another busy day followed on the 17th. The ORB records that the pilots flew to Hornchurch before carrying out a number of shipping patrols throughout the afternoon. At 19.05 12 Spitfires took off and joined forces with aircraft from 54 and 611 Squadrons from Hornchurch and climbed to 21,000 feet over Dungeness before sweeping between Boulogne and Cap Gris Nez four times, each time losing height before climbing back into the sun. No enemy aircraft were sighted.

On 17/18 June shipping/offensive patrols were mounted. All consisted of pairs. No enemy aircraft were encountered. The pilots reported conditions to be generally hazy and thin cloud at 28,000 feet. By now Sheep Gilroy had amassed a total of 468 hours on Spitfires and a grand total of 682 hours 30 minutes flying time.

At 19.00 hours on 19 June 12 Spitfires took off from Rochford and rendezvoused with 611 Squadron over Gravesend and three Blenheims over Detling at 'Angels' 2. 603 consisted of: S/L Smith (W3130), F/L Scott-Malden (R7300), P/O McKelvie (R7299), P/O Delorme (R7333), P/O Falconer (R7227), Sgt Cook (W3123), F/L Gilroy (X4669, XT-X), P/O Newman (R7272), P/O Blackall (X4665), F/O Stewart-Clark (W3110), Sgt Lamb (R7305), and Sgt Hurst (R7221).The pilots flew above the formation over Dungeness where they split into sections and provided 'low cover' for what was a bombing raid on shipping.

Five 109s dived on to the formation. F/O Stewart-Clark fired at long range without result. Sheep recorded in his log book that during a dogfight he fired at two 109s.

On returning to base P/O Delorme had trouble landing owing to oil on his windscreen which prevented him from seeing clearly. First contact with the airfield was heavy and the port oleo leg broke away. He immediately throttled-up and took off for another circuit before making a good landing on one wheel and, eventually, one wing tip. The aircraft was repaired on station.

On 20 June five uneventful shipping patrols were carried out. At 05.15 on the 21st Scottie (R7300) and P/O McKelvie (R7299) took off and carried out a patrol over Barrow Deep before landing again at 06.25. At 12.05, 12 Spitfires took off as part of a Target Support Wing for an attack on St Omer: F/L Gilroy (X4669, XT-X), F/O Stewart-Clark (R7345), P/O Blackall (R7223), Sgt Salt (R7221), P/O Newman (W3184), Sgt Hurst (R7229), F/L Scott-Malden (R7300), Sgt Jackman (R7227), Sgt Neill (W3123), P/O Mycelia (R7299), P/O Delorme (W3130), P/O Falconer (R7224).

Sgt Jackman destroyed a Bf109-E, which was seen to explode, and damaged another. Sheep and Scottie together with Sgt Pilot Neill each damaged 109s.

Dudley Stewart-Clark's Spitfire was badly shot-up and he was forced to crash-land in the sea over Goodwin Sands. On being hit he had hastily unfastened his seat harness in preparation for baling out, but on realising he had insufficient height to jump he remained with his aircraft. Unfortunately, his harness was still undone when he landed in the sea and on impact with the surface he was thrown forward against the windscreen frame resulting in a gashed forehead and a lacerated thumb. He managed to climb out of the cockpit and into his dinghy which, he was relieved to discover, had inflated adequately on the choppy surface. Meanwhile, Sheep Gilroy maintained vigilant guard overhead and continued to circle until, low on fuel, he landed at Manston. With tanks hastily refilled he took off again and continued his vigil for a further 30 minutes until he saw his colleague picked up by a motor launch of the rescue services. On landing back at Rochford Sheep completed his paperwork and went on leave until the 29th.

Following a patrol over Barrow Deep at first light, 603 Spitfires were in action again between 15.45-17.15 hours for a Forward Support Wing sweep which took them over Cap Gris Nez: P/O Blackall (X4669), F/O Douglas (W3110), Sgt Salt (R7223), P/O Newman (R7272), Sgt Stone (R7305), S/L Smith (W3130), F/L Scott-Malden (R7300), Sgt Jackman (R7335), P/O Falconer (R7226), P/O Mycelia (R7299), and Sgt Jury (W3132).

Sgt Jury crash-landed but was unhurt. During the operation Scottie claimed a 109 damaged and F/O Bill Douglas shot down another which was seen on fire.

On 22 June P/O Newman left to attend a medical board at The Queen Mary Hospital, RAF Halton, the next morning. At 15.10, 11 Spitfires took off from Rochford on a Target Support Wing operation over Hazebrouck, flown by: S/L Smith (W3130), Sgt Cook (R7335), F/L Scott-Malden (R7300), P/O Delorme (R7399), Sgt Hurst (R7226), Sgt Jackman (R7299), Sgt Jury (R7236), F/O Douglas (X4469), Sgt Stone (R7272), Sgt Lamb (R7223), and Sgt Salt (R7271). Due to technical problems a twelfth Spitfire, X4665, flown by P/O Blackall did not take off.

As the formation climbed, they rendezvoused with a Hurricane squadron over the aerodrome. As the Spitfires crossed the coast they split into sections, as had become the practice when they were about to go into combat. As they approached Hazebrouck they spotted a number of 109s and climbed to attack; unfortunately they lost sight of them but P/O Delorme saw one 109 go down in flames over the target. Sgt Pilot Lamb came across two others and managed to squeeze-off a three-second burst with no visible results. During the trip back to Rochford, Lamb shot up an enemy gun position and a white motorboat before landing with the rest of the Squadron.

At 18.30 P/O Delorme (R7339) and Sgt Salt (R7221) carried out another patrol over Barrow Deep landing again at 19.20 and 19.30 respectively.

While the two Spitfires were airborne a larger force of 603 Spitfires took off from Rochford at 19.15 for what was an uneventful shipping patrol, landing after just 15 minutes. Thirty-five minutes later the pilots were once again ordered into the air for a further shipping patrol and later that evening they carried out two further patrols over Barrow Deep. Both without incident.

On the 23rd the Station Medical Officer ordered Dudley Stewart-Clark on 14 days sick leave following his exploits on the 21st. Stewart-Clark was eventually posted to 72 Squadron but was shot down and killed on 19 September as a Flight Lieutenant. He is buried in Pihen-les-Guines Communal Cemetery, France.

At 12.55 ten 603 Spitfires joined forces with those of 54 and 611 Squadrons at Hornchurch and carried out a Target Support Wing operation over Boulogne, sweeping in over the French coast at Gravelines: F/O Douglas (W3110), Sgt Lamb (R7223), Sgt Stone (R7229), P/O Blackall (X4665), Sgt Hurst (R7305), S/L Smith (W3130), Sgt Jury (R7339), F/L Scott-Malden (R7300), P/O McKelvie (R7299), P/O Delorme (W3121), and Sgt Cook (R7335).

54 Squadron pilots were first to spot a number of 109s and with 603 close behind, they dived to attack. As various dogfights ensued Sgt Lamb's aircraft was hit by a cannon shell which exploded in the fuselage. He managed to nurse his Spitfire back over the English coast before crash-landing near Dover. He was fortunate to have escaped unhurt. Bill Douglas was less fortunate. Bounced from above by four 109s he was hit in both legs and one arm by cannon shell splinters. His injuries were not serious and he managed to recover English soil before landing near Hawkinge. Later that evening an offensive patrol over Dunkerque and Murdyck went without incident.

At 19.55 hours on 24 June, 12 603 Spitfires were part of a Target Support Wing over Gravelines with their now familiar company of 54 and 611 Squadrons. P/O Falconer (R7226), Sgt Cook (R7335), Sgt Neill (R7227), P/O Mycelia (W3121), S/L Smith (W3130), F/L Scott-Malden (R7339), F/O Prowse (X4669), P/O Newman (R7221), Sgt Hurst (R7305), Sgt Hunter (X4665), Sgt Lamb (W3364), and Sgt Stone (R7229).

Combat with enemy fighters ensued and P/O Newman destroyed a Bf109E and, once again, Sgt Pilot Lamb's Spitfire was shot-up and he force-landed near Walmer. Following this sweep P/O Kenneth J. McKelvie was reported missing, later presumed dead. He had last been seen by his colleagues north of the coast off Gravelines. At first light the following morning the CO, S/L Smith (W3123) and P/O Newman (X4663) carried out a search of the Channel 'off Clacton' with little hope of finding any sign of young McKelvie. His body was never found. The 19-year-old son of 603 Squadron's first Commanding Officer, Jimmy McKelvie, Kenneth is commemorated on the Runnymede Memorial, Panel 33.

At 11.55 on the 25th nine Spitfires took part in an offensive sweep with 54 and 611 Squadrons, crossing the French coast at 12.29. They circled Hazebrouck between 12.35 and 12.44 remaining alert throughout for enemy aircraft. Non appeared and when the bombers arrived the Spitfires escorted them in to the target and out again. The ORB reads:

1 Blenheim and 2 Spitfires crash landed on aerodrome, 1 Spitfire belonged to 611 Squadron and 1 to 222 Squadron. The Blenheim was from 21 Squadron and had been severely shot up. On landing they crashed into a petrol bowser. The pilot was injured only slightly but 2 of the crew were badly hurt.

15.50: Together with 54 and 611 Squadrons 7 of our A/C conducted a sweep over St Omer which was reached at 16.32. They left at 16.42 hours. No E/A were near enough to fire at.

On 26 June 11 Spitfires took off from Hornchurch on a sweep over the French coast described in the ORB as a 'Dunkerque Cover Wing': Sgt Hunter (X4663), Sgt Salt (X4665), P/O Newman (R7272), Sgt Cook (W3213), Sgt Stone (W3113), Sgt Jury (R7227), P/O Falconer (R7226), F/L Scott-Malden (R7300), Sgt Neill (R7299), P/O Delorme (W3118), S/L Smith (W3130), and F/O Prowse (R7339).

They intercepted a number of 109s and dogfights followed. F/O Harry Prowse and P/O Delorme each damaged a Bf109E. On landing at Rochford P/O Newman was reported missing last seen over the coast of France. At 15.20 ten aircraft took off on a standing patrol over Manston at 'Angels' 16. Nothing was seen.

At 20.51 on the 27th 12 aircraft joined up with 54 and 611 Spitfires and crossed the English coast over Deal at 'Angels' 13 with 603 'on top'. Climbing all the way over the Channel they crossed the French coast east of Gravelines, reaching the target at 21.38 hours. The weather conditions were described as misty and light flak was observed further inland than usual. Having circled the target once in wing formation they then split into sections for combat. However, no enemy aircraft were encountered. Back at Rochford new arrivals P/O N.H.C. Keable and Sgt Pilot Wood arrived from 41 Squadron at Catterick and 64 Squadron at Drem, respectively.

At 07.55 hours on 28 June 12 603 Spitfires took off on a Target Support Wing operation, again joining forces with 54 and 611 Squadrons over the aerodrome at 'Angels' 13. From over North Foreland a wide sweep was made to 24,000 feet. By 08.30 the formation was over Gravelines. At 08.33, halfway to Lille, the Squadron met another formation coming from the west, joined up with them and flew on to the target. Fires were seen in and around Lille but no enemy aircraft were encountered. Later that morning Sergeants Lamb and Hurst carried out a shipping patrol.

Following eight two-ship patrols throughout the morning of 30 June, 11 Spitfires formed part of a support wing with Lens as the target. at 17.40: S/L Smith (W3130), P/O Delorme (W3118), Sgt Jackman (R7335), Sgt Paget (R7226), Sgt Neill (R7123), F/L Gilroy (R7221), Sgt Stone (W3213), Sgt Lamb (W3369), Sgt Hunter (R7305), P/O Blackall (X4665), Sgt Salt (W3138), and F/O Prowse (W3184). For technical reasons Blackall didn't get off the ground.

En route they were attacked by Bf109s. F/O Harry Prowse destroyed a Bf109E but this was tempered by the loss of Sgt L.E.S Salt who was reported missing following this mission. He was last seen over the coast north of Gravelines. During the day the following sergeant pilots reported for duty: W.B. Rudd and G.W. Tabor from 152 Squadron, Portreath, W.J. Archibald from 111 Squadron, Dyce, A.C. Hendry from 602 Squadron, Ayr (detached Montrose) and D.J. Prytherch from 72 Squadron at Acklington.

July 1941

The beginning of the month was warm and brought with it cloudless skies that gave the slow Blenheims no protective bolt holes should the Luftwaffe find them. But it also brought haze and a thundery, heavy feel to the air.

Pilots operational with 603 during the second half of 1941, included: Squadron Leader Smith, Flight Lieutenants Duncan Smith, Scott-Malden and Gilroy, Flying Officer Prowse, Pilot Officers Delorme, Falconer, Blackall and Keable, Sergeants Lamb, Hunter, Jackman, Tabor, Prytherch, Ruchwaldy, Archibald, Rudd, Paget, Neill, Cook and Stone.

Spitfires used included R7300, R7335, W3136, W3112, R7299, X4669, X4665, W3138, W3113, W7221, W3213, W3184, X4663, W3369, R7221, R7227, W3118, R7229, R7227.

P/O Nigel Keable.

From left to right: Cpl B.Robb, Sgt Ruchwaldy and E. Moffat. Hornchurch, 1941.

Tuesday 1 July started with two convoy patrols over Barrow Deep just after breakfast, and then in the evening, 12 Spitfires took part in a Circus which had been postponed from the morning because of the weather. Led by S/L Smith, they took off from Rochford at 17.40 as part of the Target Support Wing with 54 and 611 Squadrons who they met over Gravesend. Visibility was still poor and there were misgivings about continuing with the operation. The escorts should have rendezvoused with the Blenheims over Canterbury but they met them over the North Foreland instead. The bombers decided that visibility wasn't good enough to go on, so they aborted the operation, but didn't tell the escorting fighters. By now, 603 had lost sight of the bombers in the heat haze and they circled for a while over Calais then made for Gravelines where they again orbited, searching for the bombers, but being unable to find them, returned to Rochford landing at about 19.15. One Spitfire, X4663, flown by P/O Keable returned early, landing at 17.50.

The 2nd and 3rd were similar – hot and sultry – with the Squadron operating over the nearby French coast. At lunchtime on the 2nd, six Spitfires were tasked with a Lysander escort. Lysanders were high winged monoplanes with a fixed undercarriage – ungainly looking aircraft – but robust and slow flying which made them ideal to act in an air/sea rescue role. They searched for downed aircrew and dropped them dinghies if needed. On the 3rd, after five early morning convoy patrols, there were two Circus operations – 30 and 31 – to Hazebrouck with 603 in the target support role for them both. The ops were in the late morning and the early afternoon which meant that the pilots returned from the first at about 12.15 and were off again at 14.45. The same pilots and many of the same aircraft flew on both so it would be a busy couple of hours for the turnaround.

There was some success in the morning. After taking off at 11.00, they once again met 54 and 611 Squadrons and left the English coast 25 minutes later at Deal at a height of 19,000 feet. At 11.30 they crossed the enemy coast west of Gravelines. Five minutes later, nearing Hazebrouck they observed some flak below them but it caused no problems. They split into three sections, in pairs and line astern. Red and Green Sections spotted the Blenheims on their way out from having bombed and gathered protectively behind them. They were back at Gravelines at 11.45 but headed up the coast towards Dunkerque where they understood some 'friendlies' were coming out at low level. No enemy aircraft were met. P/O Blackall reported a parachute on the sea about a mile off Gravelines. But Yellow Section met some 109s near Hazebrouck:

Yellow 3, Sgt Neill saw an Me109 coming towards him in a slight dive, and turned after it losing the rest of the section. He then climbed and saw an Me.109 in a climbing turn. He fired at it, as it started to dive, at extreme range, no results were seen. Yellow 1 and 2, Flying Officer Prowse and Pilot Officer Falconer dived after 5 Me.109's 1,000 feet below them in echelon starboard. Yellow 1 attacked the right hand E/A which started climbing. He closed to 350 yds. And fired a short burst from astern. E/A put his nose down and Yellow 1 followed, but his engine cut and E/A had drawn away to 500 yds and started climbing. Yellow 1 and Yellow 2 then at 15,000 feet, turned to port and saw an Me109F flying South near St. Omer.

Yellow 1 got onto his tail. E/A climbed, Yellow 1 was catching it up and fired from 350 yds. E/A put his nose down, Yellow 1 followed but was slightly outdived. Yellow 2 flew level waiting for E/A to climb again. E/A climbed again followed by Yellow 1, and Yellow 2 fired a five second burst, from underneath Yellow 1, at E/A from 300 yds as E/A was on top of his climb. E/A then dived. Yellow 1 and Yellow 2 followed, and by this time were at 9,000 feet over Fruges. E/A then dived to 0 feet, Yellow 1 followed, and Yellow 2 stayed above. E/A then climbed, but Yellow 2 when within range was prevented from firing by his windscreen oiling up. Yellow 1 then gave E/A a final burst. Throughout this engagement E/A was emitting puffs of black smoke, mostly when climbing. These gradually increased in duration and density until E/A was last seen diving towards a wood with continuous thick black smoke. The E/A is claimed as a probable.

Yellow 1 and 2 then went NW heading for Boulogne. They passed over Desvres, along the south perimeter of the aerodrome at 300 feet. They saw no gun posts or personnel, but about 12 'houses' with slits in the front through which they saw the airscrews of E/A. Each 'house' was between two trees which overhung the roof. They then passed a gun post on their left just NW of Samer, and saw people standing about in their shirt sleeves who ran to the gun but did not fire. Then North of Alprech, they saw heavy guns and M.G.'s, the guns were pointing SE. Men were inside the enclosures, 4 men to each gun, they wound the guns round and fired. M.G. bullets fell into the sea behind Yellow 1 and Yellow 2 and black flak bursts were seen accurate to height but 200 yards behind. The apparent speed of the fusing astonished Yellow 1 and Yellow 2.

Sgt Jackman claimed an Bf109F destroyed and Prowse and Falconer another as a probable.

The above extract is taken from the report produced by the 603 Intelligence Officer, Flying Officer 'Spy' Blackbourn, on the operation. It's worth noting that whilst 603 was flying in the much disliked line astern, the pilots reported seeing four Bf109s in echelon, which was a superior combat formation. The level of detail recorded is also interesting, but is countered by the lack of understanding of the operations as a whole by the individual pilots. One pilot commented that it was only after the war and when reports were made public, that he understood just what was going on. Even the complexity of the Circus operations was not fully understood, each pilot did what he had to do being told only what he needed to know.

During the second Circus, P/O Paul Delorme claimed another 109F as a probable.

On the 3rd some pilots flew three sorties – a convoy patrol and two Circuses – and there was no let-up on the 4th and, although there were no morning convoy patrols, 603 was on operations again after lunch. Early in the morning at 05.21 Wing Commander Hughie Edwards was leading nine Blenheim IVs of 105 Squadron off from RAF Swanton Morley to join six from 107 Squadron from RAF Great Massingham on a low-level daylight raid on docks, railways and factories in the German city of Bremen in the north of the country. The operation was codenamed 'Wreckage'. Both Squadrons lost two Blenheims and the surviving aircraft all landed back at their bases by about 11.00 hours. A daring and audacious raid, it incurred significant losses for the attackers, but inflicted great damage on the enemy.

Meantime, Circus 32 was being laid on for the afternoon. The target was a power station and the Kuhlmann chemical plant at Chocques, a small French town a few miles west of Béthune not far from the Dutch border. The raiding force comprised 12 Blenheims – six each from 21 and 226 Squadrons. 226 Squadron based at RAF Wattisham had already flown an operation against Nordenay that morning as a diversionary raid in support of the attack on Bremen.

It was a full blown Circus operation with 14 fighter squadrons – including 603 – in support roles. The Hornchurch and Tangmere Wings provided target support – 54, 611 and 603 from the former and 145, 610 and 616 from the latter. Escort cover was the Biggin Hill Wing with 74, 92 and 609 Squadrons; close escort was provided by 24 Hurricanes from 71 and 242 Squadrons based at North Weald and finally rear support came from 12 Group – 56, 65 and 601 Squadrons. The weather at North Weald was 'fair with good visibility'.

Whilst not directly concerning 603, it is of passing interest that a number of subsequently well-known pilots were flying, including 'Sailor' Malan, Paul Richey, and Dickie Barwell from Biggin Hill – indeed they flew on many of the operations that 603 were flying at that time. The Hornchurch

Station Commander, Group Captain Harry Broadhurst was flying with 54 Squadron. He often flew on operations and this particular sortie would be one that he wouldn't forget. Douglas Bader, the Tangmere Wing Leader, also flew on many of the operations that 603 was involved in.

21 Squadron were based at RAF Watton in mid-Norfolk and they took off at 13.45 and headed for Southend to meet their escort. At 14.15, the 24 Hurricanes of 71 and 242 Squadrons left North Weald whilst 54 and 611 Squadrons took off from Hornchurch and 603 departed Rochford. 603 was led by S/L Smith (W3130) with: F/L Gilroy (W3113), F/O Prowse (R7379), P/O Delorme (W3118), P/O Falconer (R7380), P/O Keable (X4663), P/O Blackall (X4665), Sgt Jackman (R7299), Sgt Prytherch (R7335), Sgt Hunter (W3184), Sgt Tabor (W3138) and Sgt Archibald (W3369).

54 and 611 Squadrons reached the rendezvous at 14.27 and joined up with 603. In the meantime, the close escort Hurricanes also met up with the Blenheims and the escort cover squadrons from Biggin and at 14.30, the 'bee-hive' set course for France. 603 went with them, but for some reason, 54 and 611 Squadrons failed to leave although they noticed 603 going, but hadn't appreciated that they were going with the bombers. They continued to orbit for another five minutes then hastened after the others now making for Gravelines where they crossed the coast about 15 minutes later.

The Luftwaffe reacted strongly. I and III Gruppen of JG26 scrambled with one of the JG2 Gruppe and a series of running dogfights started shortly after the RAF aircraft crossed the coast. The Bf109s attacked in strength but were held at bay by the various escort squadrons and the bombers were able to reach the target area unmolested.

At 14.45, south west of Hazebrouck at 17,000 feet 603 Yellow Section spotted some 109s below them and Yellow 1 and Yellow 2 dived to attack. Pilot Officer Delorme, Yellow 3, decided to orbit to cover them but saw another two 109s in line abreast ahead of him and slightly below. He closed to 100 yards of the 109 on the port side and gave it a series of long bursts, closing all the while until he reckoned he was within 50 yards of it. The 109 turned and went into a gentle dive trailing black smoke. Delorme continued to fire at it, eventually seeing the starboard wing disintegrate at the root. The 109 fell out of the sky, the smoke thickening.

Its companion broke and managed to get behind the Spitfire, but before it could do any damage, Delorme made an aileron turn and in the dive that followed, the 109 was out of range. Delorme made a beeline for some cloud at 5,000 feet and slipped the 109. Having lost contact with the rest of the Squadron, he returned to base at zero feet. He claimed the 109 as destroyed.

The escort cover squadrons from Biggin Hill were also busy with the 109s which gathered at the back of the formation in an attempt to get to the bombers, but the Blenheims reached the target area unscathed at about 15.00 although the 109s eventually managed to get at them over Chocques. Heavy cloud cover made it difficult for the bombers to hit the target with any degree of accuracy. They did however go for the power station which was their primary target, then turned away to start the flight home. Most of the fighter squadrons were in action, including the Hurricanes from North Weald. The dogfights continued unabated.

Group Captain Harry Broadhurst, flying Red 1 with 54 Squadron, found himself in trouble with some 109s which were trying to get at the Blenheims. He attacked one which was on a climb and observed flames coming from its starboard wing root, then engaged another whose wing fell off. In the middle of another melee, he was hit by more enemy fire which damaged his Spitfire severely and wounded Broadhurst on his left side in the thigh and arm. The damage was such that he turned for home and landed back at Hornchurch with the wheels up.

One of the other victims was 603's F/O Harry Prowse. P/O Falconer saw him diving low over the airfield at St Omer and called him up on the R/T. Prowse replied that he was 'OK', but he didn't return and was posted as missing. But on 16 July the Squadron learnt that he was uninjured and a prisoner when Flight Sergeant Scott said that he had been listening to a German propaganda broadcast by 'Lord Haw-Haw' who had mentioned that Harry Prowse had been captured! The official notification came on the 20th when the Air Ministry sent a signal stating that a telegram had been received from the Red Cross to the effect that '42358 F/O Harry Prowse is a Prisoner of War, unwounded'. It was considered to be 'Grand news'!! In July 1985, Harry reflected on this incident:

My departure from 603 was somewhat similar to the start, but in a small field near St Omer. The damage was even greater both to the Spitfire and me. However, before hitting the ground I had remembered to turn off my ignition switches (magneto switches) as well as blow up the IFF unit, all in accordance with standard regulations. This particular Blenheim bomber escort flight had all the premonitions of disaster from the start. Squadron Leader Smith was leading the Squadron at the time, I was acting A Flight Commander. From the time we took off to the time I was shot down we saw neither the rest of the Hornchurch Wing nor the Blenheims we and the rest of the Wing were supposed to be escorting. Milling around in the air above Galland's airfields was not the healthiest place to be at that time. 603, according to my log book, lost four pilots including me during the ten days prior to my farewell on July 4th 1941. A date never to be forgotten by me.

Initially he coped well in captivity. An early letter home confirms this:

I hope this will reach you before the normal channels start moving. I was offered the opportunity to write by the CO of the squadron which shot me down. I am perfectly sound in wind and limb and so far being treated like one of them, excellently.

It wasn't long, however, before his time as a PoW became fraught, as his letters home indicated. On 15 July, well before 603 received official notification of his incarceration, he wrote:

Well, I've now been twelve days in captivity and it seems like twelve years. The time goes so very slowly with nothing to do all day but read and think. The food isn't so hot, but is nevertheless always welcome as it breaks the monotony somewhat. The weather has been very hot which is a good thing until some clothes arrive.

By the 29th things had improved:

GEFANGENENNUMMER: 1626.
ZIMMER -NR.17.
LAGER-BEZEICHNUNG: OFLAG VIIc.
DEUTCHSLAND.

Harry Prowse.

Here we are again not much news but enough to fill this miserable piece of monthly ration. I'm just dying to receive a letter from home. Another three weeks should see the first roll in. The days are going by faster now and things aren't so bad as my first letter and cards written in violent fits of depression made them out to be. I'm in the orchestra now and rehearsals take up half the day. There is a good library and I've started to learn some more Spanish. Much of the day is spent in washing out dirty clothing and washing up dirty dishes (I'm becoming quite an expert). I've sent off a card to Capt. Skinner and another to the Dutch Red Cross with the possibility of being 'adopted' by some kind-hearted Dutchman. We RAF types are still hounded out by the Army for news of home and there are several Army officers here who know people in the RAF I am acquainted with. One Scots captain is a great friend of my old C.O. [George Denholm] many an hour has passed in swapping yarns, and some of the stories they have to tell of their capture and first few months of imprisonment are very interesting. They had a terrible time at the beginning. There is more to tell but no more room for it.

He was freed on 2 May 1945, and returned to England on the 8th. Following a lengthy period of leave, Prowse attended a flying refresher course at 5(P) AFU, at Atcham, from 16 October 1945 until 23 January 1946, flying Harvards. Having been released from the RAF, Prowse decided to return to flying duties for a year and on 18 June was sent to 61 OTU, Keevil, for a refresher course on Spitfires. From 18 June 1946 until 6 June 1947, when he was released again, he remained at Keevil as an instructor. Of his time with 603 Squadron he recalled:

I was very young and found life exciting. I hated the transfer or loss of friends from the Squadron but life in general was good with little to worry about, for me at any rate. In particular I recall with nostalgia the period between Dec 17th 1940 and May 16th 1941, during the Squadron's 'rest period' at Drem and Turnhouse. Even a Sassenach like myself seemed to receive the same generous treatment from the people of Edinburgh as any other member of the Squadron.

I had taken some photographs of the Squadron, but these had vanished by the time I got back from Germany, also a war artist sketch of A Flight which I remember being dominated by 'Razz' Berry's moustache... It really was superb.

I lost touch with all ex-members of the Squadron. When Queen Elizabeth visited Brazil I received an invitation from the Sao Paulo branch of the Royal British Legion to be a member of the Guard of Honour at a reception in Sao Paulo. I knew Archie Winskill would be there too, in his official capacity, but even so it was impossible for me to get down to Sao Paulo at the time. At the Guildhall in 1980 I was delegated to stand with ex-266 Squadron members, but exchanged a few words with 'Sheep' Gilroy. Archie looked too busy to bother. 'Sheep's' opening words summed up my situation. Quote: 'I thought you were dead!'*

Also on 4 July, 226 Squadron lost one of their Blenheims (V6365). Records show that it crashed near Dunkerque. Two of the crew – Sergeant A. Smith and Sergeant W.R. Mathias were killed and are buried nearby, but Sergeant F.J. Hynes survived to become a PoW. The Hurricanes reported seeing a Blenheim crash into the sea off Gravelines. One badly damaged Blenheim was escorted to a safe landing at Manston. All of the 21 Squadron Blenheims returned safely, landing at 16.10.

The Hurricanes landed back at North Weald at 16.05, 611 and 54 Squadrons arrived at Hornchurch between 15.45 and 16.00 and 603 touched down at Rochford between 15.40 and 16.00.

It had been a successful operation and had lured the Germans up as intended. Enemy losses far outweighed the British, despite the old problem of over-claiming.

On the 5th there were no convoy patrols, but another Circus, number 33, was laid on to Lille, this time using three Stirling bombers for the first time. On the way back, 603 were attacked several times by 109s, but there were no claims. Four 603 Spitfires landed at Manston short of fuel. There were Spitfires from other squadrons all trying to get into Manston at the same time, with the same problem. During the day, F/O David Scott-Malden returned from leave having been confirmed in his post as a flight lieutenant the day before and the CO left for a well earned seven days' break which he planned to spend north of the border.

For the rest of July and August, the operations were similar – not so many convoy patrols, but usually one, and often two Circus-type operations each day and always over the same part of France with targets in and around Lille, Hazebrouck, Le Touquet, Béthune, Chocques the norm. The pilots quickly became familiar with the topography and no doubt soon got to the point that they knew it so well, they didn't need maps to find their way about.

On the 6th, after an operation to Lille, the Station Commander at Southend, Squadron Leader Henderson, held a party for the squadron officers (of which there were few!) and their guests with three members of the pipe band – Corporal Blake, Corporal Crooks and AC1 Wilson – 'in attendance' to play their pipes. The next day, the pipers were joined by Sergeant Cairns and three others who came down from Turnhouse to take part in 'Southend War Weapons Week'.

The fine weather continued until the 12th when there were thunderstorms during the night, but until then the continual round of offensive sweeps went on.

On the 7th, whilst escorting Stirlings again during Circus 37, P/O Delorme claimed a 109E probable and after landing, P/O Keable left for a well-earned 48-hour leave. This operation had

*In September 1947, Harry and his wife sailed for Brazil to work for the Vestey organisation as manager of a 17,000 acre farm until his retirement in December 1983, after which he continued to live in Brazil. Every two years the couple returned to the UK on what they called 'home leave'. They have a daughter living in Texas. Harry has since died.

Squadron Headquarters staff. Southend 16 June – 8 July 1941. Back row, from left to right: LAC Forrest, LAC Collins and Cpl Rennie. Front row, from left to right: Cpl Blake, LAC Meigh, 'Bruce', LAC Alison and LAC Fowler.

been to Albert which the pilots considered to be a long way south but it proved trouble free until the return when the 'beehive' was found and attacked by 109s. There was another operation in the afternoon – Circus 38 – with the target again being the Kuhlmann chemical works at Chocques. Whilst 603 spotted some 109s in the air there was no contact and none of pilots used their guns.

Twelve aircraft were taking off at 05.45 the next day on Circus 39, the core of which was three Stirlings attacking Lens/Mazingarbe. Mazingarbe is between Béthune and Lens, 50 or 60 miles south east of Calais on the French coast. The heat was stifling. The 603 Spitfires were led by F/L Scott-Malden. It was an eventful affair, particularly for Sergeant Wood. After meeting some 109s, Wood seems to have been hit by flak as he crossed the French coast at Calais on his way back home. Then he was pursued across the Channel by another 109, but when the enemy fighter turned – presumably to go back – Wood managed to get on its tail and fired at it from under 100 yards range. He saw his rounds hit the fuselage and one wing hit the water. Sgt Wood was slightly injured and headed back to the English coast but had to crash land near Canterbury at Bomford Bridge. His aeroplane – R7299 – burst into flames. Also during the operation, Sheep Gilroy and David Scott-Malden fired at, and appeared to damage Messerschmitt 109s. One Spitfire had returned to base not long after take-off, but the others were back by 07.15.

On this morning and probably in this operation, one of the bombers went down – a Stirling (N6034) of 7 Squadron from RAF Oakington – hit by flak. It exploded in mid-air with two of the crew managing to bale out and they both survived.

There was another Circus that afternoon with a single Stirling making for the power station at Lille and two for the Kuhlmann chemical works at Chocques. The Chief of the Air Staff, Air Chief Marshal Portal visited Hornchurch to see for himself a Circus operation at relatively close quarters. This time, 603 only contributed 11 aircraft, led by Sheep Gilroy and taking off at 16.30. Again, it proved to be an eventful operation. Sgt Tabor's section was attacked over the target by over a dozen 109s and Tabor found himself in a defensive circle with one of the enemy fighters. The 109 made a turn to starboard and Tabor followed it, firing. He reported the Messerschmitt crashing south west of Lille. Then he found himself on a head-on collision course with another 109. He fired a single burst and saw the enemy hit a tree. Other elements of the Squadron were also embroiled. P/O Delorme's aircraft was hit in the port mainplane by a cannon shell and his instruments were damaged but he managed to get the Spitfire back to England but short of fuel and landing at RAF Coltishall in Norfolk.

During the afternoon, 603 moved back to Hornchurch. This involved the move of eight officers, 13 sergeant pilots and 120 airmen and it clearly created some unhappiness. Each move meant that articles such as safes, stationery, correspondence, files, filing cabinets etc had to be shipped but why each station couldn't hold sufficient supplies of stationery, or even have their own filing cabinets was the question being asked by the weary airmen diverted for the moment from their normal work. In the middle of a heavy spell of operations, any way of making the moves simpler would have been welcomed.

F/O S.G.H Fawkes.

And so the daily grind continued. On the 9th morning convoy patrols followed by an operation to Lens with three Stirlings in the afternoon. Pilot Officer S.G.H. 'Guy' Fawkes arrived from 234 Squadron at RAF Warmwell. On the 10th another Circus to Chocques escorting three Stirlings again, one of them being lost. It was another from 7 Squadron at Oakington (N6017) with all the crew killed. Flight Lieutenant J.A. Thomson posted in from 11 Group. On the 12th during a Circus, the pilots met some 109s about three miles south of St Omer. Sgt Jackman claimed one destroyed and one damaged, Sgt Prytherch claimed a probable and Scottie, Sheep and P/O Delorme all claimed a damaged. By now Sheep had amassed over 500 hours on Spitfires and 780 hours total flying time.

There were no operations the next day, the 13th; the fine weather had broken. S/L Smith returned from his leave and P/O Blackall left for nine days away. There was one operation on the morning of the 14th – a Circus to Hazebrouck – during which they lost Sgt Hunter. They were attacked by 109s and Sgt Lamb reported that he saw Hunter (in X4665) going down trailing smoke, but during this, Lamb was bounced by six enemy fighters. Sgt Anthony Hunter was posted missing with his loss timed at 10.15 and five miles south of Gravelines. Twelve days later on the 25th, the good news from the Red Cross was that he had been captured. He survived the war.

CHAPTER 3

THE 1941 OFFENSIVE TAKES ITS TOLL

For the next week the operations continued in a similar vein when the weather allowed. Because of the variable haze and the intermittent clouds, each day tended to have a Circus laid on, but then see it gradually postponed over the day until cancellation in the late afternoon or early evening. As with so many other wartime activities, for the pilots there was the constant tension of anticipation of combat whilst waiting, but which was then all for nought.

On 16 July the Germans captured Smolensk but for 603 the day was taken up with convoy patrols and two Rhubarbs and the 17th by a late afternoon sweep and an evening Roadstead. Take-off was at 21.10 and they were back by 22.35 having escorted three Bristol Beauforts (from 611 Squadron) attempting to attack a sizeable ship off Brest. It wasn't successful: there was heavy flak and the Beauforts failed to hit the target. The Luftwaffe also reacted but although 603 was followed back much of the way by four 109s, they did not engage. It was however a long sea flight for the single-engine Spitfires which met the Beauforts over Dungeness and returned there on the way back.

On Monday 21 July there was an early morning Circus to Lille. 603 took off at 07.45. Over the target area a grand dogfight developed which involved the whole Squadron with P/O Delorme claiming a 109E as destroyed and Sgt Archibald another. On the way back at zero feet, Sgt Tabor claimed that he had destroyed another 109 landing at St Omer and he also shot up a convoy of lorries. He crowned it all by shooting at a man on a watchtower and then took a pot at a ship on his way back over the Channel!

There was another Roadstead in the afternoon, but it was judged to be abortive.

After the successes, the 22nd and 23rd were to be bad days for the Squadron. There was one operation on the 22nd, and during it Pilot Officer Paul Delorme was lost, but not to enemy action. The pilots were outbound at about 10,000 feet over the Channel and about ten miles off Ramsgate when his Spitfire (W3369) tipped over into a vertical dive never to be seen again. It was conjectured that he had suffered an oxygen failure and this had caused him to lose consciousness. Paul Delorme, a Canadian from Hamilton Ontario, was clearly destined for greater things had he survived.

The 23rd was worse. There were three separate sets of operations during the day and in each, one pilot failed to return.

Poor weather in the morning meant no action until 13.05 when ten Spitfires took off in what was described as a 'mopping up' sweep, but was in fact Circus 59. 603 flew at 25,000 feet and when they were about 15 miles east of Gravelines, they were bounced by half a dozen 109s. It was hazy. Sgt William Jackman was hit. The CO went to Jackman's aid but was himself attacked. Meanwhile Jackman called out that he was all right and going to bale out. His Spitfire (R7227) was seen diving into a cloud apparently under control, but Sgt Jackman had to bale out near Watten. He survived.

His experience was not untypical of what happened to many of the airmen who found themselves on enemy territory. He was captured about an hour after landing and spent the rest of the war in various PoW camps, but being a self-motivated and resourceful man he made two attempts to escape. The first was in August 1942 from Stalag VIIIB at Lamsdorf. He exchanged identities with a Palestinian lance corporal to get into a work camp where they were labouring in a stone quarry. While at Lamsdorf, Jackman had gathered some maps and odds and ends of civilian clothing and when the opportunity arose, he used them. There were four men involved in the escape attempt, a Flight Sergeant C. Rofe and two Palestinians. They made a hole in the floor of their lavatory, climbed into the cess pit beneath then out again through the pit's manhole. From there they made their way to the perimeter wire of the camp, cut it and escaped. The four travelled by night, laying up during daylight hours, and taking great care. Their methodology was that two would move forward, and if the coast was clear, the second pair followed in turn. After about six days, Rofe was caught by a gamekeeper but given four hours grace and managed to rejoin the other three. Four days after this, Rofe and one of the Palestinians were captured and not long afterwards, Jackman and the other Palestinian were caught by soldiers guarding a working party. They were returned to Lamsdorf and given 21 days in the 'cooler'.

His second escape attempt was from Stalag Luft VI at Heydekrug in October 1943. This time by tunnel. It wasn't a haphazard affair, but well organised with similar arrangements to those made famous by 'The Great Escape' from Stalag Luft III with 'stooges' and workers etc. The potential escapers were provided with food, civilian clothing, identity cards, compasses etc. They dug for two months and reached a point about 15 feet beyond the wire. They thought there was a reasonable chance of succeeding from there and a vote was taken as to whether or not it should be extended further out. The vote was to go no further. It proved to be the wrong decision. Only eleven escapers actually got out and Jackman and others were trapped in the tunnel when the guards found it. None of the eleven made it back to Britain and all were recaptured. W/O Jackman was ultimately released on 21 April 1945 from Stalag 357 at Fallingbostel by the British 7th Armoured Division and flown back to the UK a few days later.

The second operation on 23 July took off at 16.30 with nine 603 Spitfires acting as escort for a Lysander. Sheep Gilroy returned to Hornchurch after 15 minutes but the remainder continued with the sortie. For Pilot Officer Blackall, it was his first day back on 'ops' after his nine-day leave. He had already flown on the earlier Circus. Off the North Foreland at about 17.30, his engine failed. The CO told him to bale out, but Blackall replied that he would rather try to bring the Spitfire (R7341) down in the sea. He seemed to make a good landing but his colleagues thought that he took a long time to get out of the cockpit, and when he appeared on the surface he wasn't moving and seemed to be unconscious with no sign of a dinghy. The CO, still above, thought that he might bale out himself to help, but eventually tried to drop his own dinghy. Managing to separate it from his harness, he found that it was impossible to judge the right moment to let it go. He made a number of passes above the downed pilot but without releasing it. Eventually an ASR launch arrived but it took almost an hour for Blackall to be picked up. He was still alive but died shortly after being landed at Margate. In the meantime, Smith's situation was not ideal with an unusable parachute and the dinghy pack impeding his movement in the cramped cockpit, but he made it back safely.

P/O Hugh Blackall, 26, was married to Dorothy from Uckfield and the son of the Reverend Lewis and Gertrude Blackall. He is buried at Brookwood Military Cemetery in Surrey near Pirbright. He had total of 200 flying hours to his credit with 127 of these on Spitfires.

But the day had yet to finish. At 19.30, there was another Circus – 60 – this time to Béthune escorting six Blenheims. 603 provided eight Spitfires as escort cover taking off at 19.30. Sgt Wood's aeroplane developed an oil leak and he returned early, landing at 20.25. Meanwhile, the 'beehive' continued to the target. The Luftwaffe reacted strongly. Many 109s were encountered on the way in and vigorous dogfights started – not just for 603 but other escorting squadrons too. Sheep and Sergeants Stone and Neill managed to reach the target with the bombers but lost contact with the rest of 603 and they came back with 611 Squadron.

It was a ferocious operation and when all had returned, it was found that Sgt Tabor was missing. No one saw him going down and it was assumed that he had been hit during one of the dogfights.

Flight Sergeant George William Tabor was from Woodford Bridge in Essex and is buried in Longuenesse (St Omer) Souvenir Cemetery at the Pas de Calais in France. He was 21 years old and had been flying Spitfire W3184.

The remaining six aircraft were back at Hornchurch by 21.30, but the groups who gathered in the various billets would be subdued. Three pilots were suddenly gone and the others weren't to know at that time that Sgt Jackman had in fact survived. The losses were significant – both in the actual numbers and in the experience they represented. The Circus operations were taking their toll and 603 was very much in the front line of the battle to win the Second World War.

Sgt McKelvie returned on the 22nd. There was no let up, the next day another Circus to Hazebrouck, with 603 only able to muster seven aircraft. They were led by the Hornchurch Wing Commander Flying, Frederick S. Stapleton, who made up an eighth. It was relatively quiet. Although they saw enemy aircraft on the way in, the Germans didn't engage and it was only on the way back when they were just south of Dunkerque that they found some 109s in a vulnerable position below them that they attacked. Only the Wing Commander and the CO fired their guns, but Stapleton claimed a 109E destroyed.

This was the CO's last operation with 603. He was posted to Station HQ. The Operations Record Book records his leaving and that as Squadron Leader 'Hiram' Smith was 'a trusted leader and a popular Commanding Officer his departure will be greatly felt'. On 1 August he was admitted to Romford Hospital suffering from an abscess in his jaw.

Sgt A.C. Hendry was posted to No 1 Delivery Flight, 24 Squadron at Hendon.

Poor weather over the next few days meant that 603's next operation wasn't until the 28th which gave them a chance to lick their wounds and recover. In the interim, there were several movements of pilots. On the 25th, Squadron Leader M.J. 'Johnny' Loudon arrived from 242 Squadron to take command. He was another Battle of Britain veteran having been a Flight Lieutenant with 141 Squadron but wounded on 19 July 1940. 141 Squadron flew Boulton-Paul Defiants – the aircraft which looked not unlike a Hurricane, but with a bomber-type gun turret behind the cockpit and no forward-firing armament. Briefly successful when first in combat because the enemy pilots assumed it to be a conventional fighter and vulnerable from the rear, but after the truth was out, the Defiants were no match for the Messerschmitts. On this particular day in 1940, F/L Loudon and his gunner, Pilot Officer Farnes were flying L7001 on a convoy patrol at 12.45 when they were attacked by a Messerschmitt 109 of JG51 and shot down.

S/L M.J. 'Johnny' Loudon.

Loudon was wounded but Farnes survived unscathed although the Defiant was lost along with no less than six others from 141 that day. The Defiants had had to be rescued by Hurricanes of 111 Squadron and it was very clear that they weren't up to the task. They were soon withdrawn as day fighters and turned to the night-fighter role.

The same day as the new CO arrived, Flying Officer R.V.L. Griffiths turned up from 145 Squadron at Tangmere, and Pilot Officer R.K. Marland from 222 Squadron at Coltishall was also posted in.

On 26 July, 603 exchanged Sgt Johnny Hurst for Pilot Officer H.G. Niven from 602, and on the 27th, Pilot Officer R.A. Thomas arrived from 92 Squadron at Biggin. On the 28th, Flight Lieutenant J.A. Walker reported from 57 OTU to take over as B Flight commander.

One of the departures from 603 at that time was that of F/L Sheep Gilroy who left to take over as squadron commander with 609. This was a 'knock-on' from the resting of 'Sailor' Malan as the Biggin Hill Wing Leader. He was being replaced by 609's Micky Robinson whose post, in turn would be filled by Sheep. It marked the end of an era. 609's gain was 603's loss, but all wished

F/O Griffiths.

him well in his new post. Although it might have been seen as appropriate if he had been made the CO of 603 to replace S/L Smith, he eventually became 603's squadron commander after the war. At the same time, some in 609 were wondering why Paul Richey hadn't been promoted to squadron commander.*

On 30 July, Sgt Wood was posted away sick because of the injuries he had received when he crash landed at Bomford Bridge on the 8th. Sgt Budd left for 222 Squadron. Also on the 30th, 603 received a visit from the Scottish press corps.

And so July drew to a close. There were convoy patrols once the weather improved and on the 31st, ten Spitfires from 603 provided rear cover to a Roadstead operation, but no enemy aircraft were seen – an uneventful end to an eventful and costly month.

---

*Following his move Sheep continued to achieve success. He claimed a Bf109 damaged on 21 July and two Bf109s destroyed on 27 October, with another on 8 November. He was awarded the Croix de Guerre (Belgium) on 3 March 1942 and claimed a FW 190 damaged on the 8th. He destroyed a FW 190 on 15 April but on 31 May was posted away. He received a Bar to his DFC on 23 June 1942. In November after a rest from operations he was posted to 325 Wing in East Africa, but on the 29th he took over the Wing Leader position in 324 Wing on the Tunisian front. On the 30th he damaged a Ju88, a Bf109 on 6 December and on the 16th he destroyed three 109s on the ground. On the 28th he shot down a brace of Hs129s. On 2 January 1943, Sheep claimed a Bf109 destroyed with a share of two others on the 11th and 18th. On 28 January 1943, he was involved in a collision with Flight Lieutenant E.B. Mortimer-Rose over the wing airfield at Souk-el-Khemis. Although slightly injured Sheep managed to bale out. Tragically, Mortimer-Rose was killed when his aircraft crashed. On 23 January 1943, Sheep probably destroyed a Bf109 and damaged another. He was awarded the DSO on 2 March 1943. On 3 April he destroyed a Bf109 and on the 22nd shared a Ju52. On the 24th he destroyed a Bf109, on 1 May he shared an He111, damaged a Bf109 on the 5th, on 13 July shared a probable Ju88 and destroyed a Mc202 on 4 September. The Spitfire wing, now comprising five squadrons, played a major role as part of the Desert Air Force and Sheep continued to lead the wing until November 1943, throughout the invasions of Sicily and southern Italy. He returned to England at the end of the year and was promoted to Group Captain, taking over the command of RAF Wittering and then RAF Blakelow. Whilst at Wittering he put a great deal of effort into organising a reunion in the officers mess of many of his pre-war/wartime 603 colleagues. He was awarded the DFC (United States) on 14 November 1944.   Sheep left the RAF at the end of the war and resumed his career as a sheep farmer at Tweedsmuir partnering his father. He named his dog Rommel. He missed the flying and comradeship which eventually led to him being offered a job he could not refuse - Officer Commanding 603 Squadron.

August 1941

August started where July finished with a mixture of poor weather which prevented flying and convoy patrols, Roadsteads and Circuses when the skies were reasonably clear.

On Friday 1 August 11 Spitfires acted as rear escort for a lunchtime Roadstead and in the evening, two carried out a short convoy patrol. What is worthy of mention is that of these Spitfires flying on the Roadstead, two were Mark Vb. Until now, 603 had been using the Mark Va which had only .303 machine guns and some of the pilots at least, thought that they were being outgunned. The Vb had wing-mounted cannon which improved matters and as the month went on, the number of Vbs on strength increased.

For 603 there was no flying on the 2nd by which time the Squadron had been credited with 124 confirmed victories with 45 probably destroyed. There was not one single pilot from the Battle of Britain still with the unit. All were casualties or had been promoted and moved to other units. There were three sergeant pilots from east Scotland, including Fife and Angus, a Canadian of Scottish parents, a flying officer who was a native of Edinburgh who had been trained in Rhodesia, and the CO was Brazilian born of Scottish parents with a typical Borders family name. Of the ground crew personnel, 50% were Scots and the 'old Adjutant' had been with 603 since 1927.

603 flew 16 patrol sorties on the 3rd and for some strange reason known only in the depths of the Air Ministry, Sergeant Johnny Hurst and the newly promoted Flying Officer Niven reversed the exchange which had taken place on 26 July when Hurst had moved to 602 and Niven had come to 603 from 602. Other changes in key personnel occurred on the 5th when 603's 'spy', Flying Officer Blackbourn, was posted to RAF Leconfield to be replaced by Pilot Officer E. Beddow from the Hornchurch HQ. Blackbourn had carried out what was at times a thankless task with dedication.

It was also on the 5th that P/O Keable went missing. During an evening Circus operation 603 were tasked with target support and they were attacked by Bf109s. Keable's Spitfire (X4663) was last seen diving in a southerly direction over the Forêt De Nieppe but he didn't arrive back at Hornchurch and was posted as missing. In fact, he'd been killed. Speculation was that he had suffered oxygen failure and blacked out. Nigel Keable was 22 years of age and is buried at Noordwijk in the Netherlands. He had been due to go on leave on the 6th.

In contrast, further news reached 603 about Harry Prowse. Prowse's father wrote to the CO reporting that two communications had been sent via the Air Attaché in Stockholm – one to say that a Swedish diplomat had passed on a message from Prowse to his mother saying that he was well and unhurt. It was some consolation for the loss of Keable.

On the 6th, there were two Rhubarbs and it was learned that F/L Scott-Malden had been awarded the DFC. The next day he left for 48 hours leave. There were two Circuses on the 7th, no flying on the 8th, two more Circuses on the 9th, convoy patrols and a Circus to Hazebrouck on the 10th and again no flying on the 11th. John Buckstone departed on four days' leave on the 9th to attend a wedding at Invergordon. It isn't known how he was getting there from Hornchurch but if he was travelling by train, the journey must surely have been tedious and long! Invergordon is near Inverness and must be close to 600 miles – a long way to travel in wartime Britain – perhaps he was allowed to fly!

The first of the two Circuses on the 9th is of passing interest for 603. It was a raid on Cosnay near Béthune by four Blenheims. The intelligence report reads:

10.35. Twelve aircraft left Hornchurch to act as escort column to four Blenheims with Gosnay four miles S.W. of Béthune as the target. They were centre Squadron at 17,000 feet with 611 above and 403 below. About 20 E/A ME109's were observed to the East about 22,000 feet as the Squadron was nearing St.Omer. 2 E/A detached and attacked green Section No's 3 and 4. Sgt Stone sustained damage to his aircraft by cannon shot through his Port plane and had a narrow escape from bullets through his tail plane and fuselage. He managed to return safely to base. The remainder landed at 12.20 hours.

A relatively normal Circus although one that Sgt Stone would no doubt remember for some time! The significance of this operation was that the Tangmere Wing Leader, Wing Commander Douglas Bader, was lost in a scrap with 109s near Béthune. There is some controversy as to just what happened, however, Bader was not the only significant loss – another being Flight Lieutenant 'Buck' Casson of 616 Squadron. Both survived and were taken prisoner although in his struggle to bale out, one of Bader's artificial legs jammed in the Spitfire rudder bar and he parachuted to earth without it. The Germans let it be known that Bader had survived but missing a leg and offered safe passage should it be decided to drop him a replacement. The Air Ministry spurned the offer but during an operation on 19 August in which 603 took part, a box containing a new leg was dropped near St Omer.

The 12th brought two more sweeps – one escorting six Handley-Page Hampden bombers. These were pre-war aircraft which had been intended for daylight raids but had suffered at the hands of the Luftwaffe in the early weeks of the war when amongst others, the famous Guy Gibson flew Hampdens. They were very narrow – only wide enough to take a man's shoulders and they were known as 'Flying Suitcases'! P/O Thomas went on leave.

No flying on the 13th or the 15th, but on the 14th in addition to the Medical Officer F/O Skene going on leave, there were two sweeps (Circus 72 and 73) both of which relatively uneventful for 603.

Saturday 16 August turned out to be a busy day, and thereafter there was more activity. The day began with two early morning patrols, the first taking off at 04.55 and the second at 05.30. The weather was fine with 5/10ths cloud between three and 7,000 feet. Then at 07.25 12 Spitfires were airborne on a sweep. The CO, S/L Loudon, had to return almost as soon as he had taken off and two others had to abort a little later with engine trouble but the rest continued and although there was a fight, it was inconclusive. The Spitfires straggled back to Hornchurch.

At midday, there was another Circus, this time to Marquise in support of Blenheims and it was uneventful. They weren't finished though, and there was yet another Circus at tea time, this time 11 aircraft escorting six Blenheims attacking the airfield at St Omer. 603 were led by Harry Broadhurst, Hornchurch's station commander. Red Section attacked two 109s and Des Ruchwaldy saw one that he attacked catch fire and ditch into the sea. They all landed back at about 19.00 at the end of a long and broadly successful day.

The 17th brought only a Roadstead in the evening in the way of operational flying:

18.50. Twelve of our aircraft left Base on Roadstead operations, for a rendezvous with three Blenheims over Manston, who had been detailed to bomb a 5,000 ton M.B. off Le Touquet. During this operation "Scottie" F/Lt. Scott-Malden shot down a ME.109E. The E/A was seen to dive into the sea. Our aircraft returned via Manston and landed at 20.10 hours.

The pilots were: S/L Loudon (P8729), F/L Walker (W3569), Sgt Lamb (W3628), Sgt Stone (W3233), Sgt Prytherch (R7305), Sgt Hurst (W3138), F/L Scott-Malden (W3632), Sgt Ruchwaldy (R7333), P/O Fawkes (W3631), Sgt Paget (W3118), Sgt Neill (R7300) and Sgt Cook (W3130). Six of the Spitfires were Va and six Vb.

The Blenheims didn't bomb the ships – apparently because the flak put up by them was too heavy.

On the 18th, there were two Circuses. For the first the pilots were: S/L Loudon (P8729), F/L Walker (W3569), Sgt Lamb (W3628), Sgt Archibald (W3226), Sgt Prytherch (R7305), P/O Marland (W3138), F/L Scott-Malden (W3632), Sgt Ruchwaldy (W3130), P/O Fawkes (W3631), Sgt Paget (W3118), Sgt Neill (R7300) and Sgt Cook (W3112). The ORB reads:

14.03. After lunch 12 of our Squadron A/C left as part of the escort cover to again rendezvous with the Blenheims over Manston, this time twelve in number and the meeting timed for 14.30 hours. Our A/C failed to locate the Bombers which must have been flying below cloud, which was 10/10th's at 10,000 feet. Our Pilots left Manston at 15.03 hours, flew to within ten miles of Gravelines and then returned to Base, arriving at 16.15 hours.

For the second operation the 11 pilots were: S/L Loudon (P8729), Sgt Hurst (W3569), Sgt Lamb (W3628), Sgt Archibald (W3226), F/O Griffiths (W3138), F/L Scott-Malden (W3632), Sgt Ruchwaldy (W3118), P/O Fawkes (W3631), Sgt Paget (R7226), Sgt Neill (R7300) and Sgt Cook (W3130). The ORB reads:

17.35. They again took off, this time eleven in number as W/Cmdr Eric [sic] Stapleton was leading them, on a Circus operation to Hardelot, West of St. Omer and Guines. Orbiting near Marquise and returning to Hornchurch via Dover. Green One (S/Ldr Louden) [sic] seeing two ME.109's attacking four Spits. Dived 1000 feet down from 27,000 on to one of them. He fired a long burst from some distance but without results. All landed.

Comparing the aeroplane numbers shows that many of them flew on both operations with the same pilots so that, by implication, the ground crews were also under pressure to turn them round in time for the next sortie.

Two more Circuses on the 19th, a morning trip (Circus 81) to the power station at Cosnay (during which Douglas Bader's new artificial leg was dropped in a box) and the second (Circus 82), in the evening to Hazebrouck. During the morning there were a number of combats with enemy 109s and Scottie and Sgt Des Ruchwaldy each claimed one destroyed. Sergeants Prytherch and Hurst each claimed a probable and Sgt Paget a damaged. All the 603 Spitfires returned safely. P/O Marland was taken off strength suffering from problems with his ears and he went into hospital at RAF Halton.

On 20 August poor weather apparently stopped any operational flying although there was some gunnery practice and comments in the ORB that they had flown operations in such conditions in the past. The CO went on 48 hours leave and Sgt Paget, a New Zealander, was posted to 485 Squadron, a Kiwi unit.

The 21st brought two more Circuses. The first was at breakfast time. At 08.30, 12 aircraft left Hornchurch to meet up with half a dozen Blenheims over Manston; the target was well known to them – Chocques. 603 was high cover at 28,000 feet with 403 and 611 below them. The French coast was crossed near Dunkerque at 09.15 and shortly afterwards a brisk engagement with six 109s took place. Sergeants Ruchwaldy and Archibald each claimed to have damaged a 109, but despite this the Blenheims did not manage to reach the target. On the way back, F/L Scott-Malden and P/O Hamish Falconer were attacked whilst still over France. Hamish later recounted the experience with great clarity:

A Hun dived on me from behind. His first burst wrecked my radio, another blew the top panels off the starboard wing. He fired again, and wrecked my instruments, damaged the throttle control and splintered the front and side windscreens. Then the petrol tank caught fire. I thought I felt blood trickling down my leg, and I was miles inside France – an unpleasant situation, one way and another.

The first thing I did after deciding not to bale out was to kick at the flames with my foot. That was not much good, but a steep side-slip set up a blast which blew the flames out. That trouble overcome, I was able then to take stock of my position. I was still several miles inside France, but the engine was going, though the flames kept shooting from the port exhaust and part of the cowling was nearly off. I had to use force to hold the damaged throttle forward to keep going.

When I was about five miles from Dover I knew I couldn't make the coast, so I tried to jump out. I was at 2,500 feet at the time, but when I used my hands to take off my helmet the Spitfire fell away out of control, and I could not pull her up until I was only 800 feet from the sea.

I unfastened my parachute, intending to pancake into the sea and then jump out. About two miles from the coast my engine seized and bits fell off through vibration.

I levelled off at 50 feet above the water, but as soon as my speed dropped below 100 miles an hour, the shattered wing stalled and I crashed sideways into the sea, turned upside down, and went down about 15 feet before I got out.

It was very dark. I climbed out and swam to the surface. The shore was about a mile and a half away and I began to swim after kicking off my boots. After 20 minutes I was still about three-quarters of a mile out, but I saw soldiers waving from the beach. When I was just about 'done', one of them swam out and began to drag me towards the shore. Later another soldier arrived and helped. We were pretty well worn out when we sighted a rescue boat, so we kept still and floated until it arrived.

Above: P/O Hamish L. Falconer, 21 August 1941.
Left: Sgt J.C. Dalley models one of the life-saving dinghies carried by pilots. Note the multi-lingual 'Board Here' sign to cater for the many nationalities operating within Fighter Command.

His rescuers were members of A Company of the 44th Battery of the Royal West Kents. They saw Falconer ditching and without hesitation, three of the gunners started swimming out to him in a courageous act to save the pilot. One had to return, but the other two, Privates F. Carter and J. Worthington reached Falconer and 'rendered assistance'. The three were picked up eventually by a rescue boat, quite exhausted, but alive. Hamish Falconer had good reason to be grateful to his rescuers and their selfless act. The incident made the Scottish newspapers. One headline read: 'Pilot Flies, Sinks, Swims and Sails to Safety!' Hamish eventually arrived back at Hornchurch, minus boots, bedraggled in his sodden RAF tunic but with his white scarf still around his neck and in good spirits. His photo (above) was taken outside the officers mess. He resumed operations about two weeks later. His luck, which had held firm, was destined to run out early the following year.

At lunchtime the Squadron flew another operation to Chocques. This time the target factory was found and hit. However, 403 Squadron lost two pilots who were seen in a turn but then not heard of again, and all for no loss to the enemy. 403 had also lost a pilot on the previous Circus so it was a particularly hard day for them.

The 22nd brought some early morning patrols and a sweep. At about 11.30, a large number of enemy aircraft took to the air over St Omer and fearing a raid, the Hornchurch Wing scrambled – firstly to patrol Maidstone, but then to sweep Calais/Dunkerque, by which time the enemy aircraft had returned to their bases. There were no losses.

F/L 'Johnny' Walker was posted to 610 Squadron at RAF Tangmere and Sergeants L.F. Webster and J.C. Dalley were posted in from 61 OTU. The day drew to a close with an unusual exercise in the evening:

17.16. In the evening ten Aircraft took off to stage a series of dummy attacks on a Hotspur Glider which was towed to a height of 8,000 feet by a Hawker Hector and then released. It was the general opinion that though the glider offered an excellent target, considerable care was necessary in approaching it, owing to the ease with which it can turn, and its ability for quick manoeuvre. Further exercises would be welcomed.

The use of airborne troops in assaults was much in vogue. The Germans used paratroops to great effect for their invasion of Crete but the British were also investigating the use of gliders to transport troops to a battle zone. They would be towed there and at an appropriate moment released so that they would be able to land at pre-designated landing grounds. The troops would disembark, fully kitted and the pilot would become another soldier having done his job. The Hotspur was an early development, able to carry seven fully kitted troops but it would never be used in anger, being overtaken by Horsas, Wacos and Hamilcars. For the troops inside, going into battle was an eerie and unsettling experience which gave them a sense of vulnerability because of the lack of engine noise and only the whisper of the air on the structure, the uncomfortably loud explosions of flak and of course the risk of attack by enemy fighters. The exercise was presumably part of the testing of the glider concept to see just how much at risk it was to a defensive fighter. The reaction of the 603 pilots is somewhat unexpected in that clearly they did not regard the glider as an easy target! Nonetheless, because it was trying to land, the pilots enjoyed the opportunity of 'beating up' the airfield legally!

On a rather more mundane (but vital) note, the 22nd was a Friday and it seems that every other Friday pay parade was held. In the time honoured way of the British services, each airman marched smartly up to the pay table and announced his name and serial number to be given his money. Clearly, the administration staff considered it a nuisance and they complained that the parade stopped the work of the station for an hour! With a strength of 154 to pay, it took up to 138 man hours to organise. 'Could not some system of 'pay envelopes' be introduced on the same lines as that in vogue in civil industry?' was the rather plaintive but unanswered, request! Whilst it seems trivial, it does illustrate that the admin staff were also under some pressure and that someone was consciously trying to find ways of easing the workloads. Later, there would be more complaints about the effort involved in moving stations – something which happened frequently to 603 in 1941.

The weather closed in again, and it wasn't until the 26th that there was any significant action – an evening Circus. 603 was tasked as escort support with 611 and 54 Squadrons. F/L Scott-Malden claimed a 109 as destroyed. Sgt Ruchwaldy claimed a 109F as a probable and one damaged. Sgt Prytherch also claimed a 109F as damaged. All 603 Spitfires made it back safely.

On the 24th, F/O Bill Douglas was attached to Hornchurch from Southend for 'ops. duties'. This was part of his recovery from the injuries he had sustained earlier in the year and presaged his return to 603.

On Wednesday 27 August, 11 603 Spitfires took off at 07.15 acting as escort cover to nine Blenheims on Circus 86 to bomb marshalling yards at Lille. Flight Lieutenant Wilfred Duncan Smith had recently joined 603 and this was his second operation with them – the first being the Circus on the evening before. Duncan Smith was a well experienced combat pilot by now. His first operational posting was to 611 Squadron at RAF Digby in October 1940 and whilst he didn't take part in the intense fighting of the Battle of Britain, action came quickly. With the RAF swinging over to the offensive, Duncan Smith had a distinguished record with 611 and stayed with it until transferring to 603. Of course, the two squadrons were involved in many of the Circus operations over that long summer of 1941, so Duncan Smith knew all about 603 and its pilots. David Scott-Malden had been with 611 although he left just before Duncan Smith joined it.

F/L W.G.G. Duncan Smith.

'Smithy' Duncan Smith.

According to F/L Duncan Smith, the sky was clear and they joined up with the Blenheims at Manston. For some reason, the bombers took completely the wrong course, leaving the target on their east and they flew to Doullens before turning back. Duncan Smith recorded that the Blenheims dropped their bombs on Amiens.

The formation was then bounced by 109s and dogfights started. Duncan Smith's aircraft (W3138) was hit:

> I was flying as Green 1 in Squadron formation when on the return journey north of Amiens we encountered upwards of 6 e/a at our own height. I turned starboard to engage these and attacked an e/a from head-on but saw no results. I then turned to port and dived to engage an Me.109 E which was manoeuvring to fire at a Spitfire. I opened fire at 150 yards on a fine quarter closing to 100 yds astern. Pieces flew off the e/a and it looked like perspex splinters whereupon the e/a rolled over to port and dived away steeply. I turned to follow but lost sight of him. After this I climbed up and rejoined the bomber escort which was some distance to the west.

Flying Officer Griffiths was Green 3 and Duncan Smith's wingman. When Green 1 went after the 109 attacking the other Spitfire, Griffiths noticed a 109F directly above him, diving as if to attack his leader. As the German fired on Duncan Smith, he pulled back hard on the stick and fired a burst at the 109. Griffith's sight of the 109 had been fleeting but his fire caught the German on the underside and blew away part of the fuselage near the cockpit floor. The 109 broke off its attack and curved away down to starboard. Griffiths thought it was a probable. The fight had allowed the rest of the formation to draw ahead and Griffiths found himself on his own although he could see the bombers in front and beneath him. He started a dive down to join them. As he did so, he found that there were two 109Fs in close line astern on his port side which evidently had the same idea – to join the bombers and attack them. He turned on the 109s and, in trying to carry out a beam attack on the leader of the pair, hit the second 109. He saw bits falling off its starboard wing and it half rolled away to port. He claimed it as a damaged.

Duncan Smith's combat report (Form 'F') does not mention that he had been hit and managed to get this Spitfire back to Manston where he made an emergency landing, by which time he had run out of fuel and had to glide in.

The CO had also been hit. His Spitfire (W3624) was damaged extensively with Loudon wounded in the face and an arm, probably in the same melee of dogfights just north of Amiens in which Duncan Smith and Griffiths had been involved. Loudon had spotted about 20 109s going across his front at about the same altitude and attacked one of the leading Messerschmitts. He closed to about 100 yards and fired a three-second burst from the starboard quarter which clearly damaged the enemy fighter. Black and white smoke poured from it, but just then his Spitfire was hit in the port wing by a cannon shell from another 109. Loudon managed to get on to its tail and fired at it but it dived away. The squadron commander then saw three Spitfires above him and decided to join them, but no sooner had he started to do so than he was attacked by another 109. Again, he managed to get on to its tail and again, as he did so it dived away from him. By this time, no British aircraft were in sight, so he descended to low level intending to head back for home, but instead was attacked by another 109. The ensuing dogfight lasted for some time – five to ten minutes – during which S/L Loudon managed to get in several good bursts with his machine guns – his cannon being out of ammo. The 109 eventually made off, but Loudon's adventures weren't over yet. A few minutes later he spotted yet another Messerschmitt (or perhaps the same one) approaching him from astern. As he turned into it, he fired, but saw no result and after a short time the German made off leaving Johnny Loudon to fly out north west of the Abbeville estuary. He managed to land safely at Manston at 09.15. Duncan Smith thought that Loudon had done a great job in getting back at all. His injuries stopped him from flying for two days although his combat report records only that he was 'slightly injured'. A lesser skilled pilot would not have survived.

The extended flight left many of the Spitfires short of fuel and about half of the Hornchurch Wing landed at either Lympne or Manston. Five of the 603 aircraft landed at Manston, two at Lympne with the other four getting back to Hornchurch, but all of them short of petrol. In addition to the long route, as escort cover they had to stick with the bombers and the slow speeds and throttle changes meant that the Merlins drank fuel at a prodigious rate. The 'bag' for 603 was recorded as three probables and a damaged, but it seems to have been a generally unsatisfactory operation which hadn't gone to plan. Fortunately the losses incurred by the wing were light.

Four 603 Spitfires took off late in the afternoon on a Rhubarb but it was cancelled after ten minutes.

On 28 August, there were five patrols in the morning to protect a convoy of about 40 vessels off Harwich. Each successive pair relieved the previous one so that there were Spitfires taking off at 09.20, 09.55, 10.30, 11.10 and 11.40 with the last pair returning at 12.55. There was no action and there was no more operational flying that day. The weather wasn't conducive to operations – stormy, with high winds.

During the day, four new pilots arrived: Sergeants W.S. Allard and C.S. Bush from 64 Squadron which was currently at Turnhouse, and Sergeants H. Bennett and A.W. Otto from 122 Squadron at RAF Ouston to the west of Newcastle-upon-Tyne.

Harold Bennett was an engineer, brought up in south-east London. He spent three years studying at Woolwich College of Engineering – now Greenwich University – and after 18 months of an engineering apprenticeship with Siemens (ironically), unbeknown to his parents, he applied for, and got a release from his studies and joined the RAFVR. In the event his parents didn't attempt to stop him, and his training was the same as many other young men at the time – EFTS at Sywell in Northamptonshire, SFTS at Hullavington and OTU at Hawarden and Wrexham. During this time he flew Tiger Moths, Masters, Hurricanes and Spitfires.

When the time came for him to be given his 'Wings', to his disappointment they weren't presented in any formal way but he was merely told that he could now 'put them up'. It took the edge off the moment for a man who is by nature of a modest disposition. And so he was posted to 122 Squadron and then to 603.

Allan Otto was a Canadian. Born 5 June 1921 to Berthold and Edla, he was brought up by his parents in Fort William, near Thunder Bay, Ontario, almost in the centre of Canada. He had a younger brother, Archie. He was a quiet, thoughtful man who took a pride in doing well anything he did do, a quality that he was to bring to his flying. He completed his schooling with top

Left: Allan Otto as a young cadet pilot under training.
Right: F/Sgt Allan Otto between August 1941 and March 1942. Possibly at RAF Fairlop.

honours and started work in a store to help the family cope with the effects of the Great Depression. He had not shown any particular interest in flying or in the RCAF and it came as a surprise to his family when he came home one day after his 19th birthday in 1940 and said that there was a recruiting team from Winnipeg in the local armoury and he proposed to join up. He hoped that his mother 'wouldn't mind'. His parents, no doubt with some apprehension, gave him their blessing and on 21 July 1940 he left home to start training at Manning Depot.

After going through the usual training process, he received his 'Wings' on 18 February 1941. Eighteen days leave followed, and shortly after Sergeant Pilot Otto found himself in Britain reporting to 57 Operational Training Unit and then to his first Squadron on 29 May – 122 Squadron based at Turnhouse. During June, he made five operational sorties, four of them convoy patrols and the other a scramble to intercept an unidentified aircraft (which proved to be friendly). The Squadron then moved to Ouston. For about two weeks, Otto was posted to RAF Catterick, but returned to 122 at Ouston on 7 August before being posted to 603 on the 27th and granted a 24 hour leave pass.

It was lucky that he was posted with Harold Bennett because the two were to become firm friends and it would be a friendship that would eventually include their families, although under tragic circumstances. While Sergeant Bennett's first operation wasn't until the 27th, Sergeant Otto's was on 17 October on a Circus operation to Marquise – he flew again on the 18th and the 21st.

For the remaining three days of August, the cycle of operations continued with Circus 88 on the 29th followed by a search of the Channel by Flight Lieutenant Scott-Malden, Sergeant Neill and Sergeant Cook for a downed pilot – Wing Commander John W. Gillan DFC AFC who had been leading the North Weald Wing in Spitfire W3715. Regretfully, he had been killed. This was the man who had flown a Hurricane of 111 Squadron from Turnhouse to Northolt in 1938 to set a new World Speed Record.

The 29th also brought another fatality for 603. LAC John Costine died whilst a passenger in a Lysander. Quite why he was flying is unclear, but the circumstances were that the Lysander – a Mark III (T1675) – was on a ferry flight from RAF Lyneham to Prestwick. It stopped off at RAF Silloth in Cumberland where it picked up LAC Costine. Over Wigtownshire, they found bad weather but instead of turning back, the pilot decided to press on and the aeroplane flew into a hill near New Luce.

On the 30th there was an early morning Roadstead against an enemy merchant ship escorted by two flak ships off Dunkerque but although the escorts were badly damaged, the three Blenheims didn't attack the merchant ship. The 31st started with another shipping attack – this time on German destroyers and E-boats off Le Touquet and an uneventful Circus at lunchtime.

Sergeant Kistruck joined on the 30th while Pilot Officer J.A.R. Falconer was declared too sick for operations and remained unfit until 8 September.

September 1941

Bad weather dogged September to such an extent that from the 5th to the 14th, no operational flying took place and not much after that. Low cloud and haze reduced the visibility to below safe operating limits. Presumably the London smog was a contributory factor.

On the 1st there were shipping patrols and on the 2nd an unsuccessful Roadstead against enemy shipping off Dunkerque. In this instance, Hurricanes of 242 Squadron were tasked with shooting up the escorting flak ships whilst the Blenheims were to attack a tanker. The flak was heavy and the Blenheims drew some criticism from the escorting fighters in that they didn't appear to press home their attack as enthusiastically as they might have. The sultry haze stopped flying on the 3rd and on the 4th there was Circus 93 to Mazingarbe which brought some excitement. Twelve 603 Spitfires were involved in the target support role and the Luftwaffe reacted strongly. Sergeants Lamb and Stone claimed a 109 each as destroyed and Sergeants Hurst and Neill a probable each. During the fights, Neill was shot in his left side, shoulder, thigh and foot. Fortunately he managed to get back to Manston where he was taken to Margate General Hospital for treatment. The other Spitfires all returned safely.

During the first fortnight there were a number of changes in personnel. One notable return to Hornchurch was that of 603 veteran, Flight Lieutenant 'Black' Morton, who arrived from Sheffield University Air Squadron on 2 September pending training as a controller. He was posted back to 603 in a supernumerary capacity on the 19th.

On the 20th, the adjutant, F/O London, left for RAF Digby on promotion to Flight Lieutenant. On the 7th, Flight Lieutenant K.C. Powell reported from 52 OTU at Aston Down as a supernumerary. The next day Acting Pilot Officer R.L. Oddy was attached as deputy adjutant for training. After taking over as adjutant, following the departure of F/O London on the 20th, he remained with 603 until 1945. Following seven days leave F/O Griffiths returned on the 11th but as he had a severe case of tonsilitis he was packed off to Rush Green Hospital with the expectation that he would be out of action for a week.

The usual rotation for leave continued. On the 1st, Scottie and flying officer Doc Skene left on seven days' leave which Skene planned to spend in Edinburgh. On the 13th, P/O Fawkes left with a three-day pass and F/L Duncan Smith left with six days' leave to look forward to.

On 19 September, F/L David Scott-Malden was posted to 54 Squadron at Hornchurch as its Commanding Officer. Having been made a flight commander in May 1941, his success with 603 had been prolific – he claimed Bf109s damaged on 7, 14 and 21 June and 8 and 12 July. On each of 17, 19 and 26 August and 18 September he destroyed 109s, was awarded the DFC (promulgated on 19.8.41) and on 4 November destroyed another Bf109.*

On 21 September Flight Lieutenant F. 'Chumley' Innes was posted in from 611 Squadron to replace Scottie as flight commander.

Although operations were limited, there was still practice flying and on 13 September an unnamed 603 pilot had an unfortunate experience whilst practicing a dusk landing. He landed heavily and decided to go round again, but on his second attempt, forgot to lower the undercarriage and made a wheels-up landing in the dark.

Another interesting development was the adoption of two Curtiss Tomahawks by 611 Squadron simulating Messerschmitt 109s. The use of dissimilar combat would be significant in the training of NATO pilots during the Cold War and this is a precursor of it. The theory is that whilst it is useful to practice combat in similar aircraft, the reality of war is that the enemy will be using aircraft with different performance regimes – different turning circles, rates of climb etc. Flying similar aircraft gives the better pilot the edge, whilst fighting against different types means that the better pilot will not necessarily be the victor. Sometimes, the aircraft used to act the part of the enemy may even have similar characteristics to the enemy type giving the pilot realistic experience as to just what he might expect to come up against. During the Cold War, the USAF based 'aggressor squadrons' in the UK and their role was to fly aircraft that were painted in Soviet-style camouflage schemes and using Soviet-style tactics to give the other NATO pilots a taste of what it would be like to fight the Warsaw Pact air forces for real.

---

*See Appendix 'Life After 603.'

Operations resumed on Monday 15 September with some convoy patrols and between the 16th and the 21st there were six Circus type incursions into the enemy territory – to Marquise, Abbeville, St Omer and Mazingarbe. All the pilots returned safely. The Squadron made a number of claims for enemy aircraft hit in combat – mainly probables. The weather closed in again and fog and poor visibility once more kept the Spitfires and their pilots on the ground. Whilst the weather over the south of England closed in, far to the east, on 19 September, the Germans captured Kiev – their Russian campaign was going well.

On the 23rd, Hornchurch was visited by senior US Navy officers and the Assistant Air Attaché from the US Embassy in London. Part of their itinerary included the 603 dispersal.

During this spell of poor weather, many of the pilots at Hornchurch fell sick to a stomach disorder attributed to a steak and kidney pie served up for lunch one day in the mess!

603 flew only one other operation in September, four days later. The 11 Group monthly operational report states that 12 Circus operations were carried out during the month and that a new tactic was tried. Sometimes two (or more) operations were being carried out at much the same time to try both to confuse the Luftwaffe controllers and to draw up as many German fighters as possible.

On Saturday 27 September, 603 flew one of these two-pronged Circuses which was designated 103, with the two separate operations called Circus 103A and 103B. 603 would fly in 103B.

Circus 103A was to be an attack on the railway marshalling yards at Amines Longueau by six Blenheims from 110 Squadron and six from 226 Squadron both based at RAF Wattisham. The operation was to start at 13.00.

Circus 103B was an attack on the power station and a petrol plant at Mazingarbe by 12 Blenheim IVs of 114 Squadron based at RAF West Raynham, in Norfolk. Mazingarbe had already been on the receiving end of several attacks including those on 9, 22 and 23 July and 20 September. The West Raynham Blenheims were to take off at the same time as those from Wattisham – the two operations needed to follow tight and concurrent time scales.

603 was tasked to fly as one of the close escort squadrons and for Sgt Harold Bennett it would be his first ever operation. He was understandably nervous, on several counts. Apart from being his first 'op', because of a shortage of aircraft he was allocated W3502, the Spitfire Va usually flown by the Station Commander, Group Captain Harry Broadhurst! Because of his status, Broadhurst had the privilege of having his initials – HB – painted on his aircraft instead of the usual squadron identification letters. It was not lost on Harold Bennett that these were his initials too! Consequently, he had his photograph taken, showing him leaning confidently against 'his' Spitfire!

The weather, for a change, was fine and warm and the 12 603 Spitfires lifted noisily into the air from Hornchurch at 13.35 led by the CO, Squadron Leader Loudon in P8729. The others were: F/L Innes (P8796), F/L Duncan Smith (P8754), P/O Falconer (W3364), P/O Marland (W3138), Sgt Cook (R7226), Sgt Bennett, Sgt Prytherch (W3631), Sgt Allard (R7221), Sgt McKelvie (R7305), Sgt Lamb (W3638) and Sgt Archibald (W3233).

The Circus 103A bombers met their escorting fighters over Hastings whilst the 103B 'beehive' formed over Manston at 14.05 (603 was forced to circle for about 15 minutes). Then they turned for France, 103B crossing the enemy coast at Mardyke, 603 at 17,000 feet. One Blenheim (V6378) of 114 Squadron encountered 'technical problems' and returned to base, landing at 15.00 hours.

The Luftwaffe rose to the bait. Elements of both JG2 and JG26 scrambled, with the latter going for the Mazingarbe raid. There were fierce running dogfights around St Omer and Hazebrouck. P/O Marland was Blue 3 and Sgt McKelvie Blue 4. At about 14.15 near St Omer the formation was attacked by about nine enemy fighters. Marland spotted four Bf109s diving towards the Blenheims from the port quarter. After calling for McKelvie to follow him, he turned towards the 109s, but having failed to get within range he started to climb back to rejoin the Squadron. Meanwhile McKelvie continued after the 109s and after noticing another three about 2,000 feet above, he called out a warning to Blue 3. As he closed in on a *Schwarm* (four) of 109s, McKelvie picked out a pair. Closing to 150 yards from above and astern he opened fire on one of the fighters. Black smoke immediately poured from the German aeroplane then it turned over and dived down vertically. He claimed it as a probable. As he broke away, he saw another 109 diving down trailing black smoke but more Messerschmitts appeared behind him, so he climbed steeply to port. Ahead of him he saw more Spitfires and several dogfights in progress so climbed up towards friendly aircraft.

At some point, Blue 3 and Blue 4 lost contact. As Blue 3 climbed back to join his colleagues in a turn to port he saw two 109s coming in from the rear, one of them within range and firing. Marland throttled back and steepened his turn, at the same time slipping violently down. The 109 overshot the Spitfire and also turned to port so that he was ahead of Marland, but slightly to starboard:

> As he overshot, I pulled the nose up, and got in a beautiful burst of about 4 secs. into his belly from below, at pt. blank range, approximately 30 to 50 yards. The e/a immediately emitted white and black smoke, bits fell away, and part of what I think was the radiator. The e/a began to do a steep spiral towards the ground, and appeared to me to be out of control. I watched it for about five thousand ft. and he made no attempt to pull out.

Marland claimed the 109, which he identified as an E, as a probable.

Meanwhile, McKelvie joined the action which he had seen above him. One Spitfire was diving down on fire and two 109s were also going down apparently out of control and trailing smoke. An aircraft which he reported as a 109E dived slowly past him and fastened on to the tail of a lone Spitfire. McKelvie in turn latched on to the tail of the 109. There were other enemy aircraft behind and above, so keeping a watchful eye on them, he closed to about 100 yards and opened fire:

> ...there was a quantity of smoke, and immediately afterwards a red flash from his engine. He appeared just to hang in front of me, burning. As I broke away, I heard cannon-fire behind me; I felt something hit my left elbow, and the aircraft yawed violently, and went into a loop on its own. I blacked out several times before regaining control at 8,000 ft. and heading for home. On the way back, I sighted an Me109F flying in the opposite direction, and slightly below. I turned round behind him, and I fired at him from astern as he dived away. As my windscreen was covered with oil, I could not use my sights, and saw no results. Four more 109s attacked me as I approached the French coast at Dunkirk, but I avoided them and they broke away before reaching the coast.

McKelvie claimed the 109 that started to burn as destroyed. Crossing the French coast at Dunkerque means that he had turned north, whilst the rest of the formation was heading south towards the target area. He made his way back to Hornchurch landing safely at 15.20.

Meantime, P/O Marland remained with the wing and whilst he rejoined the rest of 603, he then lost contact with them again.

The Blenheims pressed on to Mazingarbe, but couldn't identify either of the briefed targets so at 14.35 they bombed an alternative, a railway junction at la Bassé which is north of Mazingarbe and a few miles east of Béthune. Immediately short of the target, they met heavy intense flak which slightly damaged three of the light bombers although none of the crews were injured. The bomb loads were a mixture of 500lb HE bombs and 25lb incendiaries and bursts were observed on two long sheds at the side of the railway track, with others falling wide.

At about 14.40, F/L Innes, Green Leader, was attacked by about 12 Bf109s. Below him, and to starboard, he saw a 109E on the tail of a Spitfire and firing. He dived down to carry out a beam attack on the Messerschmitt which forced it to turn away from the first Spitfire allowing Innes a good shot in a slight dive. Closing to about 100 yards, he gave it short bursts with both cannon and machine guns and thought that he hit it in the starboard wing root and tailplane because he saw pieces fall away. The 109 pulled up to port, then fell over into a steep spiral with white smoke trailing behind it, apparently out of control. He followed it down to 10,000 feet but was set upon by other 109s, so discretion being the better part of valour, he climbed back up to join the escort. He claimed the 109 as damaged.

The bombers turned almost due west crossing out over the coast at Le Touquet. On the way back across the Channel, Marland saw one of the Blenheims flying lower than the rest and he dropped down with the intention of covering it, but before he could get there, four or five other Spifires appeared. He therefore decided to act as cover for them all, at about 8-10,000 feet. But whilst he was still about seven miles from the coast, he had another problem. His engine cut:

Spitfire V W3628, 'Oman', one of the 'Persia' gifted aircraft at Hornchurch. Back row, from left to right: Sgt Pilot G.P. Stone, P/O N.H.C. Keable, Sgt Pilot D.F. Ruchwaldy, F/O R.V.L. Griffiths and P/O R.G. Marland. Centre: P/O 'Hamish' A.R. Falconer and F/L F.D.S. Scott-Malden. Front row, from left to right: P/O Guye Fawkes, Sgt Pilot W.J. Archibald and F/O H.G. Niven.

> I tested the fuel gauge, and this read 0. Dungeness was my nearest pt. And I glided towards the beach there. I crossed the coast at approx. 1,500 ft. and landed wheels up well up the beach. The surface was loose shingle, and on landing "into wind" which was pretty strong, I think I was going fairly slowly when I touched down, and although the aircraft dug, the nose well in, it did not turn over. The damage to the aircraft as far as I could see was just of the usual wheels up nature, but I rather think I must have been hit in the petrol tank, as I was only airborne 1 hr. and 35 mins. I made the landing at 15.10 hrs.

His Spitfire was subsequently repaired and issued to 164 Squadron in October.

The various aircraft straggled back. The Blenheims landed at West Raynham between 15.50 and 16.00 and the 603 Spitfires between 15.20 and 15.30. McKelvie's Spitfire had lost its rudder and the tailplane was damaged; despite this he managed to bring it down safely. But Sergeants Allard and Archibald were missing. It was subsequently learned that Sgt Allard had been captured but Sgt W.J. Archibald had been killed. He was 21 years old.

The other Circus operation had had a similar experience, but the bombers had found the briefed target at Amines and hit it. No Blenheims were lost and they all returned to Wattisham at about 15.45.

For Sgt Harold Bennett, his first operation was over. None of the marauding Luftwaffe fighters had attacked him and he had survived, but not without a rather embarrassing problem. The Squadron still flew in line astern and being new, Harold was one of the 'tail-end charlies'. At one point, not unusually in air combat, he suddenly found himself alone in the sky, so he turned for home, aware of the needle of the fuel gauge sinking all the while:

I climbed up over the White Cliffs looking for Lympne airfield, but couldn't find it quickly enough. The engine cut-out completely. The Spitfire juddered on the point of a stall which helped me make my mind up. But I missed seeing a superb field with Army lads waving their arms. Instead, I chose a suitably sized one which turned out to be a hollow. Because it wasn't flat, I couldn't touch down quickly enough and hit trees. The wings were torn off but I got away with only facial and back bruising. I was very lucky.

His Spitfire, the one usually flown by G/C Harry Broadhurst, was repaired but was eventually lost on 10 October 1942 when it failed to return from another operation. Sgt Bennett had to explain the loss of the aircraft, but in view of the circumstances no action was taken against him!

One of the interesting points about this operation was that the claims and reports mostly identify the Messerschmitt Bf109s as the E variant but by 27 September the majority of the Messerschmitts operated by JG26 were the F variant.

Of more interest, this operation seems to mark one of the first occasions that a new German fighter was met. According to F/L Duncan Smith, one of the sergeant pilots claimed to have shot down a radial-engine Curtiss Hawk and Duncan Smith also thought that he had seen a radial engine aircraft diving through the formation. The 11 Group monthly operational report for September confirms that odd looking aircraft were being seen during that month: 'On several occasions unusual enemy aircraft – BLOCH151/2 and CURTISS Hawk – have been encountered and at least three destroyed.' Some of the pilots were sceptical of – and ridiculed – suggestions that the radial-engine aircraft might have been Bloch or Curtiss Hawk 75 aeroplanes captured by the Germans from the Armée de l' Air in 1940. Their sheer agility and performance made a nonsense of this. The Spitfire Vs should have been more than able to cope with these older fighters, but in fact, the fights had been vicious and the Spitfires had been in some difficulty.

Jack Rae, the New Zealander who flew with 603 in April 1942, first met the new fighter on 28 March 1942 near Cap Gris Nez when flying high cover with 485 Squadron, but according to Jack the shock was still evident even then:

Well below us we sighted a large force of 190s attacking some Spitfires and immediately dived on them. With the considerable advantage of height and our added speed from the dive they should have been at a distinct disadvantage. But to our shock and surprise they immediately turned, gained height in what seemed a very short space of time and were attacking us. We had attacked them at what we later learned was their rated altitude of 12,500 ft. We could still out-turn them but we found we had to be extremely careful. I had a very quick deflection shot at one that peeled off and flew downwards in a cloud of smoke. My camera shot later showed that he was at extreme range…... It was written off as a 'probable.'

The new fighter was produced by the Focke-Wulf Flugzeugbau and designated the Focke-Wulf 190. It was loved by its pilots and admired by its opponents; one that had the hallmarks of a great aircraft. It 'looked' right. The lines were sleek and simple and whilst its more 'squared off' main and tailplanes didn't have the elegant curves of the Spitfire, it was a classic thoroughbred.

The first 190s issued to the Luftwaffe could outperform the Spitfire Vs in all aspects other than tight turns and the RAF pilots found themselves heavily disadvantaged. For the British, there began another frantic race to counter the 190, which would result in the Spitfire IX, but in the meantime, the new German fighter would acquire the nickname 'the butcher bird'.

Outline concepts for the Focke-Wulf 190 – or FW 190 – were the result of an order from the *Reichsluftministerium* towards the end of 1937 for a single-seat fighter to be an alternative and successor to the Bf109. Two initial proposals were prepared, one with a BMW 139 radial engine and one with the Daimler-Benz – DB601 – which also powered the Messerschmitt 109. Rather to the surprise of the engineers, the radial option was chosen. The director of the design team was a brilliant aeronautical engineer, Kurt Tank, who as well as concentrating on the aerodynamics and performance of the aircraft, also designed it for minimal maintenance times in the field in operational conditions. It had a wide track undercarriage – approximately ten feet – and was capable of operating from grass airfields.

The first prototype was flown on 1 June 1939 by the chief test pilot Hans Sander at Bremen and it immediately became clear that the new aeroplane had great potential and it was a delight to fly. The usual round of development and trials for any new aeroplane continued through 1940, and in July 1941, the first of the new FW 190-A1 was flying with 6/JG26 from Morseele.

The powerplant for the A-1 was a BMW 801C-1 engine giving 1,600 hp and a top speed of 388 mph. Its wingspan was 34 feet and $3/4$ inch, the length 28 feet and $10^{1}/2$ inches and the wing area 196.98 square feet. It was armed with four MG17 machine guns, two in the engine cowling and two in the wing roots which were synchronised with the propeller. Pilots thought that the armament was too light and these criticisms were rectified by adding a further two 20mm cannon more conventionally placed further outboard in the mainplanes. For defence it had good armour. The windscreen was 50mm armoured glass and there was a 14 mm plate fixed to the canopy behind the pilot's head to give protection to the head and shoulders as well as an 8mm plate on the back of the seat.

By the beginning of September 1941, II/JG26 was flying the FW 190 A-1 but in the following weeks, the new fighter didn't perform well incurring a number of losses – some of which were unfortunate rather than because of the shortcomings of the aeroplane. Accordingly, the A-2 was brought quickly into service, reaching JG26 by the end of November 1941. With development, the FW 190 remained a feared and capable weapon in the hands of skilled pilots until the war finally ended in 1945.

On 27 September 1941, when Circus 103 took place, II/Gruppe JG26 operated about 30 of the A-1 variant and it was probably some of these that 603 had met.

There was yet another quirk to the operation. JG26's Hauptmann Schmid claimed to have shot down a Blenheim which had been seen floating on the water of the Channel, but of course none were recorded as being missing, or even seriously damaged by any of the bomber units. There was P/O Marland's report of seeing a Blenheim in difficulty but there is nothing else to support the claim that one was shot down, or had even sustained significant damage.

JG26 claimed ten Spitfires destroyed during the 27th with the loss of only a single Bf109F-4. This aircraft was flown by Unteroffizier Gottfried Dietze, Black 5. Wounded, he baled out of the aircraft over his Clairmarais base aerodrome.

Circus 103B was typical of the operations carried out by 603 and the other squadrons at this time. Clearly they caused damage to the enemy and were a boost to the morale of the French people under occupation. And to the British for whom it was one of the few means available at that time of taking the offensive. They also helped the Russians resisting the German invader by keeping at least some of the Luftwaffe pinned down in the west.

However, various studies suggest that they were not as effective as had been hoped. Nevertheless, the Prime Minister visited RAF West Raynham on 6 June 1941 and in a speech to the assembled airmen, he called the Blenheims of 2 Group his 'light cavalry'; an indication of how he valued and respected them, and by implication, the escorting fighters. Fighter losses were quite high. The 11 Group monthly report for September records that during the month, 58 fighter pilots were lost and compares this favourably with 83 the previous month. 11 Group claimed 111 enemy aircraft destroyed, 59 probably destroyed and 50 damaged during September with similar numbers claimed during August. The reality, though, is that these claims were overstated.

Circus 103B, in percentage terms, was quite costly for 603. Of the 12 pilots who left Hornchurch at 13.35, two failed to return – Sergeants Archibald and Allard. This represents a loss rate of 17%. At least two other pilots returned with minor injuries – Sergeants McKelvie and Bennett – representing a further 17% of the original 12. Similarly for aircraft. Two were lost – R7221 and W3233 – and a further two had to force-land and were significantly damaged – W3138 and W3502. Again this means that after the operation was over, only eight of the aircraft which took off were available for further operations. This is a reduction of a third. At the height of its campaign, Bomber Command regarded losses of over 6 or 7% as becoming unacceptable – but in context, this was of large aircraft with six or seven in a crew and which cost much more to manufacture than a single Spitfire. And they were incurring losses on nearly every operation. However, if the 17% loss rate suffered by 603 during Circus 103B was to continue, then statistically a pilot couldn't expect to survive more than about six operations of this nature. A daunting thought, if any of them looked at it in this way. (Sergeant Harold Bennett would take part in eight such operations before he was lost.)

603 A Flight. From left to right: F/Sgt Allan Otto, F/Sgt Prytherch, Sgt Dalley and Sgt Forrester. Front: F/L Bill Douglas and 'Tannoy' Jones. Possibly taken at RAF Fairlop in the autumn of 1941.

However, such losses were not being incurred on all operations and over the months, many were flown with impunity. Nonetheless, if the Luftwaffe were met, the possibility always existed that the RAF squadrons might take significant losses which they did from time to time.

It is also interesting, but not unexpected, that the losses amongst the escorting fighters were much greater than the bombers. The 11 Group report for September states that 119 Blenheims and Hampdens were escorted by 11 Group squadrons with the loss of two Blenheims and one Hampden – a loss rate of 3% which can be interpreted as a reflection on the effectiveness of the tactics employed. On the two operations making up Circus 103, no bombers were lost.

This analysis is not attempting to suggest that these operations were pointless or ineffective – far from it. They achieved much. The point is that they probably did not achieve as much as had been hoped, and that the cost in courageous airmen killed, wounded or taken prisoner in carrying them out was probably much greater than had been anticipated. They were to continue well into 1942 and would allow the Prime Minister to tell Stalin that in the absence of a Second Front in the west, they were at least pinning down some of the Luftwaffe units that might otherwise have been fighting in Russia.

For the next three days of September, there was no flying because of bad weather. On the 28th, the CO, F/L Innes and P/O Marland all left for a spell of leave. F/L Duncan Smith took command in the CO's absence. On the 30th, the Duke of Kent visited Hornchurch and 603's dispersal.

CHAPTER 4

WITHDRAWAL TO SCOTLAND

October 1941

The autumnal weather of September continued into October and although there were operations on the first three days, the mists were back. For the new and inexperienced pilots it was a time to learn. Convoy patrols were a good way to get experience. There was a routine to be followed and rules of the air to obey. The outgoing patrols flew on the south side of the Thames and returned on the north to avoid any chance of collision. Usually it worked, although Harold Bennett recalled that on one occasion when he was on his way back, the outgoing patrol was uncomfortably near. As always, approaching the shipping was a dangerous time for the Spitfires with the Navy's predilection for firing first and asking questions later. The Spitfires were fitted with IFF but it didn't always work and Bennett recalls that as they flew their first orbit of a convoy, they could see the guns – which looked as 'big as houses' following them round.

On 9 October Sergeant D. Prytherch was taken ill. In the middle of the month, the weather relented a little. On some days there were training sorties and a few Circus and intruder type operations. On Monday 13 October, there was another Circus, 108B (part of another two-pronged affair) to Mazingarbe. Twelve Spitfires took off at 13.25, crossing into France at Gravelines making for Hazebrouck and Mazingarbe. A few miles inland from Gravelines Green Section was bounced by 109s and in the ensuing fight, Sgt Alan D. Shuckburgh was shot down in X4389 and killed. The son of Sir John Shuckburgh KCMG, CB and Lilian Shuckburgh of Paddington, Alan had a brother who was a P/O with 54 Squadron flying out of Hornchurch at the same time. Alan flew on many Circus operations with 603 and was experienced at the time of his death. His loss was a blow to the Squadron. He was 23 years old and is buried at Dunkerque Town Cemetery, Plot 2, Row 2 Grave 38.

Then on the 21st came another blow; the loss of Sgt McKelvie during another Circus – this time to St Omer and Hardelot. 603 put up eight Spitfires including Sgt McKelvie (in W2132) and P/O Fawkes (W3631). Others flying were F/L Innes, P/O Buckstone and Sergeants Ruchwaldy, Otto, Hurst and Neill. It was a relatively uneventful sortie. Two enemy aircraft were seen but there was no combat and Sgt McKelvie's was involved in a mid-air collision with P/O Fawkes' Spitfire which lost about four feet from one wing in the accident. Fawkes managed to nurse it back across the Channel and made an emergency landing at Lympne. McKelvie's aeroplane sustained much more damage with no possibility of making it home. He called that he was baling out and it was assumed that he had done so, but whether he did or not, he didn't survive. Fawkes was flying operationally again on the 24th.

Sgt Pilot Bill McKelvie.

A Fifer from Dysart, Sgt William McKelvie was 24 years old and is buried at Dunkerque Town Cemetery, Plot 2, Row 2 Grave 40, just along from his erstwhile colleague, Sgt Alan Shuckburgh. He was the son of James and Elizabeth McKelvie.

In Russia, Moscow was now in a state of siege and the Soviet government evacuated to Kuibyshev. The war was not going well for the Allies.

On 16 October, before the operation which cost Sgt McKelvie his life, the CO, S/L Loudon, was detached to go on special duties to Libya – supposedly for three weeks. His brief had been to pass on to the RAF pilots fighting in North Africa the latest experience from the Channel front. In the event he stayed on leaving 603 needing yet another CO. This time the man appointed was Squadron Leader Roger Forshaw who arrived at Hornchurch on the 17th. He had no operational experience, coming to 603 from Training Command, but he was ably assisted by the more experienced Squadron pilots under his command, particularly his flight commanders. It wasn't long before he completed his first operation – a Lysander escort patrol and then a convoy patrol on the 21st – the day that Sergeant McKelvie died. He had been in the thick of it.

His first Circus operation took place on the afternoon of Saturday 25 October when 12 603 Spitfires took part in a sweep with 611 and 615 Squadrons. No enemy aircraft were seen. By this time, Sergeants Bennett and Otto were building up their experience but this was the first occasion that they flew on the same operation.

For the last week of October, there were fewer of the large Circus-type operations and more convoy patrols – even 12 Rhubarb sorties. According to the ORB the last day of the month turned out to be particularly busy:

10.35 Lack of cloud cover prevented Rhubarbs from reaching their target, only 5/10 cloud at 1,500.

12.35 603 Squadron with 611 Squadron escorted Hurricane bombers to a power station at Holques. Flying at 300 ft and rising to 1,000 ft over French coast, returning in the same way. Barges in the canals were shot up some sunk, Goods trains were attacked, flak emplacements etc. Bombs dropped scored direct hits on the power station, which was left burning, and a warehouse on a railway siding was completely destroyed. P/O Fawkes plane was badly damaged by shellfire, but he made a good landing.

Harold Bennett was flying as P/O Fawkes' number 2. He recalled that on their way home, they crossed the French coast very low and in close formation with Bennett on his leader's starboard wing. They could see people in the streets below. Their route took them straight over a heavy ack-ack battery which fired at them virtually at point-blank range. One shell passed through the middle of Fawkes' starboard wing, but didn't explode – perhaps because the fuses had been set for a greater altitude. It did however leave a huge hole in the mainplane with the metal skin bent up into the airstream like so many petals of a grotesque flower. The pair managed to limp back to Lympne where Fawkes made a very difficult, but successful landing.

In the evening there was an hour-long patrol over Clacton by 12 aircraft. Sgt Lamb flew on all three operations. The CO flew a Rhubarb and the second 'op'.

In the Atlantic, there was an event of some importance to the naval war – the American Navy destroyer *Reuben James* was sunk by a U-boat. This would have a significant effect on the way that the war was perceived in the US and lead to a more active involvement by them in the battle for the convoys.

At Hornchurch, the Circus 'season' was assumed to be finished as the weather chilled and deteriorated with the approach of winter.

November 1941

Operational flying continued to be severely curtailed by weather for most of November. The first three days were taken up with convoy patrols many of which were cut short by the poor visibility. On the 1st there were four sorties, on the 2nd eight, and on the 3rd 12. The sorties on the 3rd were a squadron scramble to tackle Dornier 215s raiding a convoy. The incident happened just after lunch with eight

Spitfires taking off at 13.45. The pilots were the CO, F/L Innes, P/O Falconer and Sergeants Farmer, Webster, Cook, Ruchwaldy and Otto. Heavy cloud cover at 2,000 feet hampered visibility but nevertheless two Dorniers were attacked by P/O Falconer and Sgt Ruchwaldy who were both sure that they had hit the German aircraft. They were each credited with a damaged although because one of the Dorniers was seen to have lost an engine and to be on fire, there was speculation that it might not have made it back to base.

The Germans invading Russia captured Kursk.

There were more convoy patrols on the 4th and a Ramrod involving 12 603 Spitfires to Le Touquet. On this occasion, the pilots were able to attack with their guns and they strafed railway trucks, buildings and signal boxes. They all returned safely to Hornchurch.

The next operational flying was on Thursday 6 November when the Squadron scrambled at 15.30 because six enemy aircraft were reported to be over the Channel near Manston. This time, nothing was found but the 12 pilots maintained a lengthy patrol, landing back at Hornchurch at 16.50.

On the 8th, a planned Circus was cancelled because of thick mist at Hornchurch but in the afternoon, at 13.10, 12 Spitfires took part in an operation to escort an ASR motor launch which lasted for almost two hours. For the next few days convoy patrols were ordered on the occasions that the weather allowed. But although the operations flown were relatively minor, during these days, bigger operations were always being ordered and planned and then cancelled or postponed so that life for the pilots and ground crew continued to be busy and hectic and not particularly relaxing.

Fairlop
On Wednesday the 12th, the Squadron moved bases yet again, this time to RAF Fairlop, a newly opened satellite of Hornchurch. The advance party had moved over by road the previous evening. The bad weather, in particular poor visibility, continued to disrupt activity and the aircraft had to wait until later in the day to make the short hop but by evening, they were settled in their home which although muddy, was thought to be an improvement on Hornchurch because of the greater room both in the billets and the dispersals. Having said that, those left at Hornchurch didn't seem to envy 603 their move, comparing the 'civilised comfort' of Hornchurch with the extensive dispersal, the damp sleeping accommodation and the ablutions half a mile away from the accommodation at Fairlop as taking some getting used to.

The Royal Naval Air Service had first used Fairlop as an airfield in 1915 during the First World War when the War Office decided that measures had to be taken to defend London from attack by German airships. Two sites very near to each other on the east side of London were chosen. Landing Ground Number II at Sutton's Farm, Hornchurch, and Landing Ground Number III at Hainault Farm near Barkingside, a few miles to the north west of Sutton's Farm. Not far to the west of Hainault Farm was another field, known as Fairlop aerodrome. It was bounded on the south by Forest Road. In the Second World War, Sutton's Farm would be known by the more familiar name of RAF Hornchurch. One of the early successes was the destruction of the airship L15 on the evening of 31 March 1916 by a pilot from Hainault Farm, 2nd Lieutenant Alfred de Bathe Brandon, using explosive darts which he dropped on to the luckless airship from above. He personally had delivered the *coup de grâce* but had not been alone, the airship having been attacked earlier in the evening by others.

At the end of the war in 1919, the Fairlop airfields were returned to agricultural use but in 1940 the expansion of the RAF meant that new airfields were needed and once again Fairlop was identified as a suitable site. It had already been considered as the location for the City of London airport. On 26 September 1940, work was started on the construction of an airfield able to accommodate 1,400 airmen and airwomen with three concrete runways in the triangular layout typical of RAF airfields of this time – one 1,600 yards long and two at 1,400 yards (Hornchurch was still a grass airfield). The long runway was oriented 06/24 with the two shorter ones 11/29 and 02/20.* Landing on the main

---

*This was not on either of the sites of the First World War airfields, but in a field to the west of Hainault Farm and to the south of the previous Fairlop aerodrome. The north boundary was Forest Road, on the east, over a field was Hainault Road and the south boundary was Painters Road. Interestingly, the west boundary was the LNER Woodford and Ilford railway branch line part of which would eventually become a London underground track - the Central Line. At the south-western corner was Barkingside Station and at the north-western corner of the airfield was Fairlop Station which have since become underground stations.

runway from the west meant crossing the railway line which ran along an embankment at this point. In windy conditions, the embankment created eddies and updrafts that bounced a Spitfire around and could make the final moments of an approach quite tricky.

The principal camp buildings were on the north side, with the main entrance off Forest Road. The ground to the north and west was urban; Barkingside, New North Road, Tomswood Hill etc with some anti-aircraft gun sites situated off the station.

Work finished in August 1941, and it was declared operational on 10 September 1941 after G/C Harry Broadhurst carried out test landings and take-offs from each of the runways on 1 September. Fairlop's first

603 Squadron ground crew, 1941, with Alsatian mascot Bruce. The aircraft is possibly Scott-Malden's.

station commander was Squadron Leader H.G.P. Ovendon.

It wasn't far from Hornchurch and the airmen and airwomen based there still had plenty to occupy them when they were off duty. The officer pilots were accommodated off camp at Hainault Lodge on Hog Hill. LAC John Wilkinson, a steward in the lodge, recalled that it was an impressive house, with an ante-room and grand piano on the first floor and the dining room on the floor above.

For all personnel, the attractions of London's West End were still easily accessible but more immediately on their doorstep was the State cinema off Barkingside High Street near to the junction with Forest Road and at least two pubs – the Fairlop Oak just over the road from the picture house and the Dick Turpin, a hotel on the southern side of the airfield in Aldeborough Road North. One of the cinema's claims to fame was that it had a downed Bf109 on display in the foyer for a spell to encourage National Savings.

Harold Bennett recalled that whilst off duty, the traditional segregation of officers and other ranks still applied – even to the aircrew. NCO pilots who were more experienced than their officer leaders, or even those leading less experienced officer pilots didn't mix with them on the ground. The officers' and sergeants' messes were strictly out of bounds to each other and even off the station, they would drink in different pubs. They only mixed when on duty.

But the new airfield seemed to find favour with its first tenants – the extra room in the billets and the dispersals would make things easier for the hard pressed ground crews and pilots and their 23 Spitfires. Although on the edge of London, Fairlop (and, as has been seen, Hornchurch) had continual problems with smog created by the smoke from power stations along the Thames, industries like the car factories at Dagenham and millions of domestic coal fires. London's ring of barrage balloons included Fairlop but it had to be modified to allow them to fly circuits from the new airfield and the kink in the ring could be clearly seen by the pilots.

It wasn't until 15 November that the weather broke and the pilots could fly. It was also colder which helped harden the mud.

The Squadron spent their first day of operations from their new home on convoy patrols. The first of these, and thus the first operational flights from Fairlop were carried out by P/O Fawkes (in P7692) and Sgt Bennett in (R7230) who took off at 08.35 and returned at 10.05. Sgt Bennett had been one of the three pilots who took off on 603's final operation from Hornchurch – also a convoy patrol. Fawkes and Bennett were destined to be lost during the same operation just over a month later.

Inevitably, the poor weather started to get people down. The diary reads:

16/11/41 Dull weather, fog, drizzle, mud in all colours and depths. A day so gloomy that it was almost amusing to see the 'brassed off' faces everywhere. No flying at all.

17/11/41 Heavy rain with squalls, developing to gale force. Convoy Patrols of two aircraft took off 08.45 and 09.30 hours, further sections abandoned task owing to weather getting worse. Gale warning in Channel, heavy rains in evening.

18/11/41 A thick mist enshrouded the Airfield early, and it seemed as if it would clear about mid-day, but hopes were unfulfilled and bad visibility prevented all flying.

F/L Duncan Smith flew one of the convoy patrols on the 17th. He blacked out after landing and a day or so later was admitted to Rush Green Hospital at Romford. The immediate diagnosis was pneumonia but it was part-and-parcel of a general wearing down from a year of incessant operations and the strain they brought. In the days before this, Duncan Smith noticed that he seemed to be tiring more easily than before and the 'g' loads he endured in steep combat turns brought on bouts of coughing. He was also sick in the morning. But he put all of his symptoms down to nervous tension. He had been due to move to Hawker to work as a production test pilot but before the move could happen, his illness prevented it and he was suddenly gone – his experience no longer available.

On 20 November the return of 603 veteran, Bill Douglas, and the arrival of Flight Lieutenant Lord David Douglas-Hamilton prompted a house-warming party in the mess during the following evening. Guests included Wing Commander Frederick Stapleton and his wife. As always, the pipers were to the fore, one of them being F/L Douglas-Hamilton. Like S/L Forshaw, Douglas-Hamilton was an excellent instructor who lacked operational experience. Unbeknown to any of them, he would play a hugely significant role in 603 over the next year.

The following evening most of the officers went over to Hornchurch for a dance, some of them not getting back to Fairlop until the small hours having had a 'wizard' time! Luckily for them, the weather was poor on the 24th and only four sorties were flown with F/O Fawkes the only officer flying that day.

Thursday 27 November brought the next major operation for 603. The original task should have been an attack by Hurricane IIB fighter bombers of 607 Squadron on an industrial target in France. 607's base was Manston and the raid was to have been launched from there with 603 in an escorting role. Accordingly, the 11 603 aircraft given the job left Fairlop at 11.35 and made their way to Manston landing at 12.00 in time for planning and briefing. The Wing Commander Flying – Frederick Stapleton – accompanied them making a twelfth and he would fly as Blue Leader. Whilst they were at Manston however, the target was changed to a small enemy convoy westbound about 11 miles north of Le Havre and close to the coast. It presumably had just been spotted. They were given ten minutes to change plans.

Both the British and German convoys moving through the Channel were at risk of attack from aircraft and ships of the other side. The convoys hugged their respective coasts for safety but because of the narrowness of the Channel they were frequently found. Both sides used fast torpedo boats – the German E-Boats and the British MTBs – which would lurk near the coasts and then speed out to attack when a convoy hove into sight. The E-Boats tended to be faster than the MTBs. At night, Royal Navy MTBs sat under French cliffs in the dark and when an enemy convoy passed, they would suddenly scythe out to cut through the convoy at right angles and high speed, launching torpedoes as they went, hoping that they would get to the English coast before the E-Boats caught up with them.

The threat of air attack was such that the Germans used armed trawlers as flak ships to protect their small convoys. A convoy of two or three small (say 1,500 tons) merchantmen might have half a dozen flak ships protecting it, and it was against one of these small convoys that 603 flew a Roadstead on the 27th. They were well used to flying over convoys when they were protecting British ones, but this would be different. The convoy in question this time comprised two merchant vessels of between 1,000 and 2,000 tons accompanied by six or eight flak ships.

The weather wasn't ideal – low cloud with visibility between two and six miles on the English coast, but out over the Channel there was about 5/10ths patchy cloud cover at 5,000 feet with visibility below this judged to be 'good'.

The Hurricane IIB variant flown by 607 Squadron differed from others in that it had a universal wing – which had been first introduced on the IIA Series 2 – so that it could carry up to 12 .303 Browning machine guns but it had options of flying with wing tanks or 250 or 500lb bombs. Carrying bombs, it had a rated speed of about 260 mph at 10,000 feet and a ceiling of just under 30,000 feet. At sea level its rated speed while carrying bombs was 217mph. Without bombs at sea level it could reach 256 mph. This compares, in general terms, with the top speed at sea level of 330 mph of a Spitfire V.

603 was given the role of suppressing the flak – they were to hit the escorts first allowing the Hurri-bombers to come in behind them and hopefully in the confusion hit the merchant ships with their 250lb bombs. The attack would be low level. Further support would be provided by the other squadrons of the Hornchurch Wing.

The Hurricanes were led by Squadron Leader H.L. Dawson and they took off from Manston at 13.10 after the 603 pilots who were: S/L Forshaw (AD503), Sgt Loudon (P8796), Sgt Neill (P8720), Sgt Ruchwaldy (AD557 XT-E), F/O Fawkes (W3631), Sgt Cook (P8786), F/L Douglas-Hamilton (AD502), Sgt Lamb (W3226), Sgt Kistruck (W3110 XT-R), F/O Douglas (R7224 XT-Q) and P/O Buckstone (P8585 XT-S). This would be Bill Douglas' first operation after being wounded on 23 June. His first few flights had been in the Squadron's Tiger Moth (T7229) in September and October with his first flight back in a Spitfire on 22 November.

603 rendezvoused with the wing over Beachy Head then turned south to fly at sea level to find the ships. 607 flew in echelon with A Flight to starboard and B Flight to port. The escorting Spitfires were on 607's starboard quarter. They sighted the French coast near Fécamp and S/L Dawson turned the formation on to a south-west heading and kept them about three miles from the coast. Some flak came up from shore batteries but it didn't cause the British pilots any problems – they only noticed it in passing. Shortly after this, they spotted the convoy travelling in the same direction and S/L Dawson signalled 'Target Ahead'.

At this, the 603 pilots opened their throttles to pull ahead of the Hurricanes. They were still low on the water, not much above 500 feet, and reached the ships at 13.40.

The flak ships were spaced out around the two merchantmen – on the flanks and with one at the front and rear. S/L Forshaw – Red 1 – fired three bursts from 500 yards and saw many hits. W/C Stapleton took Blue Section in from starboard in turn followed by Green Section. All the pilots fired.

607 B Flight meantime swung round to port then made a turn to starboard to bring them across the rear merchant ship from its port beam. They were skimming the waves – 30 feet or so high and machine gunning as they approached to drop their bombs. Having done so, they pulled up and away, just in time to let 607 A Flight come in on a similar manoeuvre but from the ships' starboard quarter. One section attacked the rear merchant vessel again, whilst the two other sections had a go at the flak ships from which there was light and desultory fire which caused no damage. Some of the Hurricane pilots thought that they saw enemy aircraft in the distance but there was no contact and they assumed that the escort had dealt with them. In fact, elements of the Luftwaffe including JG26 were scrambled but failed to meet the raid or have any contact with the RAF fighters.

It was frantic, aircraft were all over the sky and there were shrouds of smoke over the ships which obscured the view of the Hurricane pilots. Nevertheless, the escort Spitfires reported that the attacked merchantman had exploded along with one of the flak ships, and that another was badly damaged and on fire. There was a great cloud of white and black smoke coming from the centre section of the rearward merchant ship and the other was damaged too. They also reported that two of the flak ships were sunk. No 603 or 607 aircraft were damaged.

Hastily withdrawing, the Hurricanes reformed and sped back to Manston landing at 14.55. 603 streamed back to Fairlop at much the same time. Later, the Squadron received a telegram from the AOC of 11 Group with congratulations on a fine performance.

The operation marked Lord David Douglas-Hamilton's first occasion under fire. The letter he wrote to his wife Prunella expressed his exhilaration and satisfaction that he was able, at long last 'to fire in earnest'. He had had a long wait to become an operational fighter pilot, having attended the same Initial Training Wing as Richard Hillary just after war had been declared.

For 607, there was a second attack against a reported submarine in Boulogne harbour again led by S/L Dawson, back in the air 45 minutes after landing. This time three of the Hurricanes were lost. Bill Douglas wrote in his log book '1 merchantman sunk by 607. 2 flak ships sunk by 603.'

At a luncheon at Mansion House on 28 November to mark the opening of RAF Fairlop, 603's CO and Bill Douglas represented the Squadron while Squadron Leader Ovenden represented RAF Fairlop. It was foggy and wet again and there was no flying. Winter started to set in and although it wasn't necessarily cold, it brought yet more fog, rain and wind.

Dawn on Sunday 7 December, found Fairlop more 'like a seaplane base' than an airfield after a night of heavy rain, but it cleared during the day and although there was a fair old south-westerly wind, it didn't prevent some practice cannon firing at Sutton Bridge. Of far more significance that Sunday, in Hawaii, the Japanese were attacking Pearl Harbor and this would have a major impact on the progress of the war and eventually lead to the defeat of the German-Japanese Axis. For the shocked Americans and the Allies already fighting, it seemed a disaster, but it became the catalyst which mobilised the industrial power of the USA to bring it actively into the war on the side of the Allies at last.

For a change the 8th dawned a lovely winter's day – sunny and clear, cold and crisp – ideal for operations involving many aircraft although later cloud built up and the visibility was gradually reduced to between four and eight miles. For the pilots operating over the sea, the water temperature at this time of year was a potential killer if they should have to ditch.

The planners at 11 Group decided to take advantage of the conditions by laying on Low Ramrod Operation Number 15 against an alcohol distillery 25 miles south east of Le Touquet at Hesdin (Target 34 in the 'Rhubarb Operations Brochure') and issued Operation Order Number 141 for the attack. By the time the cold bright day turned to twilight, 603 would have had one of its worst days for many months which would result in it being rotated north for a rest shortly after.

As usual, the day began with a series of three convoy patrols carried out between 09.00 and 10.40 by F/L Douglas-Hamilton, P/O Falconer and Sergeants Waddy, Lamb, Thomas, Webster, Dalley and Otto. On landing there was no respite for F/L Douglas-Hamilton, P/O Falconer and Sgt Lamb and they went straight into a briefing for the Ramrod along with the CO, F/O Fawkes and Sergeants Hurst, Bush, Rawson, Bennett, Neill and Cook.

The attack on the distillery would be delivered by eight 'Hurri-bombers' of 607 Squadron from Manston. Support was to be supplied by aircraft from eleven other squadrons – including 603 who were to be part of the escort wing along with 64 and 411 Squadrons. Close support was 222 Squadron from North Weald, high cover was 401, 124 and 72 Squadrons from Biggin with 303, 308 and 315 Squadrons (all Polish) from Northolt acting as rear support. As further support, 71 Squadron from North Weald was tasked with the anti-flak role.

A Ramrod was intended not just to draw up enemy fighters, but was primarily aimed at the destruction of a specific target. In this case, the bombers were once again to be fighter bombers and not the more usual Blenheims from 2 Group which meant that the whole operation was faster, and once the bombs had been delivered, the 'bombers' were more able to defend themselves – although the Hurricanes were by now distinctly inferior in a dogfight to the Bf109 and FW190 variants in service with the Luftwaffe.

Although the weather across the south of England and the Channel was relatively clear, haze hovered over Dungeness where the squadrons would rendezvous, with haze and 2/10ths cloud rising to about 5,000 feet over France. The plan was for the Hurricanes to meet up with the escort wings then cross the Channel at 17,000 feet until they were near the French coast when they would come down to low-level to carry out the attack.

For Sgt Harold Bennett this would be a memorable operation. His first one had been the Circus to Mazingarbe on 27 September and by now he had gained valuable experience and confidence. He was allocated Spitfire Va R7333 for this operation, which by coincidence had just returned from one of the convoy patrols having been flown by his chum Sgt Allan Otto. Bennett expected to be going on a 48-hour leave but was called to the dispersal along with the other pilots for briefing. His leave would have to wait until he returned.

The eight Hurricanes of 607 Squadron departed Manston at 11.05 and headed for Dungeness. They were led by Squadron Leader N. Mowat and the pilots represented a fair sprinkling of the Allied countries with a Canadian, a South African, an American and a Frenchman all flying the operation. At much the same time, the 11 Spitfires of 603 were starting their take-off runs at Fairlop. First off was Sgt Rawson in Spitfire Vb AD557 (XT-E) and last off, 15 minutes later was Sgt Bush in another Vb P8585 (XT-S). The majority of the Spitfires were by now Vbs, but there were three Vas in the formation.

The Squadron formed up in line astern – Harold Bennett again one of the guard section – 'tail-end charlies'. They climbed to altitude making for Dungeness where they met up with the other squadrons providing the various supporting wings and the eight Hurricanes; 603 were sandwiched in the middle of the escort wing at 18 to 20,000 feet with 64 Squadron leading and 411 above.

The Ramrod formation, led by the Hurricanes, was four minutes behind schedule when it set course for France at 17,000 feet, but the rear support wing set off slightly early. Notification of the delay was broadcast to the squadrons taking part and some orbited whilst the 'bee-hive' formed but the short flight across the Channel proved uneventful and they made landfall at 11.40 about ten miles north-west of Le Touquet at about 15,000 feet, then went into a shallow dive over the estuary of the Canche, flattening off at ground level near Montreuil. The Hurricanes were in echelon of two fours with Spitfires on either side. At that stage it started to go wrong.

They followed the river valley looking for the target to the south of the Forest of Hesdin. S/L Mowat spotted what seemed to be a factory beside a railway line at the south-western end of the forest near Aubin-St Vaast and decided to machine-gun it, but accidentally let the bombs go as well. Most of the others in the Hurricane formation not unnaturally thought that this was the briefed target and six followed suit, dropping their bombs too. The site contained a large brick building and some smaller wooden structures which some of the pilots thought to be a sawmill. One of the buildings looked as if it had already been damaged by fire. The attack was accurate and bombs were seen to fall across the site and cause damage. Under the circumstances, S/L Mowat decided not to carry on to the briefed target and turned right to withdraw for home. On the way, they machine-gunned some industrial buildings and an airfield, assumed to be Bout d'Airon, with what may have been a few real Bf109s interspersed with dummy aircraft. The Hurricanes crossed the French coast two miles south of Le Touquet at Merlimont followed by some light flak and returned to Manston skimming the wave tops. They all landed safely at 12.30.

The escort wing had its own difficulties. On the way in and about five miles before reaching the French coast, it dived down to about 10,000 feet, in the process losing sight of the Hurricanes. The problem was compounded when 603 lost track of the other two squadrons of the escort wing and found itself alone over Le Touquet.

The Luftwaffe reacted in strength. 11 Group subsequently concluded that the broadcasting of information about the delay in starting off, and the need for the Squadron to orbit had been noticed by the Germans so that they were in a better position to deal with the intrusion.

At the end of September 1941, only II/Gruppe of JG26 had re-equipped with the FW 190 – the A-1 variant, but by the end of December all three Gruppen were flying the 190s – a mixture of A-1 and A-2s – with 29 Bf109F-4s still remaining in use by I/Gruppe.

The three Gruppen of JG26 all scrambled and made contact with elements of the British operation, although the Hurricane fighter bombers were not attacked. Nor was 71 Squadron, the anti-flak unit. But the escort cover, high cover and rear support wings were all engaged – reportedly by mixtures of 109s and FW 190s.

603 were also found and attacked. They were told by Control that aircraft were in the vicinity, but there was little warning of the attack when it came. Flying with the guard section, Harold Bennett had none.

Weaving again I could see nothing. My Number 1 steep-turned upwards and to starboard. As I attempted to follow him, behind me there was a crash and things went haywire. I was going down with no alternatives. I knew that I had to get out and went through the drill but the forces were holding me in. I'd got rid of the canopy and the cockpit door and tried to get a grip outside when I believe the wind got inside my helmet and pulled me out sharply.

> My 'chute opened beautifully. Didn't have time to correct the swing and went very deep with the 'chute still full. I came up and found that I had no dinghy but the Mae West did its job.

Having lost so much height, it would seem good fortune played a part in overcoming the effects of the g-Force and throwing him from his Spitfire before it was too late. Nevertheless, he was in an unenviable predicament. His boots had come off but he realised that if they hadn't they might have countered what little buoyancy he had. Without his dinghy and nothing to stop the insidious chill of the sea getting into his body, his survival time was limited.

Meanwhile what was described as a 'sharp' engagement took place. 603 were bounced by about eight enemy fighters and after managing to withdraw, P/O Falconer (in P8786) and F/O Fawkes (in P8603) were both found to be missing as well as Sgt Bennett. During the fight, Sgt Lamb (in Spitfire Va W3110) was credited with a kill – a 109 which may have been an F-4 flown by Unteroffizier Joachim Bleefe of JG26 who was wounded during the fight. However, some sources suggest that it might have been an FW 190A-1 flown by Leutnant Walter Thom who died when his parachute failed to open. The CO, F/L Douglas-Hamilton and Sgt Rawson all reported firing at enemy aircraft during the engagement but without result.

At the end of the day, the RAF claimed to have destroyed four 109s and damaged another, and destroyed one FW 190. JG26 claimed six Spitfires confirmed destroyed. In fact, the RAF lost ten and attributed this to the superiority of the FW 190. It was unusual on both sides for the numbers claimed to be less than the actual losses. Of the ten, 603 lost three.

The eight remaining 603 Spitfires straggled back home. Two landed at Manston at 12.15 (15 minutes before the Hurricanes of 607 arrived back) and the rest were all back at Fairlop by 12.45.

Sgt Bennett remained in the Channel. He doesn't know how long he was in the sea, but thinks it was probably only 15-20 minutes – quite long enough for him to already be numb with the cold and likely to die if he couldn't warm up quickly:

> I saw the top of the mast of a ship. My father had given me a police whistle and I blew it to attract their attention. It was a German armed trawler. I remember seeing them holding a pole out for me to grab and once I was on the deck, a sailor coming towards me with a big knife. At first I thought he was going to kill me, but it was to cut my clothing off to see if I was wounded. The treatment from these sailors was superb. I think they were regulars. Most of the time below deck they fed me hot coffee and using a blanket, massaged life back into my frozen limbs.

The Germans had many of these armed trawlers which were used to escort coastal convoys as flak ships and Bennett thinks that it might have been a lucky shot from the trawler that brought him down because of the lack of warning. After landing ashore, Harold Bennett was taken to hospital in St Omer. In the ambulance taking him there, he met P/O Falconer who had also survived the fight but was now a PoW as well. Hamish had broken his leg and Bennett remembers that he seemed in considerable pain. He asked Bennett to hold his leg to ease the pain and when he did so he could feel the break. Even that was too painful for Falconer who eventually asked his fellow pilot just to let the broken leg rest on its own.

F/O Fawkes, the third missing pilot, had perished. His body was never recovered. Flying Officer Stephen Guye Hawksworth Fawkes was the son of Stephen and Pauline Fawkes of Ladybrand, Orange Free State, South Africa. He was 23 when he died and he is remembered on the Runnymede Memorial, Panel 30.

Following the return of all the aircraft to their respective bases, a number of patrols were sent up to look for ditched pilots. These were carried out by 602, 452 and 485 Squadrons from Kenley and 401 and 124 from Biggin Hill. By late afternoon they were called off without having found any of the missing RAF men. 401 and 452 Squadrons came up against the Luftwaffe and one pilot of 452 Squadron was missing. He had been last seen chasing an FW 190 back towards France.

For Sgt Harold Bennett the air war was over. He never took his 48-hour leave and remained in captivity for the rest of the war. He was eventually released by the advancing Soviet Army, his German captors having fled. But Harold suffered hardship along the way, which peaked just prior to liberation.

For Lord David Douglas-Hamilton, this was his first taste of dogfighting. He had engaged 109s and 190s and whilst he fired many bursts, he didn't record any hits. Eventually he found himself 'belting along over the sea' being targeted by flak, but he wasn't hit. He vowed that he would 'do better next time'.

Wilfrid Duncan Smith was still in hospital in Romford when he heard what had befallen his old Squadron but he was led to understand that it had lost eight pilots, not three, which saddened and depressed him. He would eventually return to flying and have a distinguished career later on in the war, flying once again over France before going to Malta, becoming the Wing Leader of 324 Wing in Italy and eventually the Officer Commanding Number 1 Base Area at Naples. After that, in 1945, he attended Staff College at Bracknell. Post war he took command of 603 Squadron.

There was no more flying that day, nor on the morning of the 9th, but convoy patrols were carried out in the afternoon. There were 12 sorties between 13.20 and 16.00 with one bit of excitement. Two pairs of Spitfires took off at 14.10 – F/L Douglas-Hamilton and Sgt Waddy as one pair, and Sgt Lamb (W3242) and Sgt Thomas (W3110) as the other. At 14.35, the two sergeants were over a convoy off Clacton when Lamb's Spitfire – a Vb – developed engine problems and he had to bale out. He landed safely in the sea and was lucky to be rescued by a patrol boat within a matter of minutes and so was none the worse for his soaking. Thomas returned to Fairlop by 16.00.

The next day brought high winds with little to report. The following day Sgt Thomas had his own excitement when he made a 'wheels up' landing on the airfield. The 12th brought rain allowing only practise flying.

It was now decided that 603 Squadron should be sent back home to Scotland to a quieter area and it seems that this move may have been prompted by the losses of 8 December. Packing up started on 13 December and bad weather curtailed any further operational flying other than two uneventful convoy patrols during the morning. When P/O Buckstone and P/O Kistruck returned to Fairlop at 12.00, theirs was the final operational sortie by 603 Squadron from the aerodrome. But 1942 was to bring yet more challenges, more demands of the men of 603, more tragic losses, and, as the cycle continued, still more fresh faces to join the experienced ones. Eventually, though, with the success and sacrifice of 603 and that of the other RAF squadrons and other arms of the nations forces, came victory.

On the evening of the 14th there was a party to celebrate the move, scheduled for the next day. It was a professional, lean, well experienced Squadron with pilots who were confident in their abilities and with the results to prove it that went north. They had weathered yet another storm.

As for Fairlop, it had a distinguished, if short, history.*

---

*In 1942, for the end of January and the first couple of weeks of February, Hornchurch was waterlogged so 64, 81 and 411 Squadrons moved to Fairlop. From there they took part in the search for the three German battleships, the *Scharnhorst, Gneisenau* and *Prinz Eugen* as they made their 'Channel Dash'. Following this, squadrons based there included 313 and 122 flying operations over France - much as 603 had been doing. 64 Squadron returned for the winter of 1942/43 and in 1943 the airfield became home to 609 Squadron - another auxiliary unit - flying Typhoons. By April of that year, 182 and 247 Squadrons were in residence also flying Typhoons. From then, there was a mixture of Typhoons and 'Hurri-bombers' carrying out sweeps over France and attacking V1 sites. In 1944, a Ju88 of KG6 was brought down by anti-aircraft fire and crashed nearby in Chigwell. Reports suggest that by the time police arrived, local youngsters had reached the wreck and were playing with the aeroplane's loaded machine guns! With the V1 onslaught gathering strength, Fairlop became the site for a number of barrage balloons which were intended to bring down the small unmanned flying bombs. They were successful too and 24 Balloon Centre was credited with the destruction of about 19 although a number crashed in fields uncomfortably close to the airfield. A German PoW camp was built in Forest Road and an Italian one in the Beech Grove area. The prisoners were employed in manual work in the area and some stayed in the camps until well after the war ended. In 1945 the Balloon Centre disbanded and RAF Fairlop finally closed in August 1946. Flying wasn't quite finished though. It acted as a gliding school for the Air Training Corps for a spell and as with many other disused airfields, it saw model aircraft taking to the skies where not many years before, Spitfires, Hurricanes and Typhoons had roared off to do battle over France. Eventually, it became a country park - Fairlop Waters - with an artificial lake, a sailing school and a golf course. By then, little remained to show that it had once been an operational airfield. Concrete tank traps near the railway line and the two underground stations could still be seen at the beginning of the 21st Century and of course, there remain in nearby cemeteries the graves of young airmen who were killed whilst serving there. In 2002, Fairlop was the rendezvous point for the aircraft taking part in the flypast over Buckingham Palace to celebrate the Golden Jubilee of Queen Elizabeth II. It was perhaps fitting that this should be so and that the site of this barely remembered airfield should once again, if only fleetingly, be an important marker for the RAF aircraft taking part even if their pilots were probably not aware of its historical significance.

Dyce

At 10.30 on Monday 15 December 1941, 603's Spitfires 'set off in fine style' from RAF Fairlop and flew the 400 or so miles north to RAF Dyce near Aberdeen. Their route took them via RAF Catterick and RAF Drem and they eventually arrived at their new base in the early afternoon. 'Successful movement without a hitch was carried out both in the air and on the ground' reported the Squadron ORB.

For distances such as those, the ground crew would either be taken by air or by train – or a combination of these. Handley-Page Harrows were once again used for this purpose.

Dyce was not new to 603 – the Squadron had been based there during 1940 and whilst British attention continued to focus on the air war in the south east of England and across the Channel to France and the Low Countries, this part of Scotland was not a backwater and although the Squadron would have the chance to relax, regroup and retrain, there was almost daily activity by the Luftwaffe which needed to be monitored and countered if possible.

There were several major Royal Navy bases on the east coast – Rosyth on the Firth of Forth, Invergordon on the Moray Firth and Scapa Flow in the Orkney Islands. The ports at Aberdeen, Montrose and Arbroath saw a constant shuttling of British naval vessels of all sizes moving north and south between these bases to discharge their roles in protecting the eastern seaboard, shepherding the Russian convoys round the North Cape of Norway to Murmansk and generally 'working up'. The Navy was also aware of the constant threat of major German battleships breaking out from the North Sea or the Baltic into the Atlantic through the Iceland or Faroes Gaps to pounce on convoys fighting the 'Battle of the Atlantic' then at its height.

There were also small convoys which hugged the coast and had to be protected, and trawlers slipping out to the fishing grounds.

The coast of Norway is about 250 miles away and the Luftwaffe had aircraft based there and in Denmark. Whilst 603 was at Dyce over this period, the most common encountered were Ju88s (which, depending on type, had a range of the order of 1,500 to 2,000 miles) operating from bases such as Banak and Kristiansand.

Fighter Command structure designated Scotland north of the Tay as 14 Group with two sector stations – one at Dyce, the other at Kirkwall in Orkney. In addition, there were aircraft based at Montrose, Peterhead, Fraserburgh (a satellite of Peterhead), Castletown (near Wick), Skeabrae (also in Orkney and charged with the defence of Scapa Flow) and Tain. Often squadron flights rather than whole squadrons were sent to these other airfields.

There were other fighter squadrons who worked with 603 during this latest spell in the north. 416 (City of Oshawa) – a Canadian squadron – (code letters DN) flying Spitfire IIas and 132 (code letters FF) using Spitfire IIbs were operating from Peterhead although 132 also worked out of Dyce. Another auxiliary squadron, 611 (West Lancashire) (code letters FY), was based at Dyce flying Spitfire Mark Vbs. 331 Squadron (code letters FN), a Norwegian unit, was based in the Orkneys with Spitfire IIas. 54 Squadron (code letters KL) flying Spitfire IIbs and 123 Squadron flying Spitfire Vbs were at Castletown. Boulton-Paul Defiant Mk Is of 410 Squadron (code letters RA) were also active.

In addition to Fighter Command squadrons, Coastal Command, Bomber Command and even the Fleet Air Arm had units in the area. By 16 February 1942, 883 Squadron of the FAA had six of their Hurricanes from RNAS Yeovilton in Somerset operational at windswept Peterhead.

235 Squadron of Coastal Command flying Beaufighters (which had only recently replaced Blenheims) also called Dyce 'home'. Kinloss and Lossiemouth on the north coast near Elgin were bases for Bomber Command Operational Training Units (OTUs) 19 and 20 respectively flying Ansons, Whitleys and Wellingtons and there were OTU satellite airfields at Elgin and Nairn (Brackla).

Bomber Command kept an eye on the German battleship *Tirpitz* which reached Norway in the middle of January 1942 to lurk in the Aasfjord at Trondheim, and there was clandestine activity with the operations being undertaken to build up and support the Norwegian resistance.

Later in the war, the Strike Wing based at Banff flying Mosquitoes was very active in prosecuting activity against the German occupiers of Norway and harassing his shipping. Without a doubt, there were many different aircraft operating in the crowded airspace around Aberdeen – a number of them piloted by inexperienced trainees. And in addition, the frequent, almost daily Luftwaffe sorties added a sense of threat – albeit muted.

Dyce, 1941.

Amongst the pilots who were with 603 during their three and a half months at Dyce were: Squadron Leader Roger Forshaw, Flight Lieutenants David Douglas-Hamilton, John Buckstone and 'Bill' Douglas, Flying Officer 'Tony' Holland, Pilot Officers Paul Forster, W.I. Jones, Neville King and Stone, Flight Sergeants Cook and 'Johnny' Hurst, Sergeants C.F. Bush, 'Les' Colquhoun, Dalley, John Farmer, Kistruck, Loudon, Allan W. Otto, D. Prytherch, Rawson, Des Ruchwaldy, Thomas, Waddy, Walcott and Webster.

There were movements during this time and those mentioned above were not all on the strength for the whole period. Before they left Dyce, many of the experienced pilots would move on to other units and the number of new and inexperienced pilots was to become contentious when 603 eventually moved away. Also, as we shall discover, Flight Lieutenant David Douglas-Hamilton became the CO within a few days of their arrival, but under unfortunate circumstances.

The aircraft operated by 603 during this spell in Scotland were in the main Spitfire Vbs although there were a few Vas still in use. Some of those used were: AB144, AB184 (XT-H), AB269 (XT-E), AD502, AD557 (XT-E), AD503 (XT-K), AD449 (XT-A), BL386, BL431 (XT-N), BL510 (XT-D), BL314, BL379 (XT-J), BL748 (XT-N), BL634 (XT-B), P8784, P8720 (XT-F), P8796 (XT-D), P8585, R7226 (XT-A), R7224, R7305, W3110, W3631 (XT-L), W3647 (XT-X), W3833 and W3423. (Some have the same identification letter because they were being operated at different times.)

When he became CO, S/L David Douglas-Hamilton frequently used P8796 and R7224 was a favourite of F/L John Buckstone.

In addition, the Squadron had the use of Miles Magister (N3918) as a communications 'hack' and in support, they occasionally used a Hurricane IA (Z2641) DD-H for target towing.

Their first full day at Dyce was 16 December and there was a sense of excitement at being back in the north. 'First day at Dyce was an exhilarating experience, the clean cold air being such a great change from the foggy, sooty, air at Fairlop.' There was practice flying with some of the pilots making area familiarisation flights – 'sector reccos'. Whilst 603 wasn't involved in any operational flying the Fighter Sector ORB notes that:

2 E/A operated off Aberdeenshire coast between 1720 and 1800hrs. 1 E/A dropped 6 – 8 bombs near a trawler and the Lighthouse Tender 'PHAROS' 5 miles N.E. of Peterhead. No hits damage or casualties.' The previous evening, an 'E/A came up the coast from Fifeness in 13 Group and dropped 2 objects (probably mines) in the sea 1 mile E. of Bridge of Don. E/A turned away sharply before coming within range of A.A.

The enemy activity may not have been significant compared with the south coast, but even on their first day, the Squadron became aware that it would be no holiday.

Also on the 16th A Flight of 132 Squadron left Dyce for Montrose and B Flight of 611 returned to Drem.

Weather being a vital factor in military activity, Britain was fortunate that the prevailing weather systems moved from west to east – from the Atlantic to continental Europe – so that for air operations across the North Sea and the Channel, the likely weather conditions which would be met could be forecast with a reasonable degree of accuracy from observations of what passed overhead. (It probably has to be admitted that Bomber Command crews flying deep into Germany in later years did, on many occasions, find that the forecast weather differed significantly from the reality.)

For the Luftwaffe, the opposite was true – their operations meant that they had to fly west, into weather conditions that they had not been able to observe beforehand other than by regular daily weather reconnaissance flights towards a hostile coast. Such flights were routine. As had been the case in early 1940, they sent an almost daily morning flight to the North Sea coast near Dyce. The aircraft – usually Ju88s – would patrol out to sea and the pilots of 603 tried to anticipate the flights and intercept. The ORB for 14 February 1942 records a typical interception effort: 'F/Lt Buckstone and Sgt Colquhoun had a crack at a Junkers 88 known as "Weather Willie" who at about 0900 hrs. is plotted at distances varying from 100 to 60 miles from the coast in the North Sea. They did not make contact.' The 603 ORB records the British pilots taking off at 10.00 and being airborne for half an hour. The weather on this occasion wasn't on their side with clouds '8/10-10/10 at 3000-4000 feet' although visibility was '15-20 miles'.

The apparent time discrepancy *may* be caused by the use of British Summer Time that winter.

Two days later, on 16 February, 603 tried again to shoot down the intruder. The pilots on this occasion were S/L Douglas-Hamilton and F/L Buckstone who took off in Spitfires BL431 and R7224 at 09.30 and were airborne for 65 minutes. The weather was 'fine but hazy with slight frost' and visibility was four-six miles, although there was no cloud: 'An attempt to intercept "Weather Willie" did not prove successful, the enemy aircraft was too far out'.

During the period that 603 operated from Dyce at this time, they and other squadrons made a number of attempts to shoot down Weather Willie but with no success at all.

On 17 December things were quiet with a couple of patrols in the morning and some practice flying and dusk landings.

In mid-December, the shortest day was almost upon them and it was fully dark by late afternoon. For the aircrew operating over the north-east corner of Scotland, much of their flying time was over the North Sea, which is never hospitable and for a ditched pilot or the survivor from a sunken ship without protection, is lethally cold. Without proper protection, it can kill within a matter of 20-30 minutes. The risk to flyers was clear; ditching in the North Sea meant a thin chance of survival.

Modern-day aircrew wear immersion suits – one-piece suits made of butyl-backed nylon with latex neck and cuff seals to keep the water out and giving the downed pilot or navigator more of a chance to keep warm and survive until the rescue helicopter arrives. RAF aircrew at the end of 1941 were not as well protected. Their personal equipment, although improved, remained much the same as it had been in the '30s. Typically, they wore heavy serge blouses and trousers, which became known as 'battledress' but was issued by the RAF as flying kit with the official nomenclature 'suit, blue grey (blouse and trousers)'. It was based on the army pattern. They might wear the Irvin jacket – the much coveted heavy sheepskin jacket with its flappy collar – and some, in particular the bomber crews would also wear trousers of the same material which were often issued at the same time as the jacket. But at this stage of the war, few of the 603 pilots had been given Irvin jackets, and at the end of the war they were still in short supply and tended to be passed on from one pilot to another.

Flying Officer John Moss, who was a pilot with 603 for a short spell in 1945, recalls with some amusement the off-white aircrew sweater known as 'frock, white, aircrew' which was a woollen crew neck. It wasn't unusual to hear someone shouting "Who's pinched my 'frock'?"!

Hands were protected by thin leather gloves (typically '1941 pattern gauntlets') which were designed to be worn over thin silk liners, but were usually worn on their own. (One pilot used silk stockings as liners!) These were intended to give some protection from fire, although there was no fire retardant material in them. F/O Moss also remembers that when doing his flying training in Canada over the winter of 1942/43 he found that the official issue gauntlets had two distinct drawbacks. One was that they didn't actually keep fingers and thumbs warm enough, and secondly that if an altimeter or compass setting needed to be changed, they weren't thin enough to provide the necessary 'feel' and it became an effort to take them off and put them on again. He used wool-lined leather mitts which kept the fingers warm and could be easily 'whipped off' when a change of setting was needed.

Heavy fleece-lined boots and a lifejacket were also worn and whilst those used by the 603 pilots at Dyce were a newer type, their basic equipment was much the same as it had been during the Battle of Britain, Irvin jacket, lifejacket and boots.

Some RAF flying equipment of the period is known by its year of issue. The lifejackets worn in 1940 were '32 pattern because they had been issued first in 1932; those worn by 603 during this duty spell at Dyce were '41 pattern. These were better than the earlier pattern in a number of ways. The older version was grey which restricted its visibility in the sea and many pilots who wore them painted the front yellow to make it more easily seen. The '41 pattern was a bright yellow when issued. It had a small bottle of compressed carbon dioxide at the lower right hand side which would inflate the stole after the wearer gave a small strap a sharp tug. The '32 pattern jacket had to be inflated by blowing into a tube situated at about mouth level. The new jacket also had an inbuilt patch on the left hand side that could be ripped away to release a coloured dye into the water. This would spread out and create a more visible stain for searching aircraft. It was developed further over the months from its initial issue in the middle of 1941. Leg tapes were added to stop the jacket riding up whilst in the water and stout loops were attached to the front to help pull the ditched airman to the side of a boat with a boathook and then pull him on board. There were other pockets which held a heliograph and a yellow cotton skullcap with ties under the chin to serve a double function in helping to make the ditched airman more visible as well as protecting him from the sun in warmer climes.

Similarly, the boots worn were '40 pattern. During the Battle of Britain, those in use were often the '36 pattern, or the '39 pattern which came well up towards the knee, with a leather strap and buckle at the top to hold them securely. The '40 pattern boots were shorter, with a sealed rubber-type sole and a zip which pulled together the suede leather uppers. They were fleece lined. A major deficiency with them was that the forces encountered during an escape from a damaged aeroplane often pulled them off the airman's feet so that many a shot-down bomber crewman arrived in enemy territory in his socks. The '41 pattern tried to overcome this by providing a thin leather strap around the ankle which could be buckled tightly and hopefully would stop the boot coming off. A further disadvantage for an evader was that they were very obviously flying boots which brought an added risk of detection and capture. In later years, yet another type of boot was introduced designed to allow the fleece-lined leggings to be cut away to leave a more traditional 'Oxford'-type shoe which would be less likely to be noticed in enemy territory.

However, if the ditched pilot managed to get out of the aeroplane and into the water, the situation was perilous indeed. If he had a life raft and if he managed to inflate it, all that it would do for him would be to take him out of the chilling water. Unlike those used today which have all-round cover and doors that seal, during the war most were quite open with only a few providing any other protection. Some had a cape and apron to give some protection from a rough sea but the occupant might very well be sitting in water pooled on the floor, and of course as well as being exposed to spray, most gave no protection from the wind, rain or snow. No chance to dry out.

An ASR unit was based at Aberdeen and there were Coastal Command and other aircraft in the area which were quite capable of handling sea searches, but the fact remains that an airman who found himself in the icy North Sea in the middle of a winter's night would be fortunate to survive.

If any of the men who had come back to Scotland still retained any illusions that it would be an easy and safe posting, these must have been rudely dispelled by the time they went to bed on Thursday 18 December after the Squadron's first loss of this period at Dyce was recorded.

In mid-morning, Blue Section of 603 was scrambled (F/L Douglas-Hamilton in AD502 and Sgt Colquhoun in W3110) together with Green and Yellow Sections of 132 Squadron to patrol the coast looking for enemy aircraft thought to be in the area but nothing was found and the Spitfires all landed safely back at base at about mid-day.

There was no activity in the afternoon. In the evening after dark fell, two hostile raids were plotted near the city. Sgt Ruchwaldy (in AD 557) took off at 17.15 for 35 minutes on a 'black patrol' and to the north of Aberdeen, intercepted a Beaufighter which may have been one of the reported 'enemy' aircraft. The Coastguard and the Observer Corps claimed to have seen a Ju88, but the Beaufighter and the Ju88 were not dissimilar in appearance, and in difficult visual conditions it would have been easy to confuse them. Although in more important sectors intercepting night-fighter Beaufighters were already equipped with airborne radar, single-seat fighters had to rely on eyesight – the 'Eyeball Mark I'! It was possible on a good night to spot another aeroplane up to about 1,000 yards away but many night-fighter pilots never saw a thing – even their own 'friendlies' working the same area, perhaps a thousand feet above or below. Because of the risk of collision in the dark, night-fighter single seaters usually operated on their own, as 'singletons'.

The position of the engine exhaust stubs created a further difficulty for a Spitfire pilot operating in the dark. Whilst the hot gas was invisible during the day, at night it glared brightly which had the effect of both ruining the pilot's night vision and restricting further his vision to the front. Covers were sometimes fixed above them to try to reduce the effect, but they were never completely successful and it was always a problem.

Sgt Ruchwaldy did well to spot the Beaufighter.

After he had landed, the CO, S/L Forshaw, received permission from 14 Group to try to intercept a plot, designated 'raid 552'. He never came back.

Having taken off from Dyce a few minutes after 6 o'clock (in P8796 XT-D) he was given (and acknowledged) two vectors which, after six or seven minutes, took him to a point over the dark sea to the south and east of Newburgh and two or three miles from it. Suddenly, the radio went dead and then a minute or two later the Coastguard and Observer Corps listeners heard a loud noise variously described as a 'crash', a 'thud' or a 'bang'. No flash or any sound of any gunfire was reported so quite what happened to him will never be known.

A search was carried out that night by motor launches, a trawler and a Whitley from Lossiemouth which dropped flares but 'nothing more was seen or heard of the Squadron Leader'.

Two weeks later, on 3 January 1942, a fisherman brought up aircraft wreckage from the sea bed and it was identified as being part of his Spitfire but that was the sum total of any subsequent clues. What actually happened can only be conjectured.

Flying on his own meant that if anything should go wrong, there was no immediate help on hand – although in the pitch black, a second aircraft might not have been able to give much assistance in any case. The lack of firing or any explosion suggests that he had not found his target and the loud noise heard by the observers on the coast could have been a catastrophic structural failure or the noise of his Spitfire hitting the sea. Witnesses to air crashes often say that they heard an 'explosion' when in fact what they heard was part of the structure failing suddenly with great force.

It is difficult to judge height over water, particularly at night, and it may be that he had decided to try to spot the intruder by flying low to silhouette it against the sky. (During an incident on 31 January 1942 an attempt was made to find an intruder but because it flew low on the water it was difficult to spot.) If this is what he was doing, he may have been concentrating on looking up and inadvertently allowed the aircraft to descend into the water. 'Spatial disorientation' is not unusual at night. Or it could be that the pressure setting of the altimeter was incorrect so that the altitude reading showed a height greater than it really was.

But there are other possibilities. Although only airborne for a few minutes if, on taking off, he had put the Spitfire into a hard climb, he would have been at altitude for enough time for an oxygen failure to have caused sufficient impairment for him to lose control.

Another problem was that a particularly violent manoeuvre – whether made deliberately or not – could cause unconsciousness because of the high 'G' forces involved and unlike modern aircraft, these Spitfires did not have any mechanism for protecting the pilot from these.

Yet a further potential hazard was the life raft itself – if he had one. It was situated in a seat pack between the pilot's backside and his parachute and it wasn't unknown for it to inflate for no obvious reason in the cockpit. When this happened, the ballooning dinghy squeezed out towards the instrument panel and pushed the control column forward, putting the Spitfire into a fatal dive. Some pilots, particularly later in the war, tucked a small knife into the top of one of their boots so that they could reach it easily and stick it into the burgeoning yellow mass to recover control. (As an aside, the dinghy pack was not a comfortable seat. One pilot likened it to 'sitting on a bag of cricket balls for hours on end'.)

If he managed to get out of the cockpit, S/L Forshaw was unlikely to survive for long in the dark and the icy water. But the absence of anything other than the wreckage found by the fisherman suggests that he went down with his Spitfire.

The official 'crash card', the Form 1180, indicates that the cause of his failure to return was loss of control, engine failure or enemy action, but that the most likely reason was 'loss of control'.

There are slight differences in the official records for his sortie. The 603 ORB states that the CO took off at 18.03 or 18.05, that the plot ceased at 18.10 and the R/T stopped at 18.12. The Fighter Sector ORB has him 'plotted as being 2 miles 180 degrees' from Newburgh at 1807 hours, and the noise heard between 1808 and 1810.

The detail of times is really not important – the loss of the Squadron Leader was.

Squadron Leader Roger Gatty Forshaw (37009) was born in Berkshire on 29 December 1913. He had a wife Anne, and they lived at Chesham Bois, Buckinghamshire. At the time of his death, he had logged 1,580 hours, of which 90 were in the 'accident type'. He had also amassed 92 hours night-flying time. His death is commemorated on Panel 28 of the Runnymede Memorial. The 603 ORB marked his passing: 'S/Ldr Forshaw joined the Squadron on October 19th. 1941. In the short time that he was with us, he endeared himself to the entire Squadron by personality and enthusiasm, and he is greatly missed.'

Although not explicitly recorded, there can be little doubt that the death of the CO cast a cloud over the Squadron. They had come north for a rest, away from the stresses and tensions of the intense and dangerous strike activity in the south, expecting a less risky and slower pace. His loss under such circumstances must have been hard to reconcile.

With no good news to set down, on 19 December 1941, the ORB laconically notes: 'A/S/Ldr. Lord D. Douglas Hamilton [sic] assumed control of the Squadron, his appointment to command followed very closely.'

Lord David Douglas-Hamilton was a tall, powerful man possessing an instinctive air of authority and leadership. He had been a Scottish Heavyweight Boxing International and Captain of the Oxford University Boxing Team and was a natural leader ideally suited to pick up the reins so suddenly dropped. He did not know it, but the new CO was destined to lead 603 through one of its most critical and testing periods.

At Dyce, the enemy activity was enough to allow the Squadron to work with its new leader in situations where the operational needs were real, but not overwhelming. Setting aside the tragic circumstances which gave rise to his command, it was better that it happened when it did, rather than, say, three months later when their time in the north was about to end.

S/L Lord David Douglas-Hamilton and F/L Bill Douglas at RAF Dyce in 1942. They kept a diary of the Squadron's activities on Malta later in the year, which has been a prime source of information for this history.

On 21 December, a convoy passed through the sector and a patrol was mounted for an hour mid-morning by Sgts Cook and Rawson. In the late afternoon, Sgts Hurst and Bush (in AD502 and P8784 respectively) were scrambled to investigate plots of unidentified aircraft but nothing was found and their 45-minute sortie was classified as a 'convoy patrol'. F/L Douglas and Sgt Ruchwaldy spent an hour exercising with the Aberdeen 'ack ack' guns.

Between then and Christmas Day there was little activity – practice flying at all times of the day and night. 25 December, a Thursday, was quiet. Two enemy aircraft were in the sector between 5 and 6pm and an attempt to intercept in a Hurricane was made by a Norwegian pilot called Lieutenant Berg (who was with 331 Squadron but attached temporarily to the Fighter Sector HQ). He had difficulty in getting airborne because of a heavy shower of sleet and by the time he reached the area where the plot had been recorded, the enemy had long departed and on his way home – no doubt to a warm mess and Christmas dinner!

This was the third Christmas of the war. 603 had spent each one at a different station, although always in Scotland. It is traditional that the officers serve the 'other ranks' their Christmas dinner and this would be happening all over the world where British units were gathered and not in action. It is a chance to forget the realities, to enjoy a break and relax in the easy companionship of others thrown together by circumstance in demanding situations. But before getting down to the serious business of drinking and eating, there was a little practice flying on a cold, grey and unpleasant day.

Sgt Harold Bennett, who had been shot down into the Channel on 11 December, was now a prisoner in Stalag Luft 7a near Munich. His Christmas was in stark contrast. He recalled feeling that there seemed to be just no end in sight; that his only prospect was captivity. With the war not seeming to be going well for the Allies, and in this difficult and strange environment there seemed little hope for him.

The Allied situation was still desperate. On Christmas Day 1941, the British forces in Hong Kong surrendered to the Japanese. The Germans however were stalled in Russia to the west of Moscow. The Germans held Crete and Rommel's Afrika Korps swept all in its path. If any of the members of 603 took the time to think about it on that bleak day in December 1941, they *might* have realised that at Christmas 1940, the expectation had been for another Battle of Britain type assault in 1941, but instead, the RAF (and 603) had managed to take the battle to the Germans so that this Christmas, the tables were turning – just. But few probably did. Their thoughts were on home and what would happen to them before they would see it again.

On Boxing Day there was no enemy activity, but 603 flew some sorties in poor weather before it started to snow in the afternoon. It continued for the rest of the day, blanketing the airfield and the countryside to a depth of about two inches. A Flight of 603 left for Montrose at first light and there was some practice flying. Bill Douglas, the Flight Commander flying his favourite Spitfire (AB184) XT-H.

The week drifted on to Hogmanay and the year changed with 603 engaged in a mixture of practice flights, convoy and naval patrols and scrambles to intercept the almost daily flow of Luftwaffe aircraft coming across the North Sea.

CHAPTER 5

REST, SNOW AND 'WEATHER WILLIE'

New Year's Day 1942 dawned with fog and a visibility of 600 yards, but it cleared to reveal broken cloud which built up during the afternoon. Some German activity had been expected and two sections patrolled the coast at Collieston for an hour in the morning, although with no result. In the late afternoon at 17.05, Sgt Farmer, making what was probably a non-operational flight in (R7226) XT-A flew into Auchterhouse Hill in very poor visibility. It is 1,398 feet high, a few miles north of Dundee and north west of RAF Tealing, a training airfield. Details of the accident are sparse, but it may be that he had been on leave and was returning to his unit. In any case, Sgt John Anthony Farmer was killed and became 603's first casualty of 1942.

For the next week or so, the weather was miserable – a mixture of sleet, snow, rain and cloud – cold and depressing. Those out of doors wished they were inside – those who were inside were glad that they were. The ground crew were billeted at Dyce, but those tasked with helping with the night flying had to make do with old railway carriages. These were crawling with rats and the men, understandably, were very unhappy with this.

Dawn on Monday 12 January brought the next incident of any consequence. The weather was squally with 6/10 to 8/10 cloud cover at about 2,000 feet, sometimes 10/10 at 1,000 feet and lowering to 400 in the showers. Visibility was about 400 yards all day. The 603 ORB records:

> At 06.55 Sgt Ruchwaldy with F/Lt. Buckstone did practice dark interceptions. Sgt Ruchwaldy was unable to make home base and eventually tried to force land along the River Dee. His aircraft struck the river bank and was badly damaged. Fortunately, he was not killed, but sustained a fracture of the spine, and he is expected to make a good recovery.

He had been flying Spitfire (AD503) XT-K and force-landed at 09.10* at the small village of Drum Oak – between Peterculter and Crathes – hitting an earth bank.

As with the loss of S/L Forshaw, there can only be speculation. If the pair were practising interceptions, they are likely to have done this to the east, over the North Sea, because firstly, this was where intruding aircraft were most often found and secondly to the west, the land rises to heights greater than 2,000 feet. If the weather conditions were as bad as stated, and even if they topped out the cloud to carry out their training in clear sky above, there would be the risk of letting down through the cloud and hitting the hills.

Descending through the cloud near the coast or over the sea would give the pilots the chance to see the coastline, pick up a landmark like the River Don and follow it to the airfield at Dyce.

However, it was wartime and there was a blackout so the lights of Aberdeen and other towns wouldn't be readily identifiable. If 06.55 was 'local' time, it was an hour ahead of GMT (as Britain used British Summer Time during that winter) and it would be dark. Even at first light, at about 08.45 (BST) it would still have been dull and difficult to spot any features.

The Spitfire came down on the banks of the River *Dee*, not the *Don*. It is the Don which loops round the airfield at Dyce. The Dee is on the south side of Aberdeen. If he was using it as a landmark, Sgt Ruchwaldy *may* have mistakenly thought he saw the Don and was following it upstream hoping to find the airfield in the gloom. Alternatively, he may have realised that it was the Dee and was using it to pinpoint his position with the aim of striking north towards Dyce, or south towards Montrose. Following the river to the sea, then flying down the coast to Montrose would

---

*Again, the times recorded may be a mixture of GMT and local time.

have been a better option as the airfield there was near the sea and easier to find. In any event, he apparently ran out of fuel.

Sgt Desmond Ruchwaldy never flew with the Squadron again. He may have been 'expected to make a good recovery' from his injuries, but this would take time. He was born in Singapore in 1920 and his home was at Hurstpierpoint in Sussex. He was a bank clerk before enlisting for aircrew in July 1940 and he subsequently went on to be commissioned in 1942, being awarded the DFM in 1942 and the DFC in 1944. By then he had destroyed seven enemy aircraft.

There was a little activity later on in the morning when a Ju88 dropped three bombs at Newburgh, on the coast. Two sections of 603 were scrambled – Sergeants Prytherch (in BL319) and Loudon (P8720) at 11.30 and Sergeants Bush (W3833) and Colquhoun (AD502) at 11.38. Their patrols found nothing and they were both back on the ground by 12.45.

For the rest of the week things were quiet, with a round of training flights – one a practice Rhubarb on 14 January by Sergeants Cook and Loudon – and little enemy activity. The weather tended to be cold and miserable with low clouds, wintry showers and gusty winds. The sort of weather that makes life an ordeal for those working on aircraft in the open, or even in unheated hangars. The skin on the hands becomes parchment thin. Numbed fingers seem to attract little cuts and grazes that, once in the warmth, ache and take days to mend. It is easy to start cutting corners. Dangerous incidents can occur such as when the guns of one Spitfire were fired accidentally whilst they were being checked. Luckily, on that occasion no one was hurt.

Dyce closed for flying on the Tuesday and the Thursday (although Montrose was open and tried to intercept a reported hostile contact near Ballater) but Friday 16 January brought heavy snow at Dyce preventing flying with all available personnel turned out for snow clearing. This became a pattern for the next few days. The following extracts from the 603 Operations Record Book (ORB) set the scene:

18/1/42	Snow again, no flying possible.
19/1/42	Squadron engaged on snow clearing. No flying possible.
20/1/42	P.T. exercises helped to keep the pilots in fighting trim. There was no flying possible owing to snow, and poor visibility.
21/1/42	Snow clearing during day. No flying again possible owing to very poor visibility.
22/1/42	More snow and rain for about 30 hours, much slush and water, but snow cleared away rapidly. Flying impossible. Cloud base 10/10 at 600 feet.

The ORB for the Dyce Fighter Sector tells a similar story.

19/1/42. There was no enemy activity, though the weather behaved in a distinctly hostile manner. There was a cold S.E. wind which brought snow about 1900 hours. An aerodrome Defence Exercise scheduled for early on 20/1/42 was cancelled owing to snow.

It must have been pretty bad!!

20/1/42. A high wind, snow and visibility limited by 10/10 cloud at 1200ft made flying impossible, even if snow on the runways had not made taking off impossible. All hands set about snow clearing and before evening the aerodrome was fit for flying, though drifts on the roads were interfering with traffic. A Hun aircraft appeared off Stonehaven about 1220 and went away again from off Kinnairds Head, no hostile acts being reported.

On Friday 23 January, the weather – this time heavy rain which helped get rid of the snow – still prevented flying and nine of the pilots visited the ASR boats in Aberdeen. These were likely to have been helping in the search to find S/L Forshaw when he had gone down in the sea a month before. It would give the pilots confidence to have some contact with the crews who might very well be out searching for them in the future and to understand some of their problems.

It was misty with low cloud on Saturday 24 January. The nine pilots – presumably from B Flight at Dyce – visited the nearby RDF (Radio Direction Finding) station at Schoolhill – a Chain Home aerial.

One of the station WAAF officers, Assistant Section Officer Peterson, left Dyce to travel by road to RAF Peterhead where she had been posted. The 35 miles should only have taken a couple of hours at most but half way there the car stuck in the snow near Ellon and A/S/O Peterson was forced to abandon it in the arctic landscape and started to walk.

In the evening, the 603 officers held a Burn's Supper in the mess. 25 January is 'Burn's Night' and at the end of January, all over the world, enthusiasts of the works of 'Rabbie' Burns, the national bard of Scotland, hold formal 'suppers' to a tried and tested formula of a meal of haggis, 'neeps' (turnips) and 'champit tatties' (mashed potatoes) washed down with plenty of Scotch whisky, recitations of some of Burns' poetry, an address to the 'lassies' and a toast to the Immortal Memory of the great man himself – perhaps in Drambuie as it was 603.

Traditionally the steaming haggis is piped in to the dining room on a platter held aloft by the chef, and ceremoniously slit open after some worthy recites the address 'To a Haggis'. Rather than use a knife to open up the haggis, a ceremonial sword is sometimes used – certainly in the officers' mess at RAF Turnhouse! Having its own pipe band, there was no difficulty for the officers of 603 to find a piper and the honour on this occasion fell to Sgt Jackie Crooks.

Late that evening, the wind picked up and it started to rain. A/S/O Peterson was still somewhere between Ellon and Peterhead. By three in the morning, the rain turned to snow which continued throughout Sunday. The ORB reads:

> It was an incredible sight to see very heavy snow driven before a whole gale, with gusts reaching 65 mph. At no time throughout the entire day and onwards to mid-night did the gale or amount of snow diminish. Drifts of from two feet to four feet accumulated and all mobile traffic came to a standstill.... it was only possible to walk against (the driving snow) for short periods with great physical effort.

This became known as 'the great blizzard'. It prevented A/S/O Peterson reaching her destination until the following day, the Monday, 48 hours after she had left Dyce!

At Dyce the next few days were spent shovelling the snow to clear the runways and taxiways, but although it continued to be cold and icy, the snowfalls grew fewer and flying resumed. On 28 January, F/L Vernon of the Fighter Sector HQ was posted away to the Middle East; he was probably quite pleased to go! In the late afternoon, Red Section (F/Sgt Hurst in BL386 and Sgt Kistruck in W3647) scrambled to investigate an unknown aircraft off Montrose but it turned out to be a Coastal Command Blenheim and their sortie lasted ten minutes.

The next 'flap' happened at about 10.00 hours on Friday 30 January when the Squadron was called on to help find a Halifax of 76 Squadron MP-Q (L9581). It had taken off from RAF Lossiemouth near Elgin at about quarter past two that morning on a sortie to bomb *Tirpitz* – the German battleship – still anchored near Trondheim in Norway. The attacking force was made up of nine Halifaxes and seven Stirlings and in the event most didn't reach the Norwegian coast.

This bomber had suffered severe icing and a radio failure and was being nursed back over the North Sea by its pilot, Sgt J.W.H. Harwood, with its port inner engine u/s and getting low on fuel.

Aircraft from 416 and 603 Squadrons were scrambled to find the Halifax and escort it back to Dyce. Sgt Prytherch took off in BL510 and was airborne for 25 minutes, but almost at the coast, the Halifax lost too much height and ditched just off Aberdeen. Luckily, the entire crew survived without serious injury – possibly with the help of the ASR unit visited by 603!

Later in the day, F/O Tony Holland and P/O Forster flew to Montrose in 'the Maggie' – the 'hack' Miles Magister. The continual snow dragged spirits down: 'We are tired of shovelling snow.' The following day, the weather improved greatly, but there had been a heavy fall of snow overnight – '......once again snow clearing is the order of the day.' Late in the afternoon, F/O Holland returned to Dyce in 'the Maggie'. Also, a 'Hurricane' of 603 Squadron was reported as trying to intercept an enemy aircraft off Stonehaven, apparently looking for shipping to attack. The Hurricane was actually flown by a Norwegian pilot of 331 Squadron 'attached for night flying', and although he managed to close-in on the enemy, he was unable to see it because the German flew low, making it difficult to pick the aeroplane out against the dark sea. Although the Norwegian pilot may have been Lieutenant Berg – the same man who had taken off on Christmas Day to try to intercept a hostile plot – there was another incident a few days later on 5 February involving Lieutenant Lundsten who was attached to 603 from 331 for night flying. 331 flew Spitfires and it's unclear as to where the Hurricane came from but Hurricanes were used as target-towing aircraft and this one may have been issued to 603 for this purpose. The two flights by the Norwegian pilots were not recorded in the aircraft movement part of the 603 ORB and some incidents only appear in the Dyce Fighter Sector ORB.

Lt Lundsten had a lucky escape. He had taken off from the snowy airfield at dusk in a Hurricane to carry out a patrol. Whilst airborne, a gun panel on one wing blew up and bent back in the airflow creating the effect of an asymmetrical airbrake – pulling the aircraft round towards the side where the cover had opened. With two engines, he might have been able to reduce the effect by using the throttles to set differential engine power, but with one engine, he could only use the rudder. The stalling speed of the aeroplane rose to 140 mph and the Hurricane became almost un-flyable. But the pilot decided to try to land it rather than bale out which would have been a sensible option. With a touchdown speed of 160 mph, he pulled off a landing with the wheels up, crashing into a snow drift which helped cushion the impact, allowing him to escape with only bruising. One official account notes that the Hurricane was badly damaged – another that it 'was really very little damaged'. Whatever the state of the Hurricane, it is agreed that getting it back to Dyce and bringing it down constituted a feat of extraordinary airmanship on the part of Lt Lundsten.

At 17.00 hours the same day, there were reports that a convoy was under attack off Collieston and the readiness Spitfire – which wasn't 603 – scrambled to investigate, but found nothing. On its return, it landed whilst a lorry was on the runway laying out the flarepath and the aircraft touched it with a wing tip. There were no reports of any injuries.

For the next few days there was little out of the usual round of practice flying, patrols etc. The weather improved somewhat, becoming milder which started a thaw.

Sunday 8 February brought reasonably good weather and 603 carried out two scrambles and two convoy patrols. Eight aircraft were involved. There were also three practice Rhubarbs.

The following day, one of the few successful encounters with the Luftwaffe occurred. At 11.30 603 Red Section – F/Sgt Prytherch (in BL319) – Red 1 – and Sgt Rawson (in AB184) XT-H – Red 2 – scrambled (along with two other sections) at 11.30 to investigate a hostile and just before noon

Squadron photo taken at RAF Dyce, possibly in April 1942. Rear: P/O Stone (on prop), S/L Douglas-Hamilton and F/L Bill Douglas. Sitting on wing: P/O Murray, F/Sgt Hurst and F/L Buckstone. Front row: F/Sgt Prytherch, Sgt Loudon, F/O Holland, Sgt Thomas, Sgt Colquhoun, Sgt Waddy, Sgt Buckley, Sgt Bush, P/O Jones and P/O Neville King.

found a Ju88 about six miles to the east of Aberdeen over the sea. The weather was 7/10ths cloud at 1,500 feet with visibility six miles. The section patrolled at 1,000 feet and F/Sgt Prytherch spotted an aircraft approaching them from the rear at sea level. It passed below them and he allowed it to position itself between the two Spitfires and the coast. Red 2 moved into line astern and they dived on the unknown aircraft from the starboard quarter, identifying it as a Ju88. Red 1 opened fire and swung directly astern of the German giving it two bursts from cannon and machine gun. There was some return fire from the top dorsal gun of the bomber but it caused no damage. There were no signs of damage from Red 1's attack although splashes in the sea were seen under the Junkers.

Sgt Rawson moved in. He attacked from astern too, with a three-second burst. The Ju88 started to make its escape and turned east being harried by Rawson closing range and firing until he got to within 70 yards. He too was subjected to desultory return fire but again with no hits registering on the Spitfire. He broke away to port, then turned for another similar attack from the rear. This time, F/Sgt Prytherch, flying in line abreast saw hits on the starboard wing and smoke coming from the starboard engine. But, by now both Spitfires were out of ammunition so there was nothing more that they could do other than accompany the bomber away.

They were now about 60 miles from the coast and both British pilots saw another twin-engined aircraft flying towards them. It turned out to be a Blenheim which fired off the colours of the day and without deviating flew straight over the top of the Spitfires.

By this time, the Ju88 had drawn a mile or so ahead, so the section let it go and returned to Dyce at 12.25.

Because it wasn't seen to go down, the Ju88 was credited as a 'probable', but there were high hopes that it had been destroyed. This seemed even more likely when reports of a dinghy being seen off Kinnairds Head came in, and also late the next day, when a 'broadcast was received from Germany to say that ...a dinghy was 11 miles East of Kinnairds Head.' This was heard at about 5.30 in the afternoon but it was too late to carry out any searches, although a large part of Wednesday was spent by the Spitfires looking for it. Nothing was found and after two days of exposure in the North Sea it has to be assumed that the unfortunate German airmen perished.

Over the next few days the weather was cold but changeable. There was more snow but also some much clearer weather which encouraged flying. 14 February was particularly active with 14 Spitfires involved in patrols off Montrose and Aberdeen because of an almost constant flow of hostile plots, but with no contact with the enemy being made. There was also yet another concerted effort to bring down Weather Willie but with no success (see page 62).

On 15 February 1942 British and Commonwealth forces in Singapore surrendered to the Japanese invaders.

On 17 February, F/O Holland in W3833 was tasked with a dusk patrol and took off at 18.30 hours. The weather was cloudy, but generally good although the wind was 'very variable under 5 m.p.h.' The Fighter Sector Headquarters ORB records baldly: 'F/O Holland of 603 had an unfortunate crash on landing after this evening's routine patrol.' Tony Holland recalls that the accident was caused by a line squall which turned the wind round through 180 degrees, which in itself shouldn't have been a problem but Flying Control hadn't altered the flarepath direction. Landing with the wind behind him, Tony Holland was unable to stop the Spitfire before it ran into a bank of

RAF Dyce in 1942, possibly during Press Day. From left, Sgt Loudon, F/L Bill Douglas, S/L Douglas-Hamilton, F/L John 'Buck' Buckstone, P/O Stone and F/O Tony Holland.

solid snow – the detritus dug from the peri tracks and runways. Touching the brakes didn't help and he found himself neatly wedged between a Mosquito on the starboard side and a Beaufort – complete with torpedo – on the port! Both aircraft had suffered the same problem.*

On 18 February, a new cruiser moved through their sector and it was escorted by Spitfires of 603 led by F/L Douglas.

F/L Bill Douglas in XT-H, AB184. Probably taken 19 February 1942 during Press Day.

Time, attention and effort – particularly that of the CO – was spent on preparations for a visit by the Scottish press on Thursday 19 February when 14 journalists and photographers were duly entertained to lunch. In the afternoon a 40-minute display of flying included aerobatics and formation flying by six pilots led by the CO. The weather was perfect for such an event with clear skies and light winds. It was judged to be a great success as a public relations exercise by the RAF. Articles about the Squadron appeared in the Aberdeen *Press and Journal* and the Edinburgh *Evening Dispatch* on 25 February, both covering much the same ground but both enthusing about the Squadron and its successes since the start of the war. The flying display was reported as being particularly impressive – 'breathtaking' and 'amazing'. One Spitfire supposedly flew only three feet above the ground, with even the 'hardened' ground crew never having seen anything like it before!! There were also details of the encounter with the Ju88 on 9 February, made suitably anonymous for the censor.

Another point brought out was the mix of nationalities of the pilots. F/L Bill Douglas remained the only original pilot of 603 still with the unit. Other pilots came from the USA, New Zealand, New Guinea and one reportedly from Malaya. Sgt Rawson was one of the New Zealanders. An unnamed American pilot is quoted as saying that he would rather stay with 603 than join the Army Air Corps now that the USA was in the war – an interesting comment in the light of one of the incidents which happened during the move to Malta in April.

The positive reporting could only be a morale booster for all those in the Squadron and the readers – particularly the folk of Edinburgh. With a successful day under their belts, a good mood prevailed that night in the messes. The event was a success for 603 and S/L Douglas-Hamilton. Notwithstanding the fact that the newspapers of the day were unlikely to print a report that would not help to raise morale, there is a genuine enthusiasm for the display in the reports that were printed and the impression given that 603 was indeed a Squadron full of energy and vitality.

Two months had passed since the loss of S/L Forshaw – two months during which the new CO brought his team up to strength and ability with a spell of concentrated training complemented by some 'real' operational work. He had made a good start to his tenure as Commanding Officer.

Although the day was taken up with the press, life went on as usual as far as the Luftwaffe threat was concerned and four Spitfires scrambled at lunchtime to investigate unidentified plots which turned out to be friendly aircraft. In the evening, F/Sgt Hurst carried out a dusk patrol.

The days were getting longer. The effect of working to British Summer Time meant that dawn came later, but the light stayed until later in the evening so that the subtle lengthening of the days was

---

*There is some doubt about the date of this accident (Tony Holland's log book having been lost at sea in the Mediterranean in 1942). Other sources suggest that it might have occurred on either 6 or 22 February, but the information to hand suggests that it was probably 17 February as recorded in the Operations Record Book.

slightly more marked than usual. The weather also settled down. There weren't the extremes that had been experienced over the previous few weeks. It wasn't good weather, but days of generally light winds, broken clouds interspersed with rain, sleet and snow showers meant that flying could continue. Some of the days the weather was magnificent with clear skies and sun. The Squadron participated in varied activities – with the accent on training, but in differing roles. Operationally there was some excitement too.

On Saturday 21 February, the Fighter Sector HQ noted: '603 Squadron (and indeed all Squadrons in 14 Group Area) were brought to readiness at 1500 hrs. today. An atmosphere of tension persists.' The 603 ORB similarly records: 'At 1600 hours entire Squadron called to readiness. Night readiness also maintained.' (Again the difference in time suggests that the 603 ORB was recording 'local' time – which was BST, and the Fighter Sector was using GMT.)

The readiness state carried through the following two days 'Squadron maintained full state of readiness all day. Several scrambles but no enemy aircraft seen.' Fighter Sector: 'Squadron at full readiness at 06.23 hrs. today (1 hour before dawn).' As far as 603 was concerned, the readiness was finally reduced to one section at 16.00 on 23 February.

The various official records do not give any reason for the increased readiness state but during that period aircraft of the Fleet Air Arm flew off the carrier HMS *Victorious* to attack another German battleship, *Prinz Eugen* which, with *Admiral Scheer* was on the move from Kiel to Trondheim. Having been damaged by a torpedo from the British submarine HMS *Trident* off Trondheim, it managed to make the shelter of Bergenfjord where it joined *Tirpitz* and *Admiral Scheer*. (*Prinz Eugen*, together with *Scharnhorst* and *Gneisenau* had slipped through the English Channel under cover of bad weather from the French coast to the North Sea on 11/12 February, despite British efforts to stop them.)

At the same time, a mixed force of 15 bombers – Halifaxes, Manchesters and Stirlings – attacked four Luftwaffe airfields in Norway to divert attention from the raid on *Prinz Eugen*. The attack on the battleship wasn't a success because of poor weather.

It seems likely that the increased readiness state was in case assistance was needed – either for the returning bombers or if *Victorious* and its escorts were attacked, but no call was made on 603 or any of the other squadrons.

Another indicator of the more attacking philosophy now in place was in the form of exercises with units of the 51st Highland Division on 25 February. Six aircraft of B Flight led by the CO strafed and shot up the army units as they 'retired' towards Nairn, on the north coast of the Moray Firth to the east of Inverness.*

The next day was also busy.

Two night flight interceptions took place. 2 Aircraft of B Flight and 1 of A Flight took off and the O/C S/Ldr. Douglas Hamilton took off about mid-night to investigate an X which turned out to be a friendly aircraft. There was much practice flying and air to air firing during the day.

The CO took off in BL748 at 23.45, returning at 00.20.

*In June 1940, the 51st Highland Division had continued to fight on in France after the evacuation of the British and French troops from Dunkerque. As the Germans advanced and the situation deteriorated, the Navy planned to pull the Scots out in an evacuation from Le Havre. But, the enemy onslaught was too fast and the division became trapped at St Valéry and surrendered to General Erwin Rommel and his 7th Panzer Division on 12 June 1940. The capture of 8,000 'Jocks', with most of them remaining 'in the bag' until the end of the war, was a disaster for the Scottish Regiments and an incident that still stirs emotions 60 years later. Later in 1940, one of the territorial divisions - the 9th (Scottish) - based in the north-east of Scotland was re-numbered the 51st. During 1941 and the first quarter of 1942, it became responsible for coastal defences north of Aberdeen whilst engaged in its training. It carried out 'assaults' on local towns like Nairn and 603 provided the air element of some of the exercises. Shortly after 603 left the United Kingdom for the Mediterranean, the new 51st Highland Division moved first to Aldershot then to Egypt where its first action was the Battle of El Alamein - ironically against the Afrika Korps commanded by Erwin Rommel. It would fight across the deserts of North Africa, the dust of Sicily and then to Northern Europe and the Normandy invasion (including the return to St Valéry and ultimately the crossing of the Rhine into the German heartland.

603 airborne at RAF Dyce at the beginning of 1942 during Press Day. Back aircraft flown by Sgt Loudon and P/O Stone; Middle: F/O Holland and S/L Douglas-Hamilton; Front: Sgt Ruchwaldy and F/L Buckstone.

At this time in the war, there were great efforts being made by the Government to raise funds for weapons. The drives to sponsor Spitfires and other aircraft, the selling of bonds all brought in much needed money to the Treasury. Saturday 28 February saw the start of a week in Aberdeen to raise money for the Navy – 'Aberdeen Warship Week' and at 2.30 in the afternoon, three Spitfires performed a display of formation flying over the city along with Beaufighters of 235 Squadron. The weather was good; virtually no cloud, excellent visibility and light winds. After the display put on for the press just over a week before, there was no reason why the flying should not have been breathtaking!

And so February 1942 ended on a high note. The following is part of a 'Microgram', classified 'SECRET', dated 16 November 1943 from the Officer Commanding 603 Squadron RAF, ME to Headquarters, RAF, ME Air Staff (Operations Records):

> This Unit has no daily record with which to compile a 540* for March 1942, these records having been left behind in the U.K. We are at a loss to understand why the 540 for March has not been received by the Air Ministry, for, to the best of our knowledge, this record was forwarded in the usual way.

The 540 for March 1942 never turned up and so the activities of 603 for March and on Malta can only be reconstructed from the 540s of other units, and individual recollections and diaries. The entry from the Fighter Sector ORB – the 540 – for the first day of March sets the tone:

> There was one X raid plotted between Aberdeen and Montrose at 20,000 ft. and a section of 416 Squadron was scrambled from Peterhead but ordered to land before reaching the ordered height of 22,000 ft. when the "Doubtful" was removed.
>
> 603 and 416 Squadrons patrolled 'a naval unit' between Aberdeen and Invergordon until it was taken over by Tain.
>
> The real 'flap' came about 1900 hours when the Observer Corps reported an attack on a convoy off Rattray Head: no hostile was plotted but an 'X' was put on the board shortly after this report was received. One Spitfire of 603 Squadron was out on dusk patrol and investigated this, and several subsequent 'doubtful' plots in the same vicinity, in the process being fired on by the convoy. One ship in the convoy was machine-gunned and a report was received of a bomb being jettisoned, but the plotting was confused and confusing and this made it difficult to get the fighter near the Hun. Probably there was only one Hun. Weather was good.

---

*The Form 540 was the Operations Record Book compiled by all units - including RAF stations. For the historical researcher they are a key source of factual information and they are now held at the Public Records Office at Kew on the outskirts of London.

As always, the Navy was nervous about any aircraft above them and didn't take any chances!
The weather worsened again for the next few days. On the evening of 4 March there was more activity.

Two a/c of 603 from Dyce were on practice flying when they were ordered to patrol a convoy off Rattray Head, and F/L Douglas* of 603 Sq. on his way up from Montrose to Dyce to do the night state went up to Peterhead before landing at Dyce. A Hun appeared East of Aberdeen and flew up the coast very close in. F/L Douglas was vectored towards it and must have been very close but the dusk, the cloud and iced windscreen made vision very difficult. The two a/c over the convoy got into a position for a stern chase, but had not sufficient petrol to undertake it.

The weather was bad again for the next two days: 'A bitterly cold wind and periodical falls of snow made Dyce a very unpleasant place.' The days came and went with training flights, more attempts to intercept Weather Willie and the inevitable scrambles to find unknown plots. 9 March brought another exercise with the Army in the Forres area. Between 6 and 12 March, a German naval battle group centred round *Tirpitz* moved into the North Sea off the Norwegian coast but did little.

On Thursday 12 March, there was a sad little incident when the Naval Liaison Officer at Turnhouse asked that aircraft be sent to look at a ship to the east of Montrose. Two Spitfires were sent and found wreckage and two lifeboats 'full of men'. There is no record of who they were – other than that they were from a lost 'warship' – perhaps it had hit a mine. *Tirpitz* was not involved in any action with British surface units. One Spitfire maintained a patrol over the sailors until 'filthy weather and darkness compelled it to withdraw.' It wasn't possible to pick up the survivors that night and it wasn't until the next day that the boats came ashore – one near Newburgh 'with heavy loss of life'.

For reasons that are unclear, 416 and 603 Squadrons changed bases on 14 March.** This entailed 603 moving to RAF Peterhead and 416 moving its A Flight to RAF Dyce and B Flight to Montrose. The ground crew moved successfully, but only five of the 603 Spitfires managed to land at their new airfield because of thick fog which covered much of the north east of Scotland. One of 416's aircraft had real problems getting into Dyce and only landed with great difficulty. F/L Douglas' log book records that he tried to help the 416 pilots to land: 'Tried to bring in some of 416. A case of being safer in the air than on the ground. Fun & games by 416 'B'.' They completed the move the next day – it was still foggy, but it cleared later on. The two flights of 603 were now back together.

Some buildings, foundations of others and broken sections of roadway of what used to be the airfield at Peterhead were still to be seen in 1999. The site is just to the east of the fishing port and is slightly higher in elevation. It is on the coastal plain, only a few miles from the sea and exposed. It feels the teeth of any gales and the wind and snow can be stinging to unprotected skin. Being built in 1941 it didn't have the comforts of the stations built in the 1930s and it was bleak to say the least. Peterhead itself is a gaunt fishing town, with little for the men to do when off duty. The airfield was known locally as Longside Airfield after the small town just a few miles away.

The station became operational on 19 July 1941 with 143 Squadron which had reformed there on 7 July carrying out air defence work. At this time though, the station still had to be completed. Only two of the three planned runways had been built and the peri track wasn't finished either. Nor were the accommodation blocks finished and the airmen and women were billeted locally. On 30 November 1941, a marauding Ju88 attacked the airfield, killing one officer, injuring three airmen and damaging a Spitfire. All belonged to 416 Squadron which had arrived there about two weeks before the attack.

It may not have been one of the important, well known stations, but it had a complement of over 70 officers (including nine WAAFs) with almost 1,400 airmen and women involved in keeping over 40 aircraft flying. There were eight officers, 57 ratings and six aircraft from the Royal Naval Air Service on the camp as well.

A letter written in November 1943 states that '...the Squadron was engaged .....on Army Co-operational training mainly with Units of 51st Highland Division.' Presumably this entailed some ground-support sorties – 'mud moving' – as it became known, possibly acting as attackers for exercises.

---

*In W3631 XT-L.
**One source states that 416 went to Skeabrae in the Orkneys but the move to Dyce/Montrose is probably correct.

Fog became a feature of the next few days and it limited flying, although there were further efforts by Beaufighters of 248 Squadron to shoot down Weather Willie but again with no success: 'We'll get the devil yet!'

They didn't know it but for 603, their time in Scotland was drawing to an end; however before they left, there were two further incidents, one pleasant, the other not.

On 23 March, it was announced that Sgt Ruchwaldy, who had crashed on the banks of the River Dee back at the beginning of January had been awarded the DFM. The citation read:

> Since June, 1941, this airman has participated in a large number of operational sorties in which he has destroyed 2 and probably destroyed a further 2 enemy aircraft. He is a good pilot and he has at all times shown the greatest determination.

Then, on Thursday 26 March, P/O Jones and Sgt Walcott were carrying out some practice flying when at 11.15, they collided over the airfield. P/O Jones' Spitfire (BL510) XT-D crashed, killing him. Sgt Walcott, an American volunteer who had only been with the Squadron for a matter of days, survived. The Fighter Sector ORB entry read: 'All Dyce Fighter Sector personnel were shaken today by news from Peterhead of the death of P/O Jones of 603 Squadron.'

It is perhaps ironic that it also concludes on the same day that it was one of the quietest spells on record for 14 Group. Flying is a risky activity, but it is surely more poignant when there are deaths in so-called quiet sectors. At 15.00 on Saturday 28 March, P/O William Irvin Jones was buried at Longside Cemetery a few miles up the road from the airfield in what was surely one of the saddest of ceremonies.

The same day, 603 was classified as non-operational 'pending move overseas', and the next day B Flight of 416 flew from Montrose to Peterhead to fill the gap created by 603's departure.

It didn't take long for the move to happen and life went on as usual for those left at Dyce. The Squadron pilots left for two weeks embarkation leave during which a He111 attacked a minesweeping trawler and escaped north unmolested.

At this time the ground crews and the pilots separated, both to go to the Middle East, but the pilots to Malta and the ground crews to Egypt. The Squadron aircraft were not going with them. They would be left behind in the UK and the pilots would be flying tropicalised Spitfires instead.

The time that 603 spent in the north east of Scotland between December 1941 and April 1942 had not been the most active, or the most exciting, but it allowed them to recuperate from their efforts in the south of England during 1941 and to fly together at immediate squadron readiness in preparation for the exertions that would be required in Malta.

Albeit in a quiet zone, the Squadron had suffered losses – even deaths; S/L Forshaw in December, Sgt Farmer in January and P/O Jones at the end of March. However, they had probably shot down a Ju88 and had gained some valuable operational experience in their regular scrambles by day and night to intercept the hostile X raids, latterly the work with the Army in March and the regular convoy and naval patrols. The press day in February had been a great success and it certainly seems that the Squadron was in good fettle when the time came to move on. However, many of the pilots who had flown to Dyce from Fairlop that Monday in December had gone and 603 had lost a great deal of valuable combat experience. The sad fact was that the Squadron which left for Malta was not the same one which had arrived at Dyce four months before.

One of the veteran ground crew Angus Gillies, had just been married. Angy had to let his wife Mary know that he wouldn't be able to meet her as planned and didn't see her for three years! Nevertheless, they went on to have a long marriage, living in Edinburgh for the remainder of their lives.

On Monday 13 April 1942, the pilots set sail in the USS *Wasp* from the Clyde bound for the Mediterranean; on 15 April the ground crew sailed for Egypt. 603 Squadron was not to return to Scotland or the UK for that matter until 1945.

CHAPTER 6

THE FIRST *WASP* RELIEF FORCE

Those who first view Malta and its companion island of Gozo from the sky, often say that they look like leaves – yellow or green – floating on an azure sea. Whilst no doubt apt, this description paints an unsuitably benign picture for the situation in which the islands found themselves during April 1942, when these 'leaves' were of crushing importance to both the Allied and Axis war efforts to such an extent that it can be argued that the ultimate outcome of the war depended on which side won the battle raging around them on the seas, and above them in the air.

Malta is at the crossroads of the Mediterranean, 900 or so miles to the west lies Gibraltar and a similar but rather lesser distance to the east is Alexandria and Egypt. To the north, 60 miles away is Sicily and to the south, 260 miles away is the coast of North Africa and the port of Tripoli in Libya.

Its main axis runs roughly north west/south east and it is about 18 miles long, with a width of about eight miles. Its area is about 140 square miles; smaller than the Isle of Wight – another often quoted comparison. Gozo is about a third of the area of the main island on a continuation of the axis to the north west across a narrow channel. There is a third small island called Comino in the channel itself and to the south west, another tiny island called Filfla.

Malta has been coveted and conquered by many races and nations during its history. About 870 AD it was occupied by the Arabs who made significant changes to the farming methods used on the island with the introduction of irrigation and new types of crops. They also started the practice of surrounding the fields with small walls to reduce erosion. More than 1,000 years later these low walls would be a factor during the Second World War influencing both the prospects for an Axis glider-borne invasion and for RAF pilots trying to force-land damaged aircraft.

In 1479 it became part of the Spanish Empire. The influence and power of the Turks was perceived by the Spanish King, Charles V, to be a threat to the continuation of a Catholic Europe and in 1530, he decided as a matter of strategy to hand the islands (as well as Tripoli) over to the Order of the Knights of St John of Jerusalem who had been gradually forced farther and farther west from the Holy Lands by the Turks.

It was only a matter of time before there was a confrontation with the Turks who in 1565, laid siege to the island setting a precedent both in the siege itself and its outcome which was ultimate victory for the defenders – the Knights and the Maltese people. This became known as 'The Great Siege'.

The Knights' presence lasted for another two centuries until they passed control to the French under Napoleon in 1798. But the Maltese people found the new regime unpalatable and after forcing the French out of the countryside, they besieged them in the capital fortress of Valetta and called upon Admiral Nelson and the Royal Navy for help. This suited the aspirations of the British and as requested they blockaded the island. On 5 September 1800, the Valetta garrison surrendered and the French were ejected from Malta. Having been invited to help, the British found themselves in a quandary as to what should be done with the island. One proposal was that it should be restored to the Knights but the people were not in favour of this. Ultimately it was agreed – with the consent of the Maltese people – that it would become a British Crown Colony. Thus was formed a bond with the British in 1814 that was to last until the Second World War and beyond.

The Maltese people, who numbered about 300,000 in 1940, in the main enjoyed a co-operative and congenial relationship with the British and the British Empire which grew and strengthened with the passage of time and was based on mutual respect. English became a main language. The Royal

Malta Artillery and the King's Own Malta Regiments became valued and loyal units of the British Army. The island became an important base for the Royal Navy – the headquarters of the Mediterranean Fleet. The Grand Harbour, Sliema Creek and Marsamxett Harbour were filled with British battleships, cruisers, destroyers, submarines and all the rest. This mutual respect was to be forever expressed in the award of the George Cross to Malta in 1942 following the privations suffered by its people during its second 'Great Siege'.

In the years towards the end of the 1930s, whilst the clouds of war were lowering and thickening across northern Europe, Malta seemed to be on the edge, surrounded by countries which were apparently either on the side of the British or were neutral and with the Mediterranean dominated by the British and French navies. But that was to change.

At the start of June 1940, the main focus of the British war effort was France which was in the process of capitulating to the invading Germans. The prospects for Britain were distinctly bleak and it was at this critical time, when defeat seemed certain that Benito Mussolini – Il Duce – the Fascist dictator of Italy decided to declare war on Britain and France. Within a matter of hours of the declaration being made, on Tuesday 11 June, the Italian air force – the Regia Aeronautica – attacked the Grand Harbour at Valetta, the airfield at Hal Far and the seaplane base at Kalafrana. Italy meant to bring Malta into its empire and this attack signalled the start of the second 'Great Siege' which would continue until the end of 1942. Malta had suddenly been pitchforked into the war because of the ambitions of Mussolini and its geographical position.

Because of Britain's fears about a German invasion across the English Channel and the desperate need for fighter aircraft on the south coast of England in 1940, initially Malta's air defence was left with only the Sea Gladiators which became legends as 'Faith', 'Hope' and 'Charity'. (In fact, there were four Gladiators which were formed into a Flight to fight with great courage against vastly superior numbers of Axis aircraft – they tended to operate with three on 'readiness' at any one time.) Their story is well covered elsewhere.

Italy had interests in North Africa and it became a battleground which would draw in Germany in the shape of the Afrika Korps commanded by Erwin Rommel. Between 1940 and 1943, the North African fighting see-sawed back and forward along the coastal strip until the Allies eventually drove the Axis out in 1943 following the battle of El Alamein in the east and the invasion of French North Africa in the west in the last few months of 1942.

For the British – and the Allies – access to the eastern Mediterranean was vital. As the struggle for North Africa moved back and forward, the British forces depended on Egypt to be a secure base and a key in the logistic chain for supplying the units fighting in the desert. Further, access to the Far East was shorter via the Suez Canal – the alternative being to route south round the Cape of Good Hope which added significantly to the time. The defence of India and points east was affected by the ease or otherwise of access and again, whilst the Cape was a viable alternative, it was significantly longer.

The shortest and quickest route was through the Mediterranean. Malta, positioned half way was an important staging post for both aircraft and ships. The loss of Malta or at least the denial of the east/west sea and air route would affect Britain's ability to maintain the desert armies, to prosecute the war itself and to defend its interests even further east. To save Malta was, therefore, of utmost importance.

Necessarily, any account of 603 Squadron concentrates on the role of the defending fighters, but the offensive capability of the RAF and the Fleet Air Arm meant that there was a considerable number of aircraft types operating from Malta in different roles. Despite its size, there were three major airfields (Hal Far, Luqa* and Ta Kali) squeezed into the limited area available with several small 'strips' to augment them. The island is generally low lying – the highest point is 821 feet near Dingli at the hills on the west side. It has a typical Mediterranean climate with rainy winters and hot dry summers which affect the operation of aircraft. Much of it is limestone and the light colour becomes an uncomfortable glare in high summer.

Ta Kali was the airfield where 603 would be based. It was about four miles north west of Luqa

---

*Today the commercial airport for Malta.

– almost in the centre of the island – overlooked by higher parts of the island to the west with the town of Rabat a couple of miles to the south west.

It had started off life as a civilian airport – mainly used by Italians – and it wasn't until the end of October 1940 that it became an RAF station with the aim at that time of basing a single squadron of fighters there. By April 1942, there was a rough strip across the centre of the landing field.

On 8 November 1940 the airfield became RAF Station Ta Kali and about two weeks later 261 Squadron transferred in from Luqa to become Ta Kali's first operational unit flying Hurricanes. In May 1941, 249 Squadron also flying Hurricanes arrived and 261 was disbanded. In June 126 Squadron was formed and the two would be there when 603 arrived in April 1942 along with 185.

In December 1941, 1435 Night Fighter Flight formed from the Malta Night Fighter Unit at Ta Kali. The Flight had been originally set up in July flying Hurricanes.

By January 1942, although the British offensive aircraft on the island continued to attack the enemy, persistent bombing by the Italians and Germans, and their superiority in the air, meant that the situation was fast becoming critical. It was clear to the AOC on Malta, Air Vice-Marshal Hugh Lloyd that it was likely to become untenable and he had been flagging this up to Middle East Command Headquarters in Cairo and the Air Ministry back in London.

His concerns were acted upon by the AOC-in-C Middle East, Air Marshal Sir Arthur Tedder who commissioned a report on the situation in Malta. The man chosen to produce it was Group Captain Basil Embry – a dynamic light bomber pilot who had been shot down and captured at the beginning of the war but escaped – killing a guard on the way. He was a very able man, quite capable of assessing the situation objectively and reporting his findings unequivocally.

This he did following a visit in January 1942 and his essential conclusions were that the Hurricanes being used were outmoded, that there was a need for first class controlling and that whilst the morale of the RAF was good, the pilots particularly should not be expected to continue to fight under the unpleasant and difficult conditions currently existing, but should be changed at suitable intervals.

Fortunately for Malta, the report was acted upon quickly.

In the meantime, the bombing continued and it was wet and cold. The airfields bogged down. Messerschmitt 109s flew low across the island picking targets of opportunity. In January, none of Rommel's supply ships were sunk and the British convoys bringing vital supplies were increasingly having to fight their way in. In February, convoy operation MF5 from Alexandria failed to get through.

Meanwhile Hitler was once again considering a possible invasion of Malta – to be code named 'Operation Hercules'. Although details weren't finalised until the end of April when July was pencilled in to launch it, the possession of Malta was a pre-requisite for victory by the Afrika Korps in North Africa. Having been forced back beyond Tobruk by the 8th Army at the end of 1941, Rommel was once again advancing east towards Egypt.

As a result of Embry's report, in February over a dozen more experienced pilots – including Stan Turner, 'Laddie' Lucas and Bob Sergeant arrived by Sunderland at Kalafrana. Reaching Ta Kali and taking command of 249 Squadron, Turner wasted no time in changing the outmoded tactics that were being used and making better use of the aircraft that were serviceable. Rather than have each squadron only able to put up a couple of aircraft at a time, they were pooled. Pilot Officer Bob Sergeant would fly with 249 Squadron from Ta Kali where 603 was also to be based, and three years later, in 1945, he found himself flying with 603 when the Squadron was back in the UK.

These measures were effective, but of course, it was Spitfires that were really needed. The AOC had been pressing for these and on 28 February HMS *Eagle* and HMS *Argus* attempted to fly off the first batch, but it was a disaster. There were problems with the long-range tanks. The delivery was called off, to the great annoyance of the Navy and the acute embarrassment of the RAF. It also turned out that the cannons on the aircraft hadn't been properly adjusted, and to crown everything the spares for the aircraft weren't there.

Finally, and not without further embarrassing problems for the RAF, 15 Spitfires arrived at the island on 7 March. The sight of the Spitfires raised the morale of those below, but 15 was a mere drop in the ocean. Again, accompanied by problems caused by the RAF itself, *Eagle* made two further trips from Gibraltar on 21 and 29 March delivering nine and seven Spitfires respectively.

The RAF had come out of these first deliveries in a poor light because of the lack of preparation and planning. It had to improve.

The arrival of the Spitfires spurred the Luftwaffe to even greater efforts to destroy them. The airfields and Ta Kali in particular were subjected to fierce and constant bombing and attack. The number of fighters escorting the enemy bomber formations increased and the new British fighters were still not able to cope. Aircraft were still being lost – both in aerial combat and on the ground because of the incessant bombing.

The case for more Spitfires was being made to the Air Ministry. G/C C.A. Bouchier DFC – Station Commander at Hornchurch when 603 was there during the Battle of Britain – now the Deputy Director of Fighter Operations, produced a report on 27 March 1942 which ran to three pages and was an analysis of how pilots from the UK squadrons were selected to reinforce fighter squadrons on Malta, the Near and Far East. He concluded that if asked to choose two pilots to leave a squadron for this purpose, the CO would often 'get rid' of his poorest pilots which meant that the squadrons being reinforced were getting low quality and often inexperienced pilots who did not enjoy the esprit de corps and confidence of the units they were joining. His recommendation was that full squadrons should be sent rather than penny numbers of pilots. The squadrons did tend to be 'cliquish'. A new CO would often gather his friends and trusted colleagues from previous squadrons to join him and would be reluctant to let them go again.

But the situation on Malta was very much in the forefront of the Prime Minister's mind. *Eagle* was out of action with problems with its steering gear so it wouldn't be available for a month. A drawback with HMS *Victorious* was that the lifts from the hangars in the ship weren't large enough to take a fully constructed Spitfire and the time that it would take to build a machine on the deck using the components from the hangar below was prohibitive. There was also *Argus*, but it was small, and in any case it would be needed to provide air cover while the Spitfires were launched. Rather than dribble in small numbers of aircraft, what Malta needed was a large delivery that would turn the odds more in favour of the defenders.

On 1 April 1942, the Prime Minister wrote to President Roosevelt seeking his help. The US Navy carrier, *Wasp* was steaming for British waters and with its larger lifts and size, it could accommodate about 50 Spitfires. The President was asked if he would approve the use of *Wasp* to carry out the next delivery. He agreed and the stage was set for the pilots of 603 to leave for Malta.

After embarkation leave, and having met at RAF Abbotsinch just a few hours before, at 20.30 on Sunday 12 April 1942 the pilots of 603 arrived at Port Glasgow on the River Clyde to join *Wasp*. There were few of the experienced pilots who had flown to Dyce from Fairlop the previous December left. Many, possibly as many as 17, had been posted elsewhere and S/L Douglas-Hamilton found himself greeting about a dozen pilots who were new to 603. The dilution of the experience meant that the Squadron left for the ferocity of Malta with nine pilots who had not been in action and another 13 who had less than 25 hours flying time on Spitfires which in Bob Sergeant's view was just not adequate for what fighter pilots on Malta at that time would have to do. But there remained a core who had come down from Dyce: A Flight: F/L Bill Douglas, P/O Paul Forster, P/O Gordon Murray, F/Sgt Allan Otto and Sgt Webster. B Flight: F/L John Buckstone, F/O Tony Holland, P/O Neville King, F/Sgt Johnny Hurst, and Sergeants Buckley and Walcott.

In reality, although the recommendation that full squadrons should be sent to Malta was being implemented, the two which were about to set sail in *Wasp* had not had the chance to train and operate together sufficiently to form the cohesive units that were presumably what Bouchier had intended should be sent. All of this despite the hard work and training of S/L Douglas-Hamilton. Indeed, some of the new pilots didn't know which squadron they were posted to until joining the carrier.

The plan was for USS *Wasp* to take 52 Spitfire Vs in an operation codenamed Operation Calendar. Its aircraft lifts were large enough to accommodate a fully built Spitfire allowing them to be chocked and lashed down in the hangars below the flight deck, with others suspended from strongpoints in the deckheads above in slings for the voyage. But before reaching the aircraft carrier, there were more mundane transportation problems to be overcome.

The first 12 aircraft were to be flown in to Abbotsinch on Wednesday 8 April, followed by a further ten on each of the following four days. Fighter Command was tasked to provide 55 pilots of whom 52 were to embark in *Wasp* with the other three to remain at Abbotsinch as reserves.

The weather in Scotland at the beginning of April 1942 was atrocious with heavy rain. The original intention was that the Spitfires – all new – would be ferried from the MUs (where the final testing and gun calibration was supposedly being completed) to the airfield at Abbotsinch – near to *Wasp*. A few flew in – to clouds of spray and with instructions not to taxi for fear of bogging down. One option considered was to load them on to barge-type vessels and float them down to the carrier which would be anchored in the river, but this wasn't realistic because of the lack of suitable vessels and because the tides would only allow a working time of two hours each day.

Another idea was to move them by road but again this proved to be unworkable because the wingspan was too long to give sufficient width clearance at bridges and narrow points in the road.

However, it was thought that it might be possible to do this by a shorter route if the carrier was brought further in, so it carefully berthed in the King George V Dock on the south bank of the Clyde just downstream from Govan. The first test Spitfire moved slowly and gingerly through the streets on a modified 'Queen Mary' low loader. If the wing tips were removed, it could be done.

Because of the boggy conditions at Abbotsinch, the new Spitfires were now being flown into Prestwick on the coast near Ayr, but as luck would have it, there was another airfield at Renfrew a mile or so to the east of Abbotsinch and it seems that some Spitfires were flown there, although it too was prone to flooding. From there it was a relatively straightforward task – with the problems having been ironed out – to transport them on the Queen Marys to *Wasp* and this was done in convoys of six at a time. The Spitfires were then hoisted aboard.

The delivery of the Spitfires to *Wasp* went under the codename Newman. On 9 April, the weather was becoming a problem and a signal to the Chief of the Air Staff warned that the poor flying conditions were likely to hold up the Newman deliveries and that the met. forecast for the next few days was 'not propitious'. It raised such concern that there was a warning that it might be necessary to 'ask for a postponement of the sailing date' although in the event, there were no delays.

A typical aircraft was BP958. It was ordered from Supermarine Aviation (Vickers) Ltd on 24 October 1940 as part of contract B19713/39 for Mark Is. Constructed as a Mark Vc, it made its first flight at Chattis Hill on 19 March 1942. It arrived at 6 Maintenance Unit on 20 March and after completing its tests etc, it was flown to RAF Abbotsinch on 10 April. From Abbotsinch it was taken by road as described to *Wasp*. As will be seen, although its history prior to boarding the carrier was typical, what happened to it was not. It was the only Spitfire to launch which did not arrive on Malta and it was to be lost in circumstances which were, to say the least, unusual and unexpected.

The Vc had a Merlin 46 engine and it was 'tropicalised' for operations in the Mediterranean. Previous versions of the V could be modified to a tropicalised configuration, although this required more than two dozen major changes to be made. Visually the most obvious difference was the deep chin created by the addition of a Vokes tropical air filter across the carburetor air intake. This filtered out the dust and sand kicked up during operations in the desert and dry climates which would reduce the working life of the Merlins significantly. However, it also had the effect of increasing drag with a resulting loss in airspeed, but this was considered acceptable as part of the performance compromise. The Vc variant was fitted with the 'universal' wing which allowed greater flexibility in the armaments carried. They could carry four 20mm cannons (Hispano) and four .303 machine guns (Browning). These Spitfires had four cannon* and it was ordered that two were to be loaded with 60 rounds. A signal from the Air Ministry to AHQ Malta dated 16 April 1942 informs them that the Newman Spitfires would have belt ammunition feed to the cannons, which was different to those sent previously.

---

*The weight of four cannon reduced performance and often two were removed to give a better balance between firepower and performance.

It was reckoned that the range of a Spitfire Vc in still air was 860 nautical miles if the long-range tanks were jettisoned and 760 if they weren't.

The question of the camouflage paint scheme applied poses some interesting questions. The Spitfires taken on board *Wasp* on the Clyde may have been issued in the normal Northern European paint scheme – known as the sea temperate scheme – but there is an alternative view that they were in desert colours. Two of the 603 pilots recall that on Malta, and some weeks after 20 April their aircraft were light grey or blue in colour although they are not certain of this. (They are, however, sure that they were not brown.) Black and white photographs taken of the Spitfires being hoisted on board *Wasp* and in the carrier show that they were received with a camouflage scheme applied, but of course the actual colours are not discernible. However, the standard sea temperate scheme, introduced from August 1941, included a yellow strip along the outboard leading edge of the mainplanes and a sky-coloured band around the fuselage just forward of the tailplanes. The photographs of the Spitfires on *Wasp* quite clearly do not have these features so their camouflage was either the brown desert scheme or a non-standard sea temperate scheme.

Whether or not the Operation Calendar Spitfires were in the desert or North European scheme, before launching from *Wasp*, the top surfaces of some, if not all, were re-painted dark blue which was more appropriate for the long sea flight to Malta and for operating over the Mediterranean from Malta. (This suggests that they were brown to start with – otherwise why change a blue/grey scheme to blue?) Photographs show that this paint was applied roughly – particularly around the markings and the serial numbers – with the implication that it was done hurriedly and as a temporary measure. On 7 April, as the Calendar Spitfires were being readied for ferrying to the Clyde, the RAF HQ on Malta requested that in future, all Spitfires should be sea camouflaged to expedite getting them on line when they arrived on Malta.* It seems that the application of the blue was in response to this request.

As to the specific colour, it is difficult to be precise. If the need to change was known prior to the departure** of *Wasp* the paint may have been taken on the carrier at that time. If not, then the paint used for the American Wildcats on board may have been used. The dark blue normally applied to US Navy aircraft at this time – 'non-specular sea blue' – would be available in the carrier, but this is conjecture. The other unknown is how long the blue remained on the aircraft on Malta. The desert camouflage scheme would seem to be inappropriate for aircraft spending much of their time over the sea although many Spitfires on Malta did operate in desert brown. But some of the Spitfires which arrived on Malta with the desert scheme may have been over-painted blue and/or grey with paints available locally to make them less visible over the sea.

This would explain the recollections of the two 603 pilots who fought from Malta that their Spitfires were blue/grey.

In summary, it seems that the Spitfires hoisted aboard *Wasp* on the Clyde were probably in the desert camouflage scheme and, that on the carrier many, if not all, had their top surfaces painted dark blue for the flight to Malta.

The Spitfires did not have normal squadron markings applied. In an unusual change from the norm, instead of the familiar 'XT' codes, the 603 Spitfires were to have the number '2' applied on the left side of the fuselage roundel with a letter on the opposite side to denote the individual aeroplane – eg 2●B. In the rush to get the aircraft prepared, the letter and number were sometimes interchanged. Many weeks later on Malta, code letters appeared again to replace the numbers, but only one and for 603 it was, not surprisingly X.***

The Spitfires loaded aboard *Wasp* included: BP874, BP954, BP955, BP956, BP 958, BP961, BP962, BP963, BP964, BP965, BP966, BP969, BP970, BP973, BP974, BP975, BR116, BR117, BR120, BR121, BR123, BR124, BR125, BR126, BR129, BR176 (1●N), BR180, BR182, BR183, BR184, BR185, BR187, BR190, BR192, BR194, BR195, BR199, BR203, BR204 and BR227.

Those known to have been flown off the carrier by 603 were BR190 (2●A) by the CO, BR184 (2●C) by Tony Holland, BR124 (2●U) by Bill Douglas, BP958 by Sgt Walcott, BR185 (2●D), BR187 (2●G) and BP962 (2●R).

---

*At the time of writing, a copy of the signal had not been obtained.
**It may be that the order to re-paint the Spitfires was received after the *Wasp* had left the Clyde.
***F/L Bill Douglas first flew a Spitfire with the 'X' code on 4 June. It was X●J BR364.

603 wasn't the only squadron making the trip to Malta. On this occasion 601 would also be flying off. Its CO was Squadron Leader John Bisdee DFC, another veteran of the Battle of Britain and of the sweeps across the Channel in 1941 when he was based at Biggin Hill with 609 Squadron. They too had the same problems as the Edinburgh Squadron in that they were to sail with a complement which included many new and inexperienced pilots. For all of them, the start of the adventure would be a hazardous take-off from the carrier's flight deck – something which none of them had ever done before – other than one. This was Squadron Leader Edward 'Jumbo' Gracie who had been fighting in Malta already as the CO of 126 Squadron and had a number of kills to his credit. A forceful, forthright and efficient officer, he had returned to the UK on the instructions of the AOC Malta to tell at first hand the reality of life on the island to the senior commanders in London and to make sure that further reinforcements were sent. This would be his second carrier launch to Malta – his first having been on 21 March from HMS *Eagle*.

The weather remained overcast and gloomy. The pilots came aboard *Wasp* and found their bunks and accommodation. They were two or three to a cabin and some were sharing with American officers who were all interested in what experience the British pilots had and how many kills they had notched up. At first sight, the pilots thought the carrier vast. The grey slab sides which greeted them at the side of the dock seemed to rise impossibly to the dark sky above, and then once inside, the trek to the cabins through the companionways and watertight doors seemed interminable. The Americans, however, were very welcoming and although, as is the US Navy custom, the bar in the wardroom was dry, acquaintanceships were formed over cokes and fruit juices. The quality of the food was excellent, and for the British servicemen, the abundance of eggs and fruit came as something to savour after the privations of rationing in wartime Britain.

Despite the personnel changes made whilst the Squadron was at Dyce, S/L Douglas-Hamilton still had flight commanders who were experienced – F/Ls Bill Douglas (A Flight) and John Buckstone (B Flight), with Douglas having more operational time than Buckstone. F/L Douglas had been flying since 1940, had one kill to his credit but had been wounded over France. John Buckstone had started his time in the RAF on the ground but had volunteered to become a pilot and was taking some valuable experience gained in his sweeps across occupied France with him. He was only just married. Douglas was the only original 603 auxiliary pilot still with the Squadron and he and the CO the only Scots.*

Both Squadrons were cosmopolitan with representation from many of the Allied countries and the British Empire. There were Canadians, Englishmen, an Irishman, a South African, Americans, a Belgian and two New Zealanders. In particular, 603 was fortunate that one of the Americans was an ex-Eagle squadron pilot from 121 Squadron.

The Eagle squadrons were made up of American pilots who for one reason or another – adventure, idealism – had joined the RAF or RCAF before the United States formally entered the war. About a dozen Americans fought the Battle of Britain in British squadrons, but as the number of American pilots volunteering grew, separate squadrons were raised for them. The first was 71 Squadron, formed in the autumn of 1940, and the second was 121.

The Eagle pilots were men with flair and a sense of adventure. By 1942, many of them were becoming impatient for more action and wanted to go to Malta. Flippantly, Malta was sometimes described as a 'fighter pilot's paradise' because of the choice of enemy target aircraft and some of these Americans wanted to be part of it. Others went out to fight with other squadrons.

The former Eagle who found himself with 603 in *Wasp* that day in April 1942 was Pilot Officer Fred Almos. He had become operational after the Battle of Britain and was eventually transferred from 603 to 126 Squadron as part of that Squadron's 'American Flight' about a month after reaching Malta.

---

*The CO and F/L Douglas kept a diary which was the subject of a book written by Lord James Douglas-Hamilton - whose uncle was S/L David Douglas-Hamilton - called *The Air Battle for Malta*. This diary has been used as one of the principal sources of information about the activities of 603 whilst on Malta and in the text is referred to as the 'Diary'. There are instances where the information in the Diary and in other documents does not reconcile (eg with a pilot's log book). In such cases, if significant, the discrepancy has been highlighted rather than a decision being made as to the correctness of the sources.

Two other Americans were with 603. P/O G. Murray (who would be the first 603 pilot killed in action on Malta) and Sgt Walcott, who it will be recalled, was involved in the mid-air collision over Peterhead on 26 March when P/O Jones was killed.

603 pilots who flew off on 20 April were: S/L David Douglas-Hamilton, F/Ls W.A. Douglas, J.W. Buckstone, and L.V. Sanders*, F/O A.C.W. Holland, P/Os G. Murray RCAF, J.W. Forster, N.S. King, C.B. McLean* RCAF, O.M. Linton* RCAF, J.G. Mejon* (who was Belgian), F.E. Almos* RCAF, L.W. Watts*, J.W. Slade*, H.R. Mitchell* RNZAF, Second Lieutenant C.J.O. Swales* SAAF, F/Sgts J.D. Rae* RNZAF, J. Hurst, and Sgts. Allan W. Otto RCAF, L.F. Webster, and Walcott.

There were, however, other pilots who may have been with 603 in *Wasp* and who may have flown off on 20 April, but for one reason or another there is some doubt as to whether or not they were in the carrier, or flew off. The final intention was to send four groups of 12 Spitfires, but in the event, only 47 launched. One well researched account concludes that 603 launched only 22.

Sgt C.F. Bush was with 603 at Dyce and did fight with 126 Squadron on Malta but it isn't clear how he reached the beleaguered island. He does not appear in the photograph of 603 pilots on *Wasp's* deck. P/O G.P.B. Davies* appears in the photograph of the 603 pilots on *Wasp* but may have been one of the pilots who did not fly off. F/Sgt Buckley appears in the photograph, and he was known to have shared a cabin with Sgt Walcott. He is also listed in the Diary as having reached Malta, but it isn't clear how he got there and when. Then there is P/O Doug Booth – another American Eagle. He is listed in one book as having been with 603 and mentioned in another as having gone out with them, but his name has not been found in any of the documents which emanated from 603 itself and used to research this section of the history. Finally, a privately published history of 603 mentions Sergeant Brown, and a list from the Diary also mentions a F/Sgt Brown, a Canadian, as a pilot who served on Malta.

The operational experience of the pilots varied immensely. As well as the flight commanders, some had already proved themselves in the heat of aerial combat. F/L Sanders had 45 operational sorties under his belt, F/Sgt Rae 47 sorties and confirmed claims for one FW 190 'kill', four probables and two damaged and F/Sgt Hurst had 54 sorties and confirmed claims for one 'kill' and five probables or damaged. The CO himself had only four offensive sorties under his belt but was 'up the learning curve'. He had been one of the pilots involved in operation at the end of November 1941 when an enemy convoy was attacked in the Channel and he was blooded in aerial combat as well at the beginning of December. Others who had already flown operationally were P/Os McLean, Watts, Mitchell, Slade, and Almos, Sgt Otto and Sgts Webster and Brown.

At 10.00 on Monday 13 April, it was time to leave Britain and *Wasp* slipped its moorings and moved slowly into the Clyde for a test run, touching a screw on a sandbank. It spent the night at Greenock, then at 06.00 on 14 April, it finally departed the Clyde as the centrepiece of what was designated 'Force W'. In addition to the two American destroyers *Madison* and *Lang*, the Royal Navy would provide the battleship HMS *Renown* and the destroyers *Inglefield, Echo, Partridge* and *Ithuriel*. The next day, 15 April, the carrier was steaming south down the Irish Sea in gloomy and overcast weather. The pilots, for most of whom this was a new experience, were reassured to see the size and power of the escort considering the risks that they would be running from German U-boats in particular operating in the Atlantic.

Clearing Ireland, the ships headed out into the Atlantic with the aim of passing through the Straits of Gibraltar on the night of 18/19 April.

On 15 April, all the pilots were given a briefing by the officer who was in charge of the planning and organisation – W/C John S. McLean. He was based at Gibraltar and had been involved in the previous attempts to fly Spitfires in. He was a dynamic individual with an attention to detail that should at least minimise the problems which were likely to occur. For the first time, the pilots were now given some indication of what they were going to be expected to do. He explained that the carrier would take them into the Mediterranean beyond Gibraltar and north of Algiers, the Spitfires would be launched and they would have to fly to Malta, hugging the coast of North Africa, but avoiding trouble.

*These pilots were new to 603.

S/L Jumbo Gracie also spoke to them about what they could expect from the Spitfires with their extra fuel tanks and gave them some idea as to what life was like on Malta. Needless to say, it was not encouraging and at least some of the aircrew began to wonder just what lay ahead, although some thought he was exaggerating and 'shooting a line'. During the voyage, many of them were thinking of home, writing letters and generally trying to deal with the rising apprehension and the obvious question as to whether or not they were likely to survive. Gracie's picture of the shortages on Malta was such that the pilots stocked up with the essentials of life – soap, tobacco, razor blades etc – which were so abundant on *Wasp* but virtually non-existent on Malta. Officially they were limited to 10lbs of belongings and whilst some of the pilots stuck to this, others didn't and then had to worry about whether or not the Spitfire would be too heavy to get airborne with the short take-off run along the deck. Included in their kit, each pilot carried a sandfly net and a jar of Bamber oil, Sketofax or some other anti-mosquito cream. Their flying kit also included K type dinghies.

They were also thinking about the U-boats and on the afternoon of 16 April, the escort dropped depth charges over a suspected contact although no enemy attacks were made on the convoy.

The engineering officer in charge of the Spitfires was S/L Hughes, the man who had refused to allow previous batches of Spitfires to fly off with leaky fuel tanks and had earned the ire of the Royal Navy and the RAF in London. Yet again, fuel tanks on some Spitfires were found to be apparently 'badly made' and leaking, but Hughes and his team of 120 were trying to make sure that they would all be properly sealed before the Spitfires were launched.

Bill Douglas found the whole experience hugely exciting. On 17 April, he wrote to his family back in Edinburgh:

Just a wee note to tell you that I'm alive and kicking and having one of the most interesting experiences I ever had. Unfortunately, everything is shrouded in official secrecy, and quite rightly, so I won't bother to try to hint at anything. I do know our destination now….

And then:

It really is hard to write a letter, when you're simply bulging with news, and can't say a thing. However, you'll hear it all some day. I'm thriving, eating the best food I've had for quite some time, and basking a lot in a pleasantly warm sun.

On 18 April, in the far Pacific, another US Navy carrier was launching 'Jimmy' Doolittle's bombers on their one-way raid on Tokyo.

At 03.00 on the morning of Sunday 19 April, Force W slipped through the Straits of Gibraltar and into the Mediterranean. The passage of the Straits had been done in the dark to try to avoid the prying eyes of German agents and Spanish informants who would let it be known that the reinforcements were on their way. There was an excellent 'bush telegraph' on Malta and it wasn't unusual for supposedly secret knowledge about convoys and reinforcements to be widely discussed and rumoured in the bars – as it had been on this occasion. If it was known on Malta, it was surely known by the Germans too and no doubt they would be doing their utmost to both prevent the British units reaching Malta, and destroy those that managed to get there intact.

From Gibraltar they gathered a further strengthening of the escort in the shape of the two British cruisers *Charybdis* and *Cairo* with another five destroyers – *Wrestler, Wishart, Westcott, Antelope* and *Vidette*.

The weather on 19 April was beautiful, sunny and warm. The sea was a flaring brassy blue and the gloom and dankness of the Clyde far behind. The pilots made their final preparations, packing kit, writing letters, some visited the padre, making sure that all their preparations were complete because it would be an early start the next morning. S/L Hughes and his men checked the Spitfires again and the first 12 were on the deck in preparation for flying off by 18.00. By now they knew that the aircraft were to be sent off in four groups of 12 – mainly because only 12 could be 'spotted' at the end of the flight deck at any one time. In the event, only 47 left.

Top: A Spitfire being hoisted on board USS *Wasp*, on the way to Malta.
Bottom: 603 pilots on the deck of *Wasp*. Back row, from left to right: F/Sgt J. Hurst, F/Sgt Allan Otto, Sgt Buckley, Sgt Walcott (bareheaded), and Sgt L.F. Webster. Middle row, from left to right: P/O G.P.B. Davis, P/O F.E.Almos, P/O J.W. Slade, P/O L.W. Watts, P/O H.R. Mitchell, 2Lt C.J.O.Swales, P/O O.M.Linton and P/O C.B. McLean. Front row, from left to right: P/O G. Murray, P/O P.W. Forster, F/L L.V. Sanders, F/L W.A. Douglas, S/L Lord David Douglas-Hamilton, F/L J.W. Buckstone, P/O A.C.W. Holland, P/O N.S. King and P/O J.G. Mejon.

As darkness fell, some would be feeling sombre and worried about the next day and what it would bring, where they would be and if they would be alive. It would be difficult to sleep with a long night in prospect even though they would need to be as refreshed as possible for the long flight ahead. Sgt Walcott, the American volunteer, shared a cabin with the Canadian F/Sgt Buckley and he told Buckley during the voyage from the Clyde that he was apprehensive about Malta and in fact had no intention of going. He went to see the padre hoping that he might get some dispensation, but he was sadly disappointed.

Monday 20 April 1942 dawned bright and clear in the Mediterranean. The aircrew who were to fly off were roused at 03.45 and made their way to the wardroom for breakfast at 04.15. After that, final briefing was due at 04.45 with first engine start at 05.15. If nerves would allow, breakfast would be enjoyed fully – who would know when they would eat a full breakfast again!

The four groups of Spitfires were led by Jumbo Gracie who had made the flight a few weeks before, the two squadron commanders and F/L Bill Douglas. Gracie's group would be the first off and Bisdee with the rest of 601 would be next. David Douglas-Hamilton's group would be the third to leave with Bill Douglas leading the fourth.

S/L Douglas-Hamilton's flight plan gives the details of the route. He intended to fly virtually due east for 357 miles, taking two hours, 13½ minutes to do it. This would take them from the launch position just north of Algiers along the north coast of Africa to near Sicily where they would turn south to a track of 109 degrees. This would be held for 77 miles, taking 29 minutes. A further course change to a more southerly track of 169 degrees for 27½ minutes and a distance of 73 miles threading between Pantelleria and the mainland and then the final turn back to port on to a track of 105 degrees for the last 160 miles and hopefully Malta. In all, a flight of 667 miles taking just over four hours over the sea with virtually no chance of rescue should there be a need to ditch, and in a single-engined aircraft. The final note on the flight plan reads: 'If separated or lost – on last leg head *North*. Turn *East* on reaching land (Sicily) and follow coast to easternmost point, then set compass to 222 degrees (M) for destination.' Then a final exhortation: 'Don't <u>Flap</u> or <u>Worry</u>.'!!

Radio silence was to be observed as much as possible, certainly until near Malta. For landing, 601 would go to Luqa and 603 to Ta Kali.

The wind direction was 245 degrees and its strength Force 4. *Wasp* was at position 037 degrees 30' north. 003 degrees 20' east.

Spitfire BR124 U-2 prepared for launch to Malta on *Wasp*, 20 April 1942. Note the crudely applied paint on the upper surfaces.

For all his experience, 'Jumbo' Gracie leading the first wave made what was really an elementary mistake. His group took off at 05.45 and as his formation closed about him, he turned on to his course for the first leg, but set his compass to the reciprocal so that he was leading them back to Gibraltar rather than Malta. It wasn't until one of his group broke radio silence and asked him when he intended to set course for Malta that he realised the error and corrected, much to his embarrassment.

Denis Barnham was in the second group – 601 Squadron. His Spitfire was in the gloomy hangar below. With engines running and propellers turning invisibly, it was a dangerous place to be and just as he was being wheeled on to the lift to go up to the flight deck, he glimpsed on the deck the bloody red remains of someone (either one of the RAF ground crew or an American sailor) who had walked into a propeller.

603 was also in the hangar and would be the next to leave. They had to wait while the others were pushed over to the lift, then it was their turn, although they hadn't started engines. The huge lift rose slowly, each pilot blinking in the light of

Spitfire taking off from *Wasp* on 20 April for the long flight to Malta.

the Mediterranean morning. If they had looked to the sky, they might have seen circling above 11 of *Wasp's* Grumman F4F-4 Wildcats which had launched first at 05.30 to provide a protective screen – and to create more space on the deck.

The engines were started, and the Spitfires manoeuvred into position for the take-off pointing down the flight deck into wind. As always, the long nose of the Spitfire prevented the pilot seeing directly to his front and as *Wasp* had no steam catapults to guide the launching aircraft in the correct direction, it was up to the pilot to keep the Spitfire moving down the deck in the correct direction with the superstructure island ahead and to the right.

The length of flight deck available was not great – about 600 feet – and without the extra push from a catapult, it would be up to the Merlin engines at full power to accelerate the aircraft to flying speed before reaching the end of the deck. If it didn't the Spitfire would fall into the sea directly ahead of the moving carrier which would be unable to avoid a collision. The chances of a pilot surviving a crash and the moving carrier were indeed slim, but the Captain of *Wasp* was certain that the take-off would be 'a breeze'.

Each Spitfire was placed in position. Propeller was put in fine pitch and the throttles pushed forward until the aeroplane strained against the brakes and the tail began to lift.

The whole process was choreographed by the American launching officer. On his signal, brakes are released, throttle forward for full boost, stick gripped firmly – pushed forward. Sudden push down the deck. At 250 feet the tail is well up but still a lot of weight on the oleos. Superstructure close on the starboard side, filled with people and blurry faces. At 350 feet, the tail is up and lift is coming into the wings. At 550 feet the pilot is concentrating on the fast approaching bow and the end of the flight deck. With the Merlin roaring strongly there is some flying control but not quite enough, then off the end with a turbulent bump as the Spitfire sinks towards the water and potential disaster. Wheels up in an instant (the CO forgot for a second or two!). Stick forward keeping the nose down for a fraction to gain those extra few knots of flying speed – the pilot behind will think it's gone in as it disappears below the bow – then the controls are firm enough to gently ease the Spitfire into a climb away from the sea and into its element. At 1,000 feet change over to auxiliary tank. (Those who had limited their baggage to 10lbs made it relatively easily!)

A sluggish climb to 3,000 feet to rendezvous with the others in the group, leaving *Wasp* and her escorts dwindling on that grey sparkling sea, then to 10,000 feet on the first heading into a sun still low on the horizon. Reduce revs to 2,050 and an airspeed of 160 mph to eke out the fuel. So far so good.

Engine sounds ok, but each pilot would – consciously or not – be instantly aware of the slightest change in noise or beat which could signify a watery end. On the right, just visible in the haze is the coast of North Africa. The mountains of Algeria watching them go. Patches of cloud down on the water.*

Having led his group off at 06.25, with Flight Sergeant Jack Rae leading one of the sections, S/L Douglas-Hamilton settled down for what he hoped would be a long and uneventful flight, which it was to be. Unknown to him, not long after taking off from *Wasp*, one of his pilots was taking a different route. Douglas-Hamilton merely noticed one of his Spitfires slipping back in the formation, but thought no more of it.

Sgt Walcott, who supposedly said to F/Sgt Buckley that 'Malta would never see him', at some point in the flight disappeared and wasn't seen again. It has been alleged that he made for North Africa, flying across the Atlas Mountains to force land his Spitfire (BP958) in scrub. Quite what happened to him after that isn't clear, other than that he managed to get back to the US. The most quoted outcome is that after landing, he made his way to the office of the US Consul in Algeria, claiming that he was a civilian pilot who had been forced down and that he was subsequently re-patriated**. A second version is that a sailor whose ship – HMS *Manchester* – was sunk on one of the later Malta convoys (Operation Pedestal), found himself in a French Internment Camp in North Africa along with his crewmates. He said that one of the others in the camp was Sgt Walcott, who eventually escaped and made his back to the USA.***

Walcott seems to have been an unusual character whose actions did not surprise others. Rightly or wrongly, his departure discredited his Squadron and his colleagues, of that there is no doubt. Whilst at OTU in Northern Ireland, he had supposedly tried to get himself interned in Eire – one report**** was that he had landed there 'for no good reason' – with the aim of getting back to the US and enlisting in the American forces. On the other side of the balance sheet, he was a man who volunteered to fight the battles of a country not his own and at a time when his own homeland was not being directly threatened. Nor should the incident of 26 March 1942 when P/O Jones was killed be overlooked and its possible effect on him. Clearly it was an unfortunate start for a pilot who had just joined the unit. It is known that he was concerned about surviving in Malta – with good cause – and if he felt depressed, and possible homesick, when he found himself in the very American environment of the USS *Wasp*, it all possibly became too much for him and he took what seems to have been an easy option. Nothing suggests a technical problem, but there may have been.

Some of his fellow pilots felt strongly that he had let them down. They were annoyed and angry. After all, they were living with the same stress and facing the same possible injuries and death as Sgt Walcott, but were overcoming their fears and dealing with the situation.

Whatever his motives, Sgt Walcott's defection is a rare skeleton in 603's cupboard although he was not alone in 603 in not performing as demanded. Later, on Malta, one pilot was sent home because he had not reached an acceptable standard and another was 'stood down permanently after leaving a formation'.

---

*After launching the 47 Spitfires, *Wasp* and its escort turned back towards Gibraltar. There are reports that the Italian submarine *Velella* attacked one of the destroyers but Royal Navy reports note only that they were shadowed. The carrier would make a second, similar delivery of Spitfires on 9 May in company with HMS *Eagle*. Thereafter, she sailed back to the US on her way to the Pacific to strengthen the American Fleet there after the battles of the Coral Sea and Midway. It took part in the battle for Guadalcanal. At about 14.45 on Tuesday 15 September 1942, two torpedoes fired from a Japanese submarine struck *Wasp* near its fuel tanks and magazines. The hits were fatal and the Captain gave the order to abandon ship at 15.20, leaving the ship himself 40 minutes later. She burned for about another five hours before sliding beneath the waves at 21.00 hours. Over 1,900 of the crew survived.
**This version is quoted in *The Air Battle for Malta* by Lord James Douglas-Hamilton and *Malta – The Thorn in Rommel's Side* by 'Laddie' Lucas.
***This version is quoted in *Malta - The Thorn in Rommel's Side* by Laddie Lucas but the original source there is not revealed.
****Signal 25 Apr 42 Air Ministry to AOC Malta (AIR2/7698).

The CO was unaware of Walcott's absence until 603 arrived on Malta but by then it was too late and there was nothing that he could do about it although he was furious. A signal dated 25 April 1942 from the AOC Malta to the Air Ministry in Whitehall states that Walcott's absence was 'undiscovered for 48 hours owing to continual battle in progress.'

The flight went smoothly. There were no navigational problems and they followed the original flight plan until Malta came into view from about 120 miles away. Visibility was 'wizard'. The fourth group led by Bill Douglas flew directly overhead Tunis because of 'petrol trouble' according to his log book entry, but more likely to save petrol. As they crossed the city some French biplanes rose to intercept them, but quickly dropped away without taking any hostile action once they were close enough to see what they were up against.*

Between Pantelleria and Malta, orders were received over the R/T to change to a new course which would, in fact, have taken the Spitfires back to Pantelleria. They were given in good English but the pilots realised that it was probably the enemy trying to divert them, so the orders were ignored.

As 603 approached the island, over the radio they were advised by control that Bf109s were active, but none were seen. At that time, they probably didn't appreciate just how important the ability of the controllers to monitor enemy activity and vector the RAF's defenders on to them would be in determining whether or not 603's spell in Malta would be a success or not.

The wind blew from the east and a clear sky. At about 10.00 (local time) the CO led the Squadron to Ta Kali in a tight formation from the west – across the high ground – and not noticing the crude landing strip, brought his section of four in to land across the bomb-cratered airfield as they would have done in the UK. Observing the damage to the airfield below, the others wisely landed in pairs.

'Laddie' Lucas, with 249 Squadron, thought the sight of the formation quite amazing, partly because it had been a long time since that number of Spitfires had been in the air over Malta at once and partly because it seemed to him to be a particularly dangerous thing to do if there were 109s about – a measure of the lack of experience of the new arrivals. Another 249 pilot wrote 'Provided that they have plenty of experienced people it should work much better.'

All of the 47 Spitfires launched from *Wasp* (other than that flown by Sgt Walcott) had arrived safely so there was reason to be optimistic.

The Spitfires flown by the 603 pilots picked their way across the bomb-shattered airfield to the blast pens where they were to be parked. As they climbed down into the glare and heat of Malta, glancing around at the mauled airstrip and taking in the dusty and grimy airmen who came out to meet them, the pilots must have wondered just what lay in store for them.

The ORB for Ta Kali recorded their arrival: 'More Spitfires arrive. 20 officers (603 Squadron) accommodated.' Bill Douglas' log book entry for his three and a half hour flight is equally brief: '603 & 601 reinforce Malta. Led 11a/c. Took off with L.R. [long-range] tank from carrier 35 miles north of Algiers. 47 Spits took off. Sgt Walcott non-finisher.' Allan Otto's is even more terse: 'Took off USS *Wasp*, flew from Algiers to Takali, Malta.'

For the 46 Spitfires which reached Malta, the fuel consumption averaged 47 gallons an hour with the best consumption being 130 gallons and the worst 145. One Spitfire jettisoned its long-range tank an hour and three quarters into the flight.

On 21 April, The Admiralty signalled the Task Force congratulating them:

From the loading in the Clyde, which was finished in record time, until the arrival of all your Spitfires in Malta, operation has been one hundred per cent success. Arrival of these aircraft may make all the difference to ability of Malta to hold out against present devastating Axis air attacks.

Time would tell.

---

*According to Denis Barnham in the second group with 601 Squadron, at a point well into the flight, cloud obscured the surface and a wind got up to such an extent that the group was blown north and found itself flying along the north coast of Sicily. It was however, relatively easy to find Malta from there, although with its airfields full of enemy aircraft, this was a particularly dangerous place to be.

CHAPTER 7

LEARNING THE MALTA FORM

Despite the devastation around them, relative calm greeted the 603 pilots as they shut down the engines of their Spitfires and climbed out of the cockpits to stretch their legs after the long flight.

Over the previous days, the airfield had been attacked on many occasions but it was unusual for it to be out of action for more than a few hours at a stretch. But this was achieved only with the help of many men from other arms of the services working long hours. On 12 April, nine Ju88s dropped 35 bombs on the aerodrome, cratering the runway but not to such an extent that the airfield was unusable. The army had over 300 troops repairing the damage and they worked solidly in conditions that were both dangerous and unpleasant both day and night. Whenever a raid finished they were quickly out on to the airfield and repairing the damage. One unit which served with distinction was the 8th (Ardwick) Battalion of the Manchester Regiment. It didn't take Bill Douglas long to notice and appreciate their work. In a letter to his family on 24 April he wrote: 'The army too are grand out here, carrying on firing and filling holes under the heaviest raids.' On the same day to Elaine McClelland, who would eventually become his wife, in Edinburgh:

> I take an extraordinarily good view of the army out here. They really are a first-class crowd and it's grand to see the way they keep their guns firing even with bombs falling all round them. They just pay no attention at all. And they certainly can shoot.

There were even 13 sailors from *Breconshire* – a ship that had fought its way to Malta with its cargo of oil – attached for the foreseeable future for 'permanent duties'.

The damage to the airfield buildings meant that the accommodation had to be re-organised whilst the salvaging of equipment damaged in the raids continued. On 16 April, personnel from the night-fighter unit and others were in Rabat, the runway and maintenance crews were in Messina House, 126 Squadron at Mosta and the rest including the Station HQ staff in tents in Boschetto Gardens. The local works department couldn't cope because some of its labourers refused to work on the airfields, so in addition to keeping the airfield operational and the few aircraft serviceable, the airmen had had to prepare the accommodation at Messina themselves – erecting their own latrines and ablutions. On the previous two days, much effort had gone into preparing the blast pens which would be used by the new fighters.

The new Spitfires were being slowly refuelled and readied for action. As the pilots retrieved their bags and personal belongings, they found that the various nooks and crannies of their aircraft were being checked for 'gifts' – the cigarettes, canned fruit, Spam, small tools, soap etc which had been put there in *Wasp*.

For the pilots, one of the things which they would find to be lacking on Malta was transport. The scarcity of petrol and vehicles was such that they would eventually find themselves having to walk from their messes (which were off camp) to the airfield and back, or if they were lucky they might acquire a bike. On first arrival together with their bags, they were taken in a broken-down old bus, but eventually as fuel became even scarcer they would have to get used to walking. The Station Commander, W/C Jack Satchell DFC, who, in 1939 had been ordered to take over as CO of 603, met the present CO in his car and gave the Scot a tour of the bombed out airfield before heading for the officers' mess in the Xara Palace about a mile away in M'Dina.

The latest version of the Junkers Ju87 Stuka, the 'D' model, employed over Malta by III/StG 3.

Where possible, the NCO pilots were billeted in private houses. After the war the Xara Palace became the best hotel in Malta, but it was by no means luxurious in 1942. M'Dina is a walled city, on the high ground above the airfield. Off-duty pilots could watch the events at Ta Kali from the verandah of the Xara Palace and if they felt like it walk the walls of the bastion. They didn't have long to wait before they saw some action.

As expected, the Luftwaffe on Sicily was aware of the arrival of the new Spitfires and the first raid built up an hour or two after their arrival – Ju87s and 88s escorted by 109s. The formations soon arrived overhead giving the 603 pilots a grandstand view from the verandah of the mess. At 13.00 hours, six Spitfires of 249 Squadron led by Flight Lieutenant 'Buck' McNair scrambled to meet an incoming raid. The other pilots included 'Laddie' Lucas, 'Junior' Tayleur, Raoul Daddo-Langlois, Ronnie West and Bob Sergeant, all experienced on Malta by now.

The first indication of the arrival of the German aircraft was the bursting of a few pointer shells put up by the 'ack-ack' guns. These showed the pilots of the few Spitfires and Hurricanes scrambled to meet the attack just where the formation was. Then a full barrage ensued.

Surrounded by a sea of black explosions, the Ju88s dived down to about 1,000 feet before releasing their bombs. The 603 spectators could see the bombs and hear the whistle as they fell to explode on the airfield – and on some of the newly arrived Spitfires. The racket from the explosions of bombs and the barrage deafened them. Huge clouds of dust were thrown up and two Spitfires caught fire creating columns of thick black smoke.

Then the defending Spitfires arrived. One Ju88 was hit in an engine (reported to have come down in the sea*) and the 109s started to 'mix it' with the British fighters in a grand dogfight. The 603 pilots at the Xara Palace were excitedly shouting encouragement to their colleagues above.

As the attack on Ta Kali died down, other Ju88s and 87s headed for the Grand Harbour and the airfields at Hal Far and Luqa. The sky filled with twisting, diving, shrieking aeroplanes and exploding shells. The attacks were not accurate and the newcomers noted with some concern that bombs fell wide and struck villages and houses belonging to the Maltese, although they thought the Germans were aiming for the military targets, not the civilians.

Tayleur and Daddo-Langlois both crash-landed their aircraft after encounters with 109s. The CO was to comment later:

> For us new arrivals the sight of a first-class bombing raid from a ringside seat was the most staggering thing we had ever experienced. Many of us, including myself, had never even heard the whistle of a bomb before. Some of us had not till now even seen any enemy aircraft, and few of us had seen them in such large numbers, or been able, unmolested, to watch aerial combats from the ground.

---

*A Ju88 which was reported to be on fire did struggle back to Sicily.

By the end of the day, 14 of the Spitfires which had flown off *Wasp* had been destroyed and 48 hours later, just seven of the 46 Spitfires would be left.*

In the evening, the AOC, AVM Lloyd and G/C A.B. 'Woody' Woodhall addressed the new arrivals of both squadrons in the Xara Palace together with the other pilots who had been there for some time. Woodhall was responsible for controlling the defending fighters to meet the Axis raids and he had been posted to Malta as the Senior Fighter Controller after G/C Embry's report on the parlous state of the air defences in Malta had been circulated in London in January. He brought an impeccable pedigree to his task. A fighter pilot from the First World War, in 1940 Woodhall was the Station Commander at Duxford and the Sector Fighter Controller. He worked closely with Douglas Bader who was an advocate of the controversial 'big wing' philosophy. His low key style and calm communications with the pilots he was directing, gave them confidence in his ability to guide them to the enemy formations. On Malta, his call sign as the controller was 'Gondar', but because often there were few defending aircraft up at any one time, both he and the pilots used first names. He was one of those controllers who could translate the information he was getting into a clear mental picture. His natural feel for the tactics meant that inevitably, the defending fighters found themselves in the best possible position to deal with the attacking formations. His role was vital and Malta was fortunate to have a controller of Woodhall's quality and stature in post at this time. Stan Turner – who arrived on Malta not long after Woodhall – and the Station Commander Jack Satchell had also both been with 12 Group in the Battle of Britain so there was a reuniting of very competent airmen who knew each other of old.

It was a 'pep' talk. The AOC stressed the situation they found themselves in, that it was vital that Malta should win through, the need for a supreme effort to keep the attackers at bay etc. It was stirring stuff, delivered in Lloyd's own style, short (ten minutes), to

Air Vice-Marshal Hugh Lloyd (top) and Group Captain Woodhall.

the point and without notes. Just as he reached the climax, the assembled pilots heard the wail of the air-raid sirens warning of an approaching raid, the rising crescendo of the ack-ack guns, and then the bombs dropping, too close for comfort. One exploded very close to the palace giving many of the pilots a fright. As they brushed off the dust and picked themselves up off the floor, they found the AOC and Woodhall still on their feet grinning. Lloyd famously declared to them that in the future, whenever the Battle of Malta was mentioned they would be able to say 'I was there.' S/L Douglas-Hamilton recalled that ever after, if anyone had been through some terrifying experience, they were always told 'Never mind, you'll still be able to say "I was there"!'

Within hours it became clear to Douglas-Hamilton that the inexperience of his pilots was an issue. For the pilots who had spent weeks on Malta already – like Laddie Lucas – what they were expecting, and needed were battle-hardened types who would be able to face up to the onslaught quickly. What they actually got fell dreadfully short – through no fault of the pilots themselves. The logic as to why the inexperienced 601 and 603 should be the squadrons sent to Malta is unclear although at the time, those squadrons involved in the sweeps across the English Channel were finding themselves up against the Focke Wulf 190 which was more than a match for the Spitfire Vs and there would thus have been a natural reluctance to take experienced units away from the Channel at this time. It is of course ironic that until the previous December, 603 had been one of those very squadrons with high combat readiness and experience which were taking on the 190s.

---

*It is difficult to be precise as to when the Spitfires were lost. *The Air Battle for Malta* by Lord James Douglas-Hamilton suggests that on the morning of the 21st of April, it was difficult to find six serviceable aircraft on the airfield, although many of the unserviceable were not destroyed, but were damaged by splinters and shrapnel.

Some old Malta hands were dismayed at both the lack of experience and the way that the whole reinforcement had been handled. The Spitfires themselves were not received with suitable urgency for the conditions and most of them were unable to operate within a few days of their arrival. It soon became clear that many of them had not been prepared properly before leaving Britain and that they were far from being ready for combat. Some of them arrived with guns that were dirty and unsynchronised and had never been fired, four had radios which were u/s, four had compasses that were inaccurate, in new aircraft the windshields were often oiled up – another problem for the hard pressed pilots – and generally the level of serviceability was poor.

Stan Grant DFC watches 109s above the airfield.

603 shared Ta Kali with 249 Squadron commanded by S/L Stan Grant. Laddie Lucas and Buck McNair were the two flight commanders. S/L Douglas-Hamilton and Laddie Lucas had known each other since their days at university when Douglas-Hamilton was a boxing blue at Oxford and Lucas a golfing blue at Cambridge. When Stan Turner arrived to command 249, he had seen that it would more effective for the resources – both aircraft and pilots – to be pooled. Rather than have several squadrons operating with a relatively few aircraft each, they were allocated duties on a rotational basis using the same aircraft. There was thus an unusual precedent for squadrons to work together in a way that would have been unlikely back in the UK and Douglas-Hamilton realised that it could help 603 reach top operational readiness quickly. Knowing Lucas from the past made it easier for him too.

It was agreed that the 'new boys' of 603 would spend their first few days flying with, and as part of 249 Squadron so that they would have the chance to assimilate the knowledge and experience of their seasoned pilots. S/L Douglas-Hamilton included himself in this and would fly with 249 in this capacity.

It would have been difficult for some squadron commanders in the same situation to admit that their unit needed help to reach the appropriate level of skill and some would no doubt have balked at such a public acknowledgement. 603's CO clearly saw that for the common good – both for the sake of his men and for Malta – it was necessary for the help available from 249 to be accepted in good grace and in accepting it, he enhanced his leadership of the Squadron – not the reverse. In his book, Laddie Lucas is generous in his praise for Douglas-Hamilton, calling him unselfish, un-pompous, unspoilt and noble. It took courage to take this course, but Douglas-Hamilton displayed undoubted qualities of leadership and was determined to get his young pilots through their ordeals alive if at all possible. In this he considered himself to be not just their leader, but their guardian as well.

For the remainder of 20 April, Ta Kali was bombed intermittently. The defenders were also hampered by cannon stoppages attributed to 'bad ammunition'.

For 603, their first blooding came the following day, Tuesday 21 April. Some pilots slept under canvas in an olive grove about a mile from M'dina three or four to a tent and were rudely awakened by the noise of some 109s strafing Ta Kali. They were part of a force of 34 Messerschmitt109s and 37 Ju88s attacking – in addition to Ta Kali – Luqa and the Grand Harbour.

At 06.00 hours, the CO, F/Ls Buckstone, Douglas and Sanders were on readiness with S/L Grant and three pilots of 249 Squadron waiting for 'the off'. They had had to search the airfield to find half a dozen flyable Spitfires and reportedly there were only 27 serviceable Spitfires on the entire island. One of the 249 pilots was 'Johnny' Plagis a well respected and seasoned campaigner who had been giving S/L Douglas-Hamilton help and advice about surviving on Malta.

The usual 'form' was that the first raid came in at about 08.00. The scrambled Spitfires would fly off in pairs, climb to height then dive down on the approaching German bombers. The pilots made sure that their kit was set out so that they could pull it on quickly and easily, and then they settled down to wait – sitting near their Spitfires.

It was a beautiful morning with the heat of the sun beginning to build. The wind came from the east with 5/10ths cloud at 15,000 feet. The white buildings and ground reflected the sun brightly and the pilots watched Malta wakening up and coming to life. In the distance they could see a smudge on the horizon to the north which was Sicily and they wondered what was happening on the airfields over there.

At about 08.30 the CO and F/L Sanders* were told to 'stand to' which sent them into their cockpits and at 08.45, they were ordered to scramble with four Spitfires from 249. Control ordered the six from Ta Kali to climb to about 30,000 feet and join up with five Hurricanes and four Spitfires from the other two airfields. Luqa had been bombed by Ju88s and others were heading for Ta Kali.

Bursting ack-ack shells showed them where the enemy aircraft were and the defending British fighters dropped down looking for the enemy. In the ensuing melee, the CO and F/L Sanders didn't find the bombers and were separated from the others. They spotted some 109s which they chased, but couldn't catch so didn't even have the opportunity to fire their cannons. As the 'new boys' came in to land, Johnny Plagis and another 249 pilot circled above to protect them from any marauding 109s that might be about and looking to pick off RAF fighters landing after the action. On this occasion there were none and all of the Spitfires which had taken off landed back undamaged.

S/L Stan Grant and Johnny Plagis were credited with the joint destruction of a Ju88 and Plagis also damaged a 109. Other pilots damaged a second 109 and a Ju88.

Ta Kali had been hit by about 150 bombs cratering the airfield and roadways and damaging buildings, but the rough strip runway was still usable.

The air combats over Malta were no less furious than during the Battle of Britain and indeed over France during the summer of 1941. Many pilots reported taking 'squirts' at enemy aircraft without seeing any result, but this should not be taken to imply any deficiency in gunnery or any other skill. For the pilot, the dogfight was a kaleidoscope of blazing blue sky, flashing sea, glimpses of aircraft – our own fighters, the enemy's fighters and bombers, sparkling gunfire, a 109 sliding across the canopy, a Spitfire in a steep turn across the nose, a Cant making smoke as it trailed towards the sea, a lick of flame in an engine, the thud of cannon shells hitting the fuselage, a spray of oil up the windscreen, violent g-Forces, sweaty palms, warning cries on the R/T, one of ours going down, a pair of parachutes far below……and then suddenly, shockingly, nothing. The phenomenon well known to all fighter pilots of the sky full of twisting turning aircraft, instantly becoming quite empty. Then the search to find a companion and get back safely to base.

The terse, understated log book entries about taking 'squirts' with no results mask the reality of frantic activity and adrenaline flow. And of course, a pilot might very well take a shot at an enemy and see hits, but then lose sight of his quarry as he had to break off to defend himself from another attack, but then see an aircraft go into the water and claim it as his 'kill' where it might be another's and his own target has limped back to base – one of the reasons why with the best of intentions, claims on both sides tended to be overstated.

Having got back, according to the CO, they 'loitered' at the airfield for a period after they had landed, and as they were about to leave for the mess, the air raid siren blew its warning again and shortly after they were on the receiving end of yet another attack by 109s, Ju87s and Ju88s at 12.45. At 12.30, 249 scrambled, P/O Slade of 603 with them. P/O Watts was also scrambled at 13.20 to protect the airfield and damaged a 109.

Because of the constant air raids, pilots who were not flying, went off the camp to minimise the risk of injury or of being killed. The mess verandah overlooked the airfield from a distance and the pilots often had grandstand views of the attacks. Bill Douglas wrote:

…..there's not a lot to do but watch the raids from a safe vantage point. Actually the latter is quite an occupation, as it is very useful to be able to study the Hun's technique from the ground, and to see how the chaps and the guns are getting on.

Even there they were not always safe. On 11 May, 249's Bob Sergeant was wounded during a raid. Downstairs in the Xara Palace mess and hearing a raid going in on Ta Kali, he bounded up the stairs

---

*F/L Sanders is named in the Diary, but it may have been F/L Buckstone.

Buck McNair and Ronnie West, Xara Palace.

to the verandah. Just as he got to the top, he was hit in the front of his head by a stray German incendiary bullet falling from the sky. He raised a hand in surprise and the round fell from his head and lodged in the back of his hand from where it had to be removed surgically. It signalled the end of his spell on the island. He was flown off the island 'non-effective sick' many days later – an unfortunate end to a tour for a successful pilot. Bob Sergeant however, was not finished and would fly operationally again. The round which injured him was given to him in hospital and he kept it as a souvenir of his time on Malta for the rest of his life.

In the afternoon P/Os McLean and Mitchell with F/Sgt Rae were on readiness with 249 and were scrambled at 16.45. P/O Mitchell fired at a Ju88 and a 109 but with no observed effect, and P/O McLean was quite badly shot up by a 109 which damaged the Spitfire's rudder. P/O Mitchell and F/Sgt Rae found that their accumulators were flat which meant that they had no gunsights or petrol gauges.*

At the end of their first day, the runway was still serviceable although requiring extensive repairs, there were only four serviceable Spitfires and the rations were cut. The ORB remarks dryly: 'Difficult to feed men adequately already.' 603 was well and truly in the thick of it.

22 April brought an overcast sky – a strong south-westerly wind with 10/10ths medium cloud. As always, there were flurries of raids during the day and this pattern continued. The activities of the Squadron which are described, were interspersed with these frequent attacks – not all of which were met by the RAF defenders. The lack of aircraft meant that they had no chance to organise properly. Things were somewhat informal. In his flying career, Bob Sergeant flew a Hurricane only once – on Malta:

> I'd never flown a Hurricane. Stan Turner and I went down to the Flights and Stan said 'Come on, we'll go up.' I said 'I've never flown a Hurricane before.' and he said 'Well, it's a bloody good chance to learn'. And it was an operational trip! He didn't brief me or tell me what we were doing. We went out at low level half way to Sicily, pulled up and looked around, saw nothing and came back.

For the morning readiness, the 603 pilots were once again operating with 249 on this occasion under the command of F/L Buck McNair. The 603 pilots on readiness were F/O Holland, P/Os Murray and Linton, F/Sgt Hurst and Sgt Webster. At 09.15, four Spitfires were scrambled to meet the first raid of the day. One of them was Sgt Webster. They didn't meet the bombers, but found a reconnaissance Ju88 which they attacked. All of the four pilots had a go at it and were jointly credited with it as a probable. In fact, it belonged to 6/KG77 and never returned to base.

At about 10.10, F/O Tony Holland and P/Os Murray and Linton scrambled along with the 249 pilots. In all, seven Spitfires took off. Sgts Hurst and Webster were scrambled a little later. It was to be a significant engagement for 603.

Ten minutes later, control talked them into a position to see about 20 Ju88s coming in over St Paul's Bay which they engaged. During the fight, Johnny Hurst attacked a 109 of 9/JG53 and shot it down. He claimed it as a kill; initially it wasn't confirmed although it was learnt subsequently that the pilot had baled out into the sea so the 109 was actually lost. Although not known at the time, this was 603's first full victory from Malta – although on a strict interpretation, Sgt Webster's quarter 'kill' was the first victory of any kind.

The successes were balanced by the Squadron's first loss. At one point in the dogfight, P/O Murray (in BP970) went after one of the 88s, but he was never seen again. It was presumed that he

---

*In his autobiography, Jack Rae dates this incident on the morning of 22 April.

had fallen victim to a 109 and crashed into the sea. The loss of Pilot Officer Gordon Murray (J/7232) of the Royal Canadian Air Force was the first for 603 on Malta and is commemorated on Panel 4, Column 2 of the Malta Memorial.*

Whilst the group had been airborne, the airfield had been quite badly bombed with a concentration of damage in the centre of the airstrip. P/O Linton tried to come in across the cratered area but found himself unable to stop and finished up with the Spitfire on its nose beyond the boundary fence. F/O Holland tried to land short of the craters, but couldn't stop in time and his Spitfire tipped into one of them. Both pilots however were uninjured. Following these two accidents, the remaining Spitfires left airborne were diverted to Luqa.

For pilots coming back to land, the first thing was to see if the airfield had been bombed while they were away; setting down on the battered airstrip wasn't easy. 'You'd look down. If they'd bombed it, you'd pick a line and say "I think I can get down there". Once the nose is up you can't see and you'd be hoping against hope that you'd get it right. And occasionally the boys didn't.'

Following this raid 603 had one serviceable Spitfire left ('F' BP850) and in the afternoon F/L Douglas made the short hop to Luqa and scrambled with 126 Squadron. Six Spitfires and two Hurricanes took off. Douglas managed to tangle with some Ju88s and fired at three but without any sign of damage and he lost sight of them when his aircraft was thrown into a spin by friendly flak bursting near him. His log book entry stated: 'Flew with 126 Sqdn. P/O Jemmett killed. Me109 bother. 50 Ju88's, 20 Ju87's, Me109 escort.' The sortie lasted 65 minutes.

The Diary makes the interesting comment that 109s made 'weak, darting attacks' which the Spitfires found difficult to respond to because of the number of German aircraft involved. In a letter home, the CO commented that they found that the Germans were 'scared stiff' of Spitfires but whilst this was probably a generalisation and intended to re-assure, there is a story that the Controller – G/C Woodhall – on an occasion when a raid threatened and they weren't able to scramble a single aircraft, arranged for a pilot on the ground to be 'vectored' on to an incoming raid by radio with appropriate responses over the air. It is said that the German pilots were fooled by this and two 109s shot each other down!

Some of the German pilots were new and inexperienced as in all fighting units but they soon learned. The British had to be sparing with their ammunition and the German pilots came to realise this, so they could be quite cheeky with confidence in the knowledge that the Spitfires wouldn't fire unless being attacked. They were also well organised and were quite capable of taking opportunities to shoot down the British fighters. According to Bob Sergeant: 'You didn't try to dive away from a 109. They'd beat us in the dive all the time. Your best way of getting away was a steep climbing turn.' He didn't regard the German airmen as being frightened. Lt Kurt Lauinger of III/JG53, who was himself shot down after shooting down the Spitfire of P/O Harry Fox on 18 March, confided to his captors that he would get the Iron Cross for shooting down a Spitfire – it needed two Hurricane victories for the same award.

By the next day, the 23rd, it was clear that the additional Spitfires flown in from *Wasp* had not changed the situation or improved the ability of the RAF to defend Malta as hoped. Concerns reached the Air Officer Commanding-in-Chief, Middle East, Air Marshal Sir Arthur Tedder and he was extremely displeased at what he heard. He argued that Malta was 'no place for beginners' and that only 'fully-experienced operational pilots' should be sent. Signals were soon flying between the AOC Malta, Tedder and the Chief of the Air Staff in London.

The point being made was that within a few hours of the arrival of the Spitfires on the Monday morning, the Luftwaffe launched determined and frequent attacks on the airfields to such an extent that they were becoming unusable. There seemed little point defending convoys en route to the island because as things stood, those ships that managed to reach the Grand Harbour could not be defended from the Luftwaffe bombers by the six or eight fighters which the RAF mustered for any one sortie:

---

*The Malta Memorial is outside the King's Gate entrance to Valetta and takes the form of a marble column 15 metres high, surmounted by a gilded bronze eagle two metres high.

Bofors gun position, with a member of the crew relaxing before the next raid.

Even with full use of Wasp with 50 fighters every month we must have more. Hurricanes a liability with present strength enemy fighters. Must have 100 Spitfires a month to deal with present strength of attack in 50s every 14 days. Until air situation here satisfactory cannot accept running any convoy here as it would be destroyed in harbour.

A further criticism was in the way that the *Wasp* reinforcements had been received on the airfields. It had taken far too long for the newly arrived aircraft to be refuelled and rearmed with the result that the Luftwaffe had been able to catch them on the ground. If they hadn't been destroyed directly by the attacks, they were either damaged by splinters and shrapnel or by the collapse of the blast pens that had been built to protect them. There were criticisms of the aircraft themselves in that the cannons hadn't been air tested before arriving on Malta and there were problems with 'faulty ammunition'. On 28 April, the Ta Kali ORB has an interesting comment:

Preparations for further Spitfires to arrive. Complaint by Admin Staff that no instructions given last time until planes actually arrived – too much secrecy and ground organisation not prepared – this to be remedied.

Taken in conjunction with comments that Malta had a good rumour machine, it is curious that it appears to have been common knowledge that the delivery of Spitfires was due, and yet the RAF was apparently so singularly unprepared for it.

The Governor of Malta, Sir William Dobbie, had led the island through many difficult times, but confidence in his ability to continue with the full support of the local service commanders and the Maltese people began to wane and it was decided in London that he should be quietly replaced. Accordingly, on 7 May 1942, Field Marshal Viscount Gort VC – the man who directed the withdrawal from Dunkerque in 1940 – arrived as 'Governor and Commander-in-Chief, Malta' and Dobbie returned home to Britain.

Together with all his other concerns, the awful situation on Malta was in the Prime Minister's mind and he again approached President Roosevelt seeking agreement to use *Wasp* a second time to fly in reinforcements, on this occasion in conjunction with HMS *Eagle* which was back in service. Again, the President agreed.

But there was yet more ominous news. Photographic reconnaissance sorties of Sicily showed that areas were being cleared near Gerbini airfield – not far from Mount Etna – with the conclusion that these were most likely being prepared for gliders. The preparations were monitored and into

May, it became clear that they were well advanced, with the areas cleared sited near to railway links with the mainland. The 603 pilots knew this and that if the Germans invaded, they might very well find themselves fighting desperately on the ground – and 'to the last man'. The situation appeared to be getting worse.

On 23 April, neither 603 nor 249 were flying despite many raids by the enemy. F/Os Linton and Watts and P/O Almos were posted to 249 Squadron. P/O McLean was also to leave shortly to fly with 249 Squadron.*

After a few days and as familiarity with the new situation grew, at least some of the pilots relished the challenge although their excitement was tempered with the reality of the fighting. Bill Douglas wrote to his parents (Major and Mrs Douglas who lived in Merchiston in Edinburgh) on 24 April and his enthusiasm is palpable:

> This would be a really wonderful spot in peacetime. At the moment the climate is just right. A nice warm sun, a pleasant breeze off the sea usually to keep us cool, and an occasional white cloud to break the intensity of the blueness of the sky.
> It's jolly comfortable being able to go about in shorts and a shirt – just the thing and we get quite a lot of time off. We get quite a lot of exercise, too, as we have to walk practically everywhere.
> Life on the whole is quite enjoyable – never a dull moment, and getting on with the war.

But one paragraph in his letter is an informal will, telling his parents what should be done with his possessions should he be killed although the paragraph ends: 'Not a very cheerful subject... I'm far from pessimistic about my chances of survival.'

The next two days brought a continuation of the bombing to such an extent that the Ta Kali ORB does not record individual times and details but merely comments that there were: '…many air raids during the day.'

The raids were carried out primarily by Ju87s, Ju88s and 109s, the latter frequently carrying bombs and often strafing the targets – inevitably the Grand Harbour, the three airfields and the seaplane base at Kalafrana. The Diary entry for Friday 24 April gives an indication as to what they had had to endure:

> Two Me.109s dropped bombs on Ta Kali at 06.37 hours. Between 07.00 and 08.00 30 Ju.88s with over 30 Me.109s as escort bombed the Harbour and the aerodromes. 1 Ju.88 was probably destroyed, and a second damaged. Between 10.10 and 11.10 hours 26 Ju.88s, 14 Ju.87s and Me.109 escort dropped bombs on Ta Kali and Valetta. Between 12.56 and 14.00 hours 32 Ju.88s and 20 Me.109s bombed the Grand Harbour, Luqa, Ta Kali.

Saturday 25 April brought a cold northerly wind with 5/10ths medium cloud. 249 Squadron was on readiness in the morning and the first attacks were made between 06.30 and 08.00 but not met by the defenders. There were further raids during the morning and in the afternoon 603 took over readiness from 249. At 13.00 three Spitfires from 603 and 249 scrambled to meet a raid made up of Ju87s, 88s and Bf 109s. They joined up with two other Spitfires scrambled from Luqa. From 22,000 feet, flying in line abreast, they dived on the Ju87s attacking Luqa. Although the 603 pilots did not make any claims, the Luftwaffe did not get away unscathed, 249 claiming two kills and several damaged.

At 17.41 a formation of about a hundred Ju87s, 88s and 109s was plotted approaching the island. Two Spitfires from 603 piloted by F/L Douglas (in 2●R, BP962) and Sgt Webster took off together with four Hurricanes of 185 Squadron and another Spitfire from Luqa. Douglas suffered an R/T failure, but together with the third Spitfire from Luqa, control placed them in an ideal position and they timed their attack perfectly when the Ju88s were just pulling out of their dives. F/L Douglas destroyed one of the dive bombers and this was credited to him as a confirmed kill. Sgt Webster damaged a Ju88, but as he was pulling away after his attack not much above ground level, his aircraft caught the blast from an exploding bomb and crash landed.

---

*The 249 Squadron ORB shows Linton, McLean and Watts (not Almos) joining their new Squadron on 4 June, but it was probably earlier than this. McLean is mentioned in the 603 Diary on 11 May as being in 603 A Flight but in another source as flying with 249 on this same day. It could be that because of the way that the pilots flew with other squadrons, he may have been flying with one of the squadrons whilst strictly speaking belonging to the other.

The odds against the British pilots were huge. The Germans were coming over in formations of up to 100 strong – sometimes more – and the RAF was putting up perhaps half a dozen Spitfires and Hurricanes against them. Bob Sergeant reckoned that he never flew in a formation of more than four. The odds were often of the order of ten to one or greater, but the attacks *were* being broken up and the losses inflicted on the Germans tended to be greater than those suffered by the RAF – at least in the air. A few days after arriving on Malta, Bill Douglas commented that he had never come back from a sortie carrying unexpended ammunition. Because of the imbalance, the RAF pilots couldn't be sure as to their successes – both because they weren't able to follow a damaged aircraft down, and because a German aircraft which had been damaged, might very well crash into the sea or even limp back to Sicily and the loss would not be witnessed. One pilot estimated that about one third of the Axis aircraft damaged over Malta would not make it home.

One particularly unpleasant aspect of the air battle was the killing of defenceless aircrew either on the end of a parachute or in the sea. The RAF pilots shot down over Malta were going to land on friendly territory – as in the Battle of Britain – whereas the Germans would be captured. Unlike the Battle of Britain, the main shortage on Malta at this time was aircraft not pilots. Nonetheless it wasn't unknown for German aircraft to shoot at RAF pilots hanging on the end of a parachute. But this left evidence. Another unsavoury tactic was for the aircraft to fly close to the top of an open parachute to collapse it, sending the helpless airman underneath to his death. Nor was it one sided. On one occasion, an RAF Spitfire was seen shooting up the crew of a Ju88 in a dinghy.

The Luftwaffe used Dornier Do24 seaplanes heavily escorted by 109s to search the northern half of the channel separating Malta and Sicily for ditched airmen. The Do24 was a high wing monoplane powered by three nine-cylinder radials. Its wingspan was 88 feet 7 inches and the length 72 feet 1 inch. It had a maximum speed of 211 mph, cruise 183 mph and a range of 2,950 miles. It was capable of dropping bombs and for defence had 7.92mm machine guns and a 20mm cannon in a dorsal turret. Despite British concerns about the shooting up of defenceless pilots, the Do24s were considered legitimate targets for the Malta defenders even if they were wearing red crosses and they were attacked when the opportunity presented itself.* Some pilots heard that after one of the German rescue aircraft had been seen near the Grand Harbour mines were found in the channel and this became a legitimate reason to attack them, but it wasn't generally thought that they were being used for non-humanitarian purposes. Not all pilots knew 'the form'. The Italians used Z506B aircraft for the same purpose and on 6 June, P/O Ogilvie from 185 Squadron came across one. He wasn't sure what to do and flew alongside it trying to make the pilot fly to Malta. Whilst doing this, another RAF fighter came along and shot it down.

There was a heavy raid during the afternoon of the 26th but little action for 603. The lack of Spitfires meant a glut of pilots with time to kill. On 30 April, ten days after arriving, Bill Douglas wrote to his parents:

> We have quite a lot of time off, though there's not much to do, transport being pretty strictly rationed. 'Sandy' Sanders, a supernumerary F/LT. in my flight, and I and Paul Forster & Jack Slade went for a swim the day before yesterday. We had to walk ten miles into the bargain, which is quite a lot in the heat of the sun. However it was well worth it. The climate really is ideal just now, and I haven't felt so fit for a long time.

Their morale remained high. Later in the same letter: 'There's a grand crowd of chaps here, and I'm really beginning to enjoy myself here. We go to bed early, and get up fairly early, and there's not a lot to do…' At the same time, he wrote to Elaine that he and Neville King had started a moustache growing competition – their senses of humour clearly quite healthy!

27 April saw the raids persist all day with five alerts – one for a Do24 – but no aircraft scrambled to meet them because of the serviceability problem – a week after the arrival of the 46 Spitfires from *Wasp* not one could take to the air. The Ta Kali ORB for this day records the effects:

---

*This was not just a local policy but came from the War Cabinet.

Bombs on camp. Damage to buildings. Extensive craters. Extreme repairs carried out on aerodrome and pens. Aerodrome serviceable. No scrambles. Extensive dive bombing of camps and gun positions. Men suffering with feet trouble owing to lack of boots and shoes. Dust very trying and getting worse.

The second alert was for a routine Ju88 recce sortie which the 603 pilots called 'Steam Boat Bill'. These operations were usually accompanied by two protecting 109s.

The next day, 603 was on readiness first thing. The wind came from the south west with a haze at 15,000 feet. Between 07.56 and 09.09, over 40 Ju88s and 20 Stukas escorted by 109s attacked the Grand Harbour and some army camps. At 08.30, three 603 Spitfires scrambled. They were vectored to the raid and ran into four 109s one of which was claimed as damaged by P/O Jack Slade.

The tactics for meeting the enemy raids were for one group of defenders to act as the strike force actually to find the attackers and deal with them, whilst another two (if possible) aircraft would be responsible for defending the airfield – the 'aerodrome guard'.

603 wasn't on readiness on the morning of 29 April, but F/L Douglas and Sgt Webster were 'on state' at 13.00. P/O Forster and F/Sgt Otto were also at the dispersal but their aircraft weren't serviceable. There was high cloud – 10/10ths – and the wind was from the south west. They scrambled twice – early in the afternoon at 14.00 and just before 19.00. At 14.00 Douglas – flying 2●R BP962 – and Webster took off to act as aerodrome guard but were recalled by the controller in time to tangle with some 109s and Ju88s being attacked by other defending RAF aircraft. Douglas managed to fire at one but Webster didn't fire and to compound matters his radio failed. At 18.20, following a small raid at 17.19, F/Ls Douglas (again in 2●R BP962) and Sanders, and P/Os Forster and Slade scrambled as the strike force. It was hazy. No claims were recorded, but significantly, at a range of about 15 miles and an altitude of 20,000 feet, the pilots glimpsed a tight formation of what they took to be either Macchi or Cant bombers of the Regia Aeronautica. From the ground they had also witnessed a bombing raid carried out by five aircraft 'in beautiful Vic formation' who dropped their bombs in the normal way and not by dive bombing. The Italians were back and this could signal an easing if it meant that the Luftwaffe was withdrawing.

The Italians tended to fly in close formations rather than the fluid groups adopted by the Germans. Bob Sergeant recalled that they did 'perfect aerobatics' which were as predictable as level flight: 'They should have been sliding and skipping all over the place.' 603's CO commented:

Their escorting fighters flew in very pretty but unwarlike close formation, which we nicknamed the 'Hendon Air Pageant'. To keep such formation they obviously had to concentrate rather hard to keep position, which precluded their looking about them for our fighters. In due course they learnt their lesson through bitter experience after we had shot many of them down.

This is a particularly revealing comment illustrating the change in the outlook of the RAF pilots. The 603 pilots were learning the 'Malta form'.

With regard to the tactics employed, 'Laddie' Lucas recalls in his book that when he arrived on Malta in February 1942 with a small group of reinforcing pilots (including the redoubtable Canadian Stan Turner), one of their first sights was a vic of three Hurricanes striving to get height to tackle an incoming formation of 12 109s, which were in three sections of four, flying in line abreast. The Luftwaffe adopted a much more fluid approach using the *rotte* and *schwarm* in which their fighters flew in groups of four (the *schwarm*) made up of two pairs (the *rotte*). The two fighters in a pair flew at a distance, side by side with each pilot looking inwards – at the other – so that each could cover the sky beyond the other for enemy fighters closing in.

Before and during the Battle of Britain some pilots realised the folly of the vics and had adopted the pair tactical formation, but it was 'against the rules' and it would be some time before the rules were changed.

An astonished Stan Turner watched the Hurricanes and as they disappeared into the sky had muttered 'Good God'!

A further factor was how the defending aircraft were to be controlled. Bearing in mind that the enemy airfields were only a 20-minute flight away, it didn't give the defenders much time to scramble and climb to height. Malta had its own radar unit at RAF Station Dingli. Established in 1939 in recognition of Italy's territorial ambitions in the Mediterranean, it was a key factor in assisting the RAF fighters in getting into the best tactical position to intercept enemy raids, as had been the case during the Battle of Britain.

Despite the reputation which the Italian pilots had for not being as aggressive as they could have been, the fighters used by the Regia Aeronautica were quite potent. In 1942, 603 didn't face the by-then obsolete Fiat CR.42s which had made a few brief, disastrous, forays across the Channel during the Battle of Britain, but Reggiane 2000 and Macchi 200s and 202s. In 1943, 'Smithy' Duncan Smith, who had flown with 603 as a flight commander in 1941, became the Luqa Wing Leader and had the opportunity later to inspect captured Italian aircraft. He was particularly impressed with the Reggiane Re2001/5 which was the last in the Re2000 series.

   The Re2000 series looked not unlike the P-47 Thunderbolt with a wing that had a similar, but not as elegant, shape as the Spitfire. Reggiane was a subsidiary of Caproni and the first of the line, the Re2000 was designed in 1938 and first flew in May 1939. It had a wingspan of just over 36 feet, a length of just over 26 feet and a top speed of about 329 mph at 16,000 feet. In trials, the 2000 performed well against the Messerschmitt 109E and it was used by a number of foreign air forces, including Hungary and Sweden. The RAF had considered buying it before the onset of the war precluded this. The 2001 was an improved version with the 2001/5 being the last. Duncan Smith's opinion was that it was superior to the Bf109G and the Spitfires he was flying and on Malta, the 603 pilots remarked that 'the performance and turning ability of the Re2001 was very similar to a Spit.'

   The Macchi 200 Saetta was a single-engined, single-seat, low wing monoplane. The first one flew in December 1937 and it began to enter service with the Regia Aeronautica in 1939. Many of them had open cockpits. It had a Fiat A.74 RC38 radial engine and a wingspan of over 34 feet. It was almost 27 feet long. It could reach a maximum speed of 313 mph at just under 15,000 feet and had an excellent manoeuvrability, if somewhat under-armed and slow when compared with other fighters of the period. Able to withstand considerable battle damage, it was armed with two 12.7mm Breda-SAFAT machine guns mounted in the upper fuselage.

   The 200 was quickly being improved and developed as the 201, but this in turn was overtaken by the 202 Folgore, slightly longer than the 200, but with the incorporation of the Alfa Romeo RA 1000 RC41 engine – which was a Daimler-Benz 601A-1 built under licence – giving it a much sleeker look with the removal of the blunt radial engine. The 202 also had the more conventional canopied cockpit. Its performance was much better than the 200. It could reach a maximum speed of 370 mph at well over 19,000 feet and it achieved an operational ceiling of 37,730 feet compared with 29,200 for the 200. The 202 was introduced into service with the Regia Aeronautica in the summer of 1941. Initially, it had the same armament as the 200, but it was improved in later production machines which brought the addition of two 7.7mm wing-mounted machine guns.

   Again, it was a potent machine which in the hands of competent pilots threatened the RAF's Spitfires and Hurricanes. On 30 April – Thursday – four pilots, the CO, F/L Buckstone, P/O King and F/Sgt Hurst were on readiness at 08.00, although some serviceability issues delayed this for an hour. It was warm and hazy with a southerly wind and no cloud. At 11.00 they were scrambled to meet a raid on Hal Far and Luqa.

   As instructed, the 603 Spitfires climbed to 16,000 feet going towards the south east, but when they were 15 miles out they were vectored back to the island. Again, S/L Douglas-Hamilton timed the attack just as the Ju88s (attacking Hal Far) pulled out of their dives, closing with them head-on at 2,000 feet. One was destroyed by F/Sgt Hurst and another damaged by F/L Buckstone. The CO, Buckstone and King all suffered stoppages with their cannon attributed yet again to faulty ammunition. On his approach, Douglas-Hamilton was fired on by a 109, but it was shot down by fire from a pair of Vickers 'K' guns on the ground manned by the Station Commander – W/C Jack Satchell – an act which undoubtedly saved Douglas-Hamilton's life.

S/L Lord David Douglas-Hamilton.

Sometimes, the Germans sent 109s over from Sicily in relays to linger over the airfields hoping that they would force the RAF fighters either to land or crash as they ran low on fuel. It was nerve wracking for the British pilots to be faced with the dilemma of trying to land under fire, or waiting until the 109s circling lazily above had left to return to Sicily. The pilots returning from this particular sortie were faced with many 109s and it took a while for the 603 Spitfires to get down safely although they all did so eventually, but with Hurst's aircraft suffering some damage.

The enemy would sometimes send over an additional small raid to draw the fighters into the air, then an hour or so later vector in a major attack hoping that the few defending fighters would be on the ground refuelling and rearming. Sorting out which raids to meet became a key skill for the controllers.

The last day of April also marked the departure of Jack Satchell to HQ Mediterranean for Air Staff Duties to be replaced as the Ta Kali Station Commander by Wing Commander Jumbo Gracie who made his mark as a dynamic and efficient commander. With his brusque manner and enthusiasm, he raised the morale of the troops out on the airfield but would brook no excuses. He created controversy by declaring that anyone found stealing on the camp would be 'hanged' and to reinforce the point, had at least one gibbet erected. This action was mainly directed towards the few of the Maltese who were stealing for the 'black market' and not wholeheartedly behind the defence of their island and whilst it was the cause of great mirth around the squadrons, it eventually became noticed back in London with predictable disapproving results. But there was a serious aspect as well. There were stories that one pilot had been killed when he had baled out and his parachute failed to open. The Diary makes the comment that this happened because the silk from his parachute had been stolen by a Maltese worker and the pack padded out with paper. Another reported incident was of a new pilot whose Spitfire had been badly damaged and because he was flying without a serviceable parachute – and knew it but was unwilling to admit it – he had to crash land, being badly burned when the aircraft caught fire. He subsequently died of his injuries.

Bob Sergeant cultivated the habit of checking his parachute every day and like many others, he didn't leave it lying around out of his sight although he didn't recall anyone actually being killed in this way. *If* true, the stealing of a parachute was a particularly despicable action.

With the proximity to Italy and the potential for family links, security was surprisingly lax. One pilot commented

> We used to change our call signs frequently. One day we were out with some of the (Maltese) girls and they said 'You'll be changing your call signs tomorrow' and they told us what the new call signs would be. When we went down to the briefing the next day, the Wingco Flying said 'We're changing our call signs today.' We all shouted 'Change them again, they know those. We were told yesterday by some of the locals.'

As April drew to a close, Malta was still fighting for its very survival and the pilots of 603 were daily being thrown into new and ever more dangerous situations. But, unbeknown to the pilots, the Luftwaffe was already planning to withdraw some of its aircraft from Sicily to be re-deployed in North Africa and Crete, and within a couple of days two Gruppen would be gone. On Sunday 26 April an 'Ultra' intercept of a German 'Enigma' code message indicated that some units of Fliegerkorps II were preparing to leave Sicily and soon thereafter Ju88s of II and III/KG77 left for France. Kesselring was confident that Malta had been neutralised.

There were other more mundane problems. The accommodation in tents, the lack of a varied diet and the effects of 'Malta Dog' all conspired to make life difficult. The 'dog' was an unpleasant form of gastric upset that came from drinking water which wasn't clean, or eating fruit or vegetables which hadn't been washed – or had been washed with the dirty water. It might also have been caused by the change of diet. Some drank goat's milk. Apart from feeling awful, the main effect was diarrhoea which of course stopped the pilots flying. Once having contracted the 'dog' it tended to return at intervals and made life pretty miserable. A test for whether or not a pilot could fly after a bout was whether or not he could fart 'safely'!

Perhaps allied to the problems caused by the 'dog' the food could be monotonous and unvaried. It was invariably tinned meat – Maconachie's – cooked in many different ways to try to make it varied. Stew was another particularly regular presentation. It became the source of wry jokes and it is said that one Spitfire was called 'Maconachie's Reply'! But there were some treats for servicemen on Malta in that at various times of the year, there were tomatoes, oranges, lemons, melons, pears etc in abundance and these helped to vary the monotony of Maconachie's meat provided that they were properly washed with clean water. The Maltese kept hens, so there were often eggs to be had also – two for breakfast and two for tea – but eventually the sheer monotony of hard boiled eggs overcame the novelty of their abundance. The men did get a chocolate ration, however – two packets a week.

It was inevitable that they would lose weight. For some it made them fitter and leaner, but for others it would be a problem particularly if aggravated by the effects of illness. Some pilots noticed that their tolerance to the g-Forces lessened with the tendency for them to black out more often during combat.

There was limited alcohol, but when flying out of Luqa on 22 April, F/L Douglas noted that there seemed to be beer available in the mess as well as cigarettes and chocolate. The mess at Luqa did seem to be better provisioned than Ta Kali. Those who finished up in M'Tarfa Hospital were given a half bottle of Bass a day! There was a local beer – from the Cisk Brewery – but it was running out of the basic ingredients. (The brewery was alongside Ta Kali and its tall chimney became a good landmark for the pilots. Watching the raids from the Xara Palace verandah, a great cheer would go up from the pilots if the chimney remained standing once the dust had cleared.)

For the ground crews, the living conditions were no better. Sgt Alex Wishart, a Leith man, had joined 603 Squadron in 1937 as an auxiliary and was a fitter by trade. In November 1940 as an LAC, he was posted away from the Squadron to Malta where in 1942, when 603 arrived off *Wasp*, he had responsibility for the plant which produced oxygen for all the aircrews stationed there. He recalled that his bed was in a YMCA building taken over for the troops – large rooms with no privacy. They were always hungry and the food they got was below the subsistence level. Sometimes there would be a sausage and an apple for breakfast with a mug of tea. Dinner wasn't much better. He said 'You were always hungry, but you got used to it.' There was no alcohol for the ground crews until the siege lifted and a load of Australian beer came in. But he recalls that beer could always be found in the officers' messes.

On Friday 1 May, the wind was from the west with 8/10ths cover of high cloud. 249 Squadron was on readiness in the morning with 603 after lunch at 13.00. In addition to the CO, the pilots were F/L Buckstone, P/O Mitchell and F/Sgt Rae. At about 17.00, they scrambled to break up an attack by five Italian Z1007bis bombers at about 19,000 feet. Bert Mitchell and Jack Rae were flying as numbers 2 and 4 respectively. They thought that they had been ordered up about fifteen minutes too late.

The Spitfires circled the airfield at about 20,000 feet but lost sight of the enemy aircraft. 'Woody' Woodhall warned them of 109s in the area, and they dropped down to about 16,000 feet looking for them. Two were seen approaching from the port quarter, but passed by harmlessly although one apparently jettisoned a tank (or a bomb) when the Spitfires turned towards them. Jack Rae spotted another 109 flying slowly at 6 o'clock and reported it, knowing full well that there would probably be a second in the area. But Bert Mitchell quickly found it and called a warning to Rae to break left. Rae, flying 2●R BP962, instinctively did as instructed, ramming the throttle forward at the same time, but as he did, the Spitfire was hit. The control column took a round at its base and the aeroplane became immediately unflyable. Other shells hit the cockpit. One caught him in his boot, wounding him in the leg. Others destroyed

F/Sgt Jack Rae.

many of the instruments and the throttle was useless. The Spitfire tipped into a power dive with the g-Forces pinning the pilot inside. One of the pointers that the old hands passed on was that they often flew with their cockpit hoods open – it made the pilot cooler and more comfortable in the heat and it also could save him precious seconds if he had to get out quickly. Fortunately for Rae, he had taken their advice and when the Spitfire suddenly pitched, he was somersaulted cleanly out. But his troubles weren't over. He groped feverishly for the ripcord handle, but couldn't find it. Then, in the remarkable way that the brain works under stress, he suddenly became quite calm and recalled one of his instructors in the past telling the novice pilots that if they were ever in this predicament they should simply look for it. He did as he had been told, found the ripcord and quickly discovered himself dangling under the large silk canopy.

He was still far from safe. Out over the sea, he was aware of the danger of a 109 coming back and shooting him up. The light wind blew in the right direction, but he decided to try to steer the parachute back over the island by pulling on the risers. Whilst this had the desired effect, he found that he began to oscillate under the canopy to such an extent that he became frightened that it would collapse and felt that it would be better to leave well alone. He eventually landed safely although he was greeted by an armed Maltese farmer who thought the airman to be an enemy. Ultimately, with some help from soldiers of the 4th Buffs, Jack managed to convince him that he was friendly and all was well.

As the 109s attacked Rae's aircraft, the other Spitfires turned in to help. The CO got in a three-second burst with his cannon at one of the 109s but broke off his attack to protect Rae on the end of his parachute. The other two took shots at it – Buckstone hitting it in the tail – and the 109 was eventually reported crashing into the sea although curiously, none of the pilots claimed it. Apart from the loss of Jack Rae's Spitfire, Buckstone's was damaged by a cannon shell in the tail.

The Kiwi's injury was less serious than he might have thought. He sustained a single wound in his leg but once in plaster, he could walk on crutches, although clearly wasn't able to fly.

Much later, it was possible to re-construct what had happened. As he had feared, the single 109 he had reported had been a decoy positioned to draw the attention of the British pilots. There was another, the leader of the pair, Lt Herbert Soukop of 6/JG53 and he hit Rae's Spitfire. Mitchell's timely warning saved Rae's life. (Some reports say that Rae and Buckstone had R/T failures, but this isn't borne out by other accounts of the action.)

S/L Douglas-Hamilton visited Jack Rae in hospital the next day and was clearly upset at what had happened. Rae had the rather unusual experience of being able to discuss the action with Soukop weeks later when the German was shot down and became a prisoner and Rae could piece together the sequence of events. He also gained the impression that he was Soukop's thirteenth victim. The fact that Soukop was shot down later, confirms that his aeroplane did not crash into the sea as reported.

There was another lesson to be learned. Some British pilots were in the habit of recording their kills by painting small swastikas on their Mae Wests. But this had confused the Maltese farmer that Rae met into thinking that Rae was German. In future, the practice stopped.

The setback of losing an aircraft in what was only a skirmish indicated to 603 that they were now in a fast, ferocious, dangerous war where constant alertness in the air was vital. They had indeed been 'thrown off into the deep end' into what was possibly the most severe air war in the world at that time and for this group of brave and dedicated men, the pressure mounted.

A reduced scale of rations was introduced and all sleeping out passes were cancelled. F/Sgt Rae was promoted to W/O.

During the night there were several raids on the airfield and after midnight four Spitfires of 603 were scrambled. A 109 was seen going down into the sea to the west of the island and the CO and P/O Mitchell were credited with a joint victory.

The following day – 2 May – proved uneventful. F/L Douglas, P/O McLean and F/Sgt Otto were on readiness at dawn just before 06.00 in the only three serviceable Spitfires and although there were some desultory appearances by the Luftwaffe, nothing happened and 249 Squadron took over readiness. During their turn for duty, a raid comprising six Ju88s escorted by 16 Macchi 202s came in – another measure of the increasing involvement of the Regia Aeronautica.

On 3 May – Sunday – 603 A Flight took over readiness after lunch – F/L Sanders, P/O Slade, 2nd Lt 'Zulu' Swales and Sgt Webster. They had three Spitfires with a fourth being promised that afternoon but it never appeared. The wind was from the west with 5/10ths medium cloud. At 16.50, F/L Douglas and F/Sgt Otto relieved Sanders and Swales and without the fourth aircraft, Webster also stood down. At 17.20, the three were scrambled (Douglas flying 2●G BR187) in the airfield defence role gaining height to the north and west. It was Allan Otto's first operational flight over the island. At 23,000 feet they came upon a pair of 109s which promptly departed, but in following them, the 603 aircraft split up. They reformed over Luqa where they got into a fight with some Ju87s. Douglas damaged one. He described the fight later saying that despite one of his cannons going u/s, he'd blown the whole of the long cockpit off the aeroplane. He flew past it and saw the headless gunner sprawled in the back, with an arm over the side. He was credited with a damaged. Jack Slade's cannons also failed, but he claimed an 87 with his machine guns. Its engine seized and it crash landed near Zonqor. Allan Otto's log book for the one hour ten minute sortie has the terse note: 'Intercepted Ju88, 87 + 109's, short squirt at 88, NIL.'

Slade's Ju87 (S7 + JP) belonged to 9/Stuka Geschwader 3 and was piloted by Gefreiter Karl Haff with Gefreiter Fritz Weber the wireless operator/gunner. Haff died, but some interesting intelligence was gleaned from Weber, who had sustained only light injuries. Weber was 21 years old, had been posted to Sicily as a replacement and made his first operational flight over Malta – this last one being his seventh. Most of his sorties had been against anti-aircraft positions. From what he said, it seemed that the serviceability rate for the Ju87s was high, mainly because replacement aircraft could reach Sicily in about two days. The unit also enjoyed the luxury of having more crews than aircraft so that the raids were being carried out by reasonably fresh men. But he was judged to have low morale, and he wearied of the war. Luftwaffe airmen were not necessarily rotated and would continue to fly operationally with combat units until they were unable to do so – either because they were wounded, killed or captured, but it is of passing interest that an airman with only seven operational sorties behind him should feel this way, although clearly it was not necessarily typical of the German aircrew in Sicily.

Again the problem with the failure of Slade's cannons was attributed to faulty ammunition. On 3 May, the problem with cannon stoppages came to a head. The following day tests of the cannon on three Spitfires showed that only three guns were serviceable. Checks were carried out on the ammunition and showed that 30% were 'misfits'. The CO's comment – 'really appalling.'

On 6 May, further testing of ammunition – some at least manufactured in America – resulted in 25% of the HE rounds and 15% of the ball being set aside as unusable. Out of 60 ball rounds in one box, 50 were found to be oversize.

No doubt the results of the tests were communicated back to the Air Ministry in London, but there doesn't appear to have been any explanation given or action taken to correct this quite unacceptable level of failure. Some accounts of the RAF's campaign in Malta are unrelenting in their criticism of their incompetence – firstly with the defective long-range tanks that so affected the attempts to fly Spitfires in, and secondly with the lack of air testing and preparation of the cannons before they left the UK. On Malta, soldiers were used in some instances as armourers, and whilst they would be excellent at the task, given appropriate training, it may be that the RAF was indeed lacking in the way that the Spitfires were prepared. With regard to the ammunition faults, presumably these were manufacturing problems, caused by poor quality control – either by the failure to set suitable standards or failure to monitor and meet them.

Whatever the reasons, for the pilots fighting with their backs to the wall and the ground crews struggling under such difficult conditions, these were problems that they could have done without. In addition to depriving them of a powerful weapon, cannons which failed on only one side of the aircraft created an asymmetrical recoil on the Spitfire making it more difficult to maintain a stable gun platform.

On 4 May, the CO, F/L Buckstone, P/O King and F/Sgt Hurst were at dawn readiness at 05.30. There was a raid by Ju88s during the morning but the Squadron wasn't scrambled.

249 Squadron took over readiness from 603 at 13.00 hours. At tea time, four Spitfires from Ta Kali and three from Luqa scrambled to meet an Italian raid comprising five Cant 1007 bombers accompanied by a close escort of five Macchi 202s. As the 249 Spitfires turned in to engage, they encountered about 14 Bf109s. Douglas-Hamilton recorded:

......one pilot was shot up by a 109 – a very great loss, but he had already hit them hard, at least seven destroyed. We saw it happen from the Mess verandah. He was going straight ahead with his No.2 and the two 109s slunk up behind. He turned in time to warn the other one but did not respond in time and a streak of smoke came from his a/c. He called up on R/T that he was going to land; he circled a few times then dived straight into the deck. Conclusion: "He must have passed out".

The pilot was F/L Norman MacQueen, a flight commander with 249 Squadron acting as CO in the absence of S/L Grant who was in Gibraltar at that time to bring out another delivery of Spitfires along with Laddie Lucas, Buck McNair, Ronnie West and Raoul Daddo-Langlois – also from 249. His aircraft was hit by Unteroffizier Walter Manz of III/JG53 and came down near Naxxar exploding on impact. The official version was that his radio hadn't been working – another problem which wasn't unusual – and his number 2, the American Fred Almos (who had transferred to 249 from 603 Squadron) had been trying to warn him of the approaching danger. Some of the watchers thought that neither of the pilots had spotted the enemy aircraft because of their lack of evasive action. MacQueen's loss appears to have been felt keenly by 603 and its commander – possibly because he was one of those who had been open in his help for the newly arrived pilots and someone that they had grown to respect and admire. His loss was felt sorely by the older hands too, particularly Laddie Lucas and Bob Sergeant who had usually flown as MacQueen's number 2 but hadn't been able to since his injury stopped him flying. MacQueen and Sergeant were good friends and Sergeant (who had been an undertaker before the war) accepted the unhappy task of sorting through MacQueen's effects to send them back to his family.

On 6 May, another old Malta hand, Johnny Johnston, went down in flames, victim of a 109. He wasn't killed but was burned quite badly and finished up in hospital.

The 5, 6 and 7 May were relatively uneventful for 603, but for Malta, uneventful actually meant the continuing round of raids and scrambles to meet them. The Ta Kali ORB notes that F/L Sanders, P/O Slade and Sgt Webster all damaged a Ju88 on the 5th, but the Diary and Allan Otto's log book both date this on 6 May which is likely to be correct. There were four pilots from 603 up – as well as Sanders, Slade and Webster, F/Sgt Otto took part but returned early. On his first attempt at landing, he overshot and tried to go round again. Unfortunately he crashed and sustained bad bruising and concussion with head injuries. He was flying Spitfire AB340 and his accident occurred at 08.50. He didn't fly again for some time.

Also on 5 May, a delivery of Hurricanes had been expected from North Africa, but these didn't appear although they eventually turned up two days later along with some Beaufighters, with high cover for their arrival provided by 603.

The significance of these few days was probably in the continuing involvement of the Italians which the defenders found easier antagonists and the fact that the raids seemed to be reducing in intensity. Despite the loss of the experienced pilots like MacQueen and Johnston, the Diary does remark on the lightness of the raids – on 5 May 'brighter than we've had yet' and on 7 May 'only one raid all day' and that by Italian formations. Ta Kali was raided by Ju87s and 88s on 8 May and the CO commented that it had been the first daylight raid on the airfield 'for about a week'.

CHAPTER 8

THE SECOND *WASP* RELIEF FORCE

Lord Gort took the oath of office as 'Governor and Commander-in-Chief, Malta' on 7 May. It is significant that he received the two titles because it gave him authority over the services as well as the civilian administration. He immediately made his presence felt. On the day that he arrived, there were only six Spitfires operational. The immediate issue was the arrival of more Spitfires which were expected within the next day or so from *Wasp* and *Eagle* and the preparations to be made for them. The success of the Luftwaffe in damaging or destroying most of the Spitfires brought in by 603 and 601 on 20 April could not be allowed to be repeated and Gort insisted that the new aircraft be received and turned round quickly and effectively. This would clearly involve ensuring that they were refuelled and rearmed as soon as they landed, that there was suitable protection for them whilst they were on the ground – both air cover and blast pens – and that fresh pilots were available immediately if necessary to scramble in the event of an enemy raid and get them off the exposed airfields.

This latest delivery took the name Operation Bowery. *Wasp* had returned to the Clyde on 26 April, after flying off 603 and 601 to load up with another 50 new Spitfires. Reportedly, there were further problems with leaking fuel tanks which resulted in delays and some further embarrassment for the RAF before the carrier went to Scapa Flow before proceeding back to Gibraltar accompanied by US and Royal Navy warships as escort, still referred to as Force W. HMS *Eagle* was at Gibraltar with 17 Spitfires on board and joined Force W during the night of 7/8 May.

Meanwhile back on Malta, positive preparations were being made to receive the latest delivery of Spitfires. This time each aircraft would be guided by a runner to a pre-designated and properly constructed blast pen on touchdown where waiting for it would be an experienced pilot who would relieve the incoming pilot, and five ground crew who would refuel and if necessary rearm the Spitfire so that it would be able to scramble and take on any raids within 20 minutes of landing instead of the three hours it had taken on 20 April. Each pen would need to have a suitable amount of fuel and ammunition available. This meant getting the cans of fuel over to the pens and loading rounds into the ammunition belts. The RAF personnel worked closely with the army without whom the preparations would not have been completed successfully.

The arrangements also included the ability to repair bomb craters should the airfield be attacked, the provision of army bren carriers to pull damaged aircraft off to one side should they be blocking the runway or taxi paths, and medical teams to deal promptly and effectively with any casualties.

Orders were issued that the airfields should have absolute priority for defensive barrages whilst the new aircraft were coming in and all restrictions on the use of ammunition were lifted.

On the morning of 8 May, reveille sounded at 04.00 for the arrangements to be rehearsed. The 603 pilots were each allotted to a blast pen where they would be waiting the next day for their new aircraft to arrive. They were eventually released in the early afternoon, but not before there was a raid at 09.00 by Ju87s and 88s with an escort. This raid was met by four Spitfires and 11 Hurricanes but 603 did not scramble. One Hurricane, flown by Sgt Boyd of 185 Squadron, destroyed one of the 88s, but was badly damaged and had to make a belly landing at Ta Kali.

Another raid came over in the early afternoon. S/L Douglas-Hamilton and some of the others who were still on the airfield tumbled into an old gun-pit when it started. They had rifles and fired at the bombers as best they could during the raid – but without obvious result. Several bombs landed near them and they were showered with stones – some large enough to leave dents in their steel helmets.

Alex Wishart experienced many attacks during his time on Malta. He recalled the effects of blast after an attack on Luqa:

> I used to go into a slit trench. It had only a piece of corrugated sheeting with stones on top of it. This day I was out on the far edge of the 'drome so there was no chance of getting over. Eight Itie bombers came over surrounded by fighters. The slit trench was only a few yards from our hangar and I was sure it had got hit.
>
> I went over and looked for the trench. There was a hole where the shelter had been so I went over to it and looked in. People were huddled together. I said 'Come on, Curly, Ginger. Come on lads.' But all the twelve were dead. Killed by blast.

His recollection was that the Italian bombing was usually quite accurate – more so than the Luftwaffe.

It had always been a frustration for those on the ground that during raids they could do nothing to get back at the aircraft who created such continual harassment and the previous Station Commander, W/C Satchell, had arranged for rifles to be issued and machine guns placed on stands near the aircraft pens so that those under the bombs could vent their anger at the attackers and possibly even hit them. It will be recalled that on one occasion it had been S/L Douglas-Hamilton's life that was saved by none other than the fiery Satchell himself! Although haphazard, small arms fire en masse proved to be an effective defence which was still effective 30 or so years later against the fast jets of the American air arms in Vietnam. The 249 Squadron ORB notes that 'Airmen encouraged to fire rifles from slit trenches at low-flying enemy aircraft – many rifle brigades formed.'

Tony Holland had good reason to appreciate the effectiveness of the ground fire. He recalled later:

> I remember returning from one scramble, and when on my final approach throttled right back, wheels and flaps down, hood back about fifty feet up and only the wind whistling, suddenly being alerted by a crescendo of small arms fire coming up from the slit trenches. I thought at first they had gone mad and were firing at me. On glancing over my shoulder, there was the large yellow spinner of an ME109 already firing and that was their target. I have never turned so sharply, so slowly or so low, but that warning undoubtedly saved me on that occasion. Fortunately my beautiful Spitfire did not stall.

As well as the Spitfires themselves, spare parts and other essentials were in short supply on Malta – medical stores, food and trained ground crew to keep the Spitfires in the air. With support from the highest level – the Prime Minister and the Admiralty – the fast minelayer HMS *Welshman* prepared to make a run to the island at the same time as the Second *Wasp* Relief Force was on its way. *Welshman* was commanded by Captain W. Friedberger. He had supervised the loading of about a hundred Merlin engines, over three hundred tons of medical and other equipment including powdered milk, canned meat, ammunition and six dozen crates of smoke-making equipment. In addition, there were about a hundred RAF ground crew making the hazardous journey. Churchill was aware that the ship might very well be sunk but that the consequences of this or not even attempting to force the vital supplies through could be catastrophic for Malta.

She headed eastwards before first light on 8 May having had prefabricated plywood structures added to her superstructure and funnels during the night to give her the appearance of the large Vichy French destroyer *Leopard*.

The stage was set for what was likely to be the pivotal events in the second siege of Malta with three elements: Force W, *Welshman* and the arrangements for receiving the new aircraft on Malta. 603 would have a vital role in meeting and escorting the new arrivals safely to the airfields.

Saturday 9 May dawned with a cloudless sky, a haze and a southerly wind. Reveille at Ta Kali was once again 04.00 with the arrival of the Spitfires expected four hours later. The 603 pilots ate breakfast by candlelight in their mess.

At 06.30, north of Algiers, the two carriers were steaming into the wind, with *Eagle* a thousand yards behind *Wasp*. As before, *Wasp's* Wildcats were airborne both to clear the flight deck and to provide protection for the Spitfires taking off. This time, the launch wasn't as trouble free as on 20 April. The first Spitfire to launch from *Wasp* did so at 06.43 piloted by S/L Stan Grant. The 23rd was a Canadian, Sgt R.D. Sherrington. For some reason – possibly because he had put the propeller into coarse pitch – his Spitfire didn't achieve enough airspeed to take off safely and it crashed into the sea just ahead of the carrier's bows. Both it and the unfortunate pilot were lost when the carrier ploughed over it.

A second incident involved another Canadian – P/O Jerrold Smith. He had taken off successfully, but as he climbed to join the other Spitfires in the group, he accidentally released the long-range 'slipper' tank which fell into the sea and put him into an invidious position.* He didn't have enough fuel to reach Malta and the pilots were normally told that in such circumstances they should either fly to North Africa, attempt a force landing and hopefully make their way back to friendly territory or bale out into the sea and trust that one of the naval ships in the area would pick them up. A third, but rather 'hairy' alternative was to try to land back on *Wasp* although this was discouraged and trying to land on *Eagle* positively prohibited. The Spitfires were land-based aircraft and although taking off from carriers, were not 'navalised' with the addition of hooks etc.

Smith elected to try to land back on *Wasp* once all the Spitfires had launched and against all the odds did so successfully, although his aircraft stopped uncomfortably near to the front edge of the flight deck. It was a great achievement, duly celebrated! Later, in the wardroom, he was presented with a pair of USN 'wings' and perhaps more surprisingly, with a large scotch and soda given to him quietly by Douglas Fairbanks Jnr, one of *Wasp's* officers! For this to happen in the normally 'dry' American ship was something quite out of the ordinary.

Smith eventually made it to Malta but was killed on 10 August.

Another two aircraft didn't get through to Malta – both piloted by members of the RCAF. There are various reports as to what happened to them, one that they ran out of fuel with one crashing into the sea and the other force landing in North Africa. A second that one crashed just outside the Grand Harbour having run out of fuel. What did happen was that they were flying as a pair and attacked an Italian Fiat RS14 floatplane of 170 Squadron RM flown by Sottoten Luigi Arco. It seems that return fire from the floatplane hit one Spitfire which collided with the other – both crashing into the sea. Neither pilot survived.

As far as 603 was concerned, of the Spitfires which launched, 59 reached the island fortress and were to be escorted in. There were six serviceable Spitfires available for 603 with F/Ls Buckstone and Sanders, F/O Holland, P/O Mitchell, F/Sgt Hurst and Sgt Webster at dawn readiness. They scrambled at 09.45 to give high cover for the new arrivals. Tony Holland was flying in BR184 as the number 2 for John Buckstone in BP872. There were many 109s about. The Spitfires climbed on the south side of the island east to west. Tony Holland recalled:

> ......we were bounced by numerous ME109s at about 16,000 feet. As they passed us, we all
> fired at them and John was either hit in their attack (although I saw no strikes on his aircraft)
> or I think more likely followed one down too far and too fast.

According to Holland, Buckstone's Spitfire crashed into the sea near where the 109 he was following went in. The pilot wasn't found.

The CO had been on the ground on this occasion and was saddened by the loss of his flight commander and friend: 'So Buck had gone! It was hard to believe we should not see him again and be cheered by his lively humour.'

Flight Lieutenant John Walter Buckstone RAFVR (79626), the son of Walter and Violet Buckstone of Slough, Buckinghamshire was married to Leonie. He was 22 years old when he died. His death is commemorated on Panel 2, Column 1 of the Malta Memorial.

Despite the assumption that Buckstone had been unable to pull out of the dive, it isn't absolutely certain that he wasn't shot down. A Messerschmitt 109 pilot – Oberfeldwebel Rollwage – claimed a Spitfire at 11.05 and it may be that it was he who had hit the flight commander's aircraft, but in the confusion of battle it is difficult to be certain one way or the other.

---

*It may have been a faulty pump in the tank.

Holland and Mitchell continued to tackle the 109s and reckoned that they had shot another of them down. However, bearing in mind that Tony Holland had already seen a 109 crashing, only one Luftwaffe fighter was lost. This was 'Yellow 6' of 6/JG53 piloted by Unteroffizier Helmut Schierning.

F/L Sanders took over the duties of John Buckstone.

The incoming Spitfires were duly met, but 109s at Hal Far were giving the newly arriving Spitfires a hot reception as they tried to land, short of fuel. As usual, the Messerschmitts were hanging about the airfield, trying to catch Spitfires as they landed or as they were taxying on the airfield. Some even drifted into the circuit with their flaps and undercarriages down to confuse things further. One newly arrived Australian pilot, F/L R.H.C. Sly, who had led one of the Spitfire groups to Malta, was killed when he found himself being strafed as he tried to take off again after making a successful landing to help some of the new arrivals overhead. His aircraft couldn't reach flying speed and hit one of the blast pens.

Generally, the arrangements for receiving the Spitfires worked well. At Ta Kali they were being turned round and ready for operations within ten minutes – some in seven, some in six or less. The arrival of 59 Spitfires on the island was to prove to be a turning point – 23 of which safely reached Ta Kali – and the last one landed on Malta at about 11.00.

The newly arrived aircraft were divided out to the various squadrons and 603 had 12. The CO split them into three sections of four – Red being his own with P/Os King and Mitchell (a new arrival) and Sgt Webster, White being Bill Douglas' with P/Os Forster and Slade and F/Sgt Brown and Blue being the responsibility of F/L Sanders with F/O Holland, the other P/O Mitchell and F/Sgt Hurst.

The Luftwaffe continued to come over in force, determined once again to destroy the newly arrived Spitfires and emasculate the island's defences. At 10.55, 11 Spitfires of 249 Squadron were scrambled and then at 12.00 603 Blue Section was sent off. The four pilots were F/L Sanders, F/O Holland, P/O Mitchell and F/Sgt Hurst, climbing to about 25,000 feet. But despite the better reception arrangements, the aircraft were still not fully operationally serviceable. The radios didn't work properly. Tony Holland lost sight of the other three and not being in touch with them assumed that they had dived. He too tipped his Spitfire into a dive. As the speed built up, the Spitfire was buffeting and he found it difficult to hold it steady. Suddenly he saw three aircraft ahead and assumed that they were the others of Blue Section, but as he carefully pulled out of the dive, he realised they were 109s. He pressed on to attack and lined up the nearest, but when he pressed the 'tit' nothing happened. None of his guns fired. With no radio and no guns, he had little option other than make a run back to Ta Kali which he did, escaping his erstwhile targets and landing safely.

With Blue Section back on the ground, Red and White Sections were on 'stand-to' meaning that the pilots were in the cockpits. At mid-day it became very hot and they had to endure this for over an hour. Relief came at 13.30 when about half a dozen Ju88s shot across the airfield dropping twenty-four bombs. The pilots leapt out of the aircraft and flattened themselves on the ground or dived into nearby slit trenches. The bombs dropped around them but caused little damage.

603 scrambled twice more that day. At about 15.50 the Squadron was ordered up to 25,000 feet to meet incoming bombers, but again problems with the radios prevented them getting clear instructions from the controller. They turned back to protect Ta Kali, but the focus of the raid was Luqa and the bombers were missed. However, on coming in to land, yet again, 109s waited in ambush. They circled the airfield for some time and were fired on by some of the 603 Spitfires. F/O Holland, P/O Mitchell and F/Sgt Hurst claimed to have damaged one each.

Their final action of the day was at about 18.30. Red Section scrambled on seeing a Verey light which they had thought was green – the signal for them to scramble. They climbed to 12,000 feet but didn't spot the raiders – five Cant 1007s and seven Ju88s with escorts attacking Ta Kali. In the meantime, White and Blue Sections also scrambled but they failed to make contact with the bombers. By this time, 19.00, Red Section had returned to earth and the pilots were huddling in slit trenches. The two sections in the air found some Bf109s and during the ensuing dogfight, F/L Douglas shot one down and P/O Slade damaged another, but they were chased back to Ta Kali by the 109s where they were saved by the ack-ack guns. On landing, Bill Douglas finished up in a delayed action bomb hole with his aircraft (4●S, BR251) damaged although he was unhurt. Hurst's aircraft was also found to be badly damaged after he had landed.

At the end of the day, 603 were in a position to have eight aircraft ready for operations in the morning. They were now operating as a Squadron with their own allocated aircraft and pilots. Despite the loss of John Buckstone, the day had been an undoubted success both for 603 and for the air defence of Malta. The Axis forces on Sicily had tried to repeat their successes of 20 April when so many of the newly arrived Spitfires were put out of action but they had singularly failed on this second occasion. Some of the new aircraft were damaged, but the defenders of Malta could now take back some of the initiative. They were taking the attacks to the enemy – during the afternoon, four Spitfires of 249 Squadron had patrolled off Sicily before coming back to Malta to take on Ju87s attacking the Grand Harbour and Luqa.

Two of three elements making up the latest attempt to reinforce Malta had been executed successfully – the arrival of the Spitfires from *Wasp* and *Eagle* and the arrangements for receiving them. The third element was *Welshman*.

During 9 May, she had been making her way towards Malta running the gauntlet of the Axis forces on the way. She was challenged by two Ju88s and a Vichy French seaplane but bluffed it out so that during the night, she met a trawler to guide her through the shallow waters around the island to enter the Grand Harbour at 05.25 just before sunrise. Unloading the cargo started immediately under the supervision of the Navy but was carried out by many different units of the Army as well as the Navy and the Maltese.

Perhaps realising the significance of their failure to neutralise the newly arrived Spitfires, the Luftwaffe continued to bomb the airfields during the night and the pilots found it hard to get any meaningful sleep because of the noise. Reveille at Ta Kali on the 10th was 04.00 and the Spitfires were on readiness at 05.00. For 603, the pilots were the CO, F/O Holland, P/Os King, Slade, Forster and Mitchell, F/Ls Douglas and Sanders, F/Sgts Hurst and Brown and Sgt Webster. It will be recalled that after the previous day, there were only eight Spitfires serviceable.

Attention concentrated on the Grand Harbour with the arrival of the minelayer. It was being patrolled by defending Spitfires, but because of the importance of the cargo, the harbour anti-aircraft defences were given absolute priority – no restrictions on ammunition and the British pilots were warned that the barrage would not be stopped for them if they flew over the harbour.

As soon as *Welshman* arrived, the smoke generators were started creating a pall that could be seen across the island. The Ta Kali ORB notes: 'Cruisers in Harbour attacked by J.U 87's & 88's. ....Smoke Screen over Harbour & big barrage.'

At 05.50 four Spitfires from 249 were ordered up on patrol but returned at 07.00 with nothing to report. Similarly, at 08.20, Holland, Slade, King and Mitchell took off and carried out a patrol but again came back with nothing to report.

The weather was very hot with a light southerly wind and some haze. Mitchell's eyes were giving him some problems and he was stood down to give them a chance to recover.

Mid-morning a raid was detected and 12 Spitfires scrambled from Ta Kali at 10.50 – seven from 603 and five from 249. The 603 pilots were S/L Douglas-Hamilton with F/O Holland and F/Sgt Hurst as Red Section and F/L Douglas, F/L Sanders, P/O Forster and Sgt Webster as White Section.

Climbing to 12,000 feet they found about ten Ju88s and 20 Ju87s attacking the Grand Harbour and *Welshman*. There were also Messerschmitt 109s covering the raid. As planned, the smoke generators obscured the harbour and the intense anti-aircraft barrage continued no matter whether or not the aircraft above were friends or enemies. The Spitfires dived into attack and into the barrage. Douglas-Hamilton wrote afterwards:

> An almost solid cone of AA burst rose over the harbour from ground level to about 7000 feet. Into this the Huns were diving. Into it, too, the Spitfires dived, chasing the Huns. It never occurred to any of us that we might just as easily get hurt as the Huns. No, this was a friendly barrage, meant for the Huns, and it could not possibly do us any harm!

In all 37 Spitfires and 13 Hurricanes repulsed the attack. The 88s came out of the sun from the south east, the 87s from the east. Douglas-Hamilton chased the Stukas, but to his chagrin, the one he was following and intending to hit suddenly blew up from what he assumed was a direct hit from the barrage. He flew out of the ack-ack barrage looking for the 87s but instead found a 109 crossing to his front. He allowed for deflection and pressed the gun button but there was only a brief burst and the guns stopped. The 109 pilot realised what was happening and turned away giving the Scot a perfect shot, but when he once again pressed the gun button, nothing happened. He lost the Messerschmitt in the melee, but found another Stuka. Positioning himself for a shot, again, the guns refused to fire.

He was annoyed at the failure of the guns and decided that it was pointless to continue. As far as he could see, the Spitfires and Hurricanes were holding their own well and it would be safe to get back to Ta Kali. On his way back, he was bounced by a 109 but without any hits registering. The 109 passed across him and disappeared so he promptly landed back at base.

Douglas-Hamilton was fortunate in that for all his time in Malta and all the fighting he took part in, his aircraft was never hit or damaged in the air.

In the meantime, the other pilots of 603 were mixing it with the Germans along with the other squadrons scrambled. They all returned safely at about 11.35 with claims for probables or kills. Hurst claimed a Ju87 destroyed, Holland claimed three 109s damaged and Douglas claimed two Ju87 probables. The official record was:

Douglas: One Ju87 probable and one damaged
Hurst: One Ju87 destroyed and one damaged
Holland: Three Me109s damaged

In their accounts of the air battle both S/L Douglas-Hamilton and Sgt Paul Brennan (249 Squadron) comment on the number of Spitfires in the air – a clear sign that matters were taking a turn for the better. Bill Douglas noted: 'A really wizard dog-fight and bags of flak. 603 escorted rescue launch back to St. Paul's Bay (with no ammo).'

Under the smoke cover, unloading *Welshman* continued and was completed by early afternoon, but the ship had suffered some damage, although not enough to cause major problems. Her plates were bent and buckled, there was splinter damage, holes in the sides but above the waterline, her boats were destroyed and a load of steel had been dropped on the foredeck by blast, but she could still make way in the water and after unloading, she was pulled across French Creek for oiling at Canteen Wharf. She left Malta that evening.

In the afternoon, the Squadron was once again standing to but although there were further raids they weren't ordered off. They could see the fighting going on – the twisting and turning aeroplanes in the sky – but it wasn't until evening that they were sent aloft again.

During the day, some of the pilots who had come in from *Wasp* and *Eagle* were allocated to the squadrons and 603 received 11. It was about this time that P/O Mejon seems to have been posted from 603. He was active in Malta in the coming weeks with 126 Squadron.

Another raid was detected and Spitfires of 603 were scrambled to meet it. The eight* who took off at 18.35 were: Red Section – the CO, P/Os King and Slade, and Sgt Irwin. Blue Section – F/L Douglas, P/Os Forster and McLean and Sgt Brown.

The CO had radio problems and almost immediately returned to Ta Kali where it was fixed and he was back in the air with F/O Mitchell – one of the newly arrived pilots. The Harbour was once again the target – this time for a force composed of five Z1007bis from 500 Gruppo BT, with an escort of 20 Macchi 202s and ten Re2001s. They were followed by about 20 Ju87s with an escort of 109s. Again a furious dogfight ensued and in the confusion, King was hit in the wing although the claims made for damage to the enemy more than made up for this. Douglas and Forster claimed a Ju87 destroyed, with Douglas claiming another damaged, the new arrival Mitchell claimed an 87 destroyed and another damaged with a 109 probable. The Stuka claimed by Mitchell was possibly S7+FM of 7/StG3.

---

*The Diary records eight taking off but other sources (including the Ta Kali ORB) give the figure as ten. Further, one incident not mentioned in the Diary is that P/O Mejor was airborne in BR348 and was shot down, possibly by Oberfeldwebel Rollwage of JG53 - the man who may have shot down John Buckstone the previous day. Mejor baled out successfully and was uninjured. By this time, Mejor may very well have been posted away from 603.

They returned to Ta Kali at 19.50 and at 20.00 *Welshman* left the harbour heading for Gibraltar which it reached safely on 12 May. The Ta Kali ORB recorded the following 'score for the day':

RAF fighters claimed:

destroyed:	3 JU.88's.	9 JU87's.	2 ME.109s.	1 Cant.	1 Macchi.
probably destroyed:	4 JU.88's.	7 JU.87's.	8 ME.109's.	1 Cant.	
damaged:	3 JU.88's.	8 JU87's.	9 ME.109's.	1 Cant.	

In addition the ground rifle firing parties claimed to have damaged a 109 and the AA destroyed a Ju88, five Ju87s and a 109.

A good day's work. What was certain was that the Axis air forces had taken some considerable punishment and had not succeeded in either destroying *Welshman* and its precious cargo, or inflicting major damage to the newly arrived Spitfires. With hindsight, the claims made were probably optimistic, but whatever the true losses of the Luftwaffe were, the fighting of 10 May was highly significant and it marked a turning point in the battle for Malta. The Axis no longer controlled the skies and whilst Malta was not out of the woods, its longer term security was assured provided that the inevitable Spitfire losses which would come could be made up, and the convoys could fight through to Malta and be protected whilst in harbour.

It was apparent to all – including the Maltese – that it had been an important day and that a decisive victory had been achieved. But it wasn't over yet and there was much to do.

CHAPTER 9

CONSOLIDATION

The arrival of the new pilots allowed Douglas-Hamilton to split the Squadron into the more familiar A and B Flights and this he did on 11 May. The new flights were:

A Flight: F/L Douglas, P/Os Forster, Slade, McLean, R. Bairnsfather* and G.W. Northcott*, 2nd Lt Swales, F/Sgts Boyle*, W.R. Irwin*, Johnson* and Otto and Sgts Webster and C.A.M. Barbour*. F/Sgt Otto was still injured.

B Flight: F/L Lester Sanders, F/Os Richard A. Mitchell* and Holland, P/Os H.R. Mitchell, L.G. Barlow*, E.S. Dicks-Sherwood* and King, W/O Rae, F/Sgts Brown, Hurst, D.A. Bye* and Haggas* and Sgt Buckley.* [1]

In addition to those hailing from the home countries, there were representatives of Canada, South Africa, New Zealand, Australia and Rhodesia – but still only the two Scots, Douglas-Hamilton and Douglas.

The significance of the victory achieved on 10 May was becoming evident. 603 was now properly organised and they had their own Spitfires. The air defences of Malta could now call on several squadrons with an effective organisation that could be rotated and controlled to best advantage. The days of scraping together half a dozen Spitfires and Hurricanes were over – at least for now.

The weather on 11 May brought clear skies and a strong south-easterly wind to Ta Kali, but in the afternoon there was a thunderstorm and a build up in cloud so that towards evening there was 9/10ths cloud at 10,000 feet.

603 was on dawn readiness – the CO, F/L Sanders, F/Os Holland and Mitchell, P/Os King, Northcott, McLean and Dicks-Sherwood, F/Sgt Boyle and Sgt Webster. (Dicks-Sherwood and Boyle were 'spares'.) At 10.20, six Spitfires of 603 (Sanders, McLean, Holland, Northcott, King and Webster), eight from 249 and six from 126 scrambled to meet an incoming raid reportedly made up of 15 bombers with a large escort of 109s. 603 found no bombers, but ran into some 109s and whilst most of the 603 pilots took shots at the enemy, no claims were made.

Air Chief Marshal Sir Charles Portal inspecting 603 Squadron fighter pilots in Malta. Note the Maltese Cross emblem on the Mae West of the pilot second from the left.

---

*Pilots new to 603.

[1] This may have been F/Sgt Buckley who was one of the original pilots in *Wasp* for the 20 April reinforcement, but had not flown off at that time. Records do not show him as being part of the Second *Wasp* Relief Force. It is, however, notable that he seems to have returned to the Squadron immediately after the new reinforcements arrived with the implication that he did, in fact, fly in as part of the Second *Wasp* Force. Another alternative is that he may have come out from Gibraltar by air transport. They might, of course, have been two different individuals. Other records also suggest that P/O N.R. Fowlow RCAF. also flew in at this time and joined 603 but his name does not appear in the Diary.

Air Chief Marshal Sir Charles Portal and Air Chief Marshal Sir Keith Park, AOC Malta, chatting with 603 Squadron fighter pilots.

Prior to this, at 06.55, four 249 Spitfires were on patrol and came across enemy reconnaissance aircraft. What is interesting is that they followed the enemy back to Sicily. This seems to have been a display of confidence and aggression that was a consequence of the improvements in the air defences. The 603 version is that it was designed to 'show the flag' but the Ta Kali ORB suggests that it wasn't premeditated. Once across the water, the flight ran into some Re2001s (which the pilots identified as Macchis) and in taking evasive action to get away from Johnny Plagis, one dived into the sea.

At 17.20, seven Spitfires from 603 scrambled with one returning almost immediately, leaving F/L Douglas, P/Os Forster, Slade and Bairnsfather and F/Sgts Hurst and Haggas to look for some incoming Ju88s. They came across Bf109s instead and one was claimed as destroyed by Douglas, Forster and Bairnsfather. Unfortunately, in their enthusiasm to get the 109, Douglas (3●S BP991) and the new pilot, Bairnsfather (BP964) collided at about 4,000 feet. It seems that Bairnsfather was beneath his flight commander and hit him from below. According to one report, their Spitfires 'broke up' but the pilots both survived although somewhat bruised and suffering from shock – Bairnsfather's Sutton harness was still around him. Their target Messerschmitt reportedly crashed into the sea. Douglas made light of the incident in a letter to his family on 12 May although the loss of two Spitfires for one Messerschmitt in such an unfortunate way rankled:

> At the moment I'm in hospital with nothing worse than a sprained ankle and some skin off my knees. I'm really very lucky, as I collided with another Spit, and we both had to bale out. Neither of us are hurt – I sprained my ankle landing. We've been having terrific fun here, and I'm fed up being out of the battle for such a miserable reason.

The others landed back at 18.20. Eight bombs were dropped on the airfield slightly injuring an airman and a soldier and damaging two Spitfires – Category 2.

As well as the changes in the way that the squadrons were operating, the 11th was also notable for praise for the success of the fighters.

The Times of Malta headlined the battles of the previous day. Lord Gort sent a message congratulating the RAF on the action and Churchill sent a message to the Captain and crew of *Wasp* famously when asking the rhetorical question 'Who said a wasp couldn't sting twice?' (It was actually the bee which could only sting once.)

In a letter to his wife, Douglas-Hamilton expressed his confidence that a turning point had been reached. His view was that the Germans had lost the chance to capture Malta and whilst he fully expected the bombing and attacks to continue with undiminished ferocity, he seems to be sure that the island would be able to hold out. But there were still raids and much combat.

Tuesday 12 May was hazy, but cloudless. Eight 603 pilots were on dawn readiness – P/Os Slade, McLean, Mitchell, Forster and Northcott, 2nd Lt. Swales and Sgts Barbour and Johnson. Three were scrambled at 06.15 but found nothing so they returned at 07.20.

During the late morning, several Ju88s escorted by Bf109s came across to attack Luqa. At 11.10, 16 Spitfires scrambled from Ta Kali – eight from 249 Squadron and eight from 603. Two of the 603 aircraft (piloted by the Canadian Geoff Northcott and Johnson) returned early. The others found the raiders and a fight with the escorting 109s ensued. During this, they lost Mitchell, who had been having problems with his eyes two days before. Whilst firing at one of the Messerschmitts, he was caught by others and his Spitfire plunged into the sea. As he neared the water he rather poignantly called to the Controller – G/C Woodhall – 'Goodbye Woody. I've had it.' He was followed down by Sgt Ray Hesselyn and Sgt Brennan of 249 Squadron who fired at one of the 109s following Mitchell and Hesselyn claimed it as destroyed. Looking to see if Mitchell had survived, he saw no sign of life – Bert Mitchell was gone. There was talk that he had been shot up by 109s as he landed and later whilst in his dinghy.

Pilot Officer Herbert Robert Mitchell RNZAF (391843) was 25 years old when he died and was the son of William and Edith Mitchell of Reefton, Nelson, New Zealand.*

At 13.00 A Flight took over readiness and at 13.50 in company with four Spitfires of 249 Squadron, S/L Douglas-Hamilton and F/Sgt Hurst patrolled the coast of Sicily from Cape Passas to Cape Scalandin at 30,000 to try to entice some of the enemy fighters up but none took the bait. The Spitfires landed back at Ta Kali at 14.30.

The afternoon was quiet until 17.00 when Savoia Marchetti S.84s of the Regia Aeronautica (erroneously reported as Ju88s) were spotted coming over to bomb Ta Kali at high level with a heavy escort. F/L Sanders, F/O Richard Mitchell and P/O Eric Dicks-Sherwood scrambled. Not much later, four Ju88s were also seen and eight Spitfires of 249 scrambled at 17.45 to meet them. In addition to the involvement of 603 and 249, Spitfires of 185 and 601 Squadrons scrambled as well as some Hurricanes.

The first three 603 Spitfires found the Italians and claimed two Cant 1007s shot down, a joint claim by Sanders and Mitchell for one and the second by Dicks-Sherwood which fell in flames with parachutes coming from it. (In fact, only a single S.84 of 14ª Squadriglia, 4° Gruppo Autonomo Bombardamento Terrestre was recorded as being lost by the Italians – probably Dicks-Sherwood's – with another badly damaged bomber reaching Sicily.) They landed at Ta Kali at 18.05. Three Ju88s attacked the airfield while they were being refuelled and at 18.30 two further aircraft from 603 took off to protect the airfield from attack whilst the 249 Spitfires returned to be refuelled and rearmed. Two Spitfires and a bowser were damaged by the bombs.

It was reported during the day that 109s had shot up a British pilot in a dinghy – an act which annoyed Douglas-Hamilton greatly, particularly as it may have been Mitchell.

This was a relatively quiet period – again with the proviso that on Malta this did not mean that there was no action. The HMSO booklet 'The Air Battle of Malta' published in 1944 comments:

> The opposition indeed was disinclined to leave the pavilion in the ensuing days. During the rest of the month the enemy's activity was reduced to daily bombing by small numbers of German and Italian bombers combined with daily fighter sweeps.

On 13 May, there was no cloud and a wind from the south. Five aircraft were available for B Flight in the morning but there was no action for them until 12.30 when they scrambled along with eight Spitfires from 249 to intercept a raid by about a dozen Ju87s of III/StG3 on Hal Far. There were also reports of 18+ 109s over Malta and the Spitfires were bounced by one shortly after they had taken off. They found the enemy fighters and engaged them and whilst several of the 603 pilots

---

*At this time there were two Mitchells flying with 603, the other was F/O Richard Mitchell who arrived with the second delivery from *Wasp*.

took squirts at some of them, the only claim was a damaged by F/Sgt Brown. They returned to base at 13.40.

At 13.00, A Flight took over readiness but although German aircraft were active there was no action despite scrambles by pairs of 603 Spitfires at 16.00 and 17.15.

Whilst it can be argued that the events of 9, 10 and 11 May were key turning points in the air battle for Malta, the CO described Thursday 14 May as 'the final breaking for the time being of the German bombing offensive and confirmation of our hard-won air superiority'.

The wind came from the south west with little cloud and it was cold. 603 A Flight was on dawn readiness – the CO, P/Os Forster, McLean and Northcott, 2nd Lt. Swales, F/Sgt Bye and Sgts Webster and Barbour. At 07.30 Douglas-Hamilton, Forster, Northcott, Swales and Webster took off to carry out cannon tests (often on the 'Filfla marshalling yards') but they were vectored on to a single Ju88 at 17,000 feet. The Spitfires climbed to 21,000 feet but failed to see the raider which bombed Sliema.

At 09.00 a force of Ju88s was seen approaching the island and four 603 Spitfires and eight from 249 scrambled to intercept them. In addition to the 88s there were many 109s attacking Ta Kali as well as acting as escort to the bombers. The 603 pilots had been ordered to their aircraft when the attack came in and the CO found that his Spitfire had been damaged by a piece of shrapnel that had pierced the petrol tank. Forster, Webster, McLean and Swales managed to take off, however. In all about two dozen Spitfires were put up to defend the airfields and although the enemy were found and attacked, 603 did not lodge any claims. 249 claimed two Ju88s destroyed and two 109s damaged. The Spitfires returned to Ta Kali at 10.10.

With no more excitement during the morning, B Flight took over readiness at 13.00. At 12.35, three Ju88s of KGr 806 with a heavy escort of Italian and German fighters were discovered. At 13.00 hours, five 603 Spitfires scrambled – Sanders, Mitchell, Dicks-Sherwood, Barbour and Hurst. In all, 21 defending fighters were scrambled by the RAF to meet the raid on Ta Kali. 603 found the bombers and all three were claimed as being destroyed. But with so many fighters involved, the reality of who shot down which aircraft is confused. In addition to the attentions of the Spitfires and Hurricanes, the attacking aircraft were being fired on by the ground defences. As far as 603 were concerned, one of the Ju88s was shot down by Johnny Hurst who caught it in a petrol tank just as it started its dive. It jettisoned its bombs and crashed at the eastern dispersal in full view of those on the ground. There were gruesome reports that the pilot had been burnt to a cinder – one alleging that he had still been alive and had been 'put out of his misery' by an RAF officer when he realised that the German couldn't be rescued alive. In reality, it seems that this aircraft (M7+CH) was probably hit by several pilots of different squadrons and ground fire.

The CO, who was in a slit trench, was one of those whose curiosity took him over to look at the wreckage. He recorded that he had little sympathy for the German – nor had many of those round about. As with his comments about the 109s being frightened of Spitfires, this seems a little at odds with other recollections that the German pilots who were shot down and survived were often pitied or up to a point eventually considered as friends. However, his reaction to the downed German was probably written with public opinion in mind. It might not have been entirely acceptable if it was thought that British airmen regarded their German counterparts with anything other than patriotic dislike.

Sanders and Mitchell also claimed to have jointly shot down an 88 as did Dicks-Sherwood along with Sgt Goldsmith of 126 Squadron. It may be that they had all attacked the same aircraft as it was known to have limped back to crash on Sicily.

Sanders also claimed a 109 damaged. The Spitfires returned at 13.50.

Another raid came in at tea time. At just after 17.00 another three Ju88s attacked Safi/Hal Far and whilst 249 Squadron scrambled from Ta Kali, 603 wasn't involved.

S/L Douglas-Hamilton later commented that no Ju88s came over again in daylight for several weeks and that he never again encountered any Stukas whilst he was at Malta. In fact, Ju88s did still come over in daylight, but the enemy raids tended to be made up of a few bombers with a heavy escort of fighters against which the RAF would put up a dozen and a half or two dozen Spitfires and Hurricanes. Whilst the German bombing offensive wasn't broken, the situation had taken a distinct turn for the better for the RAF since the dark days when 603 arrived on 20 April – less than a month

A pair of Fiat BR20M bombers of 220ª Squadriglia, 55° Gruppo Aut BT, which were active by night over Malta during much of 1942.

before – and had virtually all of their aircraft either damaged or destroyed. The inexperienced pilots of 603 had most certainly learnt how to fight during the few weeks they had been on the island and were contributing greatly to the improvement in the air situation now apparent.

Douglas-Hamilton was to find the following day, 15 May, another day to remember. There was a wind from the south west and 5/10ths cloud. B Flight was on readiness in the morning and scrambled at 08.00 to meet a raid by Italian bombers escorted by Macchi 202s. F/O Mitchell attacked one of the bombers, and observed hits but without any apparent effect. They returned to base.

At 13.00 hours, A Flight took over readiness together with the CO. At about 15.30, a lone Ju88 approached the island with a heavy fighter escort. About ten minutes later, four 603 Spitfires scrambled to meet the raid – the CO, P/Os Forster and Slade and F/Sgt Irwin. They climbed to 25,000 feet and waited for half an hour. It was very cold and several of the pilots started to suffer frostbite in their fingers. Paul Forster returned to Ta Kali with radio problems. After being bounced to no effect by two 109s they were ordered down and at 10,000 feet Douglas-Hamilton saw another Messerschmitt coming in to attack his wingman – Blue 2. He shouted a warning and turned towards the 109, approaching it head on. He was determined not to break first and both started firing at each other almost simultaneously. With collision imminent, Douglas-Hamilton turned hard to starboard and as he did, he saw the Messerschmitt's port wing shear off in the middle and the damaged German fighter speed past beneath him. Looking back he saw the 109 perform a number of flick rolls, then break up, and then a parachute opened.

Irwin engaged the second Messerschmitt and it headed away from the area trailing smoke.

Meanwhile, Douglas-Hamilton's 109 hit the ground near Marsa Creek. It belonged to 6 Staffel II/Jagdgeschwader 53 and was piloted by Leutnant Herbert Soukop who was credited with shooting down Jack Rae two weeks before on 1 May. Soukop had a broken arm and had to be rescued from angry locals before finishing up in M'tarfa Hospital – in the next bed to Johnnie Johnston of 249 Squadron who had been shot down on 6 May. He was visited by Douglas-Hamilton the following day. Soukop was 21 years old and a Sudeten German, blond with blue eyes. He spoke little English but Douglas-Hamilton could talk to him in German. Soukop apparently thought that the two aeroplanes had collided and was unhappy that he had been shot down without damaging the Spitfire at all. Originally a Stuka pilot, he had managed to get a transfer to fighters. Malta was his first operational theatre but he had flown many sorties over the island and was also credited with shooting down five British aircraft (not 13 as understood by Jack Rae).

In the course of their chat Douglas-Hamilton discussed the shooting up of British pilots in dinghies but, perhaps not surprisingly, Soukop denied that this ever happened.

Not unnaturally, this victory gave Douglas-Hamilton a great boost to his confidence. Again, for a pilot with little operational experience as a fighter pilot on his arrival at Ta Kali, he had learnt quickly.

Enemy airmen who finished up in M'tarfa Hospital were treated in exactly the same way as the British and they were even in adjoining beds. After Bob Sergeant was injured, he found himself beside Lt Kurt Lauinger who had shot down Harry Fox. Lauinger had happily debated the merits of the Messerschmitt 109 with the British pilot and there were no particular security measures taken to guard the enemy PoWs.

Saturday 16 May found A Flight on readiness. A warm day was forecast with the wind from the south and no cloud. The sky was blue.

At 06.10, six Spitfires from 249 Squadron went off to try to catch the early morning recco aircraft but had no luck and they were back at Ta Kali just over an hour later.

In mid morning an attack by five bombers of the Regia Aeronautica with over 45 escorting fighters – a mixed bag of Macchis and Bf109s – launched a raid on the airfield. Of the 16 Spitfires put up to defend, four were from 603 which were scrambled at 11.05: the CO and the Australian F/Sgt Johnson as Red 1 and 2, and P/O Northcott with 2nd Lt. Swales as Blue 1 and 2. It was Johnson's first operational sortie.

Climbing to 25,000 feet they ran into many Messerschmitt 109s which they engaged. With the exception of Johnson, they all fired their guns – Northcott running out of ammunition, but claiming one of the 109s damaged. S/L Douglas-Hamilton also 'got in a long squirt' and reported strikes on another Messerschmitt. But none were claimed as kills.

Whilst landing, the CO was attacked by a 109 but managed to get down safely without damage. Johnson wasn't so lucky. His aircraft was hit by four cannon shells and he had to make a landing with the wheels up. Fortunately he wasn't injured. One Italian pilot – Massimo Salvatore – claimed to have destroyed a Spitfire whilst it was landing and this may have been Johnson's. No enemy aircraft appear to have been lost.

The raid hit the target but caused only limited damage. Two airman and a soldier were killed and a Spitfire was destroyed by fire.

Axis aircraft came over again in the afternoon. The Diary records it as a fighter sweep, but in fact it was a lone Ju88 accompanied by over 40 German and Italian fighters which attacked Kalafrana. Six Spitfires from 249 were scrambled to meet it with five from 126 Squadron scrambling rather later. Both squadrons engaged the raiders and suffered some damage in return.

Unteroffizier Dr Felix Sauer, whose 109 was damaged, baled out over the sea off Marsaxlokk Bay but his loss was noticed by others from his unit – 10/JG 53 – and a Do24 was sent out to look for him.

603 B Flight took over readiness at lunch time but it wasn't until 18.20 that Red Section (call sign 'Oxo'): F/L Sanders with F/O Mitchell, P/O Dicks-Sherwood and F/Sgt Hurst, scrambled to meet an incoming raid of six. A total of 11 Spitfires were scrambled. In fact, it was the rescue Do24 with an escort of eight 109s about 20 miles or so off the Maltese coast to the north.

The four 603 Spitfires found the Dornier and were ordered to attack it – as it tried to land to pick up the downed pilot. Sanders and Hurst in line abreast went for a pair of 109s and both reported seeing glycol streaming back. Mitchell attacked another Messerschmitt which immediately turned for Sicily. He followed it until he was about 25 miles from the enemy coast before turning back. He reported that it was trailing smoke. To the 603 pilots, the general philosophy of the German escort seemed to be to turn for home when the Spitfires arrived and leave the Do24 to its fate. Dickie Dicks-Sherwood went for the flying boat but couldn't tell if there were any strikes because of glare. The Do24 did get back to Sicily, but without picking up the downed pilot who would be in the water for many days, but would eventually be rescued and survive.

603 landed back at Ta Kali after 50 minutes. The Ta Kali ORB credits Sanders and Hurst with a probable each and Mitchell a damaged.

The pilots saw no further action that night although there was some bombing by Italian aircraft and a Ju88 was shot down in the early hours off the coast.

F/Sgts Boyle and Haggas and Sgt Barbour were posted to 126 Squadron to fill a gap caused by a number of the pilots coming down with Malta Dog.

17 May was another relatively quiet day with good weather. At 07.00 two Spitfires from 249 scrambled as on the day before to try to shoot down the regular morning Ju88 recce. This time they were successful.

At 07.30 three Spitfires from 603 – Barlow, King and Hurst – were scrambled but saw nothing. They were back at Ta Kali at 08.15. Round about this time, other squadrons were scrambled to intercept German air-sea rescue attempts and a Do24 was destroyed.

At 11.55, eight Spitfires scrambled from Ta Kali – two from 249 and six from 603 to intercept another Do24 with its escort. The 603 pilots included F/O Holland, P/Os King, Barlow, Forster and F/Sgt Hurst. They found the flying boat and attacked it. There are conflicting records as to which and how many of the pilots did actually engage the Dornier. Holland, Barlow and Hurst definitely did and it may be that Forster attacked it too. On this occasion, the Bf109s did not turn and run to Sicily but engaged in a ferocious dogfight. Tony Holland's recollection is that the four who attacked the flying boat saw no result and received a hot reception from the 109s before they managed to escape back to Malta. The local ORBs record that Barlow and Hurst damaged the Dornier but there is a Combat Report (Form F) submitted by Barlow for 17 May which reports an attack on a Do24 at 4,000 feet at 14.45 by Red Section, A Flight. The 'general report' reads: 'One Do24. Evasive tactics – gentle turns. Tracer used in returning fire. Aircraft brought down with tail on fire – fell in sea 2 miles from Salina B.' The flying boat was from Seenotst 6.

In the fighting with the Messerschmitts, Neville King claimed one damaged and Barlow's Spitfire was damaged in the fighting. They landed at 13.00.

Some of the RAF pilots were uncomfortable about attacking the German air-sea rescue aircraft despite some allegations that the Germans didn't pick up British airmen in the sea and the reports of British airmen being shot at in their parachutes or in the sea. Some were presumably less enthusiastic about these actions than others.

There was enemy activity during the afternoon and evening. 603 scrambled two aircraft at 17.15 and at 19.00 but with nothing found.

Meanwhile, far to the west at Gibraltar, a further delivery of Spitfires was getting under way, this one codenamed Operation LB. Force H – HMS *Argus* and HMS *Eagle* accompanied by *Charybdis* and six destroyers – left the safety of the harbour at 'the Rock' and turned for the departure point. This time *Argus* would provide air cover whilst *Eagle* would launch 17 Spitfires to make the hazardous flight the next day. The requirement for more Spitfires to replace those being damaged and lost had not been forgotten.

In Gibraltar, the Spitfires which were loaded on to *Eagle* had been taken there by freighters in crates and constructed by a unit called the 'special erection party' which had been established to do this. One of the men working there was 'Chic' Cessford another of the 603 auxiliaries who had been posted away from the Squadron after the Battle of Britain but was now involved in keeping them in the air over Malta – albeit at a distance!

18 May was quiet for 603. They scrambled twice, at 08.45 when P/O Slade and Sgt Webster were ordered up, and at 17.50 when six Spitfires (Sanders, Holland, Mitchell, Dicks-Sherwood, Hurst and Brown) went up to escort in the new arrivals from *Eagle* who had launched in the early afternoon – rather than in the early morning as on previous operations. On both occasions there was little to report although on the second some 109s were encountered but were chased away.

The reinforcement had gone according to plan. Many of the problems encountered on the previous occasions had been ironed out and the risky take-off and flight went well. Eight Spitfires were received at Ta Kali once again following the procedures established on 9 May. One bonus for 249 Squadron was that they now got back Laddie Lucas and Buck McNair who had gone to Gibraltar a fortnight earlier to lead in the reinforcements.

In his book, Lucas suggests that there was a subtle change in atmosphere – for the better – and he was probably right. The defenders were more than holding their own against the attacks from Sicily and the previously inexperienced pilots who had survived were now battle-hardened. 603 had been on Malta for almost a month.

In air operations, novice aircrew were more likely to become casualties than those with flying and combat experience. Bomber Command found that once their crews had flown five or six operational sorties they were more likely to survive. This was also the case during the Battle of Britain when many experienced pilots survived whilst the inexperienced were more likely to be lost (although, as many established pilots were killed, for a number of reasons this point is not nearly as clear cut as legend would have it). In more modern times, the Top Gun and Red Flag exercises run by the US forces are a legacy of the air war in Vietnam and are designed to simulate real combat, giving new crews the experience to survive that they would otherwise have to gain flying 'live' missions. On Malta, the inexperienced pilots who couldn't get to the required level of competence were identified and shipped back to Gibraltar often via the nightly BOAC flight which seemed inevitably always to get through whatever the opposition.

By 18 May, despite improvements in the air situation, Malta was still facing desperate food and supply problems. The Ta Kali ORB records: 'Consumption of water reduced to 9 gallons per head per day. Sale of bread and sandwiches in EFI Canteens to be discontinued until further notice owing to shortage of supplies.' Although surface convoys had problems getting through, vital supplies of petrol and other items trickled in by submarine – notably in previous months by HMS *Upholder* captained by Lieutenant Commander David Wanklyn VC which had been lost at the end of March. Malta was still under siege.

With the arrival of a new batch of pilots, P/Os Eddie Glazebrook, Owen Berkeley-Hill and Dudley Newman were posted to 603. Again, it is difficult to be absolutely precise about who did or did not join the Squadron. P/O R.G. Smith also may have flown in to join 603 at this time.

The days that followed fell into what might be called a pattern. The two flights took it in turns to be at readiness – one at dawn until 13.00 and the other in the afternoon and evening. But for the pilots there was little sign of regular routine. They ate, drank, flew and slept when they could. It was all the luck of the draw and they were living for the day with little thought of tomorrow.

On 19 May B Flight was on readiness at dawn and eight were scrambled at 11.15 to intercept a sweep by Messerschmitt 109s, and although some were sighted there was no contact. A Flight took over at 13.00 but weren't scrambled until 19.25 when they were ordered off to look for bombers. Again there was nothing to report.

20, 21 and 22 May were similar with some scrambles for fighter sweeps but little action. On the occasions when the Spits came near the 109s, the Germans tended to make a run for Sicily. On the evening of 22 May, six Spitfires from B Flight were scrambled. P/O Barlow was fired at head-on by another Spitfire and returned with a cannon shell in the wing.

On 23 May, Ta Kali received a visit from the Inspector General of the RAF – Air Marshal Ludlow Hewitt – and significantly, the station was stood down until 13.00. The continual round of readiness was now starting to take its toll of the pilots. However brave a public face was, most would be feeling the effects of the stress and tension caused by the hours of inactivity and the ever present threat of a violent and unpleasant death – as in the Battle of Britain when some pilots reached the point when the nervous tension caused them to be physically sick at the sound of the telephone ringing. After visiting the airfield, the Inspector General retired to the mess at M'dina where he ate an excellent lunch accompanied by Gozo wine.

At 13.00 A Flight was on readiness with F/L Douglas back in harness after his collision on 11 May. There were two scrambles – four Spitfires at 14.00 and four at 20.20 but with no result. There was some bombing during the night.

On Sunday 24 May, A Flight was sent off a number of times in the morning, but to no avail. B Flight took over at 13.00 and at 15.45 scrambled to meet a raid by the Italians. The pilots were P/Os Barlow, Glazebrook and Dicks-Sherwood. They found the enemy formation about ten miles south of Kalafrana and attacked. Dicks-Sherwood was credited with the destruction of a Macchi 202 with another damaged and Barlow also with the destruction of a Macchi. Interestingly, there is a comment in the Diary that the enemy pilots were heard over the radio to be speaking German.

Despite raids the following day, B Flight on dawn readiness only scrambled once at 05.30 but found nothing.

On 26 May, the wind was from the west and it was hazy. A Flight was on dawn readiness but little happened. In the early afternoon, with B Flight now on readiness a sweep by fighters of the Regia Aeronautica – about 15 Re 2001s – came across the island. Eight 603 Spitfires were scrambled and engaged the enemy, diving on them from 28,000 feet. F/L Sanders found himself matched by one of the enemy and a hard dogfight ensued. Eventually he managed to hit the enemy aeroplane but it escaped and he claimed it as a damaged. F/O Mitchell was credited with a kill after reporting seeing his Re 2001 streaming glycol. P/O Barlow engaged another and saw it crash in flames – he too being credited with a kill. He also reported that the pilot had baled out but seemed to have fallen out of the harness. The parachute harnesses were not entirely comfortable – although more so when standing than sitting – and perhaps this pilot had loosened the straps before take-off. The jerk when the parachute opened was enough to catapult the pilot out of the straps if they weren't too tight.

There was little action for 603 the next day. Along with a number of the other pilots, the CO succumbed to the 'dog'? It was now generally accepted that the squadrons would have eight Spitfires available but because of illness and inexperience there was a shortage of pilots to fly them which meant that care had to be taken in rotating them. The flights would now be on readiness for 24-hour periods from 12.00 each day. F/Sgt Otto, W/O Rae and P/O Bairnsfather were still not operational after their crashes and it was decided to send Otto and Sgt Buckley home and they made the seven and a half hour flight from Luqa to Gibraltar in the nightly Hudson that evening (the 27th). In a letter to his parents dated 7 July, Bill Douglas wrote:

> One of my Flight Sergeants, a young Canadian called Otto, was concussed in an accident here, and has been sent home. As I don't think he knows many people in England or Scotland I gave him our address, and told him to stay with you for a few days if he was near Edinburgh. He's an excellent chap, but he wasn't going to be fit for a wee while, and I didn't think he should start again here, so I managed to get him sent home.

In Britain, Allan Otto soon recovered and returned to flying duties. Posted to 57 OTU at Hawarden, his first flight was half an hour in a Miles Master and then back to Spits. After this, he went to Cranfield to join 3501 Servicing Unit as a test pilot. The duty was to test aircraft before they were issued to squadrons - mainly Spitfire Vs. (Testing repaired aeroplanes could be dangerous and it needed skill on the part of the pilot if something hadn't been done properly. For example, occasionally the cables to the control surfaces were reversed so that pulling the stick back to raise the nose might lower it, or trying to bank to port would produce starboard bank!) In 1943, by now a Warrant Officer, Otto was sent to North Africa to join 110 Repair and Salvage Unit. These units performed a difficult and important role in looking for, recovering and repairing aircraft that had force landed in the desert. (Arthur Carroll, one of the veteran Edinburgh auxiliary airmen was also in one of those units in North Africa at that time.) Otto continued testing repaired aircraft, flying from airfields such as Maison Blanche, Souk-el-Arba, Souk-el Khemis and Kalaa Djerda. On Sunday 16 May 1943 at about 17.00 he was taking off along a road about 21 miles east of Sbeitfe in a Spitfire Vb (EP688). It seems that a truck with troops on board turned on to the road as W/O Otto's Spitfire reached flying speed. He turned sharply and at low level to avoid hitting the truck, but a wing tip caught the top of a cable-carrying pole which sent the Spitfire crashing to the ground. It burst into flames and the quiet Canadian was badly injured and died shortly afterwards in hospital. The Unit's Engineering Officer, F/L J Gordon wrote to the family on 30 October 1943. He said of Allan Otto: '….he flew with considerable skill and finish as we say. He took a quiet interest in his work but often regretted he was not back on operational flying. He mentioned to me all about Malta.' As to his death he said: ' …..he lies amongst the honoured fallen on top of a hill overlooking the green valleys and wind swept trees - the Unit made an ash wood cross and on it we mounted a replica of R.C.A.F. Badge and Wings in brass…' He was 21 years old. Warrant Officer Class 1, Allan Walter Otto is buried in Bone War Cemetery in Algeria. His brother Archie joined the RCAF about three months after Allan's crash and served firstly as a wireless operator, then on rescue patrol boats. He survived the war. After the war was over and released from his PoW camp, Allan Otto's great friend Harold Bennett tried to discover what had happened to him and sought out his family in Thunder Bay. Both families have remained friends since and keep in close touch.

Back on Malta, in addition to all the other tribulations, flies were becoming a problem as the heat of the summer built to a climax. Combined with the stress of operations and the waiting, the living conditions were uncomfortable with the heat – and of course there were restrictions on the water for drinking. Sand flies made the men ill and caused them considerable discomfort.

28 and 29 May were relatively quiet for 603. There was some flying but nothing of consequence and on the evening of the 29th the Squadron was released early at 19.30 for an early morning show the next day – a dawn anti-shipping patrol – a precursor of the role that 603 was to take on later in the Mediterranean.

The CO led the Squadron, with 2nd Lt Swales. F/L Douglas (in 3●T, BR347) and P/O Forster. They took off at 05.10 heading north west for about 30 miles, then west but found nothing other than a patch of oil just off the coast. There was also a distant sighting of an aircraft. They landed back at 05.55.

During the day there were air raid warnings at Ta Kali at 10.15, 11.32, 17.05, 18.15, 21.50 and 23.35. Blue Section scrambled at 10.20 after a warning of a fighter sweep but found nothing and the only other action for them was at 19.25 when three Spitfires took off to escort some Hudsons flying in.

In Germany on 30 May the first of Bomber Command's 'Thousand Bomber' raids took place, this one directed at Cologne. Although in the Far East, British and Commonwealth troops had been forced to pull out of Burma on 20 May, this massive raid allowed the British to feel that they were indeed striking back and that the war wasn't all going Hitler's way.

The last day of May was Sunday with a clear sky and a wind from the south. There were five air raid warnings at Ta Kali that day. B Flight was on readiness at dawn but there was no activity. A Flight took over at 13.00 and Red and Blue Sections were scrambled at 13.40 to meet an incoming raid made up of Bf109s. Red Section comprised the CO with Swales, Webster and Bye and Blue Section was a quartet of P/Os – Forster, Slade, Northcott and Berkeley-Hill.

On take-off, Paul Forster's Spitfire taxied into a small bomb crater and broke its back. The long nose of the Spitfire would have restricted his view forward and no doubt he would feel unhappy at losing one of the precious aircraft in this way. He escaped injury.

Red Section climbed to 22,000 feet and spotted two 109s near Filfla at about 12,000 feet. They dived down to bounce them but were spotted. The 109s turned seawards and were chased until they were about 15 miles off the coast with no result. Blue Section also found the enemy and engaged them, but with no claims being made.

CHAPTER 10

SUMMER HEAT

The first day of June was remarkable in that no bombs were dropped on the island during the daylight hours and the lull in enemy air activity continued. But in concentrating on the activities of 603 at Ta Kali, it shouldn't be forgotten that Malta was not only defending itself but attacking the Axis forces too. Further, the supply situation was becoming critical again. There had been no convoy to Malta since March – before 603 arrived – and whilst there were now adequate numbers of defending aircraft available, these needed the fuel and ammunition which were being stealthily brought to Malta by the submarines. But the supplies trickling in weren't enough for the long term and if the island was to survive, the successful arrival of a substantial convoy was essential.

The general air situation eased reducing the pressure on the defenders. There may not have been any bombs dropped, but there were still Messerschmitt 109s sweeping the island, drawing up the defending RAF fighters. Both A and B Flight scrambled during the day to intercept such sweeps but with nothing to report and no action.

By now, the squadrons were so well equipped and organised that it was possible to have a duty routine that allowed them to be rested on a rotational basis every five days and the following day 603 was stood down. On such days the men usually grasped the opportunity to relax and get away from the airfield, although on such a small island this was easier said than done.

When not involved in any of the actions, there was little to do. The young aircrew were in their early twenties – an age when back in the UK they would have been chasing the girls and living it up, but on Malta there were no servicewomen, although some of the RAF pilots had Maltese girl friends. For those billeted at the Xara Palace, there were walks on the bastions. M'Dina was a Holy City and was left pretty much intact by the bombers. Alcohol was available, although at times in short supply and in any case, some pilots forsook the pleasures of drink because they realised that a hangover in the morning might very well cost them their lives despite the therapeutic effect of a few breaths of pure oxygen. Brandy and port was rumoured to be a good cure for the 'dog' and the men tried it from time to time! At Ta Kali there were few wild mess parties and limited bar stocks. They could go out for meals to hotels – the Mayfair and the Queens – and restaurants, but the offerings were usually 'pretty spartan stuff' with the food shortages. They could go to the cinema, The Coliseum where 'Sing You Sinners' with Bing Crosby and 'Destry Rides Again' with James Stewart and Marlene Dietrich were typical of the films being shown.

Letters from home were high spots. These presumably came in on the nightly Hudsons from Gibraltar but despite having an APO number (1880), not on a regular basis. Bill Douglas got his first letter (from Elaine) on 5 June and in the following two days, another ten from various friends and family – 'You've no idea how good it is to hear from you all…' Air mail letter cards which cost 3d (1½ pence) seem to have been the most reliable in getting back home, but there was a cable office in Valetta which the men could use when in the capital, and of course it allowed family at home to cable to Malta.

Some passed the time by going for long walks, but in the heat, this could be exhausting and to get relief meant doing as little physical exercise as possible. The RAF being what it was and is, pilots found that they had friends from previous postings flying with other units and they would keep in touch. Sgt Les Colquhoun flew from Luqa and he would know some of the pilots at Ta Kali from his days with 603 just a few weeks before.* As always, some of the servicemen would make friends with the locals and there would be public-spirited civilians who went out of their way to welcome the service personnel into their homes – although with so many servicemen on such a small and confined island opportunities were limited. One well known resident was Mabel Strickland, an influential lady whose hospitality was a source of respite to battle-weary airmen. And the island's vet, Dr. MacFarlane and his wife Meg who had lived on Malta for 44 years, kept 'open house' for the pilots for Sunday lunch using the chicken, eggs, fruit and vegetables which were all that many of his clients could give him to pay for the treatment of their animals. Their connection with 603 was through Bill Douglas. Dr. MacFarlane was a cousin of Elaine's mother and it was she who had introduced the young pilot to his future relatives. The hospitality offered was accepted gratefully. On Sunday 28 June, Douglas ate a hearty lunch and stayed on for tea:

> ….it was indeed good to have chicken, and caramel pudding on Sunday. What with Aunt Meg's cocktails before lunch, Gozo wine with it, and coffee and Benedictine afterwards, and an enormous meal, I retired to a sofa in the afternoon and slept till teatime!

But of course, although the men could get away from the airfields occasionally, they could rarely escape the battle. During the Battle of Britain, airmen who were being rested could find relief in some part of the country where there was little if any air activity, but this wasn't so on Malta. The raids and air battles were there for all to see and even swimming or sunbathing in some secluded cove did not always stop the sounds and sights of war with the ever-present danger of a passing 109 taking a 'squirt' at the swimmers. In Marsaxlokk Bay, a popular spot for swimming, there were the remains of a Ju87 that had been shot down in April. The gunner baled out, but the pilot remained with the aeroplane and was trapped when it crashed into the sea. The body wasn't removed for some time and the wreck became a source of passing interest to swimmers. It was said that the pilot's watch remained strapped to his wrist and the time on it could be made out. Again, the fate of the German and the spectacle of his body appears to have stirred little sympathy in the allied airmen who saw it.**

S/L Douglas-Hamilton was later to write:

> On our off days we often went away to a remote sandy beach at Ghain Tuffieha and bathed and basked in the sun all day. One could then really believe one was having a holiday in Malta, and the war would seem far away. The bathing was truly magnificent: the water was beautifully blue and clear and, above all, not too cold. In parts it was almost tepid and one could stay in indefinitely. Everybody got very brown from sun-bathing.
>
> For lunch we would go up to the local hotel and partake of 'big-eats' perhaps with a glass of Gozo wine. Unfortunately, the food shortage soon made it impossible to get any food at restaurants. Sometimes it was possible to arrange a sail in a dinghy......

On 2 June, with the Squadron stood down, seven of the pilots took the chance to go to Ghain Tuffieha. They were the CO together with 'Sandy' Sanders, Bill Douglas, Paul Forster, Neville King, Johnny Hurst and L.F. Webster. Getting there was a problem but W/C Wells took them there in his car in the morning and collected them again in the evening. They seem to have enjoyed their day. Nearby was the Riviera Hotel where they lunched and drank Italian wine. On the down side, they found two sea mines – one washed on to the beach and one stuck in a rocky crevice.

Returning to Ta Kali, they were back to making preparations to receive another batch of reinforcing Spitfires the following day from HMS *Eagle* under the codename Operation Style. They also found that P/Os McLean and Berkeley-Hill along with W/O Rae – now operational again – had

---

*When 603 left Dyce, Sgt Les Colquhoun was posted to the PRU unit on Malta (69 Squadron) where he was to be a very successful and respected pilot. He was subsequently commissioned and after Malta was also part of the PRU team at RAF Benson in the UK. He finished his career in the RAF as a S/L and died in 2001.

**The Stuka was from III/Stukageschwader 3 and was shot down by Sergeant Gordon Tweedale in a Hurricane of 185 Squadron on 23 April 1942. The pilot was Unteroffizier Jurgen Schwengers. His gunner was Gefreiter Franz Netelnbeker and there was a report that after he baled out of the stricken Ju87, he was shot up at the end of his parachute and in his dinghy by Messerschmitt 109s. (There is another report that he went down with the aeroplane.)

been posted to 249 Squadron although the move didn't actually happen until 4 June, two days later – according to the 249 Squadron ORB.

Jack Rae had a distinguished career with 249 and then 485 Squadron back in the UK. His final tally was 11 kills and two destroyed, eight probables with one shared, and six damaged. He was awarded the DFC and Bar. In August 1943, by which time he was a Flying Officer, he was brought down over France and became a PoW. Interestingly, he was an inmate of Stalag Luft III which became famous for 'The Great Escape' although he did not take part in it because he was serving time in 'the cooler' after his involvement in another escape attempt. He finished the war as a Flight Lieutenant and returned to live in New Zealand with his wife and family.*

The Ta Kali ORB sets the scene for the arrival of the reinforcements:

05.00 Parade of all personnel to explain arrangements & allocation of duties in connection with arrival of further Spitfires. Same organisation which was so successful before put into operation. Arrangements as to meals on Camp as on last "arrival day". 15 Spitfires arrived ex Carrier.

There was a fresh north-westerly wind and 5/10ths medium cloud cover on Malta. The Squadron provided 12 aircraft on readiness. Those pilots not down for flying were allocated to blast pens to take over from the newly arrived pilot.

With the problems encountered on previous occasions ironed out 31 Spitfires launched from *Eagle* in what was becoming a standardised routine. Unfortunately, on this occasion the gaggles of Spitfires were intercepted by Luftwaffe Messerschmitt 109s from II/Jagdgeschwader 53 flying from Pantelleria. They claimed five Spitfires shot down, although four was the actual number.

At 09.15, 13 arrived at Ta Kali but one crashed on landing.** The services of 603 as escort were not called upon on this occasion and the Diary includes the interesting comment '603 are quicker off the mark than 249 and manage to grab more of the new aircraft and we get 8 of them as opposed to 4 by 249.'

With the arrival of the latest batch of Spitfires, the island defence was now based on a minimum of 36 aircraft being available from five squadrons which meant that at any one time, three squadrons were 'on' and two were 'off'.

The reaction by the Luftwaffe and the Regia Aeronautica to this latest arrival was remarkably low key with only two sorties by single PR Bf109s during the afternoon. 603 Red and Blue Sections were scrambled at 13.50 to intercept but without success and they did no other flying that day.

Some of the new Spitfires were fitted with de Havilland 'Hydromatic' airscrews which gave an improved performance – particularly in the climb – but sometimes when the propeller was in coarse pitch it would suddenly change to fine and then not change back. (On 3 July, the Diary notes that two Spitfires were lost because of engine failures caused by the Hydromatic prop.) On 4 June Bill Douglas took the opportunity to try out one of the Spitfires (X●J, BR364) with the improved airscrew – 'The joy!' – which clearly met with his approval.

4 and 5 June were quiet. On 4 June, 603 received four new pilots – P/Os A.A. Glen DFC, H.W. McLeod and Guy Carlet*** and W/O Gray.****

Henry Wallace McLeod hailed from Regina, Saskatchewan and was born in December 1915. He trained originally to be a teacher, but quickly changed careers to become a travelling man, touring his native province showing films. He joined the RCAF in 1940 and was commissioned in April 1941. Interestingly, on his arrival in the UK, he was posted to 602 Squadron for a spell, then to 411. He saw little action until he reached Malta, but he was to have a remarkable career once he arrived.

B Flight was at dawn readiness and A Flight took over at 13.00. It was very cloudy with a fall of rain in the evening. Both flights were scrambled during their spells on readiness but with little action and no claims being made.

---

*See *Kiwi Spitfire Ace* by Jack Rae (Grub Street).
**The Ta Kali ORB gives the number as 15.
***'Guy Carlet' was a pseudonym for Andre Levy-Despas. For the purposes of this account, the pseudonym will be used because that is the name familiar to his colleagues on the Squadron.
****One source has Carlet and Glen arriving on the island on 9 June with the Spitfires of Operation Salient.

5 June brought rain during the day although it brightened up later. The rain came as a welcome relief from the heat and the weather curtailed flying. 249 scrambled in the early morning and at tea time but to no avail. Enemy activity was slight – only several PR sorties by pairs of 109s. 603 didn't fly.

After the clouds and rain on 5 June, on 6 June, the sky was clear and the Axis air forces took advantage of it.

603 B Flight was on dawn readiness. At first light, three Spitfires of 185 Squadron were airborne and 40 minutes later four aircraft of 249 were scrambled from Ta Kali in response to incoming plots. The enemy Ju88s were found, engaged and suffered losses before the Spitfires returned.

Shortly after, at 07.00, 603 Red Section scrambled – the CO with Swales, Glazebrook and McLeod – along with four from 249 – to intercept a raid by the Regia Aeronautica comprising five Z1007bis bombers of 50° Gruppo escorted by 24 Macchi 202s of 155° Gruppo and 12 Re2001s of 2° Gruppo. Red Section climbed to 24,000 feet into the sun to the east, then having spotted the enemy at 18,000 feet dropped down on to them. There was a fierce dogfight. Douglas-Hamilton and McLeod both attacked one of the bombers (as did other Spitfires from 249) and saw strikes, but McLeod's Spitfire was hit by return fire from it and as he broke off the attack and dived away, an Italian fighter followed him down to only a few thousand feet. Meanwhile, P/O Glazebrook took on another of the bombers but saw what was happening and cut off his attack to chase the fighter harassing McLeod. The Canadian landed safely but his tailplanes had 'negative dihedral'! In the space of 30 minutes on Malta, he had learned more about combat in the air than in the previous year.

Shortly after Red Section scrambled, Blue and White Sections were also scrambled, although White (Barlow, Johnson, Dicks-Sherwood and Brown) was too late to make contact. Blue (Sanders, Mitchell, King and Gray) however found the fight and chased the bombers out to sea. Mitchell and King both claimed probables after seeing what they assumed was glycol leaking from the Re2001s they were attacking and Eddie Glazebrook also claimed a damaged. W/O Gray, on his first operational flight with 603 claimed a 109 as damaged although actually there were no 109s in the fight. In the confusion and speed of battle, pilots often mistook the aircraft they fought against – another factor making the task of the intelligence officers difficult.

At 10.20 Blue and White Sections scrambled to search for a Do24 as they thought, but in reality they were sent after a number of Re2001s searching for ditched Italian aircrew from the previous raid. They found nothing although 249 did find the fighters and had some successes – they were having a good day!

A Flight took over readiness at 13.00. Because of the shortage of fit pilots, Ormonde Swales remained on duty with A Flight until 17.00 when he was relieved by Neville King. At 13.25, F/L Douglas with P/Os Forster, Glen and Carlet scrambled to cover the return of a PRU Spitfire to Luqa but were back at 14.00 having not found it, although it did land safely without them.

There was more activity by the Regia Aeronautica in the afternoon when a Z506B air-sea rescue seaplane escorted by Re2001s and Macchi 202s came over to look for ditched airmen from the morning raid but 603 wasn't scrambled, the intruders being chased off by 185 Squadron.

As darkness started to fall, at 19.20 Blue (Slade, King, Northcott and Bairnsfather) and White (Hurst, Webster, Newman and Irwin) Sections scrambled. Shortly after taking off, Northcott and King had to return – Northcott with oxygen problems and King with a faulty radio. The others continued and at 22,000 feet north of Gozo encountered a *schwarm* of Messerschmitt 109s which split into two *rotte* to attack the Spitfires. A fight developed but with no conclusive results on either side and eventually the 109s made off. The six Spitfires landed at 20.35, just after Bill Douglas (in X●J, BR364) and Paul Forster had taken off at 20.30.

By this time it was almost dark. The Luftwaffe sent over about two dozen Ju88s to attack Ta Kali. The pair found haze up to about 10,000 feet and climbed to 14,000. At about 20.45, Forster spotted two of the 88s 1,000 feet below silhouetted against the sunset and they dived to attack. The 88s made for the land and unfortunately, the two Spitfires lost them, and eventually each other in the haze. They both tried to intercept the raiders by following the ack-ack fire and spotted three which were illuminated by searchlights but they landed at 21.00 empty handed.

Ten minutes later the airfield was quite heavily bombed but it remained serviceable. A decoy Hurricane was destroyed.

Malta, 7 June 1942. CO (Douglas-Hamilton) under nose, Douglas to his left. Note Bill Douglas' moustache!

This raid seems to have been orchestrated by the Luftwaffe. The 603 report is that Douglas and Forster were sent off to intercept two 88s. It seems that a few 88s arrived first and dropped flares over Luqa to be followed by the others who did the bombing – pathfinders and main force. It may be that the two Spitfires were scrambled as the pathfinders arrived. In any case, there were no other RAF aircraft involved and whilst the AA guns claimed a Ju88 destroyed the German records do not show a loss.

603 was scheduled to be stood down again the next day and in the evening when they got back to the mess, they found that a party was developing with entertainment by the station band so on this occasion, they joined in enthusiastically without having to worry about a hangover in the morning.

The 7 June was a Sunday and as well as 603, the whole station stood down. A station photograph was arranged for 09.00 hours but 'nearly everbody late owing to DROs* yesterday not going up with order on it until afternoon. Enormous strip torn off all assembled pilots and Officers by Station Commander. Dress in future is to be strictly according to regulations at all times, even in mess.'

Enemy activity was limited but during the day there were some sweeps by Messerschmitt 109s and in the evening an attack by Ju88s, Italian Stukas and Z1007bis after dark. During these raids, the enemy dropped small anti-personnel butterfly bombs – known as crackers – which scattered over wide areas. Some exploded on hitting the ground whilst others didn't and they created a hazard until they were cleared. They made the airfield at Ta Kali unusable although the strip remained clear. A Maltese man picked up one of the bombs killing himself and injuring others nearby. An unpleasant and worrying tactic on the part of the enemy.

Monday 8 June dawned clear with a wind from the south. Far to the west, preparations were being made for yet another delivery of Spitfires from HMS *Eagle*, but on Malta life continued as on previous days. B Flight was on readiness at dawn. There was little action, but in the one fight that did involve 603, another pilot was lost.

*Daily Routine Orders.

At 11.05, four were scrambled to investigate a report of enemy fighters on a sweep, but they found nothing and returned to the airfield at 11.30. Twenty-five minutes later, there was a scramble of the whole Squadron – nine aircraft – again to counter a sweep by 109s.

White Section was made up of only two, P/O Dicks-Sherwood and F/O Barlow. Barlow hadn't been well – perhaps the 'dog' – and the pair were bounced by several 109s. In the ensuing fight, Barlow was hit and crashed into the sea. P/Os King and Dicks-Sherwood saw a splash which they thought to be Barlow's aircraft and although they searched the area for signs of life they found none.

It was suggested that the Rhodesian pilot hadn't been as vigorous in his manoeuvring as he would have been normally had he been fully fit and it proved fatal.

The death of Leslie George Barlow RAFVR (80276) is commemorated on Panel 2, Column 2 of the Malta Memorial.

A Flight took over readiness in the afternoon. They had no action other than a search for the missing pilot which proved fruitless.

Between the problems caused by the 'dog' and this latest loss, the Squadron could only muster 22 pilots and they were given permission to maintain a readiness of ten rather than 12 to allow the pilots some time off duty.

F/Sgt Johnnie Hurst had been commissioned and he 'put up' his P/O ring.

The main event of 9 June was the delivery of the Spitfires from *Eagle*. The weather turned out fine again with a wind from the south west. This time the delivery was codenamed Operation Salient with the basic procedure as the previous deliveries. At about 06.30, 32 Spitfires took off. They started to land at Ta Kali at about 10.00 – 16 being received there. On this occasion they weren't intercepted by the Luftwaffe or the Regia Aeronautica and all the Spitfires arrived safely. One received slight damage to its tail on take-off from the carrier and crashed on landing at Ta Kali, but otherwise the trip was uneventful.

One of the incoming pilots was Sgt George Beurling – a Canadian and a talented fighter pilot but a man who possessed a very unconventional and independent character which regularly landed him in trouble with authority. His exploits are well covered elsewhere. He went to 249 Squadron but might have served with 603 but for the hand of fate.

When the new pilots arrived on Malta, they were allocated to the squadrons, but the allocation on this particular occasion was done by the squadron and flight commanders. They were given a list of names and had to choose which pilots they wanted. This time, the allocating was to be done by the two 249 flight commanders – Buck McNair and Laddie Lucas – and 603's CO. S/L Douglas-Hamilton recalled:

> ......I had been offered the choice between him [Buerling] and another pilot for 603. Someone had told me they thought 'Screwball' was a rather crazy pilot and a line-shooter, for he claimed to have destroyed two FW 190s on his first trip over France, which would have been good enough even for an experienced pilot. Unfortunately I was swayed by this argument, for otherwise there seemed little to choose between the two pilots.

Laddie Lucas recalled the selection rather differently. According to him*, Beurling's name was at the top of the list – in alphabetical order – and they tossed a coin to see who would take first choice. 249 won, and Beurling went there.

During the morning A Flight was on readiness. At 05.30, Slade, Northcott, Webster and Irwin took off to carry out an anti-shipping patrol, returning at 06.45 having found nothing.

Things were quiet until after the arrival of the new Spitfires when a sweep by about 16 Messerschmitt 109s was detected. At 10.50, Red Section – the CO with Swales, Webster and Irwin – scrambled and 20 minutes later at 11.10, White (Slade, Bairnsfather, Northcott and Newman) and Blue (Douglas [in X●B, BP957], Forster, Glen and Carlet) Sections were also scrambled.

Blue and White Sections climbed to 20,000 but found nothing. Red Section however met the 109s and a chase ensued which took them down to sea level near the Grand Harbour, but without any hits reported. Climbing back to altitude, they were bounced again and Sgt Webster claimed hits

---

*In *Malta: The Thorn in Rommel's Side*

One of the Messerschmitt Bf109Fs which fell during the early summer fighting.

on one. Bill Douglas had an unserviceable R/T. They all landed back just before noon. In all about three dozen Spitfires took part in the action.

A Flight handed over the readiness to B Flight just after 13.00 and whilst they were on '15 minutes' for a couple of hours, there was no action until evening when a large force of Italian aircraft came over – three bombers with a fighter escort. Between 18.20 and 18.30, the whole Squadron was scrambled with Sanders, King, Glazebrook and Gray as Red Section, Mitchell, Johnson and Forster as White and Hurst, Dicks-Sherwood and Brown as Blue. On taking off, Glazebrook found that his undercarriage wouldn't retract and he immediately landed back. Other Spitfires of 126 Squadron were scrambled to give a total of 21 in the air.

White and Red Sections didn't meet the bombers, but Blue did. P/O Hurst claimed to have damaged one and the others in the section also reported firing at them – but no kills. Meanwhile, Red Section found some 109s at 25,000 feet but didn't get near enough to engage them but then came across some Italian fighters which they chased out to sea also without engaging. White Section met 109s but with no conclusive outcome.

The sortie lasted about an hour, and the returning pilots found that the airfield had been bombed whilst they were away, but this did not cause any significant damage. The Italians claimed to have shot down three of the RAF defenders, but in fact only one Spitfire of 126 Squadron was damaged. B Flight was released at 21.30 hours.

The next day, 10 June, saw little activity for 603 but there was significant activity on the island. Although the deliveries of the new Spitfires (and pilots) eased the situation for the defenders, the general position for Malta was little better – particularly with regard to essential supplies – food, fuel, ammunition etc. It was calculated that Malta could hang on until August, but much more food and fuel would be needed by then. Also, the Prime Minister was keen that Malta should once again be in a position to make things as difficult as possible for the Axis forces. But doing this required fuel – torpedoes were being flown in and this used aviation fuel. A convoy was needed, and now that the RAF was in a better position to help with the defence of ships both near Malta and in the Grand Harbour, ambitious plans were made to do this – codenamed Operation Julius. There were to be two convoys – one from the east (Operation Harpoon) and the other from the west – Operation Harpoon – to arrive at Malta in the middle of June.

Harpoon started on 4 June with convoy WS19z leaving the River Clyde. It was to be made up of six merchant ships including the American tanker *Kentucky* on its first voyage having crossed the Atlantic from Philadelphia. These merchant vessels were protected by a large naval escort many of which had been involved in the deliveries of the Spitfires to Malta – including *Eagle* and *Argus*. *Welshman* was also to be making an independent run from Gibraltar at the same time.

The merchant vessels of Operation Vigorous were given the convoy number MW11 and there were three elements to it; MW11a gathering in Haifa with five merchant ships (including *City of Edinburgh*), MW11b at Alexandria with five merchantmen and MW11c which was at Port Said with four merchant ships. These three component parts would meet in the eastern Mediterranean with a powerful escort of the Royal Navy which comprised a substantial part of the Mediterranean Fleet. The merchant ships had sailed round the Cape to reach Egypt and Palestine. The 603 service echelon reached Egypt on 4 June and there was talk in Malta that they would be in one of the merchant vessels coming with Operation Vigorous, but this was not to be – fortunately for them.

On 10 June, the convoy operations were getting under way. As part of the preparations for their passage to and survival at Malta, the RAF on the island was 'beefed up' with Coastal Command Beaufighters and torpedo-carrying Beauforts with others coming in on subsequent days too. And despite the lack of action for 603, 249 were kept busy with three scrambles of eight or more aircraft during the day and some successes in the fighting to boot.

11 June was quiet for 603. White and Blue Sections of A Flight scrambled in the morning – White, to protect some Royal Navy minesweepers off the Grand Harbour and Blue, to look for some 109s. Neither section reported any contact. B Flight had a non-eventful afternoon.

603 stood down the next day, 12 June.* There were two bathing parties – one to Sliema and the other to Ghain Tuffieha. F/Sgt J.A.H. Pinney who had come in with the latest delivery of Spitfires was posted in to 603 and Sgt Banter posted away to 249. Similarly, P/O Downes was exchanged with P/O Barbour from 126.

There was bombing in the evening with the airfield being hit. There were near misses at the officers' mess at M'dina but no damage to the RAF although there were civilian casualties at Rabat. One of the attacking Ju88s was brought down by ack-ack and one damaged.

Early on the 12th, the Harpoon convoy entered the Mediterranean through the Straits of Gibraltar where it became convoy GM4. The other part of the operation – Vigorous – was moving out from the ports in the eastern Mediterranean. They were doing this in such a way as to try to confuse the Axis commanders as to just what was to happen and with the hope that the Italian Fleet would be drawn out of port early. But it didn't work. By the 13th, when the various elements had joined up, a combination of ferocious raids by German aircraft and problems with some of the merchant ships themselves were already signalling the beginning of the end. They were fighting their way through the stretch of water between Crete and North Africa which was dominated by Axis aircraft and submarines. On the North African shore, Rommel was attacking the Eighth Army fiercely with the initial aim of capturing Tobruk. The British air forces in the desert were being hard pressed with little capacity to help protect the convoy and escort on its way to Malta, but they did so all the same. To no avail. There would be two days of hard fighting before the agony of Vigorous drew to an end and the remaining ships returned to Alexandria.

13 June was a quiet day for 603. The next day saw more action, but nothing of any significance. The Diary for the 14th noted:

A Flight on at dawn: 16 pilots on now, as Luqa squadrons are stood down while fitting up with long range tanks. A few odd scrambles, but nothing came over all day. Sandy & Mitchell did a sweep to coast of Sicily on the deck and sighted a destroyer off Cape Passara. Reports are that the Italian Fleet has left Taranto. Talk by AOC to all pilots in evening. Two convoys coming, one from East and one from West, heavily escorted. One from West is due tomorrow afternoon and we are to escort it when it comes within 60 miles. One from East is due at dawn on 16th. Choice remark by AOC: 'For its size, the Malta pilot is unsurpassed anywhere.'

'Sandy & Mitchell' carried out their Sicilian sweep in the evening, at dusk. The two departed Ta Kali at 21.10 and returned 50 minutes later after having had a non-eventful sortie.

The 15th brought medium cloud and a southerly wind. The Harpoon convoy had been under constant attack the previous day but was now near enough to be able to be protected by Beaufighters and Spitfires from Luqa with long-range tanks. But the attacks on the convoy were intense.

---

*On 12 June, Jack Rae damaged a Bf109 flying BR254 X●G.

Arming a 10(Jabo)/JG 53 Bf109F with four 50kg bombs at Gela.

603 waited impatiently until the remnants of the convoy got within their range. They started the day with 16 aeroplanes on readiness, increasing later to 20. During the day they were scrambled often – 51 sorties for 55 hours – each of the five sections scrambling at least twice. Enemy formations approaching the convoys might make a break for the island and 603's job was to pick up any that did.

At 09.55 eight were sent off with the CO leading. They found nothing and on landing, S/L Douglas-Hamilton's undercarriage collapsed although he was unhurt.

Then at 11.25, four Spitfires were ordered up to provide protection for four Fleet Air Arm Albacores returning from a raid on two Italian navy cruisers which had been attacking the convoy. Along with the Albacores were two Beauforts which arrived at the battle first. This strike force had an escort of 249 Squadron Spitfires although as they were flying without long-range tanks, they could not take the attackers to the ships and back. The Beauforts and the Albacores all attacked the Italian ships although one of the Albacores was intercepted by two Macchis from Pantelleria. The four Spitfires returned at 12.30.

At 12.10 four others scrambled and reported seeing black smoke on a bearing of 300 degrees from the airfield. This is to the north west where the action would be taking place out at sea. They made no contact and returned at 13.20 with nothing more to report.

At 14.05 another four were airborne and found a pilot who had been forced to ditch when his aircraft ran out of fuel. They guided one of the air-sea rescue launches to him and he was picked up.

In the late afternoon, a 603 patrol spotted the convoy 15 miles east of Lampedusa and they also reported seeing *Welshman* approaching it. Again there was no action for them although there were fierce battles all day. 249 was engaged again, but although 603 was flying, the aircraft were not in action. That evening, the CO patrolled over the convoy:

I looked down and saw many little ships rippling their way through the water. There were no Huns about, and everything looked so peaceful, it was hard to believe that those ships had been through such hell earlier that day and during the whole of the previous day. Only tell-tale streaks of oil on the water behind some ships indicated that all of their journey might not have been so uneventful as it then appeared. In fact, there was not a ship that had not had several near-misses, and many had been damaged.

Because of the Royal Navy's tendency to assume that any aircraft was hostile, Spitfires joining a convoy did so carefully – sometimes dropping their wheels to show that they weren't a threat.

One of the ships sunk was *Kentucky*. Only two of the Harpoon merchantmen reached the Grand Harbour – as well as *Welshman* – and sadly for 603, their personal effects and baggage which had been following them out, went down in one of the ships which was lost.

Meanwhile, the Vigorous operation had been having a torrid time fighting its way in from the east. Heavily attacked and running out of ammunition and fuel, it was ordered to give up the attempt to get to Malta and return to Alexandria.

The end result of this major attempt to fight through the two convoys was that only two merchantmen had made it to the Grand Harbour together with *Welshman*. The supplies that they brought in were invaluable – but not enough to break the siege and whilst it extended the island's ability to survive for a little longer – a few days – things were still desperate.

Fuel had to be cut back even more – for the pilots it meant they would now have to walk the mile and a half from the mess to the airfield.

In North Africa, Rommel's offensive was going well as the Eighth Army reeled back towards the east and Egypt. A few days later, Tobruk fell to the Afrika Korps but the German High Command now found itself on the horns of a dilemma. Hitler wanted the Afrika Korps to push on from Tobruk further east to Egypt but some of his generals thought that the priority should be given to invading Malta. Despite the beating that the Luftwaffe had taken on 10 May, some thought that the island was neutralised and did not pose a threat. This, together with the desire to strike at Egypt ultimately prevailed and the order was given for Rommel to continue his offensive eastwards from Tobruk rather than initiate Operation Hercules in July as had been planned originally.

After the activity surrounding the convoys, the air battle quietened down considerably until Tuesday 23 June, and this despite the desperate struggle being enacted on the desert coast far to the south east. Again, although it was quiet, limited activity by both the Luftwaffe and the Regia Aeronautica kept the defenders on their toes. And of course, Malta was still striking back at Rommel's supply ships despite the crippling shortages of fuel and weaponry.

For 603 it meant carrying out readiness duties and when necessary performing their patrols and scrambles. On the 16th, they completed 16 sorties, on 17 June there were eight sorties and this desultory activity continued for days. On 18 June P/O Turlington was posted to 603 from 249.

On the 23rd it was A Flight's turn to be on dawn readiness and at 08.20 the whole Flight of 12 aircraft was scrambled and met half a dozen Bf109s which were attacked. Blue Section chased two out across the sea towards Sicily and P/Os Slade and Glen both claimed a damaged. A 109 was reported as having been seen in the sea. Bill Douglas (in X●N, BR461) chased the two 109s but didn't catch either of them.

After further sorties in the morning and the afternoon which came to little, in the early evening things hotted up again. An incoming raid was detected – three S.84s with an escort of 27 MC202s and 18 Re2001s. At 17.50, eight Spitfires from 603 and 12 from 249 scrambled from Ta Kali to meet the raid. 249 went for the bombers leaving the fighters to 603.

F/O McLeod and P/O Dicks-Sherwood spotted a number of MC202s and dived on them from about 30,000 feet. Both pilots reported seeing hits on the enemy fighters. McLeod followed another and after eventually closing to within 100 yards and firing, the Macchi flew into the sea. White Section – P/Os Newman and Ray Smith – harried another Macchi, reporting hits. F/Sgt Parkinson of Blue Section came across them and saw what he interpreted as a 'spirited defence' by the Italian airman. He entered the battle and made a three quarter head-on attack and then as the Italian fighter turned away fired again. He saw hits on the fuselage and then the pilot baling out.

603 claimed two Re2001s destroyed and two 109s damaged – again by Slade and Glen – but in fact the only loss recorded was the Macchi which was from 360ª Squadriglia. There were no 109s in the action.

On this occasion, 603 lost an aircraft too – Spitfire BR385 flown by F/O Mitchell was hit in the fight and he too had to bale out over the sea near Kalafrana. Fortunately, he was quickly rescued by an ASR launch and went down in the books as the 100th rescue for the unit. The whole engagement lasted about an hour.

There was little action over the days until the end of the June as far as 603 was concerned. The Squadron stood down on 24 June and on 28 June with the opportunity taken to get away from the war and relax in the sea. Despite the activity and the fact that they had been on Malta in the thick of action for over two months, some of the pilots found time passed slowly when not flying. Bill Douglas wrote: 'I'm really rather bored at the moment – things are very quiet just now, and unless one is kept busy time is apt to hang heavily on one's hands.'

In the evening of the 26th at 18.15, ten Spitfires from 603 scrambled, together with others from 126, 601 and 185 Squadrons to meet an incoming Italian raid called by the pilots the 'Big Five'. This comprised five Z1007bis with an escort of 18 Re2001s and 29 MC202s. The targets appeared to be the airfield at Luqa and the Grand Harbour. 603 flew together but were bounced and split up by fighters – reported as Bf109s, but more likely Re2001s. 'Pinkie' Glen claimed a 109 damaged after he saw it go into a spiral dive and another destroyed. Sgt Irwin also claimed a 109 damaged. One of the pilots had accidentally left his R/T on transmit and so communication was impossible during the dogfight. P/O Northcott and Sgt Pinney however managed to co-operate in the attack on one of the bombers which they reported as damaged.

Sgt Stamble, who had just been posted to 603, joined in enthusiastically and took a shot at one of the bombers. He 'pranged a bit' on landing, damaging a wing tip and the pitot head of his Spitfire. Bill Douglas had no success. They landed at 19.15.

Bombs had hit Luqa killing ten civilians with a similar number injured.

As well as Stamble, Sgts. E.T. Brough and E. Budd were also posted in.

On Monday 29 June, there was a moderate to strong south-westerly wind. At 08.55 Red Section (the CO, Barbour, Swales and Stamble) scrambled to intercept eight Messerschmitt 109s. Swales returned shortly afterwards with an unserviceable radio. As the remaining Spitfires climbed to meet the 109s at 24,000 feet, one pair of 109s detached themselves from the main group and bounced the Spitfires. Barbour (in BR320) was trailing the others and became a victim. He baled out and landed in the sea a few miles off the Grand Harbour but managed to get into his dinghy and was quickly picked up by one of the ASR launches unhurt.

On the night of 30 June/1 July, there was a relatively unusual action for 603. S/L Douglas-Hamilton and F/L Bill Douglas (in W●3, BR128) were on readiness for night flying at Luqa when at 03.15 they were sent off to intercept an incoming raid estimated at 15+. Normally night flying was the domain of the Beaufighters but on this occasion there were two Spitfires up as well. The GCI preferred to work with the Beaus with the result that Spitfires were sometimes 'parked' somewhere quiet to allow the Beaufighters to operate unrestricted. The two 603 Spitfires climbed to 15,000 feet 20 miles to the north, then were sent to Gozo, then Filfla where they observed incendiaries falling on Luqa and bombs on the surrounding country. They orbited Filfla at about 10,000 feet and whilst Bill Douglas reported seeing a pair of Ju87s, he couldn't engage. The CO saw no enemy aircraft and their sortie lasted an hour and ten minutes.

The two pilots were clearly frustrated by their lack of success and they felt that the policy of leaving the defences over the island at night to the guns should be changed so that fighters could follow the flashes, but on 1 July G/C Woodhall ordered that the night flying of Spitfires should cease. On a slightly brighter note, with the mess at Luqa relatively well stocked they enjoyed their supper and the breakfast they ate after the night's exertions.

As Rommel's Afrika Korps continued their advance to the east in North Africa, the various offensive squadrons on Malta struck at his supply lines and despite the failure of Operation Julius, caused real concern to the Axis command. The decision having been taken to make the North African advance the priority, Malta could not be left to its own devices and the German and Italian air strength in Sicily was being strengthened at the end of June to start a new blitz on Malta on 1 July designed to reduce the attacks on Rommel's shipping.

Nicosia, Cyprus

Whilst the pilots were on Malta, the service echelon ground crew were marooned on Cyprus between the end of June until December 1942. The photo middle left shows the sergeants' mess with decorations. But it wasn't all play (see pages 153-154)

The Regia Aeronautica had reinforced its fighter units and for the Luftwaffe, the Ju88s from KG77 which had gone to France at the end of April, returned to Sicily to Fliegerkorps II. The Germans also pulled in extra fighters from I/JG77 from the Eastern Front to the Sicilian airfield at Comiso and the arrival of this well experienced and successful unit, meant that the weary defenders in Malta would be meeting a number of pilots who were most definitely *experten*.

The new onslaught opened on the afternoon of Wednesday 1 July. It was clear with a wind from the south, which brought heat. The sun rose at 06.45 with sunset at 21.21. A Flight was on dawn readiness and although their Spitfires scrambled twice there was no action. B Flight took over after lunch and had four Spitfires scrambled in mid-afternoon. But it wasn't until the evening that they had something to report. The island's radar picked up a large raid coming in at about 18.45, it was in two formations. The first comprised two S.84bis escorted by 22 fighters and the second was three S.84bis with about 50 Macchis and 15 Re2001s.

At 18.15, the 12 Spitfires of B Flight scrambled – Red Section: Sanders, King, Glazebrook and Ballantyne, Blue: Hurst, Parkinson, Dicks-Sherwood and Brown, and White: Mitchell, Brough, Newman and Johnson. Blue Section scrambled slightly after the other two who climbed to 28,000 feet and engaged the fighters (which they claimed to include Luftwaffe 109s). The 603 pilots thought that the Italians were acting as decoys to entice them to follow them down to let the 109s bounce them, but whatever their intention, a dogfight was the result. F/Sgt Ballantyne (in BR367) claimed a 109 destroyed and another probable. He then succumbed to another attack and had to bale out over the sea losing glycol but was rescued quickly by an ASR launch.

Mitchell claimed a 109 probable and Eddie Glazebrook a damaged.

Meanwhile, Blue Section was getting into the fight. Parkinson claimed an Re2001 as a kill. He saw it begin a vertical dive towards the sea, but then came under attack by other fighters and his last view of his quarry was of it continuing its dive at about 6,000 feet heading for the water. Johnny Hurst found one of the bombers, closed to within 300 yards and saw hits, but took hits in the radiator by return fire and had to force land.

They landed back at 19.25. They flew later in the evening but there was no action. There were air raid warnings during the night at Ta Kali and in the dark after midnight three bombs fell on Boschetto Gardens – one a direct hit on a tent occupied by airmen. Seven of them were killed and many others injured. Fires were ignited in the trees and there was considerable damage to the living quarters although the ORB comments 'Morale of men was excellent.'

At the end of the first day of the new onslaught, the RAF claimed four kills, three probables and eight damaged – but the reality was two damaged. Similarly the Italians claimed ten kills, one probable and ten damaged but in fact they had only succeeded in destroying one Spitfire and damaging three. Whilst the difference between claims and confirmed was normally quite large, these seem to be unduly optimistic – on both sides.

Thursday 2 July saw an increase in the intensity. It was warm with a wind from the south east and an almost cloudless sky. B Flight was on at dawn. Just after 08.00 a raid was detected and two sections of 185 Squadron scrambled followed at 08.15 by two of 603. The raiders were 18 Messerschmitt 109s and the Spitfires found them at 28,000 feet. A fight started. In the mêlée, F/O Mitchell reported hits, but more significantly, Johnny Hurst (in BR184*) failed to return and no one knew what had happened to him. Presumably his aeroplane crashed into the sea. Whatever the cause, the Squadron felt his loss keenly. He was one of the pilots who was coping well with the pressures and making a mark.

Tony Holland – another pilot making his mark – wrote of him later: 'Johnny had a distinguished short career on Malta, a fearless young man who had several victories, was commissioned, awarded the DFC then killed all in a few short weeks.'

He would undoubtedly have gone on to even greater things if he had not been lost. Pilot Officer John Hurst DFC, RAFVR (121463) was married to Winifred and was the son of James and Annie Hurst of Strood in Kent. He was 24 when he died. His loss is commemorated on Panel 3, Column 1 of the Malta Memorial.

---

*This was the Spitfire Tony Holland flew to Malta from the Wasp on 20 April.

British pilots who found themselves having to ditch in the sea off Malta had a dilemma. The Spitfires and Hurricanes just did not ditch well. The large radiator tended to scoop in the water as the aeroplane landed and make it plunge under the water. Ideally, the solution was to let the tail touch first, then slew the fighter round just at that moment, but of course this was easier said than done.

The two flights returned at 09.15. But in addition to the loss of Johnny Hurst, two Spitfires of 185 Squadron force landed at Ta Kali – one of the pilots being wounded.

As they were landing, eight Spitfires of A Flight (Red Section: Dicks-Sherwood, King, Glazebrook and Parkinson, and White Section: Mitchell, Ray Smith, Newman and Johnson) scrambled to meet another raid. They were joined by 249 Squadron shortly after. This raid was made up of five Z1007bis with an escort of 24 Macchi 202s and 15 Re2001s.

The two sections climbed as hard as they could to get as much height as possible. The bombers seemed to circle just off the coast before starting their attack and it allowed Red Section to get to 26,500 feet and White to 25,000. White Section spotted the raid whilst about 3,000 feet above the Italians and partly up sun. They dived to attack.

Mitchell carried out a beam attack on one of the bombers at close range. There were strikes on the fuselage and wing, and the port engine caught fire. Newman followed and also reported strikes and then he was followed by Johnson, also firing.

Red Section made to enter the fray but was attacked by the fighters (which they identified as Messerschmitt 109s). King (in BR345) and Glazebrook (in BR365) both suffered hits which damaged their glycol tanks but they both made successful forced landings at Ta Kali. Finally, Smith found himself on the tail of one of the '109s' and followed it out to sea north of the Grand Harbour before shooting it down into the water. A Macchi 202 of 351ª Squadriglia was recorded as lost about 18 miles south east of Valetta.

At 10.55 and 12.05 aircraft were out looking for the missing Johnny Hurst but to no avail. A parachute was reported to have been seen 20 miles to the east and although searches were made, he wasn't found.

A Flight took over in the afternoon but although there were other raids, they weren't scrambled and 603 was stood down on the 3rd.

There was a heavy raid during the night of 2/3 July, and bombs fell near the mess in M'dina. The mirror in S/L Douglas-Hamilton's quarters cracked eliciting the comment that it would bring 'bad luck to the Hun'! Although 603 wasn't on readiness 3 July turned into another day of raids and dogfights for the defenders which set the scene for the next day.

B Flight was on dawn readiness. Four Spitfires of Red Section took off at 06.45 for an hour looking for a lost Beaufort crew but their search was fruitless. At 08.10 ten aeroplanes from 249 Squadron scrambled to meet a raid and 603 were ordered to stand to which meant cockpit readiness. At 08.55 White Section (Sanders, Glazebrook, King and Brough) scrambled to protect one of the rescue launches and were warned that there were enemy fighters about just before being bounced by three 109s. P/O King's Spitfire sustained some damage but he landed it safely. The Messerschmitts claimed two Spitfires as kills. Another raid followed later, but 603 wasn't scrambled.

A Flight took over in the afternoon but there was no 'trade' for them. In the evening as it was getting dark at 21.30, F/L Douglas (in X●D, BR177) and P/O Slade were sent off and although they were vectored on to some approaching enemy aircraft they had no success and returned at 22.05 – all this despite the order that Spitfires were not to be used in the dark.

5 July was a Sunday – a clear sky and a westerly wind. 249 Squadron stood down. 603 A Flight was on at dawn. There had been raids during the night, one at about 03.00 causing some irritation but little damage to the airfield. At about 07.30, three Ju88s came across and dropped HE and incendiary bombs damaging one Spitfire at the western dispersal. At 07.05 Red and Blue Sections scrambled but two returned fairly promptly with faulty radios and another with an unserviceable air speed indicator. The 603 Spitfires found the enemy but although they fought, results were inconclusive. The Diary also notes that a number of 185 Squadron aircraft also had to return with serviceability problems and comments that it 'looked like sabotage'.

A pair of Junkers Ju87Rs of 102° Gruppo Tuffatori (previously B a'T). The nearest aircraft is MM7082.

Surprisingly, sabotage doesn't seem to have been a major problem on Malta but there were incidents which did make the men wonder. Alex Wishart recalled the time when a Wellington bomber suffered an engine problem on taking off and when the fault was investigated, sugar was found in the fuel.

The next significant action for 603 was at 17.40 when the whole of B Flight (together with aircraft of 185) scrambled to meet a raid made up of three Ju88s with a heavy fighter escort. They climbed to 27,000 feet but only some time later saw the bombers escaping at low level having hit Ta Kali. However, they met some of the escorting fighters on their way out and F/O McLeod claimed a 109 damaged. They were back on the ground after an hour but flying again 35 minutes later to act as escort for some minesweepers after a raid was seen coming in. F/O Mitchell had to return with a radio problem but was escorted back by P/O Smith. The remaining Spitfires had an uneventful sortie.

The third and final raid of the day was again aimed at Ta Kali and consisted of two Ju88s escorted by about ten 109s. In response, 11 603 Spitfires were scrambled at 19.40 with others from 126 Squadron. Mitchell returned early again with R/T problems and for the others, confusion in forming up the Squadron resulted in them being over Gozo whilst the 88s were overhead Ta Kali. Eventually they managed to make contact with the escorting fighters but the bombers escaped unscathed.

Four Spitfires made the hop to Luqa for night-fighting duties.

On Monday 6 July the intensity of the fighting increased. Ju88s accompanied by many fighters came over about 08.00 and at 08.10 B Flight was sent off to meet them. The following sections climbed to 22,000 feet but were kept away from the bombers by the escort: Red: Sanders, King, Ballantyne and Glazebrook; White: Mitchell, Newman and Smith; and Blue: Dicks-Sherwood, Parkinson, McLeod and Brown. F/Sgt Colin Parkinson claimed a 109 damaged. The Germans claimed a Spitfire shot down. Ta Kali was bombed by seven of the Ju88s which dropped nearly 300 bombs killing one civilian and damaging a Spitfire in a blast pen.

At 09.10 seven 603 Spitfires took off when another raid approached but this time it was to avoid being caught on the ground should Ta Kali be the target. The attack headed for Luqa and the 603 group landed back at 09.35. At 12.00 they were sent off again to meet some 109s but failed to make contact although as they passed through 15,000 feet, they saw two at a much greater altitude. The pilots thought that the order to scramble had been given too late.

In the afternoon A Flight took over and had to wait until 16.20 for action. Another raid by five Ju88s and escort came in heading for Hal Far and the strip at Safi. This time they argued with operations as to when they should go, and the pilots clearly felt that again, they were sent off too late – when the raid was too near the coast. Finally ten aircraft took off – Red Section: the CO, Slade, Bye and Barbour; White: with only Swales and Pinney; and Blue: Douglas (in X●A, BP845), Irwin, Glen and Carlet. About 17 other Spitfires from 185 were sent off to meet the German force. 603 found themselves higher than the bombers but while diving to attack them were caught up by the escort. The Diary describes the action:

> Attacked by 109s at about 5,000 feet, but Glen and Carlet managed to go on and destroy 2 88s on the way home. Pinkie got hit by return fire. Rest had dogfight with 109's and Douglas was shot up and had to crash land without flaps, unhurt. Irwin shot up that 109 and probably destroyed it. He too had a couple of bullet holes in his aircraft. Slade too was shot up and had to land at Luqa, wheels down, but unhurt. Squadron airborne 30 minutes. Several aircraft u/s after this raid.

The CO's own account of the action:

> We dived down on them, but just as we were drawing near them a number of 109s dived down on us. A terrific dogfight ensued, in which the 109s for once stayed and fought. They were good, those yellow-nosed 109s. We twisted and turned around each other, blazing away every now and then; but most of us could not get away to chase the 88s.

Luftwaffe records confirm that two Ju88s were lost. One was M7+ML from KGr 806 and the other 7T+KK of KuFlGr 606 which had to ditch near the coast of Sicily.

But there was more to come. Six Spitfires of Red and Blue Sections scrambled at 18.35 to meet a raid by the Italians – four Z1107s escorted by a horde of Macchi 202s. They climbed to 20,000 feet into the sun to the north west then managed to catch four of the bombers 3,000 feet below heading home. The Spitfires dived on the enemy formation and in the mêlée, Guy Carlet claimed one fighter destroyed with another damaged. Bill Douglas (in T●W, BR385) also claimed one of the Macchis damaged and Douglas-Hamilton, Swales, Pinney and Glen all claimed separate bombers damaged.
     Following this engagement, they carried out an unsuccessful sweep to look for a ditched airman.

The day still wasn't finished. Just after 20.00 yet another raid was plotted. This time three Ju88s with the usual heavy escort of 109s and they were making for Ta Kali. Red (the CO, Turlington, Swales and Pinney) and Blue (Douglas [again in T●W, BR385], Irwin, Glen and Carlet) Sections climbed hard to 10,000 feet then circled over the airfield waiting for the attack to arrive. Spitfires from 185 and 249 Squadrons were in the air too. 603 spotted the raiders coming from the north west and they were met head on. After the initial shock of the contact, the Spitfires half-rolled and as the 88s began their dives, followed them down, firing at them. The CO's guns jammed and he was out of it. 2nd Lt Swales managed to get behind one of the 88s and gave it a comprehensive squirt. It was chalked up to him as a kill. P/O Glen engaged another, shooting off its wing and setting it alight, then became involved with a 109 which he claimed to have shot down. P/O Carlet and Sgt Irwin both reported hitting another 88 and destroying it. F/L Douglas 'had a good squirt at an 88 from above, & nearly rammed it. No claim.' The Diary notes: 'So all 3 88's were destroyed.'
     One did get back to Sicily, one landed in the sea just off the Grand Harbour and the other ditched near Sicily, the actual tally therefore being two. Similarly, only one Messerschmitt was lost, probably shot down by Screwball Beurling.
     Turlington was hit in the engine by cannon fire and made a good belly landing at Hal Far and the only other damage was some minor hits on Carlet's machine.
     The Squadron seemed to have been pleased with its day's work – particularly A Flight which had borne the brunt of the activity during the afternoon and evening. It had seemed in the past that the enemy only came over when B Flight was on readiness. B Flight claimed it was because they had a direct line to the German commanders and knew when to expect trouble – A Flight suggested it was because the enemy were more frightened of them! Jack Slade was promoted to flight commander at Luqa with 126 Squadron.

F/L Lester Sanders of 603 Squadron *(left)* was shot down by Lt Heinz-Edgar Berres *(far left)* on 8 July 1942, ditching Spitfire BR108 in Marsalforn Bay, Gozo. It was Berres' eighth victory and his first over Malta.

603 stood down on Tuesday which was another day of heavy air raids. Three of the Squadron's Spitfires were 'loaned' to 249 for the day. Clearly, the general attrition of the Spitfires was having its effect and the numbers available were beginning to become an issue yet again. AB562 (X●R) – a 603 machine – was flown by P/O Paul Brennan on his last sortie with 249 and he shot down a 109 in it.

On the morning of 8 July, it was B Flight's turn to be on readiness. The wind came from the south east and although there was no cloud, a slight haze limited visibility.

The effects of the constant fighting and the uncertainty of the battle were making an impact. Like the Battle of Britain there were intense periods of waiting followed by short bursts of activity during which a pilot might very well die a terrifying death. The CO wrote: 'We did not always get sent up even when a raid did come over, but whatever happened, most pilots were tired and generally felt like going to sleep after a spell of readiness.'

They were not always sent up to meet a raid so that some aircraft could be held in reserve in case there was a quick follow-up by the enemy hoping to catch the newly landed Spitfires on the ground and unable to defend. Added to the stress of waiting was the frustration of sitting under a raid. Douglas-Hamilton later wrote:

In the quieter days of June it had been the rule that most pilots on readiness read books. Now it seemed harder to concentrate on reading; we just sat round in the dispersal hut and waited. Some would chat with others and argue, but conversation was generally very mundane. Everybody concentrated on doing the job in hand – none knew what the morrow would bring......

When not on readiness, there was little relief.

Some days a hot sirocco blew up from the south and nearly boiled us all. It made readiness periods very exhausting, and on our 'off' periods we would lie down naked on our beds and swelter.

Only eight Spitfires were available. They were all scrambled at 06.30 to meet the first raid of the day by seven Ju88s with the usual escort of fighters, this time Messerschmitt 109s of I/JG77 and Macchi 202s of 20 Gruppo. The two sections climbed to 25,000 feet but on this occasion – sent off early – they had to wait for an hour before the raid developed. By that time they were running low on fuel. They dived into the attack. Sanders (BR108) and King (BR198) were flying as a pair and came across a Messerschmitt which they attacked but then lost. They then found the 88s and latched on to one. Sanders fired a long burst but saw no result. The rear gunner found Sanders who took a round in the armoured windscreen of the Spitfire. The pair broke off the attack. The fight had come down to sea level. As the two turned, King's wing tip touched the water and the Spitfire broke up. Sanders could do nothing to help – he was still in trouble. He was found by two of the 109s who flew on either side of him, shooting. His aircraft was badly hit and, being too low to bale out, he decided to ditch. He did this successfully in Marsalforn Bay sustaining only a cut and bruised eye where he had been thrown forward on to the gunsight. His aircraft floated for quite some time and he was picked up safely by a small boat owned by a local family who were returning from a fishing trip shortly after the crash.*

Whilst this was going on, the others were into the fight. Glazebrook fired at one 88 seeing hits on it; then he fired at another but his guns jammed. Newman claimed to have damaged one as well, and Ballantyne, Mitchell and Smith reported hits on 109s. (James Ballantyne also reported that he had fired at a Spitfire by mistake, but without any damage being caused.) F/Sgt F.R. Johnson (an Australian who had flown in from *Wasp* with 601 Squadron) was hit and injured in an arm and leg but managed to get his aeroplane (BR183) back to Ta Kali where he made a good crash landing.

The loss of Neville King, who went down with his Spitfire, was keenly felt. Apart from his family relationship with the CO, he was a good pilot albeit slightly older than most at 29. The Irishman had been a London policeman but had given that up to join the RAF.

Flying Officer Neville Stuart King RAFVR (112178), married to Brenda was the son of Joseph and Charlotte Mary King. His death is commemorated on Panel 3, Column 1 of the Malta Memorial.

Although there were other raids during the day, 603 was not called upon and for them it ended quietly albeit there were attacks on Hal Far to such an extent that damaged Spitfires from other squadrons had to land at Ta Kali.

The defenders found little relief on 9 July. They faced another hot day with little wind and haze stepped up to 20,000 feet. 603 A Flight was at readiness in the morning.

At 08.10 they scrambled Red Section: the CO, Carlet, Northcott and Pinney; and Blue: Douglas (in UF●N, BR161) Forster, Webster and Bye, which climbed to 14,000 feet. A raid was plotted but it took about an hour before the bombers came in and in the meantime, 603 'stooged around' waiting. Just before 09.00, the raid aimed at Ta Kali came in – six Ju88s at low level with escort. On spotting the bombers, the Spitfires dived down to attack but became involved in a mêlée with the escorting fighters. But they got to the bombers. Sgt Bye made a head-on attack on one of the 88s just as it was starting its dive and Webster caught another from the beam noting hits on it. But their attacks were short lived as the 109s 'mixed it' with the Spitfires and successfully drew them away from the 88s. A bowser on the airfield was destroyed and one man admitted to hospital. In 603's opinion, the bombing had been erratic. One of the 88s was shot down by the ack-ack guns.

The next raid came in at lunch time – seven Ju88s with an escort making for the Hal Far/Safi/Luqa complex. 603 A Flight scrambled again at 12.40 with F/L Douglas leading again in BR161. The incoming bombers were at 20,000 feet and the first problem was that Douglas' oxygen supply was leaking and he eventually suffered a brief black out which could so easily have led to disaster. 126 and 249 Squadrons also had Spitfires in the air, and 603 went for the escorting fighters. Northcott and Barbour both fired at 109s with Northcott reporting hits.

Guy Carlet (in BP957) didn't return. Others reported him diving on to a Ju88 but he was never seen again and 603 presumed that he had been shot down by one of the Messerschmitts. Bill Douglas noted in his log book: 'Geoff got a 109 prob. Had a short squirt at a 109 head-on. Guy Carlet missing. Made good interception over coast, but my O2 was u/s, and had a few nasty minutes. 7 JU88's etc.'

B Flight took over readiness but had to wait until well into the evening before being scrambled at 19.50 to tackle another attack by six Ju88s. Eight Spitfires were airborne led by F/O Mitchell. Spitfires from 126, 249 and 185 were also in the air. 603 climbed to 10,000 feet and met the bombers whilst 249 held off the 109s. Mitchell latched on to one of the 88s which was reported later as crashing into the sea. In the meantime, McLeod was hit by a 109 but he and Smith also attacked an 88 which they claimed as a probable. Sgt Parkinson (in X●S, BR464) was successful too: as they

---

*Sanders' Spitfire was in relatively shallow water and in 1973 parts of it were recovered and exhibited in the National War Museum.

dived down to attack the bombers, he saw one of them with smoke pouring out of it from hits by the ack-ack guns. He followed it down and at close range gave it a squirt. The 88 promptly burst into flames and disintegrated – the Spitfire flying through the wreckage. After this, he spotted a fight in progress between Spitfires and 109s and fell in astern of one of the Messerschmitts. It pushed into a dive but Parkinson followed and fired at it. The Messerschmitt continued its dive and crashed into the sea.

However, the Luftwaffe didn't record any Messerschmitt 109s as being lost during that sortie so there is an element of doubt as to just what did take place.

On the debit side, for the second time that month the Spitfire flown by F/Sgt Ballantyne (BR364) was hit and he baled out over the sea, being picked up unhurt shortly afterwards by an ASR launch.

F/L Sanders was due to be posted home and left that evening to catch the regular night flight to Gibraltar. F/L 'Mitch' Mitchell became the new flight commander.

Dawn on Friday 10 July found B Flight on readiness. At about 07.00, 14 Ju88s attacked Ta Kali. 126 and 249 were in the air. The 603 Spitfires were scrambled, but late, and they didn't get higher than 7,000 feet. They found the airfield covered in smoke from the attack but they did manage to catch the Ju88s making for Sicily after dropping their bombs. Dicks-Sherwood claimed one destroyed after he hit it with two four-second bursts. Parkinson attacked another from the side and the rear and saw strikes, but his cannons became u/s before the results were conclusive so he only claimed a probable. (The problem with the cannons was probably caused by the faulty ammunition – still a problem which had not yet been resolved.)*

At that time Ta Kali was assessed as unusable because of the dust and smoke, and the 603 aircraft landed at Luqa, but were quickly returned to Ta Kali.

After this action, 603 could only produce four serviceable aircraft. Despite the reinforcements sent, the daily fighting was having its effect and the attrition of the Spitfires meant that there were fewer and fewer available to meet the attacks. Another delivery was under way, but it would be 15 July before new aircraft arrived.

The second raid came in after 11.00 hours and the four 603 Spitfires scrambled at 10.50. They climbed to 28,000 feet and met some of the escorting fighters. F/L Mitchell claimed a Macchi shot down – the pilot having been seen to bale out. They returned at 11.55. In the afternoon, A Flight took over. The Diary records:

Scramble at about 17.00 hours. We could just manage two sections, Red of 3 a/c and Blue of 4. One of Red had to turn back with duff R/T leaving only two. Blue climbed to 20,000 feet and Red to 23,000 feet. A 20+ raid came within 20 miles and then the plot disappeared. Apparently they thought better of coming in, and we were all in a good position to bounce them out of the sun. No 88 raid in afternoon. We hope they are licking their wounds, as to-day they have lost 4 88's, 4 109's, 3 Macchis and 3 109's damaged.

Bill Douglas was flying X●S, BR464 and saw no action – 'Froze at 29,000 for damn all.'

For once the weather relented slightly on Saturday 11 July and as the sky lightened, the island was covered in fog, but it didn't last. A Flight was on readiness but wasn't scrambled for the usual breakfast raid by Ju88s which was aimed at Ta Kali between 09.30 and 10. The pilots on this occasion had their heads down in the shelters. The raid in itself did not cause a great deal of damage, but one bomb exploded very near to a shelter in which some of the pilots – including Ormonde Swales and Geoff Northcott – were taking refuge. Nobody was hurt, but they were shaken up.

At 13.40, four 603 Spitfires scrambled to meet a suspected raid but found nothing. The afternoon raid came in at about 15.00 hours with ten Ju88s and their escort at high level – 17,000 feet. 603 scrambled eight at 14.45 but they were too late to intercept and landed back safely at 15.35.

Again, 603 wasn't able to take part in dealing with the final raid of the day and they attributed it to poor controlling. At 18.45, ten Ju88s and their attendant fighters approached the Malta coast heading for Ta Kali. By this time, 185 and 247 were in the air but 603 was not. They had been

---

*The weight of four cannon reduced performance and often two were removed to give a better balance between firepower and performance.

scrambled when the raid was plotted over Sicily but were ordered to land after being airborne for 70 minutes. When the raid finally came in, they were on the ground although clearly felt that they had sufficient fuel to stay up longer and take part in the defence of their base.

One of their aircraft (X●S, BR464) was destroyed in its pen and two more damaged. In the view of the Squadron 'Control seems to have been caught out today.....'

For 603, the pre-occupation of the moment was the regularity with which they seemed to be being caught on the ground by the bombers with its consequent frustration for the pilots and the damage to the aircraft. The Diary entry for 12 July illustrates this:

Raid at 1000 hours by 8 88's on Takali. 8 of 603 airborne. Some bombs pretty wild again, and none on the aerodrome this time. High level bombing. More sheltering under billiard table at Mess. 603 climbed up to 23,000 feet but failed to intercept owing to haze although they chased 30 miles out to sea. As they were returning, they saw 'gaggle' of enemy aircraft coming in and thought they were fighters, but there were 6 88's amongst them and they again bombed Takali, but did no damage, just after our aircraft had landed. Actually one aircraft was slightly damaged by an 8 minute D.A. dropped just in front of a pen.

Another raid by 88's about 1600 hours. 603 not scrambled in spite of repeated requests. Results:- 3 of our aircraft damaged, one Cat.II rest Cat.I, and two damaged of 249. One bomb landed slap on Western Dispersal Hut, completely destroying it and burying all flying kit etc. Some airmen in slit trench 5 yards away had a narrow shave. A D.A. landed by No. 1 pen.

And later: 'Damn poor show by Ops., and everybody feels browned off that in two days 603 has four times been bombed on the ground.'

Bill Douglas (who had been flying UF●R BR871) also made the same comment in his log book. Some became quite blasé about the delayed action bombs. One was seen behind a dispersal hut with the droll comment inscribed on the side 'u/s return to stores'.

The onslaught continued the next day (13 July). A Flight was on at dawn and scrambled at 07.30 along with 126 and 185 to meet the morning raid – a particularly strong one with 18 Ju88s attacking Luqa. The eight Spitfires of A Flight climbed to 20,000 feet with the CO leading Red Section and F/L Douglas (again in BR871) Blue. The enemy bombers came in out of the sun and the two sections were told to come down 2,000 feet – which they did. They then found themselves facing two formations of nine Ju88s coming at them head on. Geoff Northcott attacked one and saw what he took to be glycol coming from both engines and claimed it as a kill. He took return fire, but it didn't cause him any problems. 2nd Lt Swales was also hit. Douglas fired at an 88 head-on but saw no hits. One of his cannon was u/s. The CO claimed two damaged. The Spitfires landed at 08.35.

They were scrambled again for the late morning/mid-day raid which was built round seven Ju88s. The Spitfires climbed hard to 17,000 feet and met the Ju88s in the dive – then turned to get under and behind them. Sgt Irwin hit one and claimed it as a kill and P/O Northcott claimed another damaged. Despite meeting the bombers, they weren't able to stop the raid which caused some significant damage to Luqa.

At 14.00 hours four Spitfires scrambled but saw no action. It wasn't until 16.55 that they were able to muster ten aircraft to scramble to meet the late afternoon raid which came in at 17.12. Ta Kali was the target this time and the Luftwaffe sent over 15 Ju88s with escort. 603 found the bombers near Sliema and attacked. Mitchell claimed to have damaged two, and Dicks-Sherwood and Ballantyne also claimed one each damaged. They were then attacked by the escort and Blue Section ordered to hold them off. F/Sgt Parkinson got a good shot at one and claimed a probable and F/Sgt Brown claimed another probable too. F/O McLeod engaged another before his Spitfire sustained hits so that the engine had failed by the time he got back to Ta Kali. He had to make a forced landing without power and although he overshot, his aircraft wasn't seriously damaged.

CHAPTER 11

CHANGING TIMES

Change was in the air – both for the Squadron and for the command of the RAF in Malta.

Earlier in the month Woody Woodhall, accompanied by Stan Turner, met some of the pilots at the Xara Palace mess to tell them that AVM Lloyd, the AOC, would be replaced. Lloyd, a bomber man, had been on the island for 14 months. It had been a hard and uncompromising period. With his aggressive outlook he had more than succeeded in maintaining Malta's role as an offensive base against the Axis operations despite all the mishaps, setbacks and tribulations that had occurred and he would step down having achieved much.

He was now to be replaced by AVM Keith Park, the New Zealander who had been the commander of 11 Group during the Battle of Britain which had borne the brunt of the German onslaught in 1940 and under whom 603 had served at Hornchurch. In losing Lloyd, Malta was gaining a new AOC of some considerable stature and reputation and as far as the fighter squadrons were concerned, a fighter man who understood their problems.

Mention of Keith Park also recalls his bitter argument during the Battle of Britain with AVM Trafford Leigh-Mallory about the use of the big wings. Of course, the concept was strongly supported by Douglas Bader and others who were based at Duxford in 1940 including Woodhall and Turner; they were posted away from Malta shortly after Park arrived.

The new AOC wanted a more aggressive modus operandi from the defending fighters under his control. On 25 July, he issued his 'Fighter Interception Plan' instructing that the Axis formations were to be intercepted and met over the sea before they had reached the Malta coastline. This would have two advantages – firstly it would reduce the destruction on the island caused by the bombs and the crashing aircraft and secondly it would help to raise morale if the continual bombing and raiding was reduced in scale. It was probably an optimistic strategy because of the lack of time for the defenders to get airborne and climb to altitude. He also wanted to see more sweeps over the enemy's airfields on Sicily.

AVM Park took over his new command on Tuesday 14 July.

The first action for 603 on 14 July was at 09.45 when eight Spitfires scrambled to meet an attack by seven Ju88s on Luqa. 249, 185 and 126 were also up. They climbed to 24,000 feet and encountered the escorting fighters. F/Sgt Parkinson linked up with another pilot after a scrap and they came across a pair of 109s which they bounced. They saw good strikes on one which slowly dived into the sea.

Air Vice-Marshal Sir Keith Park, who took over as Air Officer Commanding on Malta from Air Vice-Marshal Hugh Lloyd; he is seen here in the cockpit of one of the island's Spitfires.

145

Smith and Ballantyne took some hits during the action but all the pilots returned safely. Two of the bombers were claimed as kills but the raiders were not prevented from reaching Luqa which sustained damage from them.

There was no further action for 603 that day. The Diary notes that Sgt Les Colquhoun who had been with the Squadron until March was awarded the DFM. With all the changes in personnel, ex-603 pilots were now flying with other units and some were making names for themselves. On the downside, other ex-603 pilots were also being injured and killed – on 12 July, F/O Owen Berkeley-Hill was killed flying with 249 Squadron.

On 15 July, another batch of Spitfires came in from *Eagle* – Operation Pinpoint. This time 32 launched, but one crashed on take-off and was pushed over the side. Standing by on Malta for the arrival of the new Spitfires were 16 pilots from 603. Just after the arrival of the first group eight pilots from 603 were scrambled at 09.50 to cover the second group in. The enemy made no attempt to destroy the newly arrived reinforcements but in the afternoon, a batch of enemy fighters approached the island and amongst others, 603 scrambled eight aircraft to engage the enemy aircraft. But without a conclusive result on either side.

The Diary makes the comment that seven of the newly arrived pilots were allocated to 603 but most of them seemed to be 'fairly inexperienced'. Presumably the need to send battle-hardened pilots was still being quietly set aside for one reason or another.

The ferocity of the previous two weeks was diminishing as the Regia Aeronautica found that it had taken a beating and for 603, the pressure began to slacken off. In conjunction with the delivery of the latest batch of Spitfires, *Welshman* was once again making for Malta. On 15 July she was spotted by the enemy and attacked by Ju87s of the Regia Aeronautica but without serious damage being sustained by her.

On the morning of 16 July, the Squadron took off at dawn to cover *Welshman* on its way in to the harbour which it reached safely, arriving in time for breakfast. A Flight took over in the afternoon and whilst there were two scrambles there was nothing significant to report.

The next action was on 17 July after B Flight had taken over readiness at 13.00. Eight 603 Spitfires scrambled at 14.20 to meet a raid by five German Ju88s on Luqa. The Squadron felt that they had been ordered up late again and had only got to 18,000 feet when the bombers came across. They managed to meet the escort and a dogfight with the Bf109s ensued. F/O McLeod claimed one of them as a kill. The 109 exploded, parts of the German fighter lodging in McLeod's wing but he saw the pilot bale out and the parachute open. McLeod watched the other pilot land in the sea and as he circled the ditched airman – Feldwebel Heinz Sauer – the Canadian could see that he was alive so he dropped him his dinghy, but whilst the German was seen to be clinging to its side, he made no move to climb into it. One of the ASR launches – HSL 128 – came out to pick him up and found that he had been badly wounded by a cannon shell in the chest and was barely able to hold on to the dinghy far less climb in. Not long after being picked up by the launch, the Luftwaffe airman died.

F/Sgt Webster was commissioned and Sgt Pinney promoted to Flight Sergeant.

The 18 July brought little action in the air, but F/L R.A. Mitchell was posted away from 603 to became the CO of 249 Squadron, and it became known that Johnny Hurst had been awarded the DFC.

There was little action on the 19th too, but the 20th brought further change and some action in the air. On this day, the CO, S/L David Douglas-Hamilton, handed over command of 603 to Acting Squadron Leader Bill Douglas. Douglas-Hamilton was to act as an assistant to the Station Commander at Hal Far with the rank of Acting W/C – as the Diary put it 'Assistant Station Master (Wg/Cdr O.C. Bomb holes!)'.

His leaving, for him, was a mixture of sadness and relief to be away from the constant danger. He wrote:

> It was very sad to leave the Squadron after so many stirring days together, but at least I could feel it was in good hands.
> On leaving Takali, I had a few days' leave at a rest camp for the RAF in St Paul's Bay. It was the first leave I had had since arriving, and it was a pleasant change of surroundings. I spent every day lying in the sun and bathing off the rocks. There was also sailing to be had in small boats.

He had achieved great things. He had been thrust unexpectedly into the role of Commanding Officer in December 1941 and had made good use of the time in Scotland to develop his Squadron. Despite the loss of so many experienced pilots and the inexperience of the unit he brought to Malta from *Wasp* – including his own lack of fighter combat experience – he had faced up to the difficulties experienced with courage and strength and most of all leadership.

Many of his peers and his own pilots had a great respect for him and his qualities. He cared for his men and tried to make sure that they were well equipped for the battle and to survive. During his tenure of command which included a period of over three and a half months of often bitter fighting, seven of his pilots were killed. He was a solid and dependable commander who rose to the challenges of commanding a fighter squadron and met them with distinction. His own score was not enormous – one and a half kills, half a probable and five damaged, but he was not a man to look for glory and it seems likely that he did not claim other certain successes – rather he wanted his men to take the credit.

He was liked by most and his departure was lamented. Leaving Malta, he eventually went on to PRU duties and was killed on 2 August 1944 landing a Mosquito at RAF Benson in England after it had been hit by flak during a sortie. Typically, he received no medals, but his contribution to, and his place in the history of 603 is assured without them.

He probably suffered from the strain of leadership and his great legacies of this period were the Diary which he and Bill Douglas kept and the article he wrote which was published in *Blackwood's Magazine* in April 1944 about his experiences on Malta. The image of him sitting writing the account stayed with his wife and it may be that for him this was a release from the stresses he had endured. Both these documents give a great deal of information on the Squadron and its actions in Malta and, as noted earlier, have been prime sources for this section of this book in the absence of so many official records.

The Station Commander changed too – W/C W.K. Le May replacing W/C Jumbo Gracie. Geoff Northcott took over B Flight and F/L George W. Swanwick,* who had flown in to Malta on 15 July with Operation Pinpoint, became A Flight commander.

The war didn't stop because of changes in command and the usual routine continued. B Flight saw little action in the morning and A Flight took over at 13.00. Just after 14.00 three Ju88s with an escort of Messerschmitt 109s came in to attack Luqa. 603 already had six aircraft in the air – two acting as an escort for some minesweepers and four out on air-sea rescue patrol. The two patrolling the minesweepers saw the attack going in but were too far away to engage. By 15.45 all the Spitfires had returned to Ta Kali. The raid was ultimately met by 185 Squadron.

Another, similar raid came in just before 16.45 – three Ju88s with 109s as escort. At 16.40, eight of 603's aircraft were scrambled. They saw '16 ME 109's in line abreast, stepped up formation' and engaged them. Sgt Irwin claimed a probable and another damaged. There were other raids later on and into the night, but 603 was not called upon.

In April S/L Douglas-Hamilton had commented that the 109s seemed to be 'scared stiff' of Spitfires and unwilling to engage. If this was truly the case, it changed in July – possibly a reflection on the quality of the Luftwaffe pilots now facing the RAF in Malta. The weather on Tuesday 21 July was good for the next delivery of Spitfires from *Eagle* – this time under the codename Operation Insect. Only 30 of 32 launched arrived safely, the two were lost because of accidents during the take-off and not by enemy action. Dudley Newman was one of the arrivals – he had gone back to Gibraltar to lead-in one of the flights of new pilots. For 603 there were a number of enemy sweeps to be met but little action.

At Luqa, 1435 Flight was reformed as a day-fighter unit with the arrival of the new Spitfires and 603 lost F/O McLeod and F/Sgt Pinney to it. McLeod was posted as one of the flight commanders – an appropriate promotion for him, but it meant the loss of two experienced pilots for 603. McLeod was awarded the DFC in September, and a second a few weeks later for shooting down six enemy aircraft in five days. He had attacked some Ju88s and although his Spitfire was hit, he went for another formation but used up all his ammunition. He managed to land his damaged Spitfire safely.

---

*Flight Lieutenant Swanwick usually flew Spitfire EN979.

Soon afterwards, McLeod was posted back to Canada to be an instructor, but he would return to Europe and finish up as the highest scoring RCAF pilot with 21 kills – 13 credited to him whilst on Malta. In September 1944 whilst commanding 443 Squadron, he was killed during a fight over the Nijmegen/Arnhem area of Holland.

Friday 24 July brought a little excitement. A Flight was on readiness in the afternoon. At 16.50 they scrambled in two sections of four and eventually found five Ju88s and four 109s. They were at 29,000 feet and one section dropped on to the 88s whilst the other took on the escort. However, whilst they were about to attack the 109s, another section of Spitfires also attacked and they were unable to claim any hits. All in all an unsatisfactory and frustrating sortie.

Paul Forster was posted to Luqa.

The next day saw the return of the Regia Aeronautica who provided part of the fighter escort for five Ju88s which were attacking Luqa and Hal Far at about 15.00 hours. Eight of B Flight's Spitfires were scrambled at 13.35. They climbed to 29,000 feet and were then directed on to the enemy raiders just as the 88s were beginning their dive-bombing attacks. Blue Section was separated but found the escort and in the mêlée, P/O Glazebrook claimed a Macchi shot down. There was another scramble at 16.20 but with no action to report.

On Sunday, there was an increase in the enemy's activity but with little success for 603 – in fact frustrating failure. In the afternoon, at 16.00, eight Spitfires were scrambled but most returned with engine trouble. The Diary entry noted: 'surging and cutting at altitude, cause indefinite, but lack of fuel supply seems indicated'. It also records six aircraft returning whilst the Ta Kali ORB records seven. There is no further explanation as to what this might have been caused by – whether it was contaminated fuel or some other cause. Whatever the reason, it was a wasted afternoon and the remaining aircraft did not engage the enemy.

603's run of bad luck continued. On 27 July, there were a number of actions. 185, 249 and 126 squadrons all had successful interceptions and engagements but for one reason or another things did not go well for 603. The Diary entry for the day illustrates:

> On 15 Mins, when the first raid came in (9 JU88's and escort) 2 aircraft were scrambled for cover over the A.S.R. launches. Takali was bombed and rendered u/s by delayed actions on the aerodrome, though it was possible to take-off. The aircraft airborne landed at Hal Far. The Squadron was scrambled late for another raid which came in about half past twelve. This was intercepted by the first Squadron off and all three 88's and 9 fighters were destroyed before they reached the West. Stout work. Five of 603 were airborne from Takali on this scramble, landed at Hal Far. Relief pilots (B Flight) were sent across by bus, but this broke down, and they did not arrive till tea time, to relieve a very hungry and disgruntled A Flight. Another scramble at 19.30, but the leader's (S/Ldr Douglas) generator packed up, and he had no R/T. A few fighters were sighted, but no proper interception took place.

Clearly an unsatisfactory day for the Squadron particularly as those which did engage the enemy achieved some success. The lunchtime raid was met by Spitfires from 126, 185 and 249 Squadrons as well as the five from 603 and it was one of the first occasions that an attempt was made to intercept in accordance with the new AOC's instructions. 126 met the 88s head on over the sea and three were claimed by them as kills. 249 met the escort and Screwball Beurling shot down his fourth enemy aircraft that day and became the top scoring pilot on Malta.

603 stood down on Tuesday 28 July, but an interesting incident occurred the following day. At 13.00, B Flight – six Spitfires – led on this occasion by P/O Dicks-Sherwood scrambled to investigate an incoming plot. About 10 miles off the coast they found a low flying Italian Cant Z506B floatplane which they promptly engaged. They reported hits on its port wing – either by Dicks-Sherwood or Sgt W. Young – and the seaplane landed on the water. One of the occupants waved something white and then the Spitfires flew off alerting the ASR unit. About an hour later, one of the ASR launches arrived and found half a dozen or so men sitting on the wing waving and drinking brandy and wine! It towed the seaplane into St Paul's Bay.

The incident has been well recorded in detail elsewhere but in summary, whilst an enemy convoy was being attacked on 28 July by some torpedo-carrying Beauforts, two crashed in the sea.

The four crewman of one of them, although with some relatively minor injuries, managed to scramble into their dinghy to be rescued by an Italian floatplane and taken to its base on the Greek mainland at Prevesa. They were well entertained during the evening and that night given rooms in the officers' mess. The following morning they were taken on board another floatplane to be taken to Taranto where the Italian airmen were due to start some leave. A member of the Carabiniere guarded them but they were not tied up or restrained; presumably to make their flight more comfortable. At one point, the Carabiniere's attention began to wander and the British airmen overpowered him. His revolver was passed to the Beaufort captain – Lt Ted Strever of the South African Air Force – who ordered the pilot to fly to Malta which he did. The rest of the crew were tied up to make them secure. No doubt the Beaufort crew would feel some remorse at having treated their erstwhile captors in such a way, after being treated so well by the Italians both during the night whilst in captivity and in the air where they were not restrained to allow them some comfort during the flight to Taranto. Be that as it may, their adventure was rewarded by the award of the DFC to Strever and another crew member and the DFM to the other two.

On Thursday 30 July, there was a northerly wind and fast moving cloud. At 08.00, eight of the Squadron's aircraft scrambled to meet what was thought to be a fighter sweep, but which turned out to include three Ju88s. The fighters were a mixture of Messerschmitt 109s and Macchi 202s. 1435 Flight and 249 also had aeroplanes in the air and 603 was acting as bottom squadron. The Ju88s did not venture over the land and the Macchis were confusing the controllers by acting as if they were a bomber raid. The 603 pilots spotted half a dozen 109s and a similar number of Macchis north of Zonqor. F/Sgt Parkinson (in BP898) found a 109 and fired hitting the German in the engine. He then followed it down and at about 500 feet, from the rear and at a distance of 50 yards, hit it again. He saw the port wing come off and the 109 crash into the sea. Other 603 Spitfires were bounced by the Macchis but there was nothing to report either in the way of enemy or own losses.

At 10.55 they scrambled again, but this time as top squadron so they climbed to 26,000 feet over the Grand Harbour. There they found seven 109s in the distance travelling fast in a dive, but waited for the bombers coming in rather than engaging the fighters. However, the bombers had turned back and after some inconsequential fights with the 109s and the Italian fighters – identified as Re2002s – they landed back after being in the air for an hour.

A Flight took over readiness in the afternoon but there was no action for them nor the next morning. However, during the afternoon of the 31st, B Flight scrambled at 14.40 to meet a fighter sweep of 109s and Macchi 202s. The pilots were S/L Douglas (in N●4, BP989), F/L Northcott, P/Os Glazebrook, Newman, Barbour and Dicks-Sherwood, F/Sgt Parkinson and Sgt Ballantyne. Newman lost his engine at 11,000 feet and returned to base escorted by Glazebrook. Ballantyne's engine also cut when he was at 20,000 feet. He attempted to force land at Luqa, but overshot resulting in some damage to his aircraft (BR562).

On the climb the two sections became separated. They weren't able to get altitude quickly enough and were bounced by the enemy fighters. Parkinson was number 2 to the CO, and saw fighters coming in behind them. He called a warning but Douglas 'took no notice' so Parkinson broke up-sun. Seeing the movement the CO also broke. Parkinson managed to fire at one and reported hits. The CO followed another two into the sun but lost them. They were back at base at 15.40.

And so ended July. This was the last major action for 603 Squadron on Malta. They flew on 1 August but nothing significant happened. P/O Glazebrook was promoted to Flying Officer, but the main news of the day centred on the rumours that the Squadron was to be disbanded with the pilots posted to become part of the air echelon of 229 Squadron which had been operational on Malta until 29 April 1942 when it had disbanded.

They were stood down the following day and on 3 August became pilots in the reformed 229 Squadron. The final mention of 603 in the Ta Kali ORB on 1 August reads: '0945-1040 Seven Spitfires of 603 Squadron on patrol, nothing to report.'

The new Squadron was commanded initially by S/L Bill Douglas and for the aircrew there was little change. They continued to fly the same sorties from the same airfield using the same aircraft but as a different squadron which was to have a distinguished record in the Mediterranean before

603 Squadron on Malta end July 1942. A new boss – Squadron Leader Bill Douglas. Back row, from left to right: Sgt Lundy, F/Sgt Brown, Sgt Francis, P/O Barbour, Sgt Parkinson (?), Sgt Ballantyne, P/O Reynolds, F/Sgt Matthews, F/Sgt Elliot, F/Sgt Garvey, F/Sgt Bye, F/O Gedge, P/O Johnson, Sgt Parks, Sgt Turner and Sgt Milligan.

returning to the UK later in the war. Many of the 603 pilots were rested or posted on within weeks: 'Zulu' Swales went to 185 Squadron on 7 August, on 19 August P/O Dicks-Sherwood departed, P/Os Geoff Northcott, Webster and Forster flew back to Gibraltar and on 6 September F/L Swannick flew to Egypt on a new posting. P/O Turlington moved away on 14 September. One early loss was P/O Newman who failed to return from a scramble on 26 August. By 1945, Canadian Geoff Northcott was W/C Flying for 126 Wing on the continent engaged in ground attack and air superiority.

Curiously, although none of the 603 Malta pilots would be left, in January 1945 when 603 in turn was reformed at Coltishall in the UK, it was 229 that disbanded to become the new 603. Although, at that time there would be none of the auxiliary pilots left with the unit, W/C Bill Douglas would be their Wing Leader for a spell – a link with the original 603 that had started the war in 1939 in Scotland.

When 603 had arrived on Malta in April, Bill Douglas wrote home that he thought he would be there for about six months and this proved to be correct – on 10 September his tour ended – the 229 Squadron ORB recording quaintly that he was posted to Ta Kali 'for disposal'. Before leaving the island, he spent some days resting. On 20 September he wrote to Elaine:

> I'm writing this on the terrace at the Rest Camp, where I've been for the past five or six days having a simply glorious holiday. There are only two of us here at the moment – the Doc and I – and we're having a grand laze – swimming, sailing, sunbathing and writing letters. It really is wizard here. We've got a very pleasant house, with the garden going down to the sea and the bathing is excellent. We've had a bit of rain this month, and the garden is really beautiful. The third crop of roses are out and there are all sorts of flowers whose names I don't know, but whose colours and perfumes are terrific. The scenery is rather like those highly coloured pictures one sees of Italian lakesides, only of course the mountains are lacking. I've absolutely forgotten all about the war here, and except for the occasional Spit flying round, there's nothing to remind me of it. The weather is more or less what it was like when we came here – a certain amount of cloud about, a cool breeze, and not the scorching heat we had in the summer months. I hope that I have another week here before I go, but I expect to get packed off at any minute now.

He finally left Malta for the UK on 22 September 1942, two days after writing his letter. On 2 October he was posted to 58 OTU, Grangemouth, as an instructor and awarded the DFC, gazetted on 4 December. He was attached to 453 Squadron at Hornchurch on 7 May 1943 and got a probable Ju 87 on the 10th. He was sent to Fighter Command School of Tactics at Charmy Down as an instructor on 7 July and on August 18 was given command of 611 Squadron at Kenley. On 10 June 1944, Douglas destroyed a Ju 88 and four days later a Bf109. In August he was appointed Wing Commander Flying at Coltishall. He destroyed a Ju 88 in September and was awarded a Bar to the DFC (26.9.44). Bill Douglas was released from the RAF on 17 December 1945, as a Wing Commander.

Having survived the war he returned to Edinburgh where he eventually took over the family business – the well known 'Gray's' of George Street – and became active in the commercial and civic life of his home city. Sadly, he died in the mid-seventies. Bill Douglas reckoned that he was the last of the original 47 who flew off the *Wasp* that fateful morning in April 1942 and who were destined to return to the UK. Of course the Diary which he and Lord David Douglas-Hamilton compiled was their great gift to 603. In a letter he wrote:

> It is pretty well a factual record, and suffers I suppose from a certain repetitiveness. It contains little except a log of the basic events which affected us day by day. They were long days, and hot….. The action is there, but not the tension of waiting, the frustration of mechanical faults or the miracle that the ground crews were able to get us safely airborne at all.

But his letters also provide an insight. It has to be remembered that they were being written to loved ones far away who worried about him, so they are upbeat and confident, although his frustration and boredom come through latterly. They are couched in the phraseology of the time – he had to 'brolly forth' when he collided with the new pilot Bairnsfather and he mentions the 'popsies' at some of the dances he went to. Some of the dogfights were 'wizard'. But whilst these are unusual to the ear of the 21st century they were expressions in common use during the 1940s – of their time – and not at all to be considered peculiar. Those to his future wife, Elaine, are similar to those to his parents and family, confident and reassuring, in contrast to some of those written by pilots in the Battle of Britain which were often much more downbeat and gloomy. His letters are a testament to his resilience and confidence in his ability. We are fortunate that they have survived. They fill some of the gaps left by the terseness and bald fact recording of the Diary.

The departure of Bill Douglas from 603 at this time was the moment when all of the original Edinburgh auxiliary officers disappeared from the Squadron for the remainder of the war and heralded a change to twin-crewed, twin-engined aircraft – Beaufighters.

Malta would survive too. The key event in August was the fighting through by the Royal Navy of the Pedestal convoy with its grievous losses but also the heroism of the tanker *Ohio*. On 11 August, HMS *Eagle* which had played such a notable part in the flying in of the reinforcing aircraft was sunk by a U-boat just after another batch of Spitfires had been flown off to Malta.

But the few Pedestal ships that reached Malta secured it sufficiently. The tide really did turn in North Africa with the Battle of El Alamein and the invasion of French North Africa in the last few months of 1942. Malta had been crucial to the Allies and the significance of the Axis mistake in not invading it and allowing it to continue to operate was stark and clear.

603 was not the top scoring squadron on Malta, but it had achieved much. The Squadron that flew off the USS *Wasp* on 20 April 1942 had been relatively inexperienced and poorly prepared for what they would be expected to do. Nevertheless, with a few exceptions, all the pilots had risen superbly to the challenges and after having had to learn quickly how to survive and be effective in the vicious air battles, they had taken the fight back to the enemy. But, as demonstrated above, the pilots would be the first to agree that they had not done it by themselves. The efforts of the ground crews – often a mixture of the RAF and others – in managing to keep aircraft flying whilst under fire and always without adequate spares, was heroic and often unsung. The role of the army in keeping the airfield open – dashing out to fill bomb craters almost with the drone of the departing attackers still in the air – was vital and acknowledged as such. And of course, the skilful and expert controlling by Woody Woodhall and his team was singular in its uncanny ability usually to get the Spitfires to the right place, at the right time and at the right height to allow the pilots to do their work with all the advantages they needed to break up the attacking formations – despite some of the

concerns about the controlling which were recorded and which decreased in the last few days before the Squadron became 229.

603 fought through some of the most critical weeks of the Malta campaign – particularly the days following the second delivery of Spitfires in May from *Wasp* which some historians judge to be the turning point in the defensive air war – and they can be rightly proud of the part they played in keeping Malta going and the contribution that the George Cross island made to the ultimate Allied victory in the Mediterranean.

One of the final entries in the Diary comments that it was the service echelon in Cyprus which would be 'keeping the Squadron going' and of course whilst the pilots of 603 had been fighting the desperate battles over Malta, this had been without the 603 service echelon whom they had last seen in Scotland at the beginning of April 1942. But the 603 ground crew were not unoccupied. It seems that the intention had been that at some point the service echelon and the aircrew would be re-united – possibly on Malta – and whilst it would happen eventually at the beginning of 1943, it would be a 603 Squadron flying Beaufighters and with a completely different complement of aircrew. When the pilots left the Clyde in *Wasp* the ground crews would not see them again.

At the beginning of June there was talk on Malta that the service echelon would arrive in one of the ships of the ill-fated Operation Vigorous – it was probably just as well for the men concerned that it turned out to be just a rumour.

CHAPTER 12

THE NORTH AFRICAN ADVENTURE: CONVOY ESCORT

The Operational Record Book for April 1942 was compiled by the ground party:

> 603 Squadron had no aircraft during this month having been withdrawn operationally from the line in March. Preparations for overseas service were in hand and after equipment (Tropical Scale) had been issued, the ground crews led by Squadron Leader P. Illingworth, entrained for Port of Embarkation early on the morning of April 13th. Squadron Leader Illingworth was posted to us w.e.f. 10.4.42 for flying duties as CO. The Squadron embarked on 13.4.42 and we put to sea on the evening of April 15th. The sea voyage was uneventful.

The Squadron entry was even more terse for May: 'This month was taken up in convoy to the Middle East. The journey was wholly uneventful.' The ground crews sailed from Peterhead in the *Aorangi* (coincidentally, early in 1940, 603's Kiwi Battle of Britain ace, Brian Carbury, had named his Spitfire 'Aorangi'). They arrived at Freetown in a tropical storm. From there they went to Durban where they stayed at Clarewood Camp. The unrationed food, including steak, was greatly appreciated.

The next stage of the journey was in the *Mauritania* which sailed from Durban to Port Tewfik in Egypt without any escort. It arrived on 4 June 1943.

Meanwhile events had been moving rapidly in North Africa. On 26 May Field Marshal Erwin Rommel launched the offensive that would take the Afrika Korps from Tobruk, across the Egyptian border past Sollum and Sidi Barrani, to El Alamein by July 1943.

The ground crews meantime travelled by train from Port Tewfik to the large tented camp at Kasfareet. They summarised subsequent events in the Form 540.

> On 4th June the Squadron, with a clean bill of health, disembarked at a Port in Egypt. We were transferred at once to a Transit Camp at Kasfareet. Soon after our arrival in Egypt Squadron Leader Illingworth was posted non-effective sick and finally posted from the Squadron to HQ RAF Middle East.
>
> Plans were made for the Squadron to move to Burg-el-Arab to assist in the Maryland Repair Unit, but the Afrika Korps' advance to El Alamein altered this plan and orders finally came through for the Squadron to move on 26th June to Cyprus by sea via Alexandria. The Squadron embarked under the Acting Command of Acting Flight Lieutenant R. Oddy the Squadron Adjutant on June 27th and disembarked at Famagusta, Cyprus on June 28th leaving at once for Nicosia main aerodrome where the Squadron remained until December 1942.

They made the short sea crossing to Cyprus in a French destroyer. Angus 'Angy' Gillies recounted that whilst they were loading up, some of their kitbags fell into the sea. Warrant Officer 'Snuffy' Prentice had told the men to keep going, but on discovering one of the kitbags was his own, hastily took steps to recover them!

Norman Wood recalls his experiences with 603 Squadron in 1942 :

> I joined 603 Squadron at Peterhead in the General Duties Trade. The main attraction while we were at Nicosia was swimming in the afternoons at Kyrenia. After 12 months we returned to Egypt and were kitted out as a fully mobile Squadron, everything wheels, and then to Gambut in the Western Desert, on arrival our Beaufighters began to arrive.

I was allotted to B Flight under Flight Sergeant Gillies and as I could drive was re-mustered as an MT driver. I drove the fuel tanker and made frequent trips to Alexandria over 50 miles away to pick up rations and to Sollum to collect water supplies.

LAC Ron Lee recalls how the Germans were not the only enemy with whom they had to contend. Ron had hoped to join the RAF as aircrew, but failed the medical examination. He joined at Acton reception centre in west London, and eventually qualified as an armourer. He was posted to 603 Squadron at Hornchurch in 1941, and remained with them until the end of the war. He recounts the loss of his friend AC2 W.J. Newman, aged 19:

We had been confined to camp in Genifa, Egypt due to an outbreak of typhus fever in the adjacent compounds of the camp. After being disinfected we, plus kit, were given the all clear. Hence our belated visit to Ismailiya in the canal Zone. We boarded the SS *Princess Marguerite*, bound for Cyprus on 25 June 1942. My friend AC2 Bill Newman became ill on the boat and, on disembarkation, went into No.57 General Hospital at Kinnot suffering from, I believe, peritonitis. He failed to survive an operation and died on 8 July 1942. Being a mate of his, I was detailed to join the burial party on 9 July, after a 24-hour petrol dump guard duty. After this I developed a touch of the common, and dreadful, sandfly fever.

AC2 Newman was married to Rosetta Newman and they lived in Birmingham. He was buried in the Nicosia War Cemetery, Cyprus.

Arriving on Cyprus on 28 June at Famagusta, they were taken to Nicosia where they would stay until December. Not having any aircraft of their own, they helped other units and these included 451 Squadron, which was part of the Royal Australian Air Force flying Hurricane Is at Lakatamia. It was only a detachment of 451 which was in Cyprus – the main squadron base in 1942 being in Syria – and it was flying stripped down Hurricanes which were being used to try to intercept high flying reconnaissance Ju86s.

A detachment went to Paphos aerodrome at the south-west end of the island to keep it in serviceable condition for both day and night flying. Others made Nicosia Main day and night operational.

On 3 August 1942, Squadron Leader F.W. Marshall was appointed Administrative Officer commanding ground party – service echelon – which was helping with the maintenance of P.40 Kittyhawks of the 65th Pursuit Squadron USAAF. These aircraft had the Packard-built Merlin engines which would also power the Spitfire XVIs used by 603 in 1945. Only a limited number of their own ground crews had accompanied 65th Squadron and 603 were happy to be working on Merlins again for the whole of the month.

Others carried on with airfield maintenance and helped move dummy Hurricanes around into realistic positions to deceive the enemy's reconnaissance aircraft. These had been devised by Jasper Maskelyne, a former partner in the great team of magicians, Maskelyne and Devant. He was responsible for advising on camouflage and deception in the Middle East and could create squadrons of aircraft and batteries of guns which fooled the most expert photographic reconnaissance.

The American unit left Cyprus in September 1942 and the men of 603 were left to continue 'general aerodrome maintenance' until in November rumours began to circulate that the Squadron was to be re-equipped with new aircraft.

Whilst the ground crews were fretting about their forced inactivity, General Montgomery was preparing his counterattack. On 23/24 October he defeated the 'Desert Fox' Field Marshal Erwin Rommel at El Alamein and began a swift westward offensive, which would project his 8th Army through Sidi Barrani, Fort Capuzzo and past Benghazi by November 1942.

On 10 December the service echelon of the Squadron was warned to prepare for a move back to Egypt. They embarked at Famagusta on 15 December and reached Port Said on the 19th. On arrival in Egypt they were based at 24 Personnel Transit Centre (PTC) at Aboukir, where they spent a very enjoyable Christmas.

Early in January 1943 they heard that they were to be re-equipped with the Beaufighter Mks IC and VIC and re-roled under the command of 201 (Naval Co-operation) Group based in Alexandria,

Egypt as a maritime strike squadron and for the next few weeks, their time was spent re-equipping and generally getting back into the ways of working as an operational squadron.

In December 1940, the Bristol Beaufighter IC had begun to replace the Blenheim VIF as a long-range fighter in Coastal Command, but it was a year before this new aircraft began to enter service with maritime squadrons in the Mediterranean, where it was first employed in the Western Desert. The machine was an adaptation of the Beaufort, but far more heavily armed, and with the crew reduced to two; the navigator performed the additional function of wireless operator. An immensely strong two-seater fighter, the Beaufighter had a maximum speed of 330 mph, a cruising speed of 207 mph and a range of 1,500 miles. Forward armament was 4 x 20mm Hispano cannons and there was a rear-firing Vickers VGO machine gun with drum feed. This was later replaced by the more modern belt-fed Browning. It was a most effective anti-shipping weapon, and became even more devastating when fitted with rocket projectiles. The Beaufighter IC was followed by the VIC; the combination of Beaufighters with torpedo-carrying Beauforts began to transform the effectiveness of daylight attacks against Axis shipping in the late summer of 1942. Then the Beaufighter TFX, specially designed as a combination fighter and torpedo bomber, began to enter service in the early summer of 1943, both in the UK and Mediterranean theatres.

The tasks that the maritime strike squadrons, including 603 Squadron, performed in the Mediterranean, were multifarious. The Beaufighter squadrons included in their collective repertoire such sorties as torpedo attacks, anti-shipping attacks, cannon and machine-gun attacks on escort vessels, fighter escorts, long-range fighter attacks against enemy air transports, bombing of ports, and even strafing of enemy ground troops and transports. Their role was almost always aggressive rather than defensive. A large number of the aggressive sorties were called 'armed rovers'. Aircrews were expected to fly 200 operational flying hours before being taken off operations or screened.

A factor which operated in favour of the Axis in January 1943 was the slowness of the Allied air forces in combining into a unified command structure. In north-west Africa at the end of 1942 there were some 1,200 aircraft of the 12th United States Army Air Force and about 450 aircraft of the Eastern Air Command of the Royal Air Force, but the main tasks of these considerable air forces were the support of the Allied armies during their advances and the protection of their supply routes. It was not until mid-January 1943 that part of the 12th USAAF was formed into an anti-shipping unit, and this did not begin operational work until the end of that month. Unified air control, under the new Mediterranean Air Command, was formed towards the end of February under Air Chief Marshal Sir Arthur Tedder.

On 25 January 1943 the ground crews moved to EDKU in the Nile Delta, having been equipped as a fully mobile squadron. Flying Officer W.G. Rogers was appointed Engineering Officer; a pre-war regular with 12 years service including five years in Aden and India.

The auxiliary ground crews had maintained a wide range of engines although for the past three years they had concentrated on Merlins. With the aid of comprehensive manuals and the assistance of 24 regulars posted to the Squadron to carry out more complicated overhauls, they soon became familiar with the Beaufighter's Bristol Hercules engines. An experienced NCO, Flight Sergeant Wilkinson, took charge of the engine fitters.

603 were lucky to secure such an experienced and resourceful engineering officer. For the next two years the Squadron would be constantly on the move. All maintenance would have to be done in the open air, often in the face of high winds, sandstorms and torrential rain. Improvisation would be essential. The Squadron had to be self-contained, relying on what it could carry in its lorries or salvage in the desert. Rogers and his team did a magnificent job and theirs was a major contribution to 603's success in the desert campaign.

The aircrews joining 603 Squadron in North Africa had a long and frustrating journey. Tom Truesdale served on the Squadron during its desert campaign flying the Beaufighter:

> Beaufighter trained aircrew direct from the Operational Training Unit (OTU), were posted to the Middle East and we sailed on 17 December, 1942 from Avonmouth on the MV *Highland Brigade*. We were under the command of Squadron Leader H.K. Laycock, who we imagined would be the Commanding Officer of the Squadron, but this proved not to be the case. We disembarked at Takoradi on the then African Gold Coast on 7 January 1943

and it was the intention that we should fly to Cairo in our Beaufighters which had arrived in crates at Takoradi. Most of us however went by different means – a Junkers Ju-52 aircraft to Lagos, Nigeria, then by train to Kano in Northern Nigeria and then by Douglas DC-3 to Maiduguri, Khartoum and finally Cairo, Egypt arriving on 16 February 1943. Following a few days in a Transit Camp at Almaza near Cairo, we were posted to 603 Squadron, then at Lake Idku, about 30 miles east of Alexandria, but on 22 February I went down with malaria and as a result did not join the Squadron until 26 April, then at Misurata West, to support Operation Husky, the invasion of Sicily. The Mediterranean had not been open long and operations in the main consisted of convoy escort and the Commanding Officer was Wing Commander H.A. Chater. I was in B Flight. Apart from convoy escort, we went in detachments of four or six aircraft to Berka III, from there we did offensive sweeps along the coast of Greece.

On 27 January 1943 the Squadron was advised that 12 Beaufighter Mk VICs would be taken on charge. On 28 January, Wing Commander Hugh A. 'Fritz' Chater, a South African from Natal, was appointed to command 603.

As a sergeant, his navigator, F/O Undrill, had survived an unfortunate experience with another squadron when his pilot had landed in Idku Lake in the Nile Delta at night. The aircraft turned over and the pilot drowned but Undrill was rescued and seemed unaffected by the incident. He was later recommended for, and granted, a commission.

The following day saw pilots and navigators posted in, some from 227 Squadron – already experienced flying Beaufighters in North Africa.

1 February 1943 was a great day for the Squadron. Its first aircraft arrived and was thoroughly checked by the ground crews. It was allocated to S/L Laycock, Commander of B Flight. He air tested it on 3 February and found it completely satisfactory. Further aircraft were allocated, some from operational squadrons, and many required extensive maintenance to bring them to operational status. F/O Rogers and his team tackled the heavy load with enthusiasm. Squadron Leader G. B. Atkinson took over A Flight. More aircrew were posted in and intensive flying training continued.

Left: W/C Hugh Chater, OC 603. 'On high!'
Below: Chater at Edku before the Squadron reformed.

W/C Hugh Chater, Pritchard and Wally Eacott at Gambut.

The 8th Army captured Tripoli on 23 January and the Royal Engineers began clearing the harbour and installations to receive supply convoys. By 2 February the first convoys arrived and commenced unloading. On 6 February however, a convoy, bound for Tripoli, was attacked by enemy aircraft based at Cagliari in Sardinia. More air cover was essential.

On 8 February, 603 was tasked to provide four aircraft for detachment to Berka III airfield at Benghazi, Libya and these were led by W/C Chater.

The following day 603 provided close cover for the Outwit convoy (12 merchant vessels, one tanker and twelve destroyers) bound for Malta via Tripoli. This was the Squadron's first operational sortie since it had been re-roled and it was uneventful. Similar cover was provided for a convoy from Misurata West on 10 February.

On 12 February the detachment returned from Berka III in time for an inspection by Air Marshal Sir Sholto Douglas, AOC-in-C Middle East. Flying training took place despite bad weather.

By 18 February the weather had improved sufficiently for S/L Atkinson to take four more aircraft to Berka III to cover a convoy consisting of 12 merchant vessels, three large tankers, one liner, eight destroyers and two corvettes. This was successfully escorted across the Gulf of Sirte on its way to Tripoli and Malta. Convoy Poker (ten merchant vessels, three tankers and escort vessels) was similarly escorted on 4 March.

On 7 March Air Marshal Sir Sholto Douglas returned to inspect the Squadron before it set off to Misurata West. He was accompanied by Prince Bernhardt of The Netherlands.

On 23 February 1943, whilst the Squadron was in North Africa, at home in Edinburgh the Lord Provost of Edinburgh, Sir William Young Darling Kt., CBE, MC, DL, JP, FRSE, LLD, had been appointed Honorary Air Commodore for a period of five years. In a telegram to the Commanding Officer, he said: 'Please accept most cordial thanks for kind congratulations from yourself, officers and airmen of Squadron on my appointment.'

Another detachment of aircraft went to El Magrun on 15 March. The Squadron was detailed to escort convoy Survey. Junkers Ju88s had been observed eight miles astern of the convoy, but had made no move to attack. Flight Lieutenant Ashby was directed against them, but could not intercept in the failing light. On his return to the convoy he was fired on by all vessels, who regarded him as hostile. He made several attempts to identify himself but the gunners were not convinced. He gave up and returned to base. Despite the hostile reception, 603 provided escorts again the following day while the main body of the Squadron set out from Idku in a convoy of 51 trucks on its epic journey across 1,200 miles of poor desert roads and rough tracks to Misurata West. Most were open 3-ton vehicles and only three had tarpaulins to provide some protection for equipment and passengers. The Squadron remained fully operational throughout, and carried all the spares and equipment it might require. The land battle was still raging in Tunisia and extended supply lines might be unreliable. Despite logistical problems, 603 would be responsible for all maintenance, except major overhauls, which would have to be carried out by properly equipped workshops in the Nile Delta.

Following a 10-day journey, they arrived at their new base, Misurata West, at 08.00hrs on 27 March, despite the dreadful conditions and the great discomfort suffered by all concerned. All living quarters and technical tents were erected during the day despite high winds and dust storms. They were now ideally situated on the North African coast some 240 miles south of Malta.

On 29 March, W/C Chater arrived with the advance party of aircraft and more aircraft arrived during the subsequent few days.

Whilst the main Squadron was moving up to Misurata West, the detachment at El Magrun had been busy providing cover to convoys Liquid, Metril and Anger.

On 1 April the AOC 201 Group, Air Vice-Marshal T.A. Langford Sainsbury, flew up to Misurata West to wish the Squadron luck – to mark the 25th anniversary of the formation of the RAF. The only sortie that day was convoy protection by two Beaufighters to convoy Rival. No enemy activity was reported.

The Squadron was now fully operational at its new base and throughout April, May and June provided escort cover for convoys with codenames such as: Nation, Outwit, Survey, Curly, Poker, Roman, Heavy, Merit, Pilot,

Top: A member of 603.
Bottom: Goodfellow at Misurata West.

Brilliant, Pump, Mammoth, Evolution, Cussed, Across, Blanker, Norfolk, Venus, Nutshell, Naval, and Datum.

There were some casualties. On 19 April Flight Sergeant Goodfellow and Sergeant L.G. Maynard in aircraft J had engine trouble and ditched. Both got out safely into their individual rubber dinghies, but in his haste Sgt Goodfellow put his foot through the thin floor and had to stay with his leg in the water.

Meantime their companions Flight Sergeant R.H. Giles and Sergeant L. Coulstock in aircraft H tried in vain to inform base. As frequently happened, they could not make contact and after carefully noting the position flew back to base to report. An ASR Westland Walrus aircraft took off and F/Sgt Giles led it to the dinghies. Both men were picked up within two hours of ditching.

On 2 May 1943 three aircraft were tasked to give last light cover to convoy Liquid heading for Tripoli. Flying Officer F. Scantlebury and Flight Sergeant B.G. James in aircraft E failed to return, probably shot down by enemy fighters as intelligence had indicated that there were ten enemy aircraft in the vicinity. No trace of the crew was ever found and they were classified 'missing in action believed killed'. Scantlebury and James are commemorated on the Alamein Memorial, Egypt.

On 13 May Marshal Messe and the 1st Italian Army surrendered. Simultaneously Von Arnim surrendered with the German forces in Tunisia. The Allied massed convoys continued to bring up supplies for the forthcoming invasion of Sicily.

The campaign to secure urgent supplies from 201 Group was every bit as arduous as the campaign against the Germans. Misurata West airstrip was built on a flint outcrop which played havoc with aircraft tyres. The Squadron engineering officer estimated that 29 landings were the safe maximum and 201 Group were informed. Nothing happened and tyre stocks began to run low. A series of aircraft on ground (AOG) demands were sent, still without acknowledgement. Finally the CO sent a telegram 'Unless our demands for tyres are actioned within 48 hours 603 Squadron will be non-operational'. The result was miraculous – within 36 hours two Dakotas and a Hudson arrived, full to capacity with the necessary tyres.

Having honoured Malta with the award of the George Cross during his visit, His Majesty King George VI departed on 21 June 1943 for Tripoli in HMS *Aurora* accompanied by three destroyers. The convoy was codenamed Ferguson. 603 Squadron had the honour of providing a six-aircraft escort – two low cover and four high cover.

On the 30th, Sergeant W.E. Powell was killed and is buried in the Heliopolis War Cemetery, Egypt.

On 2 July the Squadron escorted convoy Relax consisting of two Queen Elizabeth class battleships, an aircraft carrier and nine destroyers, which were to cover Operation Husky – the Sicily landings.

On the 8th four Beaufighter Squadrons – 227, 252, 272 and 603 – together with Lockheed P.38 Lightnings from 96 Group USAAF, escorted the convoys Investigate and Cobalt, which later made rendezvous south east of Malta at dusk on 9 July to form the main assault group for the invasion of Sicily. There was no enemy activity.

Next day two convoys were protected: Abrasion, consisting of 50 troop transports and 20 naval units and Horatius, 17 supply ships plus tank landing craft.

On the afternoon of 9 July some 2,000 vessels began moving northwards for the assembly area. The eastern part of this force was covered by Middle East Command, including 603 Squadron. Heavy gliders – Horsas and Hadrians – were massing to take part in the invasion of Sicily which began on 10 July 1943. The few enemy fighters were swamped by the overwhelming Allied air power.

Syracuse was captured on 11 July and the convoys Untrue and Budget sailed for this port.

Convoy Bowery took supplies to the beachhead on 12 July, and 603 flew 19 sorties covering it from dawn to dusk. Sergeant Downing and Sergeant Cresswell in aircraft M burst a tyre on take-off. It continued on its patrol and when this was completed made a successful wheels-up landing.

The rest of July and August saw continued convoy cover for: Burgess, Riband, Copper, Totnes, Cockatoo, Norfolk, Canteen, Carbon, Sampler, Bedspread, Avocado, Hunter, Trafford, Tryst, Nelson, Tebworth, Collar, and Battling. Both air and ground crews found the convoy escort work arduous but all were aware of how crucial 603's air support was to the invasion.

Right and below:
Missolonghi, 19
August 1943. Low
level shipping strike.

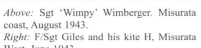
Above: Sgt 'Wimpy' Wimberger. Misurata coast, August 1943.
Right: F/Sgt Giles and his kite H, Misurata West, June 1943.
Below: F/L Rogers and F/Sgt Wilkinson, Misurata West 1943.

As the Allied forces pressed inland on Sicily the Squadron began to prepare for a more offensive role, whilst still providing convoy escorts whenever these were needed. Nearly every day there were practice low level bombing flights using 11lb practice smoke bombs.

The first of the new armed rover sorties took place on 15 August. The previous day W/C Hugh Chater had led a detachment of six aircraft from Misurata West to Berka III (Benghazi). They now carried out an offensive sweep along the southern Peloponnese from Kithera to Githion. They bombed the harbour at Matapan encountering light anti-aircraft (AA) fire. They silenced gun positions at Kalamata and bombed the airfield.

W/C Chater then returned to Misurata West, and S/L Atkinson took four aircraft to Berka III to attack shipping at Missolonghi and carry out cannon and machine-gun attacks on gun positions.

The aircraft at Misurata West continued to guard a series of convoys: Taunton, Manicure, Collins, Cockatoo, Dunnock, and Wasting.

On 19 August 1943 it was the turn of S/L H.K. Laycock in aircraft P to lead an armed rover on Missolonghi using cannon, machine guns and 250lb bombs. The aircraft's starboard engine caught fire but Laycock and Sgt R.C. Scott made a good belly landing beside the road, one mile north west of the town. They were both badly burned and were later said to be prisoners of war. Both were then reported to have died in the camp hospital on the same day, 26 August, only one week later as a result of injuries sustained in the crash. Squadron Leader Herbert Laycock and Sergeant Robert Scott are buried in the Phaleron War Cemetery, Greece.

Anti-shipping strikes continued from Berka III on 22, 23 and 30 August.

On 23 August Squadron Leader J.A. Compton and Sergeant H.G. Griffiths in aircraft R were hit by AA fire. The wing tip hit the water and the aircraft plunged into the sea, killing both men. Compton and Griffiths are buried in the Phaleron War Cemetery, Greece.

On 30 August Flying Officer A. Honig DFM and Sergeant R.G. Finlay in aircraft C were also hit by AA fire. They attempted to ditch but both were killed. Honig and Finlay have no known graves and are commemorated on the Alamein War Memorial, Egypt.

Left: Belted-up.
Above: F/L Atkinson, Borizzo, Sicily.

The 3 September 1943 saw the Allies cross the Straits of Messina and land on mainland Calabria. It was decided to move all aircraft and a supporting ground party to Sicily to provide cover to convoys destined for the mainland and to carry out offensive sweeps in the area.

W/C Chater flew to Bizerta in Tunisia to be briefed on operations in Sicily. Air Commodore Cross welcomed him and his navigator Flying Officer R.S. Undrill, and they had an unusually civilised evening – hot baths, decent drinks and an excellent meal – a great change from Misurata West. From Bizerta they flew to Borizzo in Sicily on 3 September to receive the main party, equipped with the Beaufighter XI. The same day, the ground party and their equipment, led by F/O Wyndham Rogers and F/Sgt Angy Gillies, was transported in three DC3s to Borizzo.

On 4 September, 13 Beaufighters landed at Borizzo to operate under 325 Wing, part of 242 Group Northwest African Coastal Air Force (NACAF) based in Algiers to support the 5th Army in the North African campaign. The Squadron was under the command of 62 Fighter Wing, USAAF for operational tasking and intelligence reporting. With the assistance of a further three DC3s, the move was accomplished without difficulties.

For the next three weeks 603 escorted convoys – many forming part of the fleet intended to invade Salerno. The codenames continued to multiply: Ropsley, Gladstone, Elicit, Decade, Links, Tunic, Monica, Groom, and Rockfield.

Italian forces surrendered on 8 September 1943 but the Germans continued their fierce resistance.

On 19 September the Squadron escorted a particularly interesting convoy. This included one cruiser and eight destroyers from the captured Italian Fleet, which were on their way to Grand Harbour Malta.

On the 24th, three aircraft led by W/C Chater took off at 11.56 hours on a sweep for enemy shipping evacuating Corsica: W/C Chater and F/O R.S. Undrill in aircraft E, P/O Bruce Megone and P/O J.E.D. Williams in aircraft D, and W/Os Doube and J.M. Moon in aircraft S. They sighted six Junkers Ju52s at 14.21 hours flying at sea level. In the ensuing attack Chater destroyed one and damaged another. Megone and Doube destroyed one each. Doube in aircraft S was damaged by return fire and the engagement was broken off. The other two aircraft provided escort during the return trip. Chater suddenly saw aircraft D peel off but did not realise anything was wrong. With its hydraulics shot away S belly landed, but there was no sign of D. In fact D had also been damaged in the attack and Megone found that his port inner fuel tank was on fire and headed for the nearest island – Pianosa –

LAC Ron Lee at Alexandria on leave.

where he decided the ground was level enough for a wheels-down landing and put the Beaufighter down successfully. The fire began to abate and the crew managed to put it out. The Italian population was friendly and helpful and they managed to explain that Germans from Elba visited the island each evening. Despite the damage to their aircraft Megone and Williams decided to risk taking off again rather than face captivity. Once airborne Megone crept along the coasts of Corsica and Sardinia and then across to Sicily where he landed safely. For this action he was recommended for the DFC which he was duly awarded. His citation reads :

Pilot Officer Megone is a keen and tenacious pilot. He has participated in a very large number of sorties, including a most determined attack on a large merchant ship which he bombed with destructive effect. In September 1943 he took part in an engagement against a formation of enemy aircraft, one of which he shot down. During the combat, his aircraft was hit and a fire commenced near the port main plane. Nevertheless, Pilot Officer Megone coolly flew the aircraft to the flat terrain of a small island where he effected a safe landing. Flames were still issuing from one of the fuel tanks but they were quickly extinguished. The situation was serious but, as it was clear that the island was still in enemy hands, Pilot Officer Megone took off. Displaying great skill and resolution he succeeded, after a long flight, in reaching base where he landed his badly damaged aircraft safely. His courage and resource were of a high order.

603 was now ordered to return to Landing Ground 91 (LG91) at Amariya in the Nile delta near Cairo on 4 October 1943, where the Squadron would be re-equipped with the rocket-firing Beaufighter TF Mk X prior to commencing the next phase of their operations. The party at Misurata West would make its own way, and the Borizzo party would be flown back direct. The ORB paid well deserved tribute to the ground crews:

> This concluded a hectic period in which all personnel working on aircraft had done an excellent job of work. They were handicapped by only having about one third the usual number of men, there were very limited spares and supplies, facilities were negligible and a great deal of improvisation had to be done as the detachment had moved by air and only light equipment could be taken. There was a lack of transport and refuelling difficulties were acute, much having to be done by hand from 4 gallon tins. The hours were long, commencing on most days before dawn and finishing well after dark. However, everyone worked hard and cheerfully and maintained a high enough serviceability for the Squadron to be able to fulfil all commitments, which, as far as the number of sorties was concerned, were the heaviest it had ever had in so short a period.

Tom Truesdale reflects on his time at Borizzo and the return to Gambut:

> The 603 detachment at Borizzo, Sicily was from 4 September to 6 October 1943. B Flight was commanded by Flight Lieutenant Walters since we lost Squadron Leader Laycock on 26 August. We left our Beaufighter Mk VI aircraft behind for 252 Squadron and flew in Douglas DC3 aircraft to Amariya in the Nile delta where we were re-equipped with Beaufighter Mk Xs and posted to Gambut. Operations there consisted of offensive sweeps in the Aegean Sea and its various Islands and we started converting to rockets. In February 1944, we went, a Flight at a time, to 5 Middle East Training School (METS) at Shallufa, near the Bitter Lakes, Egypt for a rocket projectile course of one week. Our Commanding Officer from November 1943 onwards was Wing Commander Ronaldson Lewis and he was still there when I left the Squadron in June 1944, though he was due to be replaced.

By March 1943, Shallufa had become 5 Middle East Training School and thereafter was the primary training centre for maritime strike crews in the Mediterranean theatre. The pilots, who were already experienced in their aircraft, were taught tactical approaches at low level on ship targets, when flying in various formations. They learned how to evade enemy fire by side-slipping, diving under the bows of their target, and then skidding away with flat turns over the surface of the sea. They also trained for night sorties, guided onto targets by their air-to-surface vessel (ASV) radar, as well as by homing devices installed in Vickers Wellington aircraft which then dropped flares to silhouette enemy ships against the skyline for torpedo attacks.

Seven DC3s flew the main Borizzo ground party and their equipment back to LG91 in the delta on 3 October, under the joint command of Flight Lieutenant Oddy and George Moore.

On 17 October 1943 the main ground party arrived at the Squadron's new base at Gambut III. They went by rail from Amariya (LG91) to Tobruk and thence by lorry to the airstrip.

On the 16th a squadron of North American B.35G Mitchells of the 310th Bombardment Group, USAAF, arrived at Gambut III. This mark of the aircraft was fitted with a 75mm cannon in the nose, firing 15lb shells. With 2 x .5 inch machine guns alongside the cannon, the aircraft was a formidable anti-shipping weapon. These aircraft made their first attack on 10 October, escorted by three Beaufighters (of 252 and 227 Squadrons). They located and attacked an R-boat and a caique near Kos, making hits on both.

The combination of Beaufighters, including 603 Squadron aircraft, and Mitchells of the 310th Bombardment Group went out each day from 24 to 29 October. The aircraft usually flew to the area of Kos in formations of about nine, attacking schooners, caiques and barges. On 27 October 1943 they attacked Antimachia airfield, the Mitchells destroying a Junkers Ju52 on the ground, while the Beaufighters blasted with cannon fire two groups of soldiers who appeared to have left the aircraft. 603 suffered no losses.

CHAPTER 13

THE ILL-FATED DODECANESE CAMPAIGN
8 SEPTEMBER – 22 NOVEMBER 1943

Both Churchill and Hitler now turned their attention to the Balkans and Aegean. Following the unconditional surrender of Italy on 8 September 1943, Allied plans were made to establish a 'second front' on southern Europe by setting up bases in the Dodecanese Islands in the eastern Aegean Sea to be used as a series of stepping stones to the Greek mainland.

The beautiful Aegean Sea is almost landlocked – bounded on the west by Greece and on the east by Turkey. Its southern approaches are guarded by mountainous Crete and Rhodes, its waters studded with hundreds of picturesque small islands.

The Germans were strongly entrenched in Greece where they had between six and seven divisions. They also had four divisions dispersed over the islands of the western Aegean, including Crete. The only weak point lay to the east in the Dodecanese, a group of islands, including Rhodes, adjoining the coast of Turkey. Throughout the Second World War, these had been garrisoned by Italian forces.

From Churchill's point of view, possession of the Dodecanese, hopefully with Italian co-operation following their surrender, offered glittering prospects. The Turks might be impressed enough to abandon their benevolent neutrality and actually join the Allies.

The land forces in the Eastern Mediterranean, under the command of General Wilson, reported directly to the Joint Chiefs of Staff in London. The Middle East Air Force of Air Marshal Sir Sholto Douglas, however, came under the command of Air Chief Marshal Sir Arthur Tedder at Eisenhower's headquarters at Algiers in the Western Mediterranean. Naval forces were similarly controlled from the Western Mediterranean by Admiral Cunningham. Eisenhower could thus veto any proposals for the strengthening of the air and naval forces required to support a Dodecanese invasion.*

Turkey could bring 46 divisions and well placed air bases to the Allied cause. This could threaten the whole of Germany's flank in south-east Europe. Control of the Dardanelles and Bosphorus would open an easier southern supply route to Russia than the dangerous and costly Arctic convoys.

However, Churchill failed to convince the Americans, who feared that such a venture might slow the advance in Italy and even divert forces destined for the invasion of north-west Europe.

---

*General Order No.20, 17 February 1943, by General Eisenhower. AHB narrative C/N11. Sir Maurice Dean, in his work 'The RAF and Two World Wars' made the following observations: 'The Dodecanese: Italy surrendered to the Allies, after some dickering between Eisenhower and Marshal Badoglio, on 8 September 1943. Clearly, Italy was now ripe for the coup de grace. But in the meantime what about picking up a few quick Greek islands occupied by a mixture of Germans and Italians such as Rhodes, possessed of useful airfields, the gateway to Greece and the close neighbour of Turkey? The origin of this idea is difficult to state but in the light of subsequent events it is difficult to believe it was not British, perhaps Churchillian. It was certainly ill conceived. A few swift calculations rapidly disposed of the idea that we had the resources necessary to capture Rhodes. So what about Leros, Kos and Samos? No sooner said than done. By mid-September 1943 they were all in British hands. And a few weeks later they were back in German hands with nothing to show for the effort on the British side save unnecessary casualties. It is difficult to see how this blunder could have been permitted. No Allied air base lay closer to (say) Leros than 400 miles. The newly acquired bases in Sicily were over 600 miles away. Yet here was Rhodes, with its German air bases, less than 100 miles away. The capture of these islands was no doubt a possible military operation, though perhaps unwise, if only the necessary resources could have been spared from the assault in the mainland of Italy which was just about to start. They could not be spared and were not spared. American suspicions, wholly unjustified, about British motives in Greece and the Balkans ruled out the possibility of their assistance in this operation. This did not help, but was scarcely a deciding factor.'

Top: Beaufighter makes low level pass.
Bottom: Armourers at work. A Flight. From left, Mansfield, Donald, Robb and Cooper.

Left: LAC Ron Lee (right) in the Middle East. *Below*: Squadron Beaufighter.

The British were therefore left to go it alone, with woefully inadequate forces over extended, vulnerable supply lines, and insufficient fighter cover to achieve air superiority over the Luftwaffe.

Hitler, on the other hand, had no one to restrain him. Months before Italy fell he had declared that the Italian peninsula could be isolated but that the Balkans were of vital importance. On 28 July 1943, he had approved a contingency plan, codenamed Axis, against possible Italian defection. This decreed that if Italy fell, all Italian forces, all Italian warships, aircraft, military installations and equipment would be disarmed, and used by the Germans. Under the pretext of training the Italians, a strong, well-armed division had already been sent to Rhodes.

Reinforcements, including Messerschmitt Bf109 fighters and Junkers Ju87 Stuka dive bombers were brought into theatre and all hope of securing Rhodes was lost.

British forces, nevertheless, occupied most of the remaining Dodecanese Islands by mid-September, including Kos and Leros. They met with very little resistance from the Italian garrisons. There was a shortage of merchant shipping and troops had to be carried in destroyers and motorised wooden sailing vessels from Cyprus and Egypt. Cargo space was restricted and only light equipment could be taken. All convoys had to pass very close to the German stronghold of Rhodes. The nearest allied air bases were however, some 330 miles away in Cyprus and North Africa. The range was too great for single-engined fighter cover and the Allied ships had to rely mainly on the protection of slower, long-range twin-engined Beaufighters. These were no match for the Bf109s operating from nearby airfields.

On 7 October 1943 an urgent call for help came from the Royal Navy. The cruisers *Penelope* and *Sirius* and the destroyers *Faulkner*, *Fury* and *Rockwood*, codenamed Force Nostril had successfully attacked a German convoy on its way to the Dodecanese. This had stirred up a hornets' nest and the warships had come under heavy attack from Junkers Ju88 bombers and Ju87 Stukas. They were now fighting their way south at high speed towards the narrow straits between enemy-held Rhodes and Scarpanto. The British, who had underestimated the speed and strength of the German reaction, were dismayed, and also concerned, about the fate of their remaining forces in the Dodecanese. Naval reinforcements, including a cruiser squadron and eight destroyers, had already been tasked from the central Mediterranean, but these did not arrive until after the fall of Kos. It was recognised that the lack of long-range fighters had been a major defect in the planning of the operation, but General Eisenhower had refused to allow any aircraft to be diverted from the campaign in Italy. However, in early October, he allowed the transfer of six squadrons of Lockheed P.38G Lightnings of the 1st and 14th Groups of the 12th USAAF, part of the Northwest African Strategic Air Force. These began operations from Gambut III on 6 October, in support of the Royal Navy, and for a brief period proved very effective in repelling attacks by the Luftwaffe. The large, long-range, high performance Lockheed P.38G Lightnings successfully drove off the attackers, shooting down one and badly damaging another. Others were forced to jettison their bombs. Unfortunately the Lightnings' fuel ran low and they had to return to their North African base. Subsequent Lightning patrols failed to locate the warships and they were withdrawn from the area to attack airfields on the Greek mainland.

Despite the risk from Bf109s, two 603 Squadron Beaufighters were now tasked to protect the naval force. They located it, and having made recognition signals closed in, only to be met by intense anti-aircraft fire from the understandably nervous naval gunners. Eventually they succeeded in establishing their friendly intentions and orbited at a respectful distance.

The cruiser *Sirius* then picked up approaching enemy bombers on her radar on 7 October 1943 and directed the two Beaufighters to intercept them. Before they could attack, Bf109 fighters swept down through the broken cloud. F/Sgts J.P. Hey and E.A. Worrall in aircraft E were hit and later ditched, killing both crew. Hey and Worrall have no known graves and are commemorated on the Alamein Memorial, Egypt. The remaining Beaufighter managed to return safely to base. *Penelope* was hit by dive bombers but all the warships eventually reached harbour.

603's next sortie into the Aegean was more successful when, on 19 October, Flight Lieutenant 'Joe' Walters and Warrant Officer F. Burrow led two aircraft from neighbouring 227 Squadron as escort to four B.25 Mitchell bombers. To the north of Crete the formation found a small enemy convoy escorted by an Arado Ar196 floatplane. A Dornier Do24 flying boat was taxiing alongside. Both aircraft were destroyed by the Beaufighters and the ships were damaged by cannon fire and bombs.

A convoy of caiques and three landing craft escorted by an armed trawler were attacked and the trawler damaged.

On 20 October, 603 escorted B.25 Mitchells in an attack on a 2,000-ton steamer and an F lighter (*marinfahrprahm* – naval ferry barges) at the entrance to Port Kalymnos.

Kos and Simi had already fallen to the German counterattack, and the loss of Antimachia airfield on Kos meant no more single-engined fighter cover. In a desperate attempt to relieve the pressure on the beleaguered Allied forces, 603 were thrown into a series of offensive strikes, which involved them in sustaining a number of casualties.

Winston Churchill now accepted Eisenhower's view:

I have now to face the situation in the Aegean. Even if we had decided to attack Rhodes on 23rd, Leros might well have fallen before that date… I propose therefore to tell General Wilson that he is free, if he judges the position hopeless, to order the garrison to evacuate by night taking with them all the Italian officers and as many other Italians as possible as well as destroying the guns and defences …I will not waste words in explaining how painful this decision is to me.*

On 24 October S/L Atkinson, together with F/O Dalziel and F/Sgt Eacott escorted three B.25G Mitchells on an offensive reconnaissance sortie. A small supply ship was damaged. Atkinson and Sgt E. Wimburger were hit by anti-aircraft fire but returned safely to base.

On 25 and 26 October, 603 escorted B.25G Mitchells in attacks on shipping at Kos and on the 27th there was a raid on Kos' Antimachia airfield when several Ju52 transport aircraft, which had just landed, were damaged and the disembarking troops attacked. Spitfires, which had been abandoned by the retreating British forces, and which the Germans were now trying to make serviceable, were also attacked.

Further raids took place on 28, 29 and 30 October. On the latter two Beaufighters of 47 Squadron, combined with two Mitchells in an attack against Naxos harbour. One Mitchell and one Beaufighter were shot down. The Beaufighter crew of F/O W. Hayter of 47 Squadron and W/O T.J. Harper of 603 managed to evade capture and eventually returned to their squadrons.

Because the runway at Gambut III was unserviceable due to bad weather, 603 operated temporarily from El Adem, some 40 miles further from their targets.

On 3 November 603 accompanied 47 Squadron torpedo Beaufighters in an attack on 13 landing craft and two E-boats.

Next day 603 flew two sorties. The first was an escort to two Beaufighters of 47 Squadron. The second was a four-aircraft cannon attack on landing craft at Kos. Hits were scored on all vessels.

On 5 November three torpedo Beaufighters of 47 Squadron, led by Wing Commander J.A. Lee Evans, were accompanied by a fighter escort of four Beaufighters of 603 led by Atkinson, on a strike against the invasion ships in Lavrion Bay, about 35 miles south-east of Piraeus. Two of the escorts turned back with engine trouble, but the remainder reached their objective. They located three merchant vessels and attacked in the face of intense and accurate flak. Lee-Evans dropped his torpedo from about 1,000 yards but his starboard engine was hit and set on fire. One torpedo was seen to be running accurately and a column of smoke rose from one of the ships. No enemy fighters were present, but other Beaufighters were hit by flak and made the long return journey with difficulty.

A further strike took place on 6 November, when Squadron Leader Ogilvie led four more Beaufighters of 47 Squadron on a cannon strafe of shipping off Paros in the Cyclades. Accompanied by four Beaufighters of 603 Squadron, they swept in from the west and scored strikes on two large barges moored in Yanni Bay. Ogilvie was chased by Bf 109s and did not return. The remainder of the formation then tackled four caiques in the small port of Naussa. They silenced gun posts in the harbour and combats took place with eight Arado Arl96s. A Beaufighter of 47 Squadron was seen to be in combat with an Arado before crashing in flames on a hillside. The crew were killed. The

---

*Mediterranean and Middle East Policy for Middle East Operations - J8 2020 AHB/11 J8/90/15A and B, RAF narrative. Operations in the Dodecanese Islands, September/November 1943 (c) AOC 391 No.19 in File AOC/262/6.

The Australian crew of a 603 Beaufighter, P/O K.J.E. Hopkins and W/O K.V. Roger, shot down an Arado Ar196 and then ditched. Fortunately, they were picked up by a submarine and taken to Malta, returning to the Squadron a week later. The remaining five aircraft returned home, but one pilot of 603 Squadron, F/Sgt T. Truesdale in aircraft M was slightly wounded and made a belly landing at Gambut III.

On 7 November S/L Atkinson led eight 603 pilots to a position off Naxos, where they sighted 17 invasion barges and other vessels. They made two attempts to attack with cannons but both were broken up by approaching Bf109s and Arado Ar196s. There were no losses on either side.

The attempts to cripple the German invasion fleet continued daily. On 9 November there were two combined armed rover sorties. In the morning, four of 603 Squadron escorted two torpedo Beaufighters of 47 Squadron to Amorgos. One torpedo aircraft turned back when a hatch blew off and damaged the tail, but the remainder found ten barges and two schooners escorted by Junkers Ju88s, Arado Ar196s and single-engined fighters. The German aircraft attacked and the Beaufighters took evasive action, returning safely to Gambut III. In the early afternoon, more 603 aircraft escorted two of 47 Squadron to Stampalia and attacked a merchant vessel and escort. No results were seen from the torpedoes, but two Ar196s were shot down into the sea. All the Beaufighters returned safely.

Four 47 Squadron torpedo Beaufighters took off on an armed rover sortie on the afternoon of 10 November, escorted by nine 603 aircraft led by Atkinson. They located a small vessel to the south of Kos and one aircraft dropped a torpedo without results. An Arado in the water was hit by cannon fire, but then the formation was attacked by 109s. A 603 Beaufighter ditched with its starboard engine on fire but the crew, P/Os W.A. 'Wally' Eacott and W.B.F. Pritchard, survived to become PoWs. The remaining aircraft returned safely.

By the time 603 had reached North Africa, it was very cosmopolitan with aircrews from all over the Commonwealth. Later, Wally Eacott recalled:

The Empire was well-represented by the aircrew on the Squadron! We heard that the Lord Provost of Edinburgh wasn't too pleased that Scotland was in the minority in that respect. We had English, Canadian, South African and Australian. Only one Scot, and his name was Sergeant R.C. Scott a Navigator who flew with Squadron Leader H.K. Laycock; both were killed after being shot down at Missolonghi in Greece on 26 August 1943.

We had some marvellous characters among the true Squadron ground crew. Chief among them was Warrant Officer Prentice, the classical 'dour' Scot who ruled with an iron rod, his son was an airman with 603 too. Flight Sergeant Gillies was another old Squadron member – truly the backbone of the Squadron.

My trusty old 'Z' for Zombie (Mk.VI) was shot up on 9th November 1943, when I had a (head-on) confrontation with Arado 196 seaplanes in the Aegean, doing their own convoy escort. I bagged one Arado and damaged the other. I had damage to aileron controls, and the next day had to use a newly-delivered aircraft for our next trip, along with about 5 mates. Somewhere north of Crete and west of Scarpanto, we were attacked by six ME109F's (we were flying at sea-level). We turned to flee, of course, discretion being the better part of valour, and a Beau being no match for a 109. To my dismay, I found my new aircraft exceedingly slow. My mates quickly shot away from me at a receding speed of 30-40 knots, and the ME's quickly shot at me, taking turns to sit on my tail and use me for target practice. All the jinking in the world only put off the inevitable. My valiant observer potted away with his scare-gun from the rear, but after a long time we caught fire and I ditched.

We both survived the war in German prisoner of war camps. I was in Stalag IVB and had a miserable Christmas. Later, I exchanged identities with a soldier and went out to a working camp, from which it was easier to escape. After suffering bread-and-water punishments for the unsuccessful attempts, I finally got away before the end and made the American lines, where after interminable delays and some interrogations I was flown home.

On 11 November 1943, three Beaufighters of 603 Squadron, led by Atkinson, accompanied three 47 Squadron aircraft and two USAAF B.25Gs on a strafing patrol over the seas around the islands, but sighted no shipping. The German invasion fleet was nearing Leros on the following night (12 November) but was not located by Allied aircraft. The landings began at Alinda Bay in the east of Leros, soon after dawn.

Soon after mid-day on the 13th, part of the invasion fleet was located by four Beaufighters of 603 Squadron and four of 47 Squadron, east of Leros. The aircraft were fired upon, but the crews thought that the warships were British destroyers, which were known to be near these waters, and did not attack. A second strike force, consisting of two 47 Squadron torpedo Beaufighters and two USAAF B.25s escorted by six 603 Beaufighters, was despatched to a convoy off the north west of Crete. They located a merchant vessel of about 3,000 tons, with one large and five small escorts. The Mitchells attacked first, followed by the torpedo aircraft but no hits were recorded. One Beaufighter was shot down. The anti-flak Beaufighters of 603 Squadron raked the vessels and also damaged two Arado Ar196s.

The Germans now attacked Leros, one of the few remaining Allied outposts, with landing craft and Junkers Ju87 Stuka dive bombers. 603 undertook offensive sweeps to counter the German bombers.

F/Sgt Yates and his observer F/Sgt Whalley recall this period during which they flew offensive patrols daily:

> On November 12, Yates was part of an escort formation attacking ships in the Western Aegean when a merchant ship and two escorts were damaged by cannon fire, and two escorting Arado Ar196 float-planes were damaged. Four days later, as the Germans made further progress in occupying Leros, Yates took part in the attack against a convoy including a Siebel ferry and flak boats.
>
> The convoy, heavily escorted by fighters, was located about 3 miles (4.8km) west of Calino and the eight Beaufighters attacked with cannon before the enemy fighters could intervene. The ferry was blown up leaving only burning wreckage and large columns of black smoke, but four Beaufighters were lost in the ensuing fight. As the situation worsened on Leros, Yates and his fellow aircrew flew daily in search of shipping, and strikes were achieved against a number of supply ships. However, by November 20 the ill-fated Dodecanese campaign had been lost.

On 13 November, five torpedo Beaufighters of 47 Squadron swept the area around Scarpanto, accompanied by four Beaufighters of 603 Squadron and two Mitchells. They found no targets to attack, but one 603 Beaufighter reported engine trouble and ditched in the sea. The Australian crew, Warrant Officers F.M. Cox and N.S. Ferguson, lost their lives. They have no known grave and are commemorated on the Alamein Memorial, Egypt.

Another sortie, consisting of four torpedo aircraft, with five of 603 Squadron and two Mitchells, took off a few minutes later. After strafing some gun posts on Leros, they were dived upon by six Bf109s when they swept round the north east of the island, and a running fight ensued. The attacks were concentrated on the B.25Gs at the rear, but the American gunners managed to beat them off.

47 Squadron Beaufighters and B.25G Mitchells were again escorted by 603 on 15 November. Three Beaufighters found two German destroyers accompanied by four Arado Ar196s and four Junkers Ju88s and led the Mitchells to them where the B.25s damaged a destroyer with their effective 75mm cannon.

The defenders on Leros were fighting against heavy odds, while the enemy had the benefit of Junkers Ju87 Stukas to act as artillery. The dive bombers would have been easy prey for the Beaufighters if they had been able to get close, but in turn the Stukas were protected by German single-engined fighters. In the early morning of 14 November, four 47 Squadron Beaufighters led by S/L Powell, accompanied by three 603 Squadron aircraft led by S/L Atkinson, took off with four B.25s from Gambut III. They sighted bomb bursts on Leros and encountered hostile anti-aircraft fire, but otherwise found no targets and all returned safely to base.

During the later morning of 14 November, five Beaufighters of 47 Squadron took off from Gambut III with three 603 aircraft and three B.25s. They sighted two enemy warships about 30 miles west of Kos, escorted by two Arado Ar196s and four Junkers Ju88s. The B.25s attacked the warships, causing a cloud of black smoke and steam to rise from one of them, but the air combat was inconclusive. All the Allied aircraft returned to base.

On 16 November six 603 Beaufighters took off in the early morning, but two returned with mechanical difficulties. The remaining four attacked two Arados, shooting down one and damaging the other. All 603 aircraft returned to base. Later in the morning, one 603 aircraft took off, together with seven Beaufighters of 47 Squadron led by S/L Powell. They located a Siebel ferry and two barges near the island of Kalymnos, escorted by seven Ar196s and four Bf109s. The Beaufighters attacked with cannons, in spite of the air cover and intense flak, blowing up the ferry and damaging the barges. The formation was attacked by 109s and three 47 Squadron Beaufighters were lost.

That evening, the defenders on Leros surrendered and the Germans took about 3,200 British prisoners, together with some 5,000 Italians. Some of the Italian officers were executed. The German casualties had been extremely heavy, with over 1,100 of the 3,000 troops who had landed killed in the campaign. During the next two days the British evacuated Samos.

Thus ended the ill-fated campaign which cost 603 dear in dead and captured aircrew.

The Americans did not approve of the Dodecanese campaign and contended that a combined operation against Rhodes would take Allied resources away from the landings on the Italian mainland. Their view prevailed and the invasion of Rhodes was postponed. Most of the land and naval assets allocated to the invasion of Rhodes, under the codename of Operation Accolade, were withdrawn.

The outcome had always been inevitable. The Germans inexorably closed in on the small Allied enclave. Only ten weeks after the Dodecanese operation commenced, all Allied forces had been driven out of the Aegean.

No less than 20 German divisions were, however, compelled to remain in Greece and the Aegean, to repel any further Allied invasions.

CHAPTER 14

THE AEGEAN CAMPAIGN:
BEAUFIGHTERS AND ROCKET PROJECTILES
1943 – 1944

Since leaving its home base at Turnhouse in August 1940, 603 Squadron had led a nomadic existence, seldom remaining anywhere more than a few weeks. On 18 October 1943, midway through the brief, ill-fated Dodecanese campaign, the Squadron settled for more than a year at a place few, if any, of its members would have chosen. Ron Lee recalls:

> There are several rivals to the claim of being the dustiest place in the Western Desert, but in any list Gambut ranks high. About 40 miles east along the coast road from Tobruk there is a battered roadhouse by the side of which a rough track turns off to the south and within a mile zigzags up the side of the escarpment. At the top it reaches a wide plateau of which the only permanent features are a small stone blockhouse and a rough stone wall, built for heaven knows what purposes, beyond which lies a vast scraped landing ground littered around the edges with tents, trucks, gunpits and big piles of crashed German and Italian aircraft. The tracks that edge this landing ground have been cut up by traffic into a foot or more of fine dust which billows in a great cloud when even a solitary car passes that way; the wake of half a dozen aircraft taking off, as they do at short intervals, is a yellow blinding fog. This is Gambut.
>
> The track meanders on farther to the south, and soon zigzags up a second escarpment on top of which it crosses the desert railway and the wide, bumpy Trigh Capuzzo. Beyond lies another vast landing ground, some more tents, guns, trucks and some more aircraft. That is Gasr el Arid.
>
> On top of both these escarpments other tracks wander off in many directions, arriving now and then at other satellite landing grounds, each with its complement of tents, guns, trucks and aircraft, for a distance of 15 miles or more. Cap the whole thing with a burnished dome of sky, blow across it periodically a hot wind from the south laden with dust storms, mix the available water with equal parts of chlorine and mud, fill the tents with thousands of cheerful young men in khaki shirts and shorts (and with several million flies) and you have the home of 603 Squadron in the Desert Air Forces.

Gambut III was perched on the edge of a shallow escarpment some 10 miles inland from the Mediterranean. To the east, south and west stretched hundreds of miles of sandy desolation.

The nearest centres of habitation were Tobruk, 40 miles to the north west, and Bardia, 30 miles to the east. In 1943, neither could be described as a town. The ebb and flow of opposing armies had left them largely ruined. Over 200 miles to the north lay Crete and the Aegean over which the Squadron were now to operate.

The ground was uneven and the engineers had created Gambut III by levelling part of the desert with bulldozers. They had then laid a thin layer of tarmac to form a single runway and a perimeter track for taxiing. Although the bulldozers had produced a reasonably flat airstrip, they had broken up the compacted surface skin and exposed the loose sand underneath. Anything more than a slight breeze raised clouds of dust which hovered sullenly over the camp whilst the surrounding desert lay clear and unruffled. This provided a useful although hardly welcoming landmark for returning aircraft.

Gambut III.

The Squadron's lorries made their way from the coastal road and slowly climbed the escarpment. The weary, travel-strained ground crews scrambled down to commence erecting yet another camp. The two-man ridge tents were by now somewhat the worse for wear. Discoloured and patched, considerable ingenuity was needed to convert them into comfortable long stay living quarters. Camp beds and chairs were made of canvas stretched over collapsible wooden frames. Sleeping bags, blankets and great coats provided protection against the bitterly cold nights.

The desert-wise stood the legs of their beds in tins of oil to discourage climbing intruders such as scorpions, which also appreciated the warmth of blankets and a human body. The more determined insects climbed up the inside of the tent anyway and dropped onto the bed from above. The less adventurous sought refuge in boots and shoes. It became second nature to shake out footwear each morning before putting it on. A temperamental generator provided enough power to light a 40-watt bulb in each tent. By sitting directly under this it was possible to read or write a letter. Most tents had hurricane lamps and candles to supplement the lighting, and as an emergency supply in the frequent event of a power failure or breakage of a precious bulb.

A limited water supply was provided by tankers. Water for washing and shaving was rationed and stored in covered tins in each tent. Wash basins were canvas stretched over a folding wooden tripod. It was easy to recycle water by placing an empty tin under the basin. The used water gradually dripped through the canvas leaving powdery sediment behind. When the bowl was empty it soon dried out and the powder could be brushed off. The water was now reasonably clear and ready for use again. Wyndham Rogers, the Engineering Officer, devised an open air shower using a discarded wing tank, used engine oil and a hand pump. The only alternative was the Navy Club at Tobruk, some 40 miles away, which was very hospitable and had ample hot water.

Surplus clothing was stored in ammunition boxes, cases or kit bags, sealed as tightly as possible against the all-pervasive sand and exploring insects.

The messes consisted of marquees, joined together to form larger structures. Battered and torn after nine months of erection and dismantling, they provided little protection from the onslaughts of the desert. The valleys between the linked tents soon filled with sand and this inexorably found its way inside. The same was true of the heavy rain so frequent during winter months.

Latrines were set up at a reasonable distance from the tented area. These were simply long wooden frames over a row of buckets. Low canvas screens provided token privacy. The buckets were emptied and liberally disinfected each morning by Bedouin labourers. The more fastidious

Top: Jim Cooper and Ron Lee, El Adem, November 1943.
Bottom: F/Sgt 'Angy' Gillies, B Flight.

timed their visits immediately after this, when the atmosphere was more acceptable.

Flight offices, armoury, parachute, equipment and orderly room tents completed the encampment.

By the end of October 1943, 603 Squadron were installed at Gambut III with a full establishment of Beaufighter TF Mk Xs, fitted with rails for the rocket projectiles (RP), which were shortly to be introduced into the East Mediterranean theatre. Almost immediately a problem arose. The heavy rains undermined the thin tarmac runway and the airstrip became unserviceable. Aircraft and essential maintenance staff had therefore to be transferred to El Adem, near Tobruk until repairs could be completed. On 19 November, 603 returned to Gambut III to consolidate.

For the following two months the health of the CO, W/C Chater, deteriorated and he was diagnosed as having jaundice. On 2 December he was replaced by Wing Commander J. Ronaldson H. Lewis DFC who had arrived the day before. Ronnie Lewis was an experienced fighter pilot who had commanded a Spitfire squadron – 504 (County of Nottingham) Auxiliary Air Force. His first priority was to review tactics and training for the missions 603 would be called on to undertake.

Left: W/C J.R.H. Lewis DFC, OC 603 1 December 1943 – 15 June 1944.
Right: Ronnie Lewis (left) and fellow officer Jack Scott.

The primary objective of the Allied Air Forces in North Africa was to degrade the fighting capability of the German garrisons in the Aegean archipelago by attacking their supply lines. These included well defended convoys; large single supply vessels; landing craft, lighters, inconspicuous wooden caiques and Junkers Ju52 transport aircraft. The Squadron would also have to attack heavily defended ground installations, airfields and radar sites.

Secondary objectives were to include armed reconnaissance over enemy territory; escorting convoys, launches and other small craft carrying out clandestine operations in the Aegean; and when possible seeking out and destroying U-boats in the Mediterranean. The type of operation would range from set piece attacks by up to 70 aircraft on large convoys to single aircraft intruding over enemy airfields at night.

The aircrews, who had joined the reconstituted Squadron in February, had mostly reached the end of their tour of duty and were now being replaced. Many of the new crews were young – in their early twenties. They were, however, enthusiastic, and fully appreciated the skill and experience of their new CO.

The tactical problems were indeed formidable. To reach enemy supply lines and bases in the Aegean, the Squadron would have to cross 240 miles of open, often stormy sea. Directly across their path lay Crete – 160 miles long with mountains rising up to 7,000 feet. To the east of Crete were the almost equally mountainous islands of Scarpanto and Rhodes. To the north west was the heavily defended mainland of Greece. There were numerous airstrips in the Aegean, many housing the Beaufighter's most formidable opposition – the Messerschmitt Bf109 fighters. Enemy radar cover was adequate and improving, and fighters could quickly be scrambled to intercept any raid which it detected.

The answer to the radar problem lay in carrying out operations below the level of the radar screen – i.e. at an altitude well under 100 feet. Rather than fly over Crete, the Squadron would enter and leave the Aegean via the narrow straits at either end of the island. It was essential for aircraft to fly at the correct height. If they were too high, they would be detected by radar. If they were too low, their slipstream might leave a wake on the water easily seen by high flying fighters. If the water was very smooth, it was difficult to judge the altitude precisely and aircraft could, and did, fly into the sea.

Countering the menace of the Bf109 was more difficult. The Beaufighters were operating beyond the range of single-engine fighter cover, even of Spitfires with long-range tanks. The 109 had a speed advantage of about 60 mph over the Beaufighter. It carried between one and three 20mm cannon and two machine guns. The Beaufighter on the other hand was immensely strong and had even more formidable armament – 4 x 20mm cannon plus a free-firing rear machine gun.

W/C Ronnie Lewis had first-hand experience of the problems a fighter faced in attacking a skilfully handled, well defended enemy formation. His answer was for the Squadron to fly in a pattern, which permitted one section to cover another should it be attacked. A typical formation for an offensive sweep of four aircraft was two pairs each flying in echelon some distance apart. If one pair was attacked, the other pair was then in a position to make a beam to quarter attack on the Messerschmitts. The pair under attack would meantime break hard (i.e. make a steep turn towards the attack). The 109s were understandably reluctant to press on when they themselves were under attack by aircraft mounting a total of 8 x 20mm cannon. They invariably broke off temporarily, and the Beaufighters gained a valuable respite. A five-mile lead needed five minutes for the 109s to close up again. If the attack took place on the return journey as it often did, the Beaufighters were heading south over open sea, and the 109s with only one engine were reluctant to continue the pursuit too far.

Both tactics demanded high flying standards, and throughout the period of his command Ronnie Lewis insisted on regular low flying training in battle formation aimed at making good a definite line of escape. Locally based Spitfire squadrons willingly co-operated.

Whilst this intensive training was under way, it had not escaped note that Christmas was approaching. Consequently, Flight Lieutenant Joe Watters paid a visit to Air Headquarters Mediterranean and Middle East (MEDME) in Cairo. He returned in an aircraft laden with fresh fruit, vegetables and other delicacies.

Living in tents far from any centre of population, it was easy to feel very isolated. There were wireless sets in the messes but as their cabinets were usually full of sand, their sound quality left much to be desired. In mid December, a Squadron news sheet was started, edited by the Intelligence Officer, Lieutenant 'The Spy' Shaw (SAAF).

The week before Christmas 1943 passed fairly quietly. 603 and 227 Squadrons were tasked to intercept and attack a U-boat, but after 30 minutes they were recalled as the submarine had been identified as friendly.

During the early morning of 15 December, four rocket projectile (RP) Beaufighters, with four gun-armed Beaufighters acting as escort, took off on an offensive sweep in the western Aegean, thus becoming the first squadron in the Middle Eastern theatre to carry out an operation armed with rockets. Nothing was sighted and the aircraft landed after a five-hour sortie.

The Navy were understandably highly suspicious of any approaching aircraft and regarded their intentions as hostile unless they could be identified. On 20 December, 603 was tasked to escort a large convoy off Benghazi. The 33 vessels were located in a compact formation with three escort vessels. The Beaufighters approached cautiously and circled at a distance, banking slowly to show their silhouette – unfortunately not dissimilar to that of the Junkers Ju88. Colours of the day were fired from the Very pistols and the letters of the day flashed by Aldis. Only when all these signals had been clearly acknowledged did the Beaufighters slowly move into a closer orbit until last light.

On the 22nd 603 had its first opportunity to use RPs when four Beaufighters attacked caiques at Amorgos and Mykonos in the eastern and central Aegean respectively. The aircraft were Flying Officer Smith in N and Sergeant Gow in Q, each carrying 60lb RPs (explosive), Flying Officer Wilson in P with 25lb RPs (armour-piercing), and Flight Lieutenant Partridge with cannon only. The first caique, one estimated to be 70-100 tons, was hit by both 25lb and 60lb rockets and left sinking. The second, a larger, three-masted ship of 150-200 tons at Mykonos, received one direct hit with a 25lb rocket and numerous cannon hits. It was left with only one mast standing and badly damaged.

After a quiet start, further successes soon followed. Harold Yates and his navigator J. Walley were in action on December 23 when their formation of four aircraft attacked a two-masted 60-ton caique with rockets and cannons before proceeding to Naxos in the central Aegean where landing barges were attacked and damaged in the face of intense flak.

In December 1943 Pilot Officers Hopkins and Giles were awarded the Distinguished Flying Cross. P/O Hopkins' citation reads:

This officer is a keen and determined pilot, whose fine fighting spirit has been evident throughout his tour. On one occasion he took part in an attack on shipping in Naxos harbour. In the face of fierce anti-aircraft fire, the attack was pressed home with great vigour and two vessels were set on fire. Pilot Officer Hopkins is a good leader, whose efforts have been most praiseworthy.

P/O Giles' citation reads:

This officer has completed many sorties and displays high courage and great devotion to duty. On a recent occasion he took part in a successful attack on a Siebel ferry. In spite of fierce opposition, Pilot Officer Giles pressed home his attack with great determination, setting a fine example.

Dining hall in the desert, Christmas 1943.

Christmas Eve saw an attack on Monemvasia harbour in the face of light flak. Fortunately there were no casualties. Everyone waited somewhat tensely for the next day.

Notwithstanding the fact that the Squadron was in a tented camp in the Western Desert, Christmas Day 1943 dawned fine and in traditional style, turkey and plum pudding were to be served. Having been conserved for some weeks beforehand, there was even a generous supply. Four aircraft were placed on early standby. High level reconnaissance aircraft had been sweeping the Aegean but no worthwhile targets were identified. The CO was in benevolent mood, and no local training was programmed. The Christmas festivities could go ahead uninterrupted.

The fine, calm weather made its own contribution. Normally, plates had to be left upside down on the trestle tables until the last possible moment to prevent them becoming covered in sand. Tins of corned beef were opened only when everyone was ready to eat. No such problems arose on Christmas Day and despite the challenges of open field kitchens, the cooks excelled themselves. The ORB recorded :

> The seasonal festivities were upheld even though this year we were in the Western Desert and entirely under canvas. The airmen's 'Dining Hall' was attractively decorated and Christmas dinner was served to the airmen by the officers and senior NCO's. The menu was the proper turkey and plum pudding with additions of soup, fish, mince pies, nuts, oranges, cigarettes and a generous supply of beer; the latter beverage having been conserved for several weeks for the occasion. General opinion was that Christmas 1943 was the best ever.

Christmas dinner was equally enjoyable in the officers mess. A hitherto unrecognised artist drew a menu surmounted by the Squadron crest and showing a Beaufighter pursuing a small helmeted demon with swastika insignia. Below were palm trees and pyramids. The bill of fare read:

Cream of Tomato Soup
***
Grilled Sole with Butter Sauce
***
Roast Turkey
Pork – Apple Sauce Stuffing
Cauliflower – Roast English Potatoes
***
Xmas Pudding with Brandy Sauce
Mince Pies – Candies – Nuts
Coffee

TF Mk Xs of 603 Squadron photographed in early 1944.

The flaming pudding was solemnly piped in by Piper Blake. The dramatic effect was only slightly marred by the sagging mess tent, which compelled him to crouch at the valleys to avoid becoming entangled in the canvas.

The Christmas break was short lived. On the 26th 603 Squadron were out in force when nine aircraft in two formations took off for offensive sweeps in the central Aegean. Six aircraft attacked shipping and harbour installations at Stampalia in the face of intense anti-aircraft fire. The second formation, consisting of the other three aircraft, followed them in. On arrival they attacked a three-masted caique of 100 tons moored alongside a jetty, and two rockets fired from the first Beaufighter blew the vessel up. Yates fired all eight rockets at the jetty and 'obliterated it in spray and debris'. The three aircraft came under intense anti-aircraft fire but escaped undamaged.

The days following Christmas were very dry, and the strong winds whipped up continual sandstorms. Eyes coated with dust became very sore and it was difficult to breathe. Hair was caked in sand. The men reacted practically. Large damp handkerchiefs were tied over mouth and nose, and gas mask cases were raided for plastic eye shields. Everyone longed for a shower of rain. The Fates were evidently in an obliging if somewhat perverse mood and days of heavy rain duly followed. Gambut III then became one gigantic great sea of mud as a result.

Flying was still possible so long as aircraft used only the runway. The perimeter track sometimes collapsed under the weight of heavy aircraft. The Beaufighters fortunately had an exceptionally sturdy undercarriage and damage was usually slight. However, these incidents could disrupt carefully timed operations.

On 30 December there was an offensive sweep over Tilos, Rhodes harbour, Symi and Stampalia. Heavy flak was encountered at Rhodes and Stampalia and light flack at Symi.

It had been known for sometime that the merchant vessel *Leopardi* was loading in Piraeus, would sail probably for Crete or Rhodes and was bound to be heavily defended. A strike was tasked for New Year's Day 1944, but since no confirmation of sailing was received from Intelligence, the sortie was cancelled. Whilst no one minded being briefed for an attack, however dangerous, it was a severe strain to sit waiting hour after hour, sometimes for several days, for the go-ahead to be given.

Despite bad weather which severely restricted flying, the Squadron carried out offensive sweeps on 6, 12 and 14 January.

603 suffered its first casualty in the Aegean campaign on 16 January 1944 when Flight Lieutenant A.P. Pringle led a formation of four aircraft on a very long sortie against the harbour installations at Khio, an island north of Samos. Flight Lieutenant G.W. MacDonnell flying in aircraft N with Flying Officer S.W. Piner, ran into the debris of an explosion and ditched not far from the Turkish coast.

F/O Piner, missing in the Agean January 1944.

Piner was seen in a dinghy, with MacDonnell swimming towards him in the calm sea. The other aircraft circled and dropped their own dinghies and other floating supplies nearby. The survivors waved and the Squadron confidently awaited news of their rescue or return. No word was ever heard of them. MacDonnell is buried in Phaleron War Cemetery in Greece and Piner has no known grave but is commemorated on the Alamein Memorial, Egypt. Aircraft H, flown by F/L Pringle, was damaged but led the rest of the formation back to base.

The desert continually surprised everyone by its constant change of mood. The rain suddenly stopped and the surface dried, and it was once again possible to set out on foot to explore the camp's surroundings. The rainfall had miraculous consequences – one small sheltered watercourse led down the escarpment towards the sea. The whole valley was carpeted with fresh green grass, and at the bottom were masses of flowers of all shades from exotic purple blossoms to drifts of little yellow and white daisies. It seemed like a long forgotten corner of England after the everlasting waste of sand and rock.

In the eastern Mediterranean, the Beaufighter squadrons needed to regroup after their heavy losses over the Dodecanese Islands and Samos in the latter part of 1943. By January 1944, four anti-shipping Beaufighter squadrons remained in the area: 227, commanded by Wing Commander J.K. Buchanan, at Berka III in Libya; 47, commanded by Wing Commander W.D.L. Filson-Young, at Gambut III in Libya; 603, commanded by W/C Ronnie Lewis, also at Gambut III; and 252, commanded by a Canadian, Wing Commander P.H. Woodruff, at Mersa Matruh in Egypt. Of these, 603 Squadron had, as noted, converted to rocket projectiles during the latter part of 1943 and 252 Squadron were in the course of converting on to them. 47 Squadron were still equipped with torpedoes, while 227 Squadron continued in the fighter/bomber role.

The rockets 603 had been equipped with could be fitted with either 60lb explosive or 25lb armour-piercing heads. They were fired manually in four pairs, or by a device nicknamed 'Mickey Mouse' which fired a timed salvo, theoretically giving a spread across the target. For an attack on a large vessel, both 25lb and 60lb heads were loaded onto the same aircraft. The object was to aim the armour-piercing heads just short of the vessel, thus hitting the hull below the water line. The 60lb heads would be fired immediately after and aimed above the water line at the superstructure and any guns. This was not an easy task. With cannon, the pilot could observe the fall of shot and make necessary corrections. With rockets, he had no such opportunity. The last pair was in the air before the first had struck. No one in the eastern Mediterranean theatre had any experience of rockets and the accuracy of their use was a matter of trial and error.

During this time it was 603 Squadron that pioneered the use of rocket projectiles in this theatre of war. Flying Officer King, a navigator, was on 603 Squadron at this time and recalls:

In 1943 I was trained on rocket projectiles being fired from Beaufighter aircraft and in November 1943, I was posted to 603 Squadron at Gambut in the Western Desert because it had been decided to convert the squadron to rocket firing. The rockets were either 25 lb armour piercing (and having an underwater trajectory) or 60 lb high explosive (HE) heads. The Squadron trained for two weeks firing rockets at wrecks in the Tobruk area with later operational training in the Aegean Sea beginning on 15 December 1943. This was the first time for rocket projectiles to be carried on operations in the Middle East. A formation of eight Beaufighters led by Wing Commander Ronaldson Lewis went on an offensive sweep around the islands of Seriphos, Thermia and Melos. Two Me109s were sighted but no shipping was encountered. On 23 December strike sorties were undertaken against shipping at Leros and Samos. My log book notes read 'sighted one Arado 196 float plane at Leros and destroyed it with cannon fire. Heavy flak at Leros and Samos'. During this period the squadron also undertook convoy escort duties, including convoy Blanket on 29 December which comprised 28 motor vessels, one tanker, six naval escorts and one cruiser.

The Squadron continued its maritime strike role attacking ships and harbours by night and day with great success until 13 February 1944 when 603 flew to Shallufa in the Suez Canal Zone for additional training. The strategy was to keep attacking Luftwaffe airfields on Crete and shipping in harbours in the Aegean Sea with the objective of creating the possibility in German minds that an attack on the soft underbelly would be made through Greece. The German garrisons became beleaguered and supplies were not getting through. On 6 May 1944, four Beaufighters escorted by Spitfires of 94 Squadron attacked a German Leonda radar site on Crete and destroyed it. This enabled allied aircraft to approach Crete undetected thereafter. It was known that in Greece a German convoy was being assembled to make a determined effort to reach Crete with essential supplies.

F/O King left 603 Squadron on 22 June 1944 after 40 operational sorties. John Saunders also recalls the conversion to rocket projectiles:

I was posted to the Squadron in August 1943 as NCO I/C the electrical section, and remained with it until 27 November 1943. During this time we were equipped with cannon-equipped Beaufighters and based at Gambut III and moved to a place just outside Tripoli. The Squadron took part in the invasion of Sicily, although I missed that being sick with malaria in Tripoli. I was heavily involved modifying the gun-firing system to adapt for single and salvo rocket firing. A Flight Lieutenant Pringle was the pilot who test flew the system and he would take me on his test runs (firing dummy rockets at the sunken shipping in Tobruk harbour) standing behind his seat; not a pleasant experience when climbing to avoid the effect of our own rocket strikes.

I remember I eventually adapted a bomb distributor system to be able to fire in pairs at preset intervals. The modification was approved by the Air Ministry and re-issued with my wiring and re-wiring diagrams as an official modification for all Beaufighters.

On 24 January, four aircraft led by F/L Pringle in aircraft A carried out an offensive sweep over the Kithera – Serephos – Thermia – Syros – Siphonos – Milos area. A 200-ton caique was encountered off Thermia and, in the first operational use of RP using radar ranging, it was hit and left sinking.

Poor weather was limiting operations during the first weeks of the New Year, but offensive sweeps were launched when possible and limited success was achieved. Sergeants Yates and Whalley scored further success on January 25, 1944 when they scored rocket and cannon hits on a 100-ton caique near Samos, but came under intense and accurate light anti-aircraft fire from shore batteries before they had to evade enemy fighters. They landed after a five-and-a-half-hour sortie.

On 27 January 1944, 603 scored one of their biggest successes to date in the Aegean campaign. Four aircraft took off on an offensive sweep over the islands of Syros and Mykonos led by F/L Pringle in aircraft H, Warrant Officer Spooner in aircraft C, Flight Sergeant Rooks in aircraft B and Flight Sergeant John Edgar in aircraft K.

Near Kithera they encountered three Junkers Ju52 float-planes escorted by three Arado Ar196 float-planes. Two Ju52s were quickly shot down in flames and the third ditched near the island of Delos. Despite spirited resistance, the three Arados were also destroyed, but not before they had damaged aircraft B flown by Rooks with Thom.

The formation shepherded Rooks back to within 40 miles of the North African coast before his aircraft finally ditched. Distress calls were sent to nearby direction finding (DF) stations and the position pinpointed. Both occupants appeared to be safe and waved to the circling aircraft. For three days, the Squadron and Air Sea Rescue units searched the area but no trace of the crew was ever found. Alan Rooks and Robert Thom have no known graves and are commemorated on the Alamein Mermorial, Egypt.

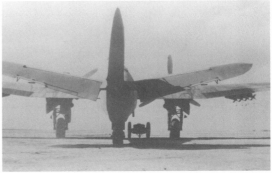

Top: A. Dornier Do24 brought down north of Crete during a sweep.

Middle left: Beaufighter TF X, Gambut. Note rocket rails under wings.

Middle right: Beaufighter FF X, Gambut, 1944.

Left: In the first six months of 1944, the Squadron's TF Mk Xs fitted with extra tanks had an endurance of eight hours. Every airfield and port in northern Greece came within range.

This incident had a surprising sequel. Almost exactly ten years later, on 22 January 1954, Mr T. Russell, a British resident in Herford, West Germany, was visited by a local architect, Herr Hermann Cremer. Herr Cremer explained that he had been the pilot of a Junkers Ju52 shot down in the Aegean and that as a token of reconciliation he wished to present a silver cigarette box to the RAF unit concerned. The gift was received by Squadron Leader Roy Schofield who was then commanding 603 at Turnhouse, and it is now in the National War Museum of Scotland in Edinburgh Castle on loan from the current 603 Squadron (see pages 319-320).

It was 40 years after the event that Herr Cremer kindly explained the reasons for his action. He wrote that he was leading the formation of Junkers Ju52s, each of which contained 21 German soldiers. After the first aircraft was shot down, he took evasive action but was hit and had to ditch at 220km per hour. With the burning wreckage of the formation scattered all round them, 11 survivors scrambled into dinghies. The Beaufighters swept low over them and Oberfeldwebel Cremer waited for them to open fire. Instead the Beaufighters flew off and the survivors were, he says, filled with new hope and gratitude. They reached a neighbouring island where they lived frugally with a shepherd for some days before being picked up by a German naval cutter.

On 30 January 1944, a combined attack took place when Wing Commander Filson-Young led six torpedo aircraft and two anti-flak Beaufighters of 47 Squadron and six Beaufighters from 603 Squadron led by F/L A.P. Pringle in aircraft H, in an attack on a small convoy off Melos consisting of a merchant vessel of about 2,000 tons being led by a U-boat with two flak ships flanking. The convoy was also well defended from the air by Arado Ar196 float-plane fighters which, although slow, were very manoeuvrable and their formidable armament included 2 x 20mm cannon, one machine gun firing forward and twin machine guns free-firing backwards. As the Beaufighters approached, the anti-aircraft fire was intense. One 47 Squadron aircraft ditched in the sea. Aircraft A crash landed at Gambut II (El Adem), Flight Sergeant Tennant in aircraft C crash landed at Gambut III. F/Sgts Yates and Walley were again in action and their aircraft, F, was damaged and they were forced to divert to Gambut II where they landed safely. F/L Pringle landed safely but ran into soft sand. One supply vessel and a flak ship were damaged.

With the reduction in the number of large enemy vessels, torpedo attacks by 47 Squadron became increasingly rare. However, 603 Squadron provided six aircraft as anti-flak escorts and fighter cover on January 30 for two 47 Squadron torpedo-armed Beaufighters.

F/Sgt Yates' aircraft was armed with rockets and cannons for the shipping strike off Melos. Two hours after take-off at dusk, a convoy made up of a 2,500-ton merchant ship, an 800-ton sloop and two 500-ton flak ships was sighted. The formation leader attacked the flak ships, scoring cannon hits as the 47 Squadron Beaufighters dropped their torpedoes. Three Arado Ar196s attacked the formation, but Yates continued his attack against an escort vessel despite intense light flak. He scored cannon strikes before achieving three rocket hits on the bow of the 800-ton vessel from which a column of black smoke rose. As the formation left there was a large explosion amidships the merchant vessel.

In the final attack Yates' aircraft was hit by flak, but, despite being extensively damaged, he attacked and damaged one of the enemy Ar196 fighters. Both he and his navigator were wounded, but Walley was able to bind up the damaged and leaking hydraulic pipes as Yates struggled to reach El Adem where he made a successful night crash-landing. Both men were admitted to hospital and did not return to operations for almost two months.

At the beginning of February 1944 there was an incident which could have proved fatal. During an offensive sweep on 2 February, Flying Officer S.J.L Smith and Flying Officer Langford in aircraft S dived to attack shipping at Port Mazelo. The target was lined up and Smith pressed the firing button. One rocket exploded in the air directly in front of him and the other burst under the wing. The aircraft was badly damaged, but Smith managed to nurse it back across the Mediterranean to a safe crash-landing. The CO thereupon decided that more systematic trials should be carried out, and he detached an aircraft to Shallufa, a training airfield, at the head of the Gulf of Suez in Egypt. Royal Engineers quickly constructed a life-sized ship target out of oil drums set into a sloping sandbank and christened it HMS *Camel*. The crew then began an extensive series of tests. The critical factors proved to be range, angle of dive and the speed of the aircraft. Various combinations were tried from 6-800 yards in a 10-degree dive at 220 knots to 8,000 yards in a 30-degree dive at 240 knots. The Beaufighter was fitted with a primitive radar, which, if properly calibrated, gave very accurate forward ranging of between 600 and 1,000 yards.

Firing conditions and point of impact were faithfully recorded and the crew spent many hours drawing up graphs showing the optimum approach under different conditions. They returned with these to the Squadron and promptly designed an appropriate crest for their own aircraft. This was a shield bearing a rocket crossed with a slide rule. The quotation underneath was from Book III of Virgil's *Aeneid* 'Incerti quo fata ferant' (Uncertain where the Fates bear us), which seemed particularly appropriate for the Aegean across which Aeneas and his companions had sailed on their way to Carthage after the fall of Troy.

During an armed rover offensive sweep over Leros on 4 February, intense AA fire damaged aircraft J piloted by Flight Sergeant E.G. Harman. A good friend of 603, Wing Commander J.K. 'Butch' Buchanan DSO, DFC (Bar), CO of 227 Squadron, was shot down during a sweep on 16 February. Butch was last seen sitting on a floating fuel tank twiddling his moustache and making rude signs to the rest of the formation circling overhead. Sadly, he was found dead from hunger, thirst and exposure some days later. In addition to a large dinghy stowed in one wing, which was supposed to inflate automatically on ditching, crew members carried personal dinghies, fishing kit, rations, water, distress flares and various escape aids. There was also an air sea rescue (ASR) radio, allegedly buoyant, which had to be cranked by hand to send either automatic or manual signals on the distress frequency. The aerial was sent aloft by a metal-framed box kite. The problems of launching a wet kite from a small dinghy tossing about in a high sea and then coaxing it to a reasonable height can easily be imagined.

Whilst there were a number of amazing escapes by aircrews following ditching in the Mediterranean, many others were not so lucky. Supplies were often washed away by the impact of ditching and one officer had a leather belt specially made in Cairo with a series of pockets secured by snap fasteners. These contained all the items likely to be needed for short-term survival.

In the early afternoon of 22 February, three of the Beaufighter squadrons, including 603 made a combined attack against a target which justified the use of torpedoes. This was the merchant vessel *Lisa* (formerly the Italian *Livenza*) of 5,343 tons, which was known to have left Piraeus the day before, bound for Heraklion in Crete, carrying a mixed cargo which included heavy guns. Wing Commander Filson-Young led six torpedo-carrying and two anti-flak Beaufighters of 47 Squadron, escorted by eight of 227 Squadron and two of 603 Squadron. Six Beaufighters of 252 Squadron were also tasked to escort the torpedo bombers, but they missed the rendezvous. Four B.25G Mitchells participated, each carrying a 75mm cannon. The formation met the enemy vessel, escorted by two torpedo boats, five Junkers Ju88s, four Bf 109s and six Arado Ar196s, near the island of Dia on the north coast of Crete.

The B.25Gs drew off the Ju88s and 109s, and shot down two for the loss of one of their number. Meanwhile, the Beaufighters passed through heavy flak from Crete and then approached the convoy. The eight Beaufighters of 227 Squadron, led by Squadron Leader D.B. Bennett, and the two of 603 Squadron, led by F/L Pringle, attacked the escort vessels and shot down one of the Arados, but three 227 Squadron aircraft were shot down.

On 29 February 1944, 603 Squadron aircraft led by Pringle in aircraft H carried out an offensive sweep over the Santorin – Nios area. A large caique under the cliffs at Santorin was attacked with cannon. A 170-foot metal lighter was attacked in Nios with rockets and cannon and was left blazing. Photographic reconnnaissance later confirmed it had sunk. F/L Pringle's aircraft was slightly damaged by return fire.

As a relaxation for the men, the only practical sport was football, and every combination of match was played: flight v flight, airmen v NCOs, NCOs v officers, officers v airmen. There were few rules and no attempt at a league table. The CO would sometimes solemnly present large iron crosses to the winners.

Destroyer *TA15* (formerly *Francesco Crispi*), sunk 8 March.

Whilst the air crews could relax there was no respite for the ground crews. All servicing had to be carried out in the open, often in sand or dust storms. There were no well equipped workshops at hand. Men stood on upturned oil drums to reach engines and control surfaces. Each rigger and fitter was intensely proud of his aircraft. If an aircraft was unserviceable the day before a planned operation, the men would work through the night rather than let their crew fly a spare aircraft. Far from the eyes of the Air Ministry or higher command, there were endless huddled discussions between ground and air crews about ways in which performance could be improved. The direction finding loops were of little use in the Mediterranean and their plastic housing resulted in unnecessary drag. They were promptly removed! Surfaces were rubbed down and polished. The armoured doors in the fuselage were heavy and many felt that if their aircraft was hit, it might need careful nursing back to base. A lighter aircraft might be that much easier and certainly faster, so the doors were often removed. Endless modifications were made to the belts feeding the rear-mounted Browning which was gradually replacing the drum-fed Vickers gas-operated machine gun. A jammed gun during aerial combat could not easily be freed.

By 8 March 1944, the weather had improved sufficiently for the Squadron to try night intruding. The Beaufighter's ASV (air to surface vessel) radar was not accurate enough for attacks in complete darkness and some moonlight was necessary to give a good chance of success. The plan was to fly along the north coast of Crete to Heraklion and lie in wait until a Junkers Ju52 transport plane came into land. Once the landing lights were switched on, it should be an easy target.

F/L Pringle and F/O A.E. Ross in aircraft H were the first of five to take off in the late afternoon on their sortie towards the eastern end of Crete. Accurate dead reckoning navigation was essential to reach the narrow entrance straits: there were no radio or long-range radar aids. At length, the rocky promontory of Crete loomed up in the darkness and the Beaufighter turned along the coast flying as low as the night visibility permitted. The moon was rising and casting a long silver path across the quiet dark waters. The island of Dia could just be seen on the right when the radar showed traces of something on the water. The Beaufighter banked away in a wide arc down moon so that whatever was there would show up in the moon path whilst the aircraft itself would be in the darker part of the sky. The radar relocated its target and the cautious stalking began. Suddenly there were dark shapes ahead, two large vessels in line astern steaming towards the harbour. Once more the Beaufighter swung away, this time to make a carefully planned attack. The correct height was reached and the dive began with the navigator calling out the range as it closed. The 'Mickey Mouse' was set for a salvo and at 800 yards, the command 'fire' was given. The glowing rocket exhausts streaked ahead and a bright yellow light suddenly appeared on the leading vessel. The Beaufighter pulled sharply away to starboard to avoid silhouetting itself against the moon. As it resumed its attack position, flames were leaping high into the air from the doomed vessel. Another attack was now made on the second ship, this time with cannon since all the rockets were gone. Some hits were observed but the damage could not be assessed in the darkness.

The other four Beaufighters saw nothing in the area, and indeed two of them abandoned their patrols in the bad weather. It was soon verified by intelligence that Pringle had hit and sunk a destroyer. This was the German *TA15* (formerly the Italian *Francesco Crispi*) of 970 tons, armed with 4 x 120mm guns as well as 20mm flak guns. Pringle was awarded an immediate Distinguished Flying Cross. His citation reads:

> On very many occasions this officer has led formations of aircraft in attacks on shipping and has contributed materially to the successes obtained. On one occasion Flight Lieutenant Pringle led the squadron in an attack on six enemy aircraft all of which were shot down, two of them by this officer. Since then, Flight Lieutenant Pringle has gained further distinction by successfully attacking a naval vessel. The ship was set on fire and eventually blew up with terrific force. This officer has set a fine example of skill, courage and devotion to duty.

The long practice flights at Shallufa had proved their worth. Air Vice-Marshal T.A. Langford Sainsbury, AOC 201 Group, arrived next day to congratulate the Squadron.

During an armed rover sweep off south-east Greece on 17 March, W/O T. Truesdale in aircraft Z had problems with his VHF radio. He was escorted back to base by Sgt Gosling in aircraft X. They were plotted as hostile and Spitfires were sent up to intercept them. Fortunately the pilots' aircraft recognition was good and they decided that the target was friendly Beaufighters, not hostile Junkers Ju88s with their similar profile.

On 22 March, two 80-ton caiques were sunk during an offensive sweep over the Nios – Paros – Naxos – Amorgos – Kalimnos area. Only light flak was encountered.

The next shipping attack was on 30 March at Nios. The pilots encountered intensive light flak and Flight Sergeant J.N. Bowen in aircraft C was hit and force landed at base.

On 2 April, the AOC-in-C Mediterranean and Middle East, Air Marshal Sir Keith Park KBE, CB, MC, DFC, an old friend of 603 from Hornchurch and Malta days, flew in to congratulate the Squadron on the sinking of the German destroyer on 8 March.

Bad weather prevented further flying until 8 April when there was an attack on three Ems-class lighters in Karlovissi harbour. Sergeants Herbert Lacey and John Foster in aircraft B were hit by flak and ditched on the way home. An article in the *Sunday Telegraph* on 5 November 1995 described the experiences of John Foster:

> Foster, an ex-Lanarkshire police constable aged 22 in April 1944, was called up on February 13 1942 into the RAFVR and following aircrew training, with his pilot Flight Sergeant Bert Lacey, was posted to 603 Squadron based at Gambut in Libya flying Beaufighters in the maritime strike role in the eastern Mediterranean.
>
> April 8 was supposed to be a day off. Foster recounts 'I was watching the ground crew at work when Bert came up and said: Johnny, we're flying'. Our target was E-boats – small and fast, lots of nasty stuff on board – which had been sighted in Vathy harbour, Samos in the Aegean. After a quick briefing we were off.
>
> Flying low level, skimming the waves at about 180 miles an hour, the Beaufighter flew around the eastern tip of Samos, over a hill and down over Vathy harbour. Foster takes up the story 'We were at the back of the queue so it was pretty stirred up by the time we went in, the air was full of black clouds of heavy ack-ack. We just let off our stuff and got out.'
>
> After five minutes of the return journey the plane was hit. 'I noticed the tip of the port wing slicing through the water. Next thing we were in the water. Somehow Bert had turned a cart-wheeling crash into a ditching. Believe me, that was first class flying.'
>
> The heavily armed aircraft sank within seconds. As it went down, a rescue dinghy freed itself from the port wing and auto-inflated on contact with the water. 'I saw the dinghy, lifted the cupola and stepped into it. Didn't even get my feet wet.' Lacey, whose Mae West had been damaged, was not to so lucky. Foster heard him cry out then watched helpless as he

F/Sgt John Foster.

drowned some 20 yards away. He finds little consolation in the probability that Lacey was wounded: 'Bert's skill had saved my life, but I couldn't save his.'

Foster had a deep gash below his left knee which he bandaged with a dirty handkerchief. By holding up the dinghy's rubber apron he was able to sail before the north wind, and in this way covered more than 100 miles in three days. He eventually reached the coast of a small island, where he was towed in by a fisherman and given retsina wine and figs. Foster had interrupted morning prayers in the chapel on the island of Sirina. Sirina's entire population was there: an old man known as Barbayanni, three sons, a young woman called Maria, and a baby. Barbayanni sent one of his sons, whom Foster came to know as Tom, down to the water. 'Tom carried me up the hill on his back to the chapel, where the old man welcomed me.' The fisherman translated Barayanni's first words to the wounded flier: 'Yesterday I had three sons, today I have four.'

Foster could not have chosen a better land fall. Inhabited, yet too small to have its own occupying German garrison, Sirina was a well known bad-weather anchorage and hiding place for Greek resistance boats. German patrols from nearby Astipalea also called in from time to time, which meant it was safer for Foster to sleep in the sheep fold.

Sometimes Foster would go down to the sea to watch the youngest boy fishing, using gelignite from a sea mine that had floated in. 'Crazy! I always thought he was going to blow himself up.' After eight days, Captain Andreas Lassen VC* and his commando raiding party sailed into Sirina Bay, en route for Santorini (from their Turkish base near Bodrum) on the 20 April, and rescued Foster. As a token of gratitude to the Greek family who had risked their lives to shelter him, Foster gave Tom his broken watch and Maria, his precious wedding ring. 'I had nothing else to give', recounts Foster. Foster completed the war flying less dangerous sorties in the Mediterranean, returning to Glasgow in 1946. In 1995, Foster and his wife returned to Sirina to find and thank the Greek family.

No trace was found of Herbert Lacey who has no known grave and is remembered on the Alamein Memorial, Egypt.

On 9 April the night was clear and F/L Pringle in aircraft H set out on a night-intruder sortie over Crete. The aircraft found no shipping and it was decided to stand by off Maleme airfield in the hope of intercepting a Junkers Ju52. Nothing happened and H cautiously approached the airfield. As it reached the circuit the flare path lit up and red Very lights were fired. No other aircraft was in the area and the Germans presumably thought the Beaufighter was friendly. To dispel this illusion Pringle flew over the flare path and fired its 60lb rockets at the airport buildings.

On 11 April 1944, another Beaufighter was shot down when four of 603 Squadron investigated a landing strip being built on the island of Paros. Both the Australian pilot, Warrant Officer Edward T. Lynch, and the RAF navigator, Flight Sergeant Cyril L. Sykes, in aircraft L, were hit by flak. Lynch tried to ditch, but at about 20 feet one engine burst into flames. The aircraft stalled and exploded on hitting the water. They have no known graves and are remembered on the Alamein Memorial in Egypt.

---

*Major A.F.E.S. Lassen VC, MC, SAS, was killed on 9 April 1945 during a raid on the north shore of Lake Comachio, Italy. He is buried in the Argenta War Cemetery, Italy. Commonwealth War Graves Commission.

April 1944. Ken Tennant, Eric Harman (KIA May 1944), Al Burgess and Taffy Hopkins (KIA May 1944).

W/C Ronnie Lewis' insistence on practice formation flying and making good a definite line of escape was fully vindicated on 13 April.

Four aircraft were searching for a reported lighter when they were attacked by three Bf109s six miles south of Cape Matapan. The Beaufighters were in two sections of two, so that either could cover the other if it was attacked.

Sergeants R.T. Gosling and S.A. West in aircraft N were flying No.2 in the second section. Unfortunately it straggled out of formation and was promptly shot down by one of the enemy fighters. The other two 109s attacked the leader of the section, Warrant Officer T.J. Harper and Sergeant T. Cook in aircraft F, severely damaging the aircraft. Reginald Gosling and Stanley West were both killed and have no known graves. They are commemorated on the Alamein Memorial in Egypt.

F/L Pringle, leading the first section in aircraft H, then made a beam to quarter attack on the enemy fighters. As the leading fighter broke behind H it came under fire. Reluctant to face a resolute formation of heavily armed aircraft, the three 109s broke off the attack and headed for home. The Squadron were fortunate; three 109s operating a few miles from their base should have been quite capable of shooting down three Beaufighters operating at the extremity of their range.

Also on 13 April, 603 provided an escort to a motor launch for a clandestine operation into the Aegean codenamed Complaint. A number of attacks were carried out on Paros where suspicious construction work had been noted. In one, Flight Sergeant Gow in aircraft V was damaged by AA fire but returned safely to base.

On 16 April F/L Pringle in aircraft R had a lucky escape. Aircrew and ground staff were always working over their aircraft, trying to streamline and lighten them to get more speed. A constant source of argument was over the heavy armoured doors behind the pilot and in the tail. On this particular sweep aircraft H was unserviceable and another aircraft complete with doors was used. In an attack on an armed caique off Nios there was extensive light flak and F/L Pringle was hit by cannon and machine guns. He reached base safely only to find that a cannon shell had exploded in the tail section, but that all fragments had been contained behind the armoured doors.

In summarising operations for the month of April the Operational Record Book noted: 'A tendency has become evident for enemy caique traffic to use more northerly routes and as fewer vessels have been discovered at the former anchorages it has been found necessary to explore islands more distant than usual.' Besides being factually correct, this alteration in tactics offered material advantages to the Squadron. The more northerly islands off the Turkish coast could be brought into range if aircraft returned to Cyprus which was slightly nearer to these targets. They could then refuel before setting off once more for Gambut. They could also bring back eggs, fruit, fresh vegetables, brandy and Cypriot wines. It was easy to tell if an aircraft thus laden was coming back from Cyprus – the landing was so smooth that not one egg was cracked!

The Squadron ORB entry for April 1944 also noted that another base for Bf109s was being constructed in the Aegean.

> Early in the month a report that a landing strip was under construction half a mile north of Marmora village on Paros was investigated and obliques taken of the area. On subsequent visits the work has been subjected to cannon and RP attacks. It is felt strongly that every effort must be made to prevent completion of this landing strip in such a strategic position.

Paros lies halfway between Athens and Rhodes, almost in the centre of the Aegean. Fighters based there would pose a serious threat to any Beaufighter missions in the central Aegean.

Another threat to squadron operations was the presence of radar direction finding (RDF) stations on the southern ends of Crete. Looking south towards the North African coast they could detect all but very low flying aircraft approaching the Aegean.

On 5 and 6 May 1944, eight Beaufighters led by F/L Pringle, recently awarded the DFC (2.5.44), in aircraft H carried out Operation Blackeye against an enemy Wasserman RDF station at Palaiokhora on the south-west coast of Crete. The tower, buildings and gun emplacements were attacked with rockets and cannon (Wellingtons of 162 Special Duties Squadron subsequently confirmed that the station was out of action). As 603 were not operating as far as the Aegean, they had the luxury of an escort of Spitfires from 94 Squadron. There was intense flak of all types – 20mm, 37mm and .303. Aircraft D was damaged but returned safely.

Flight Sergeants Yates and Whalley recalled their participation in this operation:

> The marauding Beaufighter units had taken such a heavy toll of enemy shipping that the German troops on the Aegean islands were running short of supplies and all types of ships were pressed into service. The caiques would endeavour to hide during daylight hours and sail at night, but the Beaufighters ferreted them out with daily sweeps around the islands and night intruder sorties over the sea-lanes. Due to the earlier successes, many of these long-range sorties resulted in no sightings.
>
> With fewer ships to attack, 603 Squadron turned its attention to the main radar site in southern Crete when a large-scale attack, Operation Blackeye, was mounted on April 5 and 6 against the Wasserman and Wurzburg early warning radars at Palaiokhora and Leonda. Two sections of four aircraft, escorted by Supermarine Spitfire IXs of 94 Squadron, carried out the attacks.

Yates was flying in the first section and strikes by four rockets were seen to hit the base of the 30ft (37m) high Wasserman tower at Palaiokhora, while others fell near the Wurzburg radar and gun positions. The attack at Leonda by the second section was more difficult as the target lay close to a ridge of higher ground, but rocket strikes were seen amongst a group of buildings. The attacks were repeated the following day but the defences were alerted and a number of Beaufighters were damaged, though not before 40 rockets had inflicted further damage. Photographs and radio signal interceptions confirmed the success of the attacks. Yates and Walley, who had only recently recovered from his wounds and returned to flying, made a number of offensive sweeps throughout the rest of May, but targets were proving more difficult to find. On June 3 they flew their final operation together. As one of the most experienced crews on the squadron they remained for a few weeks passing on their knowledge and skills to the newly arrived crews.

Top left: 'G-George', a TF Mk X of 603 Squadron equipped with ASV radar and nose camera, taken in May 1944.
Top right: F/Sgt 'Binder' Yates.
Middle left: Beaufighter attacks the Wasserman RDF tower using RPs.
Left: Wasserman RDF tower at Palaiokhora, Crete. During operation blackout, 5 May 1944.
Bottom: May 1944. Result of the attack by 603 using RPs.

On the same day, Flying Officer Wilson in aircraft V carried out a search for a convoy believed to be leaving Portolago Bay. A destroyer was hit by rockets.

The night of 8 May 1944 was bright, and four aircraft were despatched at intervals to carry out intruder and sweep operations in the Syros – Andros – Melos area in the south-west Cyclades. One aircraft returned with its ASV radar unserviceable and another patrolled the area but made no sightings. The leading aircraft, flown by F/L Pringle DFC in aircraft W, located a convoy north of Syros consisting of one Surose lighter, one Ems lighter and six auxiliary ciaques of 60-100 tons. Pringle attacked down the moon-path using cannon on the Ems lighter. A violent explosion ensued and the vessel sank. A 100-ton caique was the next target and this also burst into flames and sank. The last attack was made on a 60-ton caique and this developed a 20-degree list. Low level shipping attacks at night by several aircraft could be very dangerous due to the risk of mid-air collisions. Conscious that three other aircraft should be following, Pringle guided the next aircraft C flown by Flying Officer Soderlund to the scene and continued on patrol. Six miles north west of Seraphos Pringle encountered another convoy consisting of one large vessel with three torpedo-boat escorts. This was moving at high speed and taking violent evasive action in an attempt to reach the safety of the coast. Pringle attacked, this time with RP and the last of the escort vessels was hit and dropped out of the formation. There was most intense and accurate light AA fire and aircraft W was slightly damaged. Pringle was forced to divert to El Adem as his base was fogged in.

In the meantime P/O Soderlund in C was wreaking further havoc on the first convoy. He attacked the Ems lighter with 60lb RP and a violent explosion followed. Air Headquarters Eastern Mediterranean described these attacks as 'an outstanding example of precision in attack and co-operation'.

On 13 May Flight Lieutenant Partridge led six aircraft in an offensive sweep over Naxia. There was intense AA fire and Partridge was wounded. He brought his aircraft back safely.

Next day Flight Lieutenant Simpson led four aircraft in an offensive sweep. They encountered three Arado Ar196s. Flight Sergeant Harrison damaged one, which was later destroyed by F/L Simpson. Flight Sergeants Blow and Simpson damaged the other Arados which escaped to safety.

On 15 May F/L Pringle DFC in aircraft R led four aircraft in an attack on the projected landing strip at Paros. On their way they encountered and sank a 100-ton caique at Tenos. The landing strip was not completed and there were no aircraft on the ground. Construction facilities were attacked in the face of intense AA fire. Flight Sergeants James E. Paddison and John C. Rhodes were in aircraft Q which was hit, broke into two and exploded on hitting the ground. Flight Sergeants Eric G. Harman and Leslie E. Hopkin in aircraft K were hit and disappeared, presumably into the sea. Aircraft C flown by Flight Sergeant John Edgar was damaged and aircraft R was also hit by extensive flak. Four Bf109s now appeared but the two remaining Beaufighters managed to cover each other and so made good their escape via Kaso. James Paddison, John Rhodes, Leslie Hopkin and Pilot Officer Eric Harman were all buried in the Phaleron War Cemetery, Greece. Harman's recommendation for a commission was approved after his death.

Other sorties during the rest of the month encountered no enemy shipping.

Gambut III, 1944. S/L C.D.Paine, W/C J.R.H. Lewis DFC and F/L A.P. Pringle DFC.

Top: 79 OTU, Nicosia, Cyprus, May to July 1944, navigators on No. 6 Course. Back row, on left, Frank Rolfe; next to him is Bert Winwood; on right is 'Geg' Richardson. Seated right is 'General' Lee.
Bottom: An Arado Ar196 climbs away from his 603 Squadron attacker.

Squadrons from many nations were now operating the Eastern Mediterranean. The RAF had Beaufighters of 47, 227, 252 and 603 Squadrons. 94 Squadron Spitfires and 213 Squadron Mustangs were available for escort duties. 162 Squadron Spitfires carried out photographic reconnaissance.

The South African Air Force provided 24 Marauders, 15 Baltimores and 16 Beaufighters. Australia was represented by the Venturas of 459 Squadron and the Baltimores of 454; and the United States Army Air Force by 310 Bombardment Group flying B.25 Mitchells armed with the formidable 75mm cannon. There were also several Hellenic squadrons.

The high degree of inter-operability and co-operation between these diverse units was graphically illustrated in a major operation on 1 June 1944.

By May 1944, the German troops in the Aegean were in difficulties, for their supplies were beginning to dwindle. Only 16 merchant ships, totalling 15,000 tons, remained seaworthy for supplying the Aegean islands, and during the latter part of the month caiques were prevented from leaving harbour by bad weather. The German naval command decided to make a major effort to re-supply Crete, by assembling in Piraeus the most important convoy since the island had been occupied. This convoy consisted of the merchant ships *Tanais* (formerly Greek) of 1,545 tons, *Sabine* (formerly the Italian *Salvatore*) of 2,252 tons, and *Gertrud* (formerly the Danish *Gerda Toft*) of 1,960 tons. These were escorted by four warships captured by the Germans from the Italians; the destroyer *TA14* (formerly *Turbine*) and the torpedo boats *TA16* (formerly *Castelfidardo*), *TA17* (formerly *San Martino*) and *TA19* (formerly *Calatafimi*). In addition, four heavily armed UJ-boats reinforced the torpedo boats, as well as R-boats. The whole convoy set sail on the evening of 31 May, bound for Heraklion. Air cover was provided by Arado Ar196s and Junkers Ju88s at dawn the following morning.

The RAF was fully aware of the composition and cargo of the convoy, from intelligence decryptions and aerial reconnaissance. The anti-shipping strike force detailed to attack 'the June 1st convoy', as it became known, was the largest of its type gathered by the Allied air forces during the war in the Mediterranean. Two waves took off to launch their attacks when the convoy was approaching its destination. The first consisted of 12 Marauders of 24 (SAAF) Squadron, together with 18 Baltimores of 15 (SAAF) Squadron and 454 (RAAF) Squadron. They were escorted by 13 long-range Spitfires of 94 and 213 Squadrons, together with four Mustang IIIs with which 213 Squadron was being equipped. This force interdicted the convoy when it was about 30 miles north of Heraklion, and went into the attack. Bombs from the Baltimores hit the afterdeck of *Sabine*, which was leading the convoy, while others fell around the UJ-boats. The Marauders' bombs fell just ahead of *Sabine*. A Baltimore of 454 (RAAF) Squadron was shot down.

The Beaufighter force would meantime enter the Aegean at low level through the straits between Crete and Scarpanto. They would then fly west along the coast and strike the convoy just after the bombing attack, when there would be maximum confusion. Four Beaufighter squadrons were involved – 252, 227, 16 (SAAF) and 603, a total of 34 Beaufighters.

Five minutes after the first strike the Beaufighter force came out of the sun to attack with rockets and cannon. The formation was led by Wing Commander Meharg of 252 Squadron at the head of ten of his squadron, two of which were in the anti-flak role. They were accompanied by eight 603 Squadron aircraft led by F/L Simpson and F/Sgt Bunn in aircraft O. They included F/Sgts R.M. Atkinson and D.F. Parsons in aircraft F; F/Sgts Cook and Blow in R; F/O Soderlund and F/Sgt Nicol in W, F/Os Thame and King in K; F/Sgts Pennie and Hinde in M; F/Os Hartley and Vaughan in S and F/Sgts Harrison and Dibbs in X. Take-off had been at 1635hrs, and the convoy was located 27 miles north of Chania at 1900hrs. Four Beaufighters of 16 (SAAF) Squadron were also in the anti-flak role, with two of 227 Squadron as fighter escorts. Flak hit Meharg's Beaufighter before he reached the convoy, and the aircraft dived into the sea beside one of the ships, with a wing on fire. He was subsequently taken prisoner of war. Aircraft F of 603 Squadron was also hit, and both Ronald Atkinson and Dennis Parsons lost their lives. They have no known graves and are commemorated on the Alamein Memorial, Egypt.

In 16 (SAAF) Squadron, a Beaufighter crewed by Captain E.A. Barrett and Lieutenant A.J. Haupt was seen to head south with the port propeller feathered, but the men made a successful force-landing on Crete and were taken prisoner. The two 227 Squadron Beaufighters tackled the Arado Ar196s.Flight

Top: Pat Pringle's Beaufighter H, NE400. Note long nose aerial plus large camera fairing. Repairs and overhaul, Gambut 1944.
Bottom: Beaufighters being serviced at Gambut. The desert conditions were harsh on the aircraft, with engines and tyres being especially vulnerable. F/O Rogers and F/Sgt Wilkinson are in the centre of the photograph.

Sergeant F.G.W. Sheldrick climbed from 200 feet and shot down one of them. The other, crewed by Flying Officers J.W.A. Jones and R.A.R. Wilson, came down off the north-east coast of Crete on the return journey. Jones was taken prisoner, but Wilson was reported as 'safe in friendly hands'.

The effect of the attack by the Beaufighters on the convoy was little short of devastating. *Sabine* was hit several times and set on fire, as was *Gertrud*. The upper works of *Tanais* were so severely damaged that some of her crew jumped overboard. The escorts also suffered from the rockets and cannon fire. Two UJ-boats were hit – burning fiercely, *UJ2105* capsized and sank at 1920 hours. *UJ2101* went down ten minutes later. The torpedo boat *TA16* was so badly damaged that she was almost incapable of steering. The merchant ship *Tanais*, with blackened superstructure, reached the inner harbour of Heraklion at 2210 hours, as did the shattered *TA16*, but nine Wellingtons of 38 Squadron attacked the harbour at 2250 hours, causing much destruction and setting fuel dumps on fire, with the loss of one Wellington. Meanwhile, the torpedo boat *TA19* had taken *Gertrud* in tow, but was relieved by a tug which brought the blazing merchant vessel into Heraklion at about 0400 hours the following morning. However, *Sabine* burnt out and was beyond assistance. She was torpedoed by one of the three serviceable German warships, which then departed for Piraeus.

The miseries of this German convoy were not at an end. Aerial reconnaissance during 2 June confirmed that a ship was burning in Heraklion harbour, with other likely targets near her. Another bombing force was despatched during the afternoon, reaching the harbour at 1740 hours. This consisted of eleven Marauders of 24 (SAAF) Squadron, nine Baltimores of 15 (SAAF) Squadron, and two Baltimores of 454 (RAAF) Squadron. Bombs from the Marauders fell on warehouses and gutted them, while some of the bombs from the Baltimores struck the unfortunate *Gertrud* amidships. The merchant ship was still on fire, and she was carrying oil, ammunition and bunker coal. The bombs caused the fires to spread and, about 90 minutes later, the merchant ship exploded. Debris flew in all directions, causing further damage to the docks and the city. The damaged torpedo boat *TA16*, which was berthed nearby, also caught the force of this explosion and sank in harbour. All the bombers returned safely. The only merchant vessel in this ill-fated convoy to survive the aerial onslaught was *Tanais*, albeit damaged. However, she did not last long, for she was sunk by a British submarine on 9 June when returning to Piraeus.

SS *Gertrud*, sunk by 252 Squadron showing the power of a rocket attack.

Top: 603 Squadron, June 1944, Gambut. *Bottom:* 603 Squadron Beaufighter and Squadron members, Gambut 1944.

On 2 June, Air Marshal Park AOC 212 Group passed on a message which read :

Air Marshal Park sends congratulations to all Squadrons which took part in the most successful attack on enemy convoy north of Crete yesterday evening, June 1st. The Baltimores that hung on to the convoy throughout the day in spite of fighter opposition deserve special mention. The whole attack by bombers, Beaufighters and their fighter escort was first class and showed excellent teamwork by all Squadrons.*

The rest of June passed quietly. There were a number of offensive sweeps and night-intruder operations but no targets were seen.

On 17 June 1944, Wing Commander Ronnie Lewis left the Squadron. On the eve of his departure, Lewis thanked both ground and air crews in a Special Order of the Day which read :

On the eve of my departure from our famous 603 Squadron, I wish to tender my sincerest thanks, and high regard, to everyone who has served with me during the last 7 months.
    To all my ground staff, who, working under the worst possible conditions on one of the worst airfields in the desert, have produced the highest serviceability beyond compare. At all times there has been efficiency, co-operation, hard work and above all cheerfulness throughout the Squadron.

---

*From HQ 212 Group Signal No A401 dated 2 June 1944, AHB.

Ju52 shot down off Syros on 4 July, with the starboard engine on fire. The aircraft burned out on the surface and was carrying the governor of the central Aegean and staff. None survived.

Without this wonderful Squadron spirit, the terrific successes waged against the enemy in the Aegean, would have been impossible.

To my air crews words fail me. High fighting quality, the ability and keenness to seek out and destroy the Hun, the highest morale and comradeship have always predominated. This can only be borne out in the results; results which bear no comparison with any other Squadron in the Middle East.

603 Squadron has a tradition to uphold which has been upheld in no small manner. Those of us who will not now be the watches look to our new comrades to continue in that spirit.

Again to all of you, I thank you very sincerely and, humbly, for the part you have played, however small. When our paths next cross, I can only hope it will be in our 'Ain' country.

Good luck and continued good hunting.

Under his leadership the Squadron had achieved many notable successes. On 15 June 1944, Wing Commander J.D.T. Revell assumed command. He had been posted in from HQ Middle East, having completed the RP course at 5 METS Shallufa.

July opened quietly with the Squadron covering a clandestine operation codenamed Operation Scrumdown. On 4 July, F/L Simpson dealt a useful blow to the German command in the Aegean. He was leading a section of two aircraft just west of Syros when he sighted a Junkers Ju52 float-plane flying due east at about 50 feet. As the Beaufighters turned to make a stern attack, the enemy dropped as if to take cover in thick mist along the coast of the island. Both aircraft attacked and crew and passengers leapt into the sea. The Ju52 careered on and burst into flames. Intelligence later reported that a seaplane carrying several officers including the governor of the Aegean had been destroyed.

This shot of an 'accident to the enemy' was taken on 4 July 1944. The Beaufighter must have been pretty low down to take it! At this time the Squadron was operating out of various airfields in North Africa, with Gambut as the main base.

Above: S/L Watters and J. Hindle (rigger) at Gambut.
Left: F/Sgt Dalziel and Sgt Davies (right).

On 5 July, whilst on a shipping sweep, the Beaufighters were flying low over the sea to avoid radar detection as was their operational tactic in the Aegean. Ten miles south east of Melos, Flight Sergeant Charles H. Dean and Sergeant Douglas W. Taylor hit the water. The aircraft bounced 30 feet into the air, crashed and burst into flames. Both were killed and have no known graves. They are commemorated on the Alamein Memorial in Egypt.

On 6 July 1944, Flying Officer Jack C. Dalziel RCAF was also killed on active service. He is buried in the Heliopolis War Cemetery in Egypt.

A shipping attack on 19 July ran into heavy flak over Fiskardhou. Sergeant Yorke and Flight Sergeant John G. Shaw in aircraft S were hit and crashed into the sea. Yorke was later reported safe but Shaw was killed and he is commemorated on the Alamein Memorial in Egypt.

At this time the two Beaufighter Squadrons, 252 and 603, were hunting the diminishing amount of supply shipping which was supporting the Germans in the Dodecanese. Sweeps were carried out, primarily against caiques, with some success and a few losses.

Seven aircraft from 603 and one from 252 Squadron combined on 21 July in an attack against a couple of small vessels east of Mykonos. AA fire was, as usual, intense. Aircraft R was hit and caught fire. It crashed into the sea killing Flight Sergeants Donald Joyce and Kenneth F. Thomas. They are commemorated on the Alamein Memorial in Egypt.

Three 603 aircraft were lost on 23 July, when six Beaufighters carried out a sweep in the central Aegean. Led by Flight Lieutenant A.G. 'Tommy' Deck, who had joined the Squadron for a second tour, they met several Arado Ar196s near Mykonos. In the ensuing air battle, the Canadian Warrant Officer L.F. Sykes and his RAF navigator, Sergeant W.H. Foxley, came down on the sea in aircraft H but were picked up by a British submarine. In the second aircraft, the navigator Flight Sergeant Jeffrey J. Rogers lost his life, but the pilot, Flying Officer K. Jenkinson, was picked up by a British destroyer after floating in his dinghy for over six days (see page 201).

The third aircraft came down in the sea with engine failure, the pilot having shot down an Arado Ar196. It was flown by Flying Officer Cas de Bounevialle, who had also returned to operational flying for a second tour. Bounevialle and his navigator, Flight Sergeant A.E. 'Gillie' Potter, were rescued from their dinghy by a Greek caique, which took them to the mainland south east of Athens. The RAF men were told to wait for partisans, but after four days nobody had arrived and they began to walk. When they at last made contact, the partisans took them to the island of Euboea, from where

Top: Gambut III, March 1944. From left, F/L Matthews, S/L Watters, W/C Lewis, F/L Oddy, S/L Paine, F/L Partridge, S/L Pringle and F/O Ross.
Bottom: A and B Flight commanders, F/O Pirie (left) and F/O Elvin at Gambut, July 1944.

a caique carried them to Izmir in Turkey. They were accommodated in the south of this town by a likeable English lady, 'Ma' Perkins, who ran a hostel for RAF internees somewhat on the lines of a seaside landlady, providing bed and breakfast. Restrictions were not severe during their short stay, and they were even able to visit the Kursaal nightclub. From Izmir, they were taken by rail to Aleppo in Syria and then flown to Cairo, from whence they were sent straight back to 603 Squadron at Gambut.

Flight Sergeant Pennie in aircraft C was also hit and he was seriously injured. Tommy Deck told Pennie to return immediately to base. F/O Jenkinson and F/Sgt Rogers in X were having trouble with the aircraft's fuel supply and were also told to return to base. Tommy detached another aircraft to escort them. After a while F/Sgt Pennie slowed down to conserve fuel and contact with his aircraft was lost. F/O K. Jenkinson, a 21-year-old pilot, had a remarkable escape. The starboard engine of X had been hit by flak. Jenkinson headed for base, but about an hour later the starboard engine gave up and the fuel feed to the port engine choked. Jenkinson brought the aircraft down, and flattened out on the water. The tail section broke off and the navigator, Rogers, was washed away and not seen again. Jeffrey Rogers has no known grave and is commemorated on the Alamein Memorial in Egypt. Jenkinson, with a deep cut in his forehead, which he bandaged with a piece of his parachute, inflated his own dinghy, and attached it to the aircraft dinghy so that they should be more easily seen from the air. With not a drop of water to drink and only two packets of chewing gum, a bar of chocolate and barley sugar sweets to eat, during the next two days aircraft passed almost overhead but did not see him. Several times he was thrown out of the dinghy into the sea. Having no water he rinsed his mouth out with sea water from time to time but did not drink it. On the seventh day he saw a convoy and, although in a dazed state, fired off his remaining distress cartridges. The convoy sailed on and he felt his last chance had gone. He had, however, been seen and HMS *Lauderdale*, one of the escorts, altered course and picked him up. He had been in the water six days and nine and a half hours. Jenkinson spent three days on the ship, a week in hospital and 14 days in a rest camp, returning to the Squadron on 28 August.

Although three aircraft ditched in the Mediterranean and one crash-landed at base, 603 were very lucky to have lost only one man from this operation.

P/O Bruce Megone examines his shrapnel-damaged mainplane.

Top: P/O Megone's shrapnel-damaged aircraft R.
Bottom: Best efforts but….the old rule still applies – any landing that you walk away from is a good one.

On 24 July 1944 it was announced that F/Sgt Harold Yates had been awarded an immediate Distinguished Flying Medal for his part in the action on 30 January. The citation reads:

> Throughout his tour of operations, this airman has displayed notable skill and great devotion to duty. He has completed very many sorties, including several successful attacks on enemy shipping. On the last of these an attack on a large merchant vessel, escorted by several naval vessels and a number of smaller armed vessels, Flight Sergeant Yates obtained hits on one of the smaller craft. In the fight, both Flight Sergeant Yates and his navigator were wounded and his aircraft was extensively damaged. Nevertheless, this gallant pilot flew safely to base and effected a masterly landing. He displayed commendable courage and resolution throughout.

High winds and rising sand prevented flying for the rest of the month. There was a tragic accident on 29 July when LAC Peter Richardson suffered severe burns in a fire which had occurred during aircraft refuelling. Flight Lieutenant Alastair MacLean, the Squadron Medical Officer, rushed him to hospital in Tobruk but he died next day. He was buried will full military honours on 31 July 1944 in the Knightsbridge War Cemetery, Acroma, Libya.

W/C Revell had only been with the Squadron six weeks but had never been fully fit. He was posted 'sick' on 2 August and Squadron Leader C.D. 'Boozy' Paine, Commander of A Flight, became acting CO. Many experienced crews had reached the end of their tour of operations and left the Squadron. During July 1944, 603 had lost six aircraft in the sea and one had been badly damaged. Besides LAC Richardson, six aircrew had been killed and one seriously wounded.

Disaster was soon to strike again. On 7 August 1944 during a practice rocket projectile firing, Flight Sergeant James W.H. Dibbs was killed by ricocheting fragments. He was buried with full military honours. Sadly, news came through a little later that he had been commissioned just before his death but he had not yet been advised. He too is buried in the Knightsbridge War Cemetery, Acroma, Libya.

Paine and Pringle.

A grim warning to the careless. The funeral of LAC Richardson.

Top: Gambut 1944. From left, Sgt Crooks, F/Sgt Burgess, F/Sgt Edgar, P/O Harper, F/Sgt Wood and Sgt Towsey.
Bottom: Gambut 1944. Beaufighters of 603 Squadron prepare to take off.

W/C Lewis (centre) and S/L Paine (right), Gambut III, 1944.

Much better was the notification on 8 August that Flight Sergeants Wilkinson and Moore had been mentioned in despatches and that F/O A.E. Ross had been awarded the DFC. Tony Ross had been F/L Pringle's observer and his citation reads:

As observer, this officer has taken part in very many sorties, including a number of attacks on enemy shipping, during which successes have been obtained. He is a gallant and resolute member of aircraft crew and his navigational skill has played a good part in the success of many operations in which he has participated. He has set a most inspiring example.

Because of the loss of aircrew and aircraft the Squadron were declared temporarily non-operational on 13 August, to give time for a full training programme for new crews.

John Edgar was awarded the DFM on 22 August 1944. His citation reads:

Flight Sergeant Edgar is a courageous and resolute pilot. He has participated in many sorties involving attacks on a variety of targets. On one occasion, he took part in an engagement against three enemy aircraft, all of which were shot down, two of them by this determined pilot. On another occasion, Flight Sergeant Edgar participated in an attack on a large fuel dump, which was set on fire. In several attacks on enemy shipping, Flight Sergeant Edgar has greatly distinguished himself, having assisted in the destruction of six supply ships, a small tanker and an E-boat.

603's ill luck continued when operational flying on a limited scale resumed on 30 August. Canadian pilot F/O H.W. Soderlund and his navigator F/Sgt I.L. Nicol in aircraft S took off on a night-intruder operation over the shipping routes north of Crete, but nothing further was heard of the aircraft. The Squadron assumed that both had been killed. It was only much later, after the war ended, that it was learnt they were both taken prisoner.

This loss was to some extent offset by the good news that two of the crews who had ditched on 23 July had been rescued. W/O Sykes and F/Sgt Foxley were reclassified 'safe' and returned to the Squadron at the end of August. F/O Bounevialle DFC and F/Sgt Potter had been picked up by a passing ship and were on their way to Aleppo. They rejoined the Squadron during September.

Below and bottom: Football match at Gambut, 1944.
Top right: 'Chiefy' Mackenzie.
Middle right: Veteran Sgt Angy Gillies (second left).

Top: The 'originals'.

Bottom: The German merchant ship *Carla* (formerly the Italian *Corse Fougier*) of 1,348 tons, under attack on 6 September 1944 south east of Athens by eight Beaufighters of 252 Squadron and four of 603 Squadron, led by Wing Commander Dennis O. Butler. The vessel was badly damaged but reached Piraeus, where she went into dry dock and was later scuttled as a blockship.

During August, the Germans realised that their hold on Greece and the Aegean had become untenable. Not only was it proving impossible to supply their garrisons on the islands by sea, but their lines of communication through the Balkans were harried by partisans and from the air. On 30 August, the Red Army entered the oil centre of Ploesti in Romania and this vital source of fuel was thereafter denied to the Germans. When the advancing Russians reached the border of Yugoslavia, the Germans decided to use their remaining ships to bring back from the Aegean as many of their troops and as much of their material as possible, and then to evacuate southern Greece.

The two maritime Beaufighter squadrons, 603 and 252 Squadrons, joined in the task of making the evacuation of the Aegean islands a difficult and costly operation. One of the remaining enemy vessels engaged on this task was *Carola*, which had undergone repairs at Port Laki in Leros. The port had been under frequent attack by bomber aircraft, but the vessel had escaped damage. On 5 September she left the island for Piraeus, escorted by two flak ships. Wing Commander D.O. Butler took off the following morning at the head of eight Beaufighters of 252 Squadron to attack the vessel at extreme range, together with four of 603 Squadron's aircraft as top cover. They located the convoy when it was nearing the Greek mainland, south east of Athens, and attacked with rockets and cannon, in the face of 37mm and 20mm flak, as well as parachute rockets. The vessels were all severely hit and left smoking, while the 603 Beaufighters chased and damaged an escorting Arado Ar196. Two Beaufighters were hit but all returned safely. The merchant vessel did not sink and reached Piraeus, but was so badly damaged that she went into dry dock. The Germans scuttled her on 10 October, as a blockship for the port.

During the morning of 9 September, W/C Butler led eight aircraft of 252 Squadron on an attack against an enemy convoy which had been spotted by 603 Squadron on the previous night. This was the submarine hunter *UJ2142* (formerly the Italian *Filio Pi*), accompanied by an armed caique. The Beaufighters interdicted the convoy between Crete and Milos, and caused severe damage with rockets and cannon, each aircraft making two runs. No aircraft were hit, in spite of return fire.

A 603 Beaufighter ditched when on a sweep of eight aircraft on 13 September, but the crew, Pilot Officer A.B. Woodier and Sergeant H. Lee, managed to evade capture.

The next attack was on the following day, when eight 252 Squadron and eight 603 Squadron aircraft made an attack on Paroekia harbour on Paros. Some of the aircraft were carrying rockets with 25lb armour-piercing warheads, while others carried 60lb HE warheads. They made a devastating attack and sank the 260-ton minesweeper *Nordstern* as well as a smaller craft. One Beaufighter was hit but all returned safely.

On 16 September 1944, S/L Tommy Deck DFC led eight aircraft on an offensive sweep. They engaged two Junkers Ju52s and an Arado Ar196 near Portolago Bay, but the enemy sought cover behind the AA, which was some of the heaviest in the Aegean. The formation then approached Leros, another very heavily defended target. Tommy Deck in aircraft R was hit, and he and Flying Officer Heide DFC crashed. It was later reported that both were safe.

A number of night-intruder operations were then carried out over enemy airfields. No aircraft were shot down but movement of transport aircraft was hampered.

On 17 September, Land Force Adriatic occupied Kithera, an important island just south of the Greek mainland, and on 20 September, the Squadron were tasked to provide aircraft for last light cover over the Naval Task Force. As they approached the convoy they were attacked by US Navy Grumman Wildcats. The pilots had been poorly briefed, their aircraft recognition was faulty and they were unduly 'jumpy'. Sergeants L. Arthurs and F.G. Richardson's aircraft M was badly damaged but they managed to crash land at base.

On the morning of 22 September 1944, a Beaufighter of 252 Squadron flown by Flying Officer D.G.R. 'Paddy' Ward took off on a five-hour reconnaissance sortie over Leros and Samos. An important target was located alongside the jetty at Port Vathi on Samos. This was *Drache*, a former Greek merchant ship of 1,870 tons which had been used by the Germans as a minelayer and which had recently made two fast passages in the Aegean as a troop transport. Eight Beaufighters of 252 Squadron, led by W/C Butler, therefore took off for Port Vathi in mid-afternoon, accompanied by four 603 Squadron aircraft. Approaching the port from the landward

Life at Gambut

Top: 603 Squadron, sergeant's mess. Gambut, August 1944.
Top right: F/L R. L Oddy, entering his fourth year as adjutant.
Middle left: The new CO S/L Paine being introduced.
Middle right: W/C Lewis and Chiefy Mac.
Bottom left: Glen Silcock (left).
Bottom right: F/O Soderlund and F/Sgt Nicholls.

Life at Gambut

Top left: F/L 'Burdie' Partridge' and F/O McDonald.
Top right: W/O Erskine.
Middle: Sgt Crooks, Battle of Britain veteran, (left) and Sgt Towsey.
Bottom: W/O Prentice with Sgt Rennie and orderly room staff. Front row: LAC Smith, LAC Jones and Cpl Samways. Back row: LAC Reeve, LAC Anderson, Prentice, Rennie and Cpl Barnes.

side, the 603 aircraft engaged the ground positions while those of 252 hit the auxiliary vessel with about a dozen rockets armed with 601b warheads. Return fire included parachute rockets, but it was inaccurate and all aircraft returned to base. A series of explosions came from *Drache*, and reconnaissance photographs the next day revealed that she was a burnt-out wreck.

Another target was located by a Baltimore of 459 Squadron (RAAF) operating from Berka III. This target was the 700-ton *Orion* which had been dispatched to the eastern Aegean to help evacuate troops. The Baltimore shadowed the vessel and observed her shelter in the island of Denusa, ten miles east of Naxos. Shortly before mid-day on 23 September, Flight Lieutenant C.W. Fowler led seven 252 Squadron aircraft to the attack, escorted by five aircraft from 603 Squadron led by F/O Cas de Bounevialle. One of the 603 aircraft turned back with engine trouble but the others received a wireless message giving the position of the enemy vessel. They located her in a small cove and successfully attacked with 251b and 601b rockets, in the face of accurate 20mm and 40mm flak. Three Beaufighters were hit and one from 252 Squadron was lost.

When the remaining aircraft were on their return journey, a large explosion and a sheet of flame were seen from the Denusa area. However, the fate of the vessel was uncertain, and a further strike force, consisting of five 252 Squadron and three 603 Squadron aircraft, was despatched before the others landed. They arrived over Denusa at 1848 hours, to find that *Orion* was beached and still burning. There was no flak, and all aircraft attacked, leaving the vessel with fresh fires. Later reconnaissance showed that she was lying broadside on to the beach, listing badly and burnt out.

Wing Commander Christopher Foxley-Norris was a former Battle of Britain pilot and had been a highly successful flight commander in 252 Beaufighter Squadron for over a year. He had spent several months as Wing Commander Operations at Gambut III and arrived to take command from S/L C.D. Paine on 23 September 1944. He later recalled his service in the desert with 603 Squadron:

603 Squadron, Gambut 1944. S/L Paine centre.

Top: German minelayer *Drache*, sunk 22 September 1944 by Beaufighters of 252 and 603 Squadrons at Port Vathi in Samos.
Left: Big bang on ammunition ship off Rhodes, 1944.
Right: German E-boat crashing after attack, 1944.

Top: Beaufighter H, piloted by R.K. Harrington with A.E. Winwood as navigator, returning from the attack on the minelayer *Drache* at Port Vathi, 22 September 1944. The photograph was taken by F/L Scott, navigator to S/L Paine when they were being escorted back after their aircraft had received damage to the CSU of one engine and flak damage to the port wheel. Despite a very close look at the wheel in mid-air Harrington could not be sure if it was damaged. In fact the tyre was flat. However, Boozy Paine made a good landing on one wheel.

Bottom: Bert Winwood (left) and Ray Harrington.

I was posted to Air Headquarters Eastern Mediterranean in December 1943 as a replacement Flight Commander after the abortive Leros campaign in late 1943, when many Beaufighters were lost, and was then appointed to command A Flight, 603 Squadron. This, I felt, appropriate as I was myself an Auxiliary Air Force Officer, having been originally a member of 500 (County of Kent) Squadron, Auxiliary Air Force, and my navigator, F/O 'Jock' Scott, was Edinburgh born and bred!

The Squadron was currently based at Gambut III airfield, on the desert escarpment about 50 miles east of Tobruk. The Officer Commanding was Ronaldson Lewis DFC, ex-Fighter Command, and the Adjutant, the cheerful and capable Flight Lieutenant Raymond Oddy. I soon realised how lucky I was to be a member of such a remarkable and courageous community.

603 Squadron was one of three Beaufighter Squadrons operating in the Aegean, and our task was to attack shipping, and any enemy aircraft that came our way except single-engined fighters. We also carried out armed reconnaissance.

The Germans were desperately trying to supply their garrisons on Aegean islands using a dwindling number of rather aged cargo steamers and coasters, and a large number of the sturdy little Greek 'caiques' – wooden sailing vessels. All these were armed to the teeth with Bofors guns and Oerliken cannon, and I remember one convoy of caiques and coasters shooting down four out of a total of eight Beaufighters attacking it.

Top: Ron Lee with 60lb and 25lb rockets.
Left: W/C C. Foxley-Norris OC 603. September 1944.
Bottom: W/C C. Foxley-Norris and ground crew. F/L Tuhill, his navigator, middle. They are standing in front of Beaufighter X, NV248.

The aircraft NE400/H had an interesting history. Its pilot was F/Lt Pat Pringle, later Squadron Leader, DFC. On 27th January 1944, Pringle was leading four Beaufighters of A Flight on a fighter sweep in the Aegean near the island of Mykonos when they encountered three Junkers Ju-52, escorted by four Arado 196s, agile little floatplanes each carrying two fixed forward-firing 20mm cannon and two machine guns.

The Beaufighters immediately attacked, and at the end of a dogfight lasting about six minutes they had disposed of all seven of the enemy. One Beaufighter was forced to ditch halfway back across the Mediterranean, and the crew were seen to take to their dinghy. Unfortunately, a very severe storm got up during the night, and though intensive searches were made during the next day, no trace of the crew was ever found.

Squadron Leader Pringle and his navigator, F/O Tony Ross flying in Beaufighter NE400/H later sank a destroyer on a pitch black night north of Crete using rocket projectiles and ranging with their Mark III ASV Radar. Only brilliant flying and radar operation could achieve such a result; F/O Ross followed his pilot in being awarded the DFC.

On one occasion a Beaufighter on reconnaissance discovered that the Germans were attempting to build an airstrip on the island of Paros, obviously for the use of the dreaded Messerschmitts and right in the middle of our patrol area!

A strike force of four Beaus was immediately dispatched, and the constructor's plant and motor roller and a nearby fuel pump were all destroyed. The Germans were unable to obtain replacement plant, so the effort was abandoned!

In May 1944 our intelligence got wind of an all-out German effort to victual their garrison on Crete by running in a large convoy using all their available cargo steamers and with a strong escort of Flakships.

Accordingly, Air Commodore Allinson at Group HQ at Benina raked up every rocket-firing Beaufighter that he could lay his hands on, and the convoy was intercepted by about 32 Beaus north of Crete on the afternoon of June 1st. Every ship in the convoy was sunk for the loss of four Beaus, one from each unit taking part. The strike leader, W/Cdr Meharg, was shot down in flames, but rescued and taken prisoner with his navigator. I had the pleasure after the war of showing him a photo of his Beaufighter going down in flames.

Losses in the Aegean, as with all anti-shipping operations, were high. I believe that the loss ratio of aircraft taking part in all anti-shipping operations was the highest in any form of aerial warfare.

I… pay tribute to the truly marvellous spirit that animated 603 Squadron. There remained with them a nucleus of about 20 of the original Auxiliary Air Force Edinburgh volunteers, spear-headed by Warrant Officer 'Snuffy' Prentice, whose official RAF age was, I believe, 57 (and had been for years), but who must have been nearer 70! These men were determined, that whatever else happened, 603 were going to acquit themselves with honour. This unquenchable spirit permeated the whole squadron, from the CO to the most junior 'erk'. The aircraft maintenance on this grim sand-storm afflicted desert airfield was literally second-to-none and the aircraft serviceability was better than any squadron which 1 have ever known before or since.

All this went with a cheerful spirit and wonderful comradeship between officers, NCOs and airmen. I remember that the airmen were allowed a small beer ration, but the officers and senior NCOs had to make do with very poor NAAFI Cyprus Brandy optimistically labelled VSOP and Egyptian Gin, very nasty at that period! The airmen, however, used to save up their beer, and when sufficient had been accumulated, throw a party for all ranks. And what parties they were. Happy days! One forgets, of course, the operational 'jitters', the loss of friends, and remembers more the comradeship and the wonderful spirit engendered when a community is combined in working for a just cause.

Air Chief Marshal Sir Christopher Foxley-Norris KCB DSO OBE recalls the enforced retirement of W/O 'Snuffy' Prentice (It was policy that all airmen over 50 years old should be sent home from the Middle East) :

Left: The cinema at Gambut.
Middle left: Tents at Gambut, August 1944.
Middle right: The cookhouse at Gambut, August 1944.
Bottom: Part of the camp site after a rain storm.

Top: 603 say goodbye to W/O 'Smithy' Prentice.
Bottom: W/O Prentice says farewell to 603, observing the rule that all airmen over 50 years of age were sent home from the Middle East; he was nearly 60. On the left is W/C Foxley-Norris. W/O Prentice shakes hands with F/L Oddy.

… I was posted once more to Glorious Gambut where after a short spell as Wing Commander Operations, I was given the command of 603 (City of Edinburgh) Auxiliary Air Force Squadron. The operational job and the aircraft were the same as on my previous tour…

By now of course, after nearly five years of war, none of the original aircrew remained on the Squadron, but a large proportion of the ground crew were pre-war squadron members, some of them even founder members of the Squadron with nearly 20 years unbroken service. The value of the continuing cohesive spirit of these tough, loyal Edinburgh men was immeasurable. It was their squadron. They had seen it through some very rough times in the Battle of Britain and in Malta; and they were quite happy to go on doing so just as long as they were needed.

The Senior Squadron Member was a splendid old man named Warrant Officer Prentice, who was the lynch-pin of the whole organization and a mine of both history and legend. He argued firmly that his age was 'just about 50' but as his son was also an NCO on the Squadron, this was a little difficult to credit (particularly as rumour had it that his grandson was also about to join us). One sad day the blow fell. Authority in Cairo ruled that, now the critical pressures had eased, the Western Desert was no place for old men to serve and that all those over 50 years of age should be posted home. We wriggled and evaded and procrastinated, but the end was inevitable. Mr Prentice was to go home to Edinburgh.

We gave him a full ceremonial farewell parade, although the uniforms were not quite of Horse Guards standard. Gambut offered few shopping facilities, so instead of a presentation piece, we had a whip-round to which every man on the squadron contributed. After months in the Desert, most pockets were pretty well lined and I had great pleasure in presenting the old man with a cheque for well over a £100; which he accepted with dignity and apparently just as great pleasure.

The ORB recorded 603's activities during September:

There were considerable intrusions over enemy airfields and the Aegean and a number of offensive reconnaissances. Two outstanding attacks were carried out which resulted in the destruction of the 'Drache' and 'Orion'. This was a severe blow to the enemy's shipping resources at a time when every available vessel was needed for the withdrawal of German Troops from the Aegean and Dodecanese. As a result of this and of the considerable losses inflicted by the Navy the enemy has been unable to evacuate his forces in any great strength.

603 Squadron ground crew. From left to right: Moffat, Wilson, Beach and Foat.

Despite bad weather at the beginning of October, ten Beaufighters of 603 Squadron accompanied by two of 252 Squadron, led by W/C Foxley-Norris, took off at mid-day on 3 October to hunt for the 2,423-ton minelayer *Zeus* off the east coast of the mainland of Greece. This vessel, the former Italian merchant ship *Francesco Morosini*, was considered a prime target, for she was playing an important part in the German evacuation. One 603 Squadron aircraft turned back with engine trouble. The formation did not find *Zeus* but located across a convoy of five small vessels to the east of Athens, which they attacked. Rockets and cannon fire damaged three of the vessels, but return fire was intense and two Beaufighters of 603 Squadron were shot down.

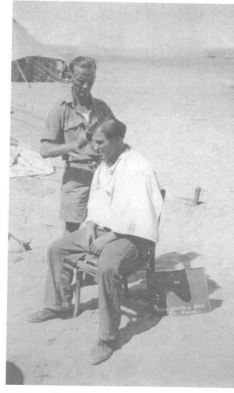

The pilot of one aircraft (P), Sergeant Desmond Harrison, was killed (he is buried at the Phaleron War Cemetery, Greece), but the navigator, Sergeant D.V. Bannister, was later reported to be 'safe in friendly hands'. The intense AA fire during this sortie damaged four aircraft: M flown by Warrant Officer Harrison and Flying Officer Silcock was damaged and Silcock was wounded. Their aircraft belly-landed at base; X flown by F/L Simpson and F/Sgt Bunn force-landed. The other aircraft (W) was crewed by F/O Cas de Bouneviall and P/O A.E 'Gillie' Potter. Bouneviall ditched with his starboard engine on fire, not far from the position where he had ditched six weeks earlier. The men were not injured, but were picked up by a UJ-boat and taken to Piraeus. From there they were escorted to Athens for a brief interrogation, and then put on a train for Yugoslavia. The train travelled only by day, since partisans were apt to attack at night. They reached Skopje and were then flown by Junkers Ju52 to Zagreb. Another train took them to Vienna and Budapest, and eventually to Frankfurt. Ending up at Stalag Luft III at Sagan in Upper Silesia, they were marched out in January 1945 and liberated by the Russians near Berlin.

Wilson and Moffat, a haircut in the desert.

Bouneviall and Potter were unlucky for, only three days after they ditched, British forces began to land on the mainland of Greece. Athens was occupied on 14 October. British landing parties also occupied Samos, and then the islands of Syros, Naxos, Lemnos and Scarpanto. On 24 October, the German garrison in a three-storeyed building in the island of Kalymnos was encouraged to surrender when five Beaufighters of 252 Squadron attacked with 601b rockets and cannon fire. The building was left on fire,

Aircraft H of F/Sgt Giles, a veteran of the Cos and Leros raids.

with black smoke, debris and dust rolling up the valley when the aircraft departed.

On 3 October, Warrant Officer John Goss flew his first operation with the Squadron:

According to my log book, my first operation was a strike on a small convoy of supply ships in the Aegean Sea, mostly caiques but with a very busy and accurate flak ship, which shot down my friend Des Harrison on his run onto a target. His navigator, Sergeant D.V. Bannister survived and was picked up by partisans who got him to Turkey. He returned back at Gambut a few weeks later. My final operational sortie was on 15 November 1944.

John Goss also recalls life at Gambut:

> Myself and my navigator lived in tents at Gambut. Sleeping on corrugated iron beds, supported on four petrol cans full of sand. My back has never been the same since! Bullybeef, sand, sandstorms, flies and brackish tasting tea and eggy-men arriving on donkeys out of the blue – ? dozen eggs for a packet of Victory V 'gaspers'! I should think El Adem was the nearest place. It all seems a hundred years ago now!

Also on 3 October, F/Sgt K.F. Pennie was awarded the DFM. His citation reads:

> Flight Sergeant Pennie has always displayed commendable skill and courage in air operations. In July 1944, he took part in an attack on an enemy convoy. In the fight, considerable anti-aircraft fire was faced. Flight Sergeant Pennie was wounded and his aircraft was hit repeatedly. Nevertheless, this gallant pilot pressed home his attack, obtaining hits on a ship.

By 14 October, British forces had occupied Athens and the island garrisons were completely isolated. There were now no shipping targets, and responsibility for providing air support for forces charged with capturing the islands passed to the newly formed Air Headquarters Greece under Air Commodore Tuttle.

On his way back home from Moscow, the Foreign Secretary, Anthony Eden, decided to visit the newly liberated city of Athens. Wing Commander Foxley-Norris led the 603 escort to Eden's plane on 25 October. There was a tumultuous welcome.

By the end of October, the whole of the coast of southern Greece was in British hands, although about 18,500 German troops were left on Crete, Rhodes, Leros, Kos and Melos, together with about 4,500 Italian Fascists. These posed no threat to the Allies and were being dealt with gradually from the air and by landings. Some of the garrisons were left to stagnate, acutely short of food and harried by the RAF and partisans, until they decided to surrender.

USAAF Mitchells, Gambut. They helped on the shipping strikes on Crete and Rhodes.

Top: P/O A.E. Arthurs and F/S F.G. Richardson.
Bottom: F/S F.Relphe and F/S A. Mackenzie.

Top: Al Burgess, Eric Harman (KIA May 1944), Ken Tennant, and Taffy Hopkins (KIA May 1944).
Right: W/C Foxley-Norris (seated centre) with officers at Gambut in autumn 1944. Note reluctant mascot.

During November 1944 the Squadron carried out a few reconnaissance sorties. The last operational reconnaissance in the Middle East was on 26 November. By December 1944, at which time operations had ceased prior to the return to the UK, over 50 vessels of varying types had been sunk (representing 7,845 tons of shipping). 603 Squadron was also credited with six probable vessels sunk (8,000 tons) and six damaged (10,992 tons). The cost was high in terms of 38 aircrew killed and two airmen. Others had been taken prisoners of war.

The Squadron were formally disbanded on 26 December 1944 and on that day sailed from Port Said to England in the *Capetown Castle*, marking the end of their tour overseas. They landed at Liverpool on 6 January 1945, and proceeded to Coltishall. Here the pilots were posted to the Mosquito Wing at Banff, but the ground crews were retained.

After well deserved leave and a warm welcome in Edinburgh the ground staff under F/L Rogers were formed into 6603 Service Echelon at Matlaske. Pilots from 229 Squadron were posted in and 603 were again a Spitfire squadron engaged on anti-V-weapon sites.

CHAPTER 15

SPIT-BOMBERS!

Towards the end of November 1944, it became known that the Squadron were to return to the UK. No doubt this news brought an extra sparkle to Christmas for men who had been abroad for months and years, knowing now that they were to disembark from Port Said on Boxing Day. Then followed almost a fortnight of sailing through the Mediterranean in the *Capetown Castle*, routing out into the Atlantic to avoid U-boats, finally arriving at Liverpool in the dark on Saturday 6 January. The change of weather from the heat of the Mediterranean to the cold and wet of an English winter must have created some mixed feelings but they were coming home, after all.

Nobody knew where they were going – including the CO, W/C Foxley-Norris – and there were some surprised faces when the 294 men found a special train waiting to transport them on the final stage of their journey. Even then they weren't told what was in store for them and there were many who tried to guess the names of the darkened stations which the train rumbled through to get a clue as to their final destination during that seemingly endless journey.

The mystery was solved when they arrived at Norwich early on Sunday morning. The 29 aircrew officers were taken to RAF Coltishall – a traditional station built in the 1930s in the countryside just north of Norwich. The facilities were good at Coltishall unlike those on some of the airfields which had been built during the war where they were a bit more primitive. The 264 ground crew were

603 reunion at RAF Wittering 1944. Seated: G/C G. McPherson, S/L A. Winskill, W/C R. Berry, G/C G. Gilroy, G/C G. L. Denholm, G/C E. Colbeck-Welch and S/L G. T. Wynne-Powell. Standing: unknown, F/L L. Martel, S/L D. Douglas-Hamilton, W/C I. Chalmers-Watson, W/C I. S. Ritchie (rear), G/C E. H. Stevens, S/L A. Barton, G/C R. J. Legg, F/L W. A. A. Read, W/C F. D. Scott-Malden, W/C J S. Morton, S/L G. Hunter, W/C A. Wallace, S/L T. C. Garden, S/L W. A. Douglas and G/C I. Kirkpatrick.

603 Squadron Coltishall, February 1945.

taken to be billeted at RAF Matlaske, one of the two satellite airfields to Coltishall.

Some of the Scots were disappointed not to be nearer home, but it was one stage closer all the same and there was the immediate prospect of leave before the unit would come together again to fly with the Coltishall Wing. Foxley-Norris recounts flippantly in his autobiography how just after arriving, he was talking to the Sector Commander, G/C Arthur Donaldson DSO, DFC, AFC, over a pint in the mess, when Donaldson asked what the Squadron codes were so that they could be painted on their new *Spitfires*!

Foxley-Norris, quite taken aback, stammered out that they flew Beaufighters – on anti-shipping strikes. Donaldson was equally bemused, saying that the Wing flew Spitfires and spent much of its time bombing V2 sites. He only then noticed – no doubt with a wry smile – that half of the 603 Squadron officers around him in the mess, wore the half wing navigator's badge. Thus, it wasn't long before the aircrew were posted – the Wing Commander to fly Mosquitoes with the Banff strike wing in the north of Scotland not far from Dyce where 603 had been based from time to time at the start of the war.

At this time the men who had flown Beaufighters disappear from the story of 603, but the CO went on to have a distinguished career in the RAF, retiring in 1974 at the age of 56 (by his own admission 'prematurely') as Air Chief Marshal Sir Christopher Foxley-Norris GCB, DSO, OBE. One of the few pilots who fought during the Battle of Britain and then flew operationally for the rest of the war – if nothing else, this was a tribute to his abilities as a pilot.

By January 1945, whilst Germany was still as powerful and dangerous as a cornered animal, the ultimate Allied victory was not in doubt, but much fighting was to be endured before peace would come – a situation in stark contrast to that when 603 had sailed from the Clyde in 1942 to the Middle East.

Then, continental Europe was firmly under occupation. Although the Battle of Britain in 1940 had stopped a German invasion, in 1941 and 1942 an equally desperate struggle was taking place across the Atlantic as the German navy – and particularly the U-boats – tried with some success to strangle the lifeline of the convoys from America bringing in food and vital war materiel to beleaguered Britain. Defeat in the Atlantic in 1942 would have meant ultimate collapse. Singapore had fallen in February and the situation in Burma was desperate with the Japanese threatening the gates of India. In North Africa, the impressive Afrika Korps led by Erwin Rommel threatened Egypt. The famous battle of Alamein had yet to be fought. But despite the ascendancy of the Axis, there were the first faint signs of things turning for the Allies although at the time they weren't tangible. America had entered the war on the Allied side following the bombing of Pearl Harbor by the Japanese in December 1941, the Red Army had halted the Wehrmacht at the gates of Moscow, RAF Bomber Command was building up the strategic air offensive against the German homeland and the

Germans were beginning to appreciate that it might not all go their way.

By January 1945, a different picture had emerged altogether. The Americans were working their way towards Japan, recovering island by island – Tarawa had been taken. The threat to India had gone. The Afrika Korps had long been cleared out of North Africa and no longer existed. Italy had surrendered to the advancing Allies, although the Germans continued to fight there. D-Day was seven months past. Paris and Brussels were liberated and the Allied armies threatened the Rhine. The Germans still resisted fiercely however. They had just made a big winter push in the Ardennes – The Battle of the Bulge – which almost caught the Allies on the hop and on New Year's Day, the Luftwaffe had mounted a huge sweep across the Allied armies catching many of their aircraft on the ground. Although the Luftwaffe had suffered huge losses of aircraft themselves the Allies had been hurt; clearly Hitler was by no means out, even if he was down.

The Allied air forces held air superiority, but not supremacy. The Luftwaffe was still potent but tiring and much of the Allied air effort was directed towards tactical support of the advancing armies – which meant ground attack.

Immediate support for the ground troops on the continent was given by the 2nd Tactical Air Force which, in December 1944, comprised two Groups – 83 and 84 – with eight wings each. These were based at airfields near the front.

603 were about to re-form in 12 Group which had its headquarters in Uxbridge.

12 Group operated primarily over Holland carrying out attacks on German rocket installations. Its main base was RAF Coltishall which had two satellites, RAF Matlaske, built in the summer of 1940 as a dispersed satellite airfield and RAF Ludham which came into use at the end of 1941 as a forward operating base. Matlaske was 12 miles to the north west of Coltishall and Ludham seven miles east south east.

These three airfields were to figure largely in the activities of 603 until April 1945 – particularly Coltishall and Ludham where the Squadron would be based. Co-incidentally, the fortunes of 603 during this period were intertwined closely with 602, with whom it had famously opened the war by shooting down the first German aircraft over the UK mainland, and also 229 which 603 had become when it disbanded in Malta in August 1942. Since then, 229 Squadron had continued to operate in the Mediterranean. Early 1944 found them based in Sicily and in April of that year, 229 had returned to the United Kingdom flying bomber escort sorties and, as a generalisation, 'armed reconnaissance' duties over France and Belgium. In October 1944, the Squadron arrived to join the Coltishall Wing.

RAF Matlaske was plagued with drainage problems and when the personnel of the 603 Service Echelon arrived, the two squadrons of Spitfires based at Matlaske – 602 and the Australian 453 – had moved their aircraft to the Mosquito base, RAF Swannington which was six or seven miles to the west of Coltishall. Swannington however wasn't able to accommodate any personnel so there was an unsatisfactory arrangement in that the daily servicing ground crew left each morning at 07.00

603 Squadron Ludham, March 1945.

by road for Swannington, with the pilots following at 09.00. Both groups were usually back at Matlaske by 18.00. At Swannington, there were three Nissen huts to accommodate them – one for the pilots and two for the ground crews and their equipment. This arrangement had been in place since the beginning of December 1944 and all concerned were getting weary of it. It was an additional complication for the two Squadrons which they could well do without.

The Coltishall Wing was busy. 229 Squadron (Squadron code 9R), well experienced in its role by the beginning of January 1945, carried out sorties virtually every day against targets mainly in Holland.

On 1 January 1945, 229 Squadron was commanded by S/L A. Patterson, and the other key personnel were:

A Flight – P/O Doidge, F/L McAndrew, F/L Sergeant, P/O Hal Grant (a Canadian), F/Sgt O'Reilly, F/Sgt Thomson, F/Sgt Wheatley (an Australian), F/O Trail and F/Sgt Green (another Australian). A Flight did not have a flight commander at that time, but F/L Jack Batchelor was posted in from 1 Squadron a few days later.

B Flight – F/L T. Rigler DFM (flight commander), F/L Welch DFC, F/L Kirkman (an Australian), P/O McConnochie (a New Zealander), P/O Van Dyck (a Belgian), W/O Cookson, F/Sgt Haupt, W/O Beckwith, F/O Sanderson and W/O Mee.

'Tommy' Rigler.

The Squadron Engineering Officer was F/O 'Spanner' Stoneman and the Intelligence Officer was P/O H. Cooper assisted by Corporal Stanners.

P/O Alfred Beckwith on leave during 1945.

The experience of the pilots varied. For example, F/L Batchelor had been flying operationally for many years. Back in 1942, he had been in a fight with a Messerschmitt Bf109 which damaged his aircraft and one of his eyes was hit by splinters. Fortunately, although his sight was affected, it wasn't lost and to correct the damage he was fitted with a contact lens which was quite large. His eye tended to become inflamed and uncomfortable and so he wore sun glasses to help reduce the glare. F/L Bob Sergeant had flown with 249 Squadron in Malta in 1942 where it will be recalled he had been wounded on the ground during a raid on Ta Kali. F/Sgt Paddy O'Reilly also had operational experience. One of his most vivid memories was when he flew fighter cover for the D-Day invasion fleet on 5 June 1944: 'I will always remember looking down and seeing these tiny black specks mirrored by the moonlight reflecting off the water, all heading for the French coast.'

Others, though, like W/O Eric Mee, W/O Alfred Beckwith, the former army sergeant PE Instructor from Leeds, and F/O Leslie Trail had little or no operational experience when they joined the unit.

Typical of the intensity of the operations being undertaken at this time, the following is an account of a mission flown on New Year's Day 1945 by 229. The targets were V2 launch sites and the support structure

– control buildings etc – of which there were many in wooded areas near the Dutch coast:

> The second operation took place at 12.25 hours when the weather at base became quite clear and settled. P/O Doidge led 4 aircraft each with 2 x 250lb GP bombs to HAGUE/HAAGSCHE BOSCH and completed a very successful mission. They approached Holland at 11,000 feet off WESTHOOFD at 14.05 hours and turned North to cross in just north of HAGUE. The target was very clearly seen in a perfectly clear day and bombed from S. to N. in dives from 10,000 to 3,000 feet. They pulled out of the dive up to 8,000 feet before crossing the coast to observe the results which were excellent. 4 bombs fell actually on the target pinpoint in the woods and 2 others fell about 200 yards South and 2 more about 150 yards to the West. A very intense curtain of flak, very accurate at about 4/5,000 feet was encountered over the whole parkland. They crossed out just North of the HAGUE at 8,000 feet at about 14.32 hours and were followed by heavy and medium accurate flak from the coastal guns at HAGUE which appear to be particularly offensive when the aircraft are about 2 miles out to sea. The Palace just North of the target was clearly seen and quite undamaged.

The various ORBs for January and February are full of references to attacks on places such as Haagsche Bosch, Hague/Hotel Promenade, Hague/Voorde, Hague Huis Te Werve, Staalduin Bosch etc. ('Bos' – pronounced 'bosch' is the Dutch for a wood. Before the war 'sch' was used for spelling, but since then 's' on its own is used. 'The Hague' should be referred to as 'Den Haag').

In addition to P/O Doidge in A, the other pilots were Flight Sergeant Thomson, F/L Sergeant and P/O Grant in Spitfires C, E and B respectively. The 'Palace' was the home of the Royal Family, and it was probably a deliberate ploy of the Germans to launch the V2s from near it in the knowledge that the Allies were unlikely to risk any serious damage to the building. The palace itself escaped being hit although there was one report that during one raid the gates had been superficially damaged.

The weather for the first week in January was cold with frosts and snows – to such an extent that a number of planned sorties had to be cancelled. For the aircrew and ground crew of 603 just returned from the warmth of the Middle East it was a jolt back to the reality of the British climate.

On 9 January, the 229 ORB records:

For some time now it has been known that 229 Squadron is to be disbanded (officially on 10th January, 1945) and on return of 603 Squadron (Beaufighters) from the Middle East we should assume their title of 603 'City of Edinburgh' Squadron. It is not quite certain whether we shall absorb their personnel and remain doing exactly the same work with Spitfires or whether on the disbandment of 229, 603 will absorb our personnel. It now appears that we shall be known as 603 Squadron, and remain exactly as we are with the same pilots and commitments but will have the old 603 Echelon whilst the Squadron 229 will just disappear. The old 603 pilots who were at Coltishall and the ground crew who were at Matlaske have now left, some on leave and some on posting

Bob Sergeant whilst with 266 Squadron before going to Malta in 1942. He flew as a flight lieutenant with 603 Squadron in 1945.

to other units. Official notification of the change has not yet been received.

On Wednesday 10 January 1945 the new A Flight Commander, F/L Jack Batchelor, was airborne at 10.05 hours to carry out an 'armed recce' but landed after 10 minutes after being caught in a heavy snow storm.

The ORB noted:

Nothing in print has yet been received confirming the report that 229 Squadron is disbanded and renamed 603 'City of Edinburgh' Squadron. As it is generally believed however to have occurred officially today this will be the first diary entry for the Squadron under that title. It is interesting to note that the Squadron has merely reverted to its original title as it is reported to have been 603 Squadron prior to the forming of 229 Squadron in August 1942 at Malta, although the Squadron does not hold any records prior to that date in confirmation of that report.

The confusion as to its identity, however, lasted for another fortnight, until 24 January:

So far this Squadron has been referred to in correspondence and communications as both 603 and 229 and for the purposes of complete clarity sometimes as 603/229 or 229/603. In spite of repeated queries from various sources the Adjutant has owing to lack of official information been unable to inform enquirers as to what really is our current Numerical Squadron Title. At last notification has been received today that we are no longer 229 Squadron but carry the title of '603 City of Edinburgh Squadron'.

As far as the pilots and the ground crew were concerned, it was generally accepted that the change took place on 10 January, but clearly there was some doubt.

Any history of a squadron must inevitably concentrate on the activities of the aircrew because that is the primary reason for it to exist. However, the preceding few pages demonstrate that by January 1945, the spirit of the original 603 Auxiliary Squadron wasn't with the pilots, but with those auxiliaries in the ground crew who had remained together in the Middle East since April 1942 and *were* 603. This isn't to say that the pilots had no feelings for their Squadron – quite the contrary. The aircrew were very much drawn together as the cutting edge of the team and would identify themselves for the rest of their lives as '603 men', no matter how long or short their spell of duty was. None of the pilots who had left the Clyde for Malta were still there but there were ground crew who had been at Fairlop and Dyce in 1941 and 1942 who were now waiting to be drawn back into the new 603.

603 in February 1945. Front row: F/L Jack Kirkman, S/L Donovan, F/L Batchelor, S/L Tommy Rigler, F/L Johnnie Welch DFC, F/L McAndrew, F/L Bob Sergeant and P/O Spy Cooper. Back row: F/O Spanner Stoneman, W/O Snowy Wheatley, P/O Bill Dodge, F/S Paddy O'Reilly, W/O Cookson, W/O Wally Haupt, and F/O McConnochie. Aloft: P/O Manivalu.

For the pilots of 229 Squadron – now 603 Squadron – there would be little obvious change. They were the same unit, flying the same aircraft from the same airfield doing the same job. Indeed, possibly the only major noticeable change for them were the 'XT' code letters which would eventually appear on their Spitfires.

So why was the change made? A possible answer goes back to 1927 when as part of the arrangements for establishing the Auxiliary Air Force, an Air Ministry Order gave auxiliary airmen (not officers) the right not be posted to another unit without their consent. If an airman didn't wish to leave 603, he couldn't be forced to do so. In simplistic terms, a new 603 Squadron would have to be created for them and this, together with the aim of having the auxiliary squadrons back in existence at their home bases after the war finished *may* have been two of the reasons to change 229 to 603. However, the eventual disbandment of the Squadron in August 1945 suggests that there may have been other reasons, or that the intentions changed with the unexpected surrender of Japan.

On returning to the United Kingdom the whole ground crew group was renamed 6603 Service Echelon until it could be decided just what was to be done with them. They were commanded by F/L Wyndham Rogers who had been with the Squadron for about two years. Arrangements were ultimately made for the men of 6603 Service Echelon to be integrated into the new Squadron, but this didn't happen immediately and in the meantime, they remained at Matlaske whilst not on leave.

Although this new 603 was substantially the re-badged pilots and ground crew of 229 Squadron, there was now a core of 603 ground crew auxiliaries to bring back the Scottishness of the unit. Whilst in the Mediterranean, they had managed to keep their bagpipes safe and also came back with two football trophies! By 1945, not one of the original auxiliary pilots was still on squadron strength. But, as we have seen, there were still about 30 of the original 603 Edinburgh auxiliary 'Jocks' together as a group, and now to be back with a 603 Squadron that flew Spitfires.

The Spitfires were Mark XVI and nearly all brand new. The XVIs were essentially Mark IXs with the American Packard-built Merlin 266 engine instead of the Rolls-Royce version, the 66, and were armed with two 20mm cannons and four .50 calibre machine guns. In addition, they were capable of carrying a significant bomb load – 1,000lbs in various combinations of 250lb and 500lb bombs. Visually the most obvious difference was that the XVIs had 'clipped wings'.

In general, the Mark XVI had a similar performance to the Mark IX with a maximum speed of about 408mph at 25,000 feet, 312mph at sea level and a normal cruising speed of 324mph at 20,000 feet. The climb to 20,000 took just over 5 minutes and it had a service ceiling of 43,000 feet. Normal stalling speed was 86mph with a touchdown speed of 76mph with flaps and undercarriage down.

The figures above are typical as all aircraft have individual idiosyncrasies and the various parameters change depending on the age of the aircraft, the condition of the paintwork and skin etc.

The standard camouflage scheme for aircraft operating in northern Europe had changed in August 1941. Instead of being dark green and dark earth on the top surfaces, the pattern was basically the same as it always had been, but the brown was now a dark grey called 'ocean grey'. The dark green was retained. Instead of the light blue on the underside, it was light grey – 'medium sea grey'. Fuselage roundels in 1945 were outlined with a thin yellow circle.

As always, because of changes in the official schemes and the availability of paint, different aircraft of all squadrons would not necessarily be painted in accordance with the official requirements or be consistent across any squadron and it wouldn't be until February before the aeroplanes were bearing the XT codes.

One of the main tasks of the Wing was to attack the launching sites of the new German V weapons the V1 and particularly the V2. The Germans were technically innovative and in some fields – especially rocketry – were ahead of the Allies. They were the first to bring a jet aircraft into service – the twin-engined Messerschmitt 262. This had been designed as a fighter – particularly to deal with the high flying daylight bombers of the USAAF 8th Air Force, but Hitler had insisted that they be used as tactical bombers – a role that they were not really suited for – and so diluted their strength. They also introduced the rocket-powered Messerschmitt 163 Komet operationally – again to counter the American daylight bombers. Interestingly, their development of atomic bombs was not nearly as far advanced as the Allies.

Arguably their most potent developments were the V1s and V2s. (The V stood for

Vergeltungswaffe or 'revenge weapon'.) The rockets had been developed at Peenemunde on the Baltic coast, and this research establishment had been the target for a major night-time, moonlit pin-point raid by Bomber Command in August 1943.

The V1 was rather like a small, simple pilotless aircraft but with the nose full of explosive. It was a simple 'cruise' missile made by Fiesler and designated the Fiesler 103, operated by the Luftwaffe.

Powered by a ram-jet and fired from a launching ramp not unlike a ski-jump sited along the continental coast and pointed towards the south east of England, many were aimed at London. Some were air launched. Usually they travelled at 350 to 400mph at a height of about 2,500 feet. General control was provided by a simple automatic pilot which kept it on course and at the correct height until it tipped into its dive when it ran out of fuel.

For those on the ground, the ram-jet sounded like a motor bike in the sky, and people in the south east of England soon became used to catching the first sound of an approaching V1, listening with rising concern as it grew nearer, hoping that it would have passed overhead before there was the sudden silence of the engine cutting out, to be followed soon after by the explosion as it hit the ground. They soon came to be known as 'doodlebugs' or 'buzz bombs'.

They were first used on 13 June 1944 possibly in retaliation for the D-Day landings in Normandy, and became a real threat to the long-suffering people of the south east and London. It was a time that was likened to the bad old days of the 'Blitz' and many civilians living in 'doodlebug alley' got back into the habit of going to the shelter at night.

The Government was very concerned by the threat posed by the V1s, and instructed that robust defences should be set up. This resulted in a layered defence system being put in place. There were four screens of defences from the Channel inwards – an outer screen of fighters over the sea, a second one of anti-aircraft guns on the coast, another of fighters further inland and finally a layer of barrage balloons.

The V2 was more ominous. It was a ballistic missile and the direct precursor of those now used to fly into space – indeed many of the German scientists (like Werner von Braun) who had worked on the development of the V weapons at Peenemunde were taken as 'prizes' by the Americans and some by the Russians at the end of the war and used to develop their space programmes. The Americans used their Germans to continue the development of the rockets whereas the Russians sucked the information and experience from theirs and continued the development themselves. Many in America were set to work initially at Fort Bliss in Texas, then in Huntsville, Alabama.

The Germans had been researching into ballistic missiles since before the war started in 1939. They developed a series of experimental rockets with an A designation and the V2 was essentially the A4 development missile with a new and more aggressive public name given to it in 1944 by the Propaganda Minister, Josef Goebbels. The first successful flight of an A4 was in October 1942 and as the V2, it had a range of over 200 miles and carried a one-ton Amatol explosive warhead with an impact fuse. The fuel was about four tons of alcohol with five of liquid oxygen to provide the necessary oxidant.

Given time, the German engineers had visions for more powerful rockets including one which would be able to hit targets as far across Britain as Glasgow and central Scotland, and ultimately one which would be capable of reaching the USA. This was to be Hitler's last throw of the dice.

The Bomber Command raid on Peenemunde was intended to kill many of the scientists and engineers involved in the project but because of a target marking error, these technical experts escaped although many of the workers were killed and damage was inflicted on the plant. Its vulnerability was exposed and production of the missiles moved to underground sites – the most important being near Nordhausen in the Harz Mountains.*

---

*This change also marked the start of the involvement of the SS in providing forced labour from the Concentration Camps. These unfortunates lived in conditions of deprivation and appalling brutality which equalled or even surpassed the camps themselves. The use of concentration camp labour was with the acquiesence - if not the encouragement - of those leading the work and was effectively brushed under the carpet by the victorious powers who fell heir to the technology. In 1984, Arthur Rudolph, who was the production manager at Nordhausen, was expelled from the USA because of his involvement in the use of forced labour but little action was taken against others. Ironically, more lives were lost producing the V2s than were killed in action.

The V2 was launched vertically, flying to an altitude of 60 miles before it fell back to earth. The problem for those in the target areas was that it made no noise – there was no warning, the explosion the only sign that it had arrived. After the first firing of two V2s against Paris (which both detonated in mid-flight) on 6 September 1944, the first one to hit the United Kingdom landed at Chiswick – Staveley Road – on Friday 8 September 1944 killing three civilians and injuring another 17. Shortly afterwards, another came down in the countryside near Epping but without causing any injuries. Because there were few signs of a V2 landing – other than the explosion – the first blast was taken, at least publicly, to have been caused by a faulty gas pipe. In reality, it was much more sinister.

The two missile attacks opened a new chapter in the history of warfare, which was not to end until 27 March 1945 when the last V2 to land on British soil arrived at Kynaston Road, Orpington. In all, of the order of 1,400 were fired against Britain. They were to kill about 2,800 people and injure over 6,200. As well as targeting London, V2s were also fired at other parts of southern England and towards targets on the continent including Paris (22), Maastricht (19), Mons (3), Lille (25), Arras (6) and Antwerp which was being used as one of the main supply ports for the Allied armies driving into Germany and had over 1,600 fired at it. A few (11) were fired at the bridge across the Rhine at Remagen after it fell into Allied hands.

The Germans assumed that the use of the rockets against towns would collapse civilian morale, but they failed to learn the lessons of the London 'blitz' and the attacks on their own cities by the RAF and the USAAF which patently failed to achieve this. Further, the small numbers of V2s fired and the size of the warhead were also to result in them being at best limited in their effect.

Because of the heights to which it flew and the speeds that it reached, no aircraft was able to catch it and no gun able to shoot it down. There was only one defence – to destroy the launch sites and the missiles before they could be fired. Many of the British pilots saw V2s launching. They left white trails in the sky and sometimes the missile itself could be seen clearly at the tip of the trail. One misty morning, Jack Batchelor saw a V2 rising in front of his Spitfire through a bank of ground mist; Paddy O'Reilly another: 'I distinctly remember seeing the shape of the rocket as it came out of the trees and then rapidly accelerated out of sight.' 'Cupid' Love of 602 Squadron reported that having just completed an attack, he saw a V2 rising like an express train from the woods directly ahead of him. He was quick-witted enough to fire at it, but it seemed to have no effect – which was probably the best result as the exploding missile was likely to have destroyed his aircraft and the others with him!

Special measures were needed to combat these missiles and Fighter Command – and 12 Group – was given the responsibility for attacking the launch sites and their support facilities in Holland.

The launchers were mobile so the missiles could be fired from heavily wooded areas and were difficult to find. The rockets were prepared at 'firing area field stores' located near the potential launch sites. These field stores normally held up to about 30 missiles but only for a few days. Lengthy storage periods resulted in greater numbers of firing failures so the aim was to launch them as quickly as possible. Liquid oxygen was manufactured locally and there were eight 'factories' in the area. The V2 with the warhead installed was taken to its chosen launch site on a *Meillerwagen* which was like a cradle on wheels which transported the rocket in a horizontal position and erected it to the vertical on a ring base – the firing table. It then took about an hour and a half for the missile, which weighed about 13 tons, to be fuelled, prepared and fired electrically. After launch, the site could be completely cleared in about half an hour. In addition, a launch needed the presence of other vehicles with the required chemicals – alcohol, liquid oxygen, hydrogen peroxide (as a tank pressurising gas) and sodium permanganate (which was a catalyst). All in all, there were a considerable number of vehicles needed to launch a V2 and a concentration of troops as well, but as far as is known, no actual launch was ever discovered and disrupted by air attack.

Wooded areas provided good launch sites because they hid the missiles and their attendant convoys and they reduced the effects of the wind which could change the launch angles. There were sites near Den Haag (Haagse Bos, Duindigt, Wassenaar and Hoek van Holland) and Hellendoorn/Dalfsen (near Zwolle) but no doubt in other wooded areas too. But the mobility of the launchers meant that sometimes V2s were launched literally from street corners.

Jan van't Hoff was a young Dutch boy who lived near the Haagse Bos. He saw many V2s being launched from near where he lived:

The Germans never stopped us going into the streets during the launches (except the curfew hours in the evenings and nights). They didn't seem to be concerned about the wellbeing of the Dutch. There was never any warning prior to the launches, but we knew since I lived so near to the Haagse Bos. There would be a sort of humming sound about thirty minutes before the launch – that is how we knew it was imminent. If, however, the noise stopped suddenly, some time later an explosion would tell us that the V2 was a failure and had exploded on the ground, thus saving British lives. If the humming sound did not stop, there would be an awful noise as the engines started and we would see the V2 rising above the treetops, accelerating and heading west if it was going to England, or later on to the south if it was heading for Antwerp.

These were very frightening moments indeed because very often they fell back to earth killing many people and destroying many houses. Sometimes they were absolutely uncontrollable and went in all directions. They could be very unpredictable ……..Lucky for London but bad for us.

One time when a V2 exploded over our house, I picked up a piece of metal from it. It could have cost me my life because within a very short time, the Germans rounded up our streets and with pamphlets warned us to hand over any piece of metal. If not the death penalty would follow. I got rid of the piece just in time! Better to survive than be a hero!!

If the attacking Spitfires weren't able to find and stop launches in progress, they could certainly disrupt the process so that launches were delayed or abandoned.

The sites were vigorously defended – often the flak was extremely heavy. It posed a real danger to the Spitfires who were dive bombing and trying to identify their targets hidden by the foliage.

The concept of dive bombing is quite straightforward – the aeroplane is rolled into a steep dive towards the target, the bomb released to be left to continue to the target, while the aeroplane is pulled out of its dive and back into the sky. Like many things, it just wasn't as easy as it seemed.

Firstly, the bombs being used in 1944/45 were what in later years would be called 'dumb' or 'iron' bombs – they had no guidance system. They were basically explosive-packed steel cylinders with a pointed nose and tail fins. They would go where they were aimed but nowhere else. Secondly, the Spitfire had no bombsight. Thirdly, releasing a bomb from the centreline of an aircraft with a single propeller runs the risk that if the dive is too steep, the bomb will pitch through the arc of the turning propeller and destroy it. (The Ju87 held its main bomb on a trapeze which rotated out below the level of the propeller so that the bomb was 'slung out' past it when it was released.) However, if the dive isn't steep enough, it becomes difficult to judge the right moment to release the bomb as the target is hidden by the nose.* Fourthly, once the bomb is in flight, it is pushed off course by any wind that happens to be blowing so the pilots had to allow for this when they pressed the button to release the bomb. More importantly, the aircraft should not be yawing or skidding as this would throw the bomb off course too. Being relatively small, the bombs had to land close to the targets if they were to have an effect, so the slightest miscalculation could render the sortie worthless. And all of this without the added distraction of heavy flak defences.

Before letting the Spitfire squadrons loose on the launch sites, the RAF decided that it was necessary to carry out trials to develop dive-bombing techniques and so in March 1944, 602 and 132 Squadrons were sent to Llanbedr in Wales to carry out the experiments. One of the 602 pilots at the beginning of 1945 was F/O Raymond Baxter (who was to become a popular presenter for the BBC for many years after the war). His recollection of the technique was that the approach was made at about 8,000 feet (depending on cloud height) but never below 5,000. On final approach to the target, the formation leader would call 'echelon starboard' (or port) and over-fly it so that it passed out of sight under the port wing, outboard of the flaps (which were retracted – not lowered). The Spitfire was then rolled to reveal the target which would be lined up in the centre of the unlocked gyro-gunsight. The Spitfire would be throttled back and trimmed into what was effectively a 'hands-off' dive. The bombs were released at 3,000 feet – no lower than 2,000 – and the aircraft was then pulled out to escape at low level. An experienced pilot could bomb accurately to within 25-30 yards.

*One 603 pilot had this happen to him, except that the bomb only took off the propeller tips and he managed to nurse the Spitfire back to safety.

This methodology would allow 12 aircraft to attack successfully. He also recalls that for low level skip bombing attacks, the gyro sight was virtually redundant.

Raymond Baxter was to fly on a number of raids when 603 and 602 operated together and was still with 602 at RAF Ludham when the two squadrons moved there in February 1945.

The recollection of the technique by 603's F/O John Moss is similar. The Spitfire was trimmed into the dive because it was inherently stable and would try to return to more level flight left to its own devices. He also remembers that on one of his first practice attempts at dive bombing, he pulled out by winding in a sudden large nose up trim which made the aeroplane swoop into a climb and caused him black-out with the high induced g-Force. When he came round a little while later, he was alone in the sky and considerably higher than he had been when he started the pull up. Pulling quickly out of a very high speed dive could create such stress on the wing surface that it deformed into ripples requiring the mainplane to be replaced. A further hazard was if the bombs on the wings 'hung up' in the dive. W/O Eric Mee had this happen to him:

> On one occasion my bombs failed to go and the loads imposed on me and the aircraft in the pull-out were terrific. The result was having to pull off a dodgy landing back at base with bombs aboard, but also having reported the malfunction, the aircraft was inspected. The mechanic who checked the wings sought me out to show me the wing supporting bolts with a considerable bend in them – the dihedral angle of the wings having altered as a result. I guess that I was lucky – I think on that occasion I must have been carrying two 250 lb bombs only.

With all that the pilots had to do, their co-ordination needed to be good. As well as just flying the Spitfire, the graticule on the gyro gunsight was controlled by a twist grip on the throttle, and the bomb-release button was on the end of the throttle lever. And on the control column there were two buttons, one for firing the cannon and the other for the machine guns.

For 603, a new chapter which couldn't have been more different to the last was opening – Mediterranean warmth to European winter, twin-engined twin-crewed Beaufighters to single-engined singled-crewed Spitfires and anti-shipping torpedo strikes to dive-bombing attack. But the new role was no less demanding in courage and skill and again involved much danger.

The coast of Norfolk is 11 miles due east of Coltishall and about 120 miles further east, across the unforgiving expanse of the North Sea, is the coast of Holland which runs roughly south/north from Rotterdam in the south near the border with Belgium to the port of Den Helder at the north. Curving round to the north and east from Den Helder are the Waddeneilanden – five long, large, narrow islands like part of a necklace which curl round to the east to the German border near Emden. The five islands, from south to north are called Texel, Vlieland, Terschelling, Ameland and Schiermonnikoog. Because these islands and the coast of Holland were often the landfall for Allied bombers making for targets deep in Europe, they were heavily defended with anti-aircraft guns and many a returning damaged British bomber was lost to them as it struggled across hoping to reach the comparative safety of the North Sea.

603 Squadron, Skeabrae, June 1945. On Spitfire: ?, ?, W/O Godfrey. On ground: F/L Staniforth, ?, ?, W/O Marsland, W/O Beckwith, F/L McAndrew, F/L Bachelor.

The weather at the beginning of January was cold and snowy and flying was curtailed by it. Unfortunately, on one of the few occasions that flying was possible, F/O Leslie S. Trail was lost and thus became the first casualty of the revamped 603. He was relatively new and had only completed two operations by then.

The incident happened on Thursday 11 January. The weather was poor – frozen snow on the ground at Coltishall with the cloud base at 700 feet giving occasional snow falls. The weather over the Dutch coast was similar. F/L Sergeant and F/O Trail were tasked with a 'Jim Crow' (sweeps to look for enemy shipping, usually carried out by a small number of aircraft) to Den Helder and Terschelling. They took off at 09.20 as Green 1 and Green 2 – in Spitfires E and C (SM306) respectively – crossing over the English coast at zero feet. A few minutes after 10.00 hours, they made landfall just a mile south of the coast of the island of Texel. F/L Sergeant climbed to gain a little altitude to turn to starboard to take the section round towards Den Helder. Trail was doing a crossover turn below his leader who was watching for him to re-appear on the other side from below, but on glancing back round and downwards he saw Trail's aircraft fly into the water and blow up. Then he saw flak coming up from the shore: 'After he'd gone in, I did a couple of orbits and they were cracking away at me from the shore – I can see it now.'

He watched clouds of smoke and flames for some minutes, but they eventually died down to leave only an oily patch on the water. The exact location of the loss was given as 52 degrees 58N, 04 degrees 42E. After finding no sign of life, he decided that Green 2 was lost and continued the Jim Crow on his own. He took a look at the port of Den Helder from about a mile out, then flew up the seaward coast of Texel until reaching the island's north end. Seeing no shipping, he returned south and again checked for a sign of Trail in the water, but all that he found was the patch of oily water. With his mission completed, he headed back to Norfolk low across the water. On the way, he tried to report the loss of the F/O but because he was so low, he couldn't make radio contact with base. Half way across the water, he spoke to a Polish squadron which was flying above him and asked them to relay the news back to Coltishall but to tell them not to send out searching aircraft. He landed back at 10.55.

Sergeant didn't know why his No.2 had crashed. They were flying low – possibly as low as 100 feet – and with Trail doing a crossover turn with one eye on the sea and the other on his leader, with a bit of slip it wouldn't have taken much for him to hit the water.

On Bob Sergeant's return, the other Squadron pilots stood ready to carry out a search for their missing colleague, but after hearing his report it was concluded that a further search was unlikely to achieve anything and it was assumed that Trail was lost. He hadn't been with the Squadron long and the young man's death was made much more poignant because he was engaged to be married and the ceremony had been planned for his next leave.

This was also the first loss sustained by the old 229 since one of their pilots was killed at RAF Manston on 2 October 1944. Flying Officer Leslie Sinclair Trail came from Wandsworth in London and he was 21 years of age when he died. His death is commemorated on Panel 268 of the Runnymede Memorial.

The weather over the next week remained poor and although some flying took place, it was limited.

There was no flying on 12 January. The pilots were entertained by a lecture given by the station armaments officer on rocket projectiles and the possibility of fitting them to Spitfires. Then they trooped across to the photographic section for a film on the daily inspection of the Spitfire.

The CO, S/L Patterson had been ill with 'stomach problems'. His illness hadn't responded to treatment and it was decided that he needed to be in hospital so he left for an expected stay of two weeks in Ely Hospital, near Cambridge.

Mosquitoes were active on several occasions to counter V1s and on 15 January, a 125 Squadron Mossie landed at Coltishall at half past midnight having returned from an intruder mission over Holland, the crew reporting that they saw a V2 rising from near Zwolle presumably from the launch site at Dalfsen at 22.13 and then another at 22.35 near Enschede where there were a number of sites in the east of Holland or over the German border. Another Mosquito crew had reported sighting a V2 launch at 19.01 hours on the same evening north of Den Haag. The V2s were coded 'Big Ben' and the launching sites etc referred to as 'Big Ben sites'.

One of the factories to produce liquid oxygen had been set up in what had been a tram depot at Loosduinen in Holland. Loosduinen is just to the south of Den Haag near the coast. Whilst destruction of the factory would have hit the Germans hard, reconnaissance and intelligence reports concluded that there were too many civilians living around it. It was felt that an air attack was likely to succeed only by a saturation-type raid which could spill over to the civilian houses and result in damage, injury and loss of life to the Dutch population that just wouldn't be acceptable.

During January, the situation was reviewed and it was decided that the factory could be attacked but only if it was done as a precision 'pin-point' attack. Accordingly, pilots from 603 were briefed a number of times for the attack, but each time it was postponed because of the flying conditions. After a number of days when it was 'on', then 'off', then 'on' again, the pilots became a bit cynical.

The attack, whenever it took place, would be planned as a Ramrod and on 13 January, the details for an attempt that day were being put together. However, because of the bad weather it was cancelled and with no other operational commitments, the officer pilots adjourned to the mess bar to celebrate the disbandment of 229 Squadron and the re-forming of 603.

Despite the weather, the squadrons continued to operate as best they might.

On 14 January, the Ramrod to Loosduinen was on again. The weather over Holland was known to be poor, but at 11.40 F/L Welch and P/O Van Dyck (in Q and V respectively) took off on a weather reconnaissance of the target area. They arrived back at 13.20 to report that there was 8/10ths cloud at 1,000 feet and 4/10ths at 15,000. At about 14.00 hours, the operation was cancelled.

The day however turned out to be quite busy. Three aircraft were requested by the army to act as simulated 'doodlebugs' – a sign of the times, and then at 15.15 there was a report that German fighters were attacking a force of American bombers returning across the North Sea. Two Spitfires were scrambled and joined up with six already in the air for formation flying practice to help drive the Germans away, but in the event, no enemy aircraft were sighted.

The ORB records that the Squadron achieved 32 hours 30 minutes practice flying with 52 sorties.

On 15 January, four Spitfires of 603 led by F/L Batchelor (in L) took off at 11.00 hours on an armed reconnaissance to Hoek van Holland and Staalduin Bos – a V2 launching site. The others were F/Sgt Haupt (in H), F/L McAndrew (in B) and F/Sgt Green (in E). They crossed the Dutch coast above the cloud level, but because of it couldn't find their target. Unable to make an attack, they set course for home at 11.50. On the way back, they sighted a twin-engined aircraft that they thought might be German heading north and jettisoned their bombs into the sea to give chase. However, it turned out to be an RAF Wellington bomber which they left to continue its sortie in peace, although a little shaken. The four landed safely at 12.30 hours in time for lunch after which the pilots sat the Fighter Command aircraft recognition test number 15 and the Squadron were then released at 15.00.

The weather on 16 January was bad and there was no flying. F/L Staniforth joined in the afternoon.

The weather the following morning, Wednesday 17 January was fine and plans were being put together yet again for the Ramrod to Loosduinen.

At 08.35 two Spitfires of 602 Squadron took off from Swannington on a Jim Crow of the Den Helder area and sighted '5 minesweeper type vessels moving west, grouped round a hulk which had neither funnels or masts, lying stationary in the centre of the Gap. About a quarter of a mile further west, 3 smaller ships were moving slowly westward. A merchant vessel of approx. 5-6,000 tons was seen moving out of Den Helder harbour and another vessel of the same type and tonnage was seen in the harbour with smoke up.' Having radioed their findings ahead, the two Spitfires landed back at Swannington at 10.00. A tempting set of targets like this couldn't be ignored and plans for a Ramrod were put aside in favour of a Roadstead against the ships.

There was a Coastal Command Strike Wing of Beaufighters based at RAF North Coates a few miles down the coast from Grimsby, and after calling ahead, the W/C (Flying), W/C Lardner-Burke DFC took off from Coltishall at 09.20 in one of the 603 Spitfires for the 20-minute flight to North Coates, 65 miles to the north west of Coltishall. After discussions, details of the Roadstead – 116 – were agreed with a time over target of about 14.05.

The plan, in simple terms, was that 72 Beaufighters of 236 and 254 Squadrons from North Coates, escorted by Spitfires of 602 and 603 Squadrons would attack the ships seen by the earlier Jim Crow after the nearby flak positions were softened up. The Beaufighter squadrons called the mission Operation Strike. The W/C returned to Coltishall at 11.20.

Confusion reigned at 603 as to fuel and bomb loads, but eventually it was decided that the Spitfires should be loaded up with 45-gallon tanks and two 250lb bombs each. At 12.45, Lardner-Burke briefed the pilots in one of the dispersal huts and the rest of the time until take-off was spent making sure that they all were fully up to speed on the detail of the operation.

In the meantime, the number of Beaufighters to take part had been reduced to 32, 16 from each squadron. The 16 from 254 Squadron were armed with cannon and those from 236 with rockets and cannon. The Beaufighter Wing was led by W/C D.L. Cartridge DFC and Bar.

The first group off were the 32 Beaufighters who were airborne from North Coates between 12.39 and 13.02.

At 13.15 hours, 12 Spitfire XVIs of 602 led by S/L Sutherland, also with two 250lb bombs each, roared off from RAF Swannington and once established in formation, turned east towards Coltishall.

At snowy Coltishall, the pilots were settling into their cockpits, tightening harnesses, fastening helmets and oxygen masks. The ground crews crouching on the mainplanes gave canopies and windscreens a final rub before jumping carefully down on to the icy ground. A last look to make sure that there were no oil or coolant leaks and then the coughing, spluttering, shattering roars as the Merlins burst into life, the air blue and smoky with exhaust gas. The 11 Spitfires of 603 taxied out to the runway, long noses fishtailing from side to side so that the pilots could see where they were going. Then on to the runway and in formation over the airfield at 13.30 to rendezvous with the other aircraft of the strike force.

The Spitfire force was led by W/C Lardner-Burke. The pilots of 603 involved were: S/L Donovan, F/Ls Sergeant, Batchelor, McAndrew, Rigler, Kirkman, Welch, P/O McConnochie, W/O Wheatley and F/Sgt O'Reilly. The three groups of aircraft joined up successfully, and at 13.35 the 23 Spitfires and 32 Beaufighters turned east towards the sea and Den Helder, two Spitfires of 602 returning early with engine trouble.

The formations crossed the Dutch coast five miles south of Den Helder, the Spitfires at an altitude of about 11,000 feet and two minutes ahead of the main strike force of Beaufighters. The two Spitfire squadrons separated and then both dive bombed the flak positions around the harbour until the Beaufighters arrived. The Spitfire attacks were highly successful and the timing was perfect. They bombed from 10,000 feet, pulling out at 5,000, strafing the gun positions and whilst some bombs fell into the sea, many found their targets. Unfortunately, Lardner-Burke's bombs 'hung-up' although he stayed in the area for the duration of the attack.

602 broke to port across the harbour as the Beaufighters flew in to start their attack just after 14.11.

The Beaufighters flashed across the water whilst the Spitfires continued to attack the flak positions now concentrating on the Beaus. The air was full of twisting aeroplanes, lines of flak rising from gun positions, smoky trails of rockets from the Beaufighters. Ruler straight lines of cannon shells walked across the water to the ships. A minesweeper-type vessel was seen burning. A flak tower was hit, and there were cannon strikes on a bridge over a canal. The Beaufighters were now taking heavy flak and two collided and crashed in fields to the south of Den Helder. Another (believed to be B of 236 Squadron) was hit in both engines. It turned on to its back and dived into the sea bursting into flames. A fourth Beaufighter also crashed into the sea near the target.

Pilots of 603 said the rusted hulk reported by the Jim Crow mission north of the harbour was putting up 'intense medium and accurate flak' although they also observed strikes on it and as they departed, it was seen to be on fire amidships creating a pall of black smoke. The Beaufighters had riddled it with rocket and cannon fire. To the north east of the docks, another vessel defending itself with heavy medium flak, which the 603 pilots thought was a destroyer (but may have been a minesweeper) was hit 'with a large red explosion' and badly damaged. There was another 'destroyer' nearer the harbour which also 'put up an intense curtain of flak' and a number of tugs or trawler-type auxiliaries were also left damaged and burning. The Beaufighters riddled a gun emplacement south west of the town and an RDF hut was hit with cannon fire.

With the Beaufighter attack well under way, the two squadrons of Spitfires withdrew south to re-form – 602 about 10 miles west of the coastal town of Egmond and 603 to the north of it. 602 set course for Swannington whilst 603 continued to orbit at 8,000 feet until they were re-joined by the surviving Beaufighters now exiting. They all then turned for home at 14.20. Whilst orbiting, two Beaufighters clearly in distress were heard on the R/T; one having been hit in a fuel tank and in flames, the other pilot – probably F/O Gaunt of D (236 Squadron) – reporting coolly that he was going to land in a field.

Bob Sergeant's radio caught fire and his cockpit was filled with smoke. He remembered flying almost below the level of the hulk: 'It was mayhem in there at that low level......masses of flak. I'd never seen anything like it.'

All the Spitfires returned safely with 602 landing at Swannington at 15.00 and 603 at Coltishall five minutes later. The Beaufighters straggled back, touching down at North Coates between 15.12 and 15.47 hours. Two of them, one from each squadron, landed at Donna Nook on the coast. One was V of 254 Squadron flown by P/O J.H. Hayes whose undercarriage wouldn't come down and had to make a belly landing. Five Beaufighters from each squadron were found to be damaged on their return, but six Beaufighters were lost. From 236 Squadron they were: R – F/L Sutehall and F/O Holvey; D – F/O Gaunt and F/Sgt Chrisp; B – F/O Middlemas and W/O Dugdale. From 254 Squadron: A – P/Os F. Trautman and N. Evans; T – F/Os G.D. Warburton and J.A. Grey; F – F/Sgts A.J. Maton and H.K. Radcliffe. The navigator of K of 254 Squadron, P/O L.G. Brown, was wounded slightly in the knee.

It was a high loss ratio and the Beaufighter squadrons couldn't afford to lose crews and aircraft in that way very often. However, the strike was considered to be a great success and there was much congratulation in the air, tinged with the news that the six Beaufighters had not returned. The pilots would be full of adrenaline and excitement as they went off to be interrogated by the Intelligence Officer, their faces lined by the tight helmets and oxygen masks but happy with their success and the fact that they had survived.

Photographs showed that the shipping had 'received rough treatment' – two minesweepers and one trawler-type auxiliary on fire as well as the hulk, and all the other vessels suffering damage from cannon fire.

The bars in the messes were busy that night, so much so that when P/Os Grant and Van Dyck left 603 for new postings, some of their fellow pilots probably didn't notice – or even remember them going.

On this day, the Red Army captured Warsaw. The noose around Germany's neck was tightening.

It was also a significant day for an ex-603 pilot who was now a PoW. Sergeant Harold Bennett had been shot down into the Channel during a Low Ramrod on 8 December 1941. Since then, he had been held in various camps in Germany but at the beginning of 1945 he was in Stalag Luft VII at Bankau in Poland. At 11.00 hours, the prisoners were told that in one hour, they should have packed their kit and be ready to leave the camp on a forced march towards the west and Berlin. Ominously, their captors told them that for any prisoner who fell out of the column, five others would be shot. The start of the march was later postponed, but only for 40 hours.

The next day, 18 January 1945 was disappointing for the pilots. Dawn brought strong winds which increased over the day until in the afternoon they were far stronger than had been forecast and flying was stopped. Just before lunch, 12 Spitfires took off with the intention of 'beating up' North Coates as a salute to the Beaufighter crews of the day before, but the turbulence was quite violent. W/O Cookson's aircraft was thrown about so roughly that he banged his head on the canopy and almost collided with a Spitfire beside him. Some pilots complained of feeling sick with the motion.

The 'beat-up' was called off, but on landing one Spitfire was caught by the wind, skidding into another which was stationary, and damaging both severely.

Some of the Beaufighter crews visited Coltishall but the events of the morning put a dampner on proceedings.

The high winds continued. On Friday 19 January there was a Jim Crow planned which set off at 10.35 but returned at 11.10 because of the weather. Two armed recces were put up in the early afternoon – each made up of four aircraft – and despite the weather both found targets.

Some pilots commented that during the dives on targets, they felt peculiar bumps which a few of them put down to flak although they weren't aware that they were being fired on. W/O Cookson's Spitfire was found to have a hole in its tailplane for no obvious reason. It was eventually decided that the most likely cause of the bumps and the damage were spent shell casings coming from the aircraft in front in the dive to attack.

In Poland at 03.30, Sgt Bennett and his fellow PoWs left the camp and the column, numbering about 1,500 men started its march to the west. Each man was given two and a half days marching rations. There was no transport for the sick and the only medical equipment was what could be carried on the men's backs. It was mid-winter and bitterly cold. On this first day, they marched 28 kilometres. Their accommodation that first night was in a number of small barns.

On the evening of 19 January, another Ramrod to the Loosduinen tram sheds was being set up for the next day. The 603 ORB for 19 January concludes: '.... as this Ramrod has recurred with varying regularity for the last 3 weeks but never been achieved it is unlikely it will occur tomorrow, particularly in view of the dismal weather forecast by Met.' As expected, it was postponed again the next morning following a very cold night with heavy frost and some snow at Coltishall. P/O Thomson arrived at Coltishall to join the unit.

That night and for the following few days there was heavy snow and hard frost which stopped single-engined aircraft flying. Three feet of snow fell overnight at Matlaske and on 20 January, the snow clearance plans were activated. The station commander was clearly concerned about the weather because the emergency rations were checked in case the roads were blocked for a lengthy period and extra heating – braziers – were lit in all ablution and toilet blocks; no doubt to make sure that pipes didn't freeze, rather than to keep the airmen warm! With no central heating, the accommodation buildings were cold and it took some effort to swing feet out of a warm bed in the dark of a January morning with the knowledge that there was a walk in the open to an ablution block for a wash and shave to look forward to. (When the thaw came, there was only one burst pipe.) Vehicles were fitted with chains.

On 25 January, Somerfield track arrived to provide a sound 'stripway' for the aircraft. It was reminiscent of the same period three years before in January 1942 when the Squadron was based at Dyce near Aberdeen and as at that time, attempts were being made to keep the pilots occupied with a mixture of training and visits to local establishments for 'educational' reasons.

On Thursday 22 January, W/C Lardner-Burke organised a visit to a local brewery – Bullard's – in Norwich. This seems to have been very successful. The ORB reports that:

> At least one hour was spent touring the building before the squadron settled down to the main objective of the visit. The draught beer was sampled and considered in a department labelled 'drink your beer quickly and get back to work' before returning to the Bottled Beer Dept. where they settled down to serious study and reflection on the art of brewing from the consumer's point of view.

One pilot said that he found the visit interesting but he:

> Could not help but pity the girls in there who had such tedious jobs. One was doing nothing but putting tops on an endless stream of bottles. What a contrast with our life on the Squadron – it may have had an element of danger but it was never boring.

In the meantime in Germany, the column of PoWs and Harold Bennett was still heading west. By 25 January, they had reached a village called Wenzen which was about half way between Hannover in the north and Kassel in the south. Their march had been very difficult. Some of it was during the night – on the night of 20 January, they were forced to cover 42 kilometres in temperatures as low as -13 degrees centigrade. There was little hot food but the British medical officer had been given a horse and cart to carry some of those who couldn't walk, but it only held six men sitting upright. One morning, the exhausted prisoners were roused at 03.00 to start marching again, and because of the time it took the men to gather their belongings together, the German troops came into the sheds and fired their rifles to move them along.

By 25 January, they had marched 138 kilometres. By this time 23 of the prisoners were missing – either escaped or lost – but thankfully, the Germans didn't carry out their earlier threat. Some of the sicker men were taken away and nothing further was heard of them.

At Coltishall, the next day, 26 January, the pilots spent the afternoon in the gym working off the effects of the previous day's 'educational tour'. During the morning, two new pilots joined the Squadron. Interestingly, they were both from India – P/O Manivalu from Taryore and P/O McGinn from Calcutta. If nothing else, the unit was quite cosmopolitan.

At Matlaske, local farmers asked the station commander for volunteers to help harvest the sugar beet crop and offered to pay them 1/3d an hour* – but there were no takers.

The Concentration Camp at Auschwitz was liberated.

On the Saturday, the Squadron were on readiness but was released at noon and in the evening the A Flight pilots put on a party for their ground crew at a nearby hotel. This seemed to be enjoyed by all.

The weather showed no signs of moderating and Sunday was as cold and frosty as ever. It was learned that S/L Patterson had been awarded the DFC.

The pilots attended a training session on the German jet aircraft the Messerschmitt 262 which was illustrated by American and RAF combat films. The 262 was appearing in increasing numbers and as the Allies advanced into Germany, there was a realistic expectation that the Spitfires might at some point be in combat with them. The 603 complement continued to be swelled with the arrival of F/Os Burrows and H.N. Machon in the morning.

Whilst on Monday 26 January, the cold seemed to lift with the hope of a thaw, it clamped back down again and for the rest of the month, there was little – if any – flying. (602 Squadron at Matlaske/Swannington was similarly restricted.)

For the pilots, the final week of January was filled with training sessions and lectures which covered many different topics. Subjects included aircraft recognition, the general history and commitments of the Squadron, the Big Ben targets, the cockpit layout of their Spitfires and the use of the gyro gunsight, air-sea rescue procedures, security and the Far East. Some more physical pursuits were also undertaken. They had a shooting competition with the pilots of the Polish 303 Squadron also based at Coltishall, spells in the gym and team games.

On 31 January, F/Sgt Webb joined the aircrew and W/C Lardner-Burke organised a visit to Norwich Cathedral. The ORB notes that the visit 'was enjoyed by all and ....some pilots even entered the building.'

The final statistics for the month were:

Total number of operational sorties	74
Total number of operational hours	96 hours 20 minutes
Total number of bombs dropped	96 x 250 lbs
Total number of non-operational hours	71 hours 15 minutes.

Flying had not been possible on 17 days justifying the figures which were considered to be low.

On 31 January, the Red Army established a bridgehead over the River Oder and was now less than 50 miles from Berlin. They were also getting closer to the column of prisoners which had set out from Stalag Luft VII just under two weeks earlier. Since 25 January, Sgt Bennett and his fellow prisoners had marched a further 62 kilometres in appalling conditions – sometimes blizzards – and with barely enough food to eat. Typically, on 29 January, the column of 1,500 was issued with 104kg of meat, a sack of salt, 25kgs of coffee and 100kg of barley. But they had been promised that transport would be available in a few days and could only hope. On 24 January a further 31 desperately sick men were taken to Sagan, where the infamous Stalag Luft III was located.

---

*One shilling and thruppence in 'old' money.

The Commanding Officer, S/L Patterson, had left Coltishall on 12 January to be admitted to Ely Hospital near Cambridge expecting to be there for about two weeks. However, he didn't respond to treatment, and on 30 January wrote what amounted to a farewell letter to the Squadron. Because of his illness, he had to be replaced and S/L Tommy C. Rigler took over and, would be with them until the end of March – almost to the end of the European war.

The ORB contains the following tribute to S/L Patterson:

'Pat' joined the Squadron in July 1944 when it was known as 229 Squadron... his exceptional energy and drive and ability has contributed very largely to the standard and reputation it now enjoys. His loss to the Squadron will be felt greatly by all who have the squadron interests at heart.

He was remembered as a bit of a loner. One pilot, W/O Eric Mee, recalled that Patterson had the windscreen of a Spitfire hanging on the wall of his office. It was starred with a bullet hole in the centre but he never found out the story behind it.

Patterson's departure and the appointment of S/L Rigler were notified on 1 February 1945. The 603 ORB confirms this.

In the morning, information was received of the posting of S/Ldr. Patterson, DFC from the Squadron to SHQ Coltishall wef 26.1.45 and F/Lt. Rigler DFM, late B Flight Commander was promoted to Acting S/Ldr. and appointed Commanding Officer of 603. This appointment was quite expected by everyone and was received with general approval as S/Ldr Rigler's career in the RAF is known to have been packed with activity and success and this promotion is regarded as his due recognition for his services.

In their latest role of ground attack and intruder type missions, 603 couldn't have had a better leader than Tommy Rigler. As a Sergeant Pilot he had taken part in many offensive operations in the summer of 1941 whilst he was with 609 Squadron – the West Riding unit of the AuxAF, based at Biggin Hill. During this time, 603 was part of the Hornchurch Wing beside 54 and 611 Squadrons. Typically, 609 and the Biggin Hill Wing would be flying on a Circus in the target support role with

S/L T.C.Rigler, February 1945.

603 and the Hornchurch Wing carrying out the same duty. The close proximity of Biggin Hill and Hornchurch meant that Rigler would at least be familiar with 603 if nothing else.

In 1941, Sgt Rigler had been awarded the Distinguished Flying Medal – promulgated in the *London Gazette* on 16 September of that year. The citation reads:

> This airman has carried out 82 sorties since March 1941. He has displayed outstanding keenness to destroy the enemy in combat and to harass him on the ground. Sergeant Rigler has destroyed at least seven hostile aircraft (three were destroyed in one sweep) and has damaged a further two.

Rigler was round faced and balding, not the image of the dashing fighter pilot but nonetheless he was clearly one of the best and was in distinguished company. At that time a number of now well known pilots were flying from Biggin Hill with one or other of the squadrons: 'Sailor' Malan, Jean Offenburg, Paul Richey, Jamie Rankin, Vicki and Christian Ortmans the Belgian brothers, Johnnie Curchin and John Bisdee.

As a flight lieutenant, Rigler had been a flight commander with 229 and 603. His tally at this time was eight confirmed kills, one probable and three damaged. As noted in the citation for his DFM he was one of only a few fighter pilots to be credited with three Bf109 'kills' during the same fight. Having become separated from his Squadron over France, he saw some aircraft in the distance – which he took to be Spitfires – and closed in to join up with them from the rear. As he did so, he realised that they were 109s. In for a penny, in for a pound he shot at the rearmost one and it went down. But as the formation broke, two of the 109s collided and both fell out of the sky as well. Rigler decided that discretion was the better part of valour and headed for England with all speed! Bob Sergeant first met Tommy Rigler when he was doing his flying training at RAF Sealand. At that time, Rigler was an LAC and Bob Sergeant had thought he was a Canadian because Rigler had been a lumberjack before joining up. He also had the enviable reputation of being able to drink 'pints of everything'!

The ORB for 1 February 1945 continues:

> The lunch hour, which extended until later in the afternoon was spent in the bar in celebration of S/Ldr Rigler's success. A slight break was made for tea when the Squadron proceeded to a hostelry at Coltishall to continue the same celebration and where it reached a soaking climax.

With all the changes that had taken place, the Squadron flying personnel were now:

S/L T.C. Rigler DFM   Commanding Officer.

A Flight – F/L Jack Batchelor (Flight Commander), P/O Bill Doidge, F/L McAndrew, F/L Bob Sergeant, F/L 'Stan' Staniforth, P/O Thomson, P/O Bala Manivalu (India), F/Sgt 'Paddy' O'Reilly, F/Sgt 'Tommy' Thomson, W/O 'Wally' Haupt, F/O Burrows, F/Sgt Johnny Green (Australian), W/O Maslen.

B Flight – F/L Johnnie Welch DFC (Flight Commander), F/L Jack Kirkman (Australian), F/O McConnochie (New Zealand), W/O Cookson, W/O 'Snowy' Wheatley (Australian), W/O Alfred Beckwith, F/O Sanderson (New Zealand), W/O Eric Mee, P/O Nelson McGinn (India), F/Sgt Laffan, F/O Machon, F/O Richmond and F/Sgt Johnnie Webb.

Despite the general bad weather in January, the intensity of the V2 attacks had increased dramatically.

On Friday 26 January, 17 were launched of which 13 landed in the London area. On a more positive note, the last air-launched V1 to hit London had done so early in the middle of the night of Saturday 13/14 January.

However, the Cabinet was getting increasingly worried about the V2s and on 27 January they decided that the attacks on the launching sites and the infrastructure of the missiles should be intensified – particularly in the area around Den Haag in Holland.

In addition to the main targets, a list of secondary or alternate targets was drawn up – attacks on these were intended to disrupt the support and logistics of the V2s rather than damage them directly. They included targets such as transport, railways – particularly junctions – storage areas, flak positions and the like.

Further, attacks were often ordered at short notice after the Dutch Resistance had passed on information about launches and potential targets.

In mid-February, orders were received that a different strategy was to be adopted. Rather than attacking as many targets as they could, attention was to be concentrated on specific ones for a week at a time. The sites allocated to 603 were important storage areas for the V2, so success now would reduce the numbers of rockets being fired at London and the other cities. The general strategy was that continual attacks on the launch site areas would upset the activities of the German troops. As the pilots couldn't see the target vehicles their orders were to bomb certain parts of the woods where V2s were thought to be operating rather than look for the actual sites themselves.

As well as the change of command, the beginning of February also brought milder weather. The airmen who made their way down to dispersal on the morning of Thursday 1 February found that there had been a fast thaw overnight and the snow had virtually gone. However, the speed of the thaw meant that the airfield was now waterlogged and it was declared unfit for flying. Friday brought gales and rain and again, flying was impossible.

Saturday 3 February saw a huge change for the better with clear blue skies and sun which allowed the resumption of operations. In fact, it was a busy day for 603. There were four armed recces and the Readiness Section was scrambled.

The armed recces were all against Big Ben targets. The first two were both to the complex at Haagse Bos where some blocks of flats were thought to be the headquarters of the rocket-firing troops. There were four Spitfires in each raid and they carried two 250lb MC bombs with .025 second tail fuses.

The first was led by the CO with F/L Staniforth, P/O Doidge and F/Sgt O'Reilly taking off at 11.05. Ten minutes out, they saw a V2 launch directly ahead of them. The formation crossed the Dutch coast at Katwijk and carried out their dive-bombing attacks at 11.45. There was some flak but it didn't cause any problems. Climbing to 8,000 feet, they patrolled inland to Utrecht but nothing of interest was seen. The four Spitfires then turned back for home and landed at 12.40.

It was quite normal to 'loiter' after an attack had been completed hoping to find 'targets of opportunity'. Raymond Baxter recalls on one occasion spotting a column of horse-drawn vehicles, but on taking his section down to attack, found that they were Dutch civilians. Expecting to be strafed, the Dutch had jumped into the ditches alongside the road, but nonetheless waved enthusiastically at the Spitfires flashing over their heads! The Germans had realised that horse-drawn carts weren't being attacked by the marauding Spitfires and they started to use them for their own transport. The Allies let it be known to the Dutch that to overcome this, they would 'buzz' the carts first so that the occupants could jump off and into safety. Once they started doing this, the Germans soon stopped the practice. The Dutch were very much with the British pilots in what they were trying to do even if it meant that there were Dutch casualties. The sight of RAF Spitfires overhead encouraged them hugely and gave them the feeling that they were not forgotten and alone. The Dutch were quite selfless and an exploding V2 or a stray bomb which might kill or injure them was regarded as a sacrifice which might help the Allies release them from their occupation. This winter was the 'hunger winter' when food was desperately short – to such an extent that ultimately RAF Lancasters were dropping food to the Dutch people in Operation Manna. The loss of an RAF Spitfire was a tragedy for the Dutch as well as for the British, but the ordinary Dutch civilians endured their hardships stoically and with enormous courage.

The second raid was led by F/L Welch with a trio of W/Os; Mee, Cookson and Beckwith and took off at 13.05 for the same target as the first. It was Eric Mee's second operational trip – in U for Urinal:

> Taking off, my plane felt a bit clumsy until the wings took the weight, and following number 3, I was soon in a 'split-arse' climbing turn to port after retracting the undercarriage as it parted company with the ground. We climbed in tight formation through several layers of thin cloud.
> Having crossed the coast, we were now at about 12,000 feet. On levelling out, the order was given to fly in open formation, this was about three or four wingspans apart so that we could relax a little and at the same time keep a good look-out.

The weather cleared as we approached the Dutch coast and the order came from the leader to 'change gear'. This was the instruction to us to switch back to our main tank and jettison the belly tank. To me this was a slight problem. To reach the release lever it was necessary for me to put my seat down to its lowest position. The trouble was that when I bent down to pull on the lever – and it often needed a hefty tug – my head would disappear below the canopy. This first caused consternation amongst my colleagues when they looked across and saw my Spitfire wobbling about with apparently no one in the cockpit. Later on they used to look on with amusement at my antics and make ribald remarks later at debriefing.

It was an exciting moment when I first crossed the enemy occupied coast, lots of neat looking fields. Then a cluster of black puff-balls blossomed to our right. The formation seemed to close up for mutual comfort as the leader changed direction a few degrees and altered our height in case it was predicted fire.

We returned to our original course which soon brought us over The Hague. The command was given 'echelon starboard go' and like well drilled ballet dancers I, together with number 3, went down under numbers 1 and 2 and came up in echelon on their right hand side.

Looking over the port wing I could see lots of houses and other buildings. Gradually the woods came into view down on our left. By this time we had dropped to about eight thousand feet with speed reduced to just under two hundred mph. As the target appeared under the trailing edge of the leader's wing, he would roll over and put the Spitfire into an almost vertical dive, closely followed by the rest of the pack.

As number 4, I was last down and was able to see the thick carpet of exploding light flak that had been aimed at the others. Then I became aware of the little red balls of fire that were coming straight at me, slowly at first, then nipping past my cockpit at a fantastic pace. No time to admire the fireworks, the task now was to pick up the target in the gunsight and fly accurately – any slipping or skidding would throw the bombs off target. Numbers 1, 2 and 3 were pulling out of their dives and it was my turn to aim at the missiles in the wood and press the bomb release. At the same time, it was necessary as the last man to operate my camera gun to record the strikes of the other chaps' bombs. This meant carrying on a little longer in the dive and the little red balls were still coming up at me, and I was all too well aware that for every one I could see there were about ten other invisible shells in between.

We pilots had a saying 'Going in you are working for the Government, coming out you are working for yourself'. This was obvious in our getaway!

After flying as accurately as possible going in, I pulled out at about three thousand feet in a 5 or 6G pullout which produced a short blackout. A good yell at this point with my feet up on the G pedals – the stick and rudder were pushed all around the cockpit to produce as erratic a course as possible, thereby hoping to confuse the gunners. I was now headed out to sea and as any wartime pilot will have experienced once having been separated for a few moments all your accompanying aircraft disappear – into thin air. Looking around on levelling out over the sea, I could not see another plane anywhere. Not to worry, though. At the briefing the leader had arranged to orbit at a pre-arranged height out to sea. Hauling back on the control column I used up my excess speed to catapult me up to the rendezvous height and sure enough there the others were, just forming up in loose formation. The return was uneventful.

They had crossed in south of Katwijk and bombed at 13.40 – their bombs falling in much the same area as the first ones along the southern edge of the woods. This time smoke and debris were seen. They also reported damaging a long white vehicle crossing a bridge in the target area and seeing white smoke and debris. Officially the flak defences were not considered to have caused them any problems. They crossed back out at 13.45 to land safely back at Coltishall at 14.25.

Bob Sergeant thought that sometimes flak was quite pretty. 'You see these black bursts and they open up into beautiful red inside.'

Many of the pilots tipped into the dive trying to ignore the little gnaw of fear of flak and hoping that it wouldn't hit them. Paddy O'Reilly remembers:

On crossing the Dutch coast we would encounter spasmodic flak but once in the area of the target there would be a solid depth of it through which you would have to dive before releasing your bombs. We got to expect this but nevertheless when diving into target and seeing this solid wall of white puffs of smoke you were diving into, you tended to flinch when you hit it.

Jack Batchelor used to try to note the position of any particularly troublesome flak batteries and if he got the chance would shoot it up later. The heaviest flak was north of Den Haag, and as was described, the Spitfires would weave to put the German gunners off their aim.

The third armed recce of the day was to a complex at Staalduin Bos at the Hook of Holland. The four Spitfires took off at 14.55 with F/L Batchelor leading F/Sgt Thomson, F/L McAndrew and F/Sgt O'Reilly. The four crossed in near the target, bombed successfully from 10,000 feet and reported causing damage. Their aiming point was a housing estate which was suspected of being used as billets and a storage area and smoke was seen rising following the attack. They found the flak to be 'very concentrated and light with red and yellow tracer' but none of the aircraft was hit. They landed at 16.30 hours.

Ironically, on the way out at 15.35 hours, they saw clouds of smoke rising from Loosduinen where the much planned Ramrod against the liquid oxygen factory had at last taken place, but without 603!!

On this occasion, 602 and 453 Squadrons at Swannington were tasked with it – Ramrod 20 – and there were two attacks that day. The first set off at 09.55 with 12 Spitfires (one returning with a mechanical failure) but the others, carrying 500lb and 250lb bombs attacked in dives from 9,000 feet to 2,500. They encountered intense and accurate light and medium flak over the target and reported that the majority of the bombs undershot although some landed near the sheds.

Permission was sought from 12 Group for another attack to be carried out, and having been granted, the Spitfires took off again at 14.55 hours – Ramrod 21. This time the results were 'fair'. Bombs were seen to fall on the buildings leaving a column of smoke that rose to 1,000 feet. Other bombs just missed the target structures but the pilots felt that blast and shrapnel damage must have been significant. They also noted the bomb craters from the first raid and it was felt that these must have caused some damage as well. On this occasion, the flak wasn't as intense as on the previous Ramrod and not as accurate. Two aircraft had returned early because of mechanical problems, but the others landed safely at 16.25.

Meanwhile, back at Coltishall, the final 603 armed recce was taking off at 15.35. This one was led again by the CO, with F/L Kirkman and W/Os Cookson and Wheatley each with two 250lb bombs. Their target on this occasion was a launch complex at Hague Langenhorst. They saw hits and left one building smoking. From there they headed over to Loosduinen at 16.15 to observe the result of the Ramrod. No damage was seen but cine photographs were taken by the CO. They then turned north over Delft crossing out north of Den Haag to land back at base at 17.00 hours.

The other operational activity that day was the scramble at 15.55 of the Readiness Section (P/O Doidge and F/L Staniforth) to investigate a report of a ditched aircraft off Southwold. Nothing was found although they reported a lot of shipping. It was later discovered that nine crew members of a Flying Fortress had been found in two dinghies with one other unaccounted for.

Despite the operational work there was also training. New pilots to a unit usually started off with flights to familiarise themselves with the local area known as 'sector reccos'. Because of the commitments of the Spifire XVIs, these training flights were carried out in Spitfire Vs – presumably 'borrowed' for the purpose.

It had been a successful day. There had been 18 operational sorties with full serviceability, nine sector reccos and five air tests. Some of the 'old lags' had flown twice on one or other of the raids, or as for Doidge and Staniforth once on a raid and once on the scramble. Staniforth also flew an air test.

For the Coltishall Wing, the tally of operational sorties was 88. The Squadron could be rightly pleased with their efforts as they settled down for the night; despite the raids on Loosduinen by 602 and 453, 603 would still have the opportunity in the coming weeks to have a crack at the factory as well.

For the next two days the weather was poor again and although some flying took place, no significant missions were undertaken. On 4 February, S/L Rigler held a conference to discuss and hopefully agree a way of bringing together the existing ex-229 (now 603) ground crew with the 6603 Service Echelon still billeted at Matlaske. Those attending the meeting included a number of officers from the old 603 Squadron – the Adjutant F/L Oddy, the Engineering Officer F/L Rogers, the Intelligence Officer, F/O Allott together with F/Ls Welch and Batchelor, F/O Stoneman who was the current Engineering Officer and P/O Cooper who was the current Intelligence Officer.

Later it was learnt that Stoneman had been posted to RAF Eshott (a training airfield near Ashington, Northumberland) and it was assumed that Rogers would once again take over as Engineering Officer.

On 5 February, the weather improved after lunch but flying was still restricted because the airfield was waterlogged. F/O Allott was posted to the Squadron in a supernumerary capacity. In the morning before lunch the pilots were given a lecture on the IFF system by the Station Signals Officer – S/L Pagram – and then in the afternoon, P/O Cooper tested them with Fighter Command aircraft recognition test 16 – one of them failing it! Following this, F/L Oddy – who was leaving to join 18 Group – gave them a talk on the history of 603 Squadron.

Deep in Germany, the long march of Allied PoWs was finally over and transport was provided for them, but whilst it was better than marching, the conditions nonetheless were, to say the least, poor. A report to the Swiss Commission as the protecting power made by the camp medical officer on 15 February 1945 describes the journey:

> On arrival at Goldberg, we were put into cattle trucks, an average of 55 men to each truck. By this time there were numerous cases of dysentery and facilities for men to attend to personal hygiene were inadequate. The majority had no water on the train for two days. When the men were allowed out of the trucks to relieve themselves, numerous of the guards ordered them back inside again and we had to be continually getting permission for the men to be allowed out. We were on the train from the morning of February the 5th until the morning of February 8th. Before commencing this journey, we were issued with sufficient rations for two days. The total distance marched was 240kms.

Their final destination was Stalag IIIA at Luckenwalde near Berlin. The medical officer concluded his report with a summary:

> As a result of this march and the deplorable conditions, the morale of the men is extremely low. They are suffering from an extreme degree of malnutrition and at present, an outbreak of dysentery. There are numerous cases of frostbite and other minor ailments. They are quite unfit for any further movement. Food and better conditions are urgently required. We left Bankau with no Red Cross supplies and throughout the march all the rations were short issued, the most outstanding being bread, which amounts to 2,924 loaves.

Sgt Harold Bennett was eventually released. He recalled that the Russians drove their tanks through the main gates of the camp to open it up. They were told to keep inside but they had to forage in the surrounding areas to get food. One day, a column of American trucks arrived to take them away, but the Russians didn't want this to happen and fired their rifles above the trucks when the prisoners tried to clamber aboard. It seems that they wanted to hold on to the British PoWs to swap them for Russians.

They were held for about a month, but eventually allowed to leave, taken by truck towards the west and then flown back to the UK; either in C47s or Lancasters – Bennett doesn't recall which. They finally landed at Blackbushe and Sgt Bennett was home after almost four years in captivity. Harold Bennett finished up as a warrant officer and on leaving the air force returned to his engineering. In 1961 he turned to teaching and in the sixties became a lecturer at Kingston College of Further Education. Content to stay in engineering, he moved to Erith College in Kent teaching computer-aided engineering design. He retired in 1988 and still lives in Kent at the time of writing.

Back in Britain, for the next few days, in fact for the rest of the month, the weather conspired to ma[ ] flying difficult – if not impossible for 603 – and there were a number of raids which were plann[ ] then cancelled – including the elusive Loosduinen tram sheds. On some of the days there was [ ] change in the way that the Squadron operated. Each sortie from Coltishall involved a double crossi[ ] of the North Sea, which was wasteful of time and fuel. Depending on the specific target, this cou[ ] be 150 odd miles – a round trip of about 300 miles. To reduce this non-effective time, some of t[ ] days were planned to make use of the airfield at Ursel (sometimes referred to as B67) position[ ] between Brugge and Ghent in Belgium. The Spitfires would carry out their raids against the targe[ ] on the Dutch coast, then fly south to land at Ursel for re-arming and re-fuelling allowing them [ ] carry out a second raid in Holland, before flying back across the North Sea to Coltishall for the nig[ ] It also meant that the reduced fuel load that was needed could be replaced by a greater bomb load[ ]

The weather on the morning of Tuesday 6 February was promising and again the Ramrod agai[ ] Loosduinen was set up for mid-day and 124 Squadron arrived at Swannington from Manston to ta[ ] part, but eventually, because of the worsening weather conditions in the afternoon, yet again it w[ ] cancelled. However, the Wing laid on a number of operations including a 12-Spitfire show by 6[ ] against the V2 sites at Haagse Bos. They carried two 250 lb bombs each and all fell in the targ[ ] area despite some intense flak.

Two days later, 603 was tasked yet again to attack the liquid oxygen factory at Loosduinen. T[ ] intention was that they would perform the raid, re-arm and re-fuel at Ursel, carry out attacks on t[ ] railway system around Utrecht and fly home. With the CO leading, 12 Spitfires took off at 10.[ ] and made for the target. Their luck, as always, was against them and it was covered by cloud. Th[ ] were unable to find a gap so turned south and found one over the storage and firing site at Staaldu[ ] Bos. Despite some heavy flak the target was bombed successfully and the aircraft all landed safe[ ] at Ursel at 11.30.

The weather closed in on them at Ursel but they took off again at 13.05 looking for t[ ] transportation targets, but because of the deteriorating conditions, they were ordered home a[ ] landed back at Coltishall at 14.05.

On Friday 9 February, they at last managed to hit Loosduinen. In the morning, after having look[ ] at the weather only an optimist would have thought that a successful operation would be possib[ ] At 08.20, a four-Spitfire armed weather recce led by F/L Batchelor took off to find stratus and c[ ] nimbus cloud in layers from 3,000 to 15,000 feet with icing conditions at 8,000 feet. The aircr[ ] came back at 09.45. A second weather recce set out again at 10.30 but reported similar condition[ ]

Finally, a third recce (of two Spitfires) which left Coltishall at 12.30 found that the cloud h[ ] blown inland and that there was a clear belt of about 40 miles over the coast.

The changed conditions allowed a Ramrod to be laid on and ten 603 Spitfires took off witho[ ] other support at 14.25. They each took with them a single 500lb and two 250lb bombs with .0[ ] second delay fuses. They were led by the CO, the other pilots being F/Os McConnochie a[ ] Sanderson, F/L Welch, W/Os Cookson and Beckwith, F/L Batchelor, P/O Doidge, F/L Stanifor[ ] and F/Sgt Thomson.

They flew directly to Den Haag, crossing in at 15.00 at 12,000 feet then turned directly [ ] Loosduinen where visibility was perfect. The Spitfires peeled off and bombed east/west fro[ ] 12,000 to 3,000 feet. The pilots reported quite a lot of damage including: 'a large orange flash a[ ] a mushroom of orange flame' coming up from one building. Flak was reported as 'meagre'.

The ten Spitfires flew on to Ursel, landing at 15.45 which they left again at 16.30 to land ba[ ] at Coltishall at 17.30. It had been a successful strike – at last!

Although some successful sorties were completed over the next few days, the weather severe[ ] limited flying and it wasn't until St Valentine's Day – Wednesday 14 February 1945 – that there w[ ] a flurry of activity for 603.The entry for the 603 ORB for the day was as follows:

Two aircraft led by F/Lt. Sergeant were airborne at 08.00 on a weather recce but both aircraft developed technical faults and were forced to return early landing at 08.25. Aircraft B was suffering from R/T transmitter trouble and the engine of F cut out when the jet tank was switched on.

At 09.25 12 Spit:XVI led by F/Lt. Batchelor and each armed with 2 x 250lb M.C. and 1 x 500lb M.C. bombs fused for airburst were airborne to attack firing and storage sites at Hague/Haagesbosch. Aircraft set course at 09.30 and flew to cross in at Gravenzamde at 11,000 ft at 10.00. Thence the formation flew straight to the target and dived from East to West from 10,500 ft down to 4,000 ft. Bombs were seen to fall along the length of the road throughout the target area, but 3 sticks fell parallel to the target about a hundred South. Black 1 (F/Lt. Welch DFC) had a hang up caused by electrical failure and jettisoned his 2 x 250 lb bombs at sea taking his 500lb bomb back to Ursel as an unsolicited gift. The aircraft experienced moderate medium flak from the whole target area and some heavy flak from the Northern Schelde islands when rendezvousing before flying to Ursel where they landed at 10.45. At 12.10 they were airborne again to attack the liquid oxygen factory at Loosduinen, flying direct from Ursel to the target and attacking it from 10,000ft in dives down to 4,000ft at 12.30 with cannon and machine guns on an E/W course. Aircraft crossed out over the Hague and returned to base landing at 13.25.

Immediately the aircraft were seized for re-fuelling and rearming as yet a third show was laid on for 16.00. While taxiing out for this F/O McConnochie in T had the misfortune to run into a tractor drawing a bomb trolley which had remained in the peri-track despite the movement of aircraft. The bump was gentle and little damage seemed to have been done on cursory examination and as the driver of the tractor baled out in time no one was hurt, but only 11 aircraft took off on the recce led by F/Lt Batchelor, which was airborne at 16.00 to attack Hague/Loosduinen. 2 aircraft developed mechanical trouble and were forced to return early landing at base at 16.40. 9 aircraft however went on to bomb the target attacking in dives from 8,000ft down to 2,000ft on an E/W course. All bombs fell in the target area at least 10 being within a hundred yards of the aiming point. ...another stick was observed to burst on the road leading through the target area. Moderate accurate flak was observed from the target area and meagre but accurate heavy from the Hook of Holland. The weather over the target was good but cloud 10/10ths at 8 – 9,000ft forced the pilots to begin their dives lower down than usual.

The day was both busy and successful. 37 operational sorties were flown for a total of 43 hours. The morning shows were both satisfactory engagements while that in the afternoon must be considered highly successful.

They landed back at 17.25. The same pilots flew all three missions so they would be feeling quite weary as night fell on Coltishall. They would also be feeling buoyed up by their successful – and much planned – attacks on the liquid oxygen factory.

It is interesting that in all the various raids undertaken, there are no encounters with enemy aircraft. The RAF seemed to be able to operate over these Dutch coastal sites almost at will despite their clear importance for Germany's defence. That isn't to say that there was no threat, but none ever materialised.

The following day, the Squadron pilots were released for training, and for the next week, a combination of foggy weather and training meant that no operations were undertaken by 603 until 21 February. The pilots, as usual in these circumstances, had their time filled in for them with lectures and ground training – some of it in the station gym.

On the afternoon of 17 February, two of the pilots who had been shot down behind enemy lines passed on their experiences. F/L Kirkman spent some time as a PoW in Italy escaping from the camp he was held in near Ravenna when Italy surrendered. The Germans were still fighting in Italy and he had had to find his way through the Appennines before finally reaching the Allies in an open boat sailing down the Adriatic to Cartona. F/Sgt Webb had been shot down just after D-Day flying a Mustang and had been a successful evader – ie, he had been able to avoid being captured by the Germans and managed to lie low until he could make contact with the advancing Allied armies.

It was during this period that the Spitfires were repainted with 603 markings.* As well as the XT codes, they each had a crest painted on the nose – the familiar 'David's Tower' which features on Edinburgh's coat of arms and on the Squadron badge. Many – if not all – the aircraft had names and each was named after a form of transport. Jack Batchelor's was called 'Batch's Buggy', Bob Sergeant's was 'Bob's Slayer', Eric Mee's was 'Curly's Caravan' on account of his nickname, and F/O John Moss, who joined the Squadron some months later at Skeabrae recalls that there was one called 'Jock's Trap' but he doesn't remember whose it was! One exception to this rule was Nick Machon, whose Spitfire was called 'Guernsey's Reply'!

Aircrew with families living in occupied countries were able to fly under assumed names in case they were captured. There had been reports of some families in Occupied Europe being cruelly treated under such circumstances. Nick Machon was one such pilot – his parents still lived in Guernsey. In 1940, he had escaped from Guernsey the day before the Nazi occupation of the island began. As a youngster, Machon had been an addict of Simon Templar – 'The Saint' – books which became popular after the war. Guernseyman Machon's middle name was Nicholle, which, when he had been instructing in the USA, had been contracted to 'Nick' by the Americans. He decided that his new identity would be Nicholas Templar! If he had been captured though, it might have been awkward explaining the name of his Spitfire!

When not flying, many of the pilots played bridge and it wasn't unusual for them to go off on a sortie leaving their bridge hands on a table in the crew room for them to continue the 'rubber' when they got back. The two flights of the Squadron often had different dispersals so there was usually a friendly rivalry between them. The dispersal huts were pretty cold and heated by coke-fired pot-bellied iron stoves that many British servicemen and women will well recall. They were difficult to get going and were usually given some encouragement with a cocktail of aircraft oil and 100 octane petrol in a can. If there were glowing embers, the method was for a 'volunteer' to open the lid of the stove, place the can on the top beside the hole, and using a long stick, tip it over so that the mixture would empty into the stove – and run like hell for the door! The other pilots had already taken the sensible precaution of being outside. There would be a tremendous 'woof' as the mixture went up with a huge flame shooting out of the chimney in the roof, and then there would be a mad dash back inside to get the best seats near the warmth.

As a variation on this, sometimes the pilots of one flight would go across to the other flight's hut and after climbing carefully and quietly on to the roof, drop a Very flare down the stovepipe chimney and into the flames! The resulting explosion would usually blow the lid of the stove around the room, giving those inside an uncomfortable few seconds.

Bob Sergeant recalled another flaming incident.

> We were cleaning the brown linoleum in the hut with petrol. We'd moved the furniture out and the petrol can was on the floor. In comes one of the W/Os who was smoking. Someone shouted 'Put that out!' and he said 'Why?' and threw the cigarette down on the floor! The place went up like a torch! We were out of the windows, packing out the doors! He realised what he had done and picked up the can to take it out but dropped it and got a bit burnt!

Most of them had bicycles, and when the weather was bad they'd practice formation or manoeuvring on their bikes – and sometimes they just had good natured mounted fights. If there was snow, there would be snowball fights with whoever happened to come along.

For the pilots flying an operational sortie it wasn't just a case of jumping into their Spitfires and going off. They had all the preliminaries before going and the post operation debriefs. At briefing they would be given target maps and photographs. One pilot recalls that on one of the stations, one wall was covered with a large photographic mosaic of Holland which was crystal clear. The target maps included the streets of Den Haag. They worked out their routes and they were marked on the flying charts. Then they were issued with an escape kit in a plastic box which held emergency rations, currency, maps printed on silk. Call signs and radio channels were written on the back of

*For example, Nick Machon flew Spitfire 9R●N on 15 February and XT●Q on 19 February.

hands. The radios had to have the right crystals put into them for the frequencies to be used. There were four channels – selected by push buttons – aerodrome base, operational control, emergency and a channel for an airfield on the continent.

At that time, RAF aircrew who were operating on the other side of the Channel were issued with revolvers and a belt of ammunition to aid their escape if shot down.

On return, the Squadron Intelligence Officer first relieved the pilots of their escape kits (particularly the currency) then they were debriefed and the IO would write up a report that would be sent 'up the line'.

The Squadron had recently moved to a different dispersal with all that that entailed, but on 16 February it became known that there was a distinct chance that it was moving to nearby RAF Ludham. This was not a popular piece of news.

It was also suggested that 602 was to move to Ludham which would mean that the two rival Scottish auxiliary squadrons might be operating from the same airfield.

On Wednesday 21 February, morning mist prevented an 07.30 weather recce and an 09.30 '12 aircraft show'. Despite the odds, it cleared later and the weather over Holland was reported as being just right for operations. A series of armed recces was set up, each to comprise four Spitfires taking off at 45-minute intervals and targeting the V2 site at Haagse Bos. The first four were airborne at 11.45 led by F/L Batchelor and concentrated on the north-east part of the launch area. They reported that all the bombs had landed in the target area with good results.

The ORB gives a vivid account of the rest of the day:

The second four were airborne at 12.30 and led by S/Ldr. Rigler DFM repeated the attack on this same target, bombs again falling in a good cluster towards the N.E. end of the target. F/O. McGinn on his first operation had trouble with his jet-tank but carried on his main tank to complete the job being forced to land at Beccles due to fuel shortage on the return. The third section led by F/Lt. Welch DFC were airborne at 13.15 and again attacked the same target. By this time the flak was dying away and again good results were obtained, 3 sticks burst in a line along the Northern edge of the target area, and 1 stick undershooting slightly fell on the road 100 yards East of the Bridge leading to the North East end of the target. The fourth section led by F/Lt. Batchelor were airborne at 14.00 to attack the same target, but to concentrate this time on the centre section. 3 sticks of bombs fell in a line dead across the centre of the target, but one stick hung up slightly and releasing as the pilot pulled out of his dive fell about 2 miles N.W. of the target at 648941. The fifth section was airborne at 14.50 to attack the same target, again concentrating on the centre of the area. This section was led by F/Lt. Kirkman and achieved some of the best bombing of the day. All the bombs fell dead on the target area, 3 sticks bursting right along its NE/SW axis and 1 stick slightly South of these.

F/Lt. Welch DFC again led the sixth formation airborne at 16.20 to attack the same target but with another switch this time back to the North Eastern part of the target. Again good bombing was achieved, 3 sticks of bombs bursting in the centre of the target, and one stick bursting in the North East corner. The seventh section was led by F/Lt. McAndrew and was airborne at 17.00 to attack the same target. Flak was more intense on both this trip and the last trip but good bombing was again achieved, all bombs falling in the target area, 2 sticks falling in the centre of the area, 1 on the southern half of the target and one in the North East corner.

The eighth formation of three aircraft was led by F/Lt. Staniforth and airborne at 17.10 for the same job. Ground mist and fairly intensive flak necessitating evasive action prevented observation of bomb bursts, but the pilots felt sure that all bombs fell in the target area.

The day was a success – 31 sorties, 43 flying hours and good bombing results.

The contribution of the ground crews mustn't be overlooked. Aircraft were being used more than once by different pilots and this needed quick re-fuelling and re-arming. 603 was operating as a team which produced the results expected of it.

The target took a real pounding. The same day, 602 was also bombing it and carried out 28 sorties against it – each Spitfire taking 2 x 250lb bombs fused for airburst. The following day concentrated attacks on the same target area were made by the two squadrons again and the German troops trying to operate the V2s must have been having an unpleasant time. On the 22nd, 603 flew 35 sorties for 41 hours and dropped 58 250lb bombs fused for airburst on the same area along with 602 carrying out similar attacks.

By this time, 602 was also flying out of Coltishall, having moved there from Swannington/Matlaske on 18 February. That was only a temporary measure and on 23 February, 602 moved to Ludham. 603 was supposed to move in that day too, but the weather was poor and after some flying in the early morning, operations were cancelled and there was no more flying. 602 seem to have managed to get their aircraft to Ludham nonetheless as presumably the weather closed in further as the day went on. S/L Rigler and some of the ground staff of 603 crossed over to Ludham by road to start the settling-in process, but it wasn't until the early afternoon of the following day that the aircraft arrived on returning from a sortie.

Ludham had had a chequered history. Until August 1943, it had been home to a number of different RAF squadrons, but it was planned to give it over to the USAAF 8th Air Force and vacated by the RAF. It was virtually unused for a year, although it proved a haven to two B17s which crash landed there returning from raids. One arrived on 27 September 1943 returning from Emden. It was from the 96th Bomb Group flying out of Snetterton and on 8 October another – 'Just a Snappin' – from the 100th Bomb Group at Thorpe Abbotts also made an emergency landing after a raid on Bremen. In August 1944 the Royal Navy took the airfield over giving it the name HMS *Flycatcher*. It was used as the headquarters of their MONABs – Mobile Naval Air Bases which were compact, mobile units used to carry out fast repairs and preparation of Fleet Air Arm aeroplanes. Five of these units were formed at Ludham before moving to Australia and also a 'transportable aircraft maintenance yard' was formed before it too went to Australia – presumably to take part in the expected fighting for Japan.

HMS *Flycatcher* moved to Middle Wallop and on 19 February 1945, S/L P.G. Ottewill GM was appointed station commander with F/O W.G. Handley as adjutant. Both arrived at Ludham at 11.00 to start the process of turning a naval air station into an RAF airfield. Although officially it was now under the control of the RAF, some functions – like the airmens' cookhouse, the officers' mess and the telephone exchange were still being operated by naval personnel. The first airmen and WAAFs arrived on 20 February, but it wasn't until 24 February – the day after the arrival of S/L Rigler and the first group from 603 – that the 700 or so naval personnel finally left.

It says a great deal about all the RAF personnel involved – including the station staff – that both 602 and 603 were each undertaking operations the day after they arrived. It must have been quite chaotic organising not just the squadrons, but the station as well. For both squadrons, it was their second move within a few days, although for 603 it had been only a change of dispersal at Coltishall and not a full blown squadron move to a new airfield.

At 07.35 on Sunday 25 February, F/L Staniforth and F/O Burrows were airborne for 603's first operational sorties from its new home – a weather recce of the Dutch coast. They returned safely at 09.45.

The weather recces were usually the first flights of the day. Paddy O'Reilly recalled:

> We would fly at sea level over the North Sea and at about a mile from the Dutch coast climb to two or three thousand feet. We would then observe the cloud density over the target area and if the area was clear of cloud we would transmit the code message 'OK for Bertie' which would tell the Ops people that the sorties could carry a 1,000 lb bomb load. If the cloud mass was 2 to 6/10ths we would transmit 'OK for Roderick' which meant that we could carry two 250lb bombs and a 90 gallon overload tank.

Bob Sergeant recalled that coming back from an early morning weather recce, the pilots looked forward to their 'aircrew breakfast' which included luxuries like bacon and eggs.

The rest of the month was taken up with operations against the same target area at Haagse Bos. In addition on 25 February, two sections of two Spitfires acted as escorts to Mustangs in the photographic reconnaissance role who were operating out of Bradwell Bay and taking photographs of the targets being attacked by 603 and 602.

On 26 and 27 February, operations were limited by the weather, but not completely curtailed and again, the same targets were being attacked. On the 26th, the Squadron was visited by the AOC of 12 Group, AVM Baker CB, MC, DFC and the Sector Commander, G/C Donaldson. On the same day, there was some excitement when no less than six USAAF B17s force landed at Ludham because they were low on fuel on their way back from a daylight raid on Berlin. Their experiences and descriptions of the destruction being visited on Berlin clearly impressed the RAF personnel who came in contact with the Americans.

28 February was extremely heavy in terms of flying. In all 36 operational sorties were completed with 47 hours and 10 minutes of flying time. The day started at 07.15 with four Spitfires carrying out an armed weather recce. Thereafter there were more attacks by sections of four Spitfires taking off at 10.15, 11.15, 12.10, 13.20, 14.15, 15.15, 16.15 and 17.05 hours. F/L Batchelor and F/L Staniforth – White 1 and 2 – on their second sortie of the day diverted in to Ursel after the attack because one of the aircraft developed engine problems. They returned to Ludham later.

As well as the attacks by 603, 602 was also carrying out similar programmes of sorties against the same targets on these days. On the 28th, 602 flew four-aircraft missions taking off at 08.55, 11.45, 12.55, 13.00, 14.35, 15.00 and 16.00 hours. Ludham was busy with Spitfires setting out and returning and the enemy troops in Holland were being given little respite. It was noticeable that on the days when the weather was poor and stopped the Spitfires flying, the Germans seemed to be able to launch more V2s.

The final statistics for operations by 603 at the end of February were:

Total number of operational sorties	277
Total number of operational hours	380 hours, 15 minutes
Total number of bombs dropped	414 x 250lbs, 33 x 500lbs
Total number of non-operational hours	146 hours and 40 minutes

These show just how much of a difference the weather had made in January. The CO commented that it had been a successful month with good bombing results. He also thought the numbers of sorties flown to be 'creditable' taking into consideration that the Squadron had moved twice during that period and that seven days had been unfit for flying.

For the record, though, 602 had flown 363 operational sorties in the same period.

The beginning of March brought little difference for the pilots and ground crew of 603 but changes were coming. In the meantime, their attacks on the V2 sites at the Haagse Bos continued.

On Thursday 1 March, the Squadron flying personnel were:

S/L T.C. Rigler DFM   Commanding Officer

A Flight – F/L Batchelor (Flight Commander), F/L McAndrew, F/L Sergeant, F/L Staniforth, F/O Thomson, P/O Manivalu, F/Sgt O'Reilly, W/O Thomson, W/O Haupt, F/O Burrows, W/O Green, W/O Maslen and W/O Godfrey.

B Flight – F/L Welch DFC (Flight Commander), F/L Kirkman, F/O McConnochie, W/O Cookson, W/O Wheatley, W/O Beckwith, W/O Eric Mee, P/O McGinn, W/O Laffan, F/O Machon, F/O Richmond and F/Sgt Webb.

The Intelligence Officer was F/O G. Allott, the Engineering Officer F/O Rogers, the Adjutant F/O Burrows and F/O Machon, as well as being a pilot, held the additional role of 'Accounts Officer'!

By the end of March, 603 would have completed 626 operational sorties, more than twice the number flown in February.

The days fell into a routine pattern of an early morning weather recce followed by up to five or six armed recces against the V2 targets. It was grinding on the pilots who were having to cope with the prospect of an unpleasant death or injury two, three or sometimes four times a day, and whilst the ground crews weren't facing the same physical dangers, they were having to turn the Spitfires round immediately on return from the missions and also carry out the routine servicing needed to keep the aircraft in good condition.

The ground crews did have their moments of danger to deal with. Arthur Inch was Sergeant Fitter/Armourer with 229 and when it became 603. One incident which happened while the Squadron was 229 illustrates the sort of problem that had to be dealt with. Snowy Wheatley's Spitfire had crashed on take-off at the start of a bombing sortie. It was loaded up with a 500lb bomb on the centreline and a 250lb bomb on each wing. The Spitfire overshot the runway and landed on its belly, ploughing a furrow in the mud before coming to a stop. The pilot popped out of it like a cork from a champagne bottle. Then came the question as to what was to be done with the bombs, still on the Spitfire and dug into the mud. Arthur Inch continues:

> All the other trades looked at the AC2 Armourer, who looked at the AC1 Armourer, who looked at the LAC, who looked at the Corporal, who looked at the Sergeant (me!) who looked at the Flight Sergeant who wasn't there and then for the W/O who wasn't there and so the buck stopped with me. I crept gingerly out to the pranged Spit, sidled carefully underneath and very carefully removed the tail fins, unscrewed the fuses and extracted them. Then with special tweezers, I removed the detonators from the three bombs and replaced them in their containers. I only then allowed the other trades to go near it.

Arthur Inch was posted from 603 in February 1945 when the 6603 Service Echelon was incorporated into the unit.

On another occasion, another pilot had an engine failure on take-off but when he crash landed, the bombs broke free, bouncing along the runway behind the Spitfire tearing along on its belly. Fortunately on that occasion there was no damage either, but the two incidents show that the ground crew had their own fair share of danger.

Often the bombs were set for airburst so that they would explode above ground. This allowed the blast to spread sideways and not upwards as it would from a ground burst. The pilots would set the bombs to 'live' and this meant that when they were released, a wire which was attached to the aircraft pulled out a pin as the bomb dropped away. At the front of each bomb was a small propeller which could turn freely in the airflow as it dropped once the pin had been pulled out. As it revolved on the way down, it would turn a screw thread in the bomb and eventually once it reached the end, the propeller dropped away, leaving the open-ended tube exposed. In this was a very thin and springy convex disc. As the air pressure built up in the tube, the disc would snap into a concave shape which in turn struck a firing pin into the bomb's detonator.

During the month, the ORB makes a specific acknowledgement of the good work of the ground crews:

> Space must be taken here to put in a word of praise for the ground crew. The stringent programme as it was left them with little time to breathe, but when it was linked to a shortage of tractors to haul the petrol bowsers, their difficulties were increased a hundred fold. The present bowsers will only re-fuel 3 Spit's, and a constant going and coming to and from the petrol point is necessary. When the tractors became U/S their work was intensified but somehow they succeeded. The arrival of the long promised and eagerly awaited 950 gallon bowser....promises even more rapid turn-rounds than have already been accomplished.

The airfield itself was a hive of activity as well. 602 were following the same sort of programme. As Spitfires from one squadron took off or landed, aircraft from the other were taking off or landing and as the weather improved with the approaching spring, the hours of daylight drew out so that there were fewer days when flying was curtailed.

The ORB for 2 March notes that the constant attacks on the launch sites at the Haagse Bos which had taken place over February and into March suggested that the intention was the complete destruction of them and there is also a comment about the reduction in the effectiveness of the flak. Of course, this was exactly what had been intended and the results were coming through.

The days saw a shift away from this target to others, although still in Holland and still designed primarily to stop the Big Ben launches.

As the Allied armies squeezed Germany between them, western Holland was being by-passed and the concentration was to drive into the enemy heartland. On 7 March, Sergeant Alex Drabik of the US Army, ran across the Ludendorff Bridge at Remagen just south of Bonn and became the first Allied soldier to reach the east bank of the Rhine. On the same day, Cologne was captured.

On Saturday 3 March, the first raid of the day took off at 08.30 to attack the Haagse Bos targets again. Six Spitfires led by F/L Batchelor were armed with two 250lb bombs each fused for airburst. One of the other pilots was F/L Bob Sergeant. On their way across the North Sea, they were told that the target was due to be attacked at the same time by 'mediums' (Mitchells) of the 2nd Tactical Air Force and it was changed to the Staalduin Bos instead. This was attacked at 09.15 and was timed between two waves of Mitchell bombers who appeared to be concentrating on houses to the south of the Haagse Bos. The 603 pilots observed that the Mitchells left the whole area burning and there was a pall of smoke rising to 2,000 feet. They also reported heavy flak which seemed to be directed at the Mitchells and not the Spitfires.

Bob Sergeant knew that the raid by the Mitchells had gone dreadfully wrong: 'We saw them going in and knew it was wrong. It was atrocious.'

The bombers were supposed to attack launch sites at Duindigt and the north-western part of the Haagse Bos in which many V2s were being stored, but there was a navigation error and the first bombs were released on the south-eastern part of the Haagse Bos instead – about two and a half kilometres out. The following bombers dropped their bombs on the fires already visible which compounded the error. The result of the mistake was that the Dutch residential area of Bezuidenhout was badly damaged and the fires were to rage for the whole day and into the evening. On the Sunday the extent of the damage was assessed. It was thought that over 1,200 houses had been hit with the deaths of almost 500 Dutch civilians. Eric Mee recalled that they could see the pall of smoke for many days as they headed over the sea towards Holland.

Jan van't Hoff was one of the many civilians caught up in the attack by the Mitchells:

On March 3 at 0900 hours I saw many Mitchell B.25 bombers and a couple of Bostons flying in our direction and was absolutely convinced that they were heading for Germany or elsewhere because bombers were not for us. We had our Spitfires. I was out in the street. All at once hell broke loose when the bombing started. It was a complete failure. Our school got three direct hits and I lost many schoolmates and teachers. Not one bomb fell on the Haagse Bos but all of them flattened this part of Den Haag.

The Spitfire squadrons were far more accurate in locating their objectives, however some lost their two 250 pound bombs too early and I remember a very scary moment when a Spit machine-gunned me with its two 20 mm guns. Luckily he missed.

Van't Hoff also recalled that the night after the bombing, a V2 crashed and exploded in Den Haag in a street which had been spared the bombing by the Mitchells.

A few days later the sites at Duindigt were attacked by the medium bombers again and damaged to such an extent that the area wasn't used again as a firing area. But the price had been heavy. Many of these wooded launch sites had been estates. The Duindigt estate had been there for 200 years. The ancient trees were destroyed as were manor houses and farms and the whole area was cratered by the Allied bombs and the V2s which hadn't successfully launched.

The Dutch were paying dearly for the privilege of having the V2s on their doorstep.

At 11.40, F/L Batchelor led the third armed recce of the day with W/Os Maslen and Haupt and P/O Manivalu to attack a different site – at Rust en Vreugd. They bombed successfully, then turned back for Ludham crossing the Dutch coast at Katwijk just after 13.00. Ten minutes later, at 7,000 feet, they spotted a USAAF B17 limping back over the sea with its inner starboard engine shot up and the starboard main undercarriage leg hanging down. The four Spitfires closed round the Fortress protectively and escorted it back to the safety of the English coast. The American pilot gave his 'little friends' a thumbs up, and as the 603 Spitfires watched, managed to pull off a successful belly landing. The Spitfires then returned to Ludham landing at 14.00 after having been in the air for well over two hours. The Americans were very appreciative of such escorts and it wasn't unusual for the crews to drive across to the RAF bases, find out who their escorts had been and buy them drinks.

Four other armed recces were carried out against the same target that day, but the last – at 16.30 – was against the Staalduin Bos, illustrating the change in concentration away from the one target area as it became less effective.

On Sunday 4 March, there were other operational changes. More use was to be made of the airfield at Ursel in Belgium, so the Spitfires took off without tanks, and carrying 1,000lbs of bombs. They would land at Ursel to refuel and re-arm, carry out their attacks and return to Ludham. This, of course had already been done on occasions in February. To minimise aircraft turnaround times on the continent, the pilots were told that they shouldn't fire their guns unless it was absolutely necessary to do so for self-protection.

The pilots recall with some affection the reaction of the liberated civilians to their arrival at airfields like Ursel. They used to line the fence and wave to the Spitfires as they taxied past to their turnrounds. Eric Mee remembers that one pilot was so engrossed in waving to the civilians – 'like royalty' – that he quite forgot what he was doing and the Spitfire ran into a vehicle, finishing up with one of its cannon embedded in its radiator! Fortunately, the only real damage was to the pilot's pride.

One of the pilots in particular had a real entrepreneurial streak. He discovered that the Dutch were desperately short of tyres for their bicycles and would 'wear' tyres around him, underneath his Mae West on the first sortie of the day. When he arrived at one of the Dutch airfields, he would nip quickly away and sell them. Sometimes, he had so many round him that his fellow pilots said he looked like a 'Michelin man'!

The first mission for Sunday 4 March operated as normal. It was airborne at 08.55, led by F/L Batchelor against a flak battery which had been causing Allied aircraft some difficulty. This was sited in sand dunes just to the south of Scheveningen near Den Haag. The plan was for the Spitfires to draw the fire of the battery by flying over it, so that its position could be spotted precisely, and then the attack carried out. This is exactly what happened and a successful mission was recorded.

At 09.30 F/L Welch with three other Spitfires bombed the V2 site at Rust en Vreugd and then flew to Ursel taking off again from there at 11.15. By the time they arrived back over Holland, cloud had thickened and they were unable to see their targets so they jettisoned their bombs and returned to Ludham. At 10.30, F/L Kirkman led a section to attack V2 sites at Ockenburg. They were successful and crossed out near Katwijk to fly down the coast to Walcheren before landing at Ursel. Whilst there, the weather deteriorated further and instead of returning with bombs to the V2 site, they went back to strafe it with their cannon and machine guns. Near Den Haag, they found the cloud down to 1,300 feet so they called off the mission and set course for home. Near the English coast, F/L Kirkman was instructed to fly north on his own to look for the crew of a downed bomber about six miles off the coast. He found the bomber in the sea, but there were no crew and no dinghies. Not long after he arrived two Thunderbolts also turned up and three small ships. As he was by now getting low on fuel, F/L Kirkman turned back for base and landed at 14.05.

For the remainder of the afternoon, the Squadron waited for the weather to improve over Holland, but it failed to do so.

Operations on 5 March followed much the same pattern with a number of different targets being hit. A total of 28 sorties were completed.

The following day, probably to everyone's relief, the Squadron were released after lunch and the pilots caught up with some well-earned rest. In the evening there was a party – as the ORB describes: '... a small "hail fellow well met" party was held at some of the local hostelries when the CO and some of the pilots entertained the Senior NCO's among the ground crew as a token of their appreciation for their hard work in servicing the aircraft and keeping them flying.' Note the party was held at a number of hostelries not just one.

In the evenings the airmen played as hard as they worked. They were young men and full of adrenaline. The war was clearly coming to an end and whilst some of the older pilots may have been able to put a perspective on it, they were still in daily danger and living for the moment. They didn't know what the next day would bring and they lived life as fully as they could. Some had cars. The flight commanders usually either had a car or had access to one and they used to try to make sure that any pilot who hadn't been off the station for a while had the chance to do so. In the village of Coltishall there were a number of pubs to visit – The Recruiting Sergeant being one.

Farther afield was Norwich with all its diversions, which also attracted 'half the American army' according to Eric Mee. He recalled that there was a NAAFI Club where he and his mate Tommy Thomson used to go:

> It was a large building with three floors. The facilities were marvellous. On the first floor there was an information desk, train and bus times etc. Cigarettes on sale and if required you could get a shower, wash and brush up, or even a hair cut. The second floor contained a large lounge with armchairs, settees, newspapers, magazines and a radiogram, the top half of the room being a dance floor. On the top floor was a cafeteria where we had very cheap but excellent meals.

W/O Johnny Green had a motor bike to get around on, but he bought a car – a Ford Eight – from a second-hand car dealer in Norwich. Eric Mee decided that he would like one as well, and having put together the necessary £60, he and Green drove into Norwich to collect it – a blue one. Mee had never driven a car before, so on the way, he was given a 15-minute lesson by the other pilot and before long found himself driving erratically back to the station without a licence in a car that had no tax, no insurance and pulled violently to the left on braking!

Johnny Green's car didn't last though. He drove it at breakneck speed and one day finished up in a ditch. Thereafter the local bobby tried to interview him, but each time he called the station, he was told that W/O Green was flying. Tommy Thomson was another with a car – an elderly Austin Seven. One day when he was flying, some of the pilots pushed it to the top of one of the walls of the aircraft blast pens. These were earth, about 12 feet high with steeply angled sides. When he came back from his 'op' he found his pride and joy perched on top 'like a monument' and he was absolutely furious. (Needless to say, the culprits helped him get it back down.)

In 229 Squadron days, Paddy O'Reilly had a red Panther motor bike and he used to go into Norwich with his room mate John Manley who had a Norton, to 'recce a dance and entertain, or be entertained by the local females.'* O'Reilly also at one time had a large black Armstrong-Siddeley that had once belonged to a funeral director to carry the mourners. Not surprisingly it became known as 'O'Reilly's hearse'.

Some of the pilots were married and some engaged. Some recall that if the soldier or airman was on operational duties there could be an unexpected difference of view with the wives about whether or not children should be born. The men were often against it because if they were killed, they didn't want to leave a widow with a youngster behind, but the wives wanted to have a child to carry on the line of the father if he should fail to return.

With the stress of operations and their 'living for the moment' philosophy, friendships were strong. Paddy O'Reilly was Snowy Wheatley's best man.

Another regular haunt was the Club at Sutton Staithe. Bob Sergeant remembers that at the end of one heavy evening the manager insisted that they sign the members' book which would make them life members. He returned many years later and sure enough, their names were still there in the book!

One pilot, a F/O, had an interesting experience one night after a heavy drinking session. He was on the ground floor of the officers' mess and during the night, managed to fall out of his bedroom window. In the dark he scrambled back in, then fell asleep again. In the morning, he awoke with a thick head, made his way over to the wash-hand basin and started to clean his teeth. His fogged mind gradually realised that the toothbrush he was using wasn't his own, and when he cast his eyes around the room, he realised that it too wasn't his!

---

*John Manley didn't fly with 603 because he was killed on a Jim Crow prior to the change. W/O O'Reilly was flying with him, saw him being hit by flak and crashing into the sea off the Dutch coast. He remained over the spot until relieved by other aircraft from the Squadron, but his friend was killed. He then had the difficult job of preparing his belongings to be sent to Manley's wife. Eventually Manley's body was washed ashore and he is buried in Bergen/Noordholland.

Meanwhile, back in Edinburgh... Sir Archibald Sinclair, Minister for Air, talking with officers of 603 Squadron. From left to right: Count Stevens, Alen Wallace, Black Morton, Lord Provost, Bill Douglas, Sinclair, Ivone Kirkpatrick, Lord Geordie Douglas-Hamilton, Tommy Garden and Ian Ritchie.

The resulting hangover in the morning could be cured by a few minutes of breathing pure oxygen in the aircraft.

Sometimes the men would write home. Bob Sergeant did so often, but not regularly. He had agreed this with his parents because he felt that if he missed a regular letter for the best of reasons, his parents would assume the worst. If they didn't get letters regularly, then on the occasions that he couldn't write, they wouldn't know and wouldn't worry.*

The daily grind continued. The recent attacks on Haagse Bos had not been troubled too much by flak and this may have been because of the pounding that the whole site had been taking, but as the Squadron expanded their list of targets, their impunity was compromised.

The first casualty was on Friday 9 March. The second armed recce of the day took off from Ludham at 10.35 led by F/L Batchelor. The target for the eight Spitfires was a storage and firing site at Wassenaar Ravelijn, a few miles north of The Hague. One of the pilots was W/O Godfrey, flying his first operational trip in Spitfire S (SM405). During the attack, it received hits from flak just behind the cockpit which severed the rudder control cables. Fortunately, along with the other aircraft, W/O Godfrey managed to fly the Spitfire back to Ursel where he landed safely at 11.45, but the aircraft was so badly damaged that it was written off. The warrant officer wasn't out of the woods though. He still had to get back to Ludham. He was flown back to Down Ampney by Transport Command but wasn't able to leave the camp as aircrew were prohibited from travelling in public wearing flying kit. Three days later, the Squadron was getting a stream of frantic messages from him to prise him from the clutches of Transport Command. But no means was available to fetch him – either in the air or on the ground and he was to remain a prisoner at Down Ampney for some days! (Things must have changed since earlier in the war. There are accounts of airmen who force landed at

---

*When he left for Malta in 1942, he had sent home a pair of good shoes for safekeeping. He'd stuffed them with newspaper and against all the rules, had put in a note to his mother saying where he was going. When he got back, he asked her if she'd got it, but she hadn't thought to look. When they looked at the shoes, the note was still there!

strange aerodromes having to travel by underground and train, carrying their kit with them to get back to their units!)

The next day was notable for several reasons. 603 flew 41 sorties with only one being aborted for 55 operational hours flown and 20,000lbs of bombs dropped. But three Spitfires suffered damage in one form or another.

At 16.20, W/O Haupt took off in A – on its third sortie of the day – as part of a section of five Spitfires to bomb launch sites at Duindigt. In the dive, he was hit in the engine by flak but he managed to drop his bombs successfully, then diverted to Knocke-Le-Zoote accompanied by W/O Green as escort. They both landed safely at 17.20.

W/O Mee in U was in the next armed recce which took off at 17.10 to attack the same target as W/O Haupt. Over the target, his aircraft was hit in the mainplane:

> Diving in from about 4,000 feet I had just released the bombs from under the wing when there was a colossal bang as a 40 mm shell went right through my wing leaving a gaping hole. Hoping desperately that it hadn't damaged the main spar, I pulled up as gingerly as height would permit and climbed back up over the sea. Reporting the incident to the Flight Commander he replied that he would fly alongside and have a look at the underside of the wing. What he saw was a much larger hole where the shell had made its exit, taking most of the bomb rack with it as it went. A split second earlier and it would have hit the 250lb bomb hanging there.
>
> We flew back to base at reduced speed with me wondering if the undercarriage and flaps would be functioning all right. The wheels came down and locked OK on the downwind leg. The flaps I had tested whilst I was high enough to spot any malfunction. The landing was quite normal and on inspecting the damage, I was amazed that the shell had torn quite a large hole through the wing without hitting anything vital – the explosion was inches away from a full magazine of cannon shells.

Finally, there was W/O Wheatley in V (SM464). The previous day, Snowy Wheatley had been forced to stay behind at Ursel when, as he was about to take off on a second armed recce, there had been a problem with the undercarriage. It wasn't until the next day that he was able to leave, lifting off from Ursel at 15.55. However, arriving back at Ludham, he found that his undercarriage wouldn't lower. A normal procedure in such circumstances was to perform violent aerobatics to try to shake the wheels down and W/O Wheatley put the aircraft through its paces for a good 20 minutes, but still the undercarriage wouldn't come down. He decided to do a belly landing. Carefully lining up his approach just to the side of the runway, he carried out an almost textbook landing on the grass. Unfortunately the aeroplane was too badly damaged to be repairable and it was struck off charge on 21 June 1945.

It had been an exceedingly eventful, but successful day and it was crowned with the news that W/O Cookson had been granted a commission. It was a popular promotion. He had been with the unit for 18 months and had flown 175 hours.

12 March was a training day, but then the daily routine resumed. On the 15th, it was learned that W/O 'Wally' Haupt had been granted his commission – another popular promotion for a man who had flown with 229 Squadron since Malta in 1943 and in the 18 months that he been with 229/603, had flown 160 operational hours. (Paddy O'Reilly was another pilot who had joined 229 on Malta not long after it had been formed from the remnants of 603.)

Meanwhile, W/O Godfrey was still not having much luck. On 16 March, the ORB states: 'W/O. Godfrey, whose absence is still on our conscience though through no fault of ours we hear today was involved in an accident yesterday as the Anson sent from Coltishall at last to fetch him, crashed (with him as passenger) at Peterborough.'

Godfrey's thoughts can only be imagined, but he must have been hoping that all his operational trips to come would be far less eventful than his first.

The next incident on 17 March resulted in tragedy – the loss of the Australian Johnny Green. By this time, the armed recces were being directed more towards the communications system rather than the launch sites. There had been a gradual shift to railway lines, roads and junctions. W/O Green was flying H (SM473) and had already completed one mission that morning attacking railway targets and along with the other 11 aircraft involved, landed at Ursel at 12.30.

There were 12 aircraft in the group and they were off again at 14.10 making for the general area of Utrecht. Johnny Green was White 2. At 14.45 they attacked the railway junction at Maartensdijk destroying lines, a signal box and a bridge. On their way back to Ursel, at 14.55, Green called that he had seen a three-ton truck going into the village of Bleskensgraaf and reported it. But he didn't use his call sign – announcing himself as 'Johnny'. F/L Jack Batchelor was leading White Section – White 1 – and thought that it was the other Flight Commander, Johnny Welch who had called and asked him to investigate. Welch was leading Blue Section. Welch however decided that it wasn't worth going after as the truck was now entering the village and as far as Batchelor was concerned, the formation continued on its way. As it swung away Johnny Green was seen to be diving down as if to attack. Some of the pilots saw intense light flak rising from the village and a cry over the R/T 'I've been hit' was heard, but because most of the pilots hadn't realised that Green had started his attack, the call wasn't attributed to him until later.

His aircraft wasn't seen to crash and there was no explosion or fire so for some time, it was hoped that he had managed to crash land and survive. Many weeks later, the Red Cross reported that an RAF pilot called Green was in a German hospital and there were hopes that it was him, but it turned out to be someone from another unit. Regretfully, he had been killed.

His friend Eric Mee shared a locker in the crew room with him. A few weeks earlier, Mee's wife had given him a good luck charm which was a gold chain with a small monkey on it and he kept it in the pocket of his Mae West. The day after Green was lost, he went to his locker, and found that his friend had taken the wrong life jacket, together with the little gold monkey on the chain.

W/O Jack Dawson Green, RAAF, was the son of Walter and Elsie Green of Camberwell, Victoria, Australia. He was 21 and is buried in the nearby village of Barendrecht. His Spitfire was uncovered by the Royal Dutch Air Force in 1972.

Eric Mee waited many years in hope before the death of his friend was confirmed. Quite why he chose to attack will never be known. Perhaps he thought that a golden opportunity was being missed. It seems that he took the decision on his own and didn't announce it. It transpired that he had been hit by a German flak battery on the Heinenoord Bridge. Jan Van't Hoff remembers seeing a Spitfire being hit by flak at the beginning of March:

> About six or seven Spits first in line abreast, tipping over and one by one diving down on Haagse bos. I was queueing up trying to get bread when I spotted our friends in the air and suddenly one of them exploded in a fireball. In spite of our own misery I felt very rotten because the pilot could never have survived.

By 1945 Jack Batchelor had been on ops for three years and so battle-hardened that he had reached a mental state where he was relatively cold about the missions. On the way to Ursel, he was checking off in his mind what would be needed to be done during the turnround and when Johnny Welch didn't leave the formation, he assumed that he had decided not to go after the truck. He still finds himself wondering that if he had pulled up Johnny Green for his lack of radio discipline rather than concentrating on what the next mission was, he might have saved the Australian's life.

Following the mission the remaining 11 aircraft flew back to Ursel where they rearmed and refuelled. At 16.45 they were airborne yet again and bombed railway targets near Den Haag before returning to Ludham at 17.30.

The events of the day illustrate the changes that had taken place in the operations since February. Firstly, the pilots were now regularly basing themselves at Ursel for the day before flying back to Ludham in the late afternoon or evening. Secondly, they were experiencing more in the way of flak damage and even casualties. Thirdly, they were now hitting the infrastructure supporting the V2s rather than the launch sites themselves.

There was some relief from the tensions of operations the next day, which was set aside for dive-bombing practice. Attention was also drawn to a B17 which forced landed at Ludham with two engines shot up.

Tuesday 20 March was a notable day for several reasons. The Sector Commander, G/C Donaldson, was leaving (to be replaced by G/C Hawtry) and he asked that the Wing put on a maximum effort – which they did by flying 165 sorties. 603 flew 57 of these for 72 hours dropping 56,000lbs of bombs and using 14 Spitfires! As Bob Sergeant said 'It was a heavy old day.' It certainly was for him.

The first operation left Ludham at 09.40 and the last landed at 19.05. The targets were the by now familiar railway and transport infrastructure, but the sorties in the late afternoon at 16.30 and 17.55 from Ursel were against a V1 launch site on the airfield at Ypenburg which was also being attacked that afternoon by 602 and the friendly rivalry between the squadrons showed.

F/L Bob Sergeant (in G) was leading a section of three – F/O Nick Machon (P) as his No.2 and F/O Thomson (R). They landed at Ursel at 17.40 having carried out an attack on Ypenburg. Sergeant recalls the decision to go again:

> We arrived and taxied in. They were refuelling 602. I saw the Intelligence Officer and he said 'Do you think you could do another run on the way back?' I said that I would have to check with the lads because it might be a dusk landing when we got back to Coltishall and they might not be night qualified. I asked them if they were happy with a dusk landing because if they were, 602 had turned it down and were going straight back. They said they would have a go so I went to see the Chiefy and said to him to come off 602 and refuel and rearm us because we would do another operational trip on the way back. He said 'Good!' and called 'Right lads, fix up 603!' – so they came off the 602 aircraft and refuelled and rearmed us!

They took off again 15 minutes after landing at 17.55 and raced back to Ypenburg. Sergeant remembered they had hit some huts and were hedge hopping across the airfield. Nick Machon was flying through the debris of the huts blown into the air. As they came round the hangars, they spotted what looked like a parade prompting Sergeant to swing round and hose the troops. They made their escape and arrived back to base at 19.05 for the dusk landing that Sergeant had anticipated. Years before when he had been doing his flying training at RAF Sealand, one evening he and six other pilots had been caught in the open in the middle of the airfield when it was attacked by an He111. The German bomber had banked round after dropping its bombs and the rear gunner had seen the seven airman and sprayed them with his machine gun. Sergeant had never forgotten the incident and he saw his attack on the parade as getting his own back!

There was no respite and 21 March was another full day of operations with an unusual incident in the morning.

At 09.55, F/L Welch led a section of six Spitfires out of Ludham each armed with a single 500lb and two 250lb bombs. Just off the Dutch coast at about 10.30, they spotted a Catalina air-sea rescue aircraft with some Spitfires trying to make a pick up from the sea. Unfortunately, they were about two miles south of Ijmuiden where the Germans had sited some coastal guns. These were in three emplacements in the dunes and were harrying the rescue attempt. The six 603 Spitfires executed one of their normal dive-bombing attacks on the emplacements and managed to silence them. However, the group came under further fire from guns near the town and eventually the Catalina turned for home.

One account is that a pilot from the Wing had to bale out and two Catalinas arrived to pick him up. One of them was damaged by the shore batteries and had to taxi back across the North Sea to safety, whilst the other wasn't able to pick up the downed pilot because of the enemy gunfire. Eventually, there was a temporary truce and a German air-sea rescue launch was allowed to pick up the British airman.

A second version is that the object of the rescue was a dinghy with the crew of a downed bomber on board and that the Catalina did manage to get them aboard eventually.

A further curious quirk is that the ORB for 602 Squadron recounts a similar incident but on 20 March, not the 21st. This version is that two Spitfires which were at Ursel were scrambled on an ASR patrol to a location about eight miles north of Den Haag where they found a downed pilot sitting in a dinghy. Shortly afterwards, a Walrus seaplane landed about 100 yards from the dinghy and it came under fire from the coastal batteries. To the frustration of the 602 pilots, it started to taxi westwards – away from the pilot in the sea – and being unable to contact it by radio, they dived across it making frantic efforts to show it where the dinghy was. But to no avail. They learned afterwards that it had damaged its rudder on landing in the rough sea.

One of the 603 pilots involved on the 21st was W/O Eric Mee who recalled:

> One of our airmen had baled out over the sea. Several gallant attempts had been made to pick him up in a Walrus and a Catalina. All had been heavily shelled by the shore batteries and damaged. Our job was to try to silence the guns by bombing and strafing. Although we silenced some of them, others that were too well hidden on the cliffs were still firing shells at the rescuers. Finally, as fuel got low, we had to return to base and another Squadron took over. Listening to the radio on the way back, I heard one of their Australian pilots say that he had been hit, and very laconically that he was 'going over the side'. Returning home, we learned that the chap in the dinghy had drifted too near the Dutch coast. All our aircraft were recalled and the Germans were contacted on an international distress frequency. A German boat bearing the Red Cross was sent to pick him up and he became a prisoner.

The ORB for this day includes a resounding appreciation of the work done by the ground crews.

> Space must be found to praise the work of the ground crews, both at base and at Ursel. They had worked hard, willingly and successfully in turning the aircraft round and the excellent serviceability speaks well for their work. The ground crews at Ursel particularly deserve credit as they do not belong to our Squadron but work as enthusiastically as if they did. The small largesse that our pilots take in the way of the days papers to them is much appreciated by them but nothing can really re-pay them for the efforts they make except the knowledge that they definitely help to increase the bomb load which the Germans in Holland receive.

This was the day of the well known and successful raid by Mosquitoes against the Gestapo headquarters at the Shellhaus in Copenhagen.

G/C Donaldson had a leaving party that night at Coltishall. S/L Rigler and the two flight commanders attended to represent 603.

The heavy flying load of the last few weeks had so impressed itself on F/L Welch, B Flight commander, that he demanded the following day off flying so that he could write up his log book! But whilst he could joke about it, for many of the pilots it had meant flying eight operational sorties in the space of 48 hours.

The next day, there was a wing attack against the Kurhaus garage at Scheveningen. This was a building that housed the vehicles used to transport the V2s to their launch sites. At 12.50, the CO led 603 off – 12 Spitfires armed with a single 500lb and two 250lb bombs. They crossed in over Den Haag at 9,000 feet and bombed east/west in three sections of four. Each section was hard on the heels of the one in front and results were good.

The aircraft recovered to Ursel for rearming and refuelling before taking off again at 16.20 to repeat the attack. Again the results were good and the Squadron were optimistic that it had been a successful day. In addition, that morning four aircraft had attacked a road bridge and railway near Gouda.

Friday 23 March saw more attacks against road and rail targets in Holland with 38 sorties being completed in 51 hours, 40 minutes. Again, the day was considered to be a success. That evening, there was an expectation of a special effort on the Saturday and 603 personnel were confined to camp. Much work was put in to have the maximum number of Spitfires serviceable for the morning and in the event, 16 were available. The pilots were in their aircraft at 04.00 sitting waiting for the off, but they sat in their freezing Spitfires until after dawn, their expectations unfulfilled. They hung around the dispersals until lunch time, but no orders were received and ultimately, in the afternoon, the time was given over to practice flying. In fact, the reason for their standby was because this was the day that the Allies were crossing the Rhine and the pilots were to be available in case 'things got sticky'.

Like many things, waiting to take-off was the worst part of the sortie for some pilots. Once they were going, there was too much to do to think about being scared and the adrenaline took over.

As Paddy O'Reilly noted:

> I must confess that I never let my mind dwell on what might lie ahead. The only time I had thoughts of what was to come was when waiting for the signal from control to start engines before escorting a bomber raid to Hamburg. It was early evening and a quiet had descended over the dispersal and having seen the fatal crash of another squadron's aircraft that same evening I wished that I could have left my Spitfire and gone home. Once the signal was given, we were too busy to dwell on what might or might not happen.

At 14.40, a section of four Spitfires was airborne led by F/O McConnochie to practise formation flying. The others were F/Sgt Webb, F/O Machon as No.3 (in SM396) and P/O McGinn as No.4 (TB396).

At 16.10, while they were performing a 180-degree crossover turn about two miles off the coast, it seems that P/O McGinn misjudged his height and/or his distance from F/O Machon and hit his aircraft from below. Both Spitfires were badly damaged. Nick Machon recounted the episode:

> I had done a forty-five minute air test on XT●P earlier in the day and I was flying the same aircraft. The practice flight with McConnochie had lasted one and a half hours when the accident happened and the weather was starting to close in.
>
> The ends of my propeller blades had gone in the collision and my starboard wing was moving up and down six to eight inches as the plane went into a spin. I tried to bale out but the cockpit hood had jammed. I got her out of the spin and switched off the engine because of the vibrations from the propeller. Almost immediately I felt a tremendous bump as the Spitfire hit the calm sea and bounced over the beach. It struck a patch of grass, bounced once again, when the starboard wing disappeared. I came to rest on mud, upside down.

The Spitfire was on the marshes at Hickling Church a few miles north of Palling and north east of Coltishall. Luckily for Nick Machon, the crash was seen by members of the local Sandell family who hastily laid planks across the mud. Nick relates the predicament they found him in:

> The cockpit hood had disappeared and I could just see a little daylight along the side of the cockpit. I would still be there had not a man and a woman come from the direction of a mill and clawed away enough mud for me to crawl out.

F/O McGinn, killed in an accident in March 1945.

The Sandells helped the pilot out of the cockpit and across the planks to safety. He was unhurt, although no doubt badly shaken.*

It was thought that P/O McGinn managed to bale out of his Spitfire, but he was too low and his parachute didn't open. The two remaining aircraft landed back a base at 16.50.

On being notified of the collision, an ASR search was started. At 16.44 F/L McAndrew and P/O Haupt took off to search for the downed pilot, but shortly afterwards, about four miles off the coast, they saw a Walrus seaplane on the water with two Thunderbolts and a Warwick circling above. They returned to base landing at 17.15 hours and flying was suspended for what was left of the day.

The body of P/O Nelson Arthur Horace McGinn was recovered from the sea by the Walrus and buried in the Cambridge City Cemetery in the early afternoon of Thursday 29 March. A Squadron formation of 12 Spitfires flew over the cemetery during the service in honour of the Royal Indian Air Force pilot who had been lost under such tragic circumstances. He was the son of Edwin and Ruth McGinn of Tiverton Down. Fortunately, Nick Machon got away with painful ribs and a nasty fright:

> My ribs were badly strained so I was taken to the Station Hospital, where a very wide bandage was stuck to my chest and round to my back. A pretty nurse gave me a sleeping draught but that had no effect. I could still see the marsh coming up at me. The nurse gave me another dose and I finally went to sleep.
>
> In spite of this I was detailed to fly five days after the accident in a practice formation and this turned out to be the Squadron's farewell to Nelson McGinn over the cemetery in Cambridge.
>
> My ribs felt OK except when I breathed heavily.

An official investigation on 9 April absolved F/O Machon of responsibility for the accident.

For the rest of the month, on the days when the weather allowed, it was back to the routine of attacks on the roads and railways which were so vital to the operation of the V2s. The war in Europe was drawing to a conclusion and on 28 March, the Squadron was given a 30-minute talk about conduct and discipline after the war had finished. In the evening, the first Ludham Station 'all ranks' dance was held using a band from Coltishall. It was well attended and judged to be 'quite a success'. Sid Phillips was stationed at Coltishall at this time and it may have been 'The Sid Phillips Band' that was playing at the dance. If so, it isn't really a surprise that everyone had a good time.

On Friday 30 March which was Good Friday, they carried out one of their last, but most difficult attacks of the period against the head office of Bataafsche Petroleum Maatschappij (the Dutch branch of Shell) in Den Haag, which had been taken over by the Germans to be used as a headquarters for the V2 attacks as well as billets.

The raid on this building – known to some of the pilots as 'the Shellhouse' – wasn't the first.

It was a large, long modern reinforced concrete structure, six or seven storeys high north of Haagse Bos with a heavily built up area on one side. On the other side was parkland, but on the opposite side of the park was a church and housing as well as office buildings. There was great concern about carrying out an attack on it as there were likely to be Dutch civilian casualties and clearly it was desirable that these should be minimised.

229 Squadron had attacked the building on 24 December 1944 and 602 Squadron was tasked with another raid on Sunday 18 March. It was a difficult target and the pilots' briefing was detailed and careful. Six Spitfires were to attack, led by the CO, S/L Sutherland. Others involved were F/L Pertwee who would become the CO of 603 in a short time and F/O Raymond Baxter. The aircraft carried a single 500lb and two 250lbs and would recover to Ursel after the raid. The raid was to be low level.

---

*In 1998, Nick Machon left his home in Guernsey and returned to the spot where he had almost been killed and presented the youngest of his rescuers in 1945, Gerry Sandell who was 14 at the time, with a traditional Guernsey milk jug as a gesture of his thanks.

602 was airborne at 13.00 and joined up with aircraft from 124 Squadron who were to make diversionary attacks on another target along with 453 Squadron. They crossed in at 2,000 feet then dropped to very low level, hedge hopping until reaching the target from the north west. They were actually below the roof level of the building when they released their bombs about 50 yards from it. Some of the pilots strafed the front of the building as they approached it. One bomb cluster overshot by about 50 yards, and another fell about 50 yards to the left of the building after the Spitfire was hit in the starboard mainplane. But the other four were all reported to have hit the building. The flak was intense and the CO's Spitfire was hit in the starboard elevator but all returned to Ursel safely where the pilots reported considerable damage to the building. Smoke and debris were seen as well as flames billowing from the east face. It was noted that the roof seemed to be intact but it was concluded by the Squadron that the inside must have been totally destroyed.

The damage assessment by the 602 pilots of their raid was correct but optimistic. The building was still usable and the Germans set about repairing it. A further raid was deemed necessary and on this occasion 603 was tasked.

The 12 pilots to fly were F/L Batchelor who would be leader, W/O Maslem, P/O Cookson, F/O Machon, F/L Welch, W/O Mee, F/L Kirkman, F/O McConnochie, F/L McAndrew, P/O Haupt, F/L Sergeant and W/O Thomson.

Nick Machon's ribs were still causing him some pain, particularly when he breathed heavily and when subjected to the g-Forces in pulling out from a dive.

They were carefully briefed, particularly about the church which might very well be full on this important Friday in the Christian calendar. Interestingly, instead of the low level attack method used by 602, 603 were to use dive bombing. The Spitfires were armed with the same bomb load though, a single 500lb bomb and two 250lb bombs. The pilots weren't entirely certain as to why they were attacking it. They knew that it had something to do with the V2s, but there were also (incorrect) rumours that the Gestapo was using it, and even that there were Dutch Resistance hostages on the top floor.

At 09.30 the Squadron lifted off from Ludham and crossed in at Den Haag at an altitude of 8,000 feet. They flew straight to the target which was clear and bombed east to west in dives from 8,000 to 1,000 feet. Moderate heavy flak was directed against them (which suggests that the building was still important to the Germans) but no aircraft were recorded as being hit.

As for the 602 raid, the bombing results were seen to be good. One cluster fell in the middle of the building producing a bright explosion and three were reported on the north-east wing. The other bombs all landed near the structure.

The Spitfires then flew directly to Ursel where they were turned round in 20 minutes and were again in the air at 11.10. They flew straight back to the same target and made an identical dive-bombing attack on it. This time no flak was experienced. Two salvos fell on the centre of the building and another three against its front. 603 departed Holland at 9,000 feet and landed back at Ludham at 12.30.

An intelligence report dated 1 April 1945 from Fighter Command HQ summarising post-attack reconnaissance photographs concludes:

After attacks by a total of thirty Fighter Command aircraft on 18th and 30th March, 1945, thirty craters are seen within a circle radius 250 yards from the centre point of the building. Damage has also occurred at points A.1, 2, 3 and 4. The target has received at least six direct hits and eight near misses.

And later: 'SORTIE 39/3033 is an oblique view of the target after attack. Five hits are seen on the roof and the concrete awning above the building has collapsed at one point.' However, the building was mainly undamaged. Reinforced concrete is notoriously difficult to destroy as some of the raids on the U-boat pens in France had demonstrated and the Squadron ORB concludes that the effectiveness of the 500lb bombs against reinforced concrete 'remains...in doubt'.

Following the attacks on the Bataafsche Petroleum Maatschappij HQ, further raids were carried out that afternoon on railway targets in Holland, the last sorties taking off at 17.50 and returning at 19.15.

The Bataafsche petrol company buildings at The Hague. Dive bombed by 603 and nine direct hits scored.

F/L Jack Batchelor was subsequently awarded the DFC and he received a signal from HQ Fighter Command at Bentley Priory on 6 June from Air Marshal Sir James Robb:

Dear Batchelor,

I am delighted to see that you have been awarded the DFC. Your skill and courage and fine leadership have been an inspiration to your Squadron, and your leading of the attack on the Bataafsche Petrol Company's building in the Hague was a magnificent piece of work.

All good wishes,
Yours sincerely,
James Robb

But things were moving on. Whilst nobody would realise it at the time, the last V2 to hit London did so on 27 March and 603's role would be altered. Another change was the posting of S/L Rigler to RAF Catfoss to take up a training role. On 30 March, it was announced that he was being awarded the DFC and this was celebrated fully on this Friday night at the end of March. The ORB is fullsome in its praise of Tommy Rigler:

> His career in the RAF has been outstanding. He has destroyed at least 8 Huns, being severely wounded twice, has risen from Sergeant Pilot to Squadron Commander and has completed over 400 operational hours as a Fighter Pilot and dive bomber pilot. Apart from his own personal work, his great experience and his personal enthusiasm have been immense factors in shaping the traditions of the Squadron and his own determination and courage in attack have inspired all the aircrew under him. We congratulate him on his well merited award and regret that he leaves us.

The citation for his DFC award read:

> This officer has completed a very large number of sorties and throughout has displayed keenness and devotion to duty worthy of the highest praise. He has led the squadron on very many low level and harassing attacks on a variety of enemy targets and much success has been achieved. By his great skill and fine fighting qualities, S/L Rigler has contributed materially to the high standard of operational efficiency of the squadron he commands.

Command of the Squadron was given to S/L H.R.P. Pertwee who immediately prior to this had been a flight commander with 602 Squadron. His posting to 603 was effective from 28 March.

The month wasn't over and with all the operations that had taken place during March, the morning of 31 March dawned with 603 needing 18 hours to complete 1,000 (operational and training) hours during the month. The weather was not ideal but there were three armed recces once more against railway targets. At 08.20, F/O McConnochie led off four Spitfires, at 09.20 F/L McAndrew and five others set off for the railway junction at Alphen and finally F/L Kirkman led two others down the runway at 12.20 on more attacks, returning at 13.35. The magic 1,000 hours was passed and the Squadron were released at 14.20.

The final statistics for their operations at the end of March were:

Total number of operational sorties	626
Total number of operational hours	889 hours, 20 minutes
Total number of bombs dropped	8385
Total number of non-operational hours	119 hours
Total hours	1,008 hours, 20 minutes

'Dickie' Pertwee was welcomed to his new command on Sunday 1 April. In many ways it was an ideal posting. He already knew the pilots and 603 knew him because of the work that they had being doing together over the previous weeks. Moving from one unit to another on the same airfield also did away with the need for major packing and unpacking so that for all concerned, it was a smooth transition. However, there were already half a dozen F/Ls on the Squadron who were quite capable of taking it over and a few of them wondered why it was felt necessary to find a CO from another unit. Pertwee was 22 years of age and came from Chelmsford in Essex. S/L Rigler was on leave.

The ending of the European war was moving ever nearer. The US First and Ninth Armies joined up, encircling the Ruhr and trapping over a quarter of a million German troops. Of more direct consequence for the two Scottish squadrons, the Germans were withdrawing from eastern Holland leaving their troops in the west cut off – all of which was to mean the end of the threat from the V2s there.

The 603 Squadron pilots at this time were:

A Flight – F/L Batchelor (Flight Commander), F/L McAndrew, F/L Sergeant, F/L Staniforth, F/O Thomson, F/Sgt O'Reilly, W/O Thomson, P/O Haupt, F/O Burrows, W/O Maslen, W/O Godfrey and W/O Evans.

B Flight – F/L Welch DFC (Flight Commander), F/L Kirkman, F/O McConnochie, P/O Cookson, W/O Wheatley, W/O Beckwith, W/O Mee, W/O Laffan, F/O Machon, F/O Richmond and F/Sgt Webb.

B Flight was awaiting a replacement for P/O McGinn.

The weather for 1 April was poor and although F/L Staniforth led off four Spitfires on an armed recce at 07.00, they couldn't make landfall and after their return to base there were no other operations that day although the pilots were kept waiting around at the dispersal in case the weather improved. The hope was that their attacks would disrupt the German withdrawal from Holland.

The following day the weather wasn't much better but it did allow some operations and at 13.55 the new CO led his first 603 operational mission which was an attack by four Spitfires on a railway junction north east of Utrecht.

The last armed recce of the day was led by F/L Kirkman at 18.30. He was accompanied by F/O Machon, F/O McConnochie and W/O Beckwith. At 19.00 they bombed a railway junction at Utrecht then returned to Ludham, landing at 20.00.

The award of the DFC to S/L Pertwee was announced that day and it was duly celebrated with a 'sortie' to Sutton Staithe.

Operations were easing for the squadrons. The entry in the 603 ORB for 3 April reads:

> As an Easter Egg both 603 and 602 Squadrons were released for the day. Breakfast ended at 10.30. and the Bar opened so pilots could recoup their strength with Guinness. At noon certain Units moved to Sutton Staithe and played darts and conversed and occasionally drank. Ten valiant souls then repaired to Potter Higham and ventured on to the Broads in two Dinghies and a Half Decker. The Dinghie crews were obviously novices and could not beat up the Broads against a gusty wind but the skilled Yachtsmen in the Half Decker tacked up for about 3 miles after one or two minor set backs (the Intelligence Officer proving that his courses are erratic in two elements) and eventually came back at a spanking rate stopping neatly alongside with a crashing of Booms and Sails. The evening was spent in a general reconnaissance of Sutton Staithe.

The 602 ORB entry for the same day is much less descriptive! 'An Easter gift in the form of a Wing release was bestowed by Group upon the two Squadrons at LUDHAM and the pilots spent a pleasant day yachting on the Norfolk Broads.' The day spent boating on the Broads signalled the end of operations entirely and it was a fitting opportunity for the pilots to recover from the exertions of the last five or six months. On 4 April, both squadrons were told that offensive operations over Holland had ended but they were to continue to maintain a defensive state – albeit a 'strong' one.

For 603, this meant having two Spitfires on 'immediate readiness' and ten at 15-minutes readiness. Just before lunch it was changed to two aircraft on immediate readiness with one flight on 15 minutes and the rest at 30.

There had been talk of a move back to Coltishall by both the squadrons and 603 had been expecting to go on Friday 6 April, but on the Wednesday at about tea time, they were told that the move was to be completed by the following day. There was immediate frantic activity and with a great deal of hard work, the ground crews managed to pack and transfer much of their equipment to Coltishall the same day although they only had the use of two Albions and a 15 cwt light truck.

The move brought the two units into 11 Group and their role would now be to act as escort for bombers.

In many accounts of the air war in Europe, the period that Fighter Command spent attacking the V2s is hardly mentioned. Accounts of the pilots who knocked the V1s out of the sky are more common, but the campaign against the rockets receives less than its fair share of attention.

Strategically, it *was* important. The War Cabinet was greatly concerned about the potential for damage which the V2s could cause and the consequences of V2s tipped with nuclear, biological or chemical warheads (which could not be discounted) being rained upon the south of England and London (and the continent) is almost too shocking to contemplate. At the beginning of 1945, the use of such weapons would have changed the whole history of the Second World War even if the end result had been the same.

V2s had been fired at Antwerp in an attempt to disrupt the Allied supply chain and at the Remagen Bridge across the Rhine to try to slow the advancing Allies. The fact that such attacks were minimised helped ensure that the final advance continued as it did.

For the pilots of all the squadrons involved – not just 603 – the missions were dangerous indeed. Until airfields on the continent became available, each sortie required a lengthy crossing of the North Sea at the beginning and end when only flying a single-engined aircraft. These flights were undertaken during the winter – when survival in the sea was unlikely even if the bale-out or crash landing was accomplished successfully. Even when the airfields in Belgium were captured and put into use, the crossing was still being made daily.

The history of the re-formed 603 follows its activities from January 1945 but the aircrew who formed 603 from 229 Squadron had been doing this work for many weeks before; as had the pilots of the other squadrons – like 602. The first strafing of V2 targets from the sector was on 23 September 1944 and the first bombs dropped by 453 Squadron on 21 November. During the period 4,750 sorties were flown with the loss of 29 aircraft and 23 pilots. By the end of the V2 attacks, having lived on a diet of two or three attacks a day, the pilots would be relieved that their hazardous daily routine was changing.

Such attacks required concentration, courage and skill. The targets were difficult to find and the methodology of the attack – dive bombing – created stresses on the body and the mind. A small misjudgement and the Spitfire might not pull out. The ever present and often heavy flak might in an instant change the plunging Spitfire into an uncontrollable mass of flame from which there would be no escape.

The ground crews too were hard pressed and critical to the success of the fight. Without their efforts, the Spitfires would not have been turned round as quickly as they were, nor would the maintenance which they needed have been carried out. The number of aircraft which aborted from sorties because of mechanical problems was small.

Those who were involved in whatever role, at least have the personal satisfaction of knowing that they contributed hugely to the ultimate victory even if public acknowledgement of their efforts is not great.

There were some official acknowledgements, however. On 10 April, the AOC of 12 Group, AVM Baker, visited the Squadron to congratulate them on their success and to bid them farewell on their departure from the Group. He also read out a letter from the Commander in Chief which included a comment that 'the peace enjoyed by London' could be attributed to them.

At the end of the war in Europe, the Prime Minister, Winston Churchill, in a broadcast on 13 May, commented particularly on the role that the RAF had played in reducing the effectiveness of the V weapons.

On the morning of Thursday 5 April, the rest of the equipment which hadn't been moved to Coltishall the previous evening was taken across and the Spitfires all made their way safely as well. The remainder of the day was spent sorting out the new dispersal which was completed by tea time.

As far as Ludham was concerned, the two Scottish auxiliary squadrons were being replaced by 91 Squadron moving up from Manston which it did on 7 April. The last sortie from Ludham was flown on 1 May 1945 and the airfield then gradually wound down to eventual closure.

On Friday 6 April, the first operation with 11 Group took place. Operations were to be under the overall command of W/C W.A. Douglas DFC – the same Bill Douglas who had been with 603 Squadron in previous years and a flight commander and the CO in Malta. They were to act as escort to a force of 54 Lancasters which was to attack shipping targets off western Holland. There were also believed to be midget submarine pens at Ijmuiden and these were targets too. It was to be a combined 603/602 operation with 12 Spitfires from 603 and 11 from 602 – and the W/C making up the 24 who took off from Coltishall at 09 05.

The weather was poor with cloud at 2,000 feet over the target. Six aircraft from 603 and nine from 602 together with Douglas reached the rendezvous with the bombers but none arrived so they continued on beyond the target to carry out a sweep which would hopefully stop any enemy activity against the bombers if they did turn up.

Meanwhile, the other six 603 Spitfires led by the CO managed to make contact with about 14 Lancasters and flew with them at 15,000 feet to the target area where after circling and being unable to see anything on the ground, the raid was abandoned. The Lancasters were escorted back out to sea, and the Spitfires turned back to Holland hoping to pick up the remaining bombers, but they weren't found. All in all a disappointing start for them in their new role.

603 did not fly operationally the following day, but the raid was repeated (by 617 Squadron) and was apparently successful on this attempt.

On 8 April, there was a briefing for an operation that was subsequently cancelled. In the afternoon, W/C Douglas led both squadrons in some practice formation flying – described as a Wing 'Balbo'. However, in the evening both 603 and 602 were ordered to airfield B.65 (which was at Maldegem,* not far from Ursel) for the night to take part in an escort operation the next day. Accordingly, at 17.20, having been fitted with 90-gallon fuel tanks, 11 603 Spitfires left Coltishall arriving at Maldegem at 18.30. 12 Spitfires from 602 were also involved.

It was a daylight raid on Hamburg by 57 Lancasters (including 17 from 617 Squadron) targeting oil storage tanks and U-boat pens. For the two auxiliary squadrons the escort was more or less non-eventful. 603 was tasked with starboard rear cover. They took off at 16.32 and flew to Egmond on the Dutch coast and met up successfully with the bombing force escorting them to near Bremen where, at 17.15, they handed over to several Mustang squadrons. The Spitfires returned to Coltishall.

During the operation, an airborne radio relay between the fighter leader and control was needed at short notice. Back at Coltishall, there was a sudden demand for two Spitfires to act in this role, and at 14.30, F/O Thomson and W/O Laffan from 603 took off arriving at Maldegem just in time to see the escort aircraft departing. On landing it was found that the W/O's aircraft had a hole in its 90-gallon tank so F/O Thomson acted in the relay role on his own, flying between Arnhem and Nijmegen at 19,000 feet. He came off patrol at 17.50, and returned to Maldegem where the other Spitfire had by now been repaired. W/O Laffan joined him in the air and the two flew back to Coltishall, landing at 19.05. During this operation, Nick Machon clocked up his 1,000 hours.

The raid on Hamburg was recorded as a success. Two Lancasters were lost bombing the oil tanks – one being brought down in the target area.**

These overnight stopovers at airfields on the continent were to become more common. The British airmen were issued with khaki battledress. The RAF blue serge battledress – which was flying kit – was the same pattern, but there was concern that if they had to bale out, some of the Allied troops on the ground might mistake the RAF blue for the grey/blue of the Luftwaffe and shoot them. Eric Mee recalled that on one occasion he and one or two others had gone for a walk into the nearby Dutch town of Leopoldsburg having a couple of hours to kill until the next sortie began. Not wearing hats, which were back in their lockers in Coltishall, they were quickly picked up by army police for being bareheaded. The Redcaps found it difficult to understand this. Leopoldsburg was a garrison town and the police were keen to maintain discipline and so in future, the pilots were told to take their hats with them. Bob Sergeant had a favourite battered old hat which no doubt was made even worse by being stuffed into a corner of the cockpit.

Sergeant also recalled that on one of the few occasions when he overnighted on the continent, they were billeted in an old monastery. During the night, he got up to relieve himself and found that the stalls had timber sides like cattle or horse stalls. In the gloom, he was startled by a shadowy shape with hood and habit who silently appeared beside him – for the same purpose.

---

*In the middle of June 1941, Maldegem was the home airfield of II Gruppe of Jagdgeschwader 26 when it was commanded by Oberstleutnant Adolf Galland. It was engaged in defending the continent against the ever-increasing Rodeos etc, some of which involved 603 in the escort role.

**They were both from RAF Skellingthorpe. NG342 of 50 Squadron (VN-S) piloted by F/O V.G. Berriman RAAF was lost near the target. RF121 of 61 Squadron (QR-J) piloted by F/L A.P. Greenfield DFC RAAF was brought down near Becklingen.

On Wednesday 11 April, 12 Spitfires set off at 08.15 to fly to B.90 – Petit Brogel* – 20 miles or so south of Eindhoven. This time they were briefed for an operation to attack railway yards in Bayreuth, but although this raid did take place, 603 was re-tasked as escort for another raid on Nuremburg. It was to be carried out by 14 Pathfinder Lancasters and 129 Halifaxes of 4 Group.

They were off again from Petit Brogel at 13.40 flying to Mannheim where they were to meet the bombers. This was achieved successfully but both the CO and F/O Burrows had to return early – the former with a radio problem and the latter with engine trouble. The force continued to Nuremburg where the bombers carried out a successful attack on the railway yards whilst the escort circled overhead. There was no reaction from the enemy and the force returned to the Rhine where the Spitfires parted company with the bombers and landed at Petit Brogel at 16.40. No bombers were lost.

The intention had been that they would return to Coltishall that night, but there wasn't enough fuel at Petit Brogel to cope with all the aircraft that had come in so their departure was delayed until the following day – rather later than expected at 13.20 because of poor weather over Norfolk.

Having arrived back at Coltishall, rumours began to circulate that they were to return to Petit Brogel in preparation for a morning show on 13 April, but it wasn't until the early evening that the order to move arrived and at 19.10, 14 aircraft from 603 and 11 from 602 flew back to Holland.

During the day, F/Sgt Paddy O'Reilly who had been with the Squadron for about a year and a half left to go to RAF Aston Down where he was to convert to Typhoons. He was a man with a good sense of humour and he was going to be missed.

That evening, with most of the Squadron in Holland, there were only a few pilots left at Coltishall – mostly those who for one reason or another were earmarked for other things. The newly arrived Sergeant Bramley wasn't considered 'operational' yet, F/L Kirkman was due to go on a course and F/L Machon was given the duty of ferrying him there. F/Os Thomson, Burrows and Cookson were 'tour expired', but whilst they were dining, they were told that 603 was to provide four Spitfires for readiness and two to carry out a recce the following day.

Although 14 aircraft had flown to Petit Brogel, there were still four serviceable aircraft at Coltishall and on the morning of Friday the 13th, they came to readiness although the recce was cancelled because of poor weather. It was reinstated later and at 09.00 Thomson and Burrows were airborne and heading east. They crossed into Holland at Katwijk, then flew south to Leiden and Gouda before turning north to Utrecht and Amersfoort. At the airfield at Soesterberg there was heavy white smoke from a dispersal east of the runways. At Amersfoort they found much wreckage and damage to the railway yards. The pair checked the coastal area for shipping targets, returning to Coltishall at 11.15 having flown at 5 to 6,000 feet in a sky that was virtually free of clouds.

F/L Kirkman eventually left for his course** – Naval Fighter Leader – and for the rest of the day, the remaining pilots kept a changing readiness state helped by 602 and 1 Squadron (which had arrived at Coltishall some days before).

Meanwhile, back at Petit Brogel, 13 aircraft led by the CO took off at 14.45 as part of a wing to meet and escort a force of bombers which was tasked to attack Swinemunde. The raid involved 34 Lancasters (from 9 and 617 Squadrons) whose target had been the harbour area where the German battleships *Prinz Eugen* and *Lutzow* were berthed. In the event, cloud prevented them seeing their targets so the raid was abandoned.

For 603, the operation was quite uneventful. They returned to Petit Brogel at 17.45 and after refuelling, landed back at Coltishall at 20.40.

The weather was changeable over the next few days with a consequent mixture of tasks for 603 – but allowing some time for recreation including two games of football against 1 Squadron – in fact a combined 602/603 team on the second occasion. The Scottish teams won both games. One of the goals was scored by Bob Sergeant.

---

*'Petit Brogel' is the name that the airfield was known by, but it is in French. To be strictly correct, it should be 'Kleine Brogel'.

**His course was at St Merryn and he was taken there in the Auster (BL299) by Nick Machon. This meant a flight of four hours with stops at Abingdon and Weston-Zoyland for fuel. Machon returned to Coltishall the next day taking just under five hours with refuelling stops at Watchfield and Waterbeach.

At 18.00 on Monday 16 April, after the second of the football matches, orders were received for aircraft from the three squadrons – 602, 603 and 1 – to move to Petit Brogel to take part in operations the next day. Accordingly, at 19.05, W/C Douglas led ten aircraft from 602, 13 from 603 and 12 from 1 Squadron to the airfield on the continent. The Spitfire flown by W/O Evans lost its 90-gallon tank and had to return to Coltishall.

The following day, Tuesday, the operation which had precipitated the move was cancelled, but the Spitfires were ordered to remain at Petit Brogel for another night to carry out escort duties 24 hours later on Wednesday 18 April. This was a raid – Ramrod 1544 – by 969 bombers – 617 Lancasters and 382 Halifaxes with 20 Mosquitoes to attack the island of Heligoland. The primary target was the naval base, but the nearby airfield and the town were also to be attacked. The Spitfires took off at 12.20 – 603 being led by the CO. On reaching the island, the wing patrolled a line to the south and east at heights between 16 and 19,000 feet from 13.30 to 13.55 until all the bombers had cleared the area. They caused immense destruction. The bombing lasted for about an hour and at its end the targets were covered by a pall of black smoke that extended 30 miles to the east. The bombed areas were heavily cratered and the raid was considered to be highly successful. The Spitfires landed back at Petit Brogel at 14.55 for re-fuelling then returned to Coltishall. Seven Halifaxes were lost.*

The format for 19 April was similar. Spitfires from the three squadrons were airborne at about 09.40 from Coltishall to fly to airfield B.86 which was at Helmond, to the east of Eindhoven. On this occasion, there were two 'boxes' totalling 36 Lancasters from 9 and 617 Squadrons which were to attack Heligoland again, this time the coastal gun positions using Tallboy bombs – Ramrod 1546. At 15.40, the Spitfire wing took off from Helmond and met up with the bombers. 603 and 1 Squadrons escorted the first group and after the bombing was finished, returned to Helmond. 602 remained in the area to cover the second 'box' of Lancasters, patrolling the area for about an hour before landing back at Helmond at 18.55.

The raid was a success and no Lancasters were lost. The enormous damage on the ground from the raid of the previous day was clearly visible and one effect of it was that the flak defences were virtually non-existent.

As part of this operation, W/O Seward had to act in the airborne relay role circling over Zwolle whilst passing messages back and forward between the fighters and control. He returned to Helmond at 19.00.

It was a successful day but the pilots were ordered to remain at Helmond overnight pending operations on 20 April. However, in the event nothing happened and although kept at 60-minute readiness, at 15.30 they were released. During the day, W/Os Laffan and Wheatley having volunteered, left Coltishall to ferry Spitfires to the Middle East – expecting to be away for about two weeks.

The Spitfires had no heating for the pilots. Loitering at 25,000 feet was cold. Sometimes the oil pressure gauge on the Packard Merlins would freeze up but the 'old hands' got to know this and when a less experienced pilot called his flight commander to say that he'd lost oil pressure and was going home, he was told not to go. Bob Sergeant's mother knitted him a short woollen polo neck sweater to supplement the warmth kept in by his issue kit – the 'frocks, white' and he also had a pair of long woolly socks that were rolled down to his flying boots when on the ground, but were unrolled to well above his knees when flying to try to keep his legs warm.

It was the following day, the Saturday that the pilots returned from Helmond to Coltishall, arriving back in the middle of the afternoon. It was learnt that W/O Alf Beckwith had been granted his commission – a promotion that was felt well justified by the other members of the unit.

---

*RG622 (MP●I) of 76 Squadron and LL556 of 347 Squadron were both involved in accidents during take-off. NP776 (EQ●R) of 408 Squadron piloted by F/L A.J. Cull RCAF, NP946 (PT●L) of 420 Squadron piloted by F/Sgt W.J. Dunnigan RCAF, PN226 (OWlN) of 426 Squadron piloted by P/O J.A. Whipple RCAF and RG564 (C8●P) of 640 Squadron piloted by P/O H.K. Pugh RCAF were lost with all crew killed. PN447 (ZA●B) of 10 Squadron piloted by F/L C.P. Smith was found to be damaged on return to base despite not apparently having been hit and after inspection was struck off charge.

Their next operation took place on the following Wednesday, 25 April. For the three days before, there had been no operational flying, but a fairly intensive and varied round of training was completed. This included air to air firing, cine gun exercises, Link trainer work, formation and low level flying.

In the morning, 603 were released for more training, but almost immediately warned that they would be needed for operations. This time it was an attack by 482 bombers on the island of Wangerooge – Ramrod 1555. The main targets were coastal batteries protecting the passage to the ports of Wilhelmshaven and Bremen which were being considered as entry points for supplies for the Allied armies. At 10.45, 13 Spitfires from 603 along with others from the wing were airborne for Petit Brogel where they landed at mid-day.

The wing took off at 15.45 and joined up with the bombing force which comprised 308 Halifaxes, 158 Lancasters and 16 Mosquitoes. Between 16.55 and 17.20 the Spitfires patrolled at 17,000 feet whilst the 'heavies' made their attacks at 14,000 feet. The weather was good with clear skies and the bombing was assessed as being accurate until the target was shrouded in smoke and dust. The defences put up moderate heavy flak which was mainly directed at the bombers.

Seven bombers were lost, six of them from collisions.* Bob Sergeant was horrified at the loss of life.

Parachutes were going down. Aircraft colliding. We just stooged around watching. There were so many of them milling about all over the place – I don't know why they weren't in a stream. It was so stupid. The war was clearly won so why carry on?

Eric Mee had similar thoughts: 'What rotten luck I thought, to get the chop with the war as good as over.'

Subsequent reports were that the raid had actually caused little damage to the guns. Regretfully, the bombing damaged a number of civilian premises including some hotels and guest houses, a church and a camp for forced workers. There were 306 casualties – a mixture of civilians, foreign workers, naval personnel and prisoners of war (French and Moroccan).

The Spitfires landed back at the airfield at 18.25 and were ordered to remain there for the night to take part in operations the next day. These were subsequently cancelled and the raid on Wangerooge turned out to be 603's last operation of the European war prior to Germany's surrender. The pilots who flew on it were F/L Batchelor, W/O Seward, F/L Staniforth, W/O Godfrey, S/L Pertwee, W/O Mee, F/L McAndrew, F/Sgt Webb, F/L Welch, Sgt Bramley, F/L Sergeant and F/O Richmond.

Whilst these 12 were away, back at Coltishall orders to move to RAF Turnhouse on the next day – Thursday – were received. 603 were at last coming home and the Edinburgh Squadron would be back in their own city.

---

*Halifax VI RG553 (MP●T) piloted by P/O G.W. Lawson RCAF and Halifax VI RG591 (MP●A) piloted by W/O J.L. Outerson RCAF, both of 76 Squadron, collided over the target and were destroyed. The only survivor was P/O Lawson who was unhurt but taken prisoner. Halifax VII NP820 (OW●N) of 426 Squadron piloted by W/O J.C. Tuplin RCAF collided with Halifax VII NP796 (EQ●M) piloted by F/L A.B. Ely RCAF over the target and there were no survivors. OW●N from 426 Squadron was also lost on the Heligoland raid on the 18th. Two Lancaster X of 431 Squadron - KB822 (SE●W) piloted by F/O D.G. Baker RCAF and KB831 (SE●E) piloted by F/L B.D. Emmet RCAF collided off Nordenay. There were no survivors. Halifax VI NP921 (L8●E) of 347 Squadron piloted by Sgt R. Mercier Free French Air Force came down on the island. There were no survivors.

CHAPTER 16

PEACE AND DISBANDMENT

The order to return home was greeted with the great enthusiasm which might have been expected, although for the current pilots, the connection with Edinburgh and the Auxiliary Air Force was somewhat tenuous. After all, none of them had been with 603 before the outbreak of the war, and whilst they were loyal to their unit, as they would be to any squadron in which they served, the special relationship with the city didn't mean that much to them. Further, many of the ground crew were in much the same situation. But for the 30 or so of the original 603 auxiliaries back with the Squadron they had an extra reason to celebrate and they did so enthusiastically.

The European war was clearly almost won, but the view at that time was that there would yet be a bloody campaign in the Pacific culminating in an invasion of the Japanese homeland which would incur huge casualties. F/O John Moss, who joined at the end of June, recalls that he had an expectation that they would be sent to the Far East – but on the other hand this possibility hadn't even crossed Bob Sergeant's mind.

EDINBURGH SQUADRON HOME AGAIN

From *The Scotsman*. Members of 603 Squadron pose on their return to Turnhouse, May 1945.

After receiving the order to move on 25 April, preparations began immediately and by the evening, they were well advanced. But most of the Squadron Spitfires were still detached at B.90 – Helmond – and weren't expected back until the next day.

The plan was that at 09.00 on Friday 27 April, 50 ground crew together with essential kit would leave Coltishall to fly north to Turnhouse in Avro Yorks* provided by Transport Command. The rest of the personnel and equipment would follow by rail.

At Helmond, on Thursday the 26th, the pilots were expecting to take part in another operation and return to Coltishall on the Friday to fly up to Turnhouse, but the operation was cancelled and the Spitfires returned to Coltishall just after 13.00 in time for lunch. This

Turnhouse, 1945. W/O Eric Mee sitting on the cowling of his aircraft S with other A Flight pilots and ground crew. F/Sgt Angy Gillies far left. Centre: F/L Welch, and Nick Machon (on Welch's left).

allowed all the kit to be finally packed in plenty of time for the morning and in the evening, the officers had a party in the mess to celebrate the move.

These carefully laid plans came to nothing. The weather was surprisingly poor for that time of year with heavy cloud and snow. The Yorks did not arrive at 09.00 as expected and the Squadron waited all day for them until in the evening they were told that the airlift was cancelled and ground personnel would be travelling by rail with the kit in lorries on Saturday.

It seemed at one point that Friday would not be completely wasted and at 17.10, 20 Spitfires left Coltishall for Turnhouse. Half an hour later they were back after it was decided that the wintry conditions at Turnhouse were so bad that they wouldn't be able to land there.

The move finally got under way successfully on Saturday morning when the main party caught the train and the transport convoy left Coltishall at 09.15. Only the aircraft remained and just before lunch, 20 took off and started the transit north. P/O Cookson in O developed engine trouble and with W/O Mee in S landed at Carnaby for repairs at 12.35. The remainder of the Spitfires arrived at Turnhouse just after 13.00 without incident.

F/L Machon in U was the last to leave Coltishall at 12.45 landing safely at Turnhouse at 14.25.

The AOCs of both 11 and 12 Groups sent signals to the Squadron thanking them for their efforts and wishing them well. From 11 Group on 28 April:

Air Officer Commanding thanks the Commanding Officer and all personnel of 603 Squadron for their participation in recent 11 Group offensive operations and wishes them all good hunting in their new role.

And from the AOC 12 Group on 26 April:

Please convey to S/Ldr Pertwee my regret that I cannot visit 603 Squadron to say goodbye. They have achieved an operational record second to none. It is a fitting heritage to carry back to their home station sector where the Squadron originally founded its fine traditions. On behalf of 12 Group I wish all ranks the very best of luck wherever they may be called upon to serve in the future.

---

*The York was a development of the Lancaster bomber, but with a squarer, chunkier fuselage and three fins. After the war it would go on to become a passenger airliner and it would be used to a great extent in the Berlin Airlift.

There was little ceremony to mark the return. On Sunday, the day was spent settling in and there was a small party in the evening to mark the moment. On Monday morning, the pilots carried out sector reccos to familiarise themselves with the local area and at 14.00 hours they were 'on state' and ready to go with two Spitfires on readiness and a further two at 30 minutes.

The only excitement was at 17.20 when a section was scrambled to investigate an X raid but it turned out to be a Coastal Command Mosquito. The ORB records the return:

> The Squadron is glad to find itself once more at its home base and engaged in the defence of its Parent City. It seems particularly fitting that the beginning and end of operations in the European zone of war should find us so engaged.

Turnhouse was a quiet sector and with the imminent ending of the war on the continent, there was little action. During April, the average number of pilots on the station was 20. Further north, Beaufighters and Mosquitoes with Mustang escorts were attacking targets in Norway, but at Turnhouse little was happening. Interceptions of unknown plots continued, but these were inevitably 'friendlies' – on 3 May for example, two 603 Spitfires were scrambled to investigate another unknown near Leuchars which turned out to be Liberator.

The attractions of Edinburgh weren't far away and on station, there were entertainments in the gym. On 26 April there was a WAAF Gang Show and the next evening a Variety Parade was put on by ENSA. There were also regular 'sorties' off the station. Nearby were the Maybury Roadhouse (a favourite of Stapme Stapleton and his colleagues in 1940), the Harp Hotel in Corstorphine and the Barnton Hotel. In town the magnet was Princes Street dominated by Edinburgh Castle on the south and with the two great railway hotels at either end – the Caledonian at the west end and the North British (or NB) at the east. Other high spots were the Grosvenor Hotel in Grosvenor Street at Haymarket and the Balmoral Rooms half way along Princes Street. Cordial relations were being established with the WAAF officers on the station too.

On 1 May 1945, the Squadron CO was S/L H.R.P. Pertwee and the aircrew were:

A Flight – F/L Batchelor (Flight Commander), F/L McAndrew, F/L Sergeant, F/L Staniforth, F/O Thomson, W/O Thomson, P/O Haupt, F/O Burrows, W/O Maslen, W/O Godfrey, W/O Evans and W/O Seward.

B Flight – F/L Welch DFC (Flight Commander), F/L Kirkman, F/O McConnochie, P/O Cookson, W/O Wheatley, P/O Beckwith, W/O Mee, W/O Laffan, F/L Machon, F/O Richmond, F/Sgt Webb and Sgt Bramley.

Of the 25 pilots on strength (including the CO), two were detached to the Middle East, three were on leave and two were tour expired (P/Os Cookson and Haupt) and left for Rednall. Only two were Scots – F/L McAndrew from Cupar in Fife and F/O Thomson from Aberdeen.

On Wednesday 2 May, a contingent of the press visited Turnhouse to gather information about the return of 603 to its home station. The weather was poor and there was no display of flying, but the day seems to have been a success. Much of the interest centred on the auxiliaries in the ground crew but nonetheless the pilots 'with blushing modesty managed to get into the pictures – in fact into many'! It was also noted that F/L Welch was seen 'running from a press photographer' but apparently merely to get his Mae West for 'an operational' photo!!

Articles appeared over the next few days in a number of Scottish newspapers – *The Scotsman*, *The Daily Express*, the *Edinburgh Evening Dispatch*, the *Daily Record* and the *Edinburgh Evening News* to name some, accompanied by suitable headlines – 'The 603 are Home Again', 'Edinburgh Squadron Home Again', 'Home Again Edinburgh's Famous Fighter Squadron'.

The articles, as would be expected, tended to give pride of place to the auxiliary ground crew who were the remnants of the original 603 that had been at Turnhouse in 1939 and provided the continuity. Those who were specifically mentioned and whose photographs appeared were W/O Erskine (the oldest member of the unit), and the Gillies brothers – but interestingly, not many of the pilots! Specifically mentioned in the article in the *Edinburgh Evening News* were Sgt Jackie Crooks, Cpl George McVie, F/Sgt Donald MacKenzie, Cpl Douglas Campbell, Sgt R. Bain, LAC Alec

W/O Eric Mee with his Spitfire 'Curly's Caravan' and his ground crew.

Cassidy and Cpl Johnnie Lee. Also mentioned and photographed was 'Bruce' the Squadron's alsation mascot, pictured sitting on the nose of one of the Spitfires! Bruce had not gone abroad when the pilots went to Malta and the service echelon to Egypt in 1942. He went south to be looked after by a former 603 officer based there. When the unit returned to the UK, G/C Ernest 'Count' Stevens arranged for Bruce to be re-united with his former friends.

After the press day, things fell into a bit of a routine. The Squadron maintained readiness but there wasn't much trade as would be expected. On the afternoon of Saturday 4 May, there was a football match on the camp – the officers against the maintenance section. F/L Sergeant and P/O Beckwith played for the officers' team and 'because of, or despite of this factor the officers won by 4 goals to 2.' In the evening, there were 'swift sorties' into Edinburgh, returning via the WAAF officers' mess.

On 5 May, a formation display was carried out over the city. The weather wasn't ideal and it wasn't right for aerobatics, but nonetheless it seems to have been an impressive show. There were 12 in the formation which took off at 14.30 and was airborne for 65 minutes. They were led by F/L Batchelor and the others who took part were W/O Maslen, F/L McAndrew, W/O Godfrey, W/O Thomson, W/O Seward, F/L Sergeant, W/O Mee, F/L Welch, F/O Richmond, F/O McConnochie and F/L Machon.

The next day it was clear that the war with Hitler was within days of finishing and a spontaneous party developed in the officers' mess. The following day, seemingly only to have just arrived at Turnhouse, 603 was ordered to move to Drem and this was achieved by the time that darkness fell. By now Drem had just been taken over by the Navy and in June would be commissioned as HMS *Nighthawk*. The ORB records: 'Apparently the war is over.'

The next day was VE (Victory in Europe) Day, but the weather was awful with mist and rain. Readiness was maintained until the evening and then 603 were released to celebrate. It is interesting that many of the Squadron can't recall just where they were or what they did on VE night! Eric Mee's recollections are typical: 'I have hazy memories of being tutored in the ritual of Highland dancing in a square, by the lads and lassies of a nearby village, all to the strain of wailing bagpipes, and to celebrate a great occasion.'

Bob Sergeant's recollections were similarly vague. As to 'the nearby village' – Haddington

F/Sgt Mackenzie (right) with other ground crew standing in front of Eric Mee's Spitfire with the Edinburgh Castle logo visible. Turnhouse, 1945.

possibly, Aberlady perhaps, Gullane or North Berwick? Details of just what happened that night are sketchy – probably just as well.

603 still had an interesting and unusual postscript to perform over the Firth of Forth – the same territory that it had covered on 16 October 1939 for their first victory.

Senior German officers representing the three services in Norway were coming to Britain to offer the surrender of the troops there and to make arrangements for the German occupation to be ended. They were to be flying over the North Sea in three white-painted Ju52s making for the Firth of Forth. This was hampered by the bad weather which had continued after VE Day. A patrol was mounted on the morning of 10 May but the Germans weren't seen and as the weather deteriorated further, flying was stopped. On the following day, patrols were carried out in the afternoon, 20 sorties in all but with nothing report. The final two patrols took off at 19.05. These were led by F/L Batchelor and F/L Sergeant.

The patrols were flown well out to sea and the three Ju52s were eventually spotted by W/O Maslen. W/O Tommy Thomson recalled that:

> …they must have fired every coloured Very flare they had to indicate that they were 'Friendly'. I was ordered to cover them from the rear with my guns cocked as a precaution against any trickery. I kept them in my sights at all times. I had to lower my flaps to maintain position as their speed was 85 mph which was my Spitfire's stalling speed!!

Eric Mee found it an odd experience:

> It was with very mixed feelings, having never actually had a German aircraft in my sights, to have three lovely fat Jerry transports all in gleaming white paint, in easy range of my loaded guns. We shepherded them into Drem, then landed. There was much press activity and our photographs together with the Germans in their long leather coats were taken.

They landed at 20.00.

The job of transporting the luggage from the Junkers to a nearby truck was given to several sailors. One sailor was absolutely disgusted at having to act as a servant to the German officers. He called over a newsreel camera and said 'I'll give you a picture of how to deal with bloody Nazi luggage.' He then stood about 5 yards away from the truck and hurled the cases in with all his might. I could see his point, though I don't think his protest appeared on the cinema news.

According to local news reports, there were 18 officers including a lieutenant colonel from the Wehrmacht and another from the Luftwaffe. They didn't remain at Drem, but were taken immediately by car to a 'mansion house' near Edinburgh which was probably Craigiehall which was the HQ of troops in Scotland and not far from the airfield at Turnhouse, arriving there at 22.00 hours. The representatives from the Kriegsmarine were taken aboard a Royal Navy ship anchored in the shadow of the Forth Bridge for interrogation, again ironical given the events of October 1939.

Despite the reaction of the sailor at Drem, the Germans were treated correctly but firmly. They were not saluted, but they were not harmed. The newspapers reported that the German officers looked sullen and frightened and stood with bowed heads. They were allowed no rest and the interrogation/conference started immediately.

On 13 May, two of the Ju52s returned to Norway from Drem taking some of the Germans back and following on from this, Allied forces returned to Norway, many of them passing through Turnhouse and with much of the major equipment – LSTs etc – going by sea from Grangemouth in the Firth of Forth. Coincidentally, from 17.00 on the same day, the Royal Observer Corps reporting system was 'stood down' and the ROC presence in the sector operations room was no longer maintained.

Despite this sign that hostilities had ceased, in the following days, 603 were still required to stand readiness which would be the source of some irritation with their navy hosts. Like all Royal Navy shore bases, HMS *Nighthawk* was run like a ship. Sailors leaving the camp went for 'a run ashore' in the 'liberty boat' and of course naval terminology was used at all times so that the toilets were 'heads', the rooms 'cabins' and the roof was a 'deckhead'. On an aircraft carrier, aircraft were picketed down if not in use and the same rule applied at Drem. The RAF pilots thought it was amusing at first, but it became petty and annoying that after having explained that being on readiness meant that they had to be able to make a quick take-off, they would still find their Spitfires picketed down.

In the way of things, they poked gentle fun at the way the station was run. On a ship, the liberty boats would leave at specific times, and HMS *Nighthawk* was no exception. Sailors were allowed out in liberty boat loads at certain times and if the time was missed, it meant hanging about waiting for the next one. The sailors would have to fall in at the guard room and be marched out in liberty boat numbers at the right time. Of course, the RAF men weren't subject to these rules so they could stroll out when they wished, accompanied by jeers and catcalls from the sailors. One night some of the pilots produced a small boat on wheels that they 'sailed' out of camp.

In general, things were very quiet. The weather remained wet and windy and when flying was possible, it was practice, practice, practice – aerobatics, formations, cross countries and cine-gun exercises when the Spitfires had dogfights and the results were analysed afterwards on film taken by them. P/O Laffan arrived back at the Squadron on 16 May. Having volunteered for ferrying work to the Middle East, he had been in the UK for the whole time because the aircraft he was to have ferried was unserviceable.

On Saturday 19 May, the morning was spent training as usual, but at 12.30 came the release for the weekend. For all, there was the chance to go to Edinburgh, or home, or just to the local pubs. The weather still wasn't good. Some would take the chance to spend the night in Edinburgh. The North British Hotel at Waverley Station was a popular place to stay and it was in the middle of town. On the Sunday morning, those who had stayed on camp had the rare chance of a long lie in and a day spent relaxing – playing bridge or snooker or just reading. It was wet and miserable.

Top: German officers at Drem having flown in from Norway. RN representative and Count Stevens representing the RAF.
Bottom: From left to right: W/O Mee (mostly out of shot), W/O Maslen, F/L Sergeant, F/Sgt Seward, F/L McAndrew, P/O Beckwith, F/L Bachelor (with sunglasses), G/C Count Stevens and three German officers who had surrendered and arrived from Norway in a Ju52 escorted in by 603.

German and British servicemen beside the Ju52, painted white to indicate surrender. Note the Ansons in background in the photograph at the bottom.

The weather remained wet and windy for the rest of May and as would be expected there was no operational flying – only the round of training. On 23 May, five new pilots arrived from the OTU at Kirton-in-Lindsey – F/Ls Keep and Dawe, F/O Bass, W/O Gilpin and Sgt Malam. F/L Jack Batchelor returned from leave on 27 May having been married. All in all it had been an anti-climatic month: 'The month has been strangely quiet after the active months of March and to a certain extent April. Scotland has treated the Squadron indifferently…' The last comment on the weather, not the people!

On Friday 1 June, the complement of pilots was:

CO: S/L H.R.P. Pertwee DFC:

A Flight: F/L Batchelor, F/L McAndrew, F/L Sergeant, F/L Staniforth, F/O Thomson, F/O Burrows, W/O Thomson, P/O Maslen, W/O Godfrey, W/O Evans, W/O Seward, F/L Keep, F/O Bass and W/O Gilpin.

B Flight: F/L Welch, F/L Kirkman, F/O McConnochie (sick at Gleneagles Hospital), F/L Machon, F/O Richmond, P/O Beckwith, W/O Mee, P/O Laffan, W/O Wheatley, F/Sgt Webb, F/Sgt Bramley, F/L Dawe and Sgt Malam.

The round of training continued. It was clear that the Squadron were being eased back into a peacetime way of operating albeit that the war in the Far East continued. On the first day of June, there was a visit by the Group Engineering Officer and in the afternoon by Air Commodore Prickman OBE the AOC of 13 Group and by G/C Parker the Station Commander at RAF Turnhouse. F/L Kirkman who had been on his naval course returned to 603 on the Sunday.

On Monday 4 June, F/L Batchelor was awarded the DFC which led to the usual round of celebrations and the following entry in the ORB: '…this award was most popular as 'Batch' in the air and on the ground has shown outstanding verve, skill and initiative and has been a constant source of inspiration to his comrades.'

The week continued with some quite intensive flying training, with F/L Kirkman passing on some of the new tactics he had learnt on his course.

The Forth rail bridge was an important landmark for pilots flying in the skies over the Firth – and it still is although there is now the road suspension bridge as well. The rail bridge is a massive cantilever design, a lattice of huge tubes and girders painted dull red. There are three large triangular-shaped sections, joined by narrow horizontal ones along which the trains run. Bob Sergeant recalled that for the skilled and audacious pilots, one of their self-imposed tests was to see if they could loop their Spitfires around the narrow sections. The consequences of a misjudgement are unthinkable – more for the bridge than the pilots! At the end of the war, many of the pilots were still fired up and the prospect of a return to the monotony of a post-war RAF probably was not the most attractive.

There were also many parties going on. It had been mooted that there would shortly be a return to Turnhouse and on 6 June, some went there to enjoy the hospitality in a foretaste of what they were anticipating. Turnhouse had agreed to postpone their VE celebrations until 603 were back in the fold and this was something they looked forward to with relish. But it was not to be – at least not just yet.

On Monday 11 June, it was learnt that they were actually being sent to the Orkney islands – off the north tip of Scotland – and this was not a popular decision. The CO and some of the others went to Turnhouse to try to find out why the change was made, but without getting any clear cut answers. The people at Turnhouse seemed to be as much in the dark as 603 and to regret the posting as much as 603. For the Edinburgh ground crew it must have been a real blow. They had only been back in the UK for five months and now they were 'overseas' again! However, there was nothing that could be done to change things, so the unit buckled down to make the move on 14 June.

The Orkney islands form a ring around a large natural harbour which is Scapa Flow and was the base of the Royal Navy's Home Fleet. The Orkneys can be rather bleak, but the islands have a gentleness which makes them attractive when the weather is good, or in the soft rains that sometimes fall. But they can also be miserable if the Atlantic storms rage across them: it was one

A Flight ground crew and air crews, Skeabrae, 1945.

such storm that exposed the prehistoric dwellings at Skara Brae which are 4,000 years old. Orkney also has prehistoric standing stones which date back 3,000 years. There is a heavy Norse influence. The capital is Kirkwall and it boasts the famous St Magnus' Cathedral dating back to 1137 when its foundations were laid, although it took three hundred years to complete.

The wreck of HMS *Royal Oak*, sunk in Scapa Flow by a German U-boat at the beginning of the war, lies there to this day as a war grave.

For air defence, the airfield at Kirkwall was the sector station, but there were a number of airfields both on Orkney and in Caithness that were involved in the defence of Scapa Flow. Skeabrae was being built in 1940 by the Admiralty, but was handed over to the Air Ministry in May to help the RAF provide fighter cover for the naval base. The first airmen arrived in August of that year. It wasn't well designed and construction in 1940 was hampered by almost incessant rain which turned the site into a mudbath. The first recorded landing was on 15 September 1940 by an aircraft belonging to the Station Communications Flight. Over the years, a number of squadrons supplied aircraft to be based there – both from the RAF and the Fleet Air Arm. These were not necessarily complete squadrons, but were sometimes detached flights. One of them was 602 Squadron at the end of 1942. Civil aircraft also used Skeabrae during the war.

After the war was over it was placed on care and maintenance and the Royal Navy disposed of it in 1957. It was never used as an airfield again, although there were NATO studies as to its possible use in the event of American forces being asked to leave Iceland and an oil company had thoughts of using it as well.

It lies on the A967 about seven miles north of Stromness and there was another airfield a few miles away which took the rather unfortunate name of a nearby village – Twatt. 603 was being sent to relieve 451 Squadron – which was Australian and also flew Spitfire XVIs – and was being sent to Turnhouse.

The rail journey to Thurso would have been rather tedious and uncomfortable for the ground element. Inverness is over 200 miles from Edinburgh and Wick a further 150 beyond. The airmen who arrived in the morning light on the 14th would be tired and weary. But they still had to face the sea crossing to Orkney which appears to have been quite rough and was undertaken in two ferries – the *Richard Grenville* and the *St Ninian*.

The 19 pilots had a much easier passage. They left Drem at 14.15 led by the CO and landed at Skeabrae at 15.40 – before the ground crew got there.

W/O Eric Mee was on leave when the move happened. He had returned to Drem to find that his colleagues had gone without him and he had to make the rail and sea journey on his own:

> The ferry was a fairly small boat which got myself and a few other passengers to Orkney with no fuss. In the Air Force, I could never understand why transport is never there to meet the boat or train, even when they know the arrival times. True to form, no transport was waiting at Kirkwall, so I had to use the time to have a look round Kirkwall and get a wee snack. It was a considerable time before the truck hove into view. The landscape looked beautiful and unspoiled, with large lakes, magnificent cliffs and a wonderful wild look about it. Once again, my good mate Tommy had secured me a bed space in the usual primitive wooden hut and I soon got settled in.

Once there, for the pilots there was the usual sector recco:

> Sent off on my own to do a 'recce' of the area, I saw even more of the ruggedness of the many islands, some of the cliffs were very high, as I found when I flew down beside that pinnacle of rock known as 'The Old Man of Hoy'. Returning to base, it was great to see that the good old 'Sally Army' had a 'tea and wads' wagon on the camp, for there seemed to be little else.

In fact, there was virtually nothing for them to do. Each morning, the pilots were subjected to PT and much of the off-duty time was spent playing various games of one kind or another. On the evening of the 19th, there was a dinner in the officers' mess to say farewell to some of the personnel who were being de-mobbed and to welcome 603. The ORB records: 'Despite the Station's valiant attempts to sabotage the team by means of a highly satisfactory dinner and no mean quantity of liquor the rugger match held at midnight, as a fitting finale to a grand evening, resulted in a clear win for the Squadron.'

Of course, in the northern latitudes, the days are much longer in the summer and a midnight rugger match was quite feasible, given the right weather conditions! The following day there was a hockey match in the afternoon.

But flying did go on and when the weather was bad, alternative training was arranged, for instance on 21 June, they had a lecture on aerodrome control. Later that day, they were visited by A/C Prickman again and the Sector Commander who was none other than G/C Jack Satchell DSO who had been the Station Commander at Ta Kali in Malta in 1942. In the evening, F/L Batchelor was presented with a silver tankard to mark his marriage.

On 26 June, F/L Kirkman and W/O Wheatley were posted to Cranfield for 'repatriation' back to Australia – actually leaving on 28 June. There were replacements coming in too, though. F/Os Lister, Moss, Underdown and Webster arrived. John Moss recalls that he and Underdown received a somewhat brusque and frosty welcome. They had been ordered to report to the Squadron at Coltishall, but on turning up there, were told that 603 had moved – but nobody knew where to. They were given a couple of days leave whilst their whereabouts were established then they made the long train journey north and the ferry trip to Orkney. Despite the fact that they had done as they had been ordered, S/L Pertwee wasn't pleased that they were arriving late and they were given a dressing down. On 28 June, the four new pilots made their first flights.

During this period, there were a number of 'long-range navigation exercises' carried out by individual pilots. In fact, these were opportunities for them to take it in turn to fly home for a day or so, and on 26 June, F/L Nick Machon took his turn. It will be recalled that he had survived the terrifying mid-air collision in which P/O McGinn was killed. To join the Air Force, Machon had escaped from Guernsey and of course hadn't had the opportunity to return home until now, when the Channel Islands were liberated. He took XT●U, the aircraft he now usually flew as his own. The flight was in three 'hops' – Skeabrae to Wittering, Wittering to Odiham and Odiham to Guernsey and took three hours 20 minutes flying. As he neared the home that he had left five years before, Nick Machon's thoughts can only be imagined. He landed safely on Guernsey and had the distinction of being the first Spitfire to do so at the end of the war. He returned to Skeabrae a few days later on 30 June via Finmere and an overnight stop at Thornaby.

One aspect of life in the Orkneys that came as a welcome surprise was the abundance of food. John Moss recalled:

One of my abiding memories was the seeming absence of any evidence of the food rationing so restricting on the mainland. I have never forgotten walking into the Mess on my first evening and seeing a whole salmon laid out on the sideboard with endless varieties of cheeses and eggs galore. I used to go into Kirkwall and send much appreciated food parcels home.

Of course, this occasion coincided with a farewell party for F/L Kirkman, so it may not have been the norm every night. Nonetheless, there was much more variety both on and off the station than on camps down south.

Eric Mee and Tommy Thomson used to go for walks along the cliffs and coves, as Eric related:

Many of the crofters were simple and kind people and would sell us eggs, home cured bacon and cheese they had produced themselves. One dear old lady asked us into her sparsely furnished living room to give us a demonstration of spinning on a real old fashioned spinning wheel. There was also a farmhouse where for about two shillings one could have as many boiled eggs, with home made bread and real butter as one could eat at a sitting.

The local pub was the most primitive that I have ever seen. Inside was a plain wooden counter in a timber panelled room with just wooden benches around the walls. There was no decoration in the room of any sort and no beer pumps at the bar. It was just opening time as Tommy and I went in and to our astonishment the liquid refreshment was brought in a galvanised iron bath and placed behind the bar. Our order was dispensed by the simple expedient of plunging a glass into the bath full of the amber nectar and plonking it on the counter. Nectar it was not, but being the only two in at the time, we felt compelled to empty our glasses and on leaving we both agreed it really was a fiendish brew.

It has to be said that the newly arriving pilots often felt a bit uncomfortable in the company of those 'old hands' who had been through so much together. One such 'put up a black' on his first flight when he did a steep climbing turn with his wheels down just after take-off. It was taken to be showing off and it was made clear to him in no uncertain terms that it wasn't the thing to do.

Despite the fact that it was summer, the weather remained consistently poor and although over the period it didn't prevent much flying, it was a factor. In June, 603 flew 365 sorties and clocked up 355 hours and 20 minutes. In addition to the Spitfires, an interesting array of other types was flown – often by F/L Staniforth. These include a Master, a Martinet, a Whitney Straight, a Tiger Moth, a Hornet Moth and the Station Proctor – which was used to give the ground crew air experience flights.

The airfield at Twatt was a Naval Air Station – HMS *Tern* – and good relationships were established with 802 Squadron which was based there flying Seafires.

On 1 July 1945, the complement of pilots in addition to the CO was:

A Flight: F/L Batchelor (Flight Commander), F/L McAndrew, F/L Sergeant, F/L Staniforth, F/O Burrows, W/O Thomson, P/O Maslen, W/O Godfrey, W/O Seward, W/O Evans, F/L Keep, F/O Bass, W/O Gilpin and F/O Webster.

B Flight: F/L Welch, F/L Machon, F/O McConnochie, F/O Richmond, P/O Beckwith, W/O Mee, P/O Laffan, F/Sgt Webb, F/L Dawe, F/Sgt Bramley, Sgt Malam, F/O Underdown, F/O Moss and F/O Lister.

Although F/O Moss was on strength, he was seconded to HQ as assistant adjutant. S/L Pertwee had been asked for a suitable junior officer to help and rather to John Moss' chagrin, he was chosen. It meant that he would miss out on any flying that was going.

On 3 July, 603 was visited by the AOC Fighter Command – Air Marshal Sir James Robb KBE, CB, DSO, DFC, AFC, accompanied by A/C Prickman – who must have been on first name terms with some of the Squadron by now – and G/C Satchell. For F/O Bass it certainly was a day to remember as he was promoted to F/L and became a father! His blushes were not spared.

During the evening of 4 July, a 603 football team beat 802 Squadron at Twatt and on the following day, which incidentally was Election Day, 603 entertained the officers from 802 to dinner in the mess. This was reciprocated on the 10th with the 603 officers being entertained in the wardroom at Twatt.

July 17 was not untypical in the flying that was carried out – although perhaps it was not altogether normal because the weather was excellent. To quote the ORB:

> The battle flight was scrambled and was airborne in $1^{1/2}$ minutes. It carried out a battle climb and three successful practice interceptions. 6 aircraft carried out a long range cross country flight individually, and other fours carried out battle formation and tail chase practise, while camera gun exercises were also being carried out.
> In the evening, a party was thrown in the Officers' Mess with dancing, eating and drinking and their usual concomitants.

More serious flying was involved in the exercises called Dodgem. These were simulated interceptions of bombers, actually Mustangs based at Peterhead. There had been attempts to do this on 9, 16, 19 and 23 July but these had been cancelled because of the weather. On this latest attempt, on 24 July, F/L Welch led 12 Spitfires off on a scramble at 11.37. They met the Mustangs successfully and there was some tail chasing before they landed back at 12.40. Eric Mee had a particularly memorable experience:

> We made a good interception and the squadron commander positioned us above them and into the sun. The order was given to go into line astern and we all came screaming down to go behind them, pull up underneath and to the rear. As I went down the Mustang formation passed beneath – all except one. He must have been lagging a long way behind, for just as I was diving vertically to the rear of the main formation, this solitary aircraft passed under my nose. We only missed each other by a few feet and I vividly remember looking down into the Mustang's cockpit. I caught a flashing glimpse of the top of the pilot's head and had a close up of his instruments. Every rivet in the fuselage showed up clearly in that fraction of a second that the plane flew underneath me.
> Shaken rigid, I came out of my dive, pulled up under my 'near miss', and gave him an imaginary long burst of cannon and machine-gun fire. To this day, I do not think he even knew I was there or how near he and I came to being mincemeat.

The following day, they were told that they were to return to Turnhouse on Saturday 28 July and on the evening of the previous day, they were all packed with 21 Spitfires ready to go.

They took their leave of Skeabrae at 09.40 in two formations – one of nine and the other of 12 and landed at Turnhouse safely at 11.00. The ground crew took the opportunity of taking eggs home and all the various nooks and crannies in the Spitfires were filled with them and the pilots were asked to be gentle in their landings.

For the ground echelon, there was the prospect of the sea and rail journey and for F/O Moss, the assistant adjutant at HQ, came the 'unkindest cut'. Anticipating that with his tenure as an office-bound administrator coming to an end, he would soon be back in his Spitfire, he was to be disappointed:

> Fondly imagining I would get back in the air again to fly back to Edinburgh with the Squadron, I was shattered to find myself detailed as officer in charge of all the Squadron ground staff who were travelling by boat and rail. Going across from Kirkwall to Thurso in

a drifter it was so rough that I was reduced to the indignity of having to lie down in a cabin – a fine example for a supposedly intrepid aeronaut!! A kindly W/O came to comfort me with some beef tea. I felt I should never live it down. At least I got airborne again back at Turnhouse, after suffering much chaffing from my pals.

John Moss is self-deprecating. He joined the RAF in February 1942 and after learning to fly – initially in the UK but then in Canada – he became an instructor. By the time he reached 603, he had over 900 hours in his log book, but had never been called upon to fly any operational sorties. He would wonder for the rest of his life how he would have coped. 'I was a fighter pilot who never fought anybody!'

The rearguard arrived at Turnhouse on the 30th and they all set about settling in, but rumours abounded to the effect that 603 were to be disbanded and this created an unsettled and unsettling atmosphere. The rumours turned out to be true.

On 1 August, the complement of pilots was:

CO: S/L H.R.P. Pertwee DFC.

A Flight: F/L Batchelor, F/L McAndrew, F/L Sergeant, F/L Staniforth, F/O Thomson, F/O Burrows, W/O Thomson, W/O Godfrey, W/O Evans, W/O Seward, F/L Keep, F/O Bass, W/O Gilpin and F/O Webster.

B Flight: F/L Welch, F/O McConnochie, F/L Machon, F/O Richmond, P/O Beckwith, W/O Mee, P/O Laffan, F/Sgt Webb, F/Sgt Bramley, F/L Dawe, Sgt Malam, F/O Moss, F/O Underdown and F/O Lister.

On 1 August, F/L McAndrew left to go on a Flying Instructor's course before he finally finished up in Canada. For the others there was more training.

The three pilots who were new to Turnhouse – F/Os Moss, Lister and Underdown – carried out 'sector recco' familiarisation flights but at 09.50, F/O McConnochie, P/O Webb, F/L Staniforth and F/O Burrows were scrambled on two separate sorties for two lost aircraft – one in the sea between the Firth of Forth and Peterhead and the other in high ground on the east coast of Scotland. They found nothing, but the wreckage of both aircraft was spotted by Mustangs – possibly those from Peterhead.

At this time, Turnhouse was also home to 164 Squadron and as it was Wednesday, in the afternoon there was a football match between them – which 603 narrowly lost 5 – 2.

The next day there was another exercise, once more entitled Dodgem. On this occasion only four 603 Spitfires were involved – F/L Staniforth, F/O Thomas, F/O McConnochie and P/O Laffan who took off at 11.40, made a successful interception and were back on the ground at 12.15.

In the afternoon, there was more flying – both formation and aerobatics. Later in the afternoon, the AOC of 13 Group arrived to have a meeting with S/L Pertwee. Whether or not there was any connection, on the following day it was confirmed that 603 were to be disbanded and 15 August was the planned date.

During this time, it must have been difficult for the men to maintain a good spirit. Apart from the disbandment, some of the long standing pilots and ground crew were leaving – either being posted on or being de-mobbed. In the previous month, Snowy Wheatley, F/L Kirkman and P/O Maslen had left, pilots who had served solidly over the last months in action. On 7 August, four of the long serving auxiliary ground crew left – W/O Erskine, Sgt Sanderson, Cpl Hunter and LAC Moffatt – heading back to civvy street.

But 9 August, Thursday, was clearly the beginning of the end. The ORB describes it as well as any:

A low mist early this morning cleared quickly and by 10.00 the weather made the Dodgem exercise possible. The Squadron was brought to Readiness at 11.00 and at 11.10 were airborne to intercept a formation of Mustangs from Peterhead. After several vectors and climbing to 11,000 ft the formation sighted 12 Mustangs on a S.E. course 2,000 ft below about 12 miles S.E. of Leuchars and dived to intercept. S/Ldr. Pertwee DFC, F/Lt. Batchelor DFC, F/Lt. Welch DFC, F/Lt. Bass, F/O. McConnochie all claimed a Mustang each destroyed and F/Lt. Machon got two. Several good dog fights were enjoyed and the whole operation seems to have been an excellent affair. The aircraft then broke and returned to base landing between 12.15 and 12.20. In the afternoon, aerobatic practice and battle formation flights were carried out.

Today the Squadron received the signal ordering them to disband from the 15th August. We can make no comment.

The following day a signal was received stating that 603 had been withdrawn from the line on 9 August, so Dodgem turned out to be the last major exercise that the Squadron made before disbanding.

There was no more flying after 9 August and the last flight of all was a four-Spitfire battle formation practice which took off at 14.45. The pilots were W/O Thomson in XT●C, W/O Seward in XT●L, F/L Bass in XT●G and W/O Gilpin in XT●K. They touched down after an hour, at 15.45 and 603 were non-operational.

No time was wasted in stripping the Squadron and on 10 August, late in the evening the first five Spitfires were flown away by ATA pilots. These were XT●A which was the Spitfire usually flown by F/L Batchelor, XT●F, XT●L, XT●C and XT●S which was Eric Mee's aircraft. As a souvenir, he managed to keep the crowbar which was clipped across the flap door to the cockpit. The pilots had by this time all had their photographs taken beside their Spitfires and with their ground crew.

They were sad to see the Spitfires flying into the darkening sky – no doubt to be broken up for scrap. Most of the others were away by 13 August.

14 August was VJ Day and again, those of the pilots who remember the evening celebrations can only do so through a haze. F/O Moss can recall being taught how to dance the Highland Schottische by young ladies in Princes Street but not much more about the celebrations that carried on back at Turnhouse.

The 15th, as well as being the first day of world peace, was the day that 603 finally ceased to exist.

The final unofficial act in the disbandment of 603 Squadron was the dinner that was held on Thursday 16 August in the Balmoral Restaurant in Princes Street. Past 603 members also attended.

Bill Douglas flew up from Hutton Cranswick for the event and stayed on for a few days. Others who were there were G/C Count Stevens, G/C 'Uncle' George Denholm and W/C 'Sheep' Gilroy. Despite the undoubted enjoyment and camaraderie, the event must have generated a mixture of emotions. For many, there would be memories of those who had been killed or injured, of good times at summer camps before the war as well as the kinship of combat and shared hardships.

There would be no little sadness when the party ended as the men, in their blue uniforms, walked into the darkness of the Princes Street evening.

Many of the pilots now had to wait on events. Bob Sergeant was told one day that he should have been de-mobbed about two weeks earlier, and within hours was on his way south. John Moss was posted to 164 Squadron on 28 August, which meant for him there was only a short journey across the airfield. He would finally be de-mobbed on 23 March 1946 and make a successful career in the theatre – much of it in South Africa. Eric Mee and his 'oppo' Tommy Thomson to their great delight were both posted to 165 Squadron, now based at Trondheim in Norway. At least some of the pilots would continue to fly their beloved Spitfires for a little longer. Jack Batchelor returned to his family business as did Bill Douglas.

G/C George Denholm post war with son Paul.

George Denholm and Sheep Gilroy enjoying a walk.

The transition back to civilian life was not necessarily easy. Bob Sergeant returned to his family undertaking business near Hull. He was a firm Christian and had been a lay preacher in the Methodist Church before joining the RAF. He recalled that when he went back, it was almost as if the neighbours and friends expected everything to go back to the way it had been before the war started. The church wanted him to take up his old role again, but for Bob it wasn't possible. Things had changed. He had changed. He was now a married man with a family and he had killed other men – not least the Germans on parade on the airfield at Ypenburg who he and Nick Machon had strafed on their way past. Whilst Bob Sergeant could reconcile these actions in his own mind, others had to accept that he was not the same man that had left so many years ago. And many young men returning from the war would have to deal with similar problems.

Bob Sergeant was to rejoin the air force a few years later and served until the end of the sixties.

After demob, Nick Machon signed on for another 18 months and was immediately sent to 151 OTU at Peshawar, India (now in Pakistan), flying Spifire VIIIs with the Indian Air Force. From there he went to 5 Squadron flying Tempests at Poona. On final demob he returned to his old newspaper, the *Guernsey Star* of which he was editor for many years.

For Turnhouse itself, life went on. The Turnhouse ORB for 15 August simply states: '603 Squadron was disbanded at Turnhouse.' On the same day, 611 Squadron disbanded at Peterhead and there was an 'all ranks dance' at Turnhouse.

On 15 September, there was a RAF 'At Home' Day to commemorate the 5th Anniversary of the Battle of Britain and the next day, a church service at Turnhouse was broadcast over the Scottish Regional Programme of the BBC. The sermon was given by Rev J. Rossie Brown of Murrayfield Parish Church and the lessons read by G/C George Denholm and Sir William Y. Darling who was Honorary Air Commodore, 603 Squadron. Many friends and relatives of members of 603 Squadron attended. It was a fitting finale.

Before the Squadron could officially disband, a bureaucratic formality had to be completed. The Air Ministry was still constrained by Air Ministry Order (AMO) dated 1927 which stated 'When a recruit has been posted to a unit, he cannot be removed and posted to another without his consent.' Consequently a form (dated circa 13 September 1945) was sent to each auxiliary airman as follows:

LIMITED CERTIFICATE OF WILLINGNESS TO BE POSTED TO RAF STATION TURNHOUSE

In accordance with RAF Records Gloucester postagram reference 267 J/32182 undated I, No.................Rank....................Name..of 603 Squadron, Auxiliary Air Force, hereby declare that I am willing to be posted to RAF Station Turnhouse, on disbandment of No.603 Squadron, Auxiliary Air Force, under authority of the above quoted postagram.

Signed

Turnhouse Witnessed.   Date

603 Squadron finished the war with a formidable list of achievements:

Aircraft
Confirmed destroyed: 250, Probably destroyed: 121.3, Damaged: 167 (Top scoring squadron during Battle of Britain : 58.5 Kills)

Shipping
Confirmed sunk: 50 vessels (7,845 tons), Probably sunk: 6 (8,000 tons), Damaged: 6 (10,992 tons)

Battle Honours
These include:

Home Defence	1940-42	Fortress Europe	1941	Sicily	1943
Battle of Britain	1940	Malta	1942	South East Europe	1943-44
Channel and North Sea	1941	Mediterranean	1943	France and Germany	1945

To gain these prestigious Battle Honours the Squadron paid a high price with 90 air and ground crew being killed in action. 603 finished the war with a creditable number of honours and awards:

22	Distinguished Flying Crosses (DFC), including one Bar
5	Distinguished Flying Medals (DFM)
1	Member of the British Empire (MBE)
1	British Empire Medal (BEM)
2	Mentioned in Despatches (MID)

On 16 August 1945 the Squadron Operations Record Book (Form 540) reported:

Tonight a farewell party for all the Squadron was held in the Balmoral Restaurant, Princes Street, Edinburgh. Many of the former Squadron personalities attended including Group Captain Stevens, Group Captain Denholm DFC, Group Captain Gilroy DSO, DFC, Wing Commander W. A. Douglas DFC and everyone voted the function a complete success and a fitting end to the Squadron activities.

On 17 November 1945, only three months after disbandment a Reunion Dinner for all ranks was held at the North British Station Hotel, Edinburgh. The Guest of Honour was John L. Falconer, The Lord Provost. The Chairman was Sir William Y. Darling CBE, MP, who had been the Honorary Air Commodore of the Squadron. Other notable personalities attending were: G/C The Earl of Selkirk AFC, G/C G.L. Denholm DFC, G/C G.K. Gilroy DSO, DFC, W/C J.L. Jack MBE, MC, and S/L the Reverend J. Rossie Brown. Also present was Bruce, the mascot. The dinner menu was as follows:

603 Squadron Dinner
Chairman
Sir WILLIAM Y DARLING, CBE, MP
Guest of Honour
The Right Hon. LORD PROVOST
MENU
Hors d'oeuvre
Thick Lentil Soup

****

Roast Turkey
Roast Potatoes
Brussels Sprouts

****

Apple Melba
Coffee

North British Station Hotel, Edinburgh

17th November 1945

An article in *The Scotsman* gave the following account of the evening:

Group Captain Denholm proposed the toast 'The City of Edinburgh'.

The Lord Provost, replying, said that the feeling in the heart of the City of Edinburgh was one of enduring gratitude towards the Squadron and of thankfulness for what they did at the beginning of the war.

Lord Selkirk, proposing '603 Squadron', said that the time was now ripe for a full recognition of the work achieved by the Auxiliary Air Force in general, and this Squadron in certain details. Some years before the war, during the early period of intensive extension of the Royal Air Force, for a considerable period the Auxiliary Squadrons through the dilution caused by the expansion, were trained to a higher pitch of efficiency than any home-based Regular Squadron, and when the war did come, Auxiliary units were able to take their place in the front line in defence of this island a full week before the outbreak of hostilities. All these Squadrons were manned almost exclusively by non-regular personnel. What perhaps was not so well known was that the Auxiliary Air Force Squadrons constituted roughly 50 per cent of the home-based Fighter Force, and over and above that there were three or four Squadrons in Coastal Command.

The Auxiliary Air Force had enabled that continuity of spirit within a squadron which had always been difficult to maintain in Regular Squadrons through the exigencies of posting, and it was that spirit, under the inspiring and magnificent leadership of Group Captain Denholm, which had enabled the Squadron to play its part, and a full part at that, even among the Few, in the moment of supreme crisis to this country.

Lord Selkirk recalled that it was his own younger brother who led the Squadron from the American aircraft carrier USS *Wasp* to land on Malta flying Spitfire Mk.VC during Operation Calendar on the 20th April 1942.

There was loud applause when Lord Selkirk said he welcomed the Air Ministry decision to reform 603 Squadron. Although, he hoped it would carry the strong ingredients of those who had served before, it must be given a new life which was primarily intended for the training and opportunity of the new generation who must in course of time take their place.

Following the dinner, Lord Selkirk proposed the formation of a 603 (City of Edinburgh) Squadron Association. A provisional committee was elected to form an association, and the Honorary Secretary was Squadron Leader Ian S. Ritchie, of Messrs Mackay and Young, Edinburgh. The first meeting of the association was held in the North British Station Hotel, Edinburgh on 21 February 1946. The Earl of Selkirk presided. An Advisory Committee was established to assist ex-603 Squadron members in their resettlement back into civilian occupations and adapting to the post-war environment. The association would also act as a means of access to the trustees of the 603 (City of Edinburgh) Squadron Benevolent Fund for ex-members and their dependants. At a meeting held on 29 April 1946 in the Edinburgh City Chambers, the Trustees of the Benevolent Fund were elected. They were:

> Lord Provost John I. Falconer (Chairman), Councillor Sawers, Councillor Robert E. Douglas, Sir William Y. Darling, CBE, MP, Honorary Air Commodore of the Squadron, Group Captain The Earl of Selkirk, OBE, AFC, Group Captain Ernest H. Stevens OBE, Group Captain George L. Denholm DFC, Group Captain George K. Gilroy DSO, DFC, C de G, Wing Commander Tommy Garden (Honorary Secretary) and Wing Commander James L. Jack MBE, MC, (Honorary Treasurer).

The Squadron Association and the Benevolent Fund was well received by the Edinburgh community with generous practical support and donations by city companies, in particular the donation of two Memorial Cottages at 63 Broomhouse Road by Messrs MacTaggart and Mickel Ltd. of Corstorphine, on 29 May 1945. The Squadron Association also purchased a house in Trinity Crescent in August 1946.

CHAPTER 17

REFORMATION – THE NEW GENERATION

1946

An article in *The Edinburgh Evening Dispatch* in January 1946 reported the possibility that 603 Squadron may be reforming and speculated on the manning levels and possible trades. On 15 February 1946, Marshal of the Royal Air Force Lord Tedder was given the Freedom of the City of Edinburgh. He paid this tribute: 'Your Squadron, 603, has a record of being in the middle of the business everywhere which, I think, is practically unique'.*

Along with other flying squadrons and ground units of the Auxiliary Air Force, 603 were reformed on 10 May 1946** under Reserve Command, which had been reformed on 1 May 1946, returning to White Waltham on 7 October. This was part of the decision to re-establish the successful pre-war concept of reserve, ie part-time forces – 'to maintain and train adequate reserves of flying and ground personnel'. The Scottish Auxiliary Air Force squadrons were under the control of 66 (Scottish) Reserve Group, based at RAF Turnhouse, with 603 being based at its traditional home of RAF Turnhouse under the command of S/L George Gilroy DSO, DFC(US) and Belgian Croix de Guerre. As a pre-war member of the Squadron with a distinguished war record, Sheep finished the war in the rank of Group Captain. Once reformed, two flights were organised and re-occupied the ancestral Town Headquarters at 25 Learmonth Terrace, 'the most sumptuous house in Edinburgh', the house having first become the Town HQ for 603 in 1925.

RAF Turnhouse post war. George Gilroy, George Denholm, Jim Morton and James Jack.

---

*Air Ministry Bulletin Directorate of Public Relations 1946.
**Air Ministry Authority A.800061/45/F8(Sec).

The operational flight would be equipped with nine Spitfire Mk XVIEs and the training flight would have four Spitfire Mk XVIEs and two Harvard IIBs. Sir William Darling Kt, CBE, MC, DL, JP, FRSE, LLD, resumed his post as Honorary Air Commodore.

On 7 July, regular airmen began to arrive intermittently and a 603 orderly room was established in a vacant wooden building.

Two Harvards were flown over Macmerry Airport by regular officers during August on the occasion of its opening. In addition two Harvards participated in the air display at Loch Leven. On 1 October 1946, the operational control of Turnhouse was transferred from Fighter to Reserve Command, with 603's adjutant Flight Lieutenant Sowery assuming the role of temporary station commander.

On 3 October 1946, General Dwight D. Eisenhower was given the Freedom of the City of Edinburgh and 603 took part in the parade.

An official announcement in the *Royal Air Force Review* during the period 1946-47 entitled 'Auxiliaries Back in Action' stated the terms and conditions of service:

Reformed again after seven years magnificent service with the RAF, the Auxiliary squadrons are now looking for the right type of men from those who are being released from war service to carry on their fine traditions.

The difference between the pre-war 'A' [Auxiliary] squadrons and those of today is that whereas before the war those who were accepted into the squadrons were 'raw' recruits drawn from civil life, today only trained men who gained their skill and experience in the Service are being taken on to man the Force. There are to be no 'passengers'; every member of the squadron comes in fully trained and able to tackle his particular job from the start. Service in the Auxiliaries will keep him up to scratch and abreast of all the latest technical developments and new methods of training as they come into effect.

The object, of course, is to have a fully trained and immediately operational force always on call for front-line action with the RAF proper in the event of hostilities.

The present composition of the Auxiliary Air Force is 20 operational squadrons. These are divided into day and night fighter and strategic light bomber squadrons. Each will have its full establishment of commissioned and non-commissioned pilots, navigators (where necessary) and ground crews. There will be an Adjutant (or Admin. Officer), an Equipment Officer, Intelligence Officer, Engineer Officer and Medical Officer for each squadron. All will be recruited from men who have served in the Royal Air Force. Applicants will be required to attend before a Selection Board and pass a medical examination before acceptance. The maximum age limit for aircrew is 30, and for ground crew 38. Admin, Equipment and Medical Officers will be accepted up to 50 years of age, and Technical Officers up to 35. The normal period of service with the AAF for officers is five years, with a further five on the Reserve, and for airmen the term is four years with the option of a further four years maximum afterwards. Those who do not wish to commit themselves for the normal periods of service may apply to serve for shorter terms if they wish. As service in the AAF is part-time, training is in the evenings and at week-ends – no pay is issued. Instead, a retainer of £35 annually is paid to aircrew and a Bounty of £5 annually to airmen in ground trades, who can also qualify for an additional Supplementary Bounty of £3 per year if they put in extra training hours. In addition to these payments, all AAF personnel (airmen and officers) are paid from ls. 6d. to 9s. per day to cover expenses during training. Full RAF rates of pay are, however, paid during the 15 days annual camp which all Auxiliaries are expected to attend.

Uniform which, for the time being, will be battle dress, is issued free to airmen; officers, of course, pay for their own. Although for the time being, until the Force expands, only a limited number of men will be able to find their way into the 'A' squadrons, it is open to all who wish to serve to apply for entry; but owing to the present limited establishments it is obvious that there will be many more applicants than there will be vacancies.

The Auxiliaries have behind them a record of high efficiency and a fighting spirit second-to-none, and they can only maintain those by recruiting the best and keenest men.'

603 pilots at Turnhouse at the time of the reformation in 1946.

By 20 October, the first candidates for AAF commissions were being interviewed by the CO.

The first Spitfire arrived on 27 October 1946 and on 2 November Wing Commander G.E. Hughes DSO, DFC was appointed Station Commander, Turnhouse.

Recruiting started in earnest on 8 November but the initial response was poor. By 9 November it was clear that there were ample applicants for flying but few for ground staff. This was understandable. Most of the ground crews had been away from home for seven years with only intermittent returns to Edinburgh. They had now to make new lives in an austere and difficult post-war environment.

Conditions for ground staff were onerous and the financial compensations were far from generous. Airmen had to be aged between 17 and 37. The maximum period of engagement was four years but engagements were allowed for one, two, three or four years at a time. On discharge, airmen who had rendered not less than two years satisfactory service were eligible to enlist in the Auxiliary Air Force Reserve. New recruits entered with the rank of aircraftman 2nd class and were promoted, when qualified, as vacancies arose.

Ground staff were required to attend 15 days continuous training, plus between 30 hours and 78 non-continuous training during evenings and weekends, according to their qualifications and progress and the training facilities available. They could, in addition, do up to 60 hours voluntary, non-continuous training. When training continuously for more than eight hours, ground staff received pay at current RAF rates for their rank and trade. For periods of training not qualifying for pay, eg in the evening, sergeants and above were paid 1s. 3d. per hour (6p), corporals 1s. (5p) and airmen 9d (4p). No payment was made for less than 2 hours training.

Non-commissioned pilots had to attend for 15 days continuous training and up to 196 hours non-continuous training at evenings and weekends. The training requirement included at least 125 hours flying. They received the same 1s.3d. per hour as other NCOs for non-continuous training periods.

On 22 November a second Spitfire arrived.

In an endeavour to boost recruitment, invitations were sent out to all ex-603 members to an 'At Home' at Town Headquarters on 23 November. More than 70 attended. By the 24th the Squadron

HAC inspection by Rt Hon Sir William Darling. HAC talking to Duncan McIntosh AFC at Turnhouse with CO Sheep Gilroy (left) and George Mullay (right).

had received 50 applications for flying posts and 50 for ground positions. Candidates for commissions and potential aircrew began to attend at Turnhouse for interviews.

By December 1946, the Air Ministry had announced that recruiting for the Auxiliary Air Force would be open to civilian candidates with no previous military service.

1947

By the beginning of 1947, 603 Squadron's regular staff consisted of three officers and 35 airmen. Recruiting was still poor in January.

There was heavy snow in February but, despite this, the first post-war auxiliary flying took place, as F/L Kingsford took R.B. Thompson up in a Harvard to practice circuits and bumps.

On 1 April the Squadron possessed two Harvards and six Spitfires, and four more Spitfires were promised. The runway was unserviceable and the Squadron had to use the grass. The rain then softened this to the point where flying was not possible.

An intensive one-week recruiting drive was now launched with the full support of the Editors of *The Scotsman*, *The Evening Dispatch* and *The Edinburgh Evening News*. A press conference was held at the HQ of the Territorial and the Auxiliary Forces Association of the City and Country of Edinburgh, the Lothians and Peebles on 10 May. Its Secretary, Brigadier F.L. Johnson read a message from Sir William Darling:

> The reconstitution of 603 Squadron is a momentous thing; momentous to those who can cast their eyes back as well as for those who look forward. We recall the triumphs of the Squadron during the war. We are now at another stage in the organisation and reorganisation of national defence, the basis of which must be citizens working through the Territorial Army and the Auxiliary Air Force.

The Town HQ ante-room now became available and the Squadron silver was collected from the Commercial Bank, Haymarket, where it had been kept secure throughout the war.

By 17 May 1947 the weather had again rendered Turnhouse unserviceable. Fortunately it improved by the 24th when the airfield was opened for Empire Day. As the *Air Reserve Gazette* for July 1947 reported :

> More than 8,000 citizens of Edinburgh accepted the invitation of 603 (City of Edinburgh) Fighter Squadron to visit them 'At Home' on Whit Saturday 1947. Turnhouse Airport was thrown open, free of charge, and big crowds followed the proceedings of the afternoon with the utmost interest. Air Commodore E.S. Burns, Air Officer Commanding 66 (Scottish Reserve) Group, RAF inspected 603 Squadron drawn up in front of its Spitfire aircraft, together with a detachment of Edinburgh Air Training Corps (ATC) cadets. Music was provided during the inspection by the Edinburgh Wing ATC and Edinburgh City police pipe bands. The air programme opened with a display of aerobatics by Flight Lieutenant R.S. Kingsford, the Squadron's Assistant Adjutant and test pilot, in a Spitfire, hidden at times by cloud. A gliding display by 6 (Scottish) Gliding School, ATC thrilled the crowd, who expressed surprise at the glider's rate of climb when towed off by a winch. On the ground the ATC demonstrated signals and armament equipment. The Royal Observer Corps showed their methods of signalling and plotting aircraft movements. Link trainer, parachute and dinghy sections on the station were open; and a gun crew demonstrated the 40mm. Bofors light AA guns which will eventually be manned by the new 2603 (City of Edinburgh) Squadron, AAF Regiment.

The weather improvement continued throughout June, with local and cross country flying possible.

July saw the move to 603's first post-war summer camp. This was at Woodvale near Liverpool, the home of 611 (West Lancashire) Squadron.

The lorries were loaded on 1 July and next day six airmen left with a bowser and two three-ton lorries. The main ground party left by train on 5 July. This consisted of 22 NCOs and 26 men under the command of the veteran Sergeant Prentice. Eight Spitfires and two Harvards took off later in the day followed by the CO in his own Spitfire. Four pilots made their way in their own cars.

Three Spitfires took part in an air display over Blackpool. One of the organisers was Wing Commander 'Ras' Berry DSO, DFC, who had been with the Squadron from 1939 to 1941.

Training included formation and local flying, lectures and firing on the Isle of Man ranges at Jurby. The target drogues were towed by Miles Martinets. 612 (County of Aberdeen) Squadron arrived during the second week and joint exercises were carried out.

The Squadron returned to Turnhouse two days early, in order to attend the laying up of the Ensign. The Operations Record Book noted:

> Laying up of 603 Squadron Ensign in St. Giles Cathedral, Edinburgh 20th July 1947. Text by Charles L. Watt, Dean of the Thistle and Chapel Royal.
>
> "Except the Lord build a house they labour in vain that build it. Except the Lord Keepeth the City the Watchmen waken but in vain."
>
> St. Giles Cathedral was to receive the Squadron Ensign. Marshal of the Royal Air Force, Lord Tedder, on behalf of the Royal Air Force was to present it. King George and Queen Elizabeth were witness to its final resting-place in the Sanctuary of the Cathedral.
>
> It was a fitting climax to nineteen years of endeavour and the unsurpassed Battle Honours won in the comparatively short life of the Squadron.
>
> The Squadron has been reformed and, as it grows, slowly at first as in the older days, but gaining momentum, fully aware of the past and mindful of the future.
>
> John A Sowery, Flight Lieutenant and Adjutant.

In presenting the Standard to the Minister of St Giles, Lord Tedder said :

> With Humble gratitude to Almighty God for His many and great mercies, I present this Ensign to St. Giles Cathedral and I ask that in honour of the Royal Air Force it may be received and accepted and given safe custody here.

The Minister replied :

> On behalf of the Cathedral Board I promise for this Ensign Safe Custody within this Church.

We gratefully receive and accept this honoured Ensign, formerly flown in the service of the King and Empire and through the perils and hazards of war in Malta, Cyprus, North Africa, Sicily, Italy and North West Europe from 1942-1945. Here it will find a secure and worthy resting place and will be held in lasting veneration.

May all who look upon it in days to come find in it a sign and symbol of God's presence with them in all dangers and distresses and have increase of faith and hope in Him who is the King of King and Lords of Lords.

```
                              PLAQUE

                  The Ensign of 603 (City of Edinburgh)
                     Squadron – Auxiliary Air Force

                    Malta, Cyprus, North Africa, Sicily
                   And North-west Europe – 1942 – 1945
                     Handed over by Marshal of the Royal
                       Air Force, The Right Honourable
                       Lord Tedder, GCB 20th July 1947

                    Their Majesties The King and Queen
                 Their Royal Highnesses The Princess Elizabeth and
                      The Princess Margaret and Lieutenant
                      Philip Mountbatten, RN, being present
```

Wing Commander Jack Meadows DFC, AFC, AE, an experienced aviator and fighter pilot who gained his licence in 1937, and became a founder member of both the post-war 600 (City of London) and 603 (City of Edinburgh) Squadrons, recounted the spirit of 603 Squadron in the immediate post-war years:

In August 1947, I got a letter from Norman Hayes, a pre-war 600 (City of London) Squadron pilot and later my airfield commander at Amiens in 2nd Allied Tactical Air Force (ATAF) . Had I heard the Auxiliary Air Force flying squadrons were to be reformed, initially on a one-flight basis? He had been asked to reform 600 Squadron, flying Spitfires from Biggin Hill. Would I be his first flight commander?

I went to Biggin Hill and flew a Harvard with him. Then my firm moved me to Edinburgh. That was that. Except that Togs Melleresh, 600's adjutant wrote to John Sowrey, adjutant of 603 in Edinburgh, and told him to contact me. After a boozy 'selection board' in L' Aperitif in Rose Street, with John, Count Stevens and another 603 'old boy', both ex-group captains, in early 1948 I became Flying Officer J.P. Meadows, AAF. Dropping several ranks was happily accepted by ex-regulars and auxiliaries at that time.

603's CO was Sheep Gilroy, a pre-war member, wartime Spitfire wing leader in North Africa and Italy and, later, group captain and station commander. Now he was back sheep-farming in the borders.

The AAF was reformed initially in Reserve Command, before taking its proper place in Fighter Command as part of the front line defence of the realm. Quickly the routine was established as before, flying every weekend, with two evenings a week ground school at Town Headquarters (THQ).

I had long accepted the peacetime rules and the need to be checked out again on a Harvard (on which I had taught numerous people to fly) by pilots much less experienced than me. Then it was Spitfires again, initially XVIs with Packard-built Merlins. Later they were replaced by Spitfire Mk 22s, with Rolls-Royce Griffons.

I had known Turnhouse slightly from wartime visits. Its hangar, messes and offices were almost all ours. One reasonable runway started just over the railway line on the east. It was a delightful place to fly from, with Edinburgh, Arthur's Seat, the Forth Bridge (no road bridge then) and mountains near but not too near! Out in the Firth of Forth, the Bass Rock seabird colony off North Berwick got plenty of visits from noisier, faster fliers.

Our numbers were building quickly, all experienced pilots in various forms. It was almost like an Operational Training Unit (OTU) as we worked up to a reasonable level of close and battle formations, crossover turns, tailchases and dogfights. To some it was very strange; Hector Monro, for instance, (later a Tory Cabinet Minister, Honorary Air Commodore of an Auxiliary Regiment Squadron and Honorary Inspector General RAuxAF) found cavorting around in a Spitfire dogfight rather different from four-engined Sunderland flying boats.

Two weeks' 'summer camp' was an essential part of the training year. After months of planning, weeks of talk and preparation, on 5 July 1948 the pilots were all ready for a 1015hrs take-off for our first post-war camp, waiting in the crew room for Sheep. At 1030hrs we crashed into John's office. At 1045hrs he nervously rang Sheep's home. Luckily, he was not up a mountain tending his sheep.

'Yes John, what can I do for you?'

'Are you coming out today, Sir?'

'I hadn't planned to; why do you ask, is there anything special?'

'Well actually, sir , the troops all left by road this morning and we're waiting to fly off, as planned, to Woodvale, to summer camp.'

'Really? Why on earth didn't someone tell me about all this before? I suppose I'd better come out; you all go on ahead, leave my aeroplane and I'll follow you.'

As a formation leader Sheep was an inspiration, and full of ideas. There was an airshow at nearby Squire's Gate, Blackpool. Our formation of Spitfires, unscheduled, opened the display with a beat-up and stream landing. Late that evening, after too much beer, we flew back more sedately.

Sheep led Squadron visits to the School of Air Fighting at West Raynham, and to Manchester Ringway to call on 613 (City of Manchester) Squadron. Biggin Hill during the week was very quiet; after take-off my hood blew off and there was an uncomfortable fumey and windy trip back to Woodvale. We returned to Turnhouse via the Isle of Man (engine as usual running rough again over the sea, although formation flying kept one's mind off it) and Prestwick.

502 (Ulster) Squadron from Aldergrove visited us in their Mosquitoes. We visited 612 (County of Aberdeen) Squadron at Dyce, and 602 (City of Glasgow) at Abbotsinch. Edinburgh itself felt a close association with us, and we 'showed the flag' overhead on many occasions. We took part in exercises defending the Forth Bridge. In the September Battle of Britain Day display at Turnhouse, I gave the solo aerobatic display. *The Scotsman* reporter who met me climbing out afterwards, in my shirt sleeves and pouring with sweat, commented only on that and not on the flying.

We had occasional dining nights in the Turnhouse mess, where the port was piped in in proper Scottish military ceremony. Our piper was an ex-Black Watch sergeant, who was on our establishment as an AC.2 cook and did very little but pipe. Before the war the Squadron had its own kilted pipe band which, by order of the Duke of Hamiliton (via the Monarch) the CO of 602 Squadron wore the Grey Douglas tartan. Now there were no musicians and no money for them.

We were inspected by the AOC, by the C-in-C, then by the Deputy Chief of Air Staff, then by Tedder (by then Marshal of the RAF), and put on flypasts for them all. Our Honorary Air Commodore, Sir William Y. Darling MP, always came, wearing brown shoes with his uniform instead of the regulation black.

When the King and Queen, with Princess Elizabeth and Prince Philip, visited Edinburgh, we mounted the guard of honour outside St. Giles Cathedral.

We again defended the Forth Bridge in the air exercises that year. Later, flying south to West Raynham as reinforcements, we were forced back by bad weather – to my relief, since a nasty smell of hot electrics was upsetting me and the instruments were wild. I broke from formation for an emergency landing at base just in time for the crew to remove the red-hot smouldering battery before it burst into flames.

In the course of all this, the part-timers had once more worked-up to a pretty efficient fighter squadron.

Then my firm moved me back to London. A quick letter to Norman Hayes produced the information he was handing over 600 Squadron to David Proudlove, who had replaced me as first flight commander when I moved north, and that they would like to see me.

Auxiliary squadrons were at times accused of being snobbish, but any exclusivity was because of deeper reasons. So much was demanded of members, particularly officers and NCOs, that it was essential for them to fit in well with other members, and seriously be prepared to give up most of their spare time. All this was quite apart from qualifications, experience and potential. So applicants (including those wanting to transfer from other squadrons) who seemed suitable were invited to THQ to meet squadron members and allow a consensus to develop. Probably no more rejections resulted than refusals from those realising more would be asked of them than they would give.

So for me there followed another boozy evening, at Finsbury Barracks, at the end of which I found myself, three years late, as 600's Flight Commander.

On 16 December 1947 the Auxiliary Air Force was honoured with the prefix 'Royal' by His Majesty King George VI in recognition of its distinguished wartime record. His Majesty assumed the position of Air Commodore-in-Chief.

The Squadron were now equipped with the Spitfire LF XVIe with North American Harvard T2Bs being used for training. The Mk XVIs were operated until the end of 1947, when the Griffon-powered F.Mk 22 was introduced.

1948

On 12 June 1948 a crowd of 8,000 attended a Squadron 'At Home' at Turnhouse and a welcome visitor was Air Marshal Sir Hugh Walmsley, Deputy Chief of the Air Staff, who had been the Squadron's adjutant from 1928 to 1931. During the event, 603 Squadron made a particular effort to recruit personnel for ground trades.

The July summer camp was at Tangmere, Sussex. The ground crews left by train from Waverley Station on 2 July and the nine aircraft flew down, refuelling at Acklington en route. During the camp there were cross-country flights, practice interceptions and air-firing exercises. A highlight for the ground crews was an outing to the Isle of Wight.

From left to right: Sheep Gilroy, Hector Monroe, John Scott, Sandy Kent, Andy Anderson, Jack Meadows, Bill Moncur, Dick Kennedy and Ian Forbes.

Summer camp at RAF Tangmere, 1948. From left to right: Johnny Mears, Jack Meadows, Bill Moncur, Bert Davidson, Dick Kennedy, Leo Scott, Sheep Gilroy, Hector Monro, Joe McCulloch, Jimmy Tweedham and Duncan McIntosh.

Left: Summer camp at Tangmere, 1948. A shot of 603 ground crew, including George Mullay far left.

Bottom: Spitfire F22s of 603 at summer camp, 1948. Group photo includes a number of veterans. Front row: F/Sgt Prentice (fifth from left), S/L Ian Forbes DFC (fifth from right, and 'uncle' of author David Ross). Sheep Gilroy is standing to left of prop blade and Hector Monroe to the right.

Ground Support Units

In the immediate post-war period, a number of ground units were formed to support the auxiliary flying squadrons. Two such units were formed at Turnhouse and Edinburgh became the first Scottish city to raise a squadron of the Royal Auxiliary Air Force Regiment and an air defence unit.

On 23 May 1947, 2603 (City of Edinburgh) Light Anti-Aircraft (LAA) Regiment Squadron was formed, based at RAF Turnhouse. The primary role of the Squadron was airfield defence equipped with light anti-aircraft guns (40mm Bofors). Its secondary role was local ground defence.

2603 were affiliated to and operated with 603 Fighter Squadron, and shared its HQ Town Headquarters. The Squadron provided trained and qualified gunners, signallers, drivers, despatch riders, cooks, storemen, clerks and medical orderlies. In common with the other Light AA Regiment squadrons, 2603 was disbanded on 10 March 1957. In March 1948, 3603 (City of Edinburgh) Air Defence Unit were formed at RAF Turnhouse, sharing a hut with 2603 LAA Squadron. However in May 1948 the unit moved to the newly opened Sector Operations Centre of 12 Fighter Group RAF at Barnton Quarry, Edinburgh, and later supported the operations bunker at RAF Anstruther on the Fife coast. In November 1948, the designation was altered to Fighter Control Unit (FCU).

The unit's primary function was to train male and female fighter plotters, radar operators, fighter and interception controllers and radar mechanics. On 10 February 1950, the responsibility of the GCI Station at Dirleton was transferred to 3603 FCU. The unit's Town Headquarters were opened during 1953 at 16 Royal Terrace, Edinburgh. The unit was also presented with its badge on 10 May 1953. The badge shows a triple-towered castle representing Edinburgh Castle on a 16-pointed star, the star symbolising the guidance given by the unit to fighter aircraft and the direction given to all points when enemy aircraft are to be sought out. The motto is *Per obscura ad metam*, 'Through darkness to the goal'. Following the disbandment of 603 Squadron on 10 March 1957, the FCU occupied 25 Learmonth Terrace as their Town Headquarters and continued to provide fighter controllers until being disbanded on 1 November 1959.*

1949

Following the usual Christmas stand down the Squadron resumed training at Town HQ on 6 January 1949. By February its auxiliary strength was 14 officers, four airmen pilots and 50 other ranks.

13 February 1949 saw the start of the annual recruiting week. This concluded with a concert in the new Victoria Cinema on 20 February, introduced by His Grace The Duke of Hamilton and Brandon, Honorary Air Commodore of 602 Squadron, whose three brothers had all served with 603 Squadron.

An article in *The Scotsman* described the first major RAF recruiting and flying display in Edinburgh since before the war :

> Over 150 applications from potential recruits were received at the Royal Air Force recruiting centre in Alexanders' Showrooms, Lothian Road, in the course of last week's intensive recruiting campaign in Edinburgh. The inquiries numbered 102 for the Royal Auxiliary Air Force, 31 for the RAFVR, and 18 for the Regular Air Force.
>
> Early on Saturday afternoon saw the start of the biggest air display seen in Edinburgh since before the war. Six Meteor IV jet fighters flew singly over the city for the best part of an hour, but, owing to complaints received after their low-flying demonstration on Wednesday, the pilots were instructed to keep above 1000 feet. The Meteors were followed by a flight of five Lincolns of 1 Group, Bomber Command, which flew up from Binbrook in Lincolnshire.
>
> A formation flight of about 20 Spitfires from Scottish RAuxAF squadrons flew over Princes Street, coinciding with the RAF procession of tableaux vehicles, towed Bofors guns, and a mobile radar unit. The procession assembled in Castle Terrace and moved along Princes Street, preceded by the RAF Central Band, to Regent Terrace. A marching contingent were drawn from RAF Kirknewton.

---

*Details obtained on Nos. 2603 and 3603 via the Late Flight Lieutenant Marjory Drummond AE, RAuxAF, fighter controller on 3603 1949-59, then member of No.2 MHU. Her historical research into the City of Edinburgh RAuxAF units is acknowledged.

Spitfires of 603 with the 'RAJ' code, c. 1950.

Spitfire XVI E at Turnhouse, c.1950.

XVI Es over Musselburgh, c. 1950.

The flying programme ended with five De Havilland Vampire day fighters flying over the city in formation. The Vampires were from 605 (County of Warwick) Auxiliary Squadron, and arrived at Turnhouse from Honiley, near Birmingham, taking only 45 minutes to complete the 290-mile journey. The formation was led by the regular Station Adjutant, Flight-Lieutenant J. Button, DFC and one of the Auxiliary pilots was I.H. Louden, of 602 (City of Glasgow) Squadron.

A demonstration of gun drill and a show of equipment was given by 2603 LAA Squadron, RAuxAF. Regiment, and Territorial Army units at the Mound car park.

6 March 1949 was a sad day for the Squadron. 603 were taking part in an air defence exercise 'Forth and Clyde' with their Spitfire F.Mk22s and some of the flying was from Leuchars. They were working closely with both 2603 Light Anti-Aircraft Regiment Squadron and 3603 Fighter Control Unit at Barnton Quarry and 612 (County of Aberdeen) Squadron who also participated in the exercise. During the exercise 612 and 603 Squadron aircraft were scrambled to investigate or oppose the approach of all aircraft in the Forth/Clyde area. The Squadron's ground crews worked long hours to achieve aircraft serviceability. When the first 603 section took off, they were played into the air by Pipe-Major Thomson playing 'Scotland the Brave' and 'Cock o' the North'. Adverse weather conditions over central Scotland on 5 March prevented flying, but one American Boeing B.29 Superfortress flew over unopposed at 15,000 feet; the crew later claimed to have 'bombed' Dunblane. During one day Flight Lieutenant Jas Storrar was unable to take part and his place was taken by Flying Officer J.M. Mears. During the exercise a 'haar' (sea fog) came down and Mears was killed while attempting to land his Spitfire F.22 (PK214). His funeral took place with full military honours on 8 March at Warriston Crematorium.

Spitfire XVI Es at Turnhouse, March 1949. Note Squadron markings.

On 9 June 603 was delighted to learn that Warrant Officer 'Snuffy' Prentice had been awarded the British Empire Medal (BEM). Snuffy's age was a closely guarded secret. He had joined more than 20 years earlier as a sergeant and had been a well loved, if sometimes feared, figure throughout his service.

On 25 June 1949, eight pilots flew to Horsham St Faith to take part in Exercise Foil, a major air defence exercise. The following day was the Turnhouse 'At Home' and visitors included the familiar figure of Air Marshal Sir Hugh Walmsley as well as the AOC-in-C Fighter Command.

Auxiliary strength on 603 Squadron was now 12 officers, five airmen pilots and 68 other ranks, totalling 85.

The 1949 summer camp was at Horsham St Faith in July and Battle of Britain Day at Turnhouse was a great success with over 30,000 visitors attending. Elsewhere, F/L Jas Storrar had been competing in the heats for the auxiliary 'Cooper Trophy' air race – a handicap race open to all auxiliary squadrons regardless of aircraft type.* His Spitfire F.22 had supercharger trouble and he was forced to withdraw, however.

On 23 September, 603 said goodbye to a pre-war member and popular CO, S/L Sheep Gilroy DSO, DFC, who, once again, returned to farming.

Following the death of his first wife, Evelyn, whom he had met during a spell of duty in South Africa, Sheep had married Jane. The couple lived in a number of farms but Sheep came to realise that the land he had was insufficient for his ambitions so he purchased Auchencairn House from the local MP, with extra land, situated near the village of Auchencairn in Kirkcudbrightshire – a wonderful red-stone castle/estate house overlooking Auchencairn Bay, the Solway Firth and across to Maryport. Sheep was very shrewd and he established a successful business when he diversified his interests to include cereal crops and gained a reputation for breeding Galloway cattle which he pursued until he retired. By 1960 he owned four farms and 1,500 sheep.

Sheep's first marriage produced a son, Pieter, who eventually took over the family business and today lives in Auchencairn House. His second marriage to Jane produced a son, Jamie, and a daughter. Jamie runs a farm close to Pieter.

---

*Cooper Trophy - a bronze figure of an athletic young man holding aloft the RAF's flying badge, presented by Wing Commander G. Cooper in commemoration of the sacrifice and devotion of the Auxiliary Air Force during the Battle of Britain; it was awarded to recognise flying excellence.

George Mullay, 603 Battle of Britain veteran, refuelling a Spitfire, during post-war '8-day Forth/Clyde Air Exercise'.

Sheep maintained a very close friendship with his best friend and colleague, George Denholm, up until his death. Post war, George and Betty visited Sheep at his Tweedsmuir home and then later at Auchencairn. When George Denholm visited Auchencairn House for the first time Sheep asked his friend's opinion. 'It's hardly a farm house. Pull it down and start again,' was the advice his former CO offered after viewing the building! The two veterans found comfort in each other's company. Whilst George was not inclined to discuss his wartime experiences with anyone other than Betty, Sheep did talk about it with his own family although Pieter recalls '…he was no raconteur.' Both sons recall him being a very difficult man to live with as a result of his experiences but they, being only too aware of the root of the problems, were sympathetic.

During 1960, Sheep was interviewed by Robert Vacha of *The Edinburgh Evening Dispatch* who visited Auchencairn during harvest, a busy time for the Gilroy household and their employees. He refused to talk about his part in the Battle of Britain: 'those harrowing days and nights – and his own heroism – were best put aside. The aftermath of the war has brought disillusionment to Sheep Gilroy,' wrote Vacha. 'It's terribly sad, terribly sad, old chap' Sheep said. Viewing the world situation as it is to-day, and particularly Britain's Welfare State, Sheep commented without bitterness, just disillusionment: 'This is not what these young lives were sacrificed for. Everybody seems to expect something for nothing. We fought for country, King and Empire, now look at what we've got. We're just living on capital now. There's no income.' Of the complete disbandment of the Auxiliary Air Force he said: 'Whatever the situation, infantry still have a role to play and to play it effectively, they must have a manned air striking force. That's where the auxiliaries come in.' He emphasised the lack of ground crew, essential for the proper maintenance of the aircraft: 'There's absolutely nothing', he said sadly in his gentle voice. On a lighter note, Pieter recalled his father once commented on the contrast of having travelled to school in a horse and cart, flown a Spitfire in the Battle of Britain and watched the first men land on the moon, stating 'What a time to live!'

When it was announced that the original site at Turnhouse was to be closed and developed, naturally, great concern was expressed as to the future of the 603 Spitfire memorial opposite the main gate. Discussions got underway and the suggestion was made to move 'XT-A' to the main entrance of the modern airport on the other side of the airfield from the original site and mount the brass memorial plaque in a dry stone wall in the facia of the plinth on which it stood. This idea met with approval and the plans were well underway when it was realised the memorial plaque was actually owned by the 603 Association and George Denholm should be consulted. George, however, expressed concern that the plaque would be vulnerable to theft if mounted in a dry stone wall and would not give his permission for it to be moved. By that time, though, it was already in its new position beneath 'XT-A'! George was again approached and informed that a dry stone was a secure and appropriate place for the plaque and reminded of the fact that his friend, Sheep Gilroy, was the President of the Dry Stone Wall Association. George duly granted permission for the plaque to be removed, stating that it could be moved only on the condition it was mounted in a dry stone wall! He was guest of honour at the unveiling ceremony.

Sheep died on 25 March 1995, at the age of 79. He was godfather to Caroline Morton, Black's daughter who described him as an '…extraordinary eccentric with a red/purple complexion and very likeable' and by Group Captain 'Cocky' Dundas as: '….Dour, serious in his habits, uncompromising of men in his judgement of their actions, but also possessed of a quick and puckish sense of humour.' Betty Denholm described him as an: '…absolutely exceptional character. Occasionally he drove us all to fury. He was a real eccentric!' Sheep was a tough, no nonsense man, an outstanding pilot and leader whose final score stood at 14 destroyed and ten more shared destroyed, two shared probables, five and four shared damaged and three shared destroyed on the ground by the end of the conflict.

Sheep's place in 603 was taken by Squadron Leader J.W.E. 'Joe' Holmes DFC, AFC who had been with the Air Staff at 12 Group, Fighter Command Headquarters.

The new CO was given a clear directive on 24 September by Reserve Command; a big effort was required so far as instrument training was concerned, to remedy 603's lamentable lack of instrument rating endorsements.

The weather was bad at the beginning of October and this caused cancellations of Exercise Northex.

On 1 November 1949, with plenty of operational training in hand and good serviceability records to show, all the RAuxAF flying squadrons were transferred from Reserve Command to 12 Group Fighter Command; the squadrons were now affiliated to front line squadrons for training purposes.

1950

Concern for the future of world peace was brought into sharp focus by the outbreak of the Korean war on 25 June and the subsequent declaration of war by the United Nations on 27 June 1950. It was far too early to judge whether this would have any effect on the Royal Auxiliary Air Force but everyone prepared for their continuous training with greater determination.

On 1 July the two-week summer camp began at Horsham St Faith. The party consisted of 19 officers (including three regulars), 24 NCOs and 97 airmen.

The Battle of Britain open day at Turnhouse on 16 September attracted 25,000 visitors.

On 7 October 1950, F/L Jas Storrar led seven Spitfires to Middle Wallop for Exercise Emperor. En route they refuelled at Linton-on-Ouse. The regular and auxiliary ground crews plus the two remaining pilots flew down in two Valettas. Although the weather was perfect and the Squadron at readiness, no Spitfires were called on to fly. The Harvards managed some instrument flying. In the end the pilots took off on their own initiative and did some formation flying.

The drive to improve 603's instrument flying continued and on 4 November, three Harvards were available for most of the day and pilots completed ten hours of flying. Most disliked the amber screens and blue goggles now commonly used. Nearly everyone preferred the obsolete hood for simulation, but best of all, instrument flying in cloud, without artificial restraint of any kind.

F22 Spitfires of 603 Squadron and AOP Auster of 666 (Scottish) Squadron. RAuxAF at Turnhouse.

On 1 December the Squadron held a 25th Anniversary Dance at Town Headquarters, 25 Learmonth Terrace, Edinburgh.

The year ended on a high note when Joe Holmes' drive and enthusiasm resulted in 13 pilots obtaining current instrument ratings – more than any other auxiliary fighter squadron in the country. The final touch was the unofficial report that 603 had won the Esher Trophy for the most efficient auxiliary squadron.

His task accomplished, Joe Holmes DFC, AFC, left on 1 December 1950 and his place was taken by Squadron Leader Peter J. Anson DFC, another regular RAF officer who had joined the RAFVR in April 1940 and, after serving throughout the war, had been granted a permanent commission in October 1948.

1951

The 603 Operations Record Book recorded a light-hearted start to 1951:

> 1st January New Years Day. Nuff said. 6th January. Only two sorties could be flown today before the weather clamped – snow, mist, low cloud. We gave in gracefully and after lunch a much needed lesson was held in dancing the eightsome reel. It is normal for the officers of the Squadron to dance an eightsome reel at parties, especially when in England. Far too many of the present officers have been so badly educated that they are ignorant of the steps of even the most popular Scottish Highland dances. A notable step forward was taken this afternoon. For two exhausting hours we learnt the reel.

The Korean war had now been raging for six months and the Chiefs of Staff were considering the possibility that it might be intended to divert Western Alliance Forces to the Far East, thus leaving Western Europe more vulnerable to a possible surprise attack. As part of the measures to strengthen forces in Europe it was therefore decided to bring reserve forces nearer to front line standards.

Mr Attlee announced plans for calling up reservists. One decision, which came as a complete surprise to 603, was that all auxiliary squadrons would be called up for three months. It was felt that three months regular service would mean a great deal to the Squadron and all its members. The primary purpose of the call-up was to reduce, as far as possible, the time required after mobilisation for them to take their place with maximum efficiency in the front line.

In February 1951, 603 received official confirmation that it had won the Esher Trophy* for 1950. The Squadron gained 458.2 points out of a possible 475 points during the competition year. The Squadron had last won this coveted trophy, awarded annually for the most efficient all-round flying performance

S/L P. J. Anson DFC and members of 603 Squadron, possibly during summer camp, 1951. In front of Spitfire F22.

*Esher Trophy - a bronze figure of Perseus presented by the Late Viscount Esher in 1926, now held by the RAF Museum, Hendon; originally awarded to the best all-round unit amongst the auxiliary flying squadrons.

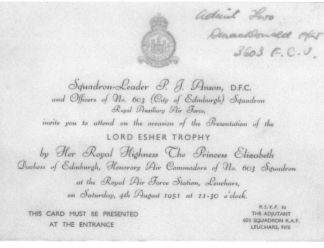

Admiral Louis
DonaldMacDonald 19/45
3603 F.C.U.

Squadron-Leader P. J. Anson, D.F.C.
and *Officers of No. 603 (City of Edinburgh) Squadron*
Royal Auxiliary Air Force,
invite you to attend on the occasion of the Presentation of the

LORD ESHER TROPHY

by *Her Royal Highness The Princess Elizabeth*
Duchess of Edinburgh, Honorary Air Commodore of No. 603 Squadron
at the Royal Air Force Station, Leuchars,
on Saturday, 4th August 1951 at 11-30 o'clock.

THIS CARD MUST BE PRESENTED
AT THE ENTRANCE

R.S.V.P. to
THE ADJUTANT
603 SQUADRON R.A.F.
LEUCHARS, FIFE

Top: S/L J. Anson DFC, CO of 603 Squadron, with the Esher Trophy, won by the Squadron in 1950, but presented by Her Majesty The Queen, (when Princess Elizabeth), in August 1951.
Above: Invitation on the occasion of the presentation of the Esher Trophy.

of an auxiliary squadron, in 1938 – the last occasion on which it was presented before the outbreak of war. Friday afternoon was promptly declared a holiday and there was an impromptu party at Town Headquarters.

As in the pre-war years, inter-squadron rivalry was intense, and in the main, good-natured. However, on occasions things could get out of hand. Air Commodore R.H. Crompton OBE, BA, RAF (Ret), recalls that when he was adjutant of 604 (County of Middlesex) Fighter Squadron, based at North Weald, who had won the coveted Lord Esher Trophy for the first post-war presentation in 1949, 604 sought that the presentation would be made by the Air Commodore-in-Chief, His Majesty King George VI, the ceremony taking place in the grounds of Buckingham Palace in the first half of 1950. 603 wrested the trophy from 604 Squadron in the next presentation year and the 604 adjutant was advised of this in January 1951 at North Weald. It so happened that over the Christmas/New Year period some thieves had taken the Stone of Scone from beneath the throne in Westminster Abbey. The fact that it had not at that time been recovered caused the OC of 604 Squadron, the late Squadron Leader Keith Lofts, and the adjutant to play a prank on 603 by composing a suitable Post Office telegram which the adjutant subsequently dictated over his telephone. According to Air Commodore Crompton, the message read something like:

1 July 1951. Pilots of the 'E' formation.

HRH Princess Elizabeth inspecting the Squadron at RAF Leuchars, 4 August 1951, during the Esher Trophy presentation.

Congratulations on your victory in the Lord Esher Trophy competition. Recommend that like 604 you should seek presentation from hands of Air Commodore-in-Chief. In advance of formal presentation, however, would suggest an informal handing over ceremony here at North Weald when we shall be pleased to entertain you, but only providing you bring with you the Stone of Scone in exchange, thereby showing your undoubted allegiance to our Monarch?

Both the OC and adjutant of 604 Squadron retired for the night and thought no more of the event until reaching their offices the next morning, when F/L Crompton had an enraged adjutant of 603 on the telephone – 'You bastards', he said, 'they think we've got the damn thing here. They've been ransacking our offices at Turnhouse since 06.30'.

Happily, all ended amicably. The Stone of Scone was returned (not by 603) and the Esher Trophy was handed over informally, the prize being duly collected from 604 Squadron at North Weald and flown up to Turnhouse in the back seat of a Harvard.

At the end of February the Scottish auxiliary squadrons flew to Leuchars to train for a new Wings weekend scheme. They were visited by Arthur Henderson, Secretary of State for Air, who was accompanied by Air Marshal Sir Basil Embry AOC-in-C Fighter Command.

The Squadron now began to realise the full implications of the three-months call up. Government naturally pressurised employers to release staff and it was felt that most auxiliaries could make suitable arrangements. Some, inevitably, could not. Those to whom a three-month call up would mean undue loss or hardship were, therefore, given an opportunity to appeal for exemption. A tribunal of five, including the CO, S/L Anson, sat at Town Headquarters to hear appeals. There were only 13 from the total of 115 auxiliaries. This was very low compared with other squadrons. The tribunal forwarded its recommendations to the Air Ministry for their final decision.

Some National Service pilots now began to near the end of their full-time service and were being considered for enrolment in auxiliary squadrons. One of these, Pilot Officer Don Knight, was on leave and came to Turnhouse on 4 April for one hour of local flying in the Harvard. Later that week he was sent solo in a Spitfire.

603 had mixed feelings when on 23 April 1951 work began on the Turnhouse runway. It was proposed to extend it from 1,330 yards to 2,000 yards, which would enable Vampires to land. At the end of May, three Vampires Vs were allocated to the Squadron and delivered to Leuchars pending completion of the runway extension. Meantime the aircraft would be serviced by 502 Squadron. The Operations Record Book sadly recorded 'Three of our well beloved Spitfires have been offered up for disposal'.

S/L Anson went over to Leuchars and flew 603's first sortie in one of its own Vampires. He was quickly followed by Flight Lieutenants Scott and Allen and Flying Officer Still.

1 July 1951. Princess Elizabeth consented to become Honorary Air Commodore of 603 Squadron. An 'E' was formed above the control tower at Turnhouse to mark the occasion.

June 1951 was a month of pride and tragedy. It started with the award of the BEM to Flight Sergeant Erskine and the King's Commendation to Flight Lieutenant 'Red' Allen.

Tragedy struck on 23 June, when 26-year-old Pilot Officer Andrew Anderson, a teacher, took off on his first solo in a Meteor 7 (VW 438) in beautiful weather. An unexpected sea fog came in, rapidly covering the field with a layer of low stratus. P/O Anderson did not reply to a recall and later, when he returned, a GCA (ground controlled approach) was unsuccessfully attempted. Very shortly afterwards he ran out of fuel and crashed amongst the trees at Inverdovat Farm, near Newport, Fife, being killed instantly. This was the first fatal accident since Mears had died in somewhat similar circumstances on 6 March 1949. It was the more tragic as P/O Anderson, a Second World War fighter pilot, was killed on his first solo flight on a jet aircraft. He was buried on 26 June in his home village of Currie. The Squadron provided an escort and firing party and P/O Anderson was buried with full military honours.

Sadness turned to pride when at 1830 hours on 29 June 1951 it was announced that HRH Princess Elizabeth, Duchess of Edinburgh, had graciously accepted the appointment as Honorary Air Commodore of 603 Squadron with effect from 16 June 1951 (in addition to becoming the Honorary Air Commodore for Nos.2603 LAA Squadron and 3603 FCU).

1 July 1951 marked the end of a long and honourable era. The Operations Record Book noted :

Today was the last day of Spitfire flying in the Squadron and it is with regret that we see the passing from Squadron service of an aircraft which has served us so well. The re-equipment of the Squadron with Vampire FB5s is now being accelerated and it is expected that by the time the Squadron moves to Leuchars for the three month training period it will be equipped to strength with ten Vampire 5s and two Meteor 7s.

A formation of ten Spitfire Mk F22s of 603 Squadron flew over the city from west to east along Princes Street, led by S/L Peter Anson DFC, the Officer Commanding. After making a wide sweep east of Arthur's Seat it changed into an E formation to represent the first letter of the name of the Squadron's new Honorary Air Commodore and crossed, once more, over the city. That same day Air Vice-Marshal R.L.R. 'Batchy' Atcherley, Air Officer Commanding 12 Group, Fighter Command, visited Turnhouse.

The Spitfires were now offered up for disposal and would soon be flown away.

CHAPTER 18

603 ENTERS THE JET AGE

On 16 July 1951 the move was made to Leuchars to commence a three-month call up and begin the conversion to the Vampire. The station's arrangements for accommodation and messing were first class and all ranks settled in quite happily. The Squadron's auxiliary strength was 13 officers and four sergeant pilots; four officers, 13 senior NCOs and 70 airmen ground staff. The regular staff included three officer pilots, one ground staff officer, ten NCOs and 61 airmen. 603 now had seven Vampires FB5s, two Meteor T7s and three Harvard IIBs as training aircraft. In addition three Vampires were attached from 602 Squadron.

Everyone settled down to a period of intensive training. Pilots who had only flown propeller-driven aircraft found the change to jets interesting and invigorating.

The dual-control Meteor provided a useful transition from the Spitfire to the de Havilland Vampire with which the Squadron were now equipped. The Vampire had twin jets and distinctive twin booms. The first production aircraft had made its maiden flight on 20 April 1945. 603's two FB5 variants had been introduced in 1949. This was a close-support ground-attack fighter/bomber. The wing-span had been reduced by two feet, producing square cut wing tips. It had a maximum speed of around 540mph.

603's first aircraft had been a de Havilland DH9A; so it was appropriate that another de Havilland aircraft should be their last. Curiously the wing span of the Vampire was eight feet less than that of the DH9A. Its take-off speed was about the same as the DH9A's maximum performance. The culmination of the training at RAF Leuchars was Exercise Pinnacle during which the Squadron acquitted itself well. Embodiment ended on 14 October, and the auxiliaries returned to their homes.

DH Vampire FBV, WA 398–M, at Leuchars. On three-months call out during July 1951.

The Squadron's new Honorary Air Commodore, HRH The Princess Elizabeth, Duchess of Edinburgh had agreed to present the Esher Trophy at RAF Leuchars. This was to be the first time the men would meet their new Honorary Air Commodore and they were determined to show that their performance on the ground was no less perfect than that in the air.

The great day finally arrived on 4 August 1951. The Royal aircraft, a Viking of the King's Flight, appeared in the circuit at 12.08 hours. Her Royal Highness was received on arrival by Air Marshal Sir Basil Embry, AOC-in-C Fighter Command. After inspecting the Guard of Honour provided by the station on the parade ground, accompanied by Air Marshal Sir Basil Embry, Lieutenant General Sir Frederick Browning and Group Captains Robinson and Brown, she inspected 603 Squadron (Squadron Leader P.J. Anson DFC), 3603 (City of Edinburgh) Fighter Control Unit (Wing Commander M. Pearson) and 2603 (City of Edinburgh) Light Anti-Aircraft Squadron (Flight Lieutenant J. Burgess vice Squadron Leader H. Edwards).

After the Inspection, Her Royal Highness addressed the parade before the presentation of the trophy:

> The Squadron has a record of service second to none, and the great traditions of service which you built in the last war still inspire you today. You are giving freely of your spare time – which I know in these days to be a thing of great value – so that you may be always ready if we are ever again called upon to defend ourselves. That you are indeed ready is shown by the award of the Lord Esher Trophy to 603 (City of Edinburgh) Squadron.

The Princess also spoke of her great pleasure on learning that HM King George VI had approved her appointment as the Squadron's Honorary Air Commodore: '… a personal link of which I shall always be very proud.' Referring to the Esher Trophy Award, Her Royal Highness said:

> This trophy is given each year to the most efficient unit in the whole of the Royal Auxiliary Air Force, and I am very proud that, at our first meeting, it should be my privilege to present it to you.

She then presented the trophy to S/L Anson. The Squadron marched off and the officers made a hurried dash to the mess where, before lunch, they were presented to the Princess. At 14.30 hours Her Royal Highness left for Balmoral.

The Squadron now returned to a normal training routine. From 1 to 15 September they went to an armament practice camp at Acklington. From 15 September to 13 October they returned to Leuchars to practice night flying on Meteors and Vampires and to carry out air firing exercises. Finally came a return to Turnhouse to complete the final phase of the call-up programme, which ended on 31 October. Following that, their former role of 'weekend fliers' was resumed and the *Weekly Scotsman* ran a two-page photographic article describing their training activities accompanied by contemporary photographs.*

Meantime one of 603's most experienced flight commanders, Flight Lieutenant 'Jas' Storrar DFC (Bar) had been sent to Acklington on a Fighter Leader's course for the period of his 'call up'.

1952

The year 1952 started with 603 being scrambled to intercept six Washingtons flying at 17,000 feet. Whilst the Squadron were airborne the weather at Turnhouse closed in and visibility dropped to 300 yards. The aircraft landed at Leuchars.

Flight Lieutenant Mike E. Hobson arrived on 5 February to take over as regular adjutant from Flight Lieutenant 'Red' Allen.

6 February 1952 was a sad day not only for the men of 603, but for the entire nation as it was the day HM King George VI died. On 12 February Flying Officer Alex Peddell took a party of 14 airmen, both auxiliary and regular, to Uxbridge for drill practice to prepare for their place in the late King's funeral procession on Friday 15 February. The *Air Pictorial – Air Reserve Gazette* for March 1952 reported:

---

*Weekend fighter pilots - Edinburgh's Flying Auxiliaries, *Weekly Scotsman*, 29 November 1951.

Leading the procession on the occasion of the funeral of His Late Majesty King George VI were a composite detachment of over 350 officers and men representing all the home Commands of the RAF, the RAF Regiment and the Royal Auxiliary Air Force, headed by the Royal Air Force Central Band.

A particularly close link with the Royal Family was established by the representation in the funeral procession of the Royal Auxiliary Air Force. Men were selected from 603 Squadron, 2603 (City of Edinburgh) Squadron of the RAuxAF Regiment, and 3603 (City of Edinburgh) Fighter Control Unit, of all of which the Queen is Honorary Air Commodore, and from 600 (City of London) Squadron and 2600 (City of London) Squadron, RAuxAF Regiment, of which the Queen Mother is Honorary Air Commodore.

Wing Commander Jack Meadows recalls the preparations for the King's funeral procession as a significant contribution of both 600 and 603 Squadrons:

King George VI would, I am confident, have understood how his funeral came to provide one my proudest memories of the Royal Auxiliary Air Force.

When 600 (City of London) Squadron assembled at our Town Headquarters, beside the Honourable Artillery Company in Finsbury Barracks, on the evening after the King's death in 1952, we remembered that 600 with 601 (County of London) and 604 (County of Middlesex), the (then) Hendon Squadrons, had at King George V's funeral been part of the forces lining London streets.

Apart from a small cadre of regulars we were all civilians, 'week-end fliers'. 600 flew its Meteors at weekends from Biggin Hill, trained at THQ on week-day evenings. As part of Fighter Command, the front line defence of the country, we prided ourselves that we flew as much as our brother regular squadrons, and that some of ours were even better at the job than they were!

That particular evening normal training was promptly replaced by practicing the little known funeral drills; reversing arms, resting on arms reversed, changing reversed arms on the slow march.

At Biggin on Saturday I was shown a surprise signal from Air Ministry; no street lining for the RAuxAF this time. Instead, 600 and 603 (City of Edinburgh), the two Squadrons then with Royal Honorary Air Commodores – the former Queen and the new Queen respectively – were to provide a detachment of sixty men to march in the procession itself. We quickly obtained our share of keen volunteers ready to desert their paid-employment for four days and accept this honour. On arrival at Uxbridge on Monday they drew rifles and bayonets while I reported to the Group Captain commanding.

'What bad luck for you, old boy; I know your chaps can't possibly be trained in time in all these strange drills; I've had the regulars, two squadrons each of 120 men, drilling away here since last Thursday, but you've only got two days now. It's impossible for you to be good enough in such a short time, so I'm going to hide your chaps down the middle of the six-abreast columns where they won't show.'

He meant it kindly and expected me to be grateful.

I politely pointed out my orders were to command the quite separate detachment of the Royal Auxiliary Air Force, that we were perfectly capable of giving a good show, that if necessary Air Ministry and the Inspector of the RAuxAF would confirm this.

'No good, old boy; I've already told Air Ministry the problem and they've agreed my plan, given me full authority. We've got lots of experience of these things, we know what we're talking about.'

I continued to protest. Finally he said:

'Right, just to satisfy you, you can train separately and be an independent unit at the dress rehearsal on Wednesday afternoon. If you're bloody good then you can stay that way, otherwise – and that's what's bound to happen – your chaps will be hidden up between the regulars. OK?'

There was no choice but to accept, with as much grace as possible.

'You can have any help you want,' he said.

I asked for the loan of two drill sergeants to help our own senior NCOs. With 603's officer, the second in command, I went to explain to our combined troops what had happened – I had served a while with 603 and found some old friends from earlier Turnhouse days. There was no doubt of the views of both squadrons. The Uxbridge drill sergeants arrived, already knew the position and entered into the challenge with great heart. In miserable weather until eleven p.m. and again all next day and evening and the following morning the chaps drilled. In the rain and the dark they used open-sided draughty tin sheds with just enough dim electric light to enable us to keep at it.

The dress rehearsal was at 2 pm. on Wednesday. As the junior branch of the junior service the auxiliaries would be right in the van, only the Central Band of the RAF ahead. In that order we slow-marched round and round the square with arms reversed, halted, did arms drill, repeated the march. After another half an hour of this came a halt, the parade was stood at ease and the order came: 'Fall out Squadron Commanders'. The three of us marched over to the Group Captain. He called the Uxbridge Station Warrant 0fficer over, always the most feared person in the Air Force, a magnificent figure of a man with an enormous voice and a long service career devoted to the finest points of ceremonial drill.

'Well Mister, what's the verdict, which was the best of the three squadrons?'

'No doubt about it. Sir, the auxiliaries were the best.'

The Group Captain grinned at me:

'You win, well done.'

That night I went round the barrack blocks to congratulate the chaps again as they polished boots and brass, blancoed webbing. Next morning we marched to Uxbridge tube station and were on a special train by six am. Detraining at Trafalgar Square we marched halfway up the Mall to the head of the procession which wound back through Admiralty Arch down Whitehall to Westminster Abbey and had its tail somewhere down Victoria Street. There was then more than an hour's further wait before we at last set off at the slow-march, Mendelssohn's Dead March from Saul echoing and re-echoing; up St James St, down Piccadilly through the Park, Marble Arch, Edgware Road, to Paddington station where the coffin of our late Monarch would go by train to Windsor. Despite changing arms frequently we were after all this slow-marching a pretty stiff bunch of chaps by the time, in Paddington station, our part in the proceedings was completed and we could break into a quick-march, slope arms and move away. Worse was the demand from our bladders which had not been relieved since we left Uxbridge about five hours before. One or two men could not wait for our arrival at tents in Hyde Park with latrines and lunch, and were allowed to fall out and knock frantically on doors in Sussex Gardens begging for relief.

I lived then just across the Park. It was an anticlimax to have to go back by RAF bus to Uxbridge to collect civilian clothes and car. Meanwhile we were proud indeed of having done well some small thing to honour our dead King and Honorary Air Commodore-in-Chief, and to have supported our Honorary Air Commodores in their sorrow.

A former member of 603 Squadron, the late Wing Commander W.G. Duncan Smith DSO (Bar), DFC (2 Bars), arrived to take command at Turnhouse on 25 February 1952.

A steady trickle of National Service pilots now began to join, or apply for membership. An initial interview was followed by appearance before a Selection Board, chaired by the CO and including the adjutant, the regular flying training officer and an auxiliary flight commander. Candidates judged suitable then attended at Turnhouse for two or three weekends. The CO and flying training officer flew with them to assess their capability. If accepted, they joined for a probationary period after which they became fully fledged members. Very few NCO pilots were recruited.

With the advent of jets, the training of the ground staff became more intricate. Those with wartime service were accustomed to servicing piston-engined aircraft and there were not the staff nor facilities to train them in more advanced technologies. More of the burden fell on the shoulder of the regular airmen. In certain areas, such as armament, auxiliaries such as W/O Erskine were as competent as any regular.

By mid 1952, the RAuxAF flying squadrons were now equipped either with Meteor F8s or Vampire F5s, the only changes being the introduction into five Vampire squadrons of a few Vampire F9s.

The perceived threat to Fighter Command in the early 1950s was massive daylight assault upon mainland United Kingdom by formations of Soviet bombers. Only a large force of fighters supported by a ground-based air defence system could hope to counter such a threat. The fighter squadrons of the RAuxAF would play an important role in the defence of the UK Air Defence Region (UKADR) by Fighter Command. To allow the squadrons to attain a high state of operational capability, the policy of HQ Fighter Command was to call up up to four squadrons for three months of intensive training. In some squadrons, although not 603, attendance was waning and to make the RAuxAF more attractive to potential recruits and encourage retention of valuable trained personnel, overseas detachments were introduced as recognition of those which demonstrated high performance. 603 was to have two annual camps in West Germany (Celle 1952 and Sylt 1953), and two in Gibraltar (1955, 1956).

June saw the Squadron participating in a large NATO Exercise codenamed Castanets. The weather was bad but convoy patrols were possible on 22 June.

On the 25th the Squadron displayed their formation flying capabilities when Her Majesty Queen Elizabeth II again visited Edinburgh. The formation flew down Princes Street at 800 feet just as the Queen came out of the station to enter her car. The first was a V formation and this was changed into an E for the return flight. It was led by S/L Pete Anson and included Flight Lieutenants Duncan McIntosh, Bill Moncur and Mike Hobson, Flying Officer Furse, Pilot Officers Tim Ferguson, George Ballingall and Don Knight and Flight Sergeant J.C. Inglis.

On her accession to the throne Her Majesty became Air Commodore-in-Chief of the Royal Auxiliary Air Force (succeeding her late father HM King George VI who had assumed the title in December 1936 following the abdication of HM King Edward VIII) but it was her express wish that she should retain her appointment as Honorary Air Commodore of 603 Squadron, 2603 LAA Squadron and 3603 FCU.

The summer camp at Celle was between 5 and 19 July and as part of the preparations for what was their first overseas camp, everyone was vaccinated and inoculated. External wing tanks now arrived for the long flight to Germany and 603 carried out practice flights in advance of the trip to assess their effect on the flying characteristics of the Vampires.

The formation flight of ten Vampires was to have been led by the CO, S/L Anson, but while he was briefing the pilots on the previous evening, a blackboard fell on his foot and broke three toes! He went by Hastings instead.

At Celle, the Squadron were allocated one small permanent building consisting of two rooms for aircrew and flying equipment and four large tents for technical, administration and equipment sections. Flying training included cine-gun exercises and practice battle formations. There were six night flying sorties in Vampires and two in Meteors. The stay at the camp finished with three mass formations with the regular squadrons and 616 (South Yorkshire) Squadron. The first two, with 32 aircraft, were battle formations at height and the third, with 28 aircraft, was low level, tight formation. The correspondent for *The Edinburgh Evening Dispatch* was Ronald Robson, who provided excellent press coverage.

On 19 July 1952, the Vampires donned their wing tanks once more for their return to Turnhouse. The summer camp had been of great value to the ground crews as well as to the pilots. The Operations Record Book commented:

Most encouraging sign was the large reduction effected in turn-round times. The intensive flying enabled the Auxiliary ground crews to tighten up their refuelling and pre-flight inspection drills. On one occasion a formation of 10 aircraft landed and was airborne again within 20 minutes. Serviceability was maintained at a high level throughout.

Wing exercises in August concluded with a flypast over Edinburgh Castle for the Military Tattoo, and 603 continued their liaison with the Royal Observer Corps.

In September 603 took part in Exercise Ardent, the largest post-war air defence exercise to date. The cities of Edinburgh and Glasgow were singled out for major night raids during this exercise, where

Exercise Ardent, October 1952.

the 'enemy' consisted of 150 bombers composed of Washingtons, Lincolns and Canberras, which approached the cities from the east. More than 200 sorties were flown by the defending fighters, in which the Vampires of both 602 and 603 Squadrons participated.

Poor weather conditions during November and December affected flying training at Leuchars, with few sorties being flown.

1953

The officers' mess dined out Sir William Young Darling Kt, CBE, MC, DL, LLD, MP, Honorary Air Commodore from 1943 to 1951, at the Caledonian United Services Club in Edinburgh. Past and present members were present.

On 22 March S/L Pete Anson DFC left to take up a post as OC Flying at RAF Church Fenton, and his place as Commanding Officer was taken by Squadron Leader Robert Lloyd Rees Davies DFC (known as Lloyd Davies), who had previously been Training Officer of 600 (City of London) Squadron, and had been awarded the DFC as a Mosquito night-fighter pilot during the war when with 25 Squadron.

The next two months saw intensive practice for the flypast during the Royal visit to Edinburgh planned for

March 1953, Turnhouse. S/L R. Lloyd Davies DFC (left) takes over command of 603 from S/L P.J. Anson DFC (right).

Left: 22 March 1953. From front left, clockwise: Jock, Pete, Lloyd (C/O), Duncan, Mitch, Mike, Ron, Harry, Tony, George, John, Andy, Johnny and Don.
Right: 'Two worried planners', 4 July 1953. Alex and Mike Hobson at Manston, each after having landed with a little less than no fuel.

June. One diversion was a simulated attack on corvettes in the Forth as part of a Royal Observer Corps exercise in May.

Despite the Squadron's best endeavours, the Royal Flypast was to be dogged with difficulties. When the Queen arrived on 22 June, 'Auld Reekie' lived up to its name. The pilots were strapped in their aircraft and ready for take-off when word of cancellation came through. The Operations Record Book noted that it was doubtful if the pilots could have found Edinburgh, let alone Princes Street, and even if they could, it would have been impossible to land back at Turnhouse.

To make up for the disappointment, the whole Scottish Wing – 603, 602 and 612 (County of Aberdeen) Squadrons – led by a former 603 pilot, W/C W.G.G. Duncan Smith DSO, DFC***, flew their DH Vampires in perfect formation over Hampden Park on 25 June. The formation was led by the Glasgow Squadron, flanked by 603 on the right, led by S/L Davies and 612 on the left, led by Squadron Leader McLean. Alas, the Queen had been delayed by eight minutes, and was not at the review stand as the wing flew overhead. She sent a special message to say that she and the Duke of Edinburgh had seen it clearly from their car, though.*

On 4 July 1953, ten Vampires and two Meteors flew to the Squadron's summer camp at Westerland on Sylt, West Germany, to be held between 4 and 18 July – coincidentally the airfield from which the Junkers Ju88s of KG/30 had taken off from on 16 October 1939 when they launched their attack against the Royal Navy shipping in the Firth of Forth and met stern opposition from 602 and 603 Squadrons.

The 603 Vampires took off at 08.10 hours and most had landed in Germany by 10.00. One section had feed trouble with its overload tanks and had to divert to Marham before going on to Sylt. The Meteors refuelled at Manston. Apart from the fuel problem the move was made without incident. The ground crews flew across in three Valettas.

The whole summer camp was devoted to air-to-air firing. Four ranges were in operation, with a Hawker Tempest towing a target over each range for periods of an hour at a time. A total of 15,940 rounds was fired, for only ten stoppages.

Sylt was a holiday resort, and everyone enjoyed the camp, but it was marred by tragedy. On 10 July, the CO, S/L Davies DFC, was driving a land rover across the airfield at night with four members of the Squadron as passengers when their vehicle was involved in a collision with a Volkswagen. In addition to two of the three occupants of the Volkswagen, Davies was killed when he was impaled on the steering column of the land rover. Flight Lieutenants Hobson, Mitchell and Anderson and Pilot Officer Cruickshank were also injured. Although badly injured, Mike Hobson

---

* 'E' pilots up early over Edinburgh, *Evening Dispatch*, 22 June 1953.

Top: 4-18 July 1953, summer camp in Sylt, Germany. Joe, Mike, Alex, Lloyd, Duncan, George, Tony, Doug, John, Tim, Andy, Mitch, Jimmy and Keith.

Middle: Summer camp at Sylt, 1953.

Bottom: 603 Squadron pipe band, 1953.

managed to make his way across the airfield to summon help for his injured colleagues. Alas, Lloyd Davies was beyond help.

Once again, Ronald Robson of *The Edinburgh Evening Dispatch* reported on the activities of the summer camp, including the sad demise of their Commanding Officer.

Mike Hobson, the 603 adjutant, assumed temporary command and sent sincerest sympathies to Mrs Davies and her three young sons.

It was announced on 27 July 1953, that a truce had been declared in the Korean war.

The new Commanding Officer was Squadron Leader Roy A. Schofield. Born in Argentina, he had joined the RAF in 1942 and in 1950 won the King's Commendation for Brave Conduct for assisting another pilot in a crash.

Exercise Momentum, an air defence exercise in August, showed the limitations of the Vampires. The Squadron were scrambled against high flying Canberras and Boeing B45s. Even when these were seen, they could seldom be caught.

During the annual Battle of Britain open day at Turnhouse, 603 Squadron performed a flypast in the shape of an E, but the main attraction was the breaking of the sound barrier creating a 'double-boom' by a Royal Canadian Air Force F86A Sabre, the first 'faster than sound' flying display to be seen in Scotland.

1954

This was a less eventful year but the flying training programme continued whenever the weather permitted.

On 29 January, HM Queen Elizabeth II, approved the affiliation of 603 Squadron with 4 Otago (Territorial) Squadron, Royal New Zealand Air Force which had been equipped with DH Tiger Moths, North American Harvards and the P.51 Mustangs reactivated from storage since the end of World War II. (Continually faced with a shortage of air and ground crews, the Royal New Zealand Territorial Air Force was finally disbanded in 1957.)

In April, F/L Mike Hobson left for Amman, Jordan, and he was replaced as regular adjutant by Flight Lieutenant W.G. Bill Holmes, a Yorkshireman from Catterick, who had taken part in the Korean war and then flown North American F86 Sabres in Germany. Before he joined Fighter Command, he had served with Transport Command and flew regularly on the Berlin Airlift.

An interesting reminder of wartime days was a letter from a former Luftwaffe pilot, Herr Hermann Cremer of Herford, West Germany. This reads, in translation:

Herford 20/1/54

As a sign of international understanding and a genuine gesture from one pilot to another, I am trying to get in touch with a former fair opponent in an air battle.

I am handing this souvenir of an air battle in the Eastern Mediterranean on 27/1/44 in which I took part as a pilot, to Mr Russell, British Resident. I am asking Mr Russell to hand over this article on the tenth anniversary to the leader of the English Squadron who on the above named day gained a victory in an air battle with a German sea transport Squadron.

Hermann Cremer

In a second letter, the ex-Luftwaffe pilot thanked HQ 2nd Tactical Air Force for tracing the Squadron.

The gift from Herr Cremer was a handsome silver cigarette box measuring eight inches by six inches. It is lined with wood, surmounted by a German flying badge and is inscribed: 'Dem Fairen Sieger in Luftkampf. Östliches Mittelmeer, 27 Januar 1944. Hermann Cremer 27/1/54.' – 'To the Fine Victor in Air Combat, Eastern Mediterranean, 27.1.44 Hermann Cremer 27.1.54.'

The Squadron had to move to Leuchars for six weeks whilst the runways at Turnhouse were being repaired.

On 10 June 1954, in celebration of Her Majesty The Queen's birthday, when she returned after the Trooping the Colour Parade, a ceremonial flypast by 27 aircraft comprising 18 DH Vampire and nine Meteors from squadrons of the Royal Auxiliary Air Force took place over Buckingham Palace,

Top left: The silver cigarette box given to the Squadron by ex-Luftwaffe pilot Hermann Cremer of Herford, West Germany. The gift is now displayed in the National War Musuem in Edinburgh Castle.
Top right: S/L Roy Schofield.
Left: F/Sgt C.E. Erskine BEM (left) and F/Sgt D. Mackenzie BEM. 26 and 20 years' experience respectively.

London. Squadrons represented were 603; 501 (County of Gloucester), of which HRH The Duke of Gloucester was Honorary Air Commodore, and 500 (County of Kent), of which Mr Anthony Eden was Honorary Air Commodore.

The Squadron was led by its Commanding Officer, S/L Roy Schofield, with F/Ls Duncan McIntosh AFC and Alex Peddell AFC, F/Os Jimmy Ewing, John Taylor, Sam Milne and Tim Ferguson of 603 Squadron all flying Vampires, and followed by nine Meteors of 500 Squadron and nine Vampires of 501 Squadron. Full-scale rehearsals were held on June 8 and 9 and the 603 pilots had flown to Biggin Hill the previous day. The formation was guided by flares placed on the roof of ShellMex House in the Strand.

The aircraft flew over Buckingham Palace at precisely 13.00 hours and the Queen was on the balcony to receive the RAF salute. The formations joined up over Sheerness and flew a route over Clacton, Colchester, Chelmsford, Fairlop, Wanstead, Leytonstone, Hackney, Aldwych and the Mall, breaking away one mile beyond Buckingham Palace. Ceremonial flypasts honouring the sovereign's official birthday were normally done by the operational commands of the RAF, and this was the first time that one had been undertaken by the Royal Auxiliary Air Force. It was controlled by the Air Officer Commanding, 11 Group, Fighter Command, Air Vice-Marshal H.L. Patch, CB, CBE.

Flight Lieutenant Mike Hobson, the former Squadron adjutant, was honoured in the Queen's Birthday Honours List with the award of the Queen's Commendation for Valuable Services in the Air.

The summer camp for 1954 was held at RAF Tangmere in July, during which the pipe band, under the musical direction of Pipe Major G. Wilson, entertained the Chairman of Bognor Regis Council and the public.

1955

No flying was possible between 9 and 24 January and even when the ice had been cleared there was very low cloud for four days.

During March two more officers were gazetted: Pilot Officers Frank Mycroft and Alexander. The difference in ages between veterans of the 1939-45 war and the new arrivals was now becoming noticeable with the new pilots and it was clear that there would be difficulties in choosing future flight commanders. A careful balance would have to be struck between age, experience and the requirements of the job.

Plans were now well in hand for the summer camp, which was to be in Gibraltar. Khaki drill uniforms were issued, medical examinations carried out and inoculations given.

It was now learned that Her Majesty The Queen would present the Squadron Standard at the end of June. The ceremony had been postponed from the previous year due to an outbreak of polio. Her Majesty's schedule for her stay in Edinburgh was very tight, and instead of going to Turnhouse she had invited 603 Squadron to the Palace of Holyroodhouse – a great honour. Flying was therefore curtailed on Sunday, as this was the only day on which all auxiliaries were available for drill practice.

April flying included practice interceptions, and an exercise with the Royal Observer Corps. It was marred by a tragic accident on the 17th when Flying Officer S. Milne let down through low cloud, apparently thinking he was over the sea. In fact he was over land and he crashed in the Lammermuir Hills and was killed. The Form 540 recalled that Milne was always a very 'press-on' pilot and felt that with more experience he would have become an outstanding pilot. He was buried with full military honours at Corstorphine Cemetery on Thursday 21 April.

Every Sunday during May drill was practised under the eagle eye of Flight Sergeant Miller, a regular from Leuchars. Arrangements were made for the standard party to go to the depot at Uxbridge for intensive instruction.

The main flying event in May 1955 was a Conship/Conshore exercise Summer Able on the 22nd. 603 Squadron and 609 from Church Fenton augmented sector fighters. The exercise was very valuable, and the quality of the ship-controlled interceptions very good. Squadron aircraft had the

role of protecting the fleet from air attack. The Vampires operated in pairs, either on standing patrols in the fleet area or on scramble from the readiness platform to intercept specified raids. The 'enemy' aircraft were Sea Hawks and Avengers from HMS *Fulmer*-RNAS Lossiemouth.

All aircraft had now been permanently fitted with long range tanks, and Command had ruled that each pilot must fly two cross-country flights of 640 nautical miles each, in preparation for the transit flights to and from Gibraltar.

At the Palace of Holyroodhouse, Edinburgh, on 30 June, the Queen presented the Squadron Standard to 603, of which unit Her Majesty had now been HAC since 1951.*

Inspection, 30 June 1955, Holyrood Palace, when Her Majesty received the 603 brooch.

---

*A commemorative booklet '603 (City of Edinburgh) Squadron, Royal Auxiliary Air Force, Presentation of the Standard by Her Majesty The Queen, Honorary Air Commodore, 603 Squadron, at the Palace of Holyroodhouse, on 30th June 1955'.

HM Queen Elizabeth II. Photograph taken at Holyrood Palace, 30 June 1955, following the presentation of the Squadron Standard.

The Standard was created by His late Majesty King George VI to mark the 25th anniversary of the RAF in 1943. It was awarded only to squadrons of 25 years' standing, or with a history of special outstanding operations. The Standard consists of a fringed and tasselled silken banner, mounted on a pike which is crowned by a golden eagle. Eight selected battle honours surround the Squadron badge, and a decorative border contains the rose, leek, thistle and shamrock, beautifully embroidered. The battle honours on the 603 Standard are: Home Defence 1940-42, Battle of Britain 1940, Channel and North Sea 1941, Fortress Europe 1942, Malta 1942, Mediterranean 1943, Sicily 1943 and South-East Europe 1944.

The parade also provided the occasion for the presentation to the Queen of a diamond and ruby brooch replicating the Squadron's original badge.

Led by their pipes and drums, and carrying the cased Standard, 603 marched on to the lawn and formed up facing the palace. Shortly afterwards, escorted by Air Marshal Sir Dermot A Boyle, the Queen walked from the palace door and was received with a Royal Salute. Her Majesty, attended by the CO, S/L Roy Schofield, then inspected the Squadron.

Following the inspection was the consecration and blessing of the Standard, which had been uncased and laid on piled drums. At the end of the religious ceremony W/C W.G.G. Duncan Smith handed the Standard to Her Majesty, who then made the presentation; the bearer was Flight Lieutenant J.D.A. Henshaw.

In an address following the presentation, The Queen said:

It is, I think very fitting that I should present a Standard to the City of Edinburgh Squadron of the Royal Auxiliary Air Force, of which I am Honorary Air Commodore, here at Holyroodhouse, which is my home in Edinburgh, and which has been so intimately connected with the life of the Scottish capital throughout its history.

The award of the Standard marks an important milestone in the life and traditions of the Squadron which received it. The road which you have travelled to reach this point has indeed been one of valour and distinction, for you played a notable part in the defence of our country in the Battle of Britain, in the heroic defence of Malta, and in seven other campaigns of the Second World War. The price you paid was heavy, for many good companions fell by the way. Their loss is mourned, but their sacrifice is remembered with pride and gratitude.

In committing the Standard to your charge, I am confident that you will be worthy of the trust in peace, and if need be in war, and that in the future you will add further lustre to the good name of your Squadron and the City of Edinburgh.

In his reply, S/L Schofield said:

Your Majesty, all members of the Squadron are deeply conscious of the great honour bestowed upon it by your award of the Standard. We are very proud that Your Majesty has been able to make the presentation in person. The consecration of our Standard today is a symbol of the achievement and sacrifice of former members of the Squadron and I am sure that every officer, NCO and airman serving in the Squadron today, and those who will serve in the future, will uphold the Squadron tradition and will receive inspiration from the standard. I feel sure that the former members of the Squadron must feel proud that their Squadron has been so honoured.

Stepping up on the dais, the Squadron commander continued:

Your Majesty, on behalf of the present and former members of the City of Edinburgh Squadron, I humbly ask you to accept this brooch fashioned in the shape of the original Squadron badge, as a token of our love and gratitude to you, our Sovereign Lady and Honorary Air Commodore.

At the close of the parade S/L Schofield led the Squadron in giving three cheers for Her Majesty. The cost of the brooch had been subscribed to by present and past members of the Squadron.

After the parade, Her Majesty was escorted to the Royal Pavilion by the AOC-in-C Fighter Command, Air Marshal Sir Dermot Boyle, and S/L Schofield. Her Majesty was joined by Lady Boyle, the Lord Provost of Edinburgh and the Lady Provost. Distinguished guests were then presented to Her Majesty by S/L Schofield who later presented the officers of 603 and their wives, a small number of past officers, six serving non-commissioned officers, airmen and their wives and a small number of past non-commissioned officers, airmen and their wives.

A photograph of Her Majesty and the Squadron was taken at the east side of the garden. The standard presentation was extensively reported in the Scottish and national press. Following the ceremony, a luncheon was held in the Adam Rooms of the George Hotel in Edinburgh.

It had been planned that the Vampires would fly to Tangmere on 1 July and take off for Istres (Marseilles) at 07.30 hours on 2 July en route for summer camp in Gibraltar between 2 and 16 July.

603 Squadron summer camp, Gibraltar.

The weather was, however, unfavourable and they left Turnhouse instead at 07.00 hours on 2 July. The aircraft flew in three groups, two of four aircraft and one pair. The latter was intended to pick up any stragglers. The leg to Istres was uneventful and, after lunch and refuelling, the course was set for Gibraltar.

The next day 603 said goodbye to one past member and welcomed another when Wing Commander Archie Winskill DFC (Bar) took over as Station Commander from W/C Duncan Smith DSO, DFC.

On 15 July, 603 Squadron came under the operational control of 13 Group, Fighter Command.

The pilots participated in Exercise Beware, an air defence exercise covering the coastline from Inverness to Plymouth, from 23 September to 2 October. Twenty auxiliary flying squadrons took part and it involved 603 Squadron intercepting high-flying intruders operating between 35-40,000 feet. It became apparent that the Vampire could not reach this operational ceiling, nor could it intercept the 'enemy' targets due to their speed. Consequently, some interceptions only resulted in visual sightings. However, 603 Squadron acquitted themselves well with good performances by both air and ground crews, gaining second place among the interceptions by auxiliary squadrons.

'We were spot on time!' The boss, Pete Anson DFC.

Down From The Sky...

More came Kenneth More star of the Douglas Bader film "Reach for the sky" straight into the cockpit of a 603 Squadron Vampire jet fighter. Smile from the tarmac is from co-star of the film Muriel Pavlow.

Kenneth More, star of the Douglas Bader film *Reach for the Sky*, in the cockpit of a 603 Squadron Vampire jet fighter. A smile from the tarmac from co-star Muriel Pavlow.

1956

Flight Lieutenant Roy Skinner completed his conversion to Hawker Hunters and Flight Lieutenant W.G. Holmes commenced his course. It was decided that auxiliary pilots could also convert to Hunters – the total number of 603 pilots converting to the type was six at this stage.

Flight Sergeant J. 'Dinger' Bell had been awarded the BEM in the New Year's Honours List, which was presented by the AOC 13 Group, Fighter Command Air Vice-Marshal W.G. Cheshire at Turnhouse. The flying programme in March was interrupted to hold drill rehearsals for the ceremony. After the presentation, the AOC met F/Sgt Bell's wife and two daughters who had been proud spectators.

Flying Officers Frank Mycroft and J.D.A. Henshaw commenced their Hawker Hunter conversion course with 43(F) Squadron at Leuchars on 19 March. By the end of the month each had completed about seven hours on Hunters. 603 Squadron was the guinea-pig for conversion of auxiliary pilots to Hunters and it was hoped that more would have the opportunity.

May 1956 saw participation in air defence Exercise Rejuvenate. Phases I and II were on 5 and 6 May. They consisted of scrambles against high level 'enemy' aircraft penetrating the sector from the north west. Sightings and interceptions were very low due to the extreme altitude and speed of the bomber aircraft. The shortcomings of the Vampire in the day-fighter role were again revealed. Each succeeding exercise only served to emphasise the deficiencies of the Vampire to intercept high-altitude targets. A fleeting glimpse was obtained of a Boeing B47 bomber before it opened up and departed hastily southwards. Phase III was on Sunday the 6th. There was too much low and medium cloud to allow full use of the reporting system.

On 12 May, a former adjutant, S/L Mike Hobson AFC, arrived to take over as CO from S/L Roy Schofield. Later, Group Captain Mike Hobson CBE, AFC, recalled his return to Turnhouse as OC 603:

> On returning from my almost two-year tour at Habbaniya [in Iraq], I was granted a couple of weeks' disembarkation leave, with instructions that I was then to present myself at Headquarters 13 Group, Fighter Command at Ouston, to be informed of my posting. Following an interview with the AOC, Air Vice-Marshal Walter G. Cheshire, I assumed command of 603 Squadron on 12 May 1956, and a few weeks later the AOC carried out his annual inspection of the Squadron…
>
> Returning to Edinburgh and to Turnhouse felt very much like coming back home again. Our ex-officio quarter, Aeroville Lodge*, in which we had lived for the odd soot-laden week in 1952, awaited us after being vacated by another Squadron Leader and his wife, since Roy Schofield was a bachelor and had been living in the mess, although shortly afterwards he married Joan who was working for British Airways in the airport building.
>
> We now possessed a car in which there was no longer any sense of adventure, as one could be reasonably certain of arriving at one's destination without any form of mechanical failure, unlike anything that we had owned before. On being posted to Iraq in 1954 I had left the Fiat with Barbara who managed to sell it at a fair price. To give it its due, it never once let us down after the initial problem of coming to a grinding halt surrounded by heavy traffic in Lancaster Gate, and having to have a new engine installed. The proceeds of the sale, plus the money that we had obtained from selling our caravan home when we last left Turnhouse, we had put into a Building Society, and now used this princely sum to buy a second-hand Ford Prefect which Barbara's father had found for us shortly before our return. This was a modern car which actually had a heater in it, though a primitive one by today's standards, for it consisted of an electric element and a fan to spread the warm air around one's feet, with no controls other than 'on' and 'off'. It was the only black car that we have ever had, but there was little choice in those days and the colour seemed to suit its lines; it served us well for two and a half years without ever letting us down. The only minus point was that Ford, at that time, installed windscreen wipers that worked on a vacuum principle from the engine, which meant that whenever the engine was taxed for extra output the wipers stopped working, so if you put your foot down in wet weather to overtake a lorry that was throwing up clouds of spray, you suddenly found that you had lost all forward vision and were flying on instruments! This gave rise to some very interesting situations, as there were few dual carriageways in those days.
>
> The station and the mess** had altered very little, and the Mills were still running the latter as mess manager and caterer. The Station Commander was Wing Commander Archie Winskill, who later became Captain of the Queen's Flight, and visited us several times at Coltishall. He had a delightful French wife, Christianne, and was himself a very smooth individual who was quite a ladies' man. I got on very well with him, as he never interfered with the running of the Squadron although he always seemed to know exactly what was going on. At my initial interview with him on arrival, he spoke to me rather like a Dutch uncle, realising that I had still not quite got used to my extra thin ring, and said something like 'Don't stand any nonsense from older subordinates – remember that you are the

*Sadly demolished shortly after to make way for the new runway of Edinburgh Airport.
**Several years later completely destroyed by fire started by a decorator's blowlamp.

Squadron Commander and what you say goes'. He always supported me fully all along the line and I later had cause to be grateful for this. He also once told me that a very worthwhile hobby was the study of senior officers, and I appreciated this advice and tried to apply it forever afterwards. The Squadron personnel had changed very little, though Flight Lieutenant Bill Moncur had taken over as Flight Commander from Flight Lieutenant Duncan McIntosh who was now running his own airline, Loganair, serving the Western Isles. Duncan's younger brother, Dave, was still on the Squadron, as were most of the pilots who had been members when I had left just two years previously.

The ground crew officers were still the same, and there had been little movement amongst the auxiliary airmen, although there had been quite a few changes amongst the regulars. My regular adjutant was Bill Holmes, who had taken over from me, and my regular training officer was Roy Skinner, who had succeeded Alex Peddell shortly after I had left. We were to come across Roy and Joyce Skinner again at Coltishall, by which time he was in the Air Traffic Control Branch, having had a few medical problems. The hand-over from Roy Schofield to myself was a very brief one, as I probably knew as much about everything to do with the Squadron as he did, so I felt at home straight away.

Being CO of the Squadron, I was, ex-officio, OC flying at Turnhouse. The other service flying units based there were the Edinburgh University Air Squadron (of which I had been a member in 1944/5), flying De Havilland Chipmunks, 666 Air Observation Post Squadron, [Royal Auxiliary Air Force] flying Taylorcraft Austers [with Territorial Army pilots and RAuxAF ground crews], and the Station Communications Flight consisting of an Avro Anson and several Airspeed Oxfords.

The airfield was joint civil/military, with the air traffic control officers also being composed of both civil and military personnel, and the Senior Air Traffic Control Officer (SATCO) (Jock Hunter) being a civilian. There was also a civilian airport manager (Jock Halley), so both Archie Winskill and myself had quite a delicate path to tread at times, requiring a good deal of diplomacy. Fortunately we all got on reasonably well as individuals, and although inevitably we had our differences of opinion from time to time, these were invariably solved amicably, and I do not recall anything ever having to be referred to higher authority. It was convenient that the military flying was at its most intense at weekends, when there were not quite as many civilian movements as during the week. Despite the many different types of aircraft flying in the circuit and in the vicinity of the airfield, both civil and military, there was never a 'near miss' during my time, which speaks volumes for the skill and ability of the air traffic controllers.

An interesting event occurred one evening when I was OC Night Flying and in air traffic control at the beginning of the evening's programme. British European Airways had recently introduced the Vickers Viscount on its London to Edinburgh and London to Glasgow schedules, and one of the daily flights used to land at Turnhouse at 18.30hrs each day. On this particular evening the Viscount pilot had made contact with us and we were expecting him to call that he was over the outer marker*, which he duly did. He then called that he was over the inner marker and was given permission to join the circuit downwind, as the landing direction was opposite to the heading on which he was now approaching the airfield. His next call was 'downwind' and he was cleared onto 'finals', although none us could see his navigation lights. He then called 'finals, three greens'** and was given permission to land whilst we were still straining to see his lights. Just as the controller was about to call him to ask him his position the operations telephone rang and the air traffic controller at Renfrew asked if we were expecting a Viscount by any chance, because if so it had just landed unannounced at his airfield! The only answer to this little mystery that we could think of was that both pilots must have been quite 'switched off' and thought that they were on the London to Glasgow run, and had in fact passed over the Renfrew outer and inner markers,

---

*Outer and inner markers were radio beacons, enabling pilots to be correctly lined-up and at the right height for their approach to an airfield.
**Indicating that all three wheels were down and locked.

and not the Turnhouse ones. The aircraft then took off from Renfrew and flew to Turnhouse, but what the passengers were told we never did discover.

On another occasion Archie Winskill rang my office to say that Roy Falconer, a chum of his, was flying one of the prototype Bristol Britannias in the area and had offered to land at Turnhouse to give him a ride, so if I would like to come along I should make my way to the air terminal building poste haste. This I did just as the Britannia was on 'finals', and having landed it taxied up to the terminal, where the steps were pushed up to the door for Archie and myself to climb in, the door was closed, and off we went. We then spent about thirty minutes on the flight deck, circling around Edinburgh and the Forth before landing back at Turnhouse where we hopped out and the aircraft flew back to Filton. I must therefore have been one of the very first passengers (although a slightly unorthodox one) to fly in a Britannia, little knowing that some seven years later I was to have a very 'hairy' flight in one when we lost engine power on two engines over the China Sea and had to make an emergency landing at Seoul.

On 31st May 1956 *The Times* published the names of those featuring in the Queen's Birthday Honours List, and I was astonished to read that I had been awarded the Air Force Cross. On the same day I received an OHMS telegram from the Commander-in-Chief Middle East Air Force, sending me his congratulations, so I presumed that it must be a fact. It was not until 23rd October, however, that the Queen held the Investiture 'at which your attendance is requested' and, having left Anthony with Barbara's parents in Ipswich, Barbara, my mother and myself proceeded to London to attend the ceremony at Buckingham Palace.

Since one is never told the reason for any award, it is only possible to make one's own assumptions. My name was obviously put forward towards the end of my tour as a Flight Commander on 6 Squadron at Habbaniya, during which time I formed a formation acrobatic team and gave many displays, including one before the Crown Prince of Iraq, and also took a flight of Venoms down the length of Africa through seven different countries, none of which had seen the Venom before, giving formation aerobatic displays in each country, and beating the Cape to Pretoria record by nine minutes on our return flight. A few months later we spent several days at the Nairobi Agricultural Show, giving displays each day, for which the RAF was awarded the Challenge Cup. Otherwise it seemed to me a fairly normal, but highly enjoyable, squadron tour, during which 6 Squadron was awarded the Lloyd Trophy for the best all-round performance in MEAF, and the lmshi Mason Trophy for the highest weapons scores in MEAF.

The 1956 summer camp proved to be 603's last and most memorable. It was again at Gibraltar and held between 30 June and 14 July. Ten Vampires were taken and W/C Winskill flew his own. They left for Tangmere on the evening of Friday 29 June and set out for Gibraltar early next morning.

The flight took three hours 50 minutes via Istres, Marseilles. The ground crews flew out direct in Handley-Page Hastings and arrived well before the Vampires. They had settled in and were ready to remove the drop tanks as soon as the Squadron's aircraft arrived. The air correspondent for *The Scotsman*, Scott Kennedy, a long-standing pre-war supporter of the Squadron, reported 603's activities during the summer camp, including the fact that the 603 Squadron pipe band took part in the 'Retreat' at Casemates Square, Gibraltar, led by Drum Major Beaton.

603 Squadron DH Vampire FBVs over Algeciras Bay, 1956.

Top and bottom: DH FBVs of 603 at Gibraltar, summer camp 1956.

North Front, Gibraltar was a Coastal Command Station and 603 was one of the nine auxiliary squadrons doing their annual continuous training in succession.

The flying training concentrated on air-to-air firing. The white, light canvas drogues were towed by Meteors at the end of some 600 feet of nylon rope. Colour-marked ammunition indicated hits scored by individual pilots. After each practice the shot-up drogue was dropped on the beach (or in the sea!) and picked up by a 'flag party' under Sergeant Miller. There was an effective air-sea rescue service including launches and Shackletons. The ground crews were kept busy refuelling, rearming and changing camera gun magazines to ensure as many sorties as possible in the time available. Mike Hobson later reflected on the camp:

> Three months after I had taken over the Squadron we flew to Gibraltar for the two weeks of our summer camp, the ground-crew and surplus aircrew following on in a Valetta. The last summer camp that I had been on with the Squadron was in 1953 when we had lost our CO, Squadron Leader R.L.R. 'Lloyd' Davies, in a motor accident on the airfield at Sylt.

Royal Gibraltar Yacht Club. Archie Winskill and Mike Hobson relaxing during summer camp.

The runway at Gibraltar had a fascinating characteristic, in that if the wind was blowing from the direction of the Rock (as it frequently did), it divided itself so that it swept round both sides, and then joined up to carry on its journey. This meant that you usually had to land somewhat downwind until half-way along the runway when you were then met with a headwind! Needless to say, this produced some interesting air currents on the approach, and having negotiated the turbulence, you had to touch down as near to the start of the runway as possible to avoid eventually running off into the sea. It is to the credit of all the pilots that we had no incidents on landing, though just short of the beginning of the runway there was a severely damaged Vampire left behind from a previous camp by 602 (City of Glasgow) Squadron who had not been quite so lucky or, as we liked to think, so skilful. The sight of this aircraft every time that one came in to land concentrated the mind wonderfully!

For the period of the RAuxAF summer camps, RAF Gibraltar had appointed a Liaison Officer (Flight Lieutenant Chris Stone) to ensure the smooth running of the organisation, and on the first day he whisked me off in a land rover to the Governor's residence to sign the book. Little did I know that in just over thirty years time I should again be signing that book, but this time as the guest and friend of the Governor Air Chief Marshal Sir Peter Terry. Whilst Peter was Governor he gave permission for the SAS to come onto the Rock when an IRA plot had been uncovered to detonate a bomb alongside the Governor's residence (the 'Convent') during the weekly changing of the guard, when there would have been a large crowd present and Peter himself would have been on the balcony. Three members of the IRA were tailed, and when challenged appeared to be drawing their weapons and so were shot dead. It was a brilliant piece of detective work, skilfully executed, but several years later, in 1990, an IRA assassin shot at Peter as he was reading in his study, leaving him with nine bullets in him, and Betty, his wife, with a badly damaged eye. It was a miracle that he survived, but only nine months later they came to stay with us and he was able to walk short distances with the aid of a stick, and could once more eat properly, as he had lost all his teeth and half of his tongue in the attack. An interesting sideline to their visit was that during their stay we also had as our guests six Special Branch policemen during the day, and two at night, all armed, so we put our caravan in the drive as extra accommodation.

Left: S/L Mike Hobson outside Buckingham Palace on 23 October 1953 after having been awarded the AFC. *Right*: Archie Winskill and Mike Hobson during a fancy dress ball at Turnhouse, 31 October 1956.

Chris Stone also took one or two of us on a tour of the inside of the Rock. This was fascinating, for over the years so many passages and caverns of cathedral-like proportions have been carved out of it that it is remarkable that there is still sufficient rock to enable it to stand up! There was sufficient space for the storage of food and ammunition to last for an almost indefinite siege.

One interesting incident occurred whilst I was flying a Meteor 7 as a tug for the banner during an air-to-air firing exercise which was our main training activity whilst at Gibraltar. This took place several miles off the coast of what was then Spanish Morocco, and consisted of flying a 'race-track' pattern with, usually, two pairs of Vampires coming up to take turns in shooting at the banner (the ammunition was tipped with different colours of non-drying paint so that the holes in the banner could be attributed to the appropriate pilot). On this particular occasion I had just reached the range and was settling down to fly on the correct course at 10,000 feet, when a small black cloud appeared a little to one side, which seemed odd. It was only when a second black cloud suddenly appeared almost immediately in front of me that the penny dropped and I realised that I was being shot at! I immediately instructed the two approaching Vampires to return to base, jettisoned the banner, and dived smartly towards the water and back to the Rock at sea level. Apparently official enquiries were made about the incident, but the Spanish denied all knowledge, so nothing came of it. Which just goes to show that the normally somewhat boring job of towing a banner up and down can have its moments!

Archie Winskill, the Station Commander, announced to me a couple of weeks before the camp that he was taking leave over that period, and would be coming out to Gibraltar with us. He must have seen an expression of mild concern come over my face, for he followed up immediately by saying that he would be taking no part in any of the proceedings, apart from wanting to fly an aircraft there and back, and that it was I who was in charge from beginning to end. He was as good as his word, and did not interfere with us in any way whatsoever during the working day, but took part in many of our social activities in the evening, including visiting with us on many occasions a particular restaurant that produced lobster thermidors that were out of this world – in fact we ate them until they were coming out of our ears! This was all very well, as he was a great chap to have around, but he kept us up until all hours, which was fine for him, as all he did all day long was lie around at the Royal Gibraltar Yacht Club where he covered himself in olive oil and sunbathed, whilst we were starting at 0700 hours each day, flying out to the range, and doing our best to hit the banner through an alcoholic haze from the night before!

The main reason for Archie's wanting to come to Gibraltar was that during the war he had been shot down over France and had made contact with the resistance movement who led him over the Pyrenees and into Spain through which he made his way down to Gibraltar. It was from there that he boarded a ship back to the UK but not before he had visited a tailor who kitted him out with a set of clothes. I think he wanted to see if he could still find the tailor, and when he did they had quite a reunion – there was no sight of Archie that night nor for most of the following day!

On one occasion Archie very nearly led us into trouble. The French Air Force sent us an invitation to spend a night with them at their base in Oran, so one day four of us set off in our Vampires for the coast of North Africa (I flew, as usual., WA 434.) and we were given a very warm reception on our arrival. It had been anticipated that we would be well entertained, as indeed we were, so we had already decided to issue them with a return invitation to Gibraltar, and to pay for the party that we intended giving them. Archie had a brilliant idea. He knew that Scotch whisky commanded a high price in Algeria, so before we set off we visited Saccone Speed, the main agents for spirits and tobacco on the Rock, and bought several crates of Scotch in bond, distributing it amongst our four aircraft and carrying it in our ammunition bays. On landing, we were accommodated in a smart hotel in the centre of Oran, and we asked the manager to store the whisky in his safe until we found a good market for it. At this he almost threw an apoplectic fit and, looking furtively over his shoulder, ushered us quickly into his office, where he rapidly closed the door and spoke in loud conspiratorial whispers. It transpired that the previous week a traveller had been 'rumbled' by the local excise authorities who found six bottles of whisky in his luggage. He was presently languishing in jail awaiting trial at some indeterminate date – hence the panic on the part of the manager. So our Scotch whisky had now become a hot potato to be got rid of as quickly as possible. This worked to the advantage of the manager, who offered us a ridiculously small sum, which by that time we were all too ready to accept, to take the contraband off our hands. Although not making a loss, we certainly made very little profit, if any, and the return visit of the French cost us rather more than it might otherwise have done, but at least none of us went to jail!

Another visitor to our summer camp was Air Commodore M.W.S. 'Mike' Robinson, AOC Scottish Sector. He spent the last few days with us in Gibraltar, having flown over in a Meteor 7 with his adjutant, Flight Lieutenant Pete Mitchell.* Mike Robinson had an artificial eye but flew proficiently nevertheless – we had known him since our last tour with 603, for he was OC Scottish Sector as a group captain for our first year, and when all sector commander posts were upgraded to air commodore he was succeeded by Air Commodore George Lott, another proficient pilot with an artificial eye. As Mike Robinson, on promotion, then took over from George Lott we were able to say that we had had three successive sector commanders with only two eyes between them! George Lott had a slightly disconcerting trick that he would play on unsuspecting young officers in the bar. Whilst drinking his beer with them he would announce that he had to go to the toilet, whereupon he would take out his artificial eye, drop it into his tankard and hand it to the 'victim' saying 'Keep my eye on my beer for me'!

---

*Killed shortly afterwards whilst rehearsing over the airfield for an individual aerobatic display in a Meteor 8.

Over the mid-camp weekend half a dozen of us hired a minibus and drove to Granada. The party included our doctor, Tommy Adamson, Bill Moncur, Bill Holmes, Roy Skinner and Scott Kennedy, the art editor of *The Scotsman*. It was fortunate that we took Tommy with us for Scott was overcome by the heat and was seriously ill for 24 hours. Otherwise the visit was a great success and thoroughly enjoyed by all. We were particularly interested to see the Hotel Sexi on the way to Granada, but did not have the time to check the significance of its name!

603 Squadron had always sported a very good pipe band, and on one of our last evenings on the Rock we combined our pipes and drums with those of the 1st Battalion the Seaforth Highlanders to 'Beat the Retreat' at Casements Square. The salute was taken by Air Commodore Miller, AOC RAF Gibraltar, and turned out to be a most popular event, attracting a great many spectators.

Eventually the day arrived when we had to fly back home, and on 14th July we bade our farewells and took off for Istres, the first of our two staging posts back to Turnhouse. The weather was fine, but at Istres we obtained an 'actual' report for Tangmere, where we had to land to clear customs, and it was obvious that the conditions already bad, were worsening, and I decided to spend the night where we were and try again the following morning. However, the next day the conditions at Tangmere were no better, and I did not wish to run the risk of diverting and possibly having the Squadron spread around various airfields in Northern Europe, so decided that we should stay at Istres another day. This was not a popular decision with two of our number, as they wanted to return to work as soon as possible and were urging me to 'have a go at it'. However, I stood firm, and Archie took me to one side afterwards and said that he agreed 100% with my decision – support that I much appreciated. The decision was perhaps harder for some of our number to accept, as the weather both where we were, at Istres, and in Edinburgh, consisted of brilliant blue skies! Needless to say, the wives, on our return, were also very sceptical about our reasons for spending an extra day on sunny beaches in the South of France!

On 16th July the weather prospects for the south of England were brighter, and we had an uneventful flight to Tangmere and then on to Turnhouse. Roy Skinner was met by his wife Joyce who had spent all day preparing a special surprise meal for him that evening – lobster thermidor!

Auxiliary squadrons have had a unique status within the Royal Air Force and the community. As Mike Hobson so succinctly penned it:

Our social life in Edinburgh was, as ever, full to the brim, with a few more functions now to be attended as CO of the Squadron. Unlike a regular squadron, an auxiliary squadron was an entity in its own right, and was not only a part of the station, but, in our case, a part of the city of Edinburgh as well, which entailed being involved in civic functions as well as service functions, and the city took a real pride in 'their' Squadron.

Mike Hobson goes on to describe how he had an inkling of the impending demise of the flying squadrons of the Royal Auxiliary Air Force:

At the beginning of December 1956 Archie Winskill was posted to the RAF Flying College at Manby, and on my birthday, 1st December, we dined him out in the Turnhouse mess, one of the guests being Sir James Gilchrist, Sheriff of the Lothians and Peebles. At the same time we dined out Flight Lieutenant George Scott, who was being sent by his employers, the British Aluminium Company, from Fort William to Canada. George was by far the most experienced of our pilots, and was certainly the oldest, and we marked the occasion by my handing over to him a handsome silver model of a Vampire on an onyx base.

Archie's successor was, strangely enough, Dickie Haine, who had been my OC Flying at Habbaniya. He and Eve, with their children Charles, Emma and Robert (who was born since we had seen them), had made their way hack from the Middle East by ship, and had been held up en route by the Suez crisis. They arrived back in this country, because of the delay, only shortly before Christmas and wished to spend their disembarkation leave over the Christmas period which, certainly in those days, was unheard of for a Station Commander. When he applied to the AOC, Air Vice-Marshal Cheshire, he was told that he could have the

Auxiliary pilots of 603 at Turnhouse. The order of the day was little different from many years before except it was fast cars and jets not piston engines.

time off only if Squadron Leader Hobson took over the Station for the Christmas period! This was to have unforeseen consequences, for on Christmas Day I made the usual round of serving the airmen's dinner and then visiting the sergeants' mess, but at the latter my drinks were spiked, with the result that I was helped back to our quarter by two of my own NCOs, considerably the worse for wear, and was just able to clamber up the stairs and retire to bed for a few hours. It was most unfortunate that Barbara's parents were spending Christmas with us and all the family had been waiting for my return before starting our Christmas dinner! This, I am afraid, was one of the hazards of the job, but is an incident best forgotten.

There had been determined moves afoot to disband the RAuxAF flying squadrons in March 1956, but because of the Suez crisis, followed by the resignation of the Prime Minister, Sir Anthony Eden, a banding together of prominent figures was able to prevent this from being carried out. However, towards the end of the year the subject was again very much on the agenda, and this time firm steps were taken by the Government to ensure that their decision was not thwarted once more. The reasoning behind the call for disbandment was that Vampires and Meteors had become outdated as the regular squadrons had all been re-equipped with Hunters, Swifts and Sabres, and there was not the money available to re-equip the auxiliaries with similar aircraft. The theory was also put forward that the technique of flying swept-wing aircraft required an advanced degree of skill that could only come about by constantly applied effort, and that therefore it was not possible to form operational squadrons from pilots who flew only at weekends. Many of us disputed this, and indeed two of my pilots, one of whom was Frank Mycroft, attended a short conversion

Brothers Dave and Duncan McIntosh. Turnhouse, mobile air traffic control wagon.

Top: DH FBV Vampire in hangar at Turnhouse.
Bottom: RAF Leuchars. Ground crew refuelling.

course onto Hunters at RAF Leuchars, and thereafter flew these aircraft each weekend with, as far as I could tell, a fair degree of proficiency.

The die, however, was cast, and at the beginning of February it was formally announced that the twenty squadrons of the Royal Auxiliary Air Force would be disbanded on 10 March 1957, and that there was to be no flying from the date of the announcement. This condition was imposed to prevent any last minute feats of bravado by the auxiliaries, and was well founded, for one of the pilots on 501 Squadron managed to start up a Vampire on his own and took off to perform sonic stunt flying along the Avon Gorge. He had not had time to strap himself in and lost control of the aircraft, flying into the side of the gorge. A foolish act that marred the otherwise smooth, though sad, disbandment of the squadrons.

There was a great deal to be done, from the service, social and personal aspects, in the few weeks that remained from the issuing of the irreversible order by the Air Ministry, and it was also obvious that the regular element of the Squadron would need to stay on for at least a week or so afterwards to tie up the various loose ends. It was also relevant that Barbara was carrying our second child, due to be born on 22nd March, just twelve days after the official date of disbandment!

During September, the Squadron participated in air defence Exercise Stronghold in which the Vampires were to intercept incoming 'hostile' bomber aircraft. The exercise was marred by fog.

Turnhouse during an exercise. DH FBV Vampire in the process of being rearmed.

CHAPTER 20

DISBANDMENT

1957

On 6 January the Squadron heard the news which had long been dreaded; the notice of the imminent disbandment of the flying squadrons of the Royal Auxiliary Air Force. The only saving grace was that the early warning gave 603 Squadron time for a final flypast over Edinburgh. Seven Vampires and one Meteor flew in formation over the capital for the last time.

S/L Hobson went up to the Air Ministry on 10 January for a conference of COs of all units to be disbanded. The conference was to be addressed by the Secretary of State for Air, but due to a parliamentary reshuffle this was not possible. Instead the Chief of the Air Staff explained the decision. All flying was to cease forthwith and the Squadron was given until 10 March to complete disbandment. The Air Ministry then issued the following notice (Air Ministry Notice 15/1/57 No.23):

> The Air Ministry confirmed that it has been decided that most units of the Royal Auxiliary Air Force are to be disbanded. The units affected are the 20 fighter squadrons, the air observation post and regiment squadrons and nine of the 30 fighter control and radar reporting units.
>
> All flying and other training in these units ceased last weekend but, allowing for the necessary administrative work, the effective date for disbandment will be 10 March. In view of the magnificent war record of the auxiliary fighter squadrons, which fully justified the hopes of those responsible for the formation of the Auxiliary Air Force, this decision has been taken with the greatest possible regret.
>
> It was in fact decided approximately two years ago that it would not be possible to re-equip the auxiliary fighter squadrons with Hunter aircraft, and it was then announced, that, subject to review from time to time, the squadrons would assume with their Meteors and Vampires the operational role of supplementing our defence against forms of air attack other than the high altitude nuclear threat. Technical development is continually reinforcing the view that the main threat to this country is from high altitude attack; other forms of attack which might be countered by less advanced types of aircraft are in consequence less likely to materialise.
>
> It was hoped at one time that it might be possible to train selected auxiliary pilots on Hunters and so provide a reserve of individual pilots for regular squadrons. It has not however, been possible to implement this scheme owing to the need to give priority to the training of regular pilots; and the supply of trained pilots of the Royal Auxiliary Air Force is likely to be limited in future by restrictions which it has been necessary to impose on the number of national service entrants for pilot training.
>
> Finally, with the growing cost of equipment it has become clear that the auxiliary fighter squadrons could not be retained, even with their present aircraft, except at the expense of the regular units which must be regarded as of higher priority.
>
> The decision to disband the air observation post and regiment squadrons has been taken on similar grounds. These units might be of value in a prolonged global war, but there are other requirements to which it is necessary to give higher priority.
>
> The fighter control and radar reporting units provide reserves for the control and reporting system, which is a vital element in the defence organisation of the country. Recent and prospective changes in the organisations and equipment of the system now make it possible

to reduce the number of these units, and 9 units have been selected, on geographical grounds, for disbanding.

A message of thanks is being sent to all members of the units which are being disbanded. Members of these units are also being given particulars of openings in other units, such as the FCUs and RRUs which will remain in being, and the reserve flights supporting operational and other units of the Royal Air Force, in which they could continue to give voluntary service.*

AIR MINISTRY

This was accompanied by a flurry of press reporting principally in *The Scotsman* and *Edinburgh Evening News*.

In 1954, Fighter Command were about to re-equip the regular fighter squadrons with the Hawker Hunter F. Mk I, an aircraft which was very advanced for its time, and as a consequence, the future of the RAuxAF flying squadrons and their associated ground support units now had to be seriously reviewed. On economic considerations alone, the provision of 20 squadrons of Hunters or Gloster Javelins would be prohibitive. In addition, major improvements to airfields and the control organisation would be required. Air Ministry plans called for these new aircraft to carry guided weapons. Expensive to provide and certainly to train with, the new sophisticated aircraft would also require well trained specialist maintenance personnel. The Duncan Sands Defence White Paper of 1956 announced the disbandment of the RAuxAF flying squadrons and the major part of their auxiliary ground support units.

Auxiliary officers had to complete their reserve commitment. They had three courses open to them. They could transfer to the RAuxAF Reserve General List or to the RAuxAF Reserve of Officers (RAuxAFRO). Alternatively they could join a fighter control unit (FCU).

In the case of 603, one chose to go to 3603 FCU, three transferred to the RAuxAF General List and 16 to the RAuxAFRO – a total of 20.

Auxiliary NCOs and airmen had five options; to transfer to a FCU, the RAuxAF Reserve, the RAFVR, enlist in the Territorial Army (TA) or apply for discharge. In the final outcome, 47 transferred to 3603 FCU, one transferred to the RAuxAFRO and 57 applied for discharge.

Meanwhile on Sunday 17 February 603 held its last parade. It formed up in George Street, Edinburgh, under the command of S/L Mike Hobson AFC. The parade adjutant was F/L W.G. Holmes. F/L W.K. Moncur commanded 1 Flight and F/L D.M. Anderson commanded 2 Flight. The Standard Bearer was F/O J.D.A. Henshaw.

Led by its pipe band, the men marched past the Lord Provost of Edinburgh, Sir John Banks, who took the salute on the Mound as they moved to the High Kirk of Edinburgh, St Giles Cathedral.

The service was conducted by Dr H.C. Whitley and the sermon was preached by Rev. Dr A. McHardy CB, CBE, MC. Lessons were read by the Earl of Selkirk and the CO. The Standard was then received by the Dean of the Thistle and Garter, Dr Charles Warr KG.

The prayer for commemoration was read by the Principal Presbyterian Chaplain to the RAF, Reverend T. Madoc-Jones OBE, BA, QHC. (The Rev Madoc-Jones had dedicated the Standard when it was presented by the HAC, Her Majesty The Queen, in June 1955.)**

The Standard bearer's belt was to be kept in the then Edinburgh Castle Museum. The service was attended by past members of 603 and by next of kin of many deceased members.

The men were marched off by the senior auxiliary officer, F/L Bill Moncur and dismissed in Chambers Street. A plaque commemorating the laying up of the Standard is displayed in the High Kirk, St Giles' Cathedral, Edinburgh. The inscription reads:

> Queen's Standard of 603 (City of Edinburgh) Squadron, Royal Auxiliary Air Force
>
> presented by Her Majesty Queen Elizabeth II Honorary Air Commodore of 603 Squadron at the Palace of Holyroodhouse on 30th June 1955, and laid up in St Giles' Cathedral on 17th February 1957 on the disbandment of the Auxiliary Air Force Fighter Squadrons.

---

*Air Ministry Communiqué No.23 dated 15.1.57. The future of the Royal Auxiliary Air Force.
**The Form and Order of Service and Ceremony for the Laying Up of the Queen's Standard, 603 (City of Edinburgh) Squadron, Royal Auxiliary Air Force, The High Kirk of Edinburgh, St Giles Cathedral, Sunday 17 February 1957.

The last parade, 17 February 1957, Edinburgh. The Lord Provost of Edinburgh, Sir John Banks, takes the salute (top).

Top: Outside St Giles Cathedral. Bill Holmes, Bill Moncur, Andy Anderson, Roy Skinner, Wilkie Hossack, Pete McWilliam, Dane Smith, Keith Cruikshank, George Ballingall, Andy Hutchinson, Norman Alexander, Rodyer Henshaw, Mike Hobson, Pete Spinney, Harry Glover and Brian Clapp.

Left: Laying up of Squadron standard, 17 February 1957, St Giles Cathedral. Standard Bearer F/O J. D. A. Henshaw.

Two days later the 603 aircraft were ferried out to the maintenance units at St Athan and Kirkbride.

Later, G/C Mike Hobson CBE, AFC, recalled the laying-up ceremony and other events relating to the disbandment:

One of the first official matters to be dealt with before our disbandment was the laying-up of the Squadron Standard. The Air Ministry had decreed that all the Auxiliary Squadron Standards should be laid up in the Royal Air Force Church of St Clement Danes, possibly at a joint service. This seemed to me to be highly inappropriate – 603 was the City of Edinburgh Squadron and was held in the greatest affection by the city with whom it had had the closest of links since its formation in 1925. To me the only appropriate resting place for the Squadron Standard was in the city itself, in St Giles Cathedral.

There was then a hectic period of planning and organisation for a final parade through the city, ending up at the cathedral for the laying-up ceremony, and the date was fixed for Sunday, 17th February 1957, with the service starting at 1100 hrs.

The day, when it eventually dawned. was a sad but very memorable one, and I can do little better than to quote from *The Scotsman* of Monday, 18th February:

The long and illustrious history of 603 Squadron of the Royal Auxiliary Air Force is being closed in accordance with the directives of the Air Ministry, and yesterday, at St Giles Cathedral, one of the final acts of disbandment was carried through when the Queen's Standard of the Squadron was given up for safe keeping.

Many hundreds of spectators had lined the route of the procession from Charlotte Square to St Giles Cathedral to see the officers and men of the Squadron on parade in public for the last time.

After marching down George Street and into Princes Street, headed by their pipers and drummers, the salute was taken by Lord Provost Sir John G. Banks from the steps of the Royal Scottish Academy.

The parade was under the command of Squadron Leader M.E. Hobson, who later read the New Testament lesson in St Giles Cathedral.

All were eventually seated and then, its golden eagle glittering in the light, the Queen's Standard of 603 (City of Edinburgh) Squadron of the Royal Auxiliary Air Force was carried slowly up the aisle of St Giles Cathedral, borne by Flying Officer Doug Henshaw past the congregation who stood singing to Holst's inspiring music the hymn 'I vow to thee my country.'

These moments in which the Standard was given into the safe keeping of the cathedral were the last public ceremonials of the Edinburgh Squadron and symbolic of the disbandment of the Royal Auxiliary Air Force throughout Great Britain.

From the West Door the Standard bearer and his guard of three marched in slow time through the nave, the light blue silken banner swaying its folds to display at a glimpse the eight selected battle honours and the crest of the Squadron.

At the Chancel Gates the Commanding Officer, Squadron Leader M.E. Hobson CBE AFC, received the Standard from its Bearer and presented it to the dean of the Thistle and of the Chapel Royal, the Very Rev Dr Charles L. Warr, with the words 'With humble gratitude to Almighty God for His many and great mercies, I present this Standard to St Giles Cathedral, and I ask that in honour of the Royal Auxiliary Air Force it may be received and accepted and given safe custody here'. Accepting it, Dr Warr replied 'We receive this Standard into the safe keeping of God's House. May all who look upon it in days to come, find in it a sign and symbol of God's presence with them in all dangers and distresses, and have increase of faith and hope in Him who is King of kings and Lord of lords'.

Then, while the cathedral rang with the singing of 'Who would true valour seek …', the clergy and the commanding officer walked in procession through the Chancel to the Holy Table. Dr Warr took the Standard, raised it erect before the great cross upon the east wall and laid it upon the table.

The service was attended by the Lord Provost, Sir John G Banks and Lady Banks, by Air Vice-Marshal W.G. Cheshire, AOC 13 Group RAF, by the Duke of Hamilton, the Earl of

603 pipe band during a formal dinner at the Grosvenor Hotel, London. The piper is being thanked on behalf of those present and shares a dram, as is the tradition, with G/C J. M. Birkin CB, DSO, OBE, DFC, AE, ADC – Inspector RAauAF.

Selkirk, First Lord of the Admiralty, and by Air Commodore M.W.S. Robinson, Commanding Officer of Caledonian Sector RAF. There were also representatives of the sister fighting services.

The sermon was delivered by the Rev Dr Archibald McHardy, a former RAF padre and a minister strongly connected with the Edinburgh squadron, and the service was conducted by the Rev H.C. Whitley. The service closed with a fanfare sounded by the silver trumpets of the Central Band of the Royal Air Force and the singing of the National Anthem.

Other Closing Events
On Friday 1 March, we held our farewell ball in our Town Headquarters at Learmonth Terrace. It was a thoroughly enjoyable affair, despite the sadness of the occasion. We invited many guests who had been friends of the Squadron over the years, and there had been no greater friend than 'Scott' Scott Kennedy, the art editor of *The Scotsman*, who attended with his wife Ann. The ball was held exactly three weeks before the anticipated (and actual) arrival of our second child, and Barbara very gallantly attended, looking radiant and her usual sparkling self.

It was thought that we should have some fitting memorial to the Squadron, and as some surplus Spitfires were being offered as gate sentinels, I applied for one of these, only to be told that they had all been allocated. However, after much negotiation I managed to secure one from a maintenance unit, and we decked it out in the Squadron's authentic colours and markings for 1940. It was intended as a memorial to all those members of 603 Squadron who lost their lives before, during and after the Second World War, and as such we needed a plaque of some sort to place in front of it. This was obviously going to be costly, but the father of two of our pilots, Doug and Roger Henshaw, very generously offered to provide this by having it cast at his factory in Edinburgh. After much deliberation over the wording, we finally settled on 'This Spitfire is a memorial to the valour of those members of the Squadron who gave their lives in the service of their country', and added, in smaller letters at the bottom, Churchill's immortal words 'Never in the field of human conquest was so much owed by so many to so few'. This plaque was mounted on a large piece of red granite, the money for which we obtained from the 603 Squadron Association, and a dedication ceremony took place on 9 March. Attending the ceremony were Bailie D.M. Weatherstone, representing the Lord Provost, and Wing Commander Dickie Haine, the station commander. The unveiling was performed by Group Captain George Denholm, CO from September 1940 to April 1941, with his own words 'A gay and happy brotherhood: they set us a shining example of high courage and unselfish loyalty to their Sovereign and their Country. We hold them in the highest honour, and in gratitude we salute them.' It is interesting to remember that in those days one could use the word 'gay' in its true and honest meaning – what a tragedy it is that such a delightful word has been hijacked. The memorial was moved to the entrance to the civil airport in the late 1990s.

Although hardly 'events', two incidents took place on the last day before disbandment. One was that the pennant of the General Officer Commanding Scotland mysteriously disappeared from the masthead at his army headquarters, and was replaced by a Royal Air Force Ensign. The second was that the British European Airways Viscount which left Turnhouse on the morning flight to London bore on each side of its gleaming fuselage transfers of the crest of 603 Squadron, with its defiant motto 'Gin Ye Daur'. Written apologies were sent to each of the offended parties.

Final Squadron Event
It was an evening never to be forgotten for a variety of reasons.

Vampires over the officers' mess, Turnhouse 1957, marking the disbandment by a final flypast.

The evening of 9 March 1957, the eve of the official disbandment date, saw the last social event of the Squadron's official lifetime. It was a dinner in the mess at Turnhouse. As recorded in the ORB:

The final function of all was held on March 9th, when a farewell dinner took place in the officers' mess, which was attended by all present officers, plus a very good showing of past members of the Squadron, which included Gp Capt G.L. Denholm DFC, Gp Capt G.K. Gilroy DSO DFC, Wg Cdr W.A. Douglas DFC, Wg Cdr I.S. Ritchie and most of the post-war officers who have since left the Squadron. A toast to 603 Squadron, proposed by the Sector Commander, Air Commodore M.W.S. Robinson CBE, was replied to by the senior Auxiliary officer, Flight Lieutenant W.K. Moncur. The regular officers were then toasted by Squadron Leader T.L. Adamson and Squadron Leader M.E. Hobson AFC replied. The oldest bachelor, Flight Lieutenant D.M. Anderson, then proposed the Squadron Ladies, and a reply on their behalf was given by Flight Lieutenant R.M.B. Cairns DFC, the oldest married officer. Gp Capt Denholm DFC spoke on behalf of past members and finally the Commanding Officer presented an inscribed tankard to the Station PMC, Squadron Leader D. Gray AFC, in recognition of his help and co-operation in all the Squadron functions held in his mess. On retiring to the anteroom, the welcome sight of full pint tankards, one for each member of the

Top: Briefing prior to final flypast, FBV Vampire pilots of 603.
Bottom: Kitting up prior to ceremonial flypast.

Top: S/L Mike Hobson in front of the original 603 crest given in 1925 on its formation as a bomber squadron. At the farewell ball held at RAF Turnhouse on 1 March 1957. Others in photograph: F/O J. Doug Henshaw and F/L W.K. Bill Moncur. Crest is situated over the fireplace in the officers' mess.

Above: Alex Peddell, his sister Lilian Hobson and Barbara Hobson, at the farewell ball. Alex, an outstanding training officer, died 15 October 1999 aged 77.

Right: Barbara and G/C Ted Colbeck-Welch. The pre-war regular adjutant of 603 was married in Edinburgh, holding the reception in the mess at Turnhouse. He later became O/C RAF Horsham St Faith.

Squadron, and each suitably inscribed, was beheld, and these were emptied without delay. A special note should be made of the doctor's tankard: the names and dates of all the Squadron babies that he has brought into the world were inscribed, totalling 14, with space left for another arrival at the end of this month. The gloom of the occasion was well veiled by the wonderful spirit that pervaded the evening, and the party did not disperse until dawn had broken, and the Squadron had made its mark in a blaze of glory. It is thought that a firework initiated said blaze, and the consequent destruction of an already condemned hut.

Later, Mike Hobson recounted the disbandment and eventual farewell dinner:

The dinner itself was excellent and, despite the finality of the occasion, spirits were high throughout the evening. The speeches, which lasted some time, were all apt and amusing, and delivered with a good sense of humour. The toast to the Squadron was proposed by Air Commodore Mike Robinson, AOC Scottish Sector, and the reply was given by our flight commander, Flight Lieutenant Bill Moncur. Squadron Leader Tommy Adamson, our Squadron MO, then toasted the regular officers, in a very witty speech to which I replied. The final toast of the evening was to the Squadron Ladies, given by Flight Lieutenant 'Andy' Anderson, our auxiliary engineering officer, and the reply was made by our auxiliary adjutant, Flight Lieutenant Bob Cairns. It is sad to recall that by 1996, of those six speakers I was the only one remaining.

After the Dinner we retired to the bar as usual, and the evening became progressively jolly. We decorated the bar ceiling with sooty impressions of our hand and footprints (the latter with some difficulty, and not without some hilarity), and then, inevitably, fireworks were produced and let off. Next to the mess main building was a wooden construction that was used for extra accommodation, and it was also where our barman, Archie, slept when it was too late for him to go home. A few weeks previously several of us had been in the bar when the PMC (Squadron Leader Don Gray) had been gazing out of the window, bemoaning the fact that this wooden hut spoiled the view from the bar, and expressing the hope that one of these days it might burn down. Nobody quite knows whether this chance remark had anything to do with subsequent events that evening, but very soon fireworks were being let off inside the hut. At this point I took the cowardly decision that it was time for me to retire to bed and leave the auxiliaries to enjoy the rest of their final evening.

Wing Commander Dickie Haine, our station commander, had been unable to be with us at our dinner as he had had to attend a civic function in Edinburgh, and he returned when he thought that it was too late to join us all, so went straight to bed. It was just before 5 o'clock in the morning that Eve, his wife, nudged him, asking what was the strange red light in the sky. Leaping out of bed, he realised that it was a fire in the direction of the mess so threw on his clothes and dashed across to where he found the wooden hut well and truly alight. The first that I knew of it was when the telephone rang by my bed and I heard Bill Holmes, my adjutant, telling me that the station commander required my presence at the mess immediately, and that he (Bill) had already summoned the fire brigade, as there appeared to be 'a bit of a conflagration'. I dressed as quickly as I could and hastened over to the scene of action, where quite a lot had been happening. Bill Holmes and Roy Skinner, the training officer, had found the handle that operated the nearby fire hydrant, which was a T-shaped pipe standing about three feet high. They then removed the fire hose from the wall of the squash court and screwed it onto one of the arms of the T-piece, and as one of them held and directed the hose in true fireman-like manner, the other turned the stop-cock with the handle and released the flow of water. Not much water came out of the hose, but a great deal came out of the other end of the T-piece which they had omitted to blank off. This might not have been too disastrous had it not been for the fact that Dickie Haine had reached the scene at that very moment, and was directly in-line with the unstopped part of the T-piece, thus receiving the main force of the water, and it was from that point that he began to lose his sense of humour. By now the whole of the station fire-fighting section was on the scene, as well as fire engines from two stations in Edinburgh, and the fire was eventually controlled and then doused sufficiently to be left. Before going back to bed, Dickie Haine informed me that the entire Squadron was under open arrest, and was to assemble in the mess at 1100 hrs that morning in No.1 uniform.

The happenings of the next few minutes we heard about later from Eve Haine. Apparently Dickie squelched his way back to his quarter to discover that he had omitted to take his keys with him, and was unable to wake Eve who had gone back to sleep. He then had to break in through a kitchen window, and it is not known what he said about the incident.

The next morning we all assembled as ordered, and were kept waiting for about an hour before Dickie Haine arrived, looking very formal, but a little more composed than when we had last seen him. He told us that he had been talking to Group Headquarters and that there was to be a Formal Inquiry, so we were all to hold ourselves ready to give evidence as and when required over the next week. We were then dismissed. As a result of the ensuing inquiry I eventually found myself once more dressed in my No.1 uniform as I stood on the now familiar mat in front of Air Vice-Marshal Cheshire's desk at 13 Group Headquarters at RAF Ouston. This time I was not offered a seat, but somehow the AOC did not seem quite as austere as he had appeared at our first meeting, although that did not prevent him from giving me a mild (unofficial) reprimand, and 'inviting' everybody present in the mess that evening to make a token contribution towards the cost of the fire. In retrospect it was well worth it.

A Deed of Trust was drawn up and a board of trustees formed to look after the Squadron silver. This consisted of S/L D.L. Adamson, F/Ls W. K. Moncur, D. M. Anderson, G/C Denholm and W/C I.S. Ritchie. Some silver was lent to Turnhouse. Most of the rest was loaned to the Ministry of Works for display in the RAF Room in Edinburgh Castle Museum on condition that should the Squadron ever be reformed, the silver would be handed back to it. (As was the case on 1 October 1999.)

With regard to the pipe band, the pipes, drums and uniforms were all transferred to 3603 (City of Edinburgh) FCU. All the band members also transferred, enabling 3603 to have a full pipe band.

On Saturday 9 March the camouflaged Spitfire XVIE gate guardian in the gardens at RAF Turnhouse was dedicated as a memorial to the men of 603 who died in the service of their country, both in peacetime and in war.

G/C George Denholm DFC, AE, unveiled the bronze plaque, set upon a red granite block, which stands before the aircraft. He said:

A gay and happy brotherhood, they set us a shining example of high courage and unselfish loyalty to their Sovereign and their Country. We hold them in the highest honour and in gratitude we salute them.

Representing the City of Edinburgh, Baillie D.M. Weatherstone paid tribute to those commemorated and said:

The behaviour and the history of the early years of this famous Squadron reflected the high character and ideals inseparable from the volunteer spirit. The early years not only built up that glorious camaraderie and spirit of adventure which was to stand the country in such good stead during the years of war, but the years were well used.

All ranks attained a mechanical and operational efficiency which was so terribly necessary when this country was on the brink of disaster. In 1939 the situation demanded that the spirit of adventure be replaced by a cold, calculated determination that nothing should come between us and victory. Every citizen of Edinburgh is aware of the outstanding part played by 603.

Today is the last opportunity for the citizens of Edinburgh to give thanks to you all, and for you all, and on their behalf I do so with all my heart.

The ceremony of dedication was conducted by the Rev Dr A. McHardy and in attendance were Mike Hobson and Dickie Haine. Other officers and men of the Squadron with their families, and the next of kin of many remembered in the dedication, were gathered around the Spitfire for the occasion.

Scott Kennedy wrote an article in which he recalled his long and happy association with Edinburgh's auxiliary squadron.

Mike Hobson now learned that he was to become CO of 92(F) Squadron at Middleton St George at the end of March.

An all ranks' squadron dance had been held on 8 March at the drill hall, Gilmore Place, Edinburgh. This was a great success, bearing in mind the sad occasion.

The Operations Record Book for 11 March 1957 was finally completed:

At midnight on 10/11 March, the Squadron officially ceased to exist, and its health and the continuance of its spirit was drunk to in a very sober sense of sorrow. It is a very sad pen that writes these last words on the last Form 540 of the City of Edinburgh Squadron. One day the unit will rise again in a modified role to undertake once more its share in part-time voluntary defence of this country and these documents will be reclaimed from the Air Ministry archives. To the fortunate band of re-formers and present – now past-members of 603 – good luck and Gin ye Daur.

On 15 March 1957, the Court Circular announced 'Squadron Leader M.E. Hobson AFC, Officer Commanding 603 (City of Edinburgh) Squadron, Royal Auxiliary Air Force, had the honour of being received by Her Majesty'. Mike Hobson later recalled the honour of being invited to Buckingham Palace by the HAC:

Her Majesty the Queen had been the Squadron's Honorary Air Commodore since the days when she had been Her Royal Highness Princess Elizabeth, at the start of my first tour on the Squadron. It was therefore with a great sense of honour that I received (by telephone!) a command to an audition with her on 15 March 1957 at Buckingham Palace. This was a day to remember, for I was ushered into her private apartment and we talked, just the two of us, for 25 minutes. Although she had obviously been well briefed beforehand, she showed a genuine interest in the Squadron, and a great deal of knowledge about the Royal Auxiliary Air Force in general. I was wondering how I would know when it was time to go, but somehow it all occurred quite naturally as we both stood up together and I shook her hand, bowed, and made my exit.

The following day, on 16 March, Her Majesty and Prince Philip held a reception at Buckingham Palace to which all squadron commanders and flight commanders of the disbanding Royal Auxiliary Air Force were invited, so I again visited the Palace, this time with Flight Lieutenant Bill Moncur. Although it was to mark a sad occasion, the reception itself was reasonably informal and relaxed, with both Her Majesty and Prince Philip speaking to all of us, either individually or in small groups. On arrival at the Palace we queued to shake hands with both of them as we were introduced, and as I shook hands with the Queen she turned to Prince Philip and said 'This is my CO', which I thought was rather a nice way of putting it!

As each of the officers left the Palace, they was handed the following letter:

BUCKINGHAM PALACE

I have welcomed this opportunity of taking leave of the Commanding Officers and senior Auxiliary officers of the squadrons of the Royal Auxiliary Air Force which are being disbanded and of sending through them this message of appreciation and thanks to all their officers, airmen and airwomen.

The history of the Auxiliary Air Force has been a glorious one. The first Auxiliary squadrons were included in the Air Defence of Great Britain in 1925. By the outbreak of war in 1939 the Auxiliary fighter, coastal and balloon squadrons formed an integral and vital part of our forces. It was aircraft of these squadrons which shot down the first enemy bomber over this country; and Auxiliary squadrons were heavily engaged in the air over Dunkirk and throughout the Battle of Britain. Later they were to win battle honours over the Atlantic, in Malta, North Africa, Sicily and Italy, the Arakan and Burma, and in Normandy, France and Germany.

After the war the fighter squadrons were reconstituted as the Royal Auxiliary Air Force and the traditional spirit of voluntary service found new outlets with the formation of Regiment, Air OP, Fighter Control and Radar Reporting Units, some of which are to remain in being and provide further opportunities for voluntary service.

The association of the Force with my family has always been close. I was proud to become Honorary Air Commodore of Nos. 603, 2063 and 3603 (City of Edinburgh) Squadrons in 1951 and to succeed my father as Honorary Air Commodore-in-Chief of the

Royal Auxiliary Air Force in 1952. Members of my family have always treasured their association with Auxiliary squadrons as Honorary Air Commodores.

I wish as Air Commodore-in-Chief to thank officers, airmen and airwomen of the Royal Auxiliary Air Force for all that they have given to the service of the country by their enthusiasm, their spirit and their devotion to duty in peace and war. It is a sad day when it is necessary to tell so many that it is no longer possible to use their services on the duties they have assumed so willingly. I wish them to know that they can look back with pride and satisfaction to service well done.

16 March, 1957   Elizabeth R

W/C Jack Meadows DFC, AE, summed up his service with both 603 and 600 Squadrons:

Auxiliaries drew from their local association the immense advantage of continuity. The typical regular spent two or three years with a squadron before moving on. Auxiliaries spent, at least in peace, whole careers in one unit associated with a home base, which concentrated unit loyalty. Although after a year or so of war most surviving aircrews and many experienced ground crew had moved on to rest and promotion elsewhere, enough ground crew stayed with their squadron almost the length of the war to retain that special spirit. When night fighting with 604 (County of Middlesex) Squadron in 1943/4 I found just that little extra resulting unit pride. A Canadian who served about the same time with 502 (Ulster) Squadron has said the same. An incidental result in 604 was a commission from the ex-Cranwell CO to spend my spare time writing a squadron history so that everyone else should understand.

After all those years it is perhaps surprising that first personal recollections of the AAF (later to become Royal) are of ceremonies. 603 (City of Edinburgh) Squadron marched up Princes Street behind pipes and drums, provided a guard of honour at St Giles Cathedral for Princess Elizabeth (later its Honorary Air Commodore). Sir William Y. Darling was still HAC, wearing brown shoes with air force uniform.

For King George VI's funeral procession, the RAuxAF contingent came from my 600 Squadron and 603 – we had to take three days off from our civilian jobs. There was an attempt, lest we let the side down, to hide us among the specially trained regulars. Territorial and unit loyalty prevailed and we were anyone's equal as our own independent unit, slow marching with arms reversed, led the procession from The Mall to Paddington station.

The ceremonial and socialising did not interfere with our main object in life. We belonged to Fighter Command, were part of the front line defence of the country, flew the same aircraft as regular squadrons, vied with them, at times beat them at their own game.

On reformation in 1946, there was the advantage of experienced war-time pilots and ground staff. As these began to fade out we managed to train new intakes (some from university air squadrons, some ex-National Service) to just as expert a level.

Special tribute must be paid to auxiliary ground staff who, like pilots, earned their living 5 days a week elsewhere. For pilots to spend most weekends, plus an evening or two each week at Town HQ was well rewarded by unlimited flying on front-line aircraft and resultant camaraderie. Although ground crew also knew the camaraderie, it was rather different spending the same time slaving in cold hangars or open hard standings servicing, repairing, or pushing papers in offices. It was largely the unit spirit, loyalty spurred on now and again by pride in occasional public pomp and ceremony, that kept them at it.

Also to be remembered are the regular cadres. Under an adjutant, a training officer (flying instructor) and an engineer officer were about 20 men, mainly technician instructors. Their devotion to the squadron became strong. All, particularly adjutants, were carefully selected. Not only did the station commander often expect from them regular hours on the airfield, they also had to be with us at weekends and at THQ on some week-day evenings. In compensation came good career opportunities through a broadening of views and by becoming known to many more senior officers than did the ordinary regular.

We were tested each year in the annual air exercises. In 1946 *The Scotsman* reported F/Lt Meadows' flight of Spitfires destroying an 'enemy force attacking the Forth bridge. Also stealing the publicity, down south we had much more competing presence from regular squadrons. Over the year we flew as many hours per pilot, per squadron, as regular units.

This was highlighted in 1951. The Government was under pressure to support the US in its Korean war. Uniquely, unlike the Territorial Army or RAFVR which required a parliamentary vote before they could be mobilised, the AAF/RAuxAF was always part of the front line of defence and needed only the Secretary of State's order to come to full time readiness. So, in addition to sending the Gloucesters and an RA battery and some ships to Korea, and recalling some reservists, the Government made the easy gesture of embodying the RAuxAF for six months. Despite a spell at armament practice camp, in that year as a whole we did less flying than in a 'normal auxiliary' year.

The reason was simple. In that six months we worked to regular hours and rules, in five days a week flew no more hours than a normal auxiliary flat-out weekend. Then there was no 'summer camp', the annual two weeks detachment – traditionally to a station near a coastal resort, later to a German base, eventually to Malta – where two weeks intensive flying, starting at dawn, could alone total almost 1,000 hours and still leave time for afternoon, weekend and evening play.

We continued to do things in our own way when doing so did not conflict with important practice or policy. At our Town Headquarters we, like the other squadrons, regularly had formal dining nights, our guests ranging from senior officers to civic or industrial powers, peers and laity. The gospel was well preached. It was possible for a squadron CO, often with the 'demi-official' letter, to approach all sorts of senior people on all sorts of subjects.

Whatever the outcome, anyone ever connected with Boom Trenchard's bright idea of an Auxiliary Air Force of flying squadrons has cause for proud memories of something that really was quite unique.

Group Captain J.M. Birkin CB, DSO, OBE, DFC, AFC, Inspector, RAuxAF, 1952-1962,* recalls the quiet efficiency prior to its disbandment in 1957:

The secret of (the Force's) efficiency and of its success lay in the enthusiasm of the volunteer. Every man from AC2 to the commanding officer in each squadron was convinced beyond doubt that his squadron was the best of all, and that the RAuxAF as a whole 'could take on the world'. It was remarkable to see how the pre-war traditions, customs and characteristics of each squadron were retained by their successors in the post-war years.

The pilots flew because they loved flying, and loved the team spirit so abundantly found in units where postings were unknown and promotions but few. The NCOs and airmen were equally enthusiastic. Many of them after leaving their place of work would return home to put on their uniforms, then travel up to 20 or 30 miles as best they could, sometimes in appalling weather. They did this because they loved their work with aircraft and because their squadron was the best.

---

*Air Commodore J.M. Birkin CB, DSO, OBE, DFC, AFC, ADC, was born at Chilwell on 12 April 1912. The first appointment to head the new Directorate of Auxiliaries, Reserves and Air Cadets, which was set up in December 1951 to advise the Air Council on matters affecting these forces, was made to AVM W.M. Yool CB, CBE. He was assisted by Group Captain I.B. Newbiggin, DFC, as Deputy Director and by the Inspector of the RAuxAF, Group Captain J.M. Birkin. Wing Commander J.M. Birkin DSO, OBE, DFC, AFC, was appointed Inspector of the RAuxAF with the acting rank of Group Captain in January 1952. He succeeded Air Commodore Finlay Crerar CBE, who held the post from September 1950, for a year. Group Captain Birkin was a member of the Pathfinder Association, and started flying in 1933. He joined the RAFVR in 1938, and on being commissioned in 1940 served as a flying instructor. While on instructional duties he went to Montrose where he was awarded an AFC. He remained at Montrose until he became commanding officer of the Meteorological Flight at Wyton, in 1943. One afternoon in April 1944, he was told to form 571 Squadron, and on the next night the Squadron operated from Oakington with two aircraft. He was awarded a DSO and DFC during his command of 571 Squadron. When the war ended he went to the Empire Flying School where he remained until he was released, and when the RAuxAF was reformed in 1946 he became CO of 504 (County of Nottingham) Squadron until 1950. In 1951 he was awarded the OBE, becoming a CB (Military) in January 1956. In May 1956, he was appointed HAC of the Nottinghamshire units of the RAuxAF by HM Queen Elizabeth II. He was appointed Aide-de-Camp (ADC) to HM Queen in April 1957. Group Captain Birkin had business interests in a lace manufacturing company and the Stock Exchange, and was a member of the MCC.

Time and again it has been thought that owing to the introduction of new aircraft or new techniques the day of the volunteer was past, but each time, by intensive work and devotion to the cause not only has the standard been maintained but even improved, and many of our finest pilots and leaders have been auxiliaries.

The good done by these squadrons in bringing the RAF, a service at times remote from the public eye, into the life of the community, cannot be easily reckoned, but the spirit of the volunteer is an asset which should never be underrated by those in authority. Its value is beyond calculation, and it can produce deeds beyond the normal call of duty under the most adverse circumstances. Battles are won or lost in the hearts of men.

All this has not been achieved without cost. Many auxiliaries, though they would be the first to admit that it was worth it, have played their part at considerable cost to themselves both in promotion and pay in their civilian occupations. Many wives and families have given up their husbands, sons and daughters at weekends, and sacrificed family holidays during the summer months. Some members, as is inevitable in operational flying, have given their lives for their country as gallantly as did so many of their fellows during the war.

The passing of the auxiliary squadrons into history is a sad moment both for the men and for the country. They have been one of the most rewarding investments ever made in the defence of these islands. Something of tremendous value has left the RAF forever, and many patriotic and unselfish men will be heartbroken at the loss of what had become to them a way of life.

The country owes them much. May their skill, enthusiasm and devotion to duty long be remembered!

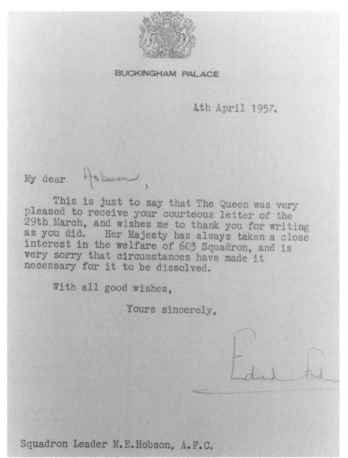

BUCKINGHAM PALACE

4th April 1957.

My dear Hobson,

This is just to say that The Queen was very pleased to receive your courteous letter of the 29th March, and wishes me to thank you for writing as you did. Her Majesty has always taken a close interest in the welfare of 603 Squadron, and is very sorry that circumstances have made it necessary for it to be dissolved.

With all good wishes,

Yours sincerely,

Edward Ford

Squadron Leader M.E.Hobson, A.F.C.

A letter from Buckingham Palace.

CHAPTER 20

THE FALLOW YEARS

The defence cut review in 1956 had led to the disbandment of flying squadrons and the light anti-aircraft regiment squadrons on 10 March 1957, followed, on 1 November 1959, by the demise of the majority of the fighter control units. The radar reporting units were disbanded between 1957 and 1961.

Following the disbandment of 603 Squadron and its associated ground infrastructure comprising 3603 (City of Edinburgh) Light AA Squadron, the force was kept in being by the foresight of Air Marshal Sir Edward Chilton, then AOC-in-C Coastal Command and his Senior Air Staff Officer (SASO), Air Vice-Marshal Wilf Oulton, who recognised the value of retaining auxiliaries as trained augmenters for the Command and Group Headquarters. Subsequently three Maritime Headquarters Units (MHUs) were formed between November 1959 and January 1960, breaking new ground for the RAuxAF by providing a maritime-oriented force to support Coastal Command Headquarters (formerly 18 Group, 11/18 Group, and currently 3 Group) at Northwood, and the former Northern and Southern Maritime Air Regions, based at Maritime Headquarters (MHQ), Pitreavie Castle, Fife (NORMAR), and the MHQ Mount Wise, Plymouth, Devon (SOUMAR), respectively. First to form was 2 (City of Edinburgh) MHU followed by 1 (County of Hertford) and 3 (County of Devon) MHUs.

3603 (City of Edinburgh) FCU Barnton Quarry, c. 1954. Note stills from Dambuster film on the wall.

Airwomen of a FCU at summer camp have a lecture from a Regular Technical Officer in the lee of a radar aircraft.

Top and bottom: 2603 (City of Edinburgh) Light AA Regiment Squadron, RAuxAF, 603 support unit with 40mm Bofors guns on exercise at Turnhouse, c.1955.

2 (City of Edinburgh) MHU was formed on 1 November 1959 and was initially manned by officers, non-commissioned officers and other ranks of the former 3603 (City of Edinburgh) Fighter Control Unit, RAuxAF, which had been disbanded the previous day under the command of Flight Lieutenant R.B. Worthington MBE, RAF.

The role of the unit at its formation was to provide operations, intelligence and communications personnel to exclusively support the joint RN/RAF MHQ at Pitreavie Castle, Fife, particularly during NATO exercises.

On 7 July 1975, HM Queen Elizabeth II, accompanied by Prince Philip The Duke of Edinburgh, visited 2 MHU at its Town HQ in Edinburgh, the ancestral home of its illustrious predecessor, 603 Fighter Squadron.

In 1986, the unit's role expanded to provide operational support to aircrew at Kinloss, Lossiemouth, Macrihanish and Turnhouse.

Later its role expanded further to provide operational, intelligence, medical, regiment, air traffic control and MT personnel to support maritime operations at Kinloss with the Nimrod MR.2 force (120, 201 and 206 Squadrons), the maritime and overland role for the Tornado GR.Mk.1Bs at Lossiemouth (12 and 617 Squadrons) and air defence activities at Leuchars with the Tornado F.Mk.3 (43(F) and 111 Squadrons). In addition, the unit provided intelligence support for the NATO/National Joint Intelligence Centre at MOC HM Naval Base Clyde, Faslane.

To train for these various roles, the unit supported the Joint Maritime Operations Training Staff (JMOTS) during Joint Maritime Courses and also provided support to overseas deployments.

2 MHU's badge was approved and awarded by HM Queen Elizabeth II in July 1963 with the motto 'Watch Weil' and the unit won the prestigious Robins Trophy* for the training years 1982-83 and 1995-96.

1957 – 1999

Following the disbandment, members of the 603 Association continued to flourish and held regular meetings at their old Town HQ. G/C Mike Hobson CBE, AFC, the last OC of 603 Squadron prior to disbandment on 10 March 1957 recalls the founding of the Guardiyen Club:

> It was agreed that, although there was a 603 Squadron Association, we should form a more intimate club of all those officers who were on the strength of the Squadron at the time of disbandment, with any previous members being offered honorary membership, and that we should meet for annual Dinner. There was some debate about what to call the Club, and it was Bill Holmes who came up with 'The Guardiyen Club', being an anagram of the Squadron motto 'Gin Ye Daur'. The Guardiyen Club has, since that day, held a dinner in Edinburgh every single year, and in 2003 held its 46th Dinner. After various venues, including hotels and Turnhouse Mess, the last to be held there, the Dinner was eventually held in our old Town Headquarters in Learmonth Terrace, by kind courtesy of the resident RAuxaF Unit, 2 (City of Edinburgh) Maritime Headquarters Unit , and continues to held there.

There were a number of significant events which involved the 603 Squadron Association and The Guardiyen Club. In 1985, 603's Diamond Jubilee was marked by a supper evening. The late Stewart Liddle, secretary of the club committee, wrote to Robert Fellowes, Her Majesty's Private Secretary, on 23 September 1985:

> Sir, Number 603 (City of Edinburgh) Squadron, Royal Auxiliary Air Force, of which Her Majesty was Honorary Air Commodore, is celebrating its 60th Anniversary, October 1925-85 at the Post House Hotel, Corstorphone, Edinburgh on Saturday 12th October 1985.
>
> We send our Loyal Greetings from all past members of the Squadron to Her Majesty, and wish to record our pride that she became Honorary Air Commodore in June 1951.

The Private Secretary replied:

---

*In 1983, the Inspector, G/C L.E. Robins CBE, AE**, ADC, DL, FIMgt, presented a trophy to be awarded to the RAuxAF unit adjudged to have done most to improve the good name and efficiency of the RAuxAF during the previous year.

Dear Mr Little, Thank you for your letter of 23rd September, addressed to Mr. Robert Fellowes, containing a message of loyal greetings to The Queen from 603 Squadron, Royal Auxiliary Air Force.

This has been laid before Her Majesty, who has commanded me to send you the attached reply.

PRIVATE SECRETARY 12th October 1985.

The enclosed note read:

The Queen sincerely thanks you, members of the committee and all former members of 603 (City of Edinburgh) Squadron, Royal Auxiliary Air Force, for your kind message of loyal greetings, sent on the occasion of the celebration of your Sixtieth Anniversary. Her Majesty, your former Honorary Air Commodore, much appreciates this message and sends her warm good wishes to you all on this occasion and for a most enjoyable evening.

Honorary Air Commodore

The evening was indeed a great success. Many past members of the Squadron from 1928 to 1957 attended. Guests included Lord James Douglas-Hamilton – nephew of an assistant adjutant of 603 and two former CO's – Air Vice-Marshal John F.H. Tetley CVO, Air Officer Scotland and Northern Ireland and Group Captain M.J. Butler ADC, OC RAF Turnhouse.

Her Majesty Queen Elizabeth continued to show her warm regard for the Squadron. On 2 July 1989, she unveiled a Scroll of Honour at Canongate Church, Edinburgh, commemorating those members of 603 who lost their lives during the Second World War.

To celebrate 603's contribution to the Battle of Britain, a large tapestry was designed by the artist Jo Barker who, together with her colleague Jill Rhind, worked on it for six months. The striking tapestry was formally hung at a ceremony attended by the Squadron's Battle of Britain veteran CO, Group Captain George Denholm DFC, AE, and other veteran pilots in a permanent exhibition at the Blackhall Library.

On 603's reformation in October 1999, Edinburgh City Council agreed that the tapestry, which had been in store, could be displayed at the Town HQ. The tapestry hung in the ballroom until December 2002 when it was returned to the Edinburgh City Council.

A colour party provided by personnel of 2 MHU, the successors to 603 Fighter Squadron, participated in the 70th Anniversary celebrations of 603 Squadron on 14 October 1995. The late Tim Ferguson MBE, an ex-603 Vampire and test pilot, was chairman of the organising committee for the day's events.

The celebrations consisted of a Thanksgiving Service at the Canongate Kirk during which the Sovereign's Colour for the RAuxAF was paraded. The Reverend Charles Robertson MA, JP, Minister of Canongate Kirk and Honorary Padre 2 MHU, officiated at the service, which was attended by the Rt. Hon. Sir Hector Monro AE, JP, DL, MP, Honorary Inspector General, RAuxAF, and former 603 Spitfire pilot; Lord James Douglas-Hamilton MA LLB MP, HAC 2 MHU; Air Commodore Dickie Duckett CVO, AFC, ADC, Air Officer Scotland and Northern Ireland; the Rt. Hon. Mr Norman Irons CBE, JP, Lord Provost of the City of Edinburgh; Group Captain Peter Igoe, Station Commander RAF Turnhouse; and Colonel R.S.B. Watson OBE, Secretary, Lowland TAVRA and Wing Commander R.G. Kemp, OC 2 MHU.

Following the thanksgiving service, a reception was held at the City Chambers Edinburgh, hosted by the Lord Provost, where G/C George Denholm gave into the charge of the City of Edinburgh a unique piece of Squadron silver in recognition of the long association between the Squadron and the city.*

A/C the Rt. Hon. Sir Hector Monro and W/C R.G. Kemp hosted an informal reception at 2 MHU's Town Headquarters for the 603 and RAuxAF veterans, and their families. In all, 250 attended.

The 70th anniversary celebrations culminated in a Ladies Guest Night for officers and NCO aircrew of the Guardiyen Club, held at the Town HQ during the evening, hosted by A/C the Rt. Hon. Sir Hector Monro and attended by many of the dignitaries present at the Thanksgiving Service. The Sovereign's Colour for the RAuxAF was exhibited, together with the 603 Standard throughout both events.

---

*Shortly before 603 flew to Leuchars in 1928 for their annual camp, it suffered its first fatal accident when P/O J.T.L. Shiells was killed in a flying accident on 7 July 1928 when he was flying an Avro 504K on a solo flight over Corstorphine. The silver presented by George Denholm was the Shiells Challenge Trophy Bowl which had been presented to 603 by Shiells' parents in commemoration of their late son.

Top: Battle of Britain pilots at Turnhouse 1985.
Bottom: Sheep and George at Turnhouse c.1990.

Top: 60th anniversary reunion in Edinburgh, 12 October 1985.
Bottom: 75th anniversary reunion.

Above: G/C G.L. Denholm was among the veterans who attended the hanging of a tapestry on 10 May 1991, to commemorate the 50th anniversary of the Battle of Britain. With George is Jill Rhind who made it.

Right: On 2 July 1989, Her Majesty Queen Elizabeth II unveiled a Scroll of Honour in the Canongate Kirk (the Kirk of Holyroodhouse) Edinburgh commemorating those members of the Squadron who lost their lives whilst serving in peace and war.

Top: A/C Rt. Hon. Sir Hector Monro (left), G/Capt George Denholm and the Rt. Hon. Norman Irons, Lord Provost, with the Shiells Trophy.
Middle: George Denholm, Mrs McCulloch, Dickie Duckett AOC, Lord Hector Monro and unknown at the City Chambers.
Bottom: Mike Hobson (front left) with Standard at the town HQ, on the 75th anniversary.

Spitfire memorial at Turnhouse.

Dedication of Spitfire Memorial

At the entrance to Edinburgh airport a replica of Spitfire LF Mk XVIE (RW393, XT-A) now stands as a memorial to the men of 603 Squadron who gave their lives whilst serving their country both in peace and war. The original aircraft and memorial had stood at the gates of RAF Turnhouse having been dedicated on 9 March 1957. The following day 603 was disbanded after 32 years service.

Following the closure of RAF Turnhouse in April 1996, the move of the Spitfire memorial from Turnhouse to Edinburgh airport owes much to the members of the 603 Association, in particular Charles 'Chic' Cessford, whose constant lobbying of both military and civil dignitaries was so successful, and to the generosity of the British Airports Authority, who provided the site and built the new memorial.

A service of re-dedication took place on Sunday 27 October 1996 at the airport. George Denholm was present together with other 603 veterans, local dignitaries, the CO and members 2 MHU, RAuxAF.

No.603 (City of Edinburgh) Squadron Locomotive Crest

On Saturday, 24 May, 1997 an important piece of 603 memorabilia, was recovered and given a permanent home in the Squadron's Town HQ thanks to the efforts of Joe McCulloh, a former 603 pilot.

The nameplate and crest were refurbished and handed over to the RAF Museum whence they were loaned to the RAuxAF unit in Edinburgh for display in Town HQ.

There was a formal unveiling ceremony by Air Commodore Lord James Douglas-Hamilton, HAC of 2 MHU on 24 May 1997 in the presence of the principal participants in the securing of the nameplate and crest. Also present were Group Captain R.T.W. Mighall, Inspector RAuxAF and W/C Bob Kemp, OC 2 MHU. Thus ended a 33-year saga (see volume one for further details).

Top: Spitfire XVI RW393 was the gate guardian at RAF Turnhouse from August 1956. It was taken to the museum at RAF Cosford where it was photographed in 1998.

Middle: The XT-A facsimile moved to Edinburgh airport in October 1996.

Bottom: The memorial plaque.

The 603 Squadron Battle of Britain class
locomotive.
Inset: The 603 nameplate.

Unveiling the nameplate. George Denholm with members of the ground crew and OC 2 MHU, W/C Bob Kemp.

Battle of Britain Honour
The RAF paid tribute in 1999 to the late G/C George Denholm DFC, AE, when it authorised that
the Battle of Britain Memorial Flight Spitfire IIA (P7350) be displayed in the colours and markings
of his aircraft (XT-D 'Blue Peter') during the Battle of Britain.

Air Commodore the Rt Hon Lord James Douglas-Hamilton, Honorary Air Commodore No 2
MHU, unveils the 603 Squadron Battle of Britain Class badge and nameplate on 24 May 1997.
Lord James' late father and two uncles had a long association with both 602 and 603 Squadrons.

CHAPTER 21

603 (CITY OF EDINBURGH) SQUADRON REFORMATION

During 1999, the Air Force Board reviewed and granted the request from the Honorary Inspector General (HIG) RAuxAF, the Rt. Hon. A/C Lord Monro of Langham AE, JP, DL that permission be given for new squadrons of the expanding RAuxAF to be allocated the numbers and badges of distinguished auxiliary flying squadrons which were disbanded on 10 March 1957. On 1 October 1999, HM Queen Elizabeth II, (Air Commodore-in-Chief, RAuxAF) gave her approval for 603 to be reformed. Thus on 1 October, 2 MHU were re-roled and re-numbered 603 (City of Edinburgh) Squadron, continuing the traditions and historic links with the city of Edinburgh over the last 75 years. The move generated much coverage in the Scottish press.

The Lord Provost of Edinburgh, the Rt. Hon. Eric Milligan, graciously granted his approval for a celebration to be held in Edinburgh on 10 March 2000 to mark the reformation of 'Edinburgh's own' Squadron, exactly 43 years after its disbandment.

Shortly after the reformation, Wing Commander Alasdair J. Beaton, OC 603 Squadron, sent a letter of greeting on behalf of all ranks to Her Majesty Queen Elizabeth II which read:

AOC-in-C RAF Strike Command, Air Chief Marshal Sir Peter Squire and Mrs Marion Morton take the salute at the 603 reformation, Princes Street, Edinburgh.

TO THE QUEEN'S MOST EXCELLENT MAJESTY

All serving and former members of No. 603 (City of Edinburgh) Squadron Royal Auxiliary Air Force and the Lord Provost and Members of the City of Edinburgh Council send you most Loyal Greetings on the occasion of the Squadron's March Past and Civic Reception in the City of Edinburgh on 10th March 2000. The Sovereign's Colour for the Royal Auxiliary Air Force will be paraded. The events publicly mark the reforming in Edinburgh of No. 603 (City of Edinburgh) Squadron on the 43rd anniversary of the Squadron's disbandment on 10th March 1957.

Her Majesty graciously replied :

BUCKINGHAM PALACE

10th March 2000

Please convey to all serving and past Members of No.603 (City of Edinburgh) Squadron, Royal Auxiliary Air Force and the Lord Provost and Members of the City of Edinburgh Council, assembled on the occasion of the Squadron's March Past and Civic Reception in the City of Edinburgh and the parading of The Sovereign's Colour for the Royal Auxiliary Air Force, my thanks for their message of loyal greetings and best wishes for a most enjoyable occasion.

ELIZABETH R

A Squadron march past down Princes Street, under the command of W/C Beaton, was led by Pipe Major Hughes and the RAF Leuchars pipe band. The salute was taken on the steps of the Royal Scottish Academy by the AOC-in-C Strike Command Air Chief Marshal Sir Peter Squire KCB, DFC, AFC, ADC, FRAeS, RAF, and Mrs Marion Morton, Deputy Convenor of the City of Edinburgh Council, representing the Lord Provost. The Sovereign's Colour for the RAuxAF was paraded.* The Colour Party was Flight Lieutenant Graeme Lyall, Warrant Officer Don McQueen, Flight Sergeant John Webster and Sergeant John Willoughby. The Squadron and the City of Edinburgh were honoured by a flypast of a 201 Squadron Nimrod MR.2 from RAF Kinloss (with 603 Squadron member, Flight Lieutenant W. Speight as Flight Engineer), four Tornado F3s from 111 Squadron, Leuchars and three Tornado GR1Bs from 617 Squadron, RAF Lossiemouth. These aircraft represented the RAF stations which the current Squadron and its predecessor, 2 MHU, had supported for many years.

Former members of 603, including Squadron Leader Gerald 'Stapme' Stapleton DFC, one of 603's Battle of Britain pilots, were honoured guests at the parade and the Civic Reception held at the City Chambers, hosted by the Deputy Convenor on behalf of the City of Edinburgh Council. The HAC, The Rt. Hon. The Lord Selkirk of Douglas and all Squadron members and their families also attended the reception, during which W/C Beaton thanked the City of Edinburgh and the Royal Air Force for honouring the Squadron. After a brief summary of the history of the Squadron until disbandment, he continued:

… and so sadly, the 10th of March 1957 came. After 31 years of loyal service, 603's flying days were over and the Squadron held their last dining in night that evening. The party broke up in a blaze of glory when an already condemned wooden hut, mysteriously burst into flames, and a BEA aircraft, departing later the following morning, was found to have a 603 Squadron Crest on its nose.

But auxiliary service continued. From 2603 and 3603, 2 Maritime Headquarters Unit was born in 1959, a formation evolved to support the Maritime Forces of Coastal Command. 2 MHU continued unbroken support for the Royal Air Force for the next 40 years, operating from its now traditional auxiliary headquarters at Learmonth Terrace and the underground bunker of Pitreavie Castle and from RAF Kinloss on the Moray Coast. The unit ultimately broadened its work to include operational ground support for RAF Lossiemouth and RAF Leuchars.

---

*The Sovereign's Colour for the Royal Auxiliary Air Force was presented at RAF Benson on 12 June 1989.

603 reformation, Princes Street, Edinburgh.

Although its initial focus was Maritime, the auxiliaries had also adapted to suit the many needs of the RAF in Scotland. This is thus my opportunity to publicly express my most grateful thanks to the station commanders of RAFs Kinloss, Leuchars and Lossiemouth who so willingly saluted their auxiliaries by authorising aircraft from their stations to overfly our parade in Edinburgh today in such spectacular style. The original members of 603 would have been very proud. And so we come to the present day. On 1 October last year, 2 Maritime Headquarters Unit were renamed 603 (City of Edinburgh) Squadron once again. The flying days of 603 are now legends of history. We cannot change the past but we can all influence the future. The operational complexity of today's modern combat aircraft demands the fullest concentration of today's regular RAF aviators. But they do need support and protection on the ground if they are to be successful in the air. Our Squadron's new expeditionary roles of deployment in Force Protection and Mission Support aim to do just that. Our Squadron has been abroad before and most recently we have deployed auxiliaries to support our armed forces, in support of operations in Kosova and one of our officers cannot be with us today because he is otherwise engaged, with the RAF in the Middle East. But our new roles will demand the same spirit of flexibility of being a 'can do' squadron that was very much part of the spirit of the original 603, and that is how we will take the Squadron forward.

And so I turn to Air Chief Marshal Sir Peter Squire, Commander-in-Chief Headquarters Strike Command. Sir, in being with us today, and accompanied by your senior officers, you have not only honoured us with your presence, you have also in representing the Royal Air Force, honoured the past and present auxiliary members of 603. I would, on behalf of all Squadron members and their families thank you most sincerely for your support, and ask you to convey to the Royal Air Force Board our gratitude for their recommendation to Her Majesty the Queen, that 603 should be reformed, thus recognising both the past and the future contributions, that this Squadron of the Royal Auxiliary Air force has already brought and will bring to our service.

In closing, I would remind you that 603 has amongst its most loyal admirers, Her Majesty the Queen. A few days ago, I therefore sent a message of loyal greetings to Her Majesty and have received her reply.

The men and women of today's 603 are very proud indeed and deeply honoured to be part of such a prestigious squadron. Squadron spirit is the very core of the RAF's team spirit and is the vehicle by which we achieve results. Above all, the common link that binds today's

ACM Sir Peter Squire, Chief of the Air Staff RAF, speaks at the reformation.

603 with those who served before, under this number, is that we are all auxiliaries, volunteers, to serve the Royal Air Force in any way we can and in our nation's best interests but with the spirit that comes from being a member of a squadron again.

Deputy Lord Provost, Commander-in-Chief, Honoured Guests, ladies and gentlemen. Thank you all so very much for your support in being with us today and I hope that you will always remember that you were present on the day when we publicly celebrated the return to Edinburgh of its own Squadron, the return of 603.

During the Civic Reception members of the 603 Association presented the CO with the 603 Squadron pipe band drum major's mace, which was first used in 1938. This is now displayed in the foyer of Town HQ.

On 8 September 2000, W/C Al Beaton, and S/L J. Bruce Blanche, Deputy OC, attended as guests the recording of the BBC's 'Songs of Praise' programme at St George's Church, RAF Halton, Buckinghamshire to celebrate the 60th anniversary of the Battle of Britain. 603 was the primary focus and theme for this commemorative programme. A massed choir was accompanied by the Central Band of the Royal Air Force. The service was attended by 350 people, including veterans and former 603 pilots. Several other members attended as ushers. G/C Bob Kemp, QVRM, AE, ADC, FRIN, Inspector RAuxAF, was also present. John Mackenzie, Chairman of the 603 Association, and Jim Renwick were the Squadron's guests. The programme was watched by 5.4 million people on its first broadcast.

The 60th anniversary of the Battle of Britain and 603's part in it generated a lot of publicity for the Squadron and its association. On 15 September, 'Battle of Britain Day', members of the current Squadron and many veterans and their families laid a wreath at the Turnhouse Spitfire memorial to mark the occasion.

The primary role for 603 since reforming on 1 October 1999 is now Survive to Operate (STO) or Force Protection (FP). Alongside logistics and air operations, Force Protection is the third vital element in the operational capacity of the RAF. A significant number of dedicated combat ready FP tasks are grouped together under STO, a concept of defence and protection of operational assets now well embedded in NATO(air) and RAF operational capabilities, to support deployed expeditionary operations. The Squadron will also continue to provide Mission Support (MS), initially for maritime forces, but also all other RAF and NATO (Air) formations or units, again where required in the concept of expeditionary warfare.

Via these roles 603 provides operational support on behalf of RAF deployed operations and exercises, with the focus of training in the mission support role will continue at Kinloss, whilst based at its Town HQ.

On 11 December 2000, 603 was greatly honoured that Her Majesty Queen Elizabeth II, the Air Commodore-in-Chief, RAuxAF, graciously reassumed the title of HAC.*

Noting Lord Selkirk's unique and important family associations with 603 and his most distinguished, effective and loyal performance as HAC of both 2 MHU and 603, Her Majesty expressed her wish that Lord Selkirk continue to act as HAC on her behalf. Thus 603 has the unique distinction of having Her Majesty Queen Elizabeth II as its HAC with Lord Selkirk of Douglas representing her on a day-to-day basis.

The vision of Marshal of the Royal Air Force The Viscount Trenchard, the 'Father' of the RAuxAF, has been amply vindicated by the achievements of the force in Edinburgh both in peace and war. The professional skill, enthusiasm and ésprit de corps of the young founder members of the 20s and 30s are matched by the men and women of today's 603 Squadron.

Inspired by their predecessors, they now take the Squadron proudly and confidently into the 21st century, honouring the traditions of the past, in building a new future as an integral element of the RAF's contribution to the defence of the United Kingdom with the confidence and pride of the volunteer.

At the time of writing, conflict in Iraq loomed and, as part of the preparations for war 603 (City of Edinburgh) Squadron, Royal Auxiliary Air Force, was called-up for the first time since the Korean war.

Operation Iraqi Freedom: 20 March – 2 May 2003

Wing Commander Al Beaton, OC 603 Squadron, outlines the level of support that 603 Squadron personnel contributed to Operation TELIC, the British codename for the joint US / UK offensive against Iraq – Operation Iraqi Freedom:

Towards the end of 2002, the political climate and the threat of war in Iraq became the nation's focus and our primary attention. Between Christmas and New Year, employers and auxiliaries were warned to prepare for the first enactment of the 1996 Reserve Forces Act and the first call-up of our reservists since 1939. Initially 65 personnel were sent their papers in early January 2003, 55 to serve in the Force Protection/Survive to Operate (STO) role and ten to serve in the mission support role to work at RAF Kinloss reflecting 603's dual operational capability. Thus on 10 February 2003, the embodiment of 60% of 603 Squadron began as 53 auxiliaries reported for duty, after only two years and four months since our reformation.

Following a two-week period of surge training at RAF Leuchars, the deployment of our personnel on Operation TELIC began. With enormous pride, our auxiliaries, some of whom had only joined us in October 2002 and including for the first time, six women, prepared to move to an operational theatre. It was a major source of concern that all of the STO group would be split up. In historical terms, auxiliary squadrons had been deployed as a whole entity. This time it was going to be different, 15 went to Al Udeid, Qatar for key point guarding and combined incident team duties, 12 joined 504 (County of Nottingham)

---

*The *London Gazette*, Tuesday 16 April 2002, Supplement No.14617: 'Her Majesty The Queen has been graciously pleased to accept the title of Honorary Air Commodore of 603 Squadron to be effective from 11th December 2000.'

Squadron RAuxAF in Jordan, for protection duties for a Harrier GR7 and Canberra PR9 detachment, seven were posted to Ali Al Salem, Kuwait, for tasks similar to those in Qatar but also including chemical and biological monitoring duties and one individual went to Prince Sultan Air Base in Saudi Arabia to join another chemical and biological threat monitoring team. In the UK, 603 Squadron personnel deployed to RAFs Honington, Leuchars and Cottesmore. In comparison to the STO element of the Squadron, the initial ten mission supporters for Kinloss commenced work as a formed unit, with a recognised rank structure. They were soon to be supplemented by a further three auxiliaries from Edinburgh. A message of Loyal Greetings was sent to Her Majesty The Queen, advising her of the Squadron's deployment. She in turn, sent her thoughts and best wishes back to the Squadron.

Hostilities broke out in Iraq soon after the deployment of our troops to the Gulf. Whilst they were not engaged in front line offensive activities, they were nonetheless in a hostile region. Back home, a series of families days were commenced to bring into the body of the Squadron those nearest and dearest to our detached personnel. It was a very steep emotional learning curve for all our auxiliaries and their families, most of whom had never been exposed to a service environment before, let alone a war. On 24 April, His Royal Highness, the Prince of Wales met family members of the 603 at a reception in Paisley for all deployed reserve formations from the three armed forces.

Within a few weeks the war was won. The Iraqi regime of Sadam Hussein had been deposed and hostilities began to subside. As formations and units returned to the UK, our auxiliaries, being supplementary to the core fighting elements of the RAF were returned home in a somewhat more haphazard programme. At the same time our mission support element were providing crucial support to the depleted manning of station operations at RAF Kinloss. It has been a baptism by fire from the very outset of our reformation with the enthusiasm and dedication of all our auxiliaries proving the immense value of their service in support of the RAF.

As the Commanding Officer, I am immensely proud of them all. In every individual contribution, our 603 Squadron members of 2003 have once again proved the case for the crucial roles auxiliary play in times of war and peace.

It has been 60 years since the personnel of 603 Squadron have been involved in a war in the desert; in 1943/44 it was the air and ground crews that flew and serviced the Bristol Beaufighters in North Africa; in 2003, Squadron personnel deployed to a different war, in a different desert, but the spirit of the Squadron was the same.

The Town headquarters has endured little change over the years and is still occupied by the Squadron where the staff still diligently go about their duties. Regular members carry out their daily tasks on a full-time basis and are joined by the auxiliaries on Wednesday evenings, alternate weekends, exercises, and Squadron functions. Within the building they rub shoulders with the spirits of those who served before them. Over the years the veterans of the Edinburgh Squadron recall with great pride their time with the unit, but it is those lost during conflict that will always generate the greatest emotion and the all-pervading spirit and presence of the many laughing, youthful souls will always serve as an example of courage and dedication to the generations who follow.

APPENDIX 1

LIFE AFTER 603

Air Commodore Ronald Berry

Ras Berry was promoted to Flight Lieutenant on 1 December 1941 and in January 1942 returned to flying, taking command of 81 Squadron at Turnhouse where they undertook convoy patrols. The pilots were a multi-national group who had just returned from Russia having left their aircraft behind. They moved to Hornchurch in May 1942 and then to Fairlop where they undertook sweeps over Europe. During the summer, while he was there, Richard Hillary paid him a visit with fellow Guinea Pig, Tony Tollemache, whom he had befriended whilst at East Grinstead. Richard was keen to fly a Spitfire again after being shot down on 3 September and asked Ras if he would allow him to do so. Aware of his responsibilities Ras turned Richard down and years later recalled the wave of sympathy he had felt for his once handsome 603 colleague and how very difficult he had found it to turn him down.

In October 1942, 81 Squadron sailed for Gibraltar where they took delivery of tropical Spitfire Vs. On 8 November the squadron became one of the first two to land in North Africa when they were put in at Maison Blanche at the start of Operation Torch landings. The next day, over the Bone area, Berry destroyed a Ju88 and shared a Ju88 and an He111. On 11 November he damaged another Ju88, a Mc200 on the 14th and two Bf109s on the 26th. On 28th he shared a 109, on 3 December he shared a FW 190 and destroyed another on the 6th. On the 10th he destroyed a SM79.

On 22 January 1943, Ras was promoted to Squadron Leader and took over from 'Dutch' Hugo as Wing Leader of 322 Wing, handing over command of 81 Squadron to the outstanding New Zealand fighter pilot Colin Gray. Ras destroyed Bf109s on 31 January and 25 February and shared another probable on 2 March 1943 on which day he was awarded a Bar to his DFC. On 13 March he took command of 322 Wing. He damaged a FW 190 on 3 April, damaged a Ju87 on the 5th and claimed a Bf109 probably destroyed on the 13th. He claimed a Bf109 damaged on 25 and 26 April and a Ju52 destroyed on the ground on 6 May. The six Bf109s destroyed on the ground the next day were his final victories in the Tunisian campaign.

On 1 June 1943 he was awarded the DSO. On returning to the UK Berry joined 53 OTU on 29 June 1943, as o/c Training Wing at Kirton-in-Lindsey. In April 1944, he served at HQ, Air Defence of Great Britain. He was sent to the Army Staff College at Camberley and then to the Fighter Leaders School. After the end of WWII he was posted to Tangmere where he formed the Central Fighter Establishment. He commanded RAF Acklington from 1945-46, and then went to 12 Group HQ as Wing Commander Operations. On 1 January 1946 he was made an OBE. In 1947 he commanded the Air Fighting Development Unit at West Raynham until the early fifties. Posted on exchange to the USAF he flew many different types on the air proving ground, and it was here that the experts discovered his amazing tolerance to g-Force and confirmed his own theory on his survival in combat. He returned to England to become Wing Commander Plans, Fighter Command. He attended the Joint Services Staff College in 1954 and graduated in 1955. He attended a bomber course prior to becoming Wing Commander Flying at Wittering on Valiant jet bombers. He then commanded 543 Squadron on Valiants at Wyton until 1959 when he became Director of Operations, Navigation and Air Traffic Control at the Air Ministry, being promoted to Group Captain.

He was made a CBE in 1965. After two years as Group Captain Ops, Bomber Command, he commanded RAF Lindholme for three months prior to promotion to Air Commodore. He then became i/c operations at the Board of Trade until he retired in 1969.

Ras and Nancy had a daughter, Annette. Some years later, Ras expressed disappointment, albeit with a little of his unique wit, when his daughter married a German! Sadly, Nancy developed multiple sclerosis and for many years the couple lived quietly at Hornsea on the Yorkshire/Humberside coast with Ras continually caring for Nancy until the task became too much and, with his own health failing, they both moved into a home near Beverley. During this period Ras frequently answered the phone, introducing himself as 'Nurse Ronald'! Ras is remembered as a devoted husband to Nancy during her years of sickness.

Over the years Ras remained in touch with a number of his former 603 colleagues including Stapme and George Denholm.

Group Captain George Denholm

In December 1941 he left Turnhouse to form 1460 Flight on Turbinlite Havocs at Acklington as part of the experiments keenly followed by Churchill. The intention behind the scheme was to blind the enemy aircraft but the experiments failed, due mainly to the short life of the batteries. During this period Betty and George lived in a flat in Mowick Hall not far from the Northumberland airfield. They were later reunited with Black and Mardi Morton when Black was posted to Acklington to take over command of 1460 Flight in February 1942, George relinquishing command to his friend on 1 March when he was promoted to Wing Commander. Despite leaving 603 Squadron Betty recalls George continued to enjoy his work.

In August 1942 George was posted to command 605 Squadron at Ford which was flying Boston Mark IIIs on night-intruder sorties. He and Betty lived at Barnham during this posting. On 25 January George flew from Ford to RAF Hunsdon in a 605 Squadron Boston III flown by Flight Lieutenant Mike Olley. Their task was to collect the ashes of F/L Richard Hillary who had been killed on 8 January in an accident at RAF Charterhall and, whilst the memorial service was underway, scatter the contents of the urn over the approximate position where he had been rescued from the North Sea after being shot down during the Battle of Britain. The mission went according to plan although George suspected that if the ashes were released from the hatch of the aircraft as planned they would inevitably be blown straight back into the aircraft by the slipstream. He said nothing but gave the task to a member of the crew instead. As the sergeant removed the lid of the urn, extended his arm into the open hatch and released the ashes, the grey cloud blew straight back in his face leaving him covered in a light dusting of powder and spitting profusely in an attempt to clear his airway. An incident which would no doubt have appealed to Richard Hillary's sense of humour! George and Betty later met Richard's parents, Michael and Edwyna Hillary, who were touched that the Denholms had named their daughter, Hillary, in memory of their son. Betty was quick to explain that had not actually been the case!

During February 1943 605 Squadron converted to Mark II Mosquitoes and on 11 March George claimed a probable when he attacked an unidentified aircraft over Gilze-Rijen while flying DZ16 UR-L. This was his last combat claim. He left 605 Squadron in May and took command of RAF North Weald which was at that time the base of the Norwegian and Danish wing. He had been sent to Copenhagen by his father in the 1930s to look after the Scandinavian end of the shipping and timber business where he gained a passable knowledge of Danish. He was able to put this to good use at a time when the Danes spoke little English. He maintained his friendship with the Norwegian CO for many years after the war. Appropriately, George was in Norway when the war came to an end and he accepted the German surrender at Garda Moen airbase, outside Oslo. A Norwegian connection also existed on Betty's side; she had spent her early childhood in the country.

Before the end of hostilities George spent some time at RAF East Fortune, East Lothian, where he and Betty lived at Athelstaneford. George was demobilised as a Group Captain in 1945 and released from the RAF in 1947, returning to his pre-war occupation, devoting himself to J&J Denholm for the next three decades and to family life. In contrast with his pre-war experience of working in the family business, post war it became something he really enjoyed and was all-consuming. He was also surrounded by good friends and family. With their support, life was fulfilling.

George and Betty had four children: Paul, the eldest and a solicitor, Hillary, Christine and Willie who works in the same business as his father, but for Denholm's of Greenock (no relation), based at Grangemouth. George became a Bo'ness town councillor and magistrate for a short period in the 1950s. He strongly opposed the decision to close Bo'ness Docks in favour of Grangemouth, but once the decision was made the firm moved to Glasgow and Grangemouth.

By the end of WWII George's final combat claims amounted to three destroyed, three shared destroyed, one unconfirmed destroyed, three and one shared probable and one damaged. It is not his achievements in combat that reflect his success so much as the effect he had on those who served initially with him and then under his command. He was a competent fighter pilot with the experience and the ability to motivate all those around him in a way that ensured there was trust and faith in following him in doing the same. Ever the paternalist, if his officers and NCOs were ever treated unfairly he was quick to leap to their defence with a show of defiance that could only be compared with that which he generated in the cockpit of his Spitfire when diving to attack German aircraft. On one occasion when praised for his successful leadership of the 603 pilots during that period he modestly replied: 'I just made sure they all got off the ground and flew in the right direction.'

Post war, George worked with James Jack and Ian Ritchie on the 603 Benevolent Fund Committee. In addition to their many achievements, at Christmas the widows of the 603 veterans received a present from the fund.

John Young was with 603 Squadron from 15 October 1939 until 14 May 1940 during which time George Denholm was his flight commander. In the years after the war the two men remained in touch. John later reminisced about his friend and former colleague:

When I was about to retire from BOAC after 28 years as a Captain, George said to me:

'For God's sake John, on your last trip don't do anything silly.'

I said 'God willing George I won't, but thank you and I will keep an eye out.'

George then said: 'Well, I recently had in front of me a customs officer on his last day after 55 years who had accepted a bottle of custom impounded whisky. He lost his entire pension as a consequence.'

I told George that I didn't think I'd do anything like that but it did alert me and during my last trip I did have an incident, or potential incident, and it may well have been George's warning that made me more alert than I would ordinarily have been.

In the post-war years the memory of the Few in the Squadron who had died weighed heavily on his mind. He never spoke of them to outsiders and was often prone to bouts of black depression, wondering, sometimes tearfully, why he had survived while so many of his dear young comrades had died, and if their sacrifice had been worthwhile – what would today be referred to as post traumatic stress disorder (PTSD), something which a number of the 603 survivors suffered from in the post-war years, including Ian Ritchie, Black Morton and George Gilroy. Betty was an eternal optimist and kept the pessimistic and blacker thoughts of her husband at bay during those trying times. Quietly formidable, George Denholm rarely talked about his exploits and the only time that his children remember him mentioning the war was after a near collision with another car: 'That was like looking down the nose of a Messerschmitt,' he joked. He flatly refused to take part in any formal interviews with the media regarding 603 Squadron, his men, and the Battle of Britain. Despite repeated requests over the years, he simply declined to take part.

On 17 October 1953, George attended the unveiling of the new Runnymede Memorial at Coopers Hill by HM the Queen.

Throughout his retirement he continued to live in Bo'ness, remained in touch with many of his 603 colleagues and attended several of the 603 reunions. Betty and George visited Sheep Gilroy on numerous occasions at Tweedsmuir and then Auchencairn. One of his greatest pleasures in the post-war years was the cottage that he and Betty had purchased for £200 in Port Appin which they restored themselves and where the family went for sailing holidays. Despite the onset of old age he continued to attend the 603 functions in Edinburgh. His last public appearance was on 27 October 1996 when he attended the re-dedication of the (facsimile) Spitfire in the markings of 603 Squadron's XT-A, along with the Squadron memorial plaque, which had formerly stood at the entrance to RAF Turnhouse and had recently been placed on a new plinth at the entrance to Edinburgh airport. George had carried out the original unveiling after Group Captain Archie Winskill, the OC, RAF Turnhouse, acquired the aircraft as a gate guardian when plans for the erection of a memorial sculpture in Edinburgh fell through. The land and funds required to move the Spitfire from the former entrance to RAF Turnhouse to the new airport entrance on the opposite side of the airfield were donated by the city airport in memory of their Squadron.

His last appearance was on 24 May 1997, the unveiling of the 603 Squadron Battle of Britain Class locomotive nameplate at Learmonth Terrace. In his 89th year on that occasion he was, as he always has been, a shy, quiet and very private man. Three weeks later George Denholm passed away in the house in Tidings Hill, Bo'ness, in which he had been born. It was Sunday 15 June 1997. He was cremated during a private ceremony in Falkirk attended by his closest friends, former squadron members and family of those now deceased with whom he had flown during the Battle of Britain 57 years before. He was cremated wearing his wedding suit and 603 Squadron tie. As a youngster, Caroline Morton (Black's daughter) recalled finding Betty Denholm 'just' wonderful but George: '…quite frightening, older, tall, serious and just unnerving.' This was not what his men felt.

As a tribute to him, for the 1999-2002 air display seasons the Battle of Britain Memorial Flight Spitfire IIa, P7350, 'Baby Spit', was repainted in the colours of George Denholm's XT-D, L1067, 'Blue Peter'.

Betty Denholm was also good friends with George's 603 colleagues and over the years remained in touch with many of the wives as well the husbands even as their numbers sadly diminished. After the war she shared his grief and played an important part in the story of the period and therefore warrants a few lines in recognition of that fact. Betty's father was a Yorkshireman, her mother a Lancastrian and she spent the early part of her childhood in Norway where her father was working to establish the gas industry. The family returned to live in Deal, Kent. After her mother died there was nobody to look after the young Betty and she was sent to boarding school. Betty eventually left college and having no time to acquire a trade, she married George. Once in Scotland like many of the other wives and girlfriends she travelled to be with George as the Squadron moved around, each time managing to find fresh accommodation, something which surprises her to this day. There was a great air of comradeship between the wives which added to the unity of 603 Squadron at that time. Although Betty remained in Bo'ness during the Battle of Britain when the Squadron was at Hornchurch, when the unit moved north again she once again travelled to be with George and continued to do so for the remainder of the war.

After George's death, Betty found the home in Tidings Hill too much to manage and moved to Kingsbarns near St Andrews and close to her eldest son, Paul. In response to the question asking why George had declined to be interviewed she explained: '…he was loath to be associated with the kudos of having survived because he had been a better pilot than his friends and colleagues who had been killed. He never saw himself as an "ace" or even as a particularly good pilot, just that he was lucky to have survived when the others did not.' Betty reflects on his ability to have coped the way he did during the battle: 'He was a strong, tough, hard man inside and this helped with the obvious effect the losses had on him, as it did the others. But he did have great inner strength.' Ultimately, it was having a wife like Betty, who had also known and been friends with those George had lost, there to provide support and understanding which helped him through each crisis and allowed him to get on with his life.

Air Commodore Brian Macnamara

Promoted to Squadron Leader on 1 December 1941, he remained with 614 Squadron until 5 August 1942 when he was posted to 296 Squadron at Hurn, a Whitley squadron specialising in moving troops in Horsa gliders. On 8 March 1943, he took command of 295 Squadron trained for similar duties. Macnamara towed the glider which carried General Gale, GOC 6th Airborne Division, to Normandy on D-Day.

In early 1945 he went to RAF Staff College, after which he was posted to the Far East. On 15 September 1945 he took command of 31 Squadron at Akyab, Burma. He was awarded the DSO on 4 June 1946 and was promoted to Wing Commander on 1 July 1947. He was made a CBE on 13 June 1957 for distinguished service in operations in the Near East during October-December 1956. He was promoted to Air Commodore on 1 January 1961 and retired from the RAF on 4 June 1965. He retired to Lymington and recently passed away.

Flight Lieutenant Bill Read

Tannoy later moved with the unit to Llandow. He was promoted to Flying Officer on 10 June 1941. In September 1941 he went to West Kirby for embarkation to Russia and he sailed aboard *River Aston* to Archangel, with RAF ground crew and crated Hurricanes. As part of Operation Shallow 151 Wing, led by Wing Commander Ramsbottom-Isherwood and flying

Hurricanes, operated near the arctic port of Murmansk. Ramsbottom-Isherwood and his pilots fought along side and instructed the 72nd Regiment of the Soviet Naval Airfleet before handing over 39 Hurricanes and returning home in November. Bill Read and his men had a narrower brief and were ordered south to Kineshma, north east of Rostov on the Volga, where the aircraft were assembled and test flown by Bill and one other pilot. The first flight was made on 3 November 1941 and the last on 13 January 1942 when Operation Shallow came to a close. Read formed five Russian squadrons and instructed the pilots. As a result of his work there he earned the nickname 'Russia' Read. Following Ramsbottom-Isherwood's and Read's missions, more than 2,900 Hurricanes were crated and sent to Russia, although many were lost as a result of attacks on the arctic convoys. Enough survived to perform an important part in Russia's struggle on the eastern front.

After returning to the UK he was posted to 51 OTU at Cranfield, Bedfordshire in April 1942. On 10 June 1942 his promotion to Flight Lieutenant was confirmed and the next day he was awarded the AFC (11.6.42). He was decorated by the King who expressed an interest in his work in Russia.

In March 1943, Bill was posted to 29 Squadron at West Malling, equipped with Beaufighters at that time, and from May the squadron flew Mosquitoes from Bradwell Bay. He moved to the Intensive Flying Development Flight at Boscombe Down in September 1943, testing the Westland Welkin which never flew operationally. In early February 1944 Bill went to the AFDU at Wittering and flew various aircraft in developing rocket projectiles.

He was seconded to BOAC in July 1944 and sent to Cairo. Bill flew as first officer on Lodestars to Istanbul and Nairobi and later on Ensigns to Calcutta. He was released from the RAF in March 1946 and eventually joined BOAC as a junior captain. In 1949 he began flying Constellations on the London-Sydney run and later Comets. On a visit to Alice Springs in 1951, Bill met Mary Hellyer, who was on holiday away from her farm in Herefordshire. They married in 1961. Bill retired from BOAC in 1963 and became a farmer. He later reflected on his part in the Battle of Britain: 'The large amounts of ammunition which I fired in the general direction of the Luftwaffe were largely ignored by them, and they shot me down at East Horsley railway station!' In May 2000, Tannoy, a nickname he enjoyed, died after a long battle with cancer aged 81 at his home in Cornwall.

Wing Commander Ian Ritchie

Bear was promoted to Squadron Leader on 1 December 1941 and by 1944 was commanding the University Air Squadron, St Andrews. Much against his will he was released from the RAF in 1945, as a Wing Commander and returned to his pre-war profession as a solicitor with Dove, Lockhart, Mackay and Young W.S. He and his wife lived at Gullane, near Drem aerodrome. As was the case with many of his colleagues, the mantle of fighter pilot was not easily discarded and it proved to be a very difficult time. During combat in the summer of 1940, he had experienced extremes of emotion and had forged deep friendships with many of those with whom he served in 603 Squadron. He also loved flying. Back in the tranquillity of his office and waiting room in York Place, he found he greatly missed both of these things. The work itself he found particularly boring after the excitement of being a fighter pilot. It is quite extraordinary, and a measure of the modesty of the man, that Bear had been reluctant to attend any Battle of Britain Memorial functions because he felt his part in the battle was insignificant. It was Uncle George who managed to persuade him to attend when he was reunited with his colleagues who had also survived the battle.

As a member of the 603 Benevolent Fund committee, Ian Ritchie ensured a high standard was achieved as they continued to provide expertise in running the fund, even after the retirement of James Jack in 1958. Throughout the 1950s the list of Trustees of the 603 Benevolent Fund was impressive. The Fund was generally quite wealthy and the wealth was well-managed with many of its members able to offer a high standard of in-house expertise and influence which they brought with them from their civilian occupations. According to Betty Denholm: 'Bear deserves far more credit for the work he undertook than he ever received.' Post war he was also a member of the provisional committee elected to form the 603 Association as Honorary Secretary. In carrying out his duties Bear felt compelled to attempt to locate the whereabouts of all 603 ground crew personnel who had served the Squadron so loyally during the Battle of Britain. With assistance from the other committee members he ensured they were not left wanting. During their time in office, and with generous and practical outside support in the form of two 'memorial cottages' donated by Messrs. MacTaggart, and Mickel Ltd., of Corstorphine, the committee provided temporary accommodation for needy veterans until such times as they were able to fend for themselves. The Association also purchased a house in Trinity Crescent to help the housing needs of its members. Ultimately, a number of successful small businesses were formed by airmen veterans thanks to the support of Bear and the Association committee members.

Bear's close friendship with a number of 603 colleagues, in particular George Denholm, continued up until his death in 1987 aged 77. Betty Denholm and Molly Ritchie have kept in touch and have represented their late husbands as popular guests at 603 Squadron/Association events.

Air Vice-Marshal David Scott-Malden

In late November 1941, Scottie was posted to HQ 14 Group, Inverness on staff duties. In March 1942, he was appointed to lead the North Weald Wing. On 28 April he claimed a probable FW 190 and on 4 May he damaged two Bf109s and on the 19th probably destroyed a FW 190. He damaged a Bf109 on the 27th. Scottie was awarded a Bar to his DFC, promulgated on 5 June 1942. On 19 and 29 June he shared in destroying FW 190s and over Dieppe on 19 August he damaged a Do217. He was awarded the DSO (11.9.42) and the Norwegian War Cross (6.10.42). Rested from operational flying, Scottie was sent on a speaking tour of the American universities flying over in a Clipper flying boat and returning in a Liberator in November when he was sent to HQ Fighter Command, and then from July until October 1943, he was a liaison officer with the US 8th Bomber Command. From 28 October 1943, Scottie was Wing Commander at RAF Hornchurch until 6 February 1944, when he was posted to a mobile GCU at Hornchurch in the 2nd TAF, preparing for the invasion of Europe, under Group Captain Gerald Edge. After D-Day, the unit moved to Normandy. In August 1944, Scottie was promoted to Group Captain and took command of 125 Wing in France. In April 1945, he was posted to the Air Ministry as Air Staff Plans 1 – working on the redeployment of air forces from Europe to the Far East – until September when he was taken ill. In 1945, he was made Commander, Order of Orange-Nassau by the Dutch at the end of the war, when he attended the Admin Training School at Digby (OATS). With the conflict over Scottie remained in the RAF as a Squadron Leader. In 1946, he went on the Selection Board for RAF Cranwell, and then became an instructor there starting a war studies course. He was in the tactics branch at the CFE, West Raynham, from November 1948, until June 1951, when he attended the RAF Staff College. From 1952 until 1954 he was Wing Commander Admin of the 2nd TAF at RAF Wildenrath, Germany after which he went to Flying College at Manby for a year. In April 1955 he was at Fighter Command as night ops and at the end of the year he joined the Joint Planning Staff at the Air Ministry, where he undertook the initial plans for the 1956 Suez operations. A period on the RAF Junior Directing Staff at the Imperial Defence College was followed by a posting to SASO, 12 Group at Horsham St. Faith, as an Air Commodore. Following the downgrading of groups to sectors, he became AOC No.12 East Anglian Sector until 1964. In April 1964, as an Acting Air Vice-Marshal, he ran 'Unison 65', a high-level Commonwealth exercise, before becoming ACS Policy at the Ministry of Defence. The constant pressure led to ill-health and on 25 September 1966 he was invalided out of the RAF with the rank of Air Vice-Marshal. On recovery he became an administrator in the Ministry of Transport until 1978, when he retired to Poringland, Norfolk. He died in 1999.

Squadron Leader Jack Stokoe

On 23 February Jack Stokoe got his wish to go back to the fighting in the south when 54 Squadron were sent back to Hornchurch where it was re-equipped with the Spitfire Mk II. He recorded in his log book: 'Back south again, Yippee!!'.

On 5 March he destroyed a Bf109 15 miles south west of Boulogne in a Spitfire II. On 17 April his Spitfire was damaged by a near-miss Flak burst. He destroyed a Bf110 10 miles south east of Clacton on 20 April but was then himself shot down. After his aircraft had been hit, but before he could bale out, the Spitfire exploded and he regained consciousness to find he was falling free of the aircraft but still strapped to his seat (Jack believes a cannon shell may have hit the armour plate/mid-section behind his seat causing the explosion and structural failure). He managed to extricate himself and pull his ripcord, remembering the great relief felt when it actually worked. Jack landed in the North Sea approximately 30 miles from land on a day when surface conditions were severe. Unable to free himself from the rigging lines and the water-laden chute, he was in danger for some time as it threatened to drag him under the choppy surface of the sea. He was eventually rescued by the crew of a minesweeper who stripped him of his wet clothing and gave him rum and a bunk in which he could spend the return journey. One of the crew photographed Jack while he was still in his partially-inflated dinghy. It was by good fortune that the minesweeper crew picked him up first. An RAF rescue launch was on its way to the area but having been beaten to the task, it headed back to port. The sea was very rough and as it entered the harbour the launch overturned with loss of life. Jack spent seven days in hospital recovering from minor injuries and hypothermia.

Back in action, on 6 May 1941, Jack damaged a Bf109 over Dover and the next day claimed a 109 probable south of Calais. On 21 June he probably destroyed a 109 over Gravelines-St Omer and on the 24th destroyed a Bf109F north of Gravelines. This was his final victory. On 27 June he was posted to 74 Squadron at Gravesend but three days later he was sent to 59 OTU at Crosby-on-Eden as an instructor. Jack was moved to 60 OTU at East Fortune, East Lothian, on 17 July. This unit was renumbered 132 OTU in November 1942. On 3 October 1943 he was posted to 1692 (R/D) Flight, also situated at East Fortune, where he instructed on airborne radar. He was awarded the DFC, promulgated on 6 June 1944. The following month he was promoted to Squadron Leader.

In late June 1945 he became Senior Admin Officer at Great Massingham and, in August, Station Commander. He was posted to HQ, Transport Command in December and in January 1946 he went to Australia to replace Squadron Leader Tony Bartley as Officer Commanding (OC) Mascot Airfield, Sydney. Mascot was in the process of closing and he went to HQ 300 Group at Melbourne, organising the closing down of the Australia-Singapore air route. He returned to the UK in May-June 1946 as OC troops aboard-ship.

Jack was released from the RAF on 21 August 1946 as a squadron leader. His total claims by the end of the war were: seven and one shared destroyed, two and one shared probable and four damaged. He regards his part in the Battle of Britain with quintessential British spirit: '…well you just got on with it, didn't you…'

With the war over he believed promotion would be slow with so many supernumerary wing commanders and group captains available. He missed the flying and rejoined the RAFVR at 20 Reserve & Flying Training School (R&FTS), Rochester, in July 1947, as a Flying Officer RAFVR, flying Tiger Moths and Chipmunks until June 1952.

Jack's parents had died before WWII leaving one younger brother and an aunt (his father's sister). With little to return to in County Durham he settled in Kent and worked at the County Council as a weights and measures inspector on trading standards and consumer protection. He was Chief Standards Trading Officer for Kent for the last 14 years. A position he was immensely proud of. He retired in 1983.

For many years after the war he had a large scar on his forehead and residual scarring to his face and hands from the burns he received. In later life the only visible sign of his wartime injuries was a crooked little finger, the result of the burns received in 1940. During the years after the war he avoided anything to do with the part he played in the conflict, but during the last few years of his life Jack became an active participant at the annual Battle of Britain anniversary functions at the Purfleet Military Heritage museum. During the 1996 function he was re-united with Stapme Stapleton after 56 years. Having suffered a severely disabling stroke some weeks before, Jack Stokoe died in his sleep on Friday 1 October 1999. He was 79. Just prior to his death he was guest of honour at the unveiling of the 'Jack Stokoe bay' at Purfleet where his log book and medals are displayed.

Jack married his sweet-heart from the north east during the war and they had a daughter, Anne. Sadly, the marriage didn't survive the war. Jack enjoyed life in the south and the couple became estranged and later divorced. Jack never returned north. At his cremation service at Rochester a Harvard (the aircraft in which Jack learnt how to fly) flew overhead in salute. Anne travelled down for the sad occasion.

Squadron Leader John Strawson

Later that month Strawson departed from Scapa Flow with his new squadron in HMS *Victorious* which was later transferred to HMS *Ark Royal* for the remainder of the journey. On 14 June 1941 the aircraft took off for Malta where they were refuelled before flying on to Egypt two days later. From Egypt they flew to Haifa in Palestine where 260 Squadron amalgamated with 450 RAAF, flying ground-attack sorties in the Syrian campaign with detachments at Beirut and El Bassa. Ground attacks continued until 16 October when the Squadron left El Bassa and travelled to the Western Desert where they provided air support for the fluctuating fortunes of the Allied ground forces, strafing enemy positions and providing fighter escort for Allied bombers. On 31 December 1941, Strawson was promoted to Flight Sergeant.

In February 1942, the Squadron withdrew to re-equip with the Curtiss Kittyhawk Mk I, returning to combat in March. Strawson was discharged on 3 March 1942 on appointment to temporary commission. He was assessed as 'Fit for commission in G.D. Branch RAFVR' on 17 March and granted a commission on the 25th. For 5 May 1942 his service record reads: 'Granted commission for the emergency, P/O on probation (ex Sgt) wef: 4.3.42.' His total service time to that date was 3 years 320 days with total qualified service being 2 years, 182 days.

August was a busy time for 260 and during the month Strawson led the unit on 23 operational sorties and 25 Squadron exercises. On 8 August he led eight Kittyhawks providing protective escort for the Lodestar taking Winston Churchill from Burg el Arab to LG97. Strawson was again promoted to Flying Officer on probation on 1 October 1942.

As a Flight Lieutenant at HQ 239 Wing he wrote home: 'Leading the Squadron is one thing but detailing the pilots who are to fly and their positions in the formation is more difficult.' When a colleague was killed he wrote: 'The other day one of my best chaps was killed in action in which I led the squadron. Not nice at all. He was married... I did not make a slip... It is just the war.' On 22 September 1942 Strawson was promoted to Acting Squadron Leader and was responsible for allocating operations to the squadrons of the wing. Several months of intense activity followed with 260's movements mirroring the advances and withdrawals of the British Eighth Army across Egypt and Libya as it came up against Rommel's Africa Korps for control of the area.

On 16 November 1942, Strawson was part of the advanced wing party which was travelling to Martuba to survey potential sites for advanced landing grounds. When manoeuvring his jeep off the road to pass a number of stationary vehicles he hit a landmine and was killed instantly. He was 26 and is buried in Plot 4, Row G, Grave 3 at the Knightsbridge War Cemetery, Acroma, Libya (25 miles from Tobruk). The cemetery is located at the intersection of the Trigh Capuzzo and Trigh Bir Hakeim desert tracks, south west of Tobruk. Following his death, Strawson's mother had her son's DFC made into a brooch which she wore in his memory. The villagers of Low Marnham presented their church with an urn engraved with Strawson's details which is still used today to fill the parish fonts. On the 60th anniversary of the Battle of Britain, W.H. 'Bill' Strawson CBE, DL, unveiled a plaque and an avenue of lime trees at Blyborough near Lincoln in tribute to his eldest brother.

It was not until 2002, that the name of Sergeant Pilot John Strawson DFC was finally included on the Master List of Battle of Britain aircrew. Details in the 603 ORB are sparse during this period with no mention of Strawson being with the Squadron at all. When attempting to discover what part he may or may not have played in the battle with the Edinburgh Squadron it was initially suggested that he might have undertaken a non-operational sortie – a sector recco or an air test – when he was shot down but when considering the pattern of the Luftwaffe sweeps it is highly unlikely that George Denholm would have even contemplated sanctioning even an experienced pilot, let alone an inexperienced one, to take an aircraft from Hornchurch into an area of enemy (and friendly) operational aerial activity.

Air Commodore Sir Archie Winskill

On 14 August he destroyed a 109 bringing his total to at least three enemy aircraft destroyed. The following day he was promoted to Flying Officer. Later that month he was shot down near Calais recalling it was: 'four days after Bader in the summer of 1941 whilst on a fighter sweep over France.' Assisted by the French Resistance, he managed to evade capture and, by December 1941, had returned to England via Spain and Gibraltar. He was awarded the DFC, promulgated on 6 January 1942. On 6 April 1942, he formed 165 Squadron at Ayr, which he commanded until August. As Flight Lieutenant he then took command of 222 Squadron at Drem until September when he became CO of 232 Squadron at Turnhouse. He was still in command when the Squadron went to North Africa in November. On 18 January 1943, he was shot down during a fighter sweep over the Mateur area, probably by FW 190s. He recalled: '...whilst attacking ground targets I was caught by some concentrated ground fire and landed behind enemy lines. Again I escaped and returned to the squadron dressed as an Arab!!' On 7 April he destroyed a Ju87 and shared another. On the 27th he damaged a FW 190 and on 7 May he destroyed a Ju88 and a Bf109 on the ground at La Sebala airfield and the next day he damaged a Bf323 on the ground. With his tour complete Winskill was awarded a Bar to his DFC, promulgated on 27 July 1943, and returned to Britain. He commanded CGS, Catfoss from September 1943 until December 1944, when, as a Squadron Leader (21.6.44) he went to the Army Staff College, Camberley. On completion of his course he was posted to a staff job at the Air Ministry in June 1945. He recalled: 'After the war I flew all the post-war jet aircraft – Vampire, Meteor, Hunter, Javelin, Canberra – in squadron service, again in an era when loss rates were still high.' From 1955-56 he was Officer Commanding RAF Turnhouse. Archie Winskill was promoted to Group Captain (1.7.59) and the following year made a CBE (11.6.60). On 18 December 1968, he retired from the RAF as an Air Commodore (1.7.63). He was Captain of the Queen's Flight from 1968 until 1972. He was created a KCVO in 1980 (CVO 1973). At the time of writing Sir Archie lives in retirement at Henley on Thames. He reflects:

In my 85th year I sometimes despair when I ponder how as young men we fought for King and Country – Country being the United Kingdom. We seem to be tearing these islands apart. Islands which created a successful empire, and a language which controls the world and a Prime Minister who could not be bothered to attend the Battle of Britain memorial service in Westminster Abbey on the 60th Anniversary!

NO.603 (CITY OF EDINBURGH) SQUADRON
ROLL OF HONOUR 1941-1955

On 2 July 1989, Her Majesty Queen Elizabeth II unveiled a Scroll of Honour in the Canongate Kirk, (the Kirk of Holyroodhouse) Edinburgh, commemorating those members of the Squadron who lost their lives whilst serving with 603 in peace and war.

1941	17 Jan	Sgt	J. Liddell	RAFVR
	17 Feb	F/L	J.C. Boulter DFC	RAF
	7 Jun	P/O	R.J. Burleigh	RAF
	20 Jun	P/O	C.A. Newman	RAFVR
	24 Jun	P/O	K.J. McKelvie	RAFVR
	30 Jun	Sgt	L.E.S. Salt	RAFVR
	22 Jul	P/O	P. Delorme	RAFVR
	23 Jul	P/O	H. Blackall	RAFVR
	23 Jul	F/Sgt	G.W. Tabor	RAFVR
	5 Aug	P/O	N.H.C. Keable	RAFVR
	29 Aug	LAC	J.T. Costine	RAFVR
	27 Sept	F/Sgt	W.J. Archibald	RCAF
	13 Oct	Sgt	A.D. Shuckburgh	RAFVR
	21 Oct	Sgt	W. McKelvie	RAFVR
	8 Dec	F/O	S.G.H. Fawkes	RAFVR
	18 Dec	S/L	R.G. Forshaw	RAF
1942	1 Jan	Sgt	J.A. Farmer	RAFVR
	26 Mar	P/O	W.I. Jones	RCAF
	22 Apr	P/O	G. Murray	RCAF
	9 May	F/L	J.W. Buckstone	RAFVR
	12 May	P/O	H.R. Mitchell	RNZAF
	8 Jun	F/O	L.G. Barlow	RAFVR
	2 Jul	P/O	J. Hurst DFC	RAFVR
	8 Jul	F/O	N.S. King	RAFVR
	8 Jul	AC2	W.J. Newman	RAFVR
	9 Jul	F/O	G.A. Carlet (Levy-Despas)	RCAF
1943	2 May	F/O	M.F. Scantlebury	RAFVR
	2 May	WO	B.G. James	RAAF
	30 Jun	Sgt	W.E.J. Powell	RAF
	23 Aug	S/L	J.A. Crompton	RAFVR
	23 Aug	Sgt	H.G. Griffiths	RAFVR
	26 Aug	S/L	H.K. Laycock	RAF
	26 Aug	F/Sgt	R.C. Scott	RAFVR
	30 Aug	F/O	A. Honig DFM	RAFVR
	30 Aug	F/Sgt	R.G. Finlay	RAFVR
	7 Oct	F/Sgt	J.P. Hey	RAFVR
	7 Oct	F/Sgt	E.A. Worrall	RAFVR
	13 Nov	W/O	F.M. Cox	RAAF
	13 Nov	W/O	N.S. Ferguson	RAAF
1944	16 Jan	F/L	G.W. MacDonnell	RAFVR
	16 Jan	F/O	S.W. Piner	RAFVR
	27 Jan	F/Sgt	A. Rooks	RAFVR
	27 Jan	F/O	M.J.R. Thom	RAFVR
	8 Apr	F/Sgt	H. Lacey	RAFVR
	11 Apr	P/O	E.T. Lynch	RAAF
	11 Apr	P/O	C.L. Sykes	RAFVR
	13 Apr	F/Sgt	R.T. Gosling	RAFVR

	13 Apr	Sgt	S.A. West	RAFVR
	15 May	F/Sgt	J.E. Paddison	RAFVR
	15 May	F/Sgt	J.C. Rhodes	RAFVR
	15 May	P/O	E.G. Harman	RAF
	15 May	F/Sgt	L.E. Hopkin	RAFVR
	1 Jun	F/Sgt	R.M. Atkinson	RAFVR
	1 Jun	F/Sgt	D.F. Parsons	RAFVR
	5 Jul	F/Sgt	C.H. Dean	RAFVR
	5 Jul	F/Sgt	D.W. Taylor	RAFVR
	6 Jul	F/O	J.C. Dalziel	RCAF
	19 Jul	F/Sgt	J.G. Shaw	RAFVR
	21 Jul	F/Sgt	D. Joyce	RAFVR
	21 Jul	F/Sgt	K.F. Thomas	RAFVR
	23 Jul	F/Sgt	J.J. Rogers	RAFVR
	30 Jul	Cpl	P. Richardson	RAFVR
	7 Aug	P/O	J.W.H. Dibbs	RAFVR
	3 Oct	Sgt	D. Harrison	RAFVR
1945	11 Jan	F/O	L. S. Trail	RAF
	17 Mar	W/O	J.D. Green	RAAF
	24 Mar	P/O	N.A.H. McGinn	RIAF
1949	6 Mar	F/O	J.M. Mears	RAuxAF
1951	22 Jun	F/O	A. Anderson	RAuxAF
1953	10 Jul	S/L	R.L.R. Davies DFC	RAF
1955	17 Apr	P/O	S. Milne	RAuxAF

This list includes all members of 603 Squadron who died while serving in war and peace. Confirmed by Air Historial Branch (RAF) and the Commonwealth War Graves Commission.

HONOURS AND AWARDS

Year	Name	Award/*London Gazette* Entry
1941	Flying Officer J.S. Morton AAF	DFC 29.4.41. 2446.
1941	Acting Flight Lieutenant F.D.S. Scott-Maldon RAF	DFC 19.8.41. 4810.
1942	Sergeant D.F. Ruchwaldy	DFM 7.4.42
1942	Pilot Officer J. Hurst RAFVR	DFC 7.7.42. 2980.
1943	Pilot Officer C.B. Megone RAFVR	DFC 12.11.43 4971
1943	Acting Squadron Leader G.B. Atkinson RAFRO	DFC 14.12.43. 5436.
1943	Pilot Officer R.H. Giles RAFVR	DFC 14.12.43. 5437.
1943	Pilot Officer K.J.E. Hopkins RAAF	DFC 14.12.43. 5437.
1944	Flight Lieutenant A.P. Pringle RAFVR	DFC 2.5.44. 2007
1944	Acting Flight Lieutenant G.J. Matthews RAFVR	DFC 7.7.44. 3188
1944	Flight Lieutenant A.E. Ross RAFVR	DFC 22.8.44. 3882
1944	Flight Sergeant Wilkinson	Mention in Despatches (MID)
1944	Flight Sergeant Moore	Mention in Despatches (MID)
1944	Flight Sergeant J.R. Edgar RAFVR	DFM 22.8.44
1944	Flight Sergeant H.B. Yates RAFVR	DFM 22.8.44
1944	Flight Sergeant E.T. Pennie RAFVR	DFM 3.10.44
1944	Flight Lieutenant D.G. Simpson (NZ) RNZAF	DFC 7.1.44. 5085
1945	Acting Squadron Leader T.C. Rigler DFM RAFVR	DFC 1.5.45. 2302
1945	Flight Lieutenant W.J. Batchelor RAFVR	DFC 1.6.45. 2793
1945	Flight Lieutenant W.G. Rogers	MBE

Post War

Year	Name	Award
1949	Warrant Officer J. Prentice RAuxAF	BEM
1951	Flight Lieutenant D. McIntosh RAuxAF	AFC
1951	Warrant Officer C.E. Erskine RAuxAF	BEM
1953	Flight Lieutenant G.W. Scott AFC RAuxAF	MBE
1953	Warrant Officer A.D. Mackenzie RAuxAF	BEM
1954	Flight Sergeant F. W. E. Day RAuxAF	BEM
1954	Flight Lieutenant M.E. Hobson RAF	Queens Commendation for Valuable Service in the Air
1956	Flight Sergeant J. Bell RAuxAF	BEM

Post Reformation

Year	Name	Award
2000	Warrant Officer D. McQueen RAuxAF	MBE
2001	Flight Lieutenant N. Daniel RAuxAF	MBE
2001	Squadron Leader J.B. Blanche AE RAuxAF	QVRM

DISTINGUISHED FLYING CROSS (DFC) 1941-1945 – *LONDON GAZETTE* ENTRIES

SCOTT-MALDEN, Francis David Stephen. Acting Flight Lieutenant (74690) RAFVR. 603 Sqn.
London Gazette: 19/8/1941: 4810

This officer has been continuously engaged in operational flying since June, 1940, leading his flight and sometimes the squadron. During the last six weeks, he has taken part in 38 offensive operations over enemy territory. A fine leader, Flight Lieutenant Scott-Malden has at all times displayed great keenness and determination in his engagements with the enemy. He has destroyed three and damaged many of their aircraft.

MEGONE, Cyril Bruce. Pilot Officer (148126) RAFVR. 603 Sqn.
London Gazette: 12/11/1943: 4971

Pilot Officer Megone is a keen and tenacious pilot. He has participated in a very large number of sorties, including a most determined attack on a large merchant ship which he bombed with destructive effect. In September 1943, he took part in an engagement against a formation of enemy aircraft, one of which he shot down. During the combat, his aircraft was hit and a fire commenced near the port main plane. Nevertheless, Pilot Officer Megone coolly flew the aircraft to the flat terrain of a small island where he effected a safe landing. Flames were still issuing from one of the fuel tanks but they were quickly extinguished. The situation was serious but, as it was clear that the island was still in enemy hands, Pilot Officer Megone took off. Displaying great skill and resolution he succeeded, after a long flight, in reaching base where he landed his badly damaged aircraft safely. His courage and resource were of a high order.

ATKINSON, Gordon Barry. Acting Squadron Leader (42091) RAFO. 603 Sqn.
London Gazette: 14/12/1943: 5436

This officer has participated in a very large number of sorties, including many attacks on shipping. On one occasion he led the squadron in a sortie during which a large ship was attacked and disabled. Squadron Leader Atkinson has displayed inspiring leadership and great determination and has played a good part in the success achieved by his squadron.

GILES, Rueben Henry. Pilot Officer (148129) RAFVR. 603 Sqn.
London Gazette: 14/12/1943: 5437

This officer has completed many sorties and has displayed high courage and great devotion to duty. On a recent occasion he took part in a successful attack on a Siebel ferry. In spite of fierce opposition, Pilot Officer Giles pressed home his attack with great determination, setting a fine example.

HOPKINS, Keith Isaac Eula. Pilot Officer (Aus 400924) RAAF. 603 Sqn.
London Gazette: 14/12/1943: 5437

This officer is a keen and determined pilot, whose fine fighting spirit has been evident throughout his tour. On one occasion he took part in an attack on shipping in Naxos harbour. In the face of fierce anti-aircraft fire, the attack was pressed home with great vigour and two vessels were set on fire. Pilot Officer Hopkins is a good leader, whose efforts have been most praiseworthy.

PRINGLE, Alexander Patrick. Flight Lieutenant (106756) RAFVR. 603 Sqn.
London Gazette: 2/5/1944: 2007

On very many occasions this officer has led formations of aircraft in attacks on shipping and has contributed materially to the success obtained. On one occasion, Flight Lieutenant Pringle led the squadron in an attack on six enemy aircraft, all of which were shot down, two of them by this officer. Since then, Flight Lieutenant Pringle has gained distinction by successfully attacking a naval vessel. The ship was set on fire and eventually blew up with terrific force. This officer has set a fine example of skill, courage and devotion to duty.

ROSS, Anthony Edward. Flying Officer (133713) RAFVR. 603 Sqn.
London Gazette: 22/8/1944: 3882

As observer, this officer has taken part in very many sorties, including a number of attacks on enemy shipping, during which successes have been obtained. He is a gallant and resolute member of aircraft crew and his navigational skill has played a good part in the success of many operations in which he has participated. He has set a most inspiring example.

RIGLER, Thomas Charles. DFM. Acting Squadron Leader (114032) RAFVR. 603 Sqn.
London Gazette: 1/5/1945: 2302

This officer has completed a very large number of sorties and throughout has displayed keenness and devotion to duty worthy of the highest praise. He has led the squadron on very many low level harassing attacks on a variety of enemy targets and much success has been achieved. By his great skill and fine fighting qualities, Squadron Leader Rigler has contributed materially to the high standard of operational efficiency of the squadron he commands.

DISTINGUISHED FLYING MEDAL (DFM)
1941-1945 – *LONDON GAZETTE* ENTRIES

RUCHWALDY, Desmond Fred. Sergeant (1281372) RAFVR. 603 Sqn.
London Gazette: 7/4/1942
Since June, 1941, this airman has participated in a large number of operational sorties in which he has destroyed two and probably destroyed a further two enemy aircraft. He is a good pilot and he has at all times shown the greatest determination.

EDGAR, Johnstone Robertson. Flight Sergeant (1349729) RAFVR. 603 Sqn.
London Gazette: 22/8/1944
Flight Sergeant Edgar is a courageous and resolute pilot. He has participated in many sorties involving attacks on a variety of targets. On one occasion, he took part in an engagement against three enemy aircraft, all of which were shot down, two of them by this determined pilot. On another occasion, Flight Sergeant Edgar participated in an attack on a large fuel dump, which was set on fire. In several attacks on enemy shipping, Flight Sergeant Edgar has greatly distinguished himself, having assisted in the destruction of six supply ships, a small tanker and an E-boat.

YATES, Harold Birchall. Flight Sergeant (1089142) RAFVR. 603 Sqn.
London Gazette: 22/8/1944
Throughout his tour of operations, this airman has displayed notable skill and great devotion to duty. He has completed very many sorties, including several successful attacks on enemy shipping. On the last of these an attack on a large merchant vessel, escorted by several naval vessels and a number of smaller armed vessels, Flight Sergeant Yates obtained hits on one of the smaller craft. In the fight, both Flight Sergeant Yates and his navigator were wounded and his aircraft was extensively damaged. Nevertheless, this gallant pilot flew safely to base and effected a masterly landing. He displayed commendable courage and resolution throughout.

PENNIE, Ernest F. Flight Sergeant (1350204) RAFVR. 603 Sqn.
London Gazette: 3/10/1944
Flight Sergeant Pennie has always displayed commendable skill and courage in air operations. In July, 1944, he took part in an attack on an enemy convoy. In the fight, considerable anti-aircraft fire was faced. Flight Sergeant Pennie was wounded and his aircraft was hit repeatedly. Nevertheless, this gallant pilot pressed home his attack, obtaining hits on a ship.

HONORARY AIR COMMODORES

The Rt. Hon. Sir William Y. Darling CBE, MC, DL, JP, FRSE, MP:
23 Feb 1943 – 15 June 1951*

HRH The Princess Elizabeth:
16 June 1951 – 31 May 1957

(HRH The Princess Elizabeth who, at her own express wish, continued as Honorary Air Commodore when she ascended the throne on 6 February 1952)

The Rt. Hon. Lord Selkirk of Douglas QC, LLB, MA:
1 October 1999 – 10 December 2000

Her Majesty Queen Elizabeth II:
11 December 2000 – Present.**

*Sir William Darling originally took over as Honorary Air Commodore for five years but in 1948 he was granted an extension in office for a further five years but resigned in June 1951 to allow HRH The Princess Elizabeth to take over as Honorary Air Commodore of 603 Squadron. He died on 4 February 1962.

** See page 368 for Lord Selkirk's role.

THE SQUADRON STANDARD
AND
BATTLE HONOURS

The Standard was created by His Late Majesty King George VI to mark the 25th anniversary of the Royal Air Force in 1943. It was awarded only to squadrons of 25 years' standing, or with a history of special outstanding operations. The Standard consists of a fringed and tasselled silken banner, mounted on a pike, which is crowned by a golden eagle.

The primary source for information regarding Battle Honours is Air Publication (AP) 3327 'Colours and Standards in the Royal Air Force'. Individual squadron details to which a squadron may lay claim, and those it actually chooses to display upon its Standard, are derived from squadron records, the RAF Forms 540 and 541. Entitlement to, and presentation of, squadron standards is usually covered by an Air Ministry Order (AMO). Once the squadron has satisfied the qualifying requirements it receives a list, from the Air Ministry (MOD) (Air) of the Battle Honours to which it is entitled, with a note of those that may be placed upon the Standard. The squadron then selects the honours which it wishes to display, to a maximum of eight, and this, along with the formal request for a standard is forwarded to the sovereign for approval.

Eight selected Battle Honours surround the Squadron badge, and a decorative border contains the rose, leek, thistle and shamrock, beautifully embroidered. The Battle Honours on the 603 Squadron Standard are:

Home Defence 1940-42
Battle of Britain 1940
Channel and North Sea 1941
Fortress Europe 1942
Malta 1942
Mediterranean 1943
Sicily 1943
South East Europe 1944.

In addition, the Squadron was also awarded the Battle Honour France and Germany 1945.

COMMANDING OFFICERS

S/L G.L. Denholm DFC, AAF	4 Jun 40 – 1 Apr 41
S/L F.M. Smith RAF	1 Apr 41 – 25 Jul 41
S/L M.J. Loudon RAF	25 Jul 41 – 17 Oct 41
S/L R.G. Forshaw RAF	17 Oct 41 – 18 Dec 41
S/L Lord D. Douglas-Hamilton RAFVR	18 Dec 41 – 20 Jul 42
S/L W.A. Douglas RAF*	20 Jul 42 – 3 Aug 42
S/L P. Illingworth RAF**	10 Apr 42 – 4 June 42
S/L F.W. Marshall RAFVR***	3 Aug 42 – 28 Jan 43
W/C H.A. Chater RAF	28 Jan 43 – 1 Dec 43
W/C J.R.H. Lewis DFC, RAFRO	1 Dec 43 – 15 Jun 44
W/C J.T.D. Revell, RAF	15 Jun 44 – 2 Aug 44
S/L C.D. Paine (Acting) RAFVR	2 Aug 44 – 23 Sept 44
Squadron disbanded 26 Dec 1944	
Squadron reformed 10 Jan 1945	
W/C C.N. Foxley-Norris RAF	23 Sept 44 – 26 Dec 44
S/L E.H.M. Patterson DFC, RAFVR****	10 Jan 45 – 26 Jan 45
S/L T.C. Rigler DFC, DFM, RAFVR	26 Jan 45 – 1 Apr 45
S/L H.R.P. Pertwee DFC, RAFVR	1 Apr 45 – 15 Aug 45
Squadron disbanded 15 August 1945	
Squadron reformed 11 June 1946	
S/L G.K. Gilroy DSO, DFC, AAF	11 Jun 46 – 23 Sept 49
S/L J.W.E. Holmes DFC, AFC, RAF	23 Sept 49 – 1 Dec 50
S/L P.J. Anson DFC, RAF	1 Dec 50 – 22 Mar 53
S/L R. R.L.R. Davies DFC, RAF	23 Mar 53 – 25 Aug 53
S/L R. Schofield, RAF	25 Aug 53 – 9 May 56
S/L M.E. Hobson AFC, RAF	9 May 56 – 10 Mar 57
Squadron disbanded 10 March 1957	
Squadron reformed 1 October 1999	
W/C A.J. Beaton RAuxAF	1 Oct 99 – Present

*Posting Notice 92/05/42 dated July 1942, then to reconstituted 229 Squadron. PMC, RAF Records Innsworth.
** Officer Commanding Ground Party.
*** Administrative Officer Commanding Ground Party.
**** Ex-229 Squadron. Non-effective sick throughout period of command.

SELECTED PEN-PORTRAITS OF COMMANDING OFFICERS
(SEE 'LIFE AFTER 603' FOR GEORGE DENHOLM)

Squadron Leader Lord David Douglas-Hamilton
18 December 41 – 20 July 42
Thrust unexpectedly into command by the loss of S/L Roger Forshaw, Lord David was to guide the Squadron through one of its most difficult and challenging operational postings on Malta whilst it was besieged by Axis forces.

He was the youngest of four brothers – Douglas, Geordie and Malcolm – all enthusiastic aviators and unique as a group in that they all commanded RAF squadrons. Prior to the outbreak of the Second World War, Geordie was the CO of 603 and Douglas CO of 602 (City of Glasgow) Squadron. Douglas also had the distinction of being the first pilot to make the hazardous flight over Mount Everest – in 1933.

David Douglas-Hamilton was a natural leader. Physically powerful – he was 6 foot 4 and captained the Oxford University boxing team – he nonetheless cared deeply for the welfare of the young men under his command and was saddened greatly by the deaths of those who fell to the guns of the enemy.

In 1938, he joined the Auxiliary Air Force and in October of that year married Prunella Stack. Prior to this, David had already amassed a considerable number of flying hours whilst training with his brother Malcolm and he was irritated to find that despite this, the RAF would still require him to complete the normal flying training process. He was further annoyed to learn that on the successful completion of his training he was to become a flying instructor at RAF Netheravon rather than go on to operations.

But he would eventually be granted his wish and in the autumn of 1941, he found himself posted to 603 as a flight commander flying Spitfires and thrust into a daily round of Circuses, Roadsteads and other operations across the English Channel. He flew his first operation on 27 November 1941 – an attack on enemy shipping.

In mid-December, two days after 603 moved north to RAF Dyce to be rested, S/L Forshaw was lost and Lord David became the CO. In April 1942, 603 flew to Malta to be a part of its defence. By this time, many of the experienced aircrew had been posted on and the group which made the hazardous flight from the USS *Wasp* to Malta contained many new and inexperienced pilots. Despite this, Lord David managed to create a successful team which distinguished itself in the most difficult of circumstances. He and one of his flight commanders, F/L Bill Douglas, kept a diary of the Squadron's activities whilst on Malta and it provides a unique record of what life was like for 603 during this dangerous and stressful period. With poor living conditions as well as the constant threat from the enemy, in some ways, the siege of Malta was worse than the Battle of Britain as far as the fighting airmen were concerned.

Lord David stood down as 603's CO in July and shortly after this, the Squadron was disbanded as a Spitfire Squadron. Possibly as a means of relieving some of the stress within him, he wrote an account of his experiences on Malta which was published in the Edinburgh-based *Blackwood's Magazine* in two instalments in 1944.

He returned to the UK and in 1943, there was a change of role. He was posted to RAF Benson near Oxford where he flew Mosquitoes on photo-reconnaissance operations over Germany and the occupied countries with 544 Squadron. On 2 August 1944 on an operation across central/southern France, his aircraft was badly shot up by anti-aircraft fire which injured (or killed) the navigator, Philip Gatehouse, and knocked out one engine. Squadron Leader Douglas-Hamilton decided to try to reach the safety of home. He managed to nurse the faltering Mosquito back almost to his base at Benson, but virtually within sight of the airfield and safety, it came down in the English countryside in what seems to have been an attempt to make a wheels-up landing. Both men were killed. Lord David was survived by his wife and two sons. His tenure of command of 603 was through one of its most testing and challenging periods and he rose to it superbly despite being modest and unassuming.

The connection of the Douglas-Hamilton family and 603 Squadron continues with the involvement of Lord James Douglas-Hamilton (now Lord Selkirk) as an Honorary Air Commodore. He is a nephew of Lord David who would no doubt be pleased to know that the family connection continues into the 21st century.

Wing Commander H.A. Chater
28 January 43 – 1 December 43
Of his time with 603 Squadron, Hugh Chater's only regret was that due to ill-health he didn't complete a full tour. On returning to the UK the large amount of flying hours he accumulated compensated for the many and varied moves he and his family had to endure. He believes his beloved Beaufighter (and the Mosquito) has never received the acclaim it deserved. This is Hugh Chater's own story:

I was born in Natal, South Africa, the third of four sons, all of whom were destined to become pilots, and three of whom were to survive the war (my eldest brother was killed in the desert in a Blenheim, returning from an operation at night). My fervent wish was to train as a doctor, like my father. I was the only one of us who wished to follow him, but the whole family was shattered when he died suddenly of a stroke in 1930. I was thirteen at the time and had just started at Public School – Michaelhouse.

On leaving school at 17, I worked for a team of accountants on the advice of my eldest brother, who was in business in Durban, and continued with my boxing, gymnastics, wrestling and rugby. I also took flying lessons at the Durban Aero Club.

Meanwhile, a year before, my eldest brother had left for England and had been accepted into the RAF, so it seemed right that I should try to do likewise. I left Durban by sea in midsummer, arriving at Southampton on 19 December 1936. Weatherwise this was a severe shock, so in the train to London, I donned my new Jaeger dressing-gown. This caused some amusement.

After interviews at the Air Ministry (and the purchase of warm clothes), I was sent to the Bristol Flying School at Yatesbury. The Tiger Moth was one up on my previous types and after we had been in the air for a while on my first trip, my instructor asked whether I had flown before. I said 'Yes, Sir.' 'Why didn't you tell me?' he asked and when I said that I didn't want to seem to be showing off, he chuckled and said 'Well done.' He taught me a great deal, not only in the air, but about life in the RAF in which he had served for many years.

From Yatesbury we were sent to Uxbridge for the course on RAF discipline and drill and to choose uniforms and other equipment from the various outfitters. We were made Acting Pilot Officers and sent to RAF Grantham, where we did the first part of our flying course on Hawker Harts. After this we went for the final part of our training to South Cerney, where we flew Harts, Audax and Fury aircraft.

I was posted to RAF Catterick for duty with 41 Fighter Squadron. This was unfortunately ended after eight months when I was posted to the RAF Central Flying School at Upavon for instructor training. I was very sad to leave 41 Squadron, but was told that more instructors were needed for the training of pilots who were being recruited for the conflict which was clearly coming.

After my course at CFS I was posted to the RAF College at Cranwell, in October 1938, where I remained until September 1940, when all flying training was to be moved to Commonwealth countries. I was then posted to No.22 Air School at Vereeniging in South Africa, where I stayed until January 1943. Then I was posted to the Middle East for operational duties. By which time I had completed 1581 hours on instructional flying.

On arriving in Cairo (M.E.H.Q.) I was sent to the so-called Operational Training Unit at Ballah, where I met a Warrant Officer Davies, a nice man, who had only one serviceable old Blenheim; the second, and only other, was being used for spares. We took off and after about 20 minutes I was sent off on my own. I flew around for a while and as I was coming downwind for a third landing the starboard engine coughed once or twice and then stopped. I completed the circuit and landed. There was no other form of instruction whatsoever. This was my operational training! However, I saw two Hurricanes outside an office tent and went over, to be warmly welcomed by two Canadians, who were in charge. I was briefed on Hurricanes and the firing of rockets and had two trips. The rocket-firing was an invigorating experience. After Ballah I reported to 201 Group in Alexandria and was told that I would be given command of 603 Squadron, with the acting rank of wing commander. Apparently the Lord Provost was concerned, quite rightly, that 603 Squadron had no pilots or aircraft and the groundcrews were in Cyprus, being used to service aircraft passing through.

I was taken to EDKU, an airfield just outside Alexandria, to await the arrival of aircraft and aircrews. The groundcrews arrived very soon from Cyprus and were able to familiarise themselves with the two early-arrival Beaufighters, which were serviceable, but fairly well-used.

The 603 groundcrews and their officers fitted in very well and were virtually the solid basis on which the Squadron was rebuilt. The Adjutant, Raymond Oddie [sic] I soon discovered was an excellent officer.

The aircrew began to arrive and pretty soon we had the full complement; a good mix of Australian, British, two Canadians and one New Zealander.

Whilst at EDKU we carried out a few operations with a squadron based at Berka. This involved a number of fairly long trips between the two airfields.

On 1 April 1943 we arrived at Misurata, in Libya – our own compact operational base for the first time.

There were two other squadrons on the other side of the airfield, one a Beaufort squadron, which flew at night, dealing with enemy submarines, using depth-charges, while the second was a redundant Hurricane squadron awaiting news of its next assignment, since the Germans had been driven out of Africa. We discovered that the Hurricane pilots were using a captured Stuka to replenish their supply of alcohol from the delta. We organised that our airmen should have the limited supplies of beer from the re-opened brewery at Tripoli – this meant that every airman received one bottle of beer a week, while the Officers and NCO's made other arrangements. There were some memorable parties including one when the crew of a visiting South African Ju52, which had had its middle engine fall out, gave us a barrel of brandy. Later that night I found a squadron commander busily driving his desert car to nowhere while its axle rested on a palm-tree stump.

I was able to tour the base weekly with our excellent Warrant Officer, Mr [Jock] Prentice. He was considerably older than the rest of us, but one of the best I have ever met. His bearing and dress were always immaculate, even in desert conditions and the airmen had a deep respect for him (I was told there had been a problem in Cyprus when his authority was brought to bear in no mean fashion and the matter sorted). Whilst at Misurata I had to deal with three Boards of Enquiry. the first was a serious fire near the fuel-dump, caused by the engine of one of the tankers being filled catching alight. Wisely the driver quickly reversed the truck away from the dump, thus avoiding a worse problem. The second was more serious and happened just after a Beaufort took off at night and had an engine-failure. The aircraft crashed into some palm trees and was completely destroyed by the ensuing fire. No bodies were found, but a boot, with a foot in it, was found some distance away. The third occurred when an airman (on this occasion it was an airman from another squadron) who worked in the Sergeants Mess managed to get drunk and tried to hit a sergeant. My adjutant was with me on all these occasions and had everything well under control.

Misurata had been a good base, but our next move was to Borizzo, in western Sicily, where it was rather sad to see vineyards being bulldozed for our aircraft by the Americans who were based there. We stayed in Sicily for a month and carried out a number of sorties, including one accompanying eight Italian destroyers and one cruiser which were being helped on their way to the Grand Harbour in Malta by the Royal Navy. We also shot down three Ju52s leaving Corsica for Italy. Other convoy duties had included one accompanying the vessel carrying King George VI from Malta to Tripoli after he presented the island with its George Cross.

On our return from Sicily we were based at Gambut 3, under 235 Wing, and from there I carried out my last sortie, as I was found to have hepatitis and was moved to a hospital in Cairo. It was a sad wrench to leave the Squadron in this way, after such a short time. I had flown 42 operational sorties with my navigator, Wally Undrill, who had been with me throughout, and we had flown many other odd trips together between February and October 1943.

On leaving hospital I was taken back to Alexandria and was lucky enough to be made Fighter Direction Officer on board HMS *Daffodil*, the leading ship of an escort flotilla, for my return to the UK.

I was welcomed aboard by the Captain and his officers and made to feel immediately at home. We sailed at once and were to meet westbound ships in the afternoon. A lieutenant showed me round the ship and told me about the Captain. It was clear that the Old Man was very highly regarded by the whole crew. I thought back to our convoy-escorts from the air and realised that this trip was giving me a wonderful insight into the naval side – different in some aspects, but with the same purpose of guarding the convoys. 603 Squadron did actually escort us on the following day.

There was much activity on board one morning in the Western Mediterranean when enemy submarines were reported in the vicinity. I was at my allotted position on the bridge and it was fascinating to watch the hunt, the attack and finally the destruction of one (and an attack on a second which was only deemed to be a probable by the Captain). I was told that this was his fifth confirmed kill. On disembarking at Gibraltar we assembled in a hotel and I was able to return their hospitality and thank them for the amazing experience.

Back in the UK I was posted to 51 Night Fighter OTU at Cranfield as Chief Instructor. I was delighted to meet Beaufighters again and also the Beaufort, which [at Cranfield] served as the dual training aircraft. However, at my initial interview with the CO, a former night-fighter himself, I had to ask if I could take the course first, as I had no night-fighting experience (I presumed I was sent there as I was experienced on Beaufighters and had done quite a lot of night-flying). The CO consulted the Air Ministry, but his was not approved and I was sent, after two very worthwhile months, to the Empire Central Flying School at Hullavington. There I flew a number of aircraft which were new to me: Stirling, Wellington, Hudson, Havoc, Spitfire and Avenger and also went to the RAF Medical Centre in London to be cleared after the hepatitis.

In August 1944, I was posted to RAF Snitterfield, No.18 (P) AFU at Kidlington as Wing Commander Training. Then, in June 1945 I was made CO of RAF Lulsgate Bottom, near Bristol, which, needless to say, was above all the surrounding country. This station ran courses for well-qualified pilots destined to instruct at Operational Conversion Units. I was awarded the AFC in September 1945.

In April 1946, I was posted to CFS at Upavon, which we then moved to Little Rissington. This was the new base for the training of Flying Instructors. In December I was sent to the Empire Flying School on the staff of the instrument weather course at Hullavington. Our students were qualified pilots from squadrons plus a few airline pilots. Those of us on the staff were, of course, qualified all-weather pilots. In addition to the aircraft already mentioned, I was lucky enough to fly the Lancaster and Buckmaster in all weathers. I managed to win the Clarkson Aerobatic Trophy while I was there and was also able to fly the Meteor (my first jet), with which I would become familiar later on.

In October 1948 I was posted to the Air Ministry Department of Air Training. My job there was to visit all the schools and keep abreast of the various aspects of training. I also flew aircraft which were kept at Hendon for the use of Air Ministry personnel.

After that, in November 1951, I was sent to join 2 Course for a year at the RAF Flying College at Manby. This course was to include lectures by all the commanders-in-chief in the RAF. The idea was to acquaint us with what was planned for the future. We flew the Vampire, Meteor, Lincoln, Valetta and Varsity. We just missed the Canberra, but I was fortunate to fly that later on.

One trip entailed a flight, under the command of our staff tutor, to Keflavik in a Lincoln. We spent the night at the US base there and took off the next morning up the east coast of Greenland to 75 degrees North before turning west across the icecap, aiming for Thule, an American base on the west coast. Unfortunately we began to take on too much ice, as the aeroplane had no de-icing system; it was therefore decided to return to Keflavik.

Towards the end of the course we were teamed into six groups to fly to different parts of the globe, taking about a month, so six Lincolns took off one after another from Manby. My luck was to go with the New Zealand group and our route was to take us to Luqa, Habbanniya, Mauripur, Negombo and Changi. Here we stopped to witness a supply drop for troops in the Malayan jungle by an Australian crew in a Dakota. The next day we continued to Darwin, Amberly, Ohakea, Wigram and Whenapua.

The visit to New Zealand was excellent. We were given a great welcome wherever we went and visited their stations and had discussions on various aspects of training and operations.

Back at Manby I was lucky enough to be in a formation of three Vampires for the end of course aerobatic display. We were led by Bobby Oxspring, who was known for leading a flight of Vampires across the Atlantic. The third member was Bruce Cole.

In March 1952 I was sent to No.203 Meteor AFS at Driffield. There the Station Commander expressed concern over the number of fatal accidents that had occurred and asked me if I could find any reason for them. After interviewing the two squadron commanders, I decided that I would fly with each instructor and get to know them in the air. Most were satisfactory, but four needed some straightening out on their performance. One of these had no Instrument Rating and I had him taken off instruction until he was qualified and altered his manner.

I left Driffield in April 1954. One student had died, on his first night solo flight. The fourth instructor who I had earlier taken off instructional duties, did an unauthorised trip to the relief landing-ground, flew down the runway at 500 feet (the cloud base was 800), and tried to do a loop from that height. He came out of the cloud to one side, hit a farm tractor and killed himself and the farmer.

My next posting was to RAF Kai Tak in Hong Kong as Wing Commander Admin, which I enjoyed (my number two briefed me well). It was good to have easy access to a Harvard, Meteor and Vampire T11 and to renew my Instrument Rating. My most important task in the few months I was there was the organising of the Battle of Britain Day. Everyone helped, including the Hong Kong Police, and the day was a great success.

A little while after this my CO told me that I was to lose my acting rank and to leave for Singapore. He could not tell me why because he did not know himself. So my family and I left by ship and I ended up at RAF Seletar, where I was to be in the Group HQ.

On my first day in the Mess the Station Commander said to me: 'Oh, so you're the chap who spent all your time on horses in Hong Kong!' I was more than somewhat surprised at this, as I had not ridden a horse since I was seventeen in South Africa. However, I happened to know that another officer of the same rank had been removed from his post in the Hong Kong Headquarters and sent back to England for spending too much time on race-horses. When I was interviewed by the AOC, Air Commodore Clouston, I mentioned this to him. He seemed surprised and told me to take up my post and he would find out what all this was about from the Far East HQ, and would send for me in due course.

The next day he sent for me and said: 'You will retain your rank and will be posted to Kuala Lumpur to join the HQ there and be responsible for the aircraft involved in the Malayan activities.' Chin Peng, the leader of the Chinese terrorists was still operating at this time and I flew to a number of jungle forts in a Pioneer and learned a lot from the British and Malayan forces about their operations. I was at Kuala Lumpur as a substantive Wing Commander until February 1957 and then returned to England.

My next post was at the A&AEE at Boscombe Down. I was delighted that my saviour in Singapore was the Commandant of this establishment, which included quite a number of civilians (mostly scientists) under a senior one, who was my counterpart, and some 2,500 Officers, NCOs and airmen, who were my responsibility.

These were the happiest three years of my career in the RAF and I worked hard. I was encouraged to fly when possible, including as a passenger with RAF Test Pilots, putting the Victor through its paces. I flew 156 hours as a pilot on five different aircraft, but mostly on Meteors. I also flew a Beverley to Lagos, then Kano, to drop a helicopter and its crew, who were to carry out tropical trials; we came back across the Sahara to Idris and so back to Boscombe.

I was sad to leave Boscombe, but had to move on to Maintenance Command, near Andover, as Air 1. My duties involved keeping in touch with all the maintenance units round the country which had aircraft in storage. This was not a particularly taxing job, but I managed to fly to the stations (including one in Northern Ireland), and discuss the matters with the pilots who checked aircraft serviceability at intervals.

My next posting was to Burma as Air Attaché. After a spell at the Air Ministry, being briefed in the various departments, and a number of visits to British aeronautical manufacturers, my family and I sailed from Liverpool in a passenger/cargo vessel. We were welcomed in Rangoon by Group Captain Cook and his wife who were handing over their respective duties to us.

The Burmese armed services had taken over the government of the country and the day after we got there they took over nearly everything else as well. We soon learned that caution was the way to proceed. Of course our telephones were tapped (my wife was once asked to wait while a tape was changed), and our house watched, but we soon got used to this and the diplomatic life was interesting to say the least.

I shared a Devon with the Air Attaché in Bangkok and so was able to visit the Burmese Air Force bases and to fly the Ambassador and other Embassy staff members, inasmuch as was permitted, round the country. My flying in Burma was 203 hours.

Our return journey to the UK took us by air to Bangkok, by train to Singapore and by ship the rest of the way. This was a memorable trip after the rather stressful diplomatic experience.

In March 1965 I arrived to take over the training at the OCTU, which was in the process of being moved from Feltwell in Norfolk to Henlow in Bedfordshire; two squadrons were at each station, so for the first four or five months I spent a great deal of time going from one to the other by car, as there were no aeroplanes available.

My time at the OCTU was the most hard and interesting period of my career. Dealing with a considerable number of staff and students meant quite a bit of midnight-oil time. Also there was a full scale Passing-out Parade every month, with Commanders-in-Chief inspecting, students and relations in attendance, followed by a formal Lunch and a Ball in the evening. Our wives contributed regularly throughout the courses.

I was concerned that some students being sent to us by the Air Ministry had crime-waivers. This appeared to me to be unacceptable for future officers in the RAF. I was reported to my C in C, Air Chief Marshal Sir William Coles. He, however, supported me and we had no more trouble.

In early 1968 I was sent to RAF Bassingbourn for six months as CO, to close it down (it had been opened in the mid-thirties). My first selfish thought was that at last I would be able to fly the Canberra, which we had just missed at Manby. However, my main task, a very sad one, was to prepare for closure. The station was in wonderful condition and I was happy to be there.

Planning for the final day required much thought and I was fortunate to have a splendid staff to carry out the arrangements. Commanders-in-Chief would be present, as would some Air Council members and local dignitaries. Our own airmen were soon being sharpened up on the parade ground and doing well.

The officers mess was too small to accommodate a large number of visitors, so I decided one of the hangars, which was heated, should be prepared. The wives came in on the act and their contribution was magnificent. The Queen's Colour Squadron and its Regiment guardians were made available to us.

On the big day the weather was reasonable and we had arranged that arriving vehicles would be routed straight through the camp and back down to the end hangar, past all the Canberras, which were parked in a line on the tarmac. This seemed an appropriate way of saying farewell.

The ladies, kitchen and bar staff, had turned the hangar into something special and my wife and I were proud to welcome all the visitors to our Station.

For the final moments we moved to chairs outside, where the Queen's Colour Squadron, the band and our own airmen finished the sad ceremony. There remained only the lowering of the Standard and the playing of the Last Post.

After Bassingbourn I was sent to Thorney Island, in charge of Administration, to complete my time in the RAF. It was a very pleasant Station and I was yet again fortunate to have an excellent staff of Officers, NCOs and airmen.

I retired in April 1972, having flown just over 4,400 hours on 52 different types of aircraft.

Two years earlier my wife and I had decided that we would like to live in this area [Tewkesbury, Gloucestershire] and had found a 250 year-old farmhouse, with five acres, on common land in a beautiful spot at the foot of the Malvern Hills. This was to be our home for eleven years.

I sought employment, but was offered only two jobs; one was monitoring a bunch of secretaries and the other was in charge of Ugandan refugees in Beverley, Yorkshire. Neither of them was very suitable, so I did voluntary work for the RAF Benevolent Fund instead.

Our home was habitable but in need of a lot of work. The RAF had provided then (and still does) a month's pre-retirement course on all sorts of activities and I had chosen House Maintenance, for which I was most grateful and for which I still have all the precis. The course included plumbing, plastering, papering (all matters except electrics). I had no wish to became a couch potato.

The pointing needed doing badly, so we bought scaffolding, cement, sand and all the necessary tools and set to work. It took us fifteen months and we became expert scaffolding erectors. When the weather outside was not suitable we dealt with all the plumbing, including baths, loos and sinks (the stone variety). Our time with these jobs was limited because we had to deal with lawns, flower and vegetable gardens, an orchard and poultry as well.

The house was ideal for our son and daughter to bring their friends from school and later college and for our friends and relations to visit us.

We now live in a smaller house, with plenty of lawns and garden and are wondering where to go next...

Air Chief Marshal Sir Christopher Foxley-Norris
W/C C.N. Foxley-Norris – 23 September-26 December 1944

Christopher Foxley-Norris took over 603 as its Commanding Officer whilst it flew Beaufighters from *Glorious* to Gambut in North Africa. His tenure lasted until the end of December 1944 when the Squadron sailed back to the UK from Egypt and to RAF Coltishall in Norfolk.

Born on 16 March 1917 and educated at Winchester and Trinity College, Oxford, his long and distinguished career in the RAF began in 1935 when he joined the Oxford University Air Squadron and successfully completed his initial flying training.

He was commissioned in 1936. Having read Law, in 1939, he left Oxford to read for the Bar and moved to London where he intended to join 615 (County of Surrey) Squadron, AuxAF. The start of the Second World War however, changed this plan dramatically and he was to be one of the relatively few RAF pilots who fought during the Battle of France in 1940 right through to the end of the war. He had a brother who also served in the RAF.

His first posting to an operational squadron was to 13 Army Co-operation Squadron based at Douai in France during the Phoney War flying Lysanders. When the Germans invaded France and the Low Countries in May 1940, the Squadron was forced to retreat by road from the advancing panzers and was eventually withdrawn back to UK by steamer from Cherbourg.

Re-roled as a coastal reconnaissance unit, 13 Squadron was briefed to look for enemy activity that might herald an invasion. But the young would-be fighter pilot wanted to be flying more exciting aeroplanes and to be contributing more fully to the defence of Britain which was clearly about to be invaded and so he was delighted to be posted to RAF Aston Down to learn to fly Hurricanes. His delight was, however, short lived when after successfully completing the conversion course, Foxley-Norris was posted to 3 Squadron then based at RAF Drem and away from the battle. In retrospect he appreciated that it was probably no bad thing that he was not thrown into the Battle of Britain immediately, but was able to build up experience in the relatively quieter air of Scotland.

He was posted south to join 615 Squadron – the Squadron he had hoped to join in 1939 as an auxiliary – at Northolt and although he has expressed disappointment at his record during the Battle of Britain, he was, nevertheless, one of the Few. Like 603, 615 was one of the squadrons that turned to a more offensive role in 1941 and Foxley-Norris was one of the pilots who flew 615's first Rhubarb across the Channel in January 1941. By March, 615 was due to be rested and it was ordered back to North Wales whilst Foxley-Norris and some of the other younger pilots were sent on instructing duties. From CFS at Upavon, Foxley-Norris moved to RAF Ternhill to take up instructing duties but no sooner having arrived, he developed an acute appendicitis which had to be removed quickly.

On recovery he was sent to Canada to a new airfield in Alberta called Penfold which was training aircrew under the Commonwealth Air Training Scheme. The risky voyage was undertaken in a fast unescorted ship. Instructing could be a hazardous occupation, but Foxley-Norris survived his spell at Penfold and at other airfields in Canada before he was returned to the UK. Having started flying single-engined aircraft, by the time he returned from Canada, most of his flying time was on twin engines so he found himself posted to 143 Squadron based in the UK flying Beaufighters on low level maritime strike operations.

Towards the end of 1943, the situation in the Aegean meant that the RAF was undertaking operations against Axis lines of communications, attempting to starve out the garrisons of many of the small islands. There was a need for pilots and Foxley-Norris joined 252 Squadron based near the Suez Canal. At this time, 252 was flying alongside 603.

The squadrons moved North African bases on a number of occasions but in September 1944, the now Wing Commander Foxley-Norris was posted to 603 as the CO after serving briefly as Wing Commander Operations. His tenure of command of 603 lasted about three months, when the aircrews and service echelon were ordered back to Britain arriving at Coltishall in the depths of winter in January 1945. It transpired that 603 was to reform flying Spitfires but with some string pulling, the Wing Commander managed to get the bulk of his pilots and navigators transferred to the Banff Strike Wing based in the north east of Scotland where he himself was given command of his old Squadron, 143 now flying Mosquitoes. The role was not unlike that which they performed in the Mediterranean but now they found themselves operating off Norway and over the icy North Sea. The award of his DSO came through whilst at Banff and he was still based there when the European war finished in 1945.

He accepted the offer of a permanent commission in the RAF which meant that he now finally gave up any aspirations as a lawyer. Other command posts followed. 14 Squadron in Germany, and in 1946 a staff post in 2 Group and then Staff College. After Staff College, he returned as CO of the Oxford University Air Squadron. After an enjoyable two and half years, his next move was as an instructor at the Staff College at Bracknell. He married his wife Joan in 1948. His next posting was as Air Planner HQ Far East Air Force based in Singapore but was disappointed it didn't involve a flying post, nonetheless the job 'had its moments' because of the fighting against the communist insurgents in Malaya; and the fighting in Korea. In the late summer of 1956 he returned to the UK still as a wing commander with ambitions to become a group captain. His next appointment though was as Wing Commander Flying at RAF West Malling then flying Meteor NF 12/14 night fighters. The appointment was short lived and three months later he found himself promoted to acting group captain and posted to HQ Fighter Command as Chief of Plans. Following this important role which involved much time spent working with the NATO allies, in 1958, his next command post was as station commander of RAF Stradishall in Suffolk, but late in 1959 because of its imminent closure, he found himself on the move again to become the station commander of West Malling. With the reduction in the British armed forces that took place in the late 50s and early 60s, it wasn't long before the RAF was making plans to pull out of West Malling. Attendance at the Senior Officers War Course at Greenwich was followed by the Imperial Defence College and promotion to Air Commodore with the appointment as Director of Organisation and Administrative Plans at the Air Ministry in central London. Whilst this post was not entirely to his taste, it paved the way for even greater things. In 1963 he became Air Vice-Marshal, Assistant Chief the Defence Staff a post which he held for 15 months. With the British military now operational in Brunei, given the opportunity in 1964, he requested, and was given the post of AOC 224 Group based once more in Singapore. It was a real operational post with a great deal of aerial activity in the region. The Group had as many as 300 aircraft under its command. Foxley-Norris flew on operations – even as an Air Vice-Marshal – and had the rather unusual experience for a man of this rank of being on the receiving end of some enemy fire.

In 1967, he returned once again to the UK to become the Director General of Organisation (RAF) and about year later, Commander-in-Chief of RAF Germany and Commander of the Second Allied Tactical Air Force – part of the NATO structure. He was by now an Air Marshal and based in Berlin. The RAF now flew Phantoms and the Air Marshal tried his hand with them and the F104 currently being flown by the Luftwaffe and the USAF.

In 1971 he took over as Chief of Personnel and Logistics in Whitehall with the rank of Air Chief Marshal but with the gradual reduction in Britain's commitments and the consequent reduction in spending he was surprised to be retired prematurely at the age of 56 in 1974.

After leaving the RAF, his life continued to be full and although he is a golfer and philatelist, he directed his energies to other things – many of them with some connection to aviation and the RAF. He became involved with the ex-RAF and Dependents Severely Disabled Holiday Trust, Chairman of Gardening for the Disabled, President of the Leonard Cheshire Housing Association, Chairman of the Cheshire Foundation, to name only a few. He is also Chairman of the Battle of Britain Fighter Association, a post which he has held for many years.

He received a number of honours being given an OBE in 1956, made a CB in 1969, KCB in 1969 and GCB in 1973. He became an Honorary Fellow of Trinity College in 1973.

Air Chief Marshal Sir Christopher Foxley-Norris GCB, DSO, OBE has enjoyed a remarkable life in the RAF and published an autobiography in 1978 called *A Lighter Shade of Blue*. His strong sense of humour is one aspect of his personality which the members of the Fighter Association recall with most fondness. 603 was fortunate to have the benefit of his experience.

Wing Commander James Ronaldson Herbert Lewis
1 December 1943 – 15 June 1944
Prior to taking command of 603 Squadron Lewis was a Squadron Leader with 227 Squadron flying Beaufighter Mk VIs in the maritime strike role based at Lakatamia. He was awarded a DFC in November 1943 whilst a flight commander with 227 Squadron. He had previously taken command of 504 (County of Nottingham) Squadron on 1 February 1942 holding the post until January 1943 flying Spitfire VBs.

His citation from the *London Gazette* (No. 5187) dated 26 November 1943 reads:

This officer has participated in many sorties, including a number of attacks on shipping during which he has damaged at least 30 caiques. In air combat he has shot down 3 enemy aircraft. Squadron Leader Lewis is a skilful and determined leader, whose excellent example has inspired the flight he commands.

Squadron Leader Thomas Charles Rigler
26 January 1945 – 1 April 1945
Squadron Leader Tommy Rigler assumed command of 603 on 26 January 1945. He had previously served with 609 (West Riding) Squadron, an AuxAF unit based at Warmwell, for 15 months (from February 1941, just prior to their move to Biggin Hill in Kent). He was awarded the DFM as a sergeant pilot flying Spitfire Mk IIAs in 1941. His citation reads:

(9044920) Sergeant Rigler. This airman has carried out 86 sorties since March, 1941. He has displayed outstanding keenness to destroy the enemy in combat and to harass him on the ground. Sergeant Rigler has destroyed at least seven hostile aircraft (three destroyed in one sweep) and has damaged a further two.

Sergeant Tommy Rigler was later commissioned, leaving 609 Squadron in May 1942.

In recognition of his leadership of 603 Squadron, Acting Squadron Leader T.C. Rigler was awarded the DFC. (see page 384 for his citation.)

Squadron Leader Harold Richard Paul Pertwee
1 April 1945 – 15 August 1945
Squadron Leader Pertwee enlisted in the RAFVR in February 1941. Prior to taking command of 603 Squadron he was a flight commander with 602 Squadron. He was awarded the DFC whilst serving with 602 at Ludham, flying Spitfire XVIs. His citation from the *London Gazette* (No.2488) dated 11 May 1945 reads:

This officer has displayed the greatest keenness for air operations and his example of determination and devotion to duty has been most commendable. He has taken part in very many sorties during which he has been responsible for the destruction of a good number of enemy mechanical vehicles. He has destroyed one and damaged several more enemy aircraft.

He was the last wartime OC of the Squadron prior to its disbandment at Turnhouse on 15 August 1945. After the war Harold Pertwee remained in the RAF and commanded 66 Squadron prior to taking command of 611 (West Lancashire) Squadron, RAuxAF, based at Woodvale near Liverpool in 1951.

Post War

Squadron Leader Joseph William Ernest Holmes
23 September – 1 December 1950

Joe Holmes was born on April 22 1916 in Yorkshire. His father had been killed on the Somme during WWI. Young Joe was educated at Normanton Grammar School, Trinity College, Carmarthen, and Carnegie Hall, Leeds.

He later taught at Holme Valley Grammar School, Huddersfield, before entering the RAF in 1939.

Commissioned in 1941, he joined 263 Squadron at Charmy Down. The next year he was posted to 137, before returning to 263 as a flight commander in 1943.

263 and 137 were the only two Westland Whirlwind fighter-bomber squadrons to fly operationally in the Second World War. The Whirlwind, a single-seat twin-engined aircraft, did not enjoy the best of reputations, but Holmes coaxed excellent results from it.

Between 1941 and 1943 the Whirlwind squadrons were engaged on cross-channel low-level raids and attacks on enemy shipping. On one occasion Holmes sank a German supply ship, the *Ost Vlanderen*, as it approached St Peter Port, Guernsey.

On another he was escorting Bristol Blenheim light bombers on a raid against Cherbourg when he was set upon by three superior Bf109 fighters: 'They did all the talking,' as he laconically noted. As a Flight Lieutenant with 263 Squadron he was awarded a DFC in 1943. His citation from the *London Gazette* (No.2729) dated 15 June 1943 reads:

> This officer has taken part in many operations during which attacks have been made on such targets as airfields, gun positions and military installations. Flight Lieutenant Holmes is a first class leader, whose skill and courage have set an excellent example.

An AFC followed shortly afterwards, in recognition of his efforts to raise standards of air-gunnery.

In February 1944 he was given command of 266 (Rhodesia Squadron) flying Typhoon IBs.

Joe Holmes was generally recognised as the pilot who wounded Field Marshal Rommel (the 'Desert Fox') as he toured German front-line positions in Normandy in July 1944. Cannon fire from a Hawker Typhoon IB fighter-bomber of 266 Squadron caused Rommel to be struck in the face by broken glass. A blow on the left temple and cheek-bone fractured Rommel's skull, and he was taken unconscious to hospital. Research later indicated that Holmes was almost certainly responsible for inflicting these injuries.

After the war a succession of postings led to command in 1950 of 603 Squadron. From 1952 he was Chief Flying Instructor at 233 Operational Conversion Unit, and in 1954 he was posted to the Far East, where he contributed significantly to the air operations which led to Britain's eventual success in the Malaysian Emergency – Operation Firedog.

During this period, while sitting in the second pilot's seat of a 1 Squadron (Royal Australian Air Force) Avro Lincoln bomber (the successor to the four-engined Lancaster), Holmes saved both crew and aircraft from disaster. The bomber hit high ground after taking off from RAF Tengah on Singapore Island, and two of its engines caught fire. Holmes seized the controls, managed to splash-down in the sea, then spurred on the crew as they swam through shark-infested waters to safety, pushing with them a dinghy in which lay the injured. He was mentioned in despatches.

In 1960, after staff work at the Air Ministry, Holmes was appointed Air Attaché in Bangkok. He was station commander at RAF Benson from 1963 and in 1965 joined Supreme Headquarters Allied Powers Europe as a senior operations officer.

He retired from the RAF in the rank of group captain and went on to teach at Victoria College, Jersey. Joe Holmes was much involved in the affairs of the island and in ex-service organisations. He died on Jersey aged 77 in 1993.

Squadron Leader Peter John Anson
1 December 1950 – 22 March 1953

Squadron Leader Peter Anson joined the RAFVR in April 1940. In 1945 he was awarded a DFC (*London Gazette* 1 October 1945 No.4858) whilst serving with 135 Squadron based in India, flying the P47D Thunderbolt Mk I. Between June and September 1945, he commanded 135 Squadron (renumbered 615 [County of Surrey] Squadron on 10 June 1945) at Vizagapatamin, India, flying the Republic P47D Thunderbolt II. He served throughout the war and was granted a permanent commission in the RAF in October 1948.

He took command of 603 on 1 December 1950, the year they won the coveted Esher Trophy for the second time. The trophy was presented to S/L Anson at RAF Leuchars on 8 August 1951, by HRH Princess Elizabeth, Duchess of Edinburgh.

On 22 March 1953 he was posted to RAF Church Fenton as OC Flying.

Squadron Leader Robert Lloyd Rees Davies
23 March – 25 August 1953

Squadron Leader Lloyd Davies was born in Bangor, Wales. He joined the RAFVR (No.63457) straight from school at Eton. Following training, he flew with 25 Squadron as a night-fighter pilot on Mosquitoes, flying bomber support sorties over Germany against enemy night fighters. He was awarded the DFC in 1944; the citation in the *London Gazette* (No.3771) dated 15 August 1944 reads:

> This officer has completed a notable tour during which he has attacked many enemy airfields and railway communications with success. He is a highly skilled and courageous pilot whose example has been inspiring. He has destroyed 3 enemy aircraft at night, 2 of them in one sortie.

Post war he became a pilot with the British Overseas Airways Corporation (BOAC), before re-joining the RAF when he was granted a permanent commission. He was appointed OC 603 Squadron 23 March 1953, having been the training officer with 600 (City of London) Squadron, based at Biggin Hill, Kent.

S/L Davies was killed in a road accident on the airfield whist at annual camp at Sylt, Germany on 10 July 1953 aged 34 (see page 317). All ranks could hardly believe that this six foot five inches tall jet fighter pilot, who had flown Mosquito night fighters during the war, should die in such a way.

Squadron Leader Roy Arthur Schofield
25 August 1953 – 9 May 1956
Roy Schofield was born on 17 May 1923 in Argentina, and was educated at Clayesmore School in Dorset. In 1942 he joined the RAF as volunteer aircrew, and commenced pilot training in Canada, gaining his wings and being commissioned into the RAFVR as a pilot in 1943. During 1943/44 he was a flying instructor in Canada. Following this he trained on DH Mosquito aircraft and joined 82 Squadron in India.

After the war, he was posted to Iwakuni, Japan in 1946 as Flight Commander, Communications Flight. In 1947 he was posted back to the United Kingdom for flying duties, and during the period 1947 to 1950 he was Flight Commander, Fighter Command Communication Squadron, Bovingdon. On 26 June 1950 he was awarded the King's Commendation for Bravery for aiding the crew of a crashed Firefly aircraft.

A tour followed from 1950 to 1953, when he was ADC and personal pilot to the C-in-C Air Forces Western Europe, Air Chief Marshal Sir James Robb, and then to three successive Inspectors General of the RAF. In 1953, following this interesting tour of duty, he became a flight commander with 257 (Burma) Squadron at Wattisham flying Gloster Meteor F8s.

S/L Roy Schofield took command of 603 Squadron following the tragic death of S/L Lloyd Davies.

Whilst officer commanding, he had the honour of receiving the Squadron's Standard from Her Majesty Queen Elizabeth II, 603s HAC at the Palace of Holyroodhouse on 30 June 1955. After the ceremony, the Queen was presented with a diamond brooch in the form of the original Squadron badge by S/L Schofield on behalf of all ranks.

He commanded 603 until 9 May 1956 when he was posted to RAF Swinderby, Lincolnshire as Chief Ground Instructor. In 1957 he was appointed the Station Commander of RAF Gan in the Maldive Islands. He was also Liaison Officer to the Government of the Maldives.

During the period 1958 to 1966, he held a number of staff appointments, becoming Deputy Personnel Staff Officer at Headquarters Fighter Command (1958), OC Administration Wing at RAF Horsham St. Faith, Norwich (1958/59), becoming Station Commander in 1959. In 1961 he was posted to RAF Wildenrath, Germany as OC Administration Wing until 1964, when he posted to the Apprentice Wing at 1 Radio School, RAF Locking, Somerset. Roy Schofield retired from the RAF as a wing commander in 1966.

On leaving the RAF he held a number of civilian appointments in Portugal 1967 to 1976. He was appointed Bursar, Glasgow Academy in 1977. He retired in 1988 and passed away early in 2003.

Wing Commander Mike Hobson
Regular Adjutant of 603 Squadron: 6 February 1952 to 15 June 1954
Commanding Officer of 603 Squadron: 9 May 1956 to 10 March 1957
Michael Edward Hobson was born on 1 December 1926 at Ainsdale, Lancashire, and attended Terra Nova preparatory school at nearby Birkdale before going on to Clifton College in 1940. The day after his 14th birthday his House received a direct hit during an air raid on Bristol, necessitating the relocation of the school to Bude, North Cornwall, for the rest of the war.

In 1944 he was accepted for a RAF Short University Course at Edinburgh, where he became a member of the Edinburgh University Air Squadron and read Pure and Applied Mathematics and Meteorology before joining the Royal Air Force at ACRC Torquay on 3 April 1945.

After various induction courses he started his flying training at 19 FTS, RAF Cranwell, on Tiger Moths and Harvards, and having graduated on 23 August 1946 he went on to complete a course on Spitfires at 61 OTU, RAF Keevil. He was then selected to convert onto jets, and in June 1947 was posted to the Meteor conversion course at 226 OCU, RAF Bentwaters, where he met Barbara, who was to became his wife, on the very first evening at his new Station.

His first squadron posting was to 92 Squadron at RAF Duxford, followed by 257 Squadron at RAF Horsham St Faith, leading to a tour at Eastern Fighter Sector Headquarters, also at Horsham St Faith, as PA to Group Captain (later Air Chief Marshal Sir Kenneth) 'Bing' Cross.

On 5 February 1952 he was posted to RAF Turnhouse as Regular Adjutant of 603 Squadron, flying Vampires. On the following day King George VI died and Princess Elizabeth, Honorary Air Commodore of the Squadron, succeeded to the throne. For this tour he was awarded the Queen's Commendation for Valuable Service in the Air.

After 603 was disbanded, there then followed a tour commanding 92 Squadron, flying Hunters at RAF Middleton St George; a three-year spell as RAF Schools Liaison Officer for Eastern Scotland (based once again in Edinburgh); twelve months at the Royal Air Force Staff College, Bracknell; then a tour as Wing Commander Flying at 229 OCU, RAF Chivenor, once more flying Hunters.

From Chivenor he moved to Latimer to attend the Joint Services Staff College course, and on promotion to Group Captain started a two and a half year tour in June 1966 commanding RAF Coltishall which then housed the 226 OCU, flying Lightnings, as well as a flight of search and rescue helicopters. He was responsible during this period for the training of the entire Saudi Arabian defence force on the Lightning. On completion of the tour he was appointed CBE and for the next three years served as Deputy Director of Operations (Air Defence) at the Ministry of Defence.

Posted to Hong Kong in April 1972 as Chief Staff Officer to the Commander of British Forces, he was afflicted with angina very soon after arrival and was flown home on a 'casevac' aircraft. After various spells in hospital he was posted to RAF Brampton as SASO Air Cadets, and retired from the service on medical grounds on 31 July 1973.

Married to Barbara Hammond in 1951, they now live in Suffolk and have three sons, the youngest of whom is currently commanding 24 Squadron at RAF Lyneham, flying the newly introduced Hercules C130-J.

Wing Commander Alasdair J. Beaton
1 October 99 – present

Wing Commander Alasdair Beaton was born and brought up in Uganda, East Africa, completing his initial education in Kampala and Nairobi. He attended George Watsons College in Edinburgh before joining the RAF as a Direct Entry commissioned pilot at RAF South Cerney in 1966. Following initial flying training at RAF Acklington, Northumberland, and the award of his pilot's brevet, he went on to complete advanced flying training at RAF Valley and weapons training at RAF Chivenor before going to RNAS Fulmer at Lossiemouth, as one of the first RAF First-Tourist pilots to be posted to the Buccaneer. On completion of the OCU on the Buccaneer Mk I and Mk II with the Royal Navy on 736 Squadron, he was posted to 12 (B) Squadron RAF in the maritime strike/attack role in 1970. A second Buccaneer tour on 16 Squadron in RAF Germany followed before he went to CFS to become an advanced flying training instructor at RAF Valley, teaching on the Gnat, the Hunter and the Hawk from 1977 to 1981 and becoming an A2 qualified flying instructor. On promotion to the rank of squadron leader he was posted back to RAF Lossiemouth as 12 Squadron's training officer before becoming a flight commander on 208 Squadron, completing ten years flying and achieving over 2,000 hours on the Buccaneer. After only one year on the ground, as the Strike/Attack Instructor at the Royal Navy's Maritime Tactics School at HMS *Dryad*, Portsmouth, he retired from the RAF aged 38. He instructed on the Alpha Jet in the Qatar Emiri Air Force in the Gulf for three years before returning to the UK to embark on a career in civil aviation flying Boeing 757s with Airtours International based at Glasgow airport. He now flies as a Captain with easyJet and is Chief Pilot for the company in Scotland.

W/C Beaton joined 2 (City of Edinburgh) Maritime Headquarters Unit in 1993 and was appointed Commanding Officer in July 1998. On 1 October 1999, he became Officer Commanding the reformed 603 Squadron.

APPENDIX 10

SQUADRON BASES
1941-PRESENT

Drem	13 Dec 1940
Turnhouse	28 Feb 1941
Hornchurch	16 May 1941
Rochford (Southend)	16 Jun 1941
Hornchurch	8 Jul 1941
Fairlop	12 Nov 1941
Dyce	15 Dec 1941
Peterhead	14 Mar 1942
Left for Middle East Ground echelon	13 Apr 1942
Ta Kali (Malta) Air echelon via USS *Wasp*	20 Apr –
	3 Aug 1942
Air echelon at Ta Kali renumbered as 229 Sqn	3 Aug 1942
Kasfareet (Egypt) Ground echelon	4 Jun 1942
Nicosia (Cyprus) Ground echelon	28 Jun 1942
Det Lakatamia/Paphos/Aboukir (Egypt)	
(No 24 PTC)	21 Dec 1942
Idku (Egypt)	25 Jan 1943
Det Berka IIIMisurata West (Libya)	27 Mar 1943
Det Berka III/El Magrun/Borizzo (Sicily)	6 Sep 1943
LG 91 (Amariya, Egypt)	4 Oct 1943
Gambut III (Libya) Det El Adem	18 Oct 1943 – 26 Dec 1944
Non-operational	19 Oct 1943 – 2 Apr 1944
Det Shallufa (5 METS)	
Det El Adem (Egypt)	
Disbanded	26 Dec 1944
En route UK via Port Said	26 Dec 1944
Reformed from 229 Sqn	10 Jan 1945
Coltishall	10 Jan 1945
Ludham	24 Feb 1945
Coltishall	5 Apr 1945
Turnhouse	28 Apr 1945
Drem	7 May 1945
Skeabrae	14 Jun 1945
Turnhouse	28 Jul –
	15 Aug 1945
Disbanded	15 Aug 1945
Reformed	10 May 1946
Turnhouse	10 May 1946
Leuchars	16 Jul 1951
Turnhouse	13 Oct 1951
	– 10 Mar 1957
Disbanded	10 Mar 1957
Reformed	1 Oct 1999
Edinburgh/Kinloss	1 Oct 1999 – Present

APPENDIX 11

SUMMER CAMPS 1947-1956

The Squadron's annual summer camps were held in the first two weeks of July during the Edinburgh Trade Fair Fortnight .

Post War 1947 to 1958

1947	Woodvale
1948	Tangmere
1949	Horsham St Faith
1950	Horsham St Faith
1951	Leuchars
1952	Celle – Germany
1953	Sylt – Germany
1954	Tangmere
1955	Gibraltar
1956	Gibraltar

APPENDIX 12

SQUADRON MARKINGS AND CODES

Before April 1939, squadron aircraft featured their identity on the fuselage, i.e. '603' together with the unofficial Squadron badge in black on the silver tailfins. Following the Munich Crisis of late 1938, Air Ministry Order (AMO) A.154/39, dated 27 April 1939, allocated two letter combinations to all the then existing squadrons, 603 was allocated the code letters 'RL' which appeared on its Gloster Gladiator Mk 1 aircraft. This code was changed to 'XT' upon the outbreak of war in September 1939, and this was retained whilst the Squadron was based in the United Kingdom.

   The Squadron codes were not used by 603 aircraft in Malta during 1942 or on the Beaufighter aircraft in the North African – Mediterranean campaign 1943-44.

   When the Squadron was reformed from 229 Squadron in January 1945 the XT codes were soon reinstated and retained until disbandment in August 1945. Being reformed as an AuxAF squadron in Reserve Command in May 1946 the Squadron's Spitfires originally carried the codes 'RAJ' but these reverted to 'XT' when the Squadron transferred to Fighter Command in November 1949. However, in 1951 the Squadron acquired an official insignia comprising a light blue/dark red check band along the side of the fuselage bordered top and bottom by a black band. This began on the Spitfires and was continued on the tail booms of the Vampires and the fuselage of the Meteor T 7s with the Squadron badge on a black disc and the aircraft letter on the nose.

1941 – 1945

Spitfire IIA	October 1940 – May 1941
Spitfire VA	May 1941 – December 1941
Spitfire VB	August 1941 – March 1942
Spitfire VC	April 1942 – August 1942
Beaufighter IC	February 1943 – November 1943
Beaufighter IF	February 1943 – November 1943
Beaufighter VIC	February 1943 – October 1943
Beaufighter XI	August 1943 – October 1943
Beaufighter X	October 1943 – December 1944

Post-War Aircraft

Reformed at Turnhouse on 10 May 1946 (under Air Ministry Authority A.800061/45/F8(Sec)) within Reserve Command and equipped in October 1946 with Supermarine Spitfire LF XVIEs (TE437/RAJ-G), NA Harvard T2Bs were used for training (KF699/RAJ-A). The Squadron re-equipped with Spitfire Mk F22s in February 1948 (PK428/RAJ-H , PK317/XT-D). In May 1951, it converted to DH Vampire FB5s (VZ864, VV 678/O); the Gloster Meteor T7s were used for training (WF838/Y) and remained until disbandment on 10 March 1957. On 1 November 1949, all the RAuxAF squadrons transferred from Reserve Command to Fighter Command, being affiliated to RAF front-line squadrons for training.

NO.603 (CITY OF EDINBURGH) SQUADRON: OPERATIONAL AIRCRAFT

Spitfires flown by 603 Squadron

<u>For P-Series Supermarine Spitfire F37/34 MkII Oct 1940-May 1941 see Volume I.</u>

VS Spitfire
MK VA : May 1941 to Dec 1941

P8603	P8720	P8784	P8786/XT-D	P8793	P8796
P9289	R7221/XT-R	R7223	R7225	R7226/XT-A	R7227/XT-E
R7229	R7230	R7270	R7272	R7293	R7299
R7300/XT:D	R7305/XT-O	R7333/XT-G	R7335	R7337/XT-J	R7339
R7341	R7345	R7350	W3110	W3111/XT:O	W3112/XT-T
W3113/XT-O	W3118/XT-G	W3121	W3123	W3130	W3136/XT-J
W3138	W3184	W3213/XT-W	W3364	W3369	W3379
X4663	X4665	X4669/XT-X			

VS Spitfire MK VB : Aug 1941 to Mar 1942

AB134	AB144/XT-G	AB184/XT-H	AB260	AB269XT-E	AB340
AB911	AD269/XT-E	AD449/XT-A	AD502	AD503/XT-K	AD557/XT-E
BL214	BL314	BL319/XT-J	BL379/XT-J	BL386	BL431/XT-N
BL478	BL510/XT-D	BL533	BL537	BL634/XT-B	BL748/XT-N
BL894	BL960	P7874	P8720/XT-F	P8784	P8796/XT-D
R7224	R7226/XT-A	R7333	W2435	W3226	W3233 W3242
W3423/XT-X	W3433	W3502	W3569	W3624/XT-I	W3628/XT- L
W3631/XT-L	W3632/XT-E	W3642	W3647/XT-X	W3711/XT-B	W3833/XT-R
X4389	X4415	X4489	X4490	X4593	X4594 X4613

VS Spitfire VC : Apr 1942 to Aug 1942

AB562	BP190/2-A	BP845	BP850	BP872	BP898/N
BP958	BP960	BP961	BP962/2-R	BP964	BP970
BP973/J	BP991	BP992	BR108	BR124	BR127/1-N
BR161	BR167	BR169	BR183	BR184	BR187
BR198	BR231	BR251	BR294	BR306	BR320
BR345	BR347	BR356	BR364	BR365	BR367/O
BR385	BR464	BR562			

Bristol Beaufighter Mk IC / IF : Feb 1943 to Nov 1943

T4700/N	T5273	V8321/V	V8322	V8372	X7708
X7741	X7760/Y	X7761/H	X7762	X7772	X7838

Bristol Beaufighter Mk VI C : Feb 1943 to Oct 1943

EL348	EL448/O	EL465	EL468/X	EL474	EL478
EL503	EL509	EL516	EL517	EL523	EL524
JL503Z	JL504/H	JL516	JL538	JL509/ W	JL537/M
JL588/S	JL625K	JL626/P	JL724	JL731	JL761
JL771	JL900	NT893/P	T5273	X8105/Y	X8144

Bristol Beaufighter Mk TFX: Oct 1943 to Dec 1944

JL900	JM407	KW346	LX783	LX864	LX869
LX872	LX949/Z	LX361/Y	LX983	LX985/M	LX998
LX977/R	LZ123	LZ127	LZ133/H	LZ135	LZ138
LZ139/S	LZ144	LZ145	LZ148	LZ150	LZ234/Z
LZ235/L	LZ239	LZ241	LZ242	LZ245/L	LZ265/Y
LZ272/F	LZ274/G	LZ275	LZ278	LZ281/K	LZ336/Q
LZ310	LZ325	LZ329	LZ330	LZ339	LZ361
LZ363	LZ372	LZ373	LZ340/P	LZ370/N	LZ376
LZ400	LZ404	LZ409	LZ465	LZ483	LZ489/A
LZ517	LZ522/J	LZ530	LZ533/R	LZ535	NE246/K
NE247	NE282/Z	NE304/W	NE311/V	NE354/W	NE363/C
NE367	NE370	NE379	NE383	NE400/H	NE413/P
NE421/L	NE494	NE499	NE517/R	NE522	NE533
NE593	NE594	NE595	NE607/Q	NE610	NE718
NT893	NT894	NT964	NT986	NV213	NV237/A
NV248	NV610				

Bristol Beaufighter Mk XI

JM268/O	JM383/X

Taylorcraft Auster I 1945
LB299 (Communications flight)

VS Spitfire LFXVIE: Jan 1945 to Aug 1945; Oct 1946 to Jun 1948

SL561/RAJ-H	SL564/RAJ-G	SL578	SL609/RAJ-M	SL611	SL719/RAJ-N
SM198	SM306	SM315	SM340	SM337	SM344
SM348	SM357	SM360	SM367	SM385	SM396
SM401	SM405	SM413	SM416	SM453	SM464
SM473	TB139	TB191	TB244	TB295	TB357
TB376	TB625/RAJ-E	TB629	TB904	TB911	TB989
TB993	TB998	TD132	TD151	TE248	TE354/RAJ-L
TE359	TE437/RAJ-J	TE457/RAJ-J	TE463/RAJ-P	TE477/RAJ-J	

VS Spitfire F 22 : Feb 1948 to Jul 1951

PK214	PK328	PK337/RAJ-A	PK341/RAJ-G	PK342/RAJ-N	PK354/RAJ-L
PK317/RAJ-D	PK411/RAJ-O	PK423/RAJ-H	PK428/RAJ-H	PK433/RAJ-Q	PK504/RAJ-P
PK396/RAJ-K	PK525/RAJ-M	PK539/J	PK570/RAJ-F	PK571/RAJ-E	PK614/RAJ-J

DH Vampire FB 3 : 1951 to Nov 1955

VT793	VF316	VT812

DH Vampire FB 5 : May 1951 to March 1957

VV567	VV606/Q	VV637/D	VV678/O	VZ269/J	VZ303
VZ812	VZ841	VZ846/ P	VZ847	VZ848/S	VZ864/C
VZ865/H	WA240/A	WA398/M	WA430/J	WA432/D	WA434/E
WA440/N	WE830	WG807	WG833	WG841/J	

DH Vampire FB 9: Jun 1956 – Jan 1957

WL518 /T	WG841/J

TRAINING AIRCRAFT

North American Harvard T2B : Jun 1946 to 1953

FS770/RAJ-A	FT342/RAJ-R	KF560/RAJ-C	KF699/RAJ-A	KF449/RAJ-B

DH Vampire T11 : 1956-1957
XE895

Gloster Meteor T 7 : May 1951 to 1957

VZ649	WF825/X	WF837	WF838/Y	WG949/Z

603 (CITY OF EDINBURGH) SQUADRON, RAUXAF GIFTED SPITFIRES

Spitfires gifted to the nation each bore a name suggested by the donor and this was marked, according to official instructions, in four-inch yellow characters on the engine cowling, but this ruling was not rigidly applied. Some limiting factor was necessary in order that camouflage was not compromised.

Most of the names are indicative of the donor, but where this is not clear and the sponsor is known, additional information is given in the remarks column. Some names were originally chosen by 603 pilots who had christened their aircraft at the start of the war with the same name being subsequently reassigned by donor or fund committee:

Mark	Aircraft	Name	Remarks
IIA	R7210	City of Liverpool IV	Lord Mayor City of Liverpool Fund (£20,000)
IIA	P7449	Bidar	Hyderabad War Purpose Fund
IIA	P7683	Londonderry	Bedford Telegraph Fund (£85,000)
IIA	P7742	N.E.M.	National Employers Insurance Ltd (£5,000)
IIA	P7749	City of Bradford IV	Bradford Fund
IIA	P7750	City of Bradford V	Bradford Fund
IIA	P8161	Leyland Leeds City	Leeds Fund (£15,000, W.F. Leyland £5,000)
IIA	P8239	Sialkot II	
IIA	P8428		New Zealand High Commission
VA	P8603	Nabha I	
VA	P8786	Auckland I	
VA	R7223	Portobello	Name suggested by the Edinburgh Spitfire Fund
VA	R7227	Port o'Leith	Name suggested by the Edinburgh Spitfire Fund
VA	R7229	B. R. C. Stafford I	
VA	R7270	Nae Bother	
VA	R7272		G. H. G. Chambers-Hughes Esq
VA	R7293	Sans Tache	
VA	R7299	The Bairn	Formerly Aitch Aitch (Lord Hirst). Name suggested by the Edinburgh Spitfire Fund
VA	R7300	The Scottish Queen	Name suggested by the Edinburgh Spitfire Fund
VA	R7333	The Kirby I	
VA	R7339	Waverley	Formerly Mah Tal (J. Latham Ltd). Name suggested by the Edinburgh Spitfire Fund
VA	W3110	Holyrood	
VA	W3113	Fiji II	
VA	W3118	Kirtlands	Formerly Fiji III. Name suggested by the Edinburgh Spitfire Fund
VA	W3123	Walter McPhail	Name suggested by the Edinburgh Spitfire Fund
VA	W3130	Edinburgh	Name suggested by the Edinburgh Spitfire Fund
VA	W3138	Corstorphine	Formerly Cawnpore I. Name suggested by the Edinburgh Spitfire Fund
VB	W3213	Cecil McKay	
VB	W3242	Crispin of Leicester	
VB	W3502	Wolds and Buckrose	
VB	W3628	Oman	Persian Gulf Forces
VB	W3631	Bahrain II	Persian Gulf Forces
VB	W3632	Bahrain I	Persian Gulf Forces
VB	W3647	Saddleworth	
VB	W3833	Holt XI	Herbert Holt and Major Andrew Holt via the 'Who's for Britain Fund', Canada

VB	X4593	Kerala	Madras Mail
VB	X4594	Andhradesa	Madras Mail
VB	X4613	Falkland Islands IX	
VB	X4665	Royal Scot	Formerly Earl Shilton. Name suggested by the Edinburgh Spitfire Fund
VB	X4669	Sir Walter Scott	Formerly Kaffraria II. Name suggested by the Edinburgh Spitfire Fund
VB	AB184	Cameroon Francais	
VB	AB911	Denbighshire	
VB	BL537	Pekalongan	

603 (CITY OF EDINBURGH) SQUADRON CHRONOLOGY, 1941 TO DATE

Date/Year	Event
27 Feb 1941	To Turnhouse
16 May 1941	To Hornchurch
May 1941	Re-equip with Spitfire VA
16 Jun 1941	To Southend
9 Jul 1941	To Hornchurch
Aug 1941	Re-equip with Spitfire VB
12 Nov 41	To Fairlop
15 Dec 1941	To Dyce
14 Mar 1942	To Peterhead
13 Apr 1942	To Middle East Command, ground echelon en route to Egypt
20 Apr 1942	Air echelon to Ta Kali, Malta via USS *Wasp*. Operation Calendar under the command of S/L Lord David Douglas-Hamilton flying Spitfire VC
3 Aug 1942	Air echelon at Ta Kali, Malta
4 Jun 1942	Ground echelon to Kasfareet, Egypt
28 Jun 1942	Ground echelon to Nicosia, Cyprus det at Lakatamia and Paphos
21 Dec 1942	To Aboukir (No 24 PTC)
25 Jan 1943	To Idku, Nile Delta Egypt
Feb 1943	Re-equip with Bristol Beaufighter IC
Feb 1943	Re-equip with Bristol Beaufighter VIC det Berka III
23 Feb 1943	The Rt Hon Sir William Y. Darling CBE MC DL JP FRSE MP appointed Honorary Air Commodore
Aug 1943	Re-equip with Bristol Beaufighter XI
6 Sep 1943	To Borizzo
4 Oct 1943	To Landing Ground 91
Oct 1943	Re-equip with Bristol Beaufighter X
18 Oct 1943	To Gambut III, Libya det El Adem
Dec 1944	En route to UK via Port Said
26 Dec 1944	Disbanded
6 Jan 1945	Ground echelon under the command of F/L W. Rogers becomes No.6603 Service Echelon based at Matlaske, Norfolk
10 Jan 1945	Reformed at Coltishall, 229 Sqn renumbered 603 Sqn, Fighter Command
Jan 1945	Re-equip with Spitfire LF XVIE
24 Feb 1945	To Ludham
5 Apr 1945	To Coltishall
28 Apr 1945	To Turnhouse
7 May 1945	To Drem assist in Luftwaffe surrender, escort to Luftwaffe Ju 52 aircraft flying to Drem
14 Jun 1945	To Skeabrae
28 Jul 1945	To Turnhouse
15 Aug 1945	Disbanded at Turnhouse
10 May 1946	Reformed at Turnhouse within Reserve Command under the command of S/L G.K. Gilroy DSO DFC

11 Jun 1946	Embodied
Oct 1946	Equipped with Spitfire LF XVIE
Feb 1948	Re-equipped with Spitfire F22
1949	To Fighter Command
May 1951	Re-equip with Vampire FB 5
16 Jun 1951	The Rt Hon Sir William Y. Darling CBE MC DL JP FRSE MP resigns as Honorary Air Commodore
16 Jun 1951	HRH The Princess Elizabeth appointed Honorary Air Commodore
16 Jul 1951	To Leuchars for three months call-out in response to Korean war
14 Oct 1951	To Turnhouse
6 Feb 1952	HRH Princess Elizabeth, at her own express wish, continued as HAC when she ascended the throne
30 Jun 1955	Presentation of Squadron Standard by HM The Queen at the Palace of Holyroodhouse
17 Feb 1957	Squadron Standard laid up at the High Kirk of Edinburgh, St Giles Cathedral
10 Mar 1957	Disbanded at Turnhouse 9 Mar 1957. Spitfire Memorial dedicated at RAF Turnhouse
1 Oct 1999	Reformed as Role Support Squadron in Edinburgh under 2 and 3 Group, RAF Strike Command under the command of Wing Commander A.J. Beaton RAuxAF from 2 (City of Edinburgh) Maritime Headquarters Unit, RAuxAF
1 Oct 1999	The Rt Hon Lord Selkirk of Douglas QC LLB MA MSP appointed Honorary Air Commodore
10 Mar 2000	Reformation Parade, Edinburgh

GROUND SUPPORT UNITS

No.2603 (City of Edinburgh) Light Anti-Aircraft Squadron, RAuxAF

Honorary Air Commodore
The Rt Hon Sir William Y. Darling CBE MC DL JP FRSE MP: 1947 – 16 Jun 1951
HRH The Princess Elizabeth: 16 Jun 1951 – 31 May 1957
(HRH The Princess Elizabeth, at her own express wish, continued as Honorary Air Commodore when she ascended the throne on 6 February 1952.)

Officers Commanding

S/L I.G. Neilson DFC RAuxAF *	23 Aug 1947
S/L C.F.H. Edwards RAuxAF	28 Feb 1948
F/L R. Grant	18 Feb 1953
S/L C.T.N. Moore MBE RAF	7 Apr 1953
F/L R. Grant	16 Apr 1956
F/L V.J.G. Cole RAF	15 Aug 1956
Disbanded 10 Mar 1957	

* During the Second World War served as a Lieutenant/Temporary Captain with the Royal Regiment of Artillery, flying as a pilot with No.652 (Air Observation Post) Squadron and was awarded the DFC in 'recognition of gallant and distinguished service in North West Europe' (*London Gazette* 12.10.1944: 4674)

No.3603 (City of Edinburgh) Fighter Control Unit, RAuxAF

Honorary Air Commodore
The Rt Hon Sir William Y. Darling CBE MC DL JP FRSE MP: 1948 – 16 Jun 1951
HRH The Princess Elizabeth: 16 Jun 1951 – 31 May 1957
(See comment above)

Officers Commanding

F/L P. W. Broom	1 Apr 1948
W/C M.G. Pearson, OBE, MA, RAuxAF	17 May 1948
W/C J.H. Scott AE, RAuxAF	26 June 1954
F/L A.H. Siminson RAF	19 Nov 1957
F/L R.B. Worthington, MBE, RAF	8 Sep 1958
Disbanded 1 November 1959	

No.2 (City of Edinburgh) Maritime Headquarters Unit, RAuxAF

Honorary Air Commodores
A/C The Rt Hon His Grace The Duke of Hamilton and Brandon KT GCVO AFC LLD, 1961 – 1967
A/C The Hon Lord Birsay KT CBE TD DL LLD FEIS QC, 1967 – 1982
A/C His Grace The Duke of Hamilton and Brandon KStJ MA, 1982 – 1995
A/C The Rt Hon Lord Selkirk of Douglas QC LLB MA MSP, 1995 – 1999

Officers Commanding

F/L R.B. Worthington MBE RAF	1 Nov 59 – 20 Dec 59
F/L W. Campbell RAF	21 Dec 59 – 13 Jul 60
W/C K. Gray RAuxAF	14 Jul 60 – 30 Oct 67
W/C P. Cook MBE AE BSc RAuxAF	1 Nov 67 – 30 Oct 75
W/C J.E. Pollington MITO AMBIM RAuxAF	31 Oct 75 – 22 Mar 80
W/C N.M. Maclean AE RAuxAF	23 Mar 80 – 12 Jul 82
W/C K.S. Rowe OBE RAuxAF	13 Jul 82 – 11 Jul 90
W/C R.G. Kemp AE MIMgt RAuxAF	12 Jul 90 – 12 Jul 98
W/C A.J. Beaton RAuxAF	13 Jul 98 – 30 Sep 99

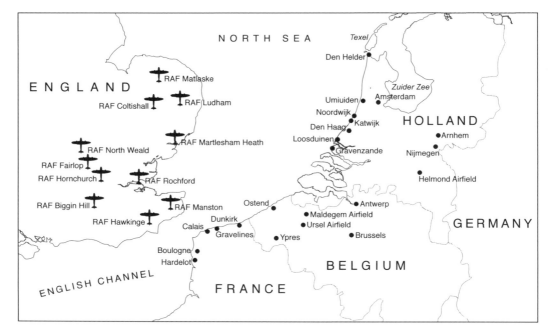

OFFENSIVE SWEEPS 1941

SELECTED BIBLIOGRAPHY

Published Sources

NB: The following is not intended as a comprehensive bibliography of 603 Squadron which would occupy an excessive number of pages. It is intended to show the primary works on which the authors have drawn in their research and to acknowledge their debt to their authors as well as provide suggestions for further reading:

Anon, *Royal Auxiliary Air Force – Information Booklet*. Air Ministry Information Division, HMSO, London, 1951.

Anon, *The Queen Presents No.603 Squadron Standard*. Flight Magazine, 8 July 1955.

Anon, *50 Years on – The RAuxAF celebrates its half-century*. Aircraft Illustrated. Vol. 8 No.1 January 1975.

Anon, *If You Dare – 603 (City of Edinburgh) Fighter Squadron At War*. Flypast Magazine No.168, July 1995.

D. Barnham, *One Man's Window*. William Kimber, 1956.

D.L. Bashow, *All the Fine Young Eagles*. Stoddart Publishing Co. 1997.

J.M. Birkin, *Goodbye RAuxAF*. Royal Air Force Flying Review, Journal of the RAF, Vol 12, No.7, March 1957.

Bruce Blanche, *Edinburgh's Own – A History of 603 Squadron*. Flypast, March 1987.

Bruce Blanche, *Royal Air Force Turnhouse – A Brief History*. Unpublished Manuscript, 1995.

Bruce Blanche, *Maritime Headquarters Units of the Royal Auxiliary Air Force*. Air Clues, Vol.50, No.4, April 1996.

Bruce Blanche, *The Week-end Flyers*. Aeroplane, August 1999.

Bruce Blanche, *RAuxAF – 75 Years' Achievement*. Air Pictorial Magazine, Vol.61, No.10, October 1999.

Bruce Blanche, *The Auxiliaries of Auld Reekie*. RAF Yearbook, 1999.

Bruce Blanche, A Booklet to Commemorate the Reformation of No.603 (City of Edinburgh) Squadron RAuxAF, 1 October 1999. Privately published. 2000.

Bruce Blanche, *History of the Maritime Headquarters Units*, Royal Auxiliary Air Force 1959 – October 1999. Journal of the Royal Air Force Historical Society. In Press.

Chaz Bowyer, *Beaufighter at War*, Ian Allan, 1976.

J.F. Bowyer, *Royal Auxiliary Air Force*. Scale Aircraft Modelling. Vol.7 No.1, 1984.

A. Boyle, *Trenchard – Man of Vision*. Collins, London, 1962.

K. Burrell, *603 Squadron Royal Auxiliary Air Force – Behind Closed Doors*. Houses and Interiors, Scotland. Issue 20, November 2001.

Donald Caldwell, *The JG26 War Diary. Volume One 1939 to 1942*. Grub Street, 1996.

N & C Carter, *The DFC and How it was Won – 1918-1995*. Vols 1 & 2. Savannah Publications, London, 1998.

W.R. Chorley, *Royal Air Force Bomber Command Losses of the Second World War, Volume 2 1941* (1993), *Volume 3 1942* (1994), *Volume 6 1945* (1998). Midland Counties Publications.

Peter V. Clegg, *Flying Against the Elements*.

Sir M. Dean, *The RAF in Two World Wars*. Cassell, 1979.

K. Delve, *The Source Book of the RAF*. Airlife, 1994.

Lord David Douglas-Hamilton, *With a Fighter Squadron in Malta*. Blackwoods Magazine Vol. 255, No.1542, April, May 1944.

Lord James Douglas-Hamilton, *The Air Battle for Malta*. Mainstream Publishing, 1981.

W.G.G. Duncan Smith, *Spitfire Into Battle*. John Murray Publishers Ltd,1981.

T. Fairbairn, *Action Stations Overseas*. Patrick Stephens Ltd, 1991.

James D. Ferguson, *The Story of Aberdeen Airport*. Scottish Airports.

C. Foxley-Norris, *A Lighter Shade of Blue*. Ian Allan, London, 1978.

C. Foxley-Norris, *Royal Air Force at War – 'Aegean Interlude'*. Ian Allan, London, 1983.

Norman Franks, *Royal Air Force Fighter Command Losses of the Second World War, Volume 1. 1939-1941* (1997), *Volume 2 1942 – 1943* (1998), *Volume 3 1944-1945* (2000), Midland Publishing Ltd.

J. Goulding, *Camouflage and Markings, RAF Northern Europe 1936-45 – Supermarine Spitfire*. Ducimus Books Ltd.

J.A. Goodson and N. Franks, *Over paid, Over Sexed and Over Here*. Wingham Press Ltd. 1991.

W. Green, *Famous Bombers of the Second World War*. MacDonald and Janes, 1959.

J.J. Halley, *The Squadrons of the RAF and Commonwealth*. Air Britain, 1980.

J.J. Halley et al (Eds), *RAF Aircraft Serial Series*. Air Britain.

J.J. Halley, *RAF Turnhouse. Aeromiiltaria No.1*. Air Britain, 1986.

I. Hayes, *Single-Seat Vampires*. Air Britain Digest, February 1976.

L. Hunt, *The Story of 603 Squadron*. Edinburgh Evening News and Dispatch. Series of three articles 5-8 April 1965.

L. Hunt, *Twenty-One Squadrons – A History of the Royal Auxiliary Air Force 1925-57.* Garnstone Press, London, 1972.

J.L. Jack. *The Record of Service and Achievements of No 603 (City of Edinburgh) Squadron, Royal Auxiliary Air Force*. Private publication, 1979.

R. Jackson, *Spitfire – The Combat History*. Airlife, 1995.

C.G. Jefford, *RAF Squadrons*. Airlife, 1988.

J. Johnstone. *Tattered Battlements, A Malta Diary by a Fighter Pilot*. Peter Davis, 1943.

A. Lake, *Flying Units of the RAF – Their Ancestry, Formation and Disbandment of all Flying Units from 1912.* Airlife, 1999.

P.B. Lucas, *Five Up*. Sidgwick and Jackson Ltd, 1978.

P.B. Lucas, *Malta: The Thorn in Rommel's Side,* Stanley Paul, 1992.

Douglas McRoberts, *Lions Rampant – The Story of 602 Spitfire Squadron*, William Kimber and Co Ltd, 1985.

J. Meadows, *The Auxiliary Tradition, Parts One to Five*. Aeroplane Monthly Vol.15, Nos. 4-8, Issues 168-172, April to August 1987.

E.L. Mee. *The Real Thing*. Private publication, 1994.

Martin Middlebrook and Chris Everitt *The Bomber Command War Diaries*. Viking, 1985.

Eric Morgan and Edward Shacklady, *Spitfire – The History*. Key Books Ltd, 1987.

M.J. Neufeld, *The Rocket and the Reich*. Harvard University Press, 1996.

R.C. Nesbit, *Armed Rovers*. Airlife, 1995.

R.A. Nicholls, *The RAF's Auxiliaries*. 1980.

D. Nimmo & G. Wake, *A History of RAF Turnhouse and Edinburgh Airport*. Airfield Review, 1998.

C.D. Paine. *'He Who Dares' – Recollections of combat flying in Beaufighters*. Aircraft Scale Models. Volume 5, No.56, May 1974.

M. Parks, *Reformation of the Royal Auxiliary Air Force*. Air Clues, December 1986.

S. Parry, *Beaufighter Squadrons in Focus*. Red Kite Publishing, Walton-on-Thames, Surrey, 2002.

G. Pitchfork, *Aegean Sea Strike Pilot: Men Behind the Medals Series*. Flypast, Key Publishing Ltd, October 2001.

K. Poolman, *Faith, Hope and Charity*. William Kimber, 1954.

A. Price, *Spitfires to Malta*. Air International, Vol 41, No.3, September 1991.

J.D. Rae, *Kiwi Spitfire Ace*. Grub Street, 2001.

RAF Benevolent Fund, *The History and War Service of the Pre-War Edinburgh Town Centre RAFVR*.

Winston G. Ramsey, *The Blitz Then and Now Volume I*. After the Battle.

J.D.R. Rawlings, *Fighter Squadrons of the RAF and their Aircraft*. MacDonald and Janes, London 1969.

B. Robertson, *Spitfire – The Story of a Famous Fighter*. Harleyford Publications Ltd, 1960.

A. Rogers, *Battle Over Malta*.

A. E. Ross, *The Queen's Squadron – The History of 603(City of Edinburgh) Squadron 1925 – 1957.* Private publication, 1989.

A. E. Ross (Ed). *75 Eventful Years – A Tribute to the RAF 1918-1993*. Wingham, 1989.

A. E. Ross (Ed). *Through Eyes of Blue – Personal Memories of the RAF from 1918*. Airlife, 2002.

David Ross, *Richard Hillary*, Grub Street, 2000.

Adrian Ruck, *Odyssey that laid wartime ghosts to rest*. The Sunday Telegraph, 5 November 1995.

Chris Shores et al, *Malta: The Spitfire Year 1942*. Grub Street, 1991.

Chris Shores and Clive Williams, *Aces High*. Grub Street, 1994.

Richard C. Smith, *Hornchurch Offensive*. Grub Street, 2001.

D.J. Smith, *Military Airfields Scotland and North East and Northern Ireland. Action Stations No 7*. Patrick Stephens Ltd, 1983.

I.G. Stott, *Edinburgh's Own – A History of No.603 Squadron, RAuxAF*. Air Pictorial, August 1977.

I. Tavender, *The Distinguished Flying Medal – A Record of Courage 1918 – 1982*. J.B. Hayward and Son, Polstead, Suffolk, 1990.

O.G. Thetford, *No.603 (City of Edinburgh) Squadron – A Short History*. Air Reserve Gazette, April 1948.

R. Woodman. *Malta Convoys*. John Murray, 2000.

J. Yoxal, *The Queens Squadron – A History of No.603 (City of Edinburgh) Squadron, RAuxAF.* Flight April/May 1954.

Press Cuttings

The authors would like to thank the Editors of the following newspapers, past and present: *The Scotsman Newspaper Group, Scottish Daily Mail, The Daily Record, Glasgow Herald, The Times, Daily Telegraph, The Bulletin and Scots Pictorial, Edinburgh Evening Dispatch*

Public Records Office (PRO) Kew

The day to day events occurring in the service of any major unit of the Royal Air Force is kept in the Operations Record Book. This consists of two main forms, Form 540, a diary of events, and Form 541, which details operational sorties carried out by the unit. Bound with these forms, or filed in a separate volume, are appendices containing copies of documents affecting the unit. These vary from combat reports to routine orders. These are kept at the Public Records Office (PRO) at Kew.

RAF Fm 540 Operational Record Books – No 603 (City of Edinburgh) Squadron: 1925 – 1945 AIR 27/2079 – 2081, 1946 – 1950 AIR 27/2506, 2507, 1951 – 1957 AIR 27/2675.

Other Unpublished Sources

The recorded memories of:

Air Commodore R. Berry DSO, OBE, DFC*; Air Commodore C.A. Bouchier CBE, DFC; Air Vice Marshal F. David Scott-Malden CB, DSO, DFC*; Group Captain Mike Hobson CBE AFC; Warrant Officer Eric Mee, Flight Lieutenant Jack Batchelor, Flight Lieutenant Bob Sergeant, Flying Officer John Moss, and Warrant Officer Tom (Paddy) O'Reilly.

Papers of the late G/C J.M. Birkin CB, DSO, OBE, DFC, ADC, via James Birkin.

The Flying Log Books of:

Alfred Beckwith, Wing Commander W.A. Douglas, Pilot Officer F.R.A. van Dyck, Group Captain George Gilroy, Flying Officer Nick Machon, Warrant Officer Eric Mee, Flying Officer John Moss, Warrant Officer Allan Otto, and Flight Lieutenant Bob Sergeant.

Correspondence between Tony Holland and Air Commodore The Rt Hon The Lord Selkirk of Douglas QC, MA, LLB, MSP contained in Lord Selkirk's research material for *The Air Battle for Malta*.

INDEX OF PERSONNEL

A

Adamson, S/L 'Tommy' 332, 342, 346
Alexander, P/O 321
Allen, F/L R. 'Red' 309, 310, 312
Allott, F/O G. 245, 251
Almos, P/O Fred V. 83, 84, 99, 107
Anderson, P/O Andrew 310
Anderson, F/L D.M. 'Andy' 317, 337, 342, 345-346
Anson, S/L Peter J. 306, 309, 310, 312, 315, 316
Adolph, Hauptman Walter 3
Allard, Sgt W.S. 41, 44, 46, 48
Archibald, Sgt W.J. 23, 26, 31, 36, 37, 44, 46, 48
Arnim, von 159
Arthurs, Sgt L. 208
Ashby, F/L 158
Atcherley, AVM R.L.R. 'Batchy' 310
Atkinson, S/L G.B. 156, 157, 162, 169-171
Atkinson F/Sgt R.M. 193

B

Bader, W/C Douglas 3, 26, 36, 37, 93, 145
Bain, Sgt R. 274
Bairnsfather, P/O R. 115, 116, 123, 128, 130, 151
Baker, AVM 251
Ballantyne, F/Sgt James H. 137, 139, 142-144, 146, 149
Ballingall, Sir John 3
Ballingall, George 315
Balthasar, Major Wilhelm 3
Banks, Lord Provost Sir John, 337, 340
Banks, Lady (Wife) 340
Banks, P/O 3
Bannister Sgt. D.V. 219
Banter, Sgt 132
Barbour, F/Sgt C.A.M. 115-118, 120, 132, 135, 140, 142, 149
Barrett, Captain E.A. 193
Barlow, P/O Leslie G. 115, 120-123, 128, 130
Barnham, F/L Denis W. 38
Barwell, Dickie 25
Bass, F/L 280, 283-286
Batchelor, F/L 'Jack' 226, 228, 230, 235, 236, 241, 244-249, 251, 253, 254, 256, 258, 263-265, 271, 274, 276, 280, 282, 283, 285, 286
Baxter, F/O Raymond 232, 233, 262
Beaton, W/C A.J. 'Al' 364-365, 367-368
Beaton, Drum Major 327
Beckwith, W/O 226, 241, 242, 246, 251, 266, 270, 274, 275, 280, 283, 285
Beddow, P/O E. 35
Bell, F/Sgt J. 'Dinger' 324
Bennett, S/L D.B. 184
Bennett, Sgt Harold 41, 42, 44, 46-48, 50, 51, 53, 56-58, 66, 237-239, 245
Berg, Lt 66
Berkeley-Hill, P/O Owen 122, 124, 126, 146
Berry, W/C Ronald 'Ras' 5, 6, 9, 12, 13, 28, 295
Berry, Nancy (Wife) 13
Beurling, Sgt George 'Screwball' 130, 140, 148
Birkin, G/C J.M. 351
Bisdee, Squadron Leader John 83, 241

Blake, Cpl 28
Blackall, P/O Hugh 8, 9, 16, 19-24, 26, 30, 32
Blackall, Dorothy (Wife) 32
Blackall, Rev Lewis (Father) 32
Blackall, Gertrude (Mother) 32
Blackbourn, P/O W.L. 25, 35
Blanche, S/L J.B. 367
Bleefe, Unteroffizier Joachim 58
Blow, F/Sgt 191, 193
Booth, P/O Douglas 84
Bouchier, G/C Cecil A. 'Boy' 9, 30
Boulter John C. 'Bolster' 5, 6, 7
Bounevialle, F/O Cas de 199, 205, 211, 219
Bowen, F/Sgt J.N. 186
Boyd, Sgt 108
Boyle, F/Sgt 115, 121
Boyle, AM Sir Dermot A. 322, 323
Boyle, Ella (Wife) 323
Bramley, Sgt 269, 271, 274, 280, 283, 285
Brandon, 2nd Lt Alfred de Bathe 52
Brennan, P/O Paul 113, 117, 141
Broadhurst, G/C Harry 19, 26, 36, 44, 47, 53
Brough, Sgt E.T. 135, 137, 138
Brown, S/L the Rev James Rossie 287, 288
Brown, P/O L.G. 237
Brown, G/C 312
Brown, Sgt 84, 111-113, 115, 118, 121, 128, 131, 137, 139
Browning, Lt Gen Sir Frederick 312
Buchanan, W/C J.K. 'Butch' 180, 184
Buckley, F/Sgt 80, 84, 87, 89, 115, 123
Buckstone, P/O John 35, 50, 55, 59, 61, 62, 67, 80, 83, 84, 94, 102, 104-106, 110, 112
Buckstone, Walter (Father) 110
Buckstone, Violet (Mother) 110
Budd, Sgt E. 34, 135
Bunn, F/Sgt 193, 219
Burgess, F/L J. 312
Burleigh, P/O 5, 16, 19
Burns, A/C E.S. 295
Burrow, W/O F. 168
Burrows, F/O 239, 241, 250, 251, 265, 269, 274, 280, 283, 285
Bush, Sgt C.F. 41, 56, 57, 61, 66, 68, 84
Butler, W/C D.O. 208
Butler, G/C M.J. 357
Button, F/L J. 302
Bye, F/Sgt D.A. 115, 118, 124, 140, 142

C

Cairns, F/L R.M.B. 342, 345
Campell, Cpl Douglas 274
Carbury F/L Brian G. 5, 153
Carlet, P/O Guy (Andre Levy-Despas) 127, 128, 130, 140, 142
Carter, Private F. 38
Cartridge, W/C D.L. 236
Cassidy, LAC Alec 275
Casson, F/L 'Buck' 36
Cessford, Charles 'Chic' 121, 360
Chater, W/C Hugh A. 'Fritz' 15, 156-158, 162, 163, 175
Cheshire, AVM W.G. 324, 325, 332, 340, 346

Chrisp, F/Sgt 237
Churchill, Prime Minister, Sir Winston S. 1, 80, 109, 116, 165, 169, 267
Colquhoun, Sgt L.R. 'Les' 61-63, 68, 126, 146
Compton, S/L J.A. 162
Compton, Sgt 5, 6, 8
Cook, F/Sgt 193
Cook, Sgt T. 5, 8, 13, 16, 19-23, 36, 42, 44, 52, 55, 56, 61, 66, 68, 188
Cookson, W/O 226, 238, 241, 242, 244, 246, 251, 263, 266, 269, 273, 274
Cooper, P/O H. 226, 245
Costine, LAC John 42
Coulstock, Sgt L. 159
Cox, W/O F.M. 171
Cremer, Hermann 183, 319
Cresswell, Sgt 159
Crompton, A/C R.H. 307
Crompton, F/L 309
Crooks, Sgt Jackie 28, 69, 274
Crosby, Bing 125
Cross, A/C 163
Cruickshank, P/O K. 317
Cunningham, Admiral Sir Andrew 165

D
Daddo-Langlois, F/L W. Raoul 92, 104
Dalley, Sgt J.C. 38, 56, 61
Dalziel, F/O J.C. 169, 199
Darling, Sir William Y. 157, 287, 290, 292, 294, 297, 316, 348
Darling, Sgt Andy S. 5, 8
Davies, P/O G.P.B. 84
Dawe, F/L 280, 283, 285
Dean, F/Sgt C.H. 199
Deck, F/L A.G. 'Tommy' 199, 201, 208
Delorme, P/O Paul 'Pug' 5, 12, 16, 19-23, 25, 26, 28, 30, 31
Denholm, G/C George L. 'Uncle George' 6, 8, 9, 19, 27, 286-289, 290, 304, 305, 342, 355, 360, 363
Denholm, Betty (Wife) 7, 8, 304, 305
Dibbs, F/Sgt J.W.H. 193, 203
Dicks-Sherwood, P/O E.S. 115, 117, 118, 120-122, 128, 130, 131, 134, 137-139, 143, 144, 148-150
Dietrich, Marlene 125
Dietze, Unteroffizier Gottfried 48
Dobbie, Sir William 98
Doidge, P/O William 'Bill' 226, 227, 241, 242, 244, 246
Donaldson, G/C Arthur 224, 251, 259
Donovan, S/L 236
Doolittle, 'Jimmy' 85
Doube, W/O 163
Douglas, Major 99
Douglas, Mrs (Wife) 99
Douglas, Mrs Elaine (née McClelland) 91, 125, 150, 151
Douglas, Councillor Robert E. 290
Douglas, W/C William A. 'Bill' 5, 7, 16, 19, 20, 21, 22, 39, 54-56, 61, 66, 72, 75, 80, 82-85, 87, 90, 91, 94, 95, 97, 99-101, 104-106, 111-113, 115, 116, 122-131, 115, 116, 122-131, 134, 135, 138, 140, 142-144, 146-151, 267, 268, 270, 286, 288, 342
Douglas, Air Marshal Sir Sholto 2, 157, 165
Douglas-Hamilton, S/L Lord David 54-56, 58, 59, 61-65, 71, 73, 80, 83, 84, 87, 89, 93, 94, 102, 105, 106, 109, 112, 113, 115, 117-120, 124, 126, 128, 130, 133, 135, 138, 140, 141, 146-148, 151
Douglas-Hamilton, Lord George Nigel, Earl of Selkirk 288-290, 340, 341

Douglas-Hamilton, A/C Lord James 355, 360, 363
Dowding, ACM Sir Hugh 2
Downes, P/O 132
Downing, Sgt 159
Drabik, Sgt Alex 252
Duckett, A/C R. 'Dickie' 355
Dugdale, W/O 237
Dundas, G/C Hugh 'Cocky' 305

E
Eacott, P/O W.A. 'Wally' 157, 169, 170
Eden, Sir Anthony 320
Edgar, F/Sgt J. 181, 191, 205
Edinburgh, H.R.H. The Duke of 297, 317, 347-349
Edward VIII, HM the King 315
Edwards, W/C Hughie 25, 312
Eisenhower, General Dwight D. 165, 169, 292
Elizabeth, H.M. The Queen (later The Queen Mother) 295, 297, 313
Elizabeth, HRH The Princess 297, 310, 312
As H.M. Queen Elizabeth II 28, 313, 315, 317, 319-322, 327, 337, 346-351, 356, 357, 366-368
Embry, A/M Sir Basil 93, 309, 312
Erskine, W/O Charlie 285, 310, 314
Evans, P/O N. 237
Evans, W/O 265, 270, 274, 280, 283, 285
Ewing, F/O 'Jimmy' 320

F
Fairbanks, Douglas Jnr 110
Falconer, P/O J.A.R. 'Hamish' 12, 14, 16, 19-24, 26, 37-38, 42, 52, 56, 58
Falconer, Mr J.A. 12
Falconer Mrs J.A. 12
Falconer, John L. 288-290
Falconer, Lord Provost Roy 327
Farmer, Sgt John A. 52, 61, 67, 76
Farnes, P/O 33
Farquar, S/L Douglas 15, 16
Fawkes, P/O S. Guye H. 30, 36, 43, 50, 51, 53-56, 58
Fawkes, Stephen (Father) 58
Fawkes, Pauline (Mother) 58
Fellowes, Robert 355
Ferguson, P/O Tim 315, 320, 355
Ferguson, W/O N.S. 171
Filson-Young, W/C W.D.L. 181, 183, 184
Finlay, Sgt R.G. 162
Forshaw, S/L Roger G. 51, 54, 55, 61, 64-65, 67, 72, 76
Forster, P/O J.W. 84
Forster, P/O Paul 61, 69, 80, 100, 101, 111-113, 115, 116, 118, 119, 121, 124, 126, 128, 130, 131, 142, 148, 150
Foster, Sgt John 186, 187
Fowler, F/L C.W. 211
Fox, F/Sgt H.J. Harry 97, 120
Foxley, Sgt W.H. 199, 205
Foxley-Norris, W/C Christopher 211, 214-216, 219, 220, 223, 224
Furse, F/O 315

G
Galland, Hauptmann Adolf 3, 27
Garden, F/L Thomas C. 290
Gaunt, F/O 237
George VI, HM The King 159, 295, 297, 298, 307, 312, 313, 315, 322, 348
Gibson, W/C Guy P. 36

Gidman, P/O 7, 8, 14
Gilchrist, Sir James 332
Giles, F/Sgt R.H. 159
Giles, P/O 177
Gillan, W/C John W. 42
Gillies, F/Sgt Angus 'Angy' 76, 153 154, 163, 170
Gillies, Mary 76
Gilpin, W/O 280, 283, 285, 286
Gilroy, W/C George K. 'Sheep' 6, 12, 16, 19, 20, 21, 23, 26, 28-30, 32, 33, 286, 288, 290, 291, 296, 297, 303, 304, 305, 342
Gilroy, Evelyn (First wife) 303
Gilroy, Jane (Second wife) 303
Gilroy, Pieter (Son) 303, 304
Gilroy, Jamie (Son) 303
Glazebrook, P/O E.H. 'Eddie' 122, 128, 131, 137-139, 141, 148, 149
Glen, P/O A.A. 127, 128, 134, 135, 140
Gloucester, HRH The Duke of 320
Godfrey, W/O 251, 256, 257, 265, 271, 274, 275, 280, 283, 285
Goebbels, Josef 320
Goldsmith, Sgt 118
Goodfellow, F/Sgt 159
Gort, Field Marshal Viscount 98, 108, 116
Gosling, Sgt 186, 188
Goss, W/O John 219, 220
Gow, F/Sgt 177, 188
Gracie, S/L Edward 'Jumbo' 83, 85, 87, 88, 103, 147
Grant, P/O 'Hal' 226, 227, 237
Grant, S/L S.B. 'Stan' 94, 95, 107, 110
Gray, S/L Don 342, 345-346
Gray, W/O 127, 128, 131
Green, Elsie (Mother) 258
Green, W/O Jack D. 'Johnny' 226, 235, 241, 251, 255, 257, 258
Green, Walter (Father) 258
Grey, F/O J.A. 237
Griffiths, Sgt H.G. 152
Griffiths, F/O R.V.L. 33, 36, 40, 41, 43

H
Haff, Gefreiter Karl 106
Haggas, F/Sgt H. 115, 116, 121
Haig, F/O John G.E. Jack 9
Haine, Dickie 332, 342, 345-346
Haine, Eve (Wife) 332, 345-346
Haine, Charles (Son) 332
Haine, Emma (Daughter) 332
Haine, Robert (Son) 332
Hall, Sgt H.K. 6, 8
Hamilton, Duke of 297, 300, 340
Handley, F/O W.G. 250
Harper, W/O T.J. 188
Harman, F/Sgt E.G. 184, 191
Harper, W/O T.J. 169
Harrison, F/Sgt 191, 193
Harrison, Sgt D. 219
Hartley, F/O 193
Harwood, Sgt J.W.H. 69
Haupt, Lt A.J. 193
Haupt, P/O 'Wally' 226, 235, 241, 251, 253, 257, 262, 263, 265, 274
Haw Haw, Lord (William Joyce) 26
Hawtry, G/C 259
Hayes, P/O J.H. 237

Hayes, Norman 296, 298
Hayter, F/O W. 169
Heide, F/O 208
Henderson, Arthur 309
Henderson, S/L 28
Hendry, Sgt A.C. 23, 33
Henshaw, F/L J.Doug A. 322, 324, 337, 340, 341
Henshaw, F/O Roger (Brother) 341
Hess, Rudolf 9
Hesselyn, Sgt R.B. Ray 117
Hewitt, AM Ludlow 122
Hey, F/Sgt J.P. 168
Hillary, Richard H. 13, 55
Hinde, F/Sgt 193
Hitler, Adolf 1, 124, 134, 165, 168, 229, 230, 275
Hobson, G/C Mike E. 312, 315, 317, 319, 320, 325, 329-333, 336, 337, 340, 342, 345, 354
Hobson, Barbara (Wife) 341
Holland, F/O A.C.W. 'Tony' 61, 69, 71, 72, 80, 84, 96, 97, 109-113, 115, 121, 137
Holmes, S/L J.W.E. 'Joe' 305, 306
Holmes, F/L W.G. 'Bill' 319, 324, 326, 332, 337, 345-346
Holvey, F/O 237
Honig, F/O A. 162
Hopkin, F/Sgt L.E. 191
Hopkins, P/O K.J.E. 170, 177
Hughes, S/L 85
Hughes, W/C G.E. 293
Hughes, Pipe Major 367
Hunter, Sgt 15, 16, 20, 22, 23, 26, 30, 56
Hunter, Cpl 285
Hurst, P/O J. 'Johnny' 6, 20-23, 33, 35-37, 43, 50 ,61, 66, 69, 72, 80, 84, 96, 102, 106, 110-113, 115-118, 120, 121, 126, 128, 130, 131, 132, 137, 138
Hurst, James (Father) 137
Hurst, Annie (Mother) 137
Hurst, Winifred (Wife) 137
Hynes, Sgt F.J. 28

I
Igoe, G/C Peter 355
Illingworth, S/L P. 153
Inch, Sgt Arthur 252
Inglis, F/Sgt 315
Innes, F/L F. 'Chumley' 43-45, 49, 50, 52
Irons, Norman 355
Irwin, F/Sgt W.R. 113, 115, 119, 128, 130, 140, 147

J
Jack, W/C James L. 288, 290
Jackman, W/O William 8, 14, 18-21, 23, 25, 26, 30-32
James, F/Sgt B.G. 159
Jamesona, Lucy 5
Jemmett, P/O F.J. 97
Jenkinson, F/O K. 199, 201
Johnson, Brigadier F.L. 294
Johnson, F/Sgt F.R. 115, 117, 120, 128, 131, 137, 138, 142
Johnston, F/L W.J. 'Johnny' 107
Jones, F/O J.W.A. 195
Jones, P/O William I. 61, 76, 83, 89
Joyce, F/Sgt D. 199
Jury, Sgt R.D. 13, 21, 22, 23

K
Keable, P/O Nigel H.C. 23, 24, 26, 28, 35
Keep, F/L 280, 283, 285

Kellett, W/C Ronald 3
Kemp, G/C R.G. 'Bob' 355, 362, 367
Kennedy, A. Scott 327, 332, 341, 346
Kennedy, Ann (Wife) 341
Kennedy, Joseph 1
Kent, The Duke of, 49
King, P/O Neville S. 61, 80, 84, 100, 102, 106, 111-113, 115, 121, 126, 128, 130, 131, 137-139, 141, 142, 180, 181, 193
King, Joseph (Father) 142
King, Charlotte M. (Mother) 142
King, Brenda (Wife) 142
Kingsford, F/L R.S. 294, 295
Kirkman, F/L 'Jack' 226, 236, 241, 244, 247, 249, 251, 254, 263, 265, 266, 269, 274, 280, 282, 283, 285
Kistruck, P/O 55, 59, 61, 69
Knight, P/O Don 309, 315

L

Lacey, Sgt Herbert 186, 187
Laffan, W/O 241, 251, 266, 268, 270, 274, 277, 280, 283, 285
Lamb, Sgt 5, 13, 14, 16, 19, 21-23, 30, 36, 43, 44, 51, 55, 56, 58, 59
Langford, F/O 183
Lardner-Burke, W/C 235, 236, 238, 239
Lassen, Captain Andreas 187
Lauinger, Lt Kurt 120
Laycock, S/L H.K. 155, 156, 162, 164, 170
Lee, Sgt H. 208
Lee, Cpl Johnnie 275
Lee, LAC Ron 154, 173
Lee Evans, W/C J.A. 169
Leigh-Mallory, AVM Trafford 2, 3, 145
Le May, W/C W.K. 147
Lendon, F/L W.W. 9, 16, 43
Lewis, W/C J. Ronnie H. 164, 175, 176, 180, 188, 196, 214
Liddle, Sgt 5
Linton, P/O O.M. 'Ossie' 84, 96, 97, 99
Lister, F/O 282, 283, 285
Lofts, S/L Keith 307
Lloyd, AVM Hugh P. 79, 145
Lloyd-Davies, S/L R. 'Lloyd' 316, 317, 319, 329
London, F/O 43
Louden, I.H. 302
Loudon, S/L M. Johnny 33, 36, 41, 44, 51
Loudon, Sgt 55, 61, 68
Love, Sgt 'Cupid' 231
Lucas, S/L P.B. 'Laddie' 79, 92, 93, 94, 101, 107, 121, 130
Lundsten, Lt 69, 70
Lyall, F/L Graeme 365
Lynch, W/O E.T. 187

M

Macdonald F/L H.K. 9
MacDonnell, F/L G.W. 179, 180
MacFarlane, Dr. 126
MacFarlane, Meg 126
Machon, F/O H. Nick 239, 241, 248, 251, 259, 261-263, 266, 268, 269, 273-275, 280, 282, 283, 285-287
MacKenzie, F/Sgt Donald 274
Mackenzie, Sgt John B.S. Tails 367
MacLean, F/L Alastair 203
Macnamara, F/O Brian R. 6
MacQueen, F/L Norman 107
Madoc-Jones, Rev T. 337
Malam, Sgt 280, 283, 285
Malan, G/C A.G. 'Sailor' 3, 25, 33, 241

Manivalu, P/O Bala 239, 241, 251, 253
Manley, F/Sgt John 255
Manz, Unteroffizier Walter 107
Marland, P/O R.K. 33, 36, 44, 46, 48, 49
Marshall, F.W. S/L 154
Martel, F/L Ludwik 5, 8
Martel, Sasha (Wife) 8
Maslen, W/O 241, 251, 253, 263, 265, 274-276, 280, 283, 285
Mathias, Sgt W.R. 28
Maton, F/Sgt A.J. 237
Maynard, Sgt L.G. 159
McAndrew, F/L 226, 235, 236, 241, 244, 249, 251, 262, 263, 265, 271, 274, 275, 280, 283, 285
McConnochie, F/O 226, 236, 241, 246, 247, 251, 261, 263, 265, 266, 274, 275, 280, 283, 285
McCulloch, Joe 360
McGinn, P/O Nelson A.H. 239, 241, 249, 251, 261, 262, 266, 282
McGinn, Edwin (Father) 262
McGinn, Ruth (Mother) 262
McHardy, Rev Dr A. 337, 341, 345
McIntosh, F/O David 326
McIntosh, F/L Duncan 315, 320, 326
McKelvie, P/O Kenneth J. 6, 9, 14, 21, 22
McKelvie, Sgt William 8, 14, 16, 33, 44-46, 48, 50, 51
McKelvie, S/L James A. (Father) 51
McKelvie, Elizabeth (Mother) 51
McLean, S/L 317
McLean, P/O C.B. 84, 96, 99, 105, 113, 115, 117, 118, 126
McLean, W/C John S. 84
McLeod, P/O Henry W. 127, 128, 134, 139, 142, 144, 146-148
McNair, F/L 'Buck' 92, 94, 96, 107, 121, 130
McNeill, Sgt 5
McQueen, W/O Don 365
McVie, Cpl George 274
Meadows, W/C 'Jack' 296, 313, 348-349
Mears, F/O J.M. 302, 310
Mee, W/O Eric 226, 233, 240, 241, 242, 248, 251, 253-255, 257, 258, 260, 263, 266, 271, 273-276, 280, 282-286
Megone, P/O C. Bruce 163
Meharg, W/C 193, 215
Mejon, P/O J.G. 84, 113
Melleresh, 'Togs' 296
Messe, Marshal 159
Middlemas, F/O 237
Mighall, G/C R.T.W. 360
Miller, F/Sgt 321
Miller, A/C 332
Miller, Sgt 329
Milligan, Mr Eric 364
Milne, F/O S. 320, 321
Mitchell, Edith 117
Mitchell, P/O H.R. 84, 96, 104, 105, 110, 111, 112, 115, 117
Mitchell, F/O Richard A. 111, 113, 115, 117-120, 121, 123, 128, 131, 132, 135, 137-139, 142, 144, 146
Mitchell, F/L Peter 'Mitch' 143, 317, 331
Mitchell, William 117
Moffatt, LAC 285
Moncur, F/L W. 'Bill' 315, 326, 332, 337, 342, 345-347
Monro, A/C Sir Hector (later Lord Monro of Langham) 297, 355, 364
Montgomery, General Sir Bernard L. 154
Moon, W/O J.M. 163
Moore, F/Sgt 205
Moore, George 164
Morton, S/L James S. 'Black' 8, 43

Morton, Caroline (Daughter) 305
Morton, Marion 367
Moss, F/O John 62, 63, 233, 248, 272, 282-286
Mowat, S/L N. 57
Müncheberg, Hauptmann Joachim 3
Murray, P/O Gordon 80, 83, 84, 96, 97
Mycelia, P/O 15, 21, 22
Mycroft, P/O Frank 321, 324, 333

N

Neill, Sgt 14, 16, 19-24, 32, 36, 42, 43, 50, 55, 56
Newman, P/O C.A. 5, 8, 9, 14, 16, 21-23
Newman, P/O Dudley 122, 128, 130, 134, 137-139, 142, 147, 149, 150
Newman, AC2 William J. 154
Newman, Rosetta 154
Nicol, F/Sgt I.L. 193, 205
Niven, P/O H.G. 33, 35
Northcott, P/O G.W. 115, 117, 118, 120, 128, 130, 135, 142-144, 147, 149, 150

O

Oddy, F/L R.L. 43, 153, 164, 214, 245
Oesau, Major Walter 4
Offenburg, F/L Jean H.M. 241
Ogilvie, S/L 100, 169
Orde, Cuthbert 6, 7, 9
O'Reilly, F/Sgt Thomas 'Paddy' 226, 231, 236, 241-244, 250, 251, 255, 257, 261, 265, 269
Ortmans, F/O Christian 241
Ortmans, F/L V.M.M. 'Vicki' 241
Ottewill, S/L P.G. 250
Otto, W/O Allan W. 41, 42, 50-52, 56, 61, 80, 84, 90, 101, 105-107, 115, 123
Otto, Archie 41
Oulton, AVM 'Wilf' 351
Ovendon, S/L H.G.P. 53, 56

P

Paddison, F/Sgt J.E. 191
Pagram, S/L 245
Paine, S/L C.D. 'Boozy' 203, 211
Paget, Sgt Ian 19, 23, 36, 37
Park, AVM Sir Keith 2, 145, 186, 196
Parker, G/C 280
Parkinson, F/Sgt Colin 134, 137-139, 142-145, 149
Parsons, F/Sgt D.F. 193
Partridge, F/L 177, 191
Patch, AVM H.L. 320
Patterson, S/L A. 226, 234, 239, 240
Pearson, W/C M. 312
Pease, F/O A. Peter 13
Peddell, F/O Alex 312, 320, 326
Peel, W/C John 3
Pennie, F/Sgt K.F. 193, 201, 220
Perkins, 'Ma' 201
Pertwee, S/L H.R.P. 'Dickie' 262, 265, 266, 271, 273, 274, 280, 282, 284, 285
Peterson, A/S/O 68, 69
Phillips, Sid 262
Piner, F/O S.W. 179, 180
Pingel, Hauptmann Rolf 3
Pinney, F/Sgt J.A.H. 132, 135, 140, 142, 146, 147
Plagis, F/L J.A. 'Johnny' 94, 95
Portal, ACM Charles 29
Potter, P/O A.E. 'Gillie' 199, 219

Potter, F/Sgt 205
Powell, S/L 171, 172
Powell, F/L K.C. 43
Powell, Sgt W.E. 159
Prentice, W/O J. 'Snuffy - Snuff Box' 153, 170, 215, 218, 225, 303
Price, Sgt R.B. 6
Prickman, A/C 280, 282, 284
Pringle, F/L A.P. 'Pat' 179-181, 183-188, 191, 205, 215
Pritchard, P/O W.B.F. 170
Proudlove, David 298
Prowse, P/O Harry A.R. 10, 14, 16, 19, 20, 22-24, 26-28, 35
Prytherch, Sgt D.J. 23, 26, 30, 36, 37, 39, 44, 50, 61, 68-71
Purdy, F/O T.B. 8

R

Radcliffe, F/Sgt H.K. 237
Rae, F/L J.D. 'Jack' 5, 47, 84, 89, 96, 104, 105, 115, 119, 123, 126, 127
Rankin, W/C J. 'Jamie' 241
Rawson, Sgt 56-58, 61, 66, 70-72
Read, P/O William A.A. 'Tannoy' 8
Renwick, Mr Jim 367
Revell, W/C J.D.T. 197, 203
Rhind, Jill 355
Rhodes, F/Sgt C. 191
Richardson, Sgt F.G. 208
Richardson, LAC P. 203
Richey, W/C Paul 25, 34, 241
Richmond, F/O 251, 266, 271, 274, 275, 280, 283, 285
Rigler, S/L Thomas 'Tommy' 226, 236, 240, 241, 245, 249-251, 260, 265
Ritchie, S/L Ian S. 'Bear' 5, 290, 354, 342
Robb, AM Sir James 264, 284
Robertson, Rev.Charles 355
Robinson, S/L Micky 33
Robinson, G/C 312
Robinson, A/C M.W.S. 'Mike' 331, 341, 342, 345-346
Robson, Ronald 315, 319
Rofe, F/Sgt C. 31, 32
Roger, W/O K.V. 170
Rogers, F/Sgt J.J. 199, 201
Rogers, F/O W.G. 155, 156, 245, 251
Rollwage, Oberfeldwebel 110
Rommel, Field Marshal Erwin 78, 79, 134, 153, 154, 224
Rooks, F/Sgt A. 181
Ross, F/O A.E. 185, 205, 215
Ruchwaldy, Sgt Desmond 19, 23, 36, 37, 39, 50, 52, 55, 61, 64, 66-68, 76
Rudd, Sgt 23
Russell, E.G.L. 19
Russell, T. 183

S

Sainsbury, AVM Langford 158, 186
Salt, Sgt L.E.S. 20-23
Salvatore, Massimo 120
Sanders, Hans 48
Sanders, F/L Lester V. 84, 94, 95, 100, 106, 107, 111, 112, 115, 117, 118, 120, 121, 123, 126, 128, 130, 132, 137-139, 141, 142
Sanderson, F/O 226, 241, 246
Sanderson, Sgt 285
Satchell, G/C W.A. 'Jack' 91, 93, 102, 109, 282, 284
Sauer, Unteroffizier Dr Felix 120
Sauer, Feldwebel Heinz 146

Saunders, John 181
Sawers, Councillor 290
Scantlebury, F/O F. 159
Schierning, Unteroffizier Helmut 111
Schmid, Hauptmann 48
Schofield, S/L A.A. 'Roy' 183, 319, 320, 322, 323, 325
Scott, F/L George 309, 332
Scott, F/O 'Jock' 214
Scott, Sgt R.C. 26, 162, 170
Scott-Malden, Francis D.S. 'Scottie' 6, 12-14, 16, 19-23, 28-30, 35-37, 39, 42, 43
Seifert, Major Johannes 3
Sergeant, F/L R.A. 'Bob' 79, 80, 92, 95-97, 100, 101, 107, 120, 226, 227, 234, 236, 237, 241, 243, 246, 248, 251, 253, 255, 256, 259, 263, 265, 266, 269-272, 274-276, 280, 283, 285, 287
Seward, W/O 270, 271, 274, 275, 280, 283, 285, 286
Shaw, Lt 'The Spy' 177
Shaw, F/Sgt J.G. 199
Sheldrick, F/Sgt F.G.W. 195
Sherrington, Sgt R.D. 110
Shuckburgh, Sgt Alan D. 50, 51
Shuckburgh, Sir John (Father) 50
Shuckburgh, Lilian (Mother) 50
Silcock, F/O 219
Simpson, F/L 191, 193, 197, 219
Skene, F/O 'Doc' 5, 8, 13, 15, 36, 43
Skinner, F/L Roy J. 324, 326, 332, 339, 345
Skinner, Joyce 326, 332
Slade, P/O J.W. 'Jack' 84, 95, 100, 101, 106, 107, 111-113, 115-117, 119, 121, 124, 128, 130, 134, 138, 140
Sly, F/L R.H.C. 111
Smith, G/C W.G.G. Duncan 23, 39-41, 43, 44, 47, 49, 54, 59, 101, 314, 322, 324
Smith, F/O S.J.L. 28
Smith, S/L F. Hiram M. 9, 12-16, 19-24, 26, 27, 30, 32-34
Smith, F/O S.J.L. 177, 183
Smith, P/O Jerrold 110
Smith, P/O R.G. 'Ray' 122, 134, 138, 139, 142, 146
Soden, P/O John F. 5
Soderlund, F/O 191, 193, 205
Soukop, Lt Herbert 119
Sowery, F/L John A. 292, 295, 296
Speight, F/L W. 365
Spooner, W/O 181
Squire, ACM Sir Peter 365, 366
Stalin, Joseph 49
Stamble, Sgt 135
Staniforth, F/L 'Stan' 235, 241, 242, 244, 246, 249-251, 265, 266, 271, 274, 280, 283, 285
Stanners, Corporal 226
Stapleton, S/L B.G. 'Stapme' 6-8, 365, 376
Stapleton, Joan (First wife) 8
Stapleton, Mike (Son) 8
Stapleton, W/C Frederick S. 33, 37, 54, 55
Stevens, G/C E.H. 'Count' 275, 286, 288, 290, 296
Stewart, James 125
Stewart-Clark, P/O Dudley 9, 12, 16, 19-22
Still, F/O 309
Stokoe, Sgt Jack 5, 6
Stone, F/L 'Chris' 329, 330
Stone, Sgt 14, 19-23, 32, 35, 36, 43, 61
Stoneman, F/O 'Spanner' 229, 245
Storrar, F/L James 'Jas' 302, 303, 312
Strever, Lt 'Ted' 149
Sutehall, F/L 237

Sutherland, S/L 236, 262
Swales, 2/Lt C.J.Ormonde 'Zulu' 84, 106, 115, 117, 118, 120, 124, 128, 130, 135, 140, 144, 150
Swanwick, F/L George W. 147, 150
Sykes, F/Sgt C.L. 187
Sykes, W/O L.F. 199, 205

T
Tabor, Sgt George W. 23, 26, 29, 32
Tayleur, Sgt J.L. 'Junior' 92, 320
Taylor, Sgt D.W. 199
Tedder, Marshal of the Royal Air Force Sir Arthur 9, 79, 97, 155, 165, 291, 295, 297
Tennant, F/Sgt 183
Terry, ACM Sir Peter 329
Terry, Betty (Wife) 329
Tetley, AVM John F.H. 355
Thame, F/O 193
Thom, F/O R. 181
Thom, Leutnant Walter 58
Thomas, F/Sgt K.F. 56, 59, 61, 199
Thomas, P/O R.A. 33, 36
Thompson, R.B. 294
Thomson, Lt 12
Thomson, F/L J.A. 30
Thomson, F/O 238, 241, 251, 259, 265, 268, 269, 274, 280, 285
Thomson, W/O Tommy 226, 227, 241, 244, 246, 251, 255, 263, 265, 274-276, 280, 283-286
Thomson, Pipe-Major 302
Trail, F/O Leslie S. 226, 234
Trautman, P/O F. 237
Trenchard, Marshal of the Royal Air Force The Viscount 349, 368
Truesdale, F/Sgt Tom 170, 186
Turlington, P/O 134, 140, 150
Turner, W/C P.S. 'Stan' 79, 93, 94, 96, 101, 145

U
Underdown, F/O 282, 283, 285
Undrill, F/O R.S. 156, 163

V
Vacha, Robert 304
Van Dyck, P/O 226, 235, 237
van't Hoff, Jan 231-232, 253, 258
Vaughan, F/O 193

W
Waddy, Sgt 56, 59, 61
Walcott, Sgt 61, 76, 80, 82-84, 87, 89, 90
Walker, F/L J.A. 33, 36, 38
Wallace, P/O Alen 'Shag' 9
Walmsley, AM Sir Hugh 298, 303
Walters, F/L 'Joe' 164, 168
Wanklyn, Lt Cdr David 122
Warburton, F/O G.D. 237
Ward, F/O D.G.R. 'Paddy' 208
Warr, Very Rev. Dr Charles 337, 340
Watson, Col R.S.B. 355
Watt, The Rev Charles L. 295
Watters, F/L 'Joe' 177
Watts, P/O L.W. 84, 95, 99
Weatherstone, Bailie D.M. 342, 346
Webb, F/Sgt 'Johnnie' 239, 241, 247, 251, 261, 266, 271, 274, 280, 283, 285

Webster, Sgt L.F. 38, 52, 96, 106, 110, 283
Welch, F/L 'Johnnie' 226, 235, 236, 241, 242, 245-247, 249, 251, 254, 258-260, 263, 266, 271, 274, 275, 280, 283, 284, 285
Wells, W/C 126
West, F/L R. 'Ronnie' 92, 107
West, Sgt S.A. 188
Whalley, F/Sgt J. 171, 177, 181, 183, 189
Wheatley, W/O 'Snowy' 226, 236, 241, 244, 251, 252, 255, 257, 266, 270, 274, 280, 282, 285
Whitley, Rev Dr H.C. 337, 341
Wick, Major Helmut 3
Wilkinson, LAC John 53
Williams, F/Sgt 155, 205
Williams, P/O J.E.D. 163
Willoughby, Sgt John 365
Wilson, AC1 28
Wilson, Sgt 5, 6, 13, 14
Wilson, Pipe Major G. 320
Wilson, F/O R.A.R. 177, 191, 195
Wimburger, Sgt E. 169
Winskill, W/C 'Archie' 5, 28, 324-327, 330-332
Winskill, Christianne (Wife) 325
Wishart, Sgt Alex 104, 108, 139
Wood, Norman 153
Wood, Sgt 23, 29, 34
Woodhall, G/C A.B. 'Woody' 93, 97, 104, 117, 135, 145
Woodier, P/O A.B. 208
Woodruff, W/C P.H. 180
Worrall, F/Sgt E.A. 168
Worthington, F/L R.B. 354
Worthington, Private J. 38
Wyndham Rogers, F/L 163, 174

Y
Yates, F/Sgt Harold 171, 177, 181, 183, 189, 203
Yorke, Sgt 199
Young, Sgt W. 148